A DICTIONARY OF

ANGELS

INCLUDING THE FALLEN ANGELS

By Gustav Davidson

THE FREE PRESS
A Division of Macmillan, Inc.
NEW YORK

Maxwell Macmillan Canada
TORONTO

Maxwell Macmillan International
NEW YORK   OXFORD   SINGAPORE   SYDNEY

The Free Press
A Division of Macmillan, Inc.
866 Third Avenue, New York, N.Y. 10022

Maxwell Macmillan Canada, Inc.
1200 Eglinton Avenue East
Suite 200
Don Mills, Ontario M3C 3N1

Macmillan, Inc. is part of the Maxwell Communication Group of Companies.

Library of Congress Catalog Card Number: 66-19757

First Free Press Paperback Edition 1971

Printed in the United States of America

printing number
   3 4 5 6 7 8 9 10

Contents

Illustrations

Introduction

Some years ago when I started "collecting" angels as a literary diversion, it was certainly with no thought of serving as their archivist, biographer, and finally as their lexicographer. Such an idea did not occur to me—indeed, could not have occurred to me—until I had corralled a sufficient number of the heavenly denizens to make a dictionary of them feasible.

At first I thought that angels, named angels, were to be found only in the Bible. I soon learned that, on the contrary, the Bible was the last place to look for them. True, angels are mentioned frequently enough in both the Old and New Testaments, but they are not named, save in two or three instances. Virtually all the named angels in this compilation are culled from sources outside Scripture.[1]

Of the books in the New Testament, while the Synoptic Gospels and the Pauline Epistles have been longtime favorites of mine, the book of Revelation always held a particular fascination for me, mainly because, I believe, of its apocalyptic imagery and involvement with angels. I read the book often. But one day, as I was leafing through its pages, my eye was arrested by verse 2, chapter 8:

> And I saw the seven angels who stand before God;
> And to them were given seven trumpets.

I laid the book aside and asked myself: who are these seven holy ones that stand before God? Has any biblical scholar identified them? Are they of the order of seraphim, cherubim, principalities, powers? And are they always the same seven who enjoy the privilege and eminence of closest proximity to the throne of Glory? And why seven? Were the seven planets the prototype? Or did the notion derive from the well-known chapter in Ezekiel 9: 2–11 which gives a terrifying picture of six "men" and a seventh "clothed in linen" whom God summoned to Jerusalem to "slay without pity"? Challenging, even intimidating, questions and ones that, I felt, ought not to be left unanswered. Meantime, the pursuit led me down many a heavenly brook. Over the years it served to unlock realms of gold I never suspected existed in Heaven or on earth.

Of the seven Revelation angels I had no difficulty in establishing the identity of three: Michael and Gabriel (in Scripture) and Raphael (in *The Book of Tobit*). The last-named angel, by a happy chance, identifies himself: "I am Raphael," he discloses to his young charge Toby, "one of the seven angels who stand and enter before the glory of the Lord." No declaration could be more authoritative or conclusive. And so, with three of the seven angels identified, the problem was to bring to light the remaining four.

---

1. The Koran names seven angels: Gabriel, Michael, Iblis or Eblis, chief jinn in Arabian mythology, counterpart of the Judaean-Christian Satan; Malec or Malik, principal angel of Hell; the two fallen angels, Harut and Marut; and Malaku 'l-maut, angel of death, identified as Azrael. Contrary to popular belief and accreditation, the Koran does not name Israfel, lord of the resurrection trumpet.

I remembered reading somewhere of an angel called Uriel and that he was a "regent of the sun." He seemed a likely candidate. I was confirmed in this feeling when I came upon Uriel in *Paradise Lost* (111, 648 seq.) and found the archfiend himself providing warrant: "him Satan thus accosts./Uriel, for thou of those seav'n spirits that stand/In sight of God's high Throne, gloriously bright," etc. Poe's Israfel, "Whose heart-strings are a lute," was (or is) an Islamic angel,[2] and I wondered if that fact might rule him out. Then there was Longfellow's Sandalphon. In the poem by that name, Longfellow described Sandalphon as the "Angel of Glory, Angel of Prayer." A great angel, certainly: but, again, was he of an eminence sufficiently exalted to entitle him to "enter before the glory of the Lord"? That was the question. Vondel's *Lucifer*, Heywood's *The Hierarchy of the Blessèd Angels*, Milton's *Paradise Lost*, Dryden's *State of Innocence*, Klopstock's *The Messiah*—all these works yielded a considerable quantity of the celestial spirits, some in the top echelons, like Abdiel, Ithuriel, Uzziel, Zephon; but I had no way of telling whether any of them qualified. Surely, I comforted myself, there must be some source where the answer could be found. Actually there were a number of such sources. I had only to reach out my hand for books in my own library. Instead, in my then state of pneumatic innocence, I looked far afield.

Since I was unacquainted at the time with anyone versed in angel lore, I decided to enter into correspondence with scholars and theologians who might help me. I picked half a dozen names at random from the faculty lists of local universities, seminaries, and yeshivas. I put the question squarely to them. The responses were a long time coming and hardly satisfying. "Not in my competence" was the way one biblical exegete put it. Another referred me to the minister of a Swedenborgian church in West Germany. From others I heard nothing. But one rather noted *maskil* came through handsomely with two sets of seven, each leading off with the familiar trio (Michael, Gabriel, Raphael), thus:

First List	*Second List*
Michael	Michael
Gabriel	Gabriel
Raphael	Raphael
Uriel	Anael (Haniel)
Raguel	Zadkiel
Saraqael	Orifiel
Remiel (or Camael)	Uzziel (or Sidriel)

I now had not only the seven angels I had been looking for but a *choice* of seven; and, in

2. Not a Koranic angel, as Poe mistakenly makes him out to be. Israfel is not mentioned in the Koran, and Poe's quotation from it must derive, presumably, from a *hadith* (traditional saying attributed to the Prophet) or from "Preliminary Discourse," George Sale's long introductory essay to his translation of the Koran. Scholars have pointed out that references to Israfel and tributes to him as the Angel of Music in Arabic lore were known to Poe as occurring in the works of the French poet, de Béranger (whom Poe quotes), and the Irish poet, Thomas Moore.

addition, the names of angels I had not heard of before.[3] In the course of further correspondence I was apprised of a branch of extracanonical writings new to me: pseudepigrapha, particularly the three Enoch books, a veritable treasure-trove! *Enoch I* or the *Book of Enoch* (also called the *Ethiopic Enoch*, from the fact that the earliest version or recension of the book was found in Abyssinia) was the most readily available. It literally rioted in angel names—many of them, as I quickly discovered, duplications or corruptions of other names.

What were Enoch's sources? Did the patriarch (or whoever the author was to whom the Enoch books have been attributed) draw on his own lively imagination? (Certainly the 12-winged kalkydri and phoenixes were his invention.) Did he conjure his angels from the "four hinges of the spirit world?" Or did they come to him, as they have and still do to initiates, after a special, mystical concentration—a gift of grace, a charisma? I left that an open question, for the time being.

The Enoch books led me on to related hierological sources and texts: apocalyptic, cabalistic, Talmudic, gnostic, patristic, Merkabah (Jewish mystic), and ultimately to the grimoires, those black magic manuals, repositories of curious, forbidden, and by now well-nigh forgotten lore. In them, invocations, adjurations, and exorcisms were spelt out in full, often grossest detail, and addressed to spirits bearing the most outlandish names. The Church was not slow in pronouncing its curse on these rituals, although the authorship of one of the most diabolic of them was credited (without warrant, it is true) to a pope, Honorius the Third, who reigned during the years 1216–1227. The work is titled *The Grimoire of Honorius the Great*, and made its first appearance in 1629, some 400 years after the death of its reputed author. Arthur Edward Waite, author of *The Book of Ceremonial Magic*, cites the grimoire as "a malicious and somewhat clever imposture, which was undeniably calculated to deceive ignorant persons of its period who may have been magically inclined, more especially ignorant priests, since it pretends to convey the express sanction of the Apostolical Seat for the operations of infernal magic and necromancy."

All these goetic tracts yielded a boundless profusion of angels (and demons), and I soon had more of the fluttering creatures than I knew what to do with. In order to keep my work within sizable limits, I started weeding out (Heaven forgive me!) what I considered to be the less important names, or the ones about which little or no data could be found.

At this stage of the quest I was literally bedeviled by angels. They stalked and leaguered me, by night and day. I could not tell the evil from the good, demons from daevas, satans from seraphim; nor (to quote from a poem composed at the time) "if that world I could not hope to prove,/Flaming with heavenly beasts, holy and grim,/Was any less real than that in which I moved." I moved, indeed, in a twilight zone of tall presences, through enchanted forests lit with the sinister splendor of fallen divinities; of aeons and archons, peris and paracletes, elohim and avatars. I felt somewhat like Dante, in the opening canto of *The Divine Comedy*, when, midway upon the journey of his life, he found himself astray in a dusky wood. Or like some knight of old, ready to try conclusions with any adversary, real or fancied. I remember one occasion—it was winter and getting dark—returning home from a neighboring farm. I had cut

---

3. Subsequently, in other lists of the seven (*Enoch I, Esdras II*, etc.), I came upon the names of the following angels: Jophiel, Jeremiel, Pravuil, Salathiel, Sariel, Zachariel, and Zaphiel.

across an unfamiliar field. Suddenly a nightmarish shape loomed up in front of me, barring my progress. After a paralyzing moment I managed to fight my way past the phantom. The next morning I could not be sure (no more than Jacob was, when he wrestled with his dark antagonist at Peniel) whether I had encountered a ghost, an angel, a demon, or God. There were other such moments and other such encounters, when I passed from terror to trance, from intimations of realms unguessed at to the uneasy conviction that, beyond the reach of our senses, beyond the arch of all our experience sacred and profane, there was only—to use an expression of Paul's in I Timothy 4—"fable and endless genealogy."

Logic, I felt, was my only safe anchor in reality; but if, as Walter Nigg points out, "angels are powers which transcend the logic of our existence," did it follow that one is constrained to abandon logic in order to entertain angels?[4] For the sake of angels I was ready to subscribe to Coleridge's "willing suspension of disbelief." I was even ready to drink his "milk of Paradise." But I was troubled. Never a respecter of authority, *per se*, particularly when it was backed by the "salvific light of revelation," I nevertheless kept repeating to myself that I was pitting my personal and necessarily circumscribed experience, logic, and belief (or nonbelief) against the experience, logic, and belief of some of the boldest and profoundest minds of all times—minds that had reshaped the world's thinking and emancipated it (to a degree, at any rate) from the bondage of superstition and error. Still, I was averse to associating myself with opinions and creeds, no matter how hallowed by time or tradition, or by whomsoever held, that were plainly repugnant to common sense. A professed belief in angels would, inevitably, involve me in a belief in the supernatural, and that was the golden snare I did not wish to be caught in. Without committing myself religiously I could conceive of the possibility of there being, in dimensions and worlds other than our own, powers and intelligences outside our present apprehension, and in this sense angels are not to be ruled out as a part of reality—always remembering that *we create what we believe*. Indeed, I am prepared to say that if enough of us believe in angels, then angels exist.

In the course of much reading in patristic lore I came upon a saying by St. Augustine. It is taken from his *Eight Questions* ("de diversis questionibus octoginta tribus"). I wrote down the saying on a piece of paper and carried it around with me for a long time, not as something I concurred in, but as a challenge. This is what Augustine said: "Every visible thing in this world is put under the charge of an angel." *Genesis Rabba*, 10, puts it somewhat differently: "There's not a stalk on earth that has not its [protecting or guardian] angel in heaven."

Here and there, wherever it suited his thesis or purpose, St. Paul found angels wicked (as in Ephesians 6, etc.). In Colossians 2:17 he warns us not to be seduced by any religion of angels. Furthermore, God himself, it appears, "put no trust in his servants . . . his angels he charged with folly" (Job 4:18). There was the further injunction in Hebrews 13, "Be not carried about with divers and strange doctrines." Sound advice! And I was fain to say to Paul, as Agrippa the king said to him (in Acts 26:38), "Almost thou persuadest me to be a Christian." But *whose*

4. Walter Nigg's article "Stay you Angels, Stay with Me," *Harper's Bazaar*, December 1962. The phrase derives from Johann Sebastian Bach's "Cantata for Michaelmas Day."

strange doctrines did Paul have in mind—Moses'? Isaiah's? Koheleth's? Peter's? St. James'? And if it is Paul who thus exhorts us in Hebrews (a book once reputedly his), one might ask: is Paul a trustworthy counselor and guide—a man who, as he himself admits, was "all things to all men," and who honored and repudiated angels in almost the same breath? One thing I soon realized: in the realm of the unknowable and invisible, in matters where a questioner is finally reduced to taking things on faith, one can be sure of nothing, prove nothing, and convince nobody. But more of this anon.

One of the problems I ran into, in the early days of my investigations, was how to hack my way through the maze of changes in nomenclature and orthography that angels passed through in the course of their being translated from one language into another, or copied out by scribes from one manuscript to another, or by virtue of the natural deterioration that occurs with any body of writing undergoing repeated transcriptions and metathesis. For example: Uriel, "presider over Tartarus" and "regent of the sun," shows up variously as Sariel, Nuriel, Uryan, Jehoel, Owreel, Oroiael, Phanuel, Eremiel, Ramiel, Jeremiel, Jacob-Isra'el. Derivations and/or variations of Haniel, chief of principalities and "the tallest angel in Heaven," may be set down in mathematical equations, to wit: Haniel = Anael = Anfiel = Aniyel = Anafiel = Onoel = Ariel = Simiel. The celestial *gabbai*, keeper of the treasuries of Heaven, Vretil, turns out to be the same as, or can be equated with, or is an aphetic form of, Gabriel, Radueriel, Pravuil, Seferiel, Vrevoil. In Arabic lore, Gabriel is Jibril, Jabriel, Abrael, or Abru-el, etc. In ancient Persian lore he was Sorush and Revan-bakhsh and "the crowned Bahman," mightiest of all angels. To the Ethiopians he is Gadreel.

Michael had a mystery name: Sabbathiel. He passed also for the Shekinah, the Prince of Light, the Logos, Metatron, the angel of the Lord, and as St. Peter (for Michael, also, like the prince of apostles, holds—or held—the keys of the kingdom of Heaven). In addition, as the earliest recorded slayer of the Dragon, Michael may be considered the prototype of the redoubtable St. George. To the ancient Persians he was known as Beshter, sustainer of mankind.

Raphael, "christened" Labbiel when God first formed him, is interchangeable with Apharope, Raguel, Ramiel, Azrael, Raffarel, etc. And, to make matters more complicated, our healing angel operated under a pseudonym, Azariah (as in *The Book of Tobit*). *The Zohar* equates Raphael with a king of the underworld, Bael.

The archangel Raziel, "chief of the Supreme Mysteries," and "author" of the famous *Sefer Raziel* (Book of the Angel Raziel), answers to Akraziel, Saraqael, Suriel, Galisur, N'Zuriel, and Uriel. The seraph Semyaza may be summoned up by the pronouncement of any of a string of variations on his name—Samiaza, Shemhazai, Amezyarak, Azael, Azaziel, Uzza.

Metatron, the "lesser YHWH" (i.e., the lesser God) and twin brother of Sandalphon, also had a mystery name, Bizbul. But Metatron had more than 100 other names (see Appendix) and in magical rites he could be invoked by any of them.

The leopard-bodied Camael (alias Shemuel, Simiel, Quemuel, Kemuel), while serving in Hell as a Count Palatine and ruler of the wicked planet Mars, served at the same time in Heaven as an archangel of the divine presence. It was Camael (Kemuel) who accompanied God with a troop of 12,000 spirits at the promulgation of the Holy Law. This is vouched for in legend.[5] According to another legend,[6] Camael was destroyed by Moses when he tried to hinder the Lawgiver from receiving the Torah at the hand of God.

Satan paraded under, or hid behind, a bewildering array of forms and incarnations. The "prince of the power of the air," as Paul picturesquely dubs him, is our best example of a quick-change artist in guises and appellatives. In Zoroastrian theosophy he is Ahriman, enemy of man and God, a kind of ur-Satan (since Ahriman antedates by 1,000 years the Judaeo-Christian image of a prince regent of evil). In Leviticus, he is Azazel, the "goat of the sin offering." In Isaiah he is Lucifer (or, rather, mistakenly identified as Lucifer). In Matthew, Mark, and Luke he is Beelzebub, "lord of flies." In Revelation he is "that dragon and old serpent, the Devil." He is Mastema and/or Beliar in *The Book of Jubilees* and *The Book of Adam and Eve*. He is Sammael in *Baruch III*, *The Chaldean Paraphrase of Jonathan*, and *The Martyrdom of Isaiah*. In *Enoch* he is Satanail and Salamiel. In *The Apocalypse of Abraham* and *The Zohar* he is Duma as well as Azazel. In Falasha lore he is Suriel, angel of death. And he is Beliar or Beliel in *The Testament of the Twelve Patriarchs*, *The Zadokite Fragments* (where Mastema also figures as an alternate to Beliar), and *The Sibylline Oracles*. In the Koran he is Iblis or Eblis or Haris. And in Jewish tradition he is Yetzer-hara, the personified evil inclination in man. To Shakespeare (*I Henry IV*) he is the "Lordly monarch of the north"; to Milton (*Paradise Regained* IV, 604) he is the "Thief of Paradise"; to Bunyan (*Holy War*) he is Diabolus.[7] But whatever his guise, the once familiar peripatetic of Heaven is no longer to be found there, as guest or resident; nor is it likely that the black divinity of his feet will ever again be sighted on the crystal battlements—unless he is forgiven and reinvested with his former rank and glory, an eventuality the Church forbids its followers to entertain as possible or desirable, since Satan and his angels have been cursed by the Savior Himself "into everlasting fire" (Matthew 25:41).

Hell itself, one adduces from *Enoch II*, *Testament of Levi*, and other apocryphal and pseudepigraphic works, is not located where one would ordinarily suppose it to be, i.e., in the underworld, but in the "northern regions of the 3rd Heaven," while Evil in its various aspects is lodged in the 2nd as well as the 3rd and 5th Heavens.[8] The first 3 Heavens, according to the *Baruch Apocalypse* (*Baruch III*), are "full of evil-looking monsters." In the 2nd Heaven the fallen angels (the amorous ones, those that coupled with the daughters of men) are imprisoned and daily flogged. In the 5th the dread Watchers dwell, those eternally silent Grigori "who, with their prince Salamiel, had rejected the Lord."[9] When Paul was caught up in the 3rd Heaven, he en-

5. *Rf.* Moses Schwab, *Vocabulaire de l'Angélologie*. According to Rabbi Abdimi, no less than 22,000 ministering angels descended on Mt. Sinai on this historic occasion (see *Midrash Tehillim* on Psalm 68).

6. Louis Ginzberg, *The Legends of the Jews* III, 110.

7. A recent writer, Jean Lhermitte (*True and False Possession*, 1963), holds that "The Prince of Darkness no longer appears as a personage . . . but disguises himself willingly, even preferably, under the appearance of corporate personalities or institutions."

8. C. E. S. Wood, the American poet, in his *Heavenly Discourse*, gives Satan's P.O. address as Washington, D.C. That was back in 1927. His Satanic Majesty may have moved since then.

9. This must have been in the "north of the 5th Heaven, for elsewhere in the same Heaven, whither Zephaniah claims a Spirit conveyed him, the Old Testament Prophet "beheld angels that are called Lords, and each had a crown upon his head as well as a throne shining seven times brighter than the sun"—quoted by Clement of Alexandria from the lost *Apocalypse of Zephaniah*.

countered there "angels of evil, terrible and without pity carrying savage weapons."[10] In a word, at least 3 Heavens, or regions of at least 3 Heavens, were the abode of the eternally damned.

Now, to find Hell in Heaven should not have surprised this writer, or anyone with a smattering of Greek mythology, for the paradisiacal Elysian Fields, "residence of the shades of the Blessed," are in the immediate vicinity of Hades. A rabbinic commentary (*Midrash Tannaim*) vouches for the fact that Hell and Paradise are "side by side." This is close to what one finds in a commentary on Psalm 90 (*Midrash Tehillim*) where it is stated that there were seven things which preceded the creation of the world, and that among the seven things were Paradise and Hell, and that "Paradise was on the right side of God, Hell on the left." In a commentary on Ecclesiastes (*Yalkut Koheleth*) we learn that the two realms are actually only "a hand-breadth apart." This carefully calibrated survey is attributed to the Hebrew sage, Rab Chanina (Kahana), of the late 3rd century C.E.[11]

How incongruous, indeed how anomalous it was to plant Hell in Heaven must have occurred finally to the Great Architect Himself for, one day, without fuss or fanfare, the entire apparatus of evil—the arsenals of punishment, the chief Scourgers, the apostate angels, the horned or aureoled spirits of wrath, destruction, confusion, and vengeance—was moved from the upper to the lower world, where (if it is not too presumptuous to say so) all such paraphernalia and personnel should have been installed in the first place.

The noted scholar R. H. Charles, in his introduction to Morfill's translation of *Enoch II*, observes in a footnote that "the old idea of wickedness in Heaven was subsequently banished from Christian and Jewish thought." True, and none too soon. For what assurance otherwise would the faithful have been given that, on arrival in Heaven, they would not be lodged in one of the enclaves of Hell?

Perhaps the best—or worst—example of the confusion to be found in noncanonical as well

10. The fact that in Paul's day there still were angels of evil in Heaven "carrying savage weapons" would lead one to suppose that the fighting on high did not end with Satan's rout, and that Michael and his hosts won a Pyrrhic victory, or at best a truce.

11. In this connection, the expression "Abraham's bosom" (Luke 16), interpreted as denoting "the repose of the happy in death," may be cited here. The Apostles' Creed affirms that Jesus descended to Hell after the Crucifixion, purportedly to liberate the "saints in chains" (the unbaptized patriarchs, Abraham among them) in order to transport them to Paradise. The parable in Luke presupposes that Abraham is already there; and the fact that the rich man in Hades (Dives) is able to converse with Abraham across the "great chasm" suggests that the chasm was not very wide, and that, hence, Heaven and Hell were very close to each other, at least within speaking distance. Purgatory, it will be noted, is not mentioned. The explanation is simple: it did not exist—not, anyway, until 604 C.E. Gregory the Great invented it. Perhaps invention is too strong a term. Gregory very likely appropriated the notion of an "upper Gehenna" from the ancient Jews, or from the empyrosis of the Greek stoics, or from the twelve cycles of purgation of Zoroaster. Be that as it may, Purgatory was made official—it was "legislated into existence"—by decrees at the Council of Lyons in 1274, at Florence in 1439, and again in the 1540's at the Council of Trent, and is today part of the religious belief of all or most Christians, except members of the Church of England which, in 1562, condemned Purgatory as "a fond thing vainly invented and grounded upon no warranty of Scripture, but rather repugnant to the Word of God." We know of no angels, fair or foul, inhabiting or frequenting the place. According to Origen, it is reserved for souls waiting to be purged of the "lighter materials" of their sins "so that they may enter the kingdom of Heaven undefiled." The duration of souls in Purgatory, an indefinable time, may be cut down by indulgences, prayers, and paid masses. Jews have their *Yiskor*, which is a prayer for the repose of the dead and is recited on Yom Kippur, Sukkot, Passover, and Shavuoth. Where these Jewish dead are reposing is not clear. The Moslems have their Al Aaraaf, a region for "those who are [found] neither good nor bad, such as infants, lunatics, and idiots"—*Reader's Encyclopedia*, "Araf."

as canonical lore is the case of Satan. The Old Testament speaks of an adversary, *ha-satan*. It is a term that stood for an office; it did not denote the name of an angel. To the Jews of Biblical times the adversary was neither evil nor fallen (the Old Testament knows nothing of fallen angels), but a servant of God in good standing, a great angel, perhaps the greatest. However, he is nowhere named. In Job he presents himself before the Lord in the company of other unnamed "sons of God." There is no question of his being evil or apostate.[12] The one instance where *ha-satan* is given as *satan* without the definite article (I Chronicles 21), is now generally conceded to be a scribal oversight. In a word, the Old Testament did not name its angels, except in Daniel, a late, postexilic book. There only two angels are named: Michael and Gabriel (names, by the way, that owe their origin to Babylonian-Chaldean sources). In the New Testament, on the contrary, Satan is unequivocally a person, so named. Here he is no longer the obedient servant of God, the "prime in splendour," but the castout opponent and enemy of God, the Prince of Evil, the Devil incarnate.

The transformation of *ha-satan* in the Old Testament into Satan in the New, and the conflicting notions that arose as a consequence, are pointed up by Bernard J. Bamberger in his *Fallen Angels*: "The classic expositions of the Jewish faith have implicitly or explicitly rejected the belief in rebel angels and in a Devil who is God's enemy. . . . The Hebrew Bible itself, correctly interpreted, leaves no room for a belief in a world of evil powers arrayed against the goodness of God. . . . Historical Christianity, on the other hand, has consistently affirmed the continuing conflict between God and Satan." This continuing conflict between God and Satan, one might add, is little more than a recrudescence, with modifications, of the dualistic system that Christianity (along with Jewish sectarians of the post-Biblical era) inherited from Zoroastrianism.

Equally difficult to deal with was the question whether (and how many) other spirits in the celestial hierarchy were good or evil, fallen or still upright, dwellers of Heaven or Hell. This was a specially baffling problem and left me wandering about in a perpetual cloud of unknowing. A case in point: In *Enoch I*, 6, Remiel is styled "one of the leaders of the rebel angels." Farther along in the same book, Chapter 18, Remiel is metamorphosed into "one of the seven holy ones whom God set over those who rise." In Revelation 9, Abaddon/Apollyon is the "angel of the bottomless pit," suggesting an evil spirit in the sense of a destroyer; but in Revelation 20, Abaddon/Apollyon is manifestly good and holy, for here he is said to have "laid hold on the dragon, that old serpent, who is the devil and Satan, and bound him a thousand years" (in *The Greater Key of Solomon* Abaddon is "a name for God that Moses invoked to bring down the blighting rain over Egypt"!). Vondel, the Dutch Shakespeare (1587–1678), tells us in his *Lucifer* that Apollyon was known in Heaven, before he joined Satan, as the hierarch "of the snowy wings." To Bunyan in *Pilgrim's Progress* Apollyon is an out-and-out devil, *the* devil, just as he is

---

12. The hasidic rabbi Yaakov Yitzhak of Pzysha, known as the holy Yehudi (d. 1814), makes this clear when he declared that "the virtue of angels is that they cannot deteriorate." See Martin Buber, *Tales of the Hasidim, Later Masters*, p. 231. The fact that the adversary challenges God or questions Him does not, *ipso facto*, make the adversary evil or an opponent of God—just as, when Abraham and Job "put God to the question," they were not, on that account, regarded as evil men, or even as presumptuous men. See Harry M. Orlinsky's *Ancient Israel*, p. 30.

in secular writings generally.[13] Other examples, to cite a handful: Ariel, "earth's great Lord" and an aide to Raphael in the curing of disease, is at the same time a rebel angel in charge of punishments in the lower world. Kakabel, a high holy prince who exercises dominion over the constellations, is in *Enoch* one of the apostates. The angel Usiel, Gabriel's lieutenant in the fighting on high, is designated a companion of the lustful luminaries who coupled with mortal women; in Zoharic cabala he is the cortex (averse demon) of Gog Sheklah, "disturber of all things." Among the rabbis the opinion is divided with regard to the 90,000 angels of destruction. Are they in the service of God or the Devil? *Pirke Rabbi Eliezer* inclines to the latter view. In the *Pirke* they are called "angels of Satan."

It is well to bear in mind that all angels, whatever their state of grace—indeed, no matter how christologically corrupt and defiant—are under God, even when, to all intents and purposes, they are performing under the direct orders of the Devil. Evil itself is an instrumentality of the Creator, who uses evil for His own divine, if unsearchable, ends. At least, such may be gathered from Isaiah 45:7; it is also Church doctrine, as is the doctrine that angels, like human beings, were created with free will, but that they surrendered their free will the moment they were formed. At that moment, we are told, they were given (and had to make) the choice between turning toward or away from God, and that it was an irrevocable choice. Those angels that turned toward God gained the beatific vision, and so became fixed eternally in good; those that turned away from God became fixed eternally in evil. These latter are the demons, they are *not* the fallen angels (an entirely different breed of recusants which hatched out subsequently, on Satan's defection). Man, however, continues to enjoy free will. He can still choose between good and evil. This may or may not work out to his advantage; more often than not it has proved his undoing. The best that man can hope for, apparently, is that when he is weighed in the balance (by the "angels of final reckoning"), he is not found wanting.[14]

Angels perform a multiplicity of duties and tasks. Preeminently they serve God. They do this by the ceaseless chanting of glorias as they circle round the high holy Throne. They also carry out missions from God to man. But many serve man directly as guardians, counselors, guides, judges, interpreters, cooks, comforters, dragomen, matchmakers, and gravediggers. They are responsive to invocations when such invocations are properly formulated and the conditions are propitious. In occult lore angels are conjured up not only to help an invocant strengthen his faith, heal his afflictions, find lost articles, increase his worldly goods, and procure offspring, but also to circumvent and destroy an enemy. There are instances where an angel or

---

13. In Jewish lore, abaddon is a place—sheol, the pit, or the grave; nowhere is it the name of an angel or demon. The term is personified for the first time in Revelation and appears as Abaddon (cap A). St. John makes Abaddon synonymous with Apollyon and declares it to be the Greek form of the same angel. The Confraternity edition of the New Testament adds here (Apocalypse 9:11): "in Latin he has the name Exterminans." On the other hand, *The Magus*, which offers a number of portraits of the archfiends in color, splits Abaddon and Apollyon into two separate and distinct "vessels of iniquity," showing Abaddon with tawny hair and Roman nose, Apollyon with russet beard and hooked beak.

14. According to Abbot Anscar Vonier in *The Teaching of the Catholic Church* (1964), angels still enjoy free will. This seems to be another or new interpretation of Catholic doctrine on the subject.

troop of angels turned the tide of battle, abated storms, conveyed saints to Heaven, brought down plagues, fed hermits, helped plowmen, converted heathens. An angel multiplied the seed of Hagar, protected Lot, caused the destruction of Sodom, hardened Pharaoh's heart, rescued Daniel from the lions' den, and Peter from prison. To come closer to our own times: it will be recalled that when Spinoza was "execrated, cursed, and cast out" from his community in Amsterdam for holding among other "heretical views" that "angels were an hallucination," the edict of excommunication against him was drawn up by the rabbis "with the judgment of the angels."

The might of angels, as made known to us in Targum and Talmud, is easily a match for the might of the pagan gods and heroes. Michael overthrew mountains. Gabriel bore Abraham on his back to Babylon, whither an unnamed angel later conveyed the prophet Habbakuk (by the hair) from Judea, to feed Daniel pottage.[15] Jewish legend tells us that, during the siege of the Holy City by Nebuchadnezzar, "the prince of the world" (Metatron? Michael? or perchance Satan?) lifted Jerusalem "high in the air" but that God thrust it down again.[16] We know from Revelation that seven angels of the wrath of God smote a "third part of the stars." The mighty Rabdos is able to stop the planets in their courses. The Talmudic angel Ben Nez prevents the earth from being consumed by holding back the South Wind with his pinions. Morael has the power of making everything in the visible world invisible. The Atlantean Splenditenes supports the globe on his back. Ataphiel (Barattiel), hierarch of Merkabah lore, keeps Heaven from tumbling down by balancing it on three fingers. The Pillared Angel (mentioned in Revelation) supports the sky on the palm of his right hand. Chayyiel, the divine angel-beast, can—if he is so minded—swallow the whole world in a single gulp. When Hadraniel proclaims the will of God, "his voice penetrates through 200,000 firmaments." It was Hadraniel who struck Moses "dumb with awe" when the Lawgiver caught sight of the dread luminary in the 2nd Heaven. As late as the 17th century, the German astronomer Kepler figured out (and somehow managed to fit into his celebrated law of celestial mechanics) that the planets are "pushed around by angels."

A brief word about the number of angels abroad in the world. Since the quantity, according to Church doctrine, was fixed at Creation, the aggregate must be fairly constant. An exact figure —301,655,722—was arrived at by 14th-century cabalists, who employed the device of "calculating words into numbers and numbers into words." This is a very modest figure if we regard stars as angels (just as the Apocalyptics did: John in Revelation, Clement of Alexandria in *Stromata* VI, etc.) and include them in the total.[17] Thomas Heywood in his *Hierarchy* cautions us metrically: "Of the Angels, th'exact number who/Shall undertake to tell, he shall grow/

15. See apocryphal additions to Daniel 5:86.
16. In 1291–1294 C.E., angels moved the house of the Virgin Mary from Nazareth to Dalmatia, thence to various parts of Italy, finally depositing it in the village of Loretto. The miraculous haulage is the subject of a canvas (now in the Morgan Library, New York), by the 15th–16th century artist Saturne di Gatti.
17. Rabbi Jochanan (Talmud *Hagiga* 14a) reminds us that, far from having ceased being formed at Creation, angels are born "with every utterance that goes forth from the mouth of the Holy One, blessed be He." The Jewish notion of a continuing act of Creation (as opposed to the *tota simul* doctrine of the early Church) is traditional in Talmud, and embraces not only angels but all things formed in the first six days. This is clear from a hymn found in *Greater Hechaloth* 4:2, where God is praised for not ceasing to create "new stars and constellations and zodiacal signs that flow and issue from the light of His holy garment."

From Ignorance to Error; yet we may/Conjecture." Albertus Magnus conjectured, and put "each choir at 6,666 legions, and each legion at 6,666 angels." But demons are winged horses of another color. Unlike the angels, these apes of God are capable of reproducing their kind. What is more, as Origen alerts us, "they multiply like flies." So today there must be a truly staggering horde of them. The problem of population explosion here is clearly something to worry about.[18]

As for the vernacular employed by angels, the odds favor Hebrew. In *The Book of Jubilees* and in *Targum Yerushalmi*, we learn that the language God used at Creation and in the Garden of Eden was Hebrew. Even the serpent spoke Hebrew, according to Midrash *Lekah Genesis* 31:1. So, inferentially, angels also spoke it, or speak it. The *Apocalypse of Paul* puts it precisely: "Hebrew, the speech of God and the angels." Indeed, in rabbinic lore, and in sundry secular writings, Hebrew is said to have been the language of all mankind up to the "confusion of tongues," an event that occurred at the building of the Tower of Babel in 2247 B.C.E. (as computed by Archbishop Ussher, noted 17th-century Irish theologian).[19]

That the Torah was originally conceived and set down in Hebrew is a widely postulated view among Jews, though disputed by Philo (who thought the language was Chaldean Aramaic) and by Muslims generally (who claim it was Arabic). St. Basil thought it was Syriac.[20] On the whole it is safe to say that the *lingua franca* of angels—of *all* spirits, in fact—is Hebrew. Some exegetes hold that angels, being monolingual, speak the holy tongue exclusively, not even understanding the closely related Aramaic (as specifically stated in *The Zohar* I, 92); other authorities contend differently. They point out that Gabriel, Metatron, and Zagzagel each had a knowledge of seventy languages.[21] In recent times, Sandalphon was overheard conversing in Yiddish, the eavesdropper being the storyteller Isaac Bashevis Singer. Furthermore, we have it on the word of the Swedish mystic Swedenborg that angels not only speak Hebrew, they also write it. In his *Heaven and Its Wonders and Hell*, he avers that "a little paper was sent to me from Heaven on which a few words were written in Hebrew." This remarkable document, so far as is known, was never produced for public scrutiny, nor has it ever turned up among Swedenborg's effects.

Are angels immortal? In the opinion of most scholars, yes. But are angels eternal? No. God alone is eternal.[22] Still, the life span of angels is a fairly long one, starting from the moment they were "willed into being" to the last crack of doom. But a number of angels have, mean-

18. Luther's followers, in a work entitled *Theatrum Diabolorum*, not satisfied with the then-current estimates of devils, raised the figure to 2.5 billion, later to 10,000 billion. A reassuring thought, provided by *Hagiga* 16a, is that while "demons beget and increase like men, like men they die."

19. At the Exodus and in the Wilderness, God also spoke Hamitic. He did this, it is said, in order to make Himself understood by the Egyptian Moses and by Hamitic-speaking Jews who made up the greater bulk of Moses' followers.

20. See *The Book of Adam and Eve*, p. 245.

21. Talmud *Sotah*, fol. 36, narrates that Gabriel taught Joseph seventy languages overnight. The angel Kirtabus (in Tyana's *Nuctemeron*) is described as a "genius of languages."

22. John of Damascus qualifies this by saying in his *Exposition of the Orthodox Faith*: "God alone is eternal, or rather, He is above the Eternal; for He, the Creator of times, is not under the dominion of Time, but above Time."

while, been snuffed out.[23] Thus God put an end to Rahab for refusing, as commanded, to divide the upper and lower waters.[24] God burned the angels of peace and truth, along with the hosts under them, as well as an entire legion of administering angels (*Yalkut Shimoni*), for objecting to the creation of man—a project the Creator had His heart particularly set on and was determined to carry through, although later He repented of the venture, as we learn from Genesis 6:6. God also annihilated a whole "globe of angels," the Song-Uttering Choristers, for failing to chant the Trisagion at the appointed hour. And there is the case of a mortal doing away with an immortal: Moses, who in fact did away with two of them—Kemuel (already mentioned) and Hemah. This Hemah was the angel of fury "forged at the beginning of the world out of chains of black and red fire." Legend has it that, after swallowing the Lawgiver up to the ankles, Hemah had to disgorge him at the timely intervention of the Lord. Moses then turned around and slew the vile fiend.

While there are numerous instances of angels turning into demons, as exemplified in the fall of one-third of the Heavenly hosts (Revelation 12), instances of mortals transformed into angels (named angels) are rare.[25] Four instances have come to light, three deriving from passages in Genesis and II Kings. The first relates to the patriarch Enoch, who was apotheosized into the god-angel Metatron. The second relates to the patriarch Jacob, who became Uriel, then Isra'el, "archangel of the power of the Lord" and chief tribune among the sons of God.[26] The third relates to the prophet Elijah, who drove to Heaven in a fiery chariot and, on arrival, was transformed into the angel Sandalphon.[27] The fourth instance, vouched for in *The Douce Apocalypse*, is that of St. Francis, who evolved into the angel Rhamiel.[28] Another instance is the transforming

23. The noted 12th-century Jewish poet and theologian, Judah ha-Levi (1085–1140) in his work called *The Book of Kuzari* (IV), taught that there were two classes or species of angels. He wrote: "As for the angels, some are created for the time being, out of the subtle elements of matter (as air or fire). Some are eternal (i.e., existing from everlasting to everlasting), and perhaps they are the spiritual intelligences of which the philosophers speak." He goes on to say: "It is doubtful whether the angels seen by Isaiah, Ezekiel, and Daniel were of the class of those created for the time being, or of the class of spiritual essences which are eternal." What were they then? one might ask. Saadia B. Joseph was of the opinion that they were visions seen during prophetic ecstasy rather than outward realities. In the view of St. John of Damascus (700?–754?), *Orthodox Faith*, angels are immortal, but "only by grace, not by nature."

24. This "angel of insolence and pride" had two lives. He was deprived of the first for the reason given above. Two thousand years later, resuscitated but still obdurate, he reappears at the Exodus. Here he is drowned by God for espousing the cause of the Egyptians, which, as that nation's tutelary angel, he was honor bound to do.

25. Origen's belief in a "final restitution," when God would forgive all his sinning creatures, even the most damned, opened the door to a return of Satan to his archangelic perch in the Heavenly purlieus. Because of this heretical belief Origen, it is said, was never canonized.

26. *Prayer of Joseph.*

27. Elijah-Sandalphon became the celestial psychopomp "whose duty it was," says *Pirke R. Eliezer*, "to stand at the crossways of Paradise and guide the pious to their appointed places."

28. According to Jewish tradition, all patriarchs, along with those who led exceptionally virtuous lives, attained angelic rank when they got to Heaven. This, however, has been disputed: "the belief that the souls of the righteous after death become angels has never been part of Jewish thought" (*Universal Jewish Encyclopedia* I, 314). That it was at one time part of patristic thinking can be deduced from Theodotus (*Excerpts*) to the effect that "those who are changed from men to angels are instructed for a thousand years by the angels, after they are brought to perfection" and that then "those who have been taught are translated to archangelic authority."

of Anne, the Virgin's mother, into the angel Anas (*q.v.*). Mention might also be made here of three Biblical psalmists—Asaph, Heman, and Jeduthun—who showed up in Heaven, with their earthly names and occupations unchanged, as celestial choirmasters.

Regarding the sex or gender of angels, I was often hard put to arrive at any conclusion in the matter, even with the help of scholars. True, angels are pure spirits and so should be presumed to be bodiless and, hence, sexless.[29] But the authors of our sacred texts were not logicians or men of science; in the main, they were prophets, lawgivers, chroniclers, poets. They did not know how to represent invisible spirits other than by giving them visible, or tangible, embodiment: accordingly, they pictured angels in their own image (i.e., in the guise of men), acting and talking and going about their business—the Lord's business—the way men do.[30] Angels in Scripture, as a consequence, were conceived of as male.[31] However, it was not long before the female of the species began putting in an appearance. In early rabbinic as well as in occult lore, there are quite a number of them: the Shekinah, for one. She was the "bride of God," the divine *inwohnung* in man, who dwelt with lawfully wedded couples and blessed their conjugal union. There was Pistis Sophia ("Faith/Wisdom"), a high-ranking gnostic aeon, said to be the "pro-creator of the superior angels." There was Barbelo, consort of Cosmocrator, a great archon, "perfect in glory and next in rank to the Father-of-All." There was Bat Qol, the "heavenly voice" or "daughter of the voice" of Jewish tradition, a prophetess symbolized as a dove, who gave warnings and counsel when the days of prophecy were over. Another female power that comes to mind is the gnostic Drop or Derdekea. According to the *Berlin Codex*, Drop used to descend to earth on critical occasions "for the salvation of mankind." And there were the six left-side emanations of God, created to counterbalance the ten male emanations that issued from God's right side.[32] And finally there was the vixen Eisheth Zenunim, angel of prostitution and mate of Sammael. In Hebrew, *eisheth zenunim* means "woman of whoredom" and the epithet applied with equal force to three other wives of Sammael: Lilith, Naamah, Agrat bat Mahlah.

29. In theology there are three classifications of spirit: (1) God, Who is divine spirit; (2) angels and demons, who are pure spirits; and (3) man, who is impure spirit.

30. In *The Zohar* (Vayera 101a) we read: "When Abraham was still suffering from the effects of the circumcision, the Holy One sent him 3 angels, in visible shape, to enquire of his well-being." And the text goes on to say: "You may perhaps wonder how angels can ever be visible, since it is written, 'Who makes his angels spirits' (Psalms 104:4). Abraham, however, assuredly did see them, as they descended to earth in the form of men. And, indeed, whenever the celestial spirits descend to earth, they clothe themselves in corporeal elements and appear to men in human shape." But it is difficult to reconcile the foregoing with the statement in *The Book of Jubilees* (15:27) that "all the angels of the presence and all the angels of sanctification" were already circumcised when they were created. On the issue of the materiality of angels, authorities have been divided. Those who believe that angels are composed of matter and form include Alexander of Hales, Bernard of Clairvaux, St. Bonaventura, Origen. Those who hold, to the contrary, that angels are incorporeal include Dionysius the Areopagite, John of Rochelle, Moses Maimonides, Maximus the Confessor, and William of Auvergne.

31. The Koran 53:27: "Those who disbelieve in the Hereafter [are those who] name the angels with the names of females."

32. In the texts of the early commentators, Moses of Burgos and Isaac Ben R. Jacob ha-Cohen, as in the supplement to *The Zohar*, there are also ten evil emanations (male), of which "only seven were permitted to endure." See Appendix.

This free-loving quartet constituted a kind of composite Jewish equivalent of the Sidonian Astarte.

Zoroastrianism, which was not averse to including females in its pantheon, had its Anahita, a lovely luminary characterized as "the immortal one, genius of fertilizing waters." Offsetting her was Mairya, evil harbinger of death, represented indiscriminately as male and female. She (or he) tempted Zoroaster with the kingdoms of the earth, just as, in Matthew 4, Satan tempted Jesus. Another angel of indeterminate sex was Apsu. In Babylonian-Chaldean mythology, Apsu was the "female angel of the abyss"; but, though female, she fathered the Babylonian gods and was at the same time the husband or wife of Tamat. She (or he) was slain finally by her (his) son Ea. A true *tumtum*![33] It seems, also, according to *Genesis Rabba* and confirmed by Milton in *Paradise Lost* I, 423–424, that angels, at least some of them, were able to change their sex at will. *The Zohar* (Vayehi 232b) phrases it this way: "Angels, who are God's messengers, turn themselves into different shapes, being sometimes female and sometimes male."

To revert to the question as to whether angels have an existence outside Holy Writ, or apart from the beliefs and testimony of visionaries, fabulists, hermeneuts, ecstatics, etc. Such a question has been a debatable one from almost the start, even before the down-to-earth Sadducees repudiated them and the apocalyptic Pharisees acknowledged and espoused them. Aristotle and Plato believed in angels (Aristotle called them intelligences). Socrates, who believed in nothing that could not be verified by (or was repugnant to) logic and experience, nevertheless had his *daimon*, an attendant spirit, whose voice warned the marketplace philosopher whenever he was about to make a wrong decision.[34] Now, to invent an angel, a hierarchy, or an order in a hierarchy, required some imagination but not too much ingenuity. It was sufficient merely to (1) scramble together letters of the Hebrew alphabet; (2) juxtapose such letters in anagrammatic, acronymic, or cryptogrammatic form; (3) tack on to any place, property, function, attribute, or quality the theophorous "el" or "irion." Thus Hod (meaning splendor, like zohar) was transformed into the angel Hodiel. Gevurah (meaning strength) burgeoned into the angel Gevurael or Gevirion. Tiphereth (meaning beauty) provided the basis for the sefira Tipherethiel. The lords of the various hierarchic orders came into being in similar fashion, Cherubiel becoming the eponymous chief of the order of cherubim; Seraphiel, the eponymous chief of the order of seraphim; Hashmal, of the hashmallim, etc. Countless "paper angels" or "suffix angels," many of them unpronounceable and irreducible to intelligent listing, were thus fabricated; they passed, virtually unchallenged, into the religious and secular literature of the day, to be accredited after a while as valid. In some cases they were given canonical or deuterocanonical status. The practice preempted no one from begetting *ex nihilo* and *ad infinitum* his

33. *Tumtum* is a Talmudic term for any spirit whose sex could not be easily determined. See M. Jastrow, *Dictionary of the Targumin, Talmud Babli and Yerusalmi*, and the *Midrashim Literature*.
34. In the Middle Ages, the most eminent scholars and divines ranged themselves on opposite sides of the question. And that is perhaps still true today; a belief in angels is part of the doctrine of three of the four major faiths—Christian (mainly Catholics), Jewish (mainly orthodox), Mohammedan.

own breed of angels, and putting them into orbit.[35] The unremitting industry of early cabalists in creating angels spilled over into the raiding of pagan pantheons, and transforming Persian, Babylonian, Greek, and Roman divinities into Jewish hierarchs. Thus the kerubim of the ancient Assyrians—those huge, forbidding stone images placed before temples and palaces—emerge in Genesis 3 as animate cherubim, guardian angels armed with flaming swords east of Eden and, later, in upper Paradise, as charioteers of God (after Ezekiel encountered them at the River Chebar). The Akkadian lord of Hell, the lion-headed Nergal, was converted into the great, holy Nasargiel, and in this acceptable guise served Moses as cicerone when the Lawgiver visited the underworld. Hermes, the good *daimon*, inventor of the lyre and master of song in Greek mythology, became in Jewish lore the angel Hermesiel and identified with David, "sweet singer of Israel." The rabbinic Ashmedai derived from the zend Aeshmadeva. Etc., etc.

The Church, let it be said to its credit, tried to call a halt to the traffic, although the Church itself at one time recognized a considerable number of angels not in the calendar, and even permitted them to be venerated.[36] Scripture, as we have seen, gives the names of no more than two or three angels. That there may well be seven named angels in Scripture is the subject of a paper by this compiler; it is a thesis on which, admittedly, no two theologians are likely to agree.

In the "orthodox" count, fixed by the 6th-century pseudo-Dionysius (otherwise known as Dionysius the Areopagite),[37] there are nine orders in the celestial hierarchy. But there are other "authoritative" lists provided by sundry Protestant writers that give seven, nine, twelve orders, including such rarely encountered ones as flames, warriors, entities, seats, hosts, lordships, etc. The Dionysian sequence of the orders, from seraphim to angels (a sequence for which there is no Biblical warrant, and which Calvin summarily dismissed as "the vain babblings of idle men") has likewise been shuffled about, some sources ranking seraphim last (rather than first), archangels second (rather than eighth), virtues seventh (rather than fourth or sixth), and so on.[38]

Miracles, feats of magic, heavenly visitations, and overshadowings are often ascribed to

35. Isaac de Acco (13th–14th century), a disciple of Nahmanides, "laid claim to the performance of miracles by a transposition of Hebrew letters according to a system he pretended to have learned from the angels." See A. E. Waite, *The Holy Kabbalah*, p. 53.

36. Certain early theologians like Eusebius (c. 263–c. 339) and Theodoret (c. 393–c. 458) opposed the veneration of angels, and a Church council at Laodicea (343–381?) condemned Christians "who gave themselves up to a masked idolatry in honor of the angels." This, despite the fact that St. Ambrose (339?–397) exhorted the faithful, in his *De Viduis*, 9, to "pray to the angels, who are given to us as guardians." In the 8th century, at the 2nd Council of Nicaea (787), there was another change of heart, for the worship of angelic beings was then formally approved. The practice, nevertheless, seems to have fallen into disuse. Today there is a trend in some ecclesiastical circles to revive it. The Dominican priest Pie-Raymond Régamey, author of *What Is an Angel?* (1960), thinks that veneration of angels is not a bad thing, but warns against the "danger of such devotion becoming superficial."

37. The time that Dionysius lived and wrote has never been satisfactorily determined. Originally his writings were attributed to one of the judges of the Greek *areopagus* (court), whom Paul converted (Acts 17:34). But scholars, finding such dating untenable, moved the time ahead to the 6th century. However, according to a French legend cited by A. B. Jameson (*Legends of the Madonna*), "Dionysius the Areopagite was present at the death of the Virgin Mary," which would place him back in the 1st century. The legend relates that "Dionysius stood around the bier beside the twelve apostles, the two great angels of death (Michael and Gabriel), and a host of lamenting lesser angels."

38. *Cf.* varying sequences of the ninefold hierarchy offered by Augustine (*City of God*), Gregory the Great (*Homilia* and *Moralia*), Isidore of Seville (*Etymologiarum*), Bernard of Clairvaux (*de consideratione*), Edmund Spenser (*An Hymne of Heavenly Beautie*), Drummond of Hawthornden (*Flowres of Sion*), etc.

different angels.[39] Thus, the three "men" whom Abraham entertained unawares have been identified as God, Michael, and Gabriel; also, according to Philo, as the Logos, the Messiah, and God. In Matthew, the news of Mary being found with child of the Holy Ghost is conveyed to her spouse Joseph by the "angel of the Lord"; in Luke it is Gabriel who does the announcing—not to Joseph but direct to Mary who, however, seems to know nothing of the matter. The overnight destruction of the army of Sennacherib, numbering 185,000 men, ascribed in II Kings to the "angel of the Lord," has been laid to the prowess of Michael, Gabriel, Uriel, or Remiel. No one has yet, to the knowledge of this investigator, identified the specific "angel of the Lord" whom David saw "standing between the earth and the heaven, having a drawn sword in his hand stretched over Jerusalem" (I Chronicles 2:16). A good guess would be Michael, for that battle-ax of God, when he is not in Heaven assisting Zehanpuryu or Dokiel in the weighing in of souls, is busy on earth lopping off the heads of the unfaithful.[40]

In their hurried exodus from Egypt, and in their encounter with Pharaoh's horsemen at the Red (Reed) Sea, the Hebrews were helped by "the angel of God, which went before . . . and behind them . . . in a pillar of fire and cloud" (Exodus 14). Here the identity of the angel of God poses no problem: he was Michael or Metatron, each the tutelary prince-guardian of Israel. However, Michael or Metatron did not fight alone: he had the aid of a swarm of "ministering angels who began hurling [at the pursuing or retreating Egyptians] arrows, great hailstones, fire, and brimstone."[41] Present also, it is reported, were hosts of "angels and seraphim, singing songs of praise to the Lord," which must have helped considerably in turning the tide of battle. On the enemy side, harrying the Hebrews, was the guardian angel of Egypt, once holy but now corrupt. It appears though that Egypt had more than one guardian angel—four in fact, and that they all showed up, armed to the teeth. Various sources identify them as Uzza, Rahab, Mastema. and Duma. The fate of Rahab we know: he was drowned, along with the Egyptian horsemen. Mastema and Duma went back to Hell, where they had unfinished business to attend to. As for Uzza, some authorities say he was actually Semyaza, grandfather of Og, a leader of the fallen angels; and that since the Red Sea episode, and after his unfortunate affair with the maiden Ishtahar (immortalized in song by Byron), he hangs head down between Heaven and earth in the neighborhood of the constellation Orion. Indeed, Graves and Patai in their *Hebrew Myths* say that Semyaza is merely the Hebrew form for the Greek Orion.

39. Miracles and magic were not always frowned upon by the Church, despite Jesus' exhortation against signs and wonders as a basis for belief (John 4:48). When Pico della Mirandola (1463–1494) declared that "no science yields greater proof of angels, purgatory, hellfire, and the divinity of Christ than magic and the Kabbalah," Pope Sixtus IV "was delighted and had the Kabbalah translated into Latin for the use of students of divinity" (Albert C. Sundberg, Jr., in *The Old Testament of the Early Church*, Harvard Theological Studies, 1964). However, a commission appointed by a succeeding pope, Innocent VIII, condemned at least ten of Pico's theses as "rash, false, and heretical." This seems to have been the attitude of the Church thereafter, the cabala being proscribed as a Jewish system of black magic, the "laboratory of Satan."

40. Tractate Beshallah, *Mekilta de Rabbi Ishmael*, vol. 1, p. 245.

41. Martin Buber, *Tales of the Hasidim, Later Masters*, chapter on Rabbi Yaakov of Sadagora. While God, naturally, rejoiced over the victory of His Chosen People, He did not like to see His angels crowing over it. Thus, the Talmudists describe God as silencing an angelic chorus that chanted hallelujahs when the Egyptian hosts met with disaster, by crying out: "How dare you sing in rejoicing when my handiwork [i.e., the Egyptians] is perishing in the sea!" [*Rf.* Ben Zion Bokser, *The Wisdom of the Talmud*, p. 117.]

Jacob's antagonist at Peniel was God, as Jacob himself finally figured out when day broke (Genesis 32:30). But our learned rabbis, after pondering the text, have concluded that the antagonist was not God but an angel of God, and that he was either Uriel, Gabriel, Michael, Metatron, or even Sammael, prince of death.[42]

When Enoch was translated to Heaven, his angelic guide, according to Enoch's own testimony, was Uriel. But later on in the same book (*Enoch I*) Uriel turns out to be Raphael, then Raguel, then Michael, then Uriel all over again. Apparently they were the same angel, for Enoch throughout speaks of "the angel that was with me." But perhaps it is too much to expect Enoch to be consistent. He is, as we have seen, notoriously unreliable. True, we do not have his original scripts, or even early copies; the writings accredited to him have come down to us in a hopelessly corrupt form, much of it clearly "doctored" to conform to the views of interested parties. Still it is hard to believe he was a clear thinker or accurate reporter, although he purports to have been an eyewitness in many of the incidents he describes.

The habitat of angels proved equally perplexing. In the opinion of Aquinas, angels cannot occupy two places at the same time (theoretically it would not be impossible for them, being pure spirits, to do so). On the other hand, they can journey from one place to another, however far removed, in the twinkling of an eye. In angelology, one comes upon instance after instance where an angel is a resident of, or presider over, two or three Heavens simultaneously. Thus, in *Hagiga* 12b, Michael is the archistratege of the 4th Heaven. Here he "offers up daily sacrifice." But Michael is also governor of the 7th and 10th Heavens. As for Metatron, he is reputed to occupy "the throne next to the throne of Glory," which would fix his seat in the 7th Heaven, the abode of God. But we find Metatron, like Michael, a tenant of the 10th Heaven, the *primum mobile*, which is likewise the abode of God—when, that is, God is not in residence in the 7th.

Gabriel, lord of the 1st Heaven, has been glimpsed sitting enthroned "on the left-hand side of God (Metatron's throne, then, must be on God's right).[43] This would indicate that Gabriel's proper province is not the 1st but the 7th or 10th Heaven (it was in the 10th Heaven that Enoch beheld "the vision of the face of the Lord"). However, according to Milton in *Paradise Lost* IV, 549, Gabriel is chief of the angelic guard placed over Paradise, and Paradise being in the 3rd Heaven, we should, accordingly, find the enthroned Annunciator camping out there.

Logically, one should look for Shamshiel, prince of Paradise,[44] in zebul or sagun (the 3rd Heaven) where Azrael, suffragan angel of death, lodges, next to the Tree of Life. But some

42. There are any number of princes or angels of death. Prominent among them, besides Sammael, are Kafziel, Kezef, Satan, Suriel, Yehudiam, Michael, Gabriel, Metatron, Azrael, Abaddon/Apollyon. They are all under orders from God. When they fail to accomplish their mission, as in the case of Moses who refused to give up the ghost, then God Himself acts as His own angel of death. According to legend (Ginzberg, *The Legends of the Jews* III, 473), after God used His best arguments to persuade the aged Lawgiver that he would be better off dead than alive, and the Lawgiver still proving stubborn, God descended from Heaven (in the company of Michael, Gabriel, and Zagzagel) and "took Moses' soul with a kiss" (Jude 9). The legend goes on to say that God then buried Moses, but "in a spot that remained unknown, even to Moses himself."
43. It is here also "on the right hand of God the Father Almighty" that Jesus sits, according to the Apostles' Creed.
44. Other princes of Paradise include Johiel, Zephon, Zotiel, Michael, Gabriel.

sources place Shamshiel in charge of the 4th Heaven (also called zebul).[45] On the other hand, if we go by *The Book of Jubilees*, Shamshiel is chief of the Watchers, and so properly he would be overseeing the 2nd or 5th Heaven, where the Watchers dwell, "crouched in everlasting despair." Furthermore, in the guise of Shemuiel (the archonic warden who stands at the windows of Heaven "listening for the songs of praise ascending from synagogues and houses of study below"), Shamshiel would be posted at the portal of the 1st Heaven. Which leaves Shamshiel where? Obviously, in an emergency, it would be difficult to locate him.

A final instance: Zagzagel or Zagzagael, prince of the Torah, "angel with the horns of glory," is the celestial guard of the 4th Heaven—let us bear in mind that Shamshiel is already in charge at this level—and Zagzagel, being at the same time seneschal of the 7th Heaven, his stewardship of the 4th Heaven poses a knotty problem. Confusion without end! One is constrained to cry out, with the dying Goethe: "More light!"

A contemporary of the great Hillel, Ben Hai Hai (identified with another noted rabbi of his day, Ben Bag Bag) used to say: "According to the labor is the reward."[46] Goethe in *Faust*, part 6, comforts his readers with a similar maxim: "Kühn das Mühen, herrlich der Lohn"— "Daring the labor, lordly the reward."

If there is any reward for the labor of compiling this Dictionary, it is in the knowledge that every effort has been made to keep the sins of commission and omission down to a minimum (and no one knows better than the author how many sins may be committed in the course of such a work). There are still many problems left unresolved here. This is due either to the inaccessibility of much of the extant material in the field or to its indecipherability, or because the wit and wisdom to provide the solutions were wanting. Future investigators, better equipped, for whom some of the underbrush has been cleared away, may be able to provide the solutions, along with the names of additional angels that no doubt will turn up in new finds. I might interpose here (to paraphrase Rabbi Nathan's famous dictum, "He who preserves a life preserves a world") that the preserving of a single angel—not one of the "suffix" creatures—is like preserving a whole hierarchy. The task certainly is not an easy one, but it may prove easier than the one confronting this voyager when he started out on his quest, primed with only the scantiest notion of the labor that lay ahead.

A good way to conclude this *Apologia pro libro suo* is to quote from a recently published paper on the guise of angels. It was there intimated that "in view of the continuing hold of the supernatural over the minds of men, and the fact that a belief in the existence of angels (and demons) is an article of faith with two of our major world religions, and part of the tradition of at least four of them (Persian, Jewish, Christian, Muslim), it is highly probable that we shall have the wingèd creatures with us for a long, long time to come." True, we may not always know whether we are in the presence of "a spirit of health or goblin damned," whether we are being fanned by "airs from Heaven or blasts from Hell," but it is best to be on guard. Even Satan, as Paul cautioned us, can show himself transformed into an angel of light.

45. In Peter de Abano, *Heptameron*, zebul is also a designation for the 6th Heaven.
46. *Pirke Aboth*, chapter 5, mishna 26.

ACKNOWLEDGMENTS

In the course of compiling this Dictionary, I availed myself of the counsel, knowledge, and help of a host of friends. Some read early versions of the text; others were generous with the loan of books; still others brought to my attention sources of information I might otherwise not have known. To all such, my gratitude and thanks. Appreciating the fact that a list of persons to whom one is indebted is hardly ever complete, I ask indulgence of those whose names are here omitted, not through any conscious act of mine, but by virtue of a faulty memory—a malady from which, I gather, many human beings suffer.

From almost the beginning, two scholars encouraged and sustained me; also, on occasion, rescued me from exegetical pitfalls: Dr. Harry M. Orlinsky, professor of Bible at Hebrew Union College–Jewish Institute of Religion, New York, and Dr. Abraham Berger, chief of the Jewish Division, New York Public Library. In acknowledging my indebtedness to these distinguished colleagues and friends, I absolve them at the same time of responsibility for any errors, oversights, theological sins, indefensible assumptions or conclusions of which I may be guilty, and which are apt to occur in a work of this kind and extent, despite every effort at rooting them out. The responsibility is solely mine. I cheerfully shoulder it. And I leave it to Hamlet's "angels and ministers of grace" to defend me.

In the Oriental Division of the New York Public Library where I was (and still am) a frequent visitor, I benefited greatly from the friendly interest and wide-ranging knowledge of Francis Paar and Zia U. Missaghi (Ray Lord). They were unsparing of their time and help. In the Rare Book Room and in the quarters of the Berg Collection at the same institution I found the directors and the staff members equally knowledgeable, obliging, and helpful.

Gershom Scholem of the Hebrew University, Jerusalem, in response to my inquiries as to the identity of the right and left emanations of God (the sefiras), generously provided me with their names, along with the sources where I might come upon them (the 16th-century texts of Jacob and Isaac ha-Cohen of Soria). I am extremely grateful to Dr. Scholem. I am grateful to Dr. Solomon Zeitlin of Dropsie College, Philadelphia, for trying to "authenticate" the seven archangels "that stand and enter before the glory of the Lord" (*The Book of Tobit*). I am indebted to Prof. Theodor H. Gaster of Columbia University for his interesting observations on the angel Suriel; and to Prof. Bruce M. Metzger of Princeton for making clear his views on Jeremiel and Uriel as being the same angel under different names. I am equally under obligation to Dr. Meir Havazelet of Yeshiva University, New York, who culled angels for me from the minor midrashim and who did not hesitate to ring me up in the middle of the night to spell out the names of winged creatures he had suddenly come across (in hechaloth or Merkabah lore) and which, he feared, I might have overlooked.

I would be remiss if I did not speak here of the help accorded me by the late H. D. (Hilda Doolittle), noted American poet long resident abroad. She was an avid reader in esoterica; also a devout believer in angels, whom she invoked by name and apostrophized in song. From Zurich, where she made her home for many years until her recent death, she sent me rare books in practical cabala "for our mutual benefit." Our friendship, though brief and late in coming, I count among my most cherished memories.

Perhaps this would be a good place to make general acknowledgment to editors, authors, publishers, heads of libraries and museums, custodians or owners of works of art, for permitting the use of illustrations over which they hold the right of reproduction. Specific acknowledgment is made throughout the Dictionary where such illustrations appear. And, for their friendly cooperation, help, patience, and indulgence, I am happy to record my gratitude to the editorial and production staffs of The Free Press and The Macmillan Company.

This would be a good place also to speak of the unwavering interest, devotion, and faith in my work on the part of my wife Mollie, who proved to be at all times my severest critic (hence, my best friend). To her I owe and acknowledge a debt of gratitude which I know I shall never be able fully to discharge.

And now, without interruption, a roster of those many others who, over the years, in greater or lesser degree, and perhaps without themselves being aware of having done so, enlivened and enhanced my labors, if only through a chance remark, an apt quotation, the verification of a date or the title of a book. Here then they are, from *A* to *Y*:

John Williams Andrews, Professor Charles Angoff, Oscar Berger, Rabbi Ben Zion Bokser, Josephine Adams Bostwick, Edmund R. Brown, Eric Burger, Vera and Eduardo Cacciatore, Herbert Cahoon, Leo Cherne, Thomas Caldecot Chubb, Frank E. Comparato, Miriam Allen De Ford, Eugene Delafield, Arto DeMirjian, Jr., Dr. Alfred Dorn, Alexis Droutzkoy, Dan Duffin, Richard Ellis, Prof. Morton S. Enslin, John Farrar, Emanuel Geltman, Dr. Jivko Ghelev, Louis Ginsberg, Dean Loyd Haberly, the late Prof. Moses Hadas, Geoffrey Handley-Taylor, Hector Hawton, Prof. Abraham Joshua Heschel, Richard Hildebrand, Calvin Hoffman, Arthur A. Houghton, Jr., James Houston, W. Carter Hunter, Sulamith Ish-Kishor, Jeremiah Kaplan, Abraham Eli Kessler, John Van E. Kohn, Surya Kumari, Myra Reddin Lalor, Isobel Lee, Dr. Elias Lieberman, Dr. Gerhard R. Lomer, Eugenia S. Marks, Prof. Alfeo Marzi, Samuel Matza, Edward G. McLeroy, Gerard Previn Meyer, Martha Mood, Prof. Harry Morris, Kay Nevin, Rabbi Louis I. Newman, Louise Townsend Nicholl, Hugh Robert Orr, Jane Blaffer Owen, Mrs. Lori P. Podesta, Jane Purfield, Prof. Joseph Reider, Mrs. R. S. Reynolds, Sr., Rossell Hope Robbins, Leighton Rollins, Liboria Romano, Sylvia Sax, Howard Sergeant, Robert Sargent Shriver, Jr., Isaac Bashevis Singer, Chard Powers Smith, the late Prof. Homer W. Smith, Sidney Solomon, Prof. Walter Starkie, Rabbi Joshua Trachtenberg, Prof. Joseph Tusiani, Valery Webb, Charles A. Wagner, Vivienne Thaul Wechter, Prof. Robert H. West, John Hall Wheelock, Estelle Whelan, Basil Wilby, Claire Williams, Prof. Harry A. Wolfson, Dr. Amado M. Yuzon.

A'albiel—an angel in the service of the archangel Michael. [*Rf.* M. Gaster, *Wisdom of the Chaldeans.*]

Aariel ("lion of God")—the name of an angel found inscribed on an Ophitic (gnostic) amulet alongside the name of the god Ialdabaoth (*q.v.*). [*Rf.* Bonner, *Studies in Magical Amulets.*]

Aba—an angelic luminary concerned with human sexuality and who may be invoked in cabalistic magical rites. Aba serves as a ministering angel to Sarabotes (who is Friday ruler of the angels of the air). [*See* Abalidoth. *Rf.* de Abano, *The Heptameron*; Barrett, *The Magus*; Masters, *Eros and Evil.*]

Ababaloy—an angel invoked in Solomonic incantation operations. Ababaloy is mentioned in the black-magic manual, *Grimorium Verum.*

Abachta (Abagtha)—in rabbinic writings, one of the 7 angels of confusion, the other 6 being Barbonah (Harbonah), Bigtha, Carcas, Biztha, Mehuman, and Zether. Abachta is also numbered among the "pressers of the winepress." [*Rf.* Ginzberg, *The Legends of the Jews* IV, 374.]

Abaddon (Abbadon, the "destroyer")—the Hebrew name for the Greek Apollyon, "angel of the bottomless pit," as in Revelation 9:10; and the angel (or star) that binds Satan for 1,000 years, as in Revelation 20. *The Thanksgiving Hymns* (a copy of which turned up among the recently discovered Dead Sea scrolls) speaks of "the Sheol of Abaddon" and of the "torrents of Belial [that] burst into Abaddon." The 1st-century apocryphon *The Biblical Antiquities of Philo* speaks of Abaddon as a place (sheol, hell), not as a spirit or demon or angel. In *Paradise Regained* (IV, 624) Milton likewise employs Abaddon as the name of a place, i.e., the pit. As far as is known, it was St. John, who first personified the term to stand for an angel. In the 3rd-century *Acts of Thomas*, Abaddon is the name of a demon, or of the devil himself—which is how Bunyan regards him in *Pilgrim's Progress*. According to Mathers, *The Greater Key of Solomon*, Abaddon is a name for God that Moses invoked to bring down the blighting rain over Egypt. The cabalist Joseph ben Abraham Gikatilla denominates Abaddon as the 6th lodge of the 7 lodges of Hell (arka), under the presidency of the angel Pasiel (*q.v.*). Klopstock in *The Messiah* calls

1

Abaddon "death's dark angel." A reference to Abaddon's "hooked wings" occurs in Francis Thompson's poem "To the English Martyrs." [*See* Apollyon.] Abaddon has also been identified as the angel of death and destruction, demon of the abyss, and chief of demons of the underworld hierarchy, where he is equated with Samael or Satan. [*Rf.* De Plancy, *Dictionnaire Infernal;* Grillot, *A Pictorial Anthology of Witchcraft, Magic and Alchemy*, p. 128.] In the latter work, Abaddon is the "Destroying Angel of the Apocalypse." In Barrett, *The Magus*, Abaddon is pictured, in color, as one of the "evil demons."

Abadon—a term for the nether world (see Abaddon). The spelling here (with one 'd') is from *The Zohar* (Deuteronomy 286a).

Abagtha [Abachta]

Abalidoth—a celestial luminary who, like the angel Aba (*q.v.*), is concerned with human sexuality. Abalidoth is a minister-angel serving King Sarabotes, Friday ruler of the angels of the air. [*Rf.* Barrett, *The Magus* II; Masters, *Eros and Evil*.]

Abalim (Arelim)—an order of angels known in Christian angelology as thrones. The equation is put thus in *The Magus*. "Thrones, which the Hebrew call Abalim, that is, great angels, mighty and strong." The chief intelligences (i.e., angels) of the order are Zaphkiel and Jophiel (*qq.v.*).

Aban—in ancient Persian lore, Aban is (or was) the angel of the month of October. He governed also the 10th day of that month. [*Rf.* Hyde, *Historia Religionis Veterum Persarum*.]

Abariel—in ceremonial magic tracts, an angel used for invoking. The name Abariel is found inscribed on the 2nd pentacle of the moon. [*Rf.* Mathers, *The Greater Key of Solomon*.]

Abaros [Armaros]

Abasdarhon—supreme ruling angel of the 5th hour of the night. [*Rf.* Waite, *The Lemegeton*.]

Abathur Muzania (Abyatur)—in Mandaean cosmology, the *uthra* (angel) of the North Star. He presides over the scales in which the human soul is weighed at the death of the body. *Cf.* Ashriel and Monker (the latter, the Mohammedan black angel), both credited with performing a similar task. [*Rf.* Drower, *The Mandaeans of Iraq and Iran*.]

Abay—an angel of the order of dominations (dominions), invoked in cabalistic conjuring rites.

Abbadon [Abaddon]

Abbadona—a fallen angel, a seraph, at one time the chosen companion of the faithful Abdiel (*q.v.*). In Klopstock, *The Messiah*, Canto 21, Abbadona, not wholly committed to the rebellion and constantly bemoaning his apostasy, is called "the penitent angel." It should be pointed out, however, that a fallen angel cannot repent—not, at least, in Catholic doctrine—for once an angel sins, he is "fixed eternally in evil" and his mind, accordingly, can think evil only.

Abbaton—a name of God or of a holy angel employed in Solomonic conjurations to command demons. [*Rf.* Mathers, *The Greater Key of Solomon*.] The word has the meaning of death and, in this sense, Abbaton is Death and a guardian spirit in Hell. [*Rf.* the Coptic *Book of the Resurrection of Christ by Bartholomew the Apostle*, segments of which are quoted by M. R. James in *The Apocryphal New Testament*.]

Abdals ("the substitutes")—in Islamic lore, the name given to 70 mysterious spirits whose identities are known to God alone, and through whose operations the world continues to exist. When one of these divine entities dies (the Abdals are not, apparently, immortal), another is secretly appointed by God to replace him. Of the 70, two score reside in Syria. (*Cf.* "The Just" in Jewish folklore, and the Lamas of India.)

Abdia ("servant")—the name of an angel that appears on the external circle of the pentagram of Solomon. Abdia is listed in Figure 156 in Waite, *The Lemegeton*. The listing of an angel in a book of black magic does not mean necessarily that he is evil. Many good and great angels are so listed; also, many good and great angels are in Hell, stationed there to serve God's purpose—just as there are evil angels in certain quarters in Heaven (the grigori, for example).

Angel with the Key of the Abyss by Albrecht Dürer. Gravure on wood, in the Bibliothèque Nationale. The angel is Abaddon/Apollyon. From Willi Kurth, *The Complete Woodcuts of Albrecht Dürer*. New York: Dover Publications, 1963.

Abdiel ("servant of God")—the earliest traceable reference to Abdiel as an angel is in *The Book of the Angel Raziel*, a Jewish cabalistic work of the Middle Ages written in rabbinic Hebrew, the authorship credited to Eleazor of Worms. In *Paradise Lost* V, 805, 896, Abdiel is the "flaming seraph" who routs Ariel, Arioc, and Ramiel (rebel angels among Satan's hosts) on the first day of fighting in Heaven. Satan himself reels from Abdiel's "mighty sword stroke." Milton hails the seraph as "faithful only hee; among innumerable false, unmov'd,/Unshak'n, unseduc'd" (896–897). West in *Milton and the Angels*, p. 124, states that Abdiel as an angel was invented by Milton; however, on p. 154, Professor West correctly points out that Abdiel is to be found in *The Book of the Angel Raziel* (*op. cit.*). In the Bible (I Chronicles), Abdiel is not the name of an angel but of a mortal, a Gedite, a resident of Gilead. This is doubtlessly the original source for the name. Abdiel figures as an angel in Anatole France's fictional *The Revolt of the Angels*. Here Abdiel is known as Arcade.

Abdizriel (Abdizuel)—in the cabala, one of 28 angels ruling the 28 mansions of the moon. [*Rf.* Barrett, *The Magus.*] For the names of all 28 angels, *see* Appendix.

Abedumabal (Bedrimulael)—in the goetic tract *Grimorium Verum*, an angel invoked in magical prayer.

Abel ("meadow")—souls on arrival in Heaven are judged by Abel, who is one of 12 powers engendered by the god Ialdabaoth (*q.v.*). He is also of the angels of the 4th Heaven ruling on Lord's Day and invoked from the east. In *The Testament of Abraham* 13:11, Abel is the angel "before whom every soul must appear for judgment after Enoch, the heavenly scribe, fetches the book containing the record of the soul in question." [*Rf.* Doresse, *The Secret Books of the Egyptian Gnostics*; Barrett, *The Magus* II.]

Abelech (Helech)—in occult lore, a name of God or of an angel invoked to command demons. [*Rf.* Mathers, *The Greater Key of Solomon.*]

Abezi-Thibod ("father devoid of counsel")—in early Jewish lore, Abezi-Thibod is another name for Samael, Mastema, Uzza, and other chief devils. He is a powerful spirit who fought Moses in Egypt, hardened Pharaoh's heart and assisted Pharaoh's magicians. He was drowned (with Rahab, *q.v.*) in the Red (i.e., Reed) Sea. With Rahab, he shares the princedom over Egypt. In *The Testament of Solomon* (*Jewish Quarterly Review*, London, 1889, XI), Abezi is the son of Beelzeboul (Beelzebub) and the demon of the Red Sea: "I am a descendant of the archangel," he declares.

Abheiel—one of the 28 angels ruling the 28 mansions of the moon.

Abiou—corresponding angel of Eiael (*q.v.*).

Abiressia—in gnostic lore, Abiressia is one of 12 powers engendered by the god Ialdabaoth. [*See* Abel. *Rf.* Doresse, *The Secret Books of the Egyptian Gnostics* II.]

Ablati—in Solomonic magical tracts, an angel invoked in the Uriel conjurations. He is "one of four words God spoke to his servant Moses," the other 3 words being Josta, Agla, and Caila. [*Rf. Grimorium Verum*; Shah, *The Secret Lore of Magic*; Waite, *The Book of Ceremonial Magic.*]

Aboezra—an angel so named in *The Book of Ceremonial Magic*—"the most holy Aboezra." He is invoked in the benediction of the Salt, as prescribed in the *Grimorium Verum*.

Abracadabra ("I bless the dead")—one of 3 holy names invoked in the conjuration of the Sword. The word is one of the most ancient in magic; it derives, so it is said, from the Hebrew "ha brachah dabarah" ("speak the blessing"). As an amulet or charm, inscribed on parchment, it was hung around the neck to ward off disease. The invocant, when chanting the word, reduced it letter by letter until he had only the final "A" left. [*See* Abraxas.]

Abrael [Abru-El]

Abragateh—a spirit or angel invoked in Solomonic prayer by the Master of the Art. [*Rf.* Mathers, *The Greater Key of Solomon.*]

Abramus [Abrimas]

Abrasiel—an angel of the 7th hour of the day, operating under the rulership of Barginiel. [*Rf.* "The Pauline Art" in Waite, *The Book of Ceremonial Magic,* p. 67.]

Abraxas (Abraxis, Abrasax, etc.)—in gnostic theogony, the Supreme Unknown; in Persian mythology, the source of 365 emanations. The name Abraxas is often found engraved on gems and used as an amulet, or for incantation. In the cabala, he is the prince of aeons. He is encountered in *The Sword of Moses, The Book of the Angel Raziel,* and other tracts of magic and mysticism. According to the older mythographers, Abraxas is, or was, a demon, and placed with the Egyptian gods. The word "abracadabra" is reputedly derived from Abraxas. Originally it was a word expressing, in the gnostic system, the aeons or cycles of creation; in a deeper sense, it served as a term for God. The gnostic writer Basilides, who is said to have invented Abraxas, according to Forlong, *Encyclopedia of Religions,* claims that Abraxas was the archon-ruler of 365 Heavens, and acted as mediator between the animate creatures of the earth and the godhead. [See pictorial representation of a cock-headed Abraxas in Budge, *Amulets and Talismans,* p. 208.]

Abrid—in occult lore, an angel of the summer equinox, effective especially as an amulet against the evil eye. [*Rf.* Trachtenberg, *Jewish Magic and Superstition,* p. 139, where Abrid is listed with half a dozen other *memunim,* i.e., deputy angels.]

Abriel—one of the angels of (or formerly of) the order of dominations, invoked in cabalistic rites. [*Rf. The Sixth and Seventh Books of Moses.*]

Abrimas—an angel invoked at the close of the Sabbath. [*Rf.* Trachtenberg, *Jewish Magic and Superstition,* p. 139.]

Abrinael [Abrunael]

Abru-El ("power of God")—the Arab equivalent for Gabriel. [*Rf.* Forlong, *Encyclopedia of Religions.*]

Abrunael—one of the 28 angels ruling over the 28 mansions of the moon. *See* Appendix for a list of all 28 ruling angels.

Absinthium—the Latin form for Wormwood (*q.v.*).

Abtelmoluchos [Temeluch]

Abuhaza—in occultism, an angel ministering to Arcan, the latter being ruler of the angels of the air on Monday. He is subject to the West Wind. [*Rf.* Barrett, *The Magus.*]

Abuionij—in *The Sixth and Seventh Books of Moses,* and other occult works, an angel serving in the 2nd Heaven.

Abuiori (Abuioro)—in ritual magic, a Wednesday angel resident in either the 2nd or 3rd Heaven (according to different sources). He is to be invoked from the north. [*Rf.* de Abano, *The Heptameron;* Barrett, *The Magus* II.]

Abuliel—in Jewish occult lore, the angel in charge of the transmission of prayer. He is mentioned in Joffe and Mark, *Great Dictionary of Yiddish Language* I. Since he is not mentioned in Margouliath, *Malache Elyon* (Heavenly Angels), or in any of the hechaloth tracts that have so far come to light, or in Trachtenberg, *Jewish Magic and Superstition,* or in any of Gershom Scholem's works, Abuliel cannot be regarded as an angel of great importance. The supreme angels of prayer are Akatriel, Metatron, Raphael, Sandalphon, Michael, and Sizouze. It is possible that Abuliel assisted one of the foregoing.

Abuzohar—one of the angels of the moon, serving on Monday and responsive to invocations in ritual magic. [*Rf. Les Admirables Secrets d'Albert le Grand.*]

Acclamations—according to Robert Fludd in his *Utriusque cosmi majoris et minoris historia,* the acclamations are one of 3 primary angelic hierarchies, each hierarchy being subdivided into 3 secondary hierarchies. Fludd calls the other 2 primary hierarchies voices and apparitions.

Accusing Angel, The—usually the accusing angel is the adversary (*ha-satan*), as in Job. He is also Sammael or Mastema (*q.v.*). The hasidic

Rabbi Zusya, in referring to *Pirke Aboth* (Sayings of the Fathers), recalls the dictum that "every sin begets an accusing angel."

Achaiah ("trouble")—in the cabala, one of 8 seraphim; he is the angel of patience and the discoverer of the secrets of nature. His corresponding angel is Chous. For Achaiah's sigil, see Ambelain, *La Kabbale Pratique*, p. 260. In the New Testament, Achaiah is a Roman province. Paul visited the churches in that region (Acts 18:12, 27).

Achamoth—one of the aeons, and a daughter of Pistis Sophia (*q.v.*). In Ophitic gnosticism, Achamoth is the mother of the evil god Ildabaoth. [*Rf.* King, *The Gnostics and Their Remains.*]

Achartiel and **Achathriel**—angelic names found inscribed on oriental charms (*kameoth*) for warding off evil. [*Rf.* Schrire, *Hebrew Amulets.*]

Achazriel—an angel who serves as usher in the celestial court. [*Rf. Deuteronomy Rabba.*]

Acheliah—an angel whose name is found inscribed on the 1st pentacle of the planet Venus. [*Rf.* Mathers, *The Greater Key of Solomon.*]

Achides—this angel has his name inscribed on the 3rd pentacle of the planet Venus. [*Rf.* Shah, *The Secret Lore of Magic*; Mathers, *The Greater Key of Solomon.*]

Achsah—a spirit of benevolence invoked in prayer by the Master of the Art in Solomonic conjurations. [*Rf.* Mathers, *The Greater Key of Solomon.*]

Achtariel [Akatriel]

Achusaton—one of 15 throne angels listed in *The Sixth and Seventh Books of Moses*. For the names of all 15, *see* Appendix.

Aciel—one of the 7 underworld planetary sub-rulers, called Electors by Cornelius Agrippa, serving under the overlordship of the angel Raphael. [*Rf.* Conybeare, *The Testament of Solomon.*]

Aclahaye—genius of gambling; also one of the genii of the 4th hour. [*Rf.* Apollonius of Tyana, *The Nuctemeron.*]

Acrabiel—an angel governing one of the signs of the zodiac. [*Rf.* Agrippa, *Three Books of Occult Philosophy* III.]

Adabiel—in *The Hierarchy of the Blessèd Angels*, one of the 7 archangels. Probably another form for Abdiel (*q.v.*). Adabiel has dominion over the planet Jupiter (other sources give Mars). He is sometimes equated with Zadkiel, or even with the king of Hades, Nergal.

Adad—in Assyro-Babylonian mythology, the divinity of thunder; also "lord of foresight." [*Rf.* Huyghe, *Larousse Encyclopedia of Mythology*, p. 59.]

Adadiyah—one of the more than 100 names of Metatron.

Adam ("man")—in *The Book of Adam and Eve* I, 10, Adam is called "the bright angel." In *Enoch II*, he is a "second angel." When he was created, Adam reached from "the earth to the firmament," according to the midrash *Bereshith Rabba*. In the cabala, Adam is the 6th sephira Tiphereth (meaning "beauty"), according to Pistorius. Adam's dust, declared Rabbi Meier, was gathered from all parts of the earth. Talmud records that Adam was originally androgynous and the exact image of God (Who was likewise conceived as androgynous). The story in *The Apocalypse of Moses* is that Adam was whisked to Heaven by Michael in a fiery chariot. Another legend is that he was fetched from Hell by Jesus and transported to Heaven along with the other "saints in chains." Still another legend, recounted in the *Revelation of Moses* (Ante-Nicene Fathers Library, 8) is that Adam was buried by 4 angels—Uriel, Gabriel, Raphael, Michael. In Mathers, *The Kabbalah Unveiled*, the 10 sefiroth, in their totality, represent or constitute the archetypal man, Adam Kadmon.

Adam's Angel [Raziel]

Adatiel—an air spirit invoked in ritual magic. In the goetic tract the *Black Raven*, Adatiel is pictured as habited in a "billowing black-and-white mantle," but in the *Magia* [*Rf.* Butler, *Ritual Magic*] he is pictured in a "billowing blue mantle."

Adeo—an angel of the order of dominations, according to *The Sixth and Seventh Books of Moses.* Adeo is invoked in magical rites.

Adernahael (Adnachiel?)—this angel was given by God a magical formula, set down in an Ethiopian amulet, for the cure of colic and stomach trouble. [*Rf.* Budge, *Amulets and Talismans,* p. 186.]

Adhaijijon—an angel of the Seal, invoked in conjuring rites. [*Rf. The Sixth and Seventh Books of Moses.*]

Adhar—one of the many names of the angel Metatron (*q.v.*).

Adiel—in hechaloth lore (*Ma'asseh Merkabah*), an angelic guard of the 7th heavenly hall.

Adimus—at a church council in Rome in 745 C.E., Adimus was one of a half-dozen reprobated angels, the others including Uriel (sic), Raguel, Simiel. The bishops who invoked these angels, or approved their veneration, were excommunicated. [*Rf.* Heywood, *The Hierarchy of the Blessèd Angels.*]

Adir (Adiri, Adiron, Adi)—an angel invoked in conjuring operations by a progressive shortening of his name; also one of the many names for God. [*See* Adiririon.]

Adirael ("magnificence of God")—one of the 49 spirits (once exalted) now serving Belzebud, sub-prince of Hell. [*Rf.* Mathers, *The Book of the Sacred Magic of Abra-Melin the Mage,* p. 108.]

Adiram—an angel invoked in the benediction or exorcism of the Salt. [*Rf. Grimorium Verum.*]

Adiriah—an angel resident in the 7th Heaven. [*Rf.* Margouliath, *Malache Elyon.*]

Adiriel—an angel resident in the 5th Heaven, according to *The Zohar.* [*See* Adiririon.]

Adirir(i)on (Adir, Adriron)—angelic chief of "the might of God;" also a name for God. Adiririon is invoked as an amulet against the evil eye. He is said to be a guard stationed at one of the halls or palaces of the 1st Heaven. According to Margouliath, *Malache Elyon,* Adiririon may be equated with Adiriel [*Rf.* Scholem, *Major Trends in Jewish Mysticism;* Trachtenberg, *Jewish Magic and Superstition.*] In *Sefer Raziel* (The Book of the Angel Raziel), Adirion or Adiririon is a "trusty healing-God, in whose hands are the Heavenly and earthly households."

Adityas—the shining gods of the Vedic pantheon, consisting of 7 celestial deities or angels, with Varuna as chief. The other 6 are: Mithra, Savitar, Bhaga, Indra, Daksha, Surya. [*Rf.* Gaynor, *Dictionary of Mysticism;* Redfield, *Gods/A Dictionary of the Deities of All Lands.*]

Adjuchas—genius of the rocks; also one of the genii of the 11th hour. [*Rf.* Apollonius of Tyana, *The Nuctemeron;* Levi, *Transcendental Magic.*]

Admael—one of the 7 archangels with dominion over the earth. Admael is stationed, for the most part, in the 2nd Heaven. [*Rf. Jewish Encyclopedia,* "Angelology."]

Adnachiel (Advachiel, Adernahael)—angel of the month of November, with rulership over the sign of Sagittarius. Adnachiel alternates with Phaleg as a ruling angel of the order of angels. [*Rf.* Heywood, *The Hierarchy of the Blessèd Angels;* Barrett, *The Magus;* Budge, *Amulets and Talismans;* De Plancy, *Dictionnaire Infernal;* Camfield, *A Theological Discourse of Angels.*)

Adnai ("pleasure")—an angel whose name is found inscribed on a pentacle of the planet Venus. [*Rf.* Mathers, *The Greater Key of Solomon;* Shah, *The Secret Lore of Magic.*]

Adnarel ("my lord is God")—in Enoch writings, one of the angelic rulers of one of the seasons (usually winter). [*See* Narel.]

Adoil ("hand of God")—a primordial essence or divine creature of light summoned out of the invisible depths and who, at God's command, burst asunder. This occurred (according to *Enoch II*) at the time Enoch was being shown around the 10 Heavens. Out of Adoil issued all things visible in the world. The name Adoil does not appear elsewhere than in *Enoch II.* R. H. Charles sees here a modification of the egg theory of the universe in ancient Egyptian myth.

Adonael—in *The Testament of Solomon*, one of the 7 archangels and the only angel who is able to overcome the demons of disease, Bobel (Bothothel) and Metathiax. [*Rf. 3 Enoch*.]

Adonaeth—by appealing to the angel Adonaeth, the demon Ichthion (who causes paralysis) can be routed. [*Rf.* Shah, *The Secret Lore of Magic*.]

Adonai (Adonay, "God")—one of the 7 elohim or angels of the presence (creators of the universe) in Phoenician mythology. Adonai is also an angel invoked in the conjuration of Wax (in Solomonic magic operations) and in exorcisms of fire. In Ophitic gnosticism, Adonai is one of 7 angels generated by Ildabaoth "in his own image." [*Rf.* King, *The Gnostics and Their Remains*.] In the Old Testament, Adonai is another word for God, as "When I have mercy on the world, I am Adonai."

Adonaios (Adonaiu, Adoneus)—in the Ophitic (gnostic) system, one of the 7 archons or potentates that constitute the Hebdomad, rulers of the 7 Heavens; also one of the 12 powers engendered by the god Ialdabaoth. [*Rf.* Origen, *Contra Celsum*; Doresse, *The Secret Books of the Egyptian Gnostics*.]

Adoniel—in Waite, *The Lemegeton*, a chief officer angel of the 12th hour of the night, serving under Sarindiel. His name is found inscribed on the 4th pentacle of the planet Jupiter, along with the name of the angel Bariel. The pentacle is reproduced in Mathers, *The Greater Key of Solomon*, plate IV.

Adossia (fictional)—a supervising archangel in Gurdjieff's cosmic myth, *All and Everything, Beelzebub's Tales to his Grandson.*

Adoth—in *The Sixth and Seventh Books of Moses*, a cherub or seraph used in conjuring rites.

Adoyahel—in the cabala, a ministering throne angel. He is one of 15, as listed in *The Sixth and Seventh Books of Moses*. For the names of all 15, *see* Appendix.

Adrael ("my help is God")—an angel serving in the 1st Heaven. [*See* Adriel.]

Adrai—in Mathers, *The Greater Key of Solomon*, an angel invoked in the conjuration of Ink and Colors.

Adram[m]elech[k] ("king of fire")—one of 2 throne angels, usually linked with Asmadai (*q.v.*). In demonography, Adramelech is 8th of the 10 archdemons; a great minister and chancelor of the Order of the Fly (Grand Cross), an order said to have been founded by Beelzebub. According to the rabbis, Adramelech manifests, when conjured up, in the form of a mule or a peacock. In Seligmann, *History of Magic*, he is pictured in the shape of a horse. In II Kings 17:31, Adramelech is a god of the Sepharvite colony in Samaria to whom children were sacrificed. He has been equated with the Babylonian Anu and with the Ammonite Moloch. In *Paradise Lost*, Milton refers to Adramelech as an "idol of the Assyrians" (the name here deriving from Assyrian mythology), and in the same work—*Paradise Lost* VI, 365, Adramelech is a fallen angel overthrown by Uriel and Raphael in combat. In Klopstock, *The Messiah*, Adramelech is "the enemy of God, greater in malice, guile, ambition, and mischief than Satan, a fiend more curst, a deeper hypocrite." See picturization in Schaff, *A Dictionary of the Bible*, p. 26, where Adramelech is shown bearded and winged, with the body of a lion. De Plancy, *Dictionnaire Infernal* (1863 ed.), shows him in the form of a mule with peacock feathers.

Adrapen—a chief angel of the 9th hour of the night, serving under Nacoriel. [*Rf.* Waite, *The Lemegeton*.]

Adriel ("my help is God")—one of the 28 angels ruling the 28 mansions of the moon. Adriel is also one of the angels of death, according to Heywood, *The Hierarchy of the Blessèd Angels*, wherein, it is claimed, he will "in the last days slay all souls then living." In *Ozar Midrashim* II, 316a and 317, Adriel is one of the angelic guards of the gates of the South Wind (also of the East Wind).

Adrigon—one of the many names of Metatron (*q.v.*).

Aduachiel [Adnachiel]

Infant angel by Titian. Reproduced from Régamey, *Anges.*

Advachiel [Adnachiel]

Aebel—one of 3 ministering angels (the other 2 were Shetel and Anush) whom God appointed to serve Adam. According to *Yalkut Reubeni* and *The Book of Adam and Eve*, the 3 angels "roasted meat" for Adam and even "mixed his wine."

Aeglun—genius of lightning and one of the genii of the 11th hour. [*Rf.* Apollonius of Tyana, *The Nuctemeron.*]

Aehaiah—one of the 72 angels bearing the mystical name of God Shemhamphorae. [*Rf.* Barrett, *The Magus* II.]

Aeon—in gnosticism, the aeon is a celestial power of a high order. It is a term used to designate the 1st created being or beings, with Abraxis as head; also, as an emanation of God, to be compared with the sefira (*q.v.*). Since Creation there have been, according to Basilides, 365 aeons (other sources give 8, 12, 24 and 30), chief among them, apart from Abraxis, being the female personification of wisdom (Pistis Sophia) and the male personification of power (Dynamis). Prior to the 6th century and the Dionysian hierarchic system, the aeons were counted among the 10 angelic orders; they were personalized by the 3rd-century Hippolytus thus: Bythios, Mixis, Ageratos, Henosis, Autophyes, Hedone, Akinetos, Nonogenes, and Macaria. As far back as the 1st and 2nd centuries C.E., Ignatius Theophorus, in his *Epistles to the Trallians*, spoke of the "mightiness of the aeons, the diversity between thrones and authorities, the preeminence of the seraphim." "The aeons," says W. R. Newbold in "Descent of Christ in the Odes of Solomon" (*Journal of Biblical Literature*, December 1912), "are the hypostatized thoughts of God," emanated in pairs, male and female, and, "taken together form the pleroma or fullness of God." There is a myth of a proud aeon (probably Abraxis) who mirrored himself on chaos and became lord of the world. Early in life, George William Russell, the Irish poet and mystic, decided to sign his writings, "Aeon." A proofreader, who could not decipher the word, queried "AE?" Russell adopted the initials and thereafter never wrote under his own name. [*Rf.* King, *The Gnostics and Their Remains*; Mead, *Fragments of a Faith Forgotten*; George William Russell (AE), *The Candle of Vision.*]

Aeshma—the basis for Asmodeus (*q.v.*). In Persian myth, Aeshma is one of the 7 archangels (i.e., amesha spentas). The name is drawn, in turn, from the Zend Aeshmo daeva (the demon Aeshma).

Angels by Dürer, detail from *Mass of St. Gregory.* Woodcut reproduction, title page of Jean Danielou, *The Angels and Their Mission.*

Aetherial Powers—a term for angels in *Paradise Regained* I, 163.

Af ("anger")—one of the angels of destruction, a prince of wrath, and a ruler over the death of mortals. With Hemah (*q.v.*), Af once swallowed Moses up to his "circumcised membrum," but had to disgorge him when Zipporah (Moses' wife) circumcised her son Gershom, thus appeasing God's wrath against the Lawgiver who had, it appears, overlooked the covenantly rite. Af resides in the 7th Heaven and is 500 parasangs tall. He is "forged out of chains of black and red fire." [*Rf.* *The Zohar*; Ginzberg, *The Legends of the Jews* II, 308, 328; *Midrash Tehillim*.]

Afafiel—in hechaloth lore (*Ma'asseh Merkabah*), an angelic guard stationed at the 7th heavenly hall.

Afarof [Afriel]

Af Bri—an angel who favors the people of Israel; he exercises control over rain. (*Cf.* Matarel.) [*Rf.* Margouliath, *Malache Elyon*.]

Affafniel—a wrathful angel, prince of 16 faces (4 on each side of his head) that constantly change their aspect. [*Rf.* *The Book of the Angel Raziel*.]

Afkiel—in hechaloth lore (*Ma'asseh Merkabah*), an angelic guard stationed at the 5th heavenly hall.

Afriel (Afarof)—an angel of force (power?) who may be Raphael in another guise. [*Rf.* Montgomery, *Aramaic Incantation Texts from Nippur*; Schwab, *Vocabulaire de l'Angélologie*.] In *The Testament of Solomon*, Afarof is reputed to possess the power of thwarting the machinations of the demon Obizuth, a female destroyer of children.

Afsi-Khof—an angel who governs the month of Av (July–August), as listed in Schwab, *Vocabulaire de l'Angélologie*.

Aftemelouchos—according to a legend told in the *Falasha Anthology*, an angel of torment who, in Heaven, carries a fork of fire on the river of fire. [*Rf. Apocalypse of Paul*.]

Aftiel—in rabbinic lore, the angel of twilight. He is mentioned in Schwab, *Vocabulaire de l'Angélologie*.

Agad—in Ambelain, *La Kabbale Pratique*, an angel of the order of powers. In one of her poems "Sagesse," the poet H.D. (Hilda Doolittle) mentions Agad.

Agaf—an angel of destruction invoked in ceremonial rites at the close of the Sabbath. [*Rf.* Trachtenberg, *Jewish Magic and Superstition*.]

Agalmaturod—in Waite, *The Greater Key of Solomon*, "a most holy angel of God" invoked in magical operations.

Agares (Agreas)—once of the order of virtues, Agares is now a duke in Hell, served by 31 legions of infernal spirits. He manifests in the form of an old man astride a crocodile and carrying a goshawk. He teaches languages and can cause earthquakes. His sigil is shown in Waite, *The Book of Black Magic and of Pacts*, p. 166. According to legend, Agares was one of the 72 spirits Solomon is reputed to have shut up in a brass vessel and cast into a deep lake (or banished to "lower Egypt").

Agason—an angelic spirit invoked in Solomonic conjurations as "thy Most Holy Name Agason." [*Rf. Grimorium Verum*.]

Agathodaemon—in gnosticism, "the seven-voweled serpent [seraph], the Christ." Derived from the Egyptian serpent Agathodaimon, the good spirit, as opposed to Kakadaimon, the evil spirit. Agathodaemon has also been designated a guardian angel or genius and identified with Hermes, "the bringer of good, the angel standing by the side of Tyche." [*Rf.* Harrison, *Epilogomena to the Study of Greek Religion*, p. 296; De Plancy, *Dictionnaire Infernal*; Spence, *An Encyclopaedia of Occultism*; Blavatsky, *The Secret Doctrine*.]

Agbas—in hechaloth lore (*Ma'asseh Merkabah*), an angelic guard stationed at the 4th heavenly hall.

Agiel—an angel's name found inscribed on the 1st pentacle of the planet Mercury. According to Paracelsus' doctrine of Talismans, Agiel is the presiding intelligence (i.e., spirit, angel) of the planet Saturn, acting in concert with the spirit Zazel. [*Rf.* Christian, *The History and Practice of Magic* I, 318.]

exorcism of demons. In addition, Agla is a name of God that Joseph invoked when he was delivered from his brothers. Agla is a combination of the 1st letters of the 4 Hebrew words meaning "Thou art forever mighty, O Lord" (*atha gadol leolam Adonai*). [*Rf.* Mathers, *The Greater Key of Solomon*; Waite, *The Book of Black Magic and of Pacts*; De Plancy, *Dictionnaire Infernal.*]

Agmatia—an angel of unknown origin, mentioned in Scholem, *Jewish Gnosticism, Merkabah Mysticism, and Talmudic Tradition.*

Agniel—in *The Zohar* (Tikkun suppl.), the 4th of the 10 unholy sefiroth.

Agrat bat Mahlat—an angel of prostitution, one of the 3 mates of Sammael (*q.v.*). The other 2 mates are Lilith and Naamah.

Agreas [Agares]

Agromiel—an angelic guard of the 6th Heaven. [*Rf. Ozar Midrashim*, I, 116.]

Aha—an angel of the order of dominations; a spirit of fire used in cabalistic magical operations. [*Rf. The Sixth and Seventh Books of Moses.*]

Ahabiel—in Montgomery, *Aramaic Incantation Texts from Nippur*, an angel invoked in love charms.

Ahadiel—an angelic enforcer of the law, as noted in Margouliath, *Malache Elyon*. [*Cf.* Akriel.]

Ahadiss—an angel who exercises dominion over the month of Heschwan (October–November). [*Rf.* Schwab, *Vocabulaire de l'Angélologie.*]

Ahaha—an angel of the Seal, used in conjuring. [*Rf. The Sixth and Seventh Books of Moses.*]

Ahaij—in *The Sixth and Seventh Books of Moses*, a spirit of the planet Mercury, summoned up in ritual magic.

Ahamniel—one of the chief angel-princes appointed by God to the Sword. [*Rf.* M. Gaster, *The Sword of Moses*, XI.]

Ahaniel—one of the 70 childbed amulet angels, as listed in Margouliath, *Malache Elyon*. [*Rf.*

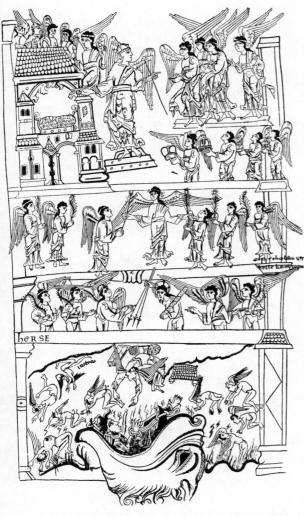

Expulsion of Lucifer from heaven. A Caedmon paraphrase. Reproduced from J. Charles Wall, *Devils.*

Agkagdiel—in hechaloth lore (*Ma'asseh Merkabah*), an angelic guard stationed at the 7th heavenly hall.

Agla—in the cabala, an angel of the Seal invoked in conjurations of the Reed; also, a spirit invoked in Monday conjurations addressed to Lucifer. In rites of exorcism, Agla is called on by lot, and here he is a magic word of power for the

The Book of the Angel Raziel; Budge, *Amulets and Talismans*.]

Ahariel—angelic ruler of the 2nd day, serving under Gabriel. [*Rf.* Margouliath, *Malache Elyon*.]

Ahassior—angelic ruler of the month of Tebet (December–January). [*Rf.* Schwab, *Vocabulaire de l'Angélologie*.]

Ahaviel—an angel's name found inscribed on an oriental Hebrew charm (kamea) for warding off evil. [*Rf.* Schrire, *Hebrew Amulets*.]

Ahiah (Hiyyah)—son of the fallen angel Semyaza (*q.v.*). [*Rf.* Ginzberg, *The Legends of the Jews* III, 340.] It should be pointed out that while angels, being pure spirits, cannot propagate their kind, fallen angels, being corrupt and demonic, are able to do so.

Ahiel ("brother of God")—one of the 70 childbed amulet angels, an assistant to the angel Qaphsiel (Kafsiel), ruler of the 7th day. [*Rf. The Book of the Angel Raziel*.]

Ahjma'il—in Arabic lore, a guardian angel invoked in rites of exorcism. [*Rf.* Hughes, *A Dictionary of Islam*, "Angels."]

Ahriman (Ariman, Aharman, Dahak, Angro-Mainyus, etc.)—the Persian prince of evil, prototype of the Christian Satan. According to Zoroaster, who was tempted by the archfiend but came off triumphant from the encounter, it was Ahriman who brought death to the world by virtue of slaying the prototype of man and beasts. [*Rf.* Forlong, *Encyclopedia of Religions*.] Ahriman was not entirely evil until Sassanid times. The Magi once sacrificed to Ahriman. He is coeval with Ahura Mazda and equally supreme in power, but will be overcome in the end by the great Persian "omniscient lord of heaven and earth."

Ahura [Asuras]

Ahzariel—an angel's name found inscribed on an oriental charm (*kamea*) for warding off evil. [*Rf.* Schrire, *Hebrew Amulets*.]

Aiavel—one of the 72 angels governing the signs of the zodiac. For the names of all 72 angels, *see* Appendix.

Aiel—an angel of the air, ruler on Lord's Day (Sunday), governor of one of the 12 zodiacal signs (Aries). He is a resident of the 4th Heaven and must be summoned from the north. He is one of the "fiery triplicities." [*Rf.* de Abano, *The Heptameron*; Waite, *The Lemegeton*.]

Ailoaios—in gnostic lore, ruler of the 2nd gate "leading to the aeon of the archons." [*See* invocation to Ailoaios in the writings of Origen, reproduced in Legge, *Forerunners and Rivals of Christianity* II, 73.]

Aishim ("the flames")—according to *The Zohar*, the aishim constitute an order of angels. The term is derived from Psalms 104:4: "who maketh his angels spirits, his ministers a flaming fire." [*See* Is(c)him.]

Aisthesis (Thelesis, "free will")—in gnosticism, a great luminary emanated from the divine will.

Akae ("oath")—according to M. Gaster, *Logos Ebraikos and the Book of Enoch*, the word Akae stands for the "ineffable name of God, the knowledge of which gives man the power of acting almost like one of the superior beings." *See* also Kasbeel, "chief of oaths." In *Enoch I* (69:14) the angel Kasbeel "places this oath Akae in the hand of Michael." It is through the power and secrets of this oath that "the sea was created and the earth founded upon the water."

Akat(h)riel Yah Yehod Sebaoth (Achtariel, Aktriel, Ketheriel, Yehadriel)—one of the great crown judgment princes placed over all the other angels. He is equated with the "angel of the Lord," a term frequently used in the Old Testament for the Lord Himself. Elisha ben Abuya, one of the 4 sages that visited Heaven during their lifetime, reported: "When I ascended into Paradise, I beheld Akatriel JHWH, Lord of Hosts, at the entrance, and 120 myriads of ministering angels surrounded him." Cabalistically, Akatriel is the name of the godhead as manifested on the throne of Glory. In an 8th-century apocalyptic tract dealing with Akatriel, Metatron appears once or twice in Akatriel's place. [*Rf.* Talmud *Berachoth* 7a; Cordovero, *Pardes Rimmonim*; Scholem,

Jewish Gnosticism, Merkabah Mysticism, and Talmudic Tradition.]

Aker—one of the 9 angels who will rule or judge "at the end of the world," according to the *Revelation of Esdras*. [*Rf. Ante-Nicene Fathers Library*, vol. 8, p. 573. For the names of the 8 angels, *see* Angels at the World's End.]

Akram(m)achamarei—in the Coptic *Pistis Sophia*, this spirit is 1st among a triad "standing high in the gnostic hierarchy of deities; master of the heavenly firmaments," and is invoked in magical rites, as revealed in a "curse" tablet reproduced by Bonner in *Studies in Magical Amulets*. Scholem, *Jewish Gnosticism, Merkabah Mysticism, and Talmudic Tradition*, p. 95, believes that Akramachamarei, because of his depiction as a sun god, "could be interpreted as a representation of the angel Ariel."

Ak(h)raziel ("herald of God")—probably another form of Raziel or Galizur (*q.v.*). Akraziel is the angel of proclamation; also guard of the last gate in Heaven. He is the angel who revealed to Adam the divine mysteries. When Moses' death was sealed and the Lawgiver pleaded for longer life, God bade Akraziel announce that Moses' prayer was not to ascend to Heaven. [*Rf.* Ginzberg, *The Legends of the Jews* III, 419.]

Akriel—angel of barrenness. Akriel is appealed to in cases of stupidity; also when reciting verses from Deuteronomy. [*Rf.* Margouliath, *Malache Elyon*; Trachtenberg, *Jewish Magic and Superstition*.]

Akteriel [Akathriel]—a great angel who, according to a Lurian but un-Jewish legend [*Rf.* Bamberger, *Fallen Angels*], was summoned by Sandalphon to reveal to him how Sammael, prince of evil, and the latter's hosts could be subdued. Nothing fruitful came of the mission even though Akteriel had the benefit of the advice of Metatron (twin brother of Sandalphon), who accompanied Akteriel. In a word, the overcoming of evil, or of the prince of evil, was not something that angels, even the greatest of them, could accomplish.

Akzariel—an angel's name found inscribed on an oriental charm (*kamea*) for warding off evil. [*Rf.* Schrire, *Hebrew Amulets*.]

Alaciel (fictional) [Nectaire]

Alad—a title applied to Nergal, lord of the dead. [*Rf.* Jobes, *Dictionary of Mythology Folklore and Symbols*.]

Aladiah—one of the 72 angels bearing the name of God Shemhamphorae. [*Rf.* Barrett, *The Magus* II.]

Alaliyah—one of the many names of the angel Metatron (*q.v.*).

Alamaqanael—one of the numerous angelic guards of the gates of the West Wind. [*Rf. Ozar Midrashim* II, 316.]

Alat—in hechaloth lore (*Ma'asseh Merkabah*), an angelic guard stationed at the 7th heavenly hall.

Alazaion—"a most holy angel of God" invoked in magical rites, especially in the conjuration of the Reed. [*Rf.* Mathers, *The Greater Key of Solomon*; Waite, *The Book of Ceremonial Magic*.]

Albim—an angelic guard of the gates of the North Wind. [*Rf. Ozar Midrashim* II, 316.]

Albion's Angel—an angel, not otherwise named, in Blake's painting "Breach in the City—in the Morning after Battle," which serves as frontispiece for the poet-painter's *Visions of the Daughters of Albion*. According to Hagstrum, *William Blake, Poet and Painter*, Albion's Angel is a "personification of the Tory Establishment under George III, or the Poetic Genius in an age of arid classicism and aristocratic art." For reproduction of Albion's Angel, see *Fogg Museum Bulletin*, vol. X (November 1943). Albion is an ancient name of England.

Albrot—one of 3 holy names (of God or angels) invoked in the conjuration of the Sword. [*Rf. Grimorium Verum*.]

Alcin—one of numerous angelic guards stationed at the gates of the West Wind, as cited in *Ozar Midrashim* II, 316.

Repose in Egypt with Dancing Angels by Vandyck. Reproduced from Anna Jameson, *Legends of the Madonna.*

Alfatha—an angel with dominion over the north. [*Rf. Gospel of Bartholomew* in James, *The Apocryphal New Testament.*] For other angels who exercise dominion over the north, *see* Gabriel, Chairoum.

Alimiel—one of the intelligences or chora (i.e., angels) of the first altitude. He is one of 5, the other 4 being Gabriel, Barachiel, Ledes, Helison. [*Rf.* Shah, *The Secret Lore of Magic*; Waite, *The Almadel of Solomon.*] In *Ozar Midrashim*, Alimiel is one of the 7 guards of the curtain or veil of the 7th Heaven. He is equated with Dumahel.

Alimon—in Mosaic incantation rites, a great angel prince who, when invoked, protects the invocant from gunshot wounds and from sharp instruments. His aides are the angels Reivtip and Tafthi. [*Rf. The Sixth and Seventh Books of Moses.*]

Almiras—in ceremonial magic, the "master and chief of invisibility." An adept must usually be in possession of the magic ring of Gyges to effect contact with the master. [*Rf. The Grand Grimoire.*]

Al Moakkibat [Moakkibat]

Almon—in hechaloth lore (*Ma'asseh Merkabah*), an angelic guard of the 4th heavenly hall.

Alphariza (Aphiriza)—an intelligence of the 2nd altitude. [*Rf.* Waite, *The Almadel of Solomon.*]

Alphun—the genius (i.e., angel) of doves. In Apollonius of Tyana, *The Nuctemeron*, Alphun figures as one of the governors of the 8th hour. [*Rf.* Levi, *Transcendental Magic.*]

Alpiel—in Hebrew mysticism, an angel or demon who rules over fruit trees. [*Rf.* Spence, *An Encyclopaedia of Occultism*; Gaynor, *Dictionary of Mysticism.*]

Altarib—an angel who exercises dominion over winter. He may be summoned in magical rites. [*Rf.* de Abano, *The Heptameron.*]

Al Ussa—in pagan Arab mythology, a female angel. Her idol was destroyed on orders of Mohammed. [*Rf.* Jobes, *Dictionary of Mythology Folklore and Symbols.*]

Al-Zabamiya—in the Koran (*sura* 74, 30), a term denoting angelic guards serving in Hell. There were 19 of them. [*Rf. The Encyclopaedia of Islam*, III, "Angels."]

Amabael—an angel who, like Altarib, exercises dominion over winter. [*Rf.* Barrett, *The Magus* II.]

Amabiel—angel of the air on Tuesday and a presiding spirit of the planet Mars. Amabiel is also one of the angelic luminaries "concerned with human sexuality." [*Rf.* Malchus, *The Secret Grimoire of Turiel*; de Abano, *The Heptameron*; Masters, *Eros and Evil*; Barrett, *The Magus* II.]

Amalek—in *The Zohar* (I) a spirit identified with Sammael as "the evil serpent, twin soul of the poison god." [*Cf.* Deuteronomy 25:19.]

Amaliel—angel of punishment; also of weakness. [*Rf.* Schwab, *Vocabulaire de l'Angélologie.*]

Amamael—in hechaloth lore (*Ma'asseh Merkabah*), an angelic guard stationed at the 3rd heavenly hall.

Amarlaii (Amarlia)—an angel invoked for the curing of cutaneous diseases. [*Rf.* Talmud *Shabbath*, fol. 67, col. 1.]

Amarlia (Amarlaii)—an angel who came out of the land of Sodom to heal painful boils, as noted in *The Sixth and Seventh Books of Moses.*

Amaros [Armaros]

Amarzyom—one of 15 throne angels listed in *The Sixth and Seventh Books of Moses.* For the names of all 15, *see* Appendix.

Amatiel—one of the 4 angels exercising dominion over spring. [*Rf.* de Abano, *The Heptameron*; Barrett, *The Magus* II.]

Amatliel—in hechaloth lore (*Ma'asseh Merkabah*), an angelic guard stationed at the 3rd heavenly hall.

Amator—in cabala, a "holy, angelic name" used in conjuring after proper investiture by the invocant. [*Rf.* Mathers, *The Greater Key of Solomon.*]

Amazaroc [Amezyarak]

Ambassadors—a term for angels, as in "the ambassadors of peace" (Isaiah 33:7) which, in *The Zohar*, is translated "angels of peace."

Amber—the term amber, occurring in Ezekiel 1:4, is taken to mean "by the ancient Hebrews, the fire-speaking being, belonging to an angelic genus, just as cherubim, seraphim, etc., denote distinct classes of angels." [*Rf.* C. D. Ginsburg, *The Essenes and the Kabbalah*, p. 242; *see* Hashmal.]

Ambriel (Amriel)—angel of the month of May and a prince of the order of thrones. Ambriel is chief officer of the 12th hour of the night, one of the rulers of the 12 zodiacal signs with dominion over Gemini. The name Amriel is found inscribed on an oriental Hebrew charm (*kamea*) for warding off evil. In the cabala (*The Sixth and Seventh Books of Moses*) Ambriel is a spirit cited for conjuring purposes under the 7th seal of the planet Mars. [*Rf.* Heywood, *The Hierarchy of the Blessèd Angels*; Waite, *The Lemegeton*; Barrett, *The Magus* II; Schrire, *Hebrew Amulets*.]

Ameratat (Ameretat)—in early Persian lore, the angel of immortality. Ameratat is one of 6 or 7 celestial powers or archangels (the amesha spentas) in the Zoroastrian system. [*Rf.* Geiger and Kuhn, *Grundriss der iranischen Philologie* III.] Some scholars see the Mohammed Marut (a Koranic fallen angel) derived from the Persian Ameratat [*Rf.* Jung, *Fallen Angels in Jewish, Christian and Mohammedan Literature*, p. 131.]

Amertati—an angel in Arabic lore; called also Mordad (*q.v.*). [*Rf.* Jung, *Fallen Angels in Jewish, Christian and Mohammedan Literature*, p. 131.]

Amesha Spentas ("holy, immortal ones"— amshashpands)—the Zoroastrian equivalents of the Judaeo-Christian archangels. Usually 6 in number, they exercised dominion over the planets. The amesha spentas are also said to be the Persian prototype of the cabalistic sefiroth. In their highest occult meaning the amesha spentas became (or originally were) the noumenal Sravah. As in the case of the sefiroth, which have their evil counterpart, so the amesha spentas have (or had) their opposites in the great demons or daevas, headed by Anra Mainya (Ahriman). The 6 "holy immortal ones" were: Armazd (chief); Ameretat (immortality); Ar(a)maiti (holy harmony, who was female); Asha (righteousness); Haurvatat (salvation); Kshathra Vairya (rulership); Vohumanah (good thought). There was also a 7th: S(a)raosha. [*Rf.* Hyde, *Historia Religionis Veterum Persarum*; Blavatsky, *The Secret Doctrine* II; Lenormant, *Chaldean Magic*; Müller, *History of Jewish Mysticism.*] In *The Dabistan*, p. 136, other amesha spentas are recorded, 4 of them said to have been "closest to the just God." They are: Bahman, Ardibahist, Azarkhurdad, Azargushtasp. The 6 "evil" archangels were Tauru, Zairicha, Khudad, Murdad, and two others. [*Rf.* Forlong, *Encyclopedia of Religions.*]

Amezyarak (Amazarec, Semyaza)—in *Enoch I* (8:2), an angel who taught conjurors and root cutters their art. He was one of 200, or one of the leaders of 200, who descended from Heaven to cohabit with the daughters of men. The Greek text of *Enoch I* reads "Semiazas" in place of Amezyarak. In R. H. Charles, *Enoch I*, the name is given as Amiziras. Eliphas Levi (*The History of Magic*) differentiates Amazarac (Amezyarak) from Semyaza in the listing of the apostate angels.

Amhiel—an angel's name found inscribed on an oriental charm (*kamea*) for warding off evil. [*Rf.* Schrire, *Hebrew Amulets.*]

Amicar—a most holy spirit (or another name for God) invoked in prayer at Vesting. [*Rf.* Waite, *The Book of Black Magic and of Pacts.*] It was not unusual for many angels, including those of the highest rank, to be impressed into the service of invocants when the latter were dabbling in black magic.

Amides—an angel, like Amicar, invoked in prayer at Vesting. [*Rf.* Malchus, *The Secret Grimoire of Turiel.*]

Amilfaton—in hechaloth lore (*Ma'asseh Merkabah*), an angelic guard stationed at the 7th heavenly hall.

Amisiel—in Waite, *The Lemegeton*, an angel of the 5th hour, operating under the rule of Sazquiel.

Amisiyah—one of the many names of the angel Metatron.

Amisor—the name of a great angel invoked in Solomonic magical rites, specifically in the invocation at fumigation. [*Rf. Grimorium Verum*; Shah, *The Secret Lore of Magic.*]

Amitiel—angel of truth, invoked as an amulet. Michael and Gabriel are credited as being such angels, along with Amitiel. In rabbinic writings, when God proposed the creation of man, the angels of truth and of peace (unnamed in the legend), as well as other angels, opposed the idea. For this opposition, the angels of truth and of peace were burned. [*Rf.* Ginzberg, *The Legends of the Jews*; Schwab, *Vocabulaire de l'Angélologie.*]

Amiziras [Amezyarak]

Ammiel ("people of God")—angel of the 4th hour of the day serving under Vachmiel. Ammiel is also mentioned as an angel of the 7th hour of the night, serving under Mendrion. [*Rf.* Waite, *The Lemegeton*, pp. 67, 69.]

Amnixiel—one of the 28 angels that rule over the 28 mansions of the moon. Amnixiel is also mentioned as an extra in the list of the 7 Electors

of Hell (which would make him, at the very least, a fallen angel). [*Rf.* Barrett, *The Magus* II; Butler, *Ritual Magic.*]

Amnodiel—like Amnixiel, Amnodiel is one of the 28 angels that rule over the 28 mansions of the moon. He also figures as an extra in the list of the 7 Electors of Hell.

Amoias—in the gnostic *Paraphrase of Shem*, one of the mysterious entities to whom the secrets of Creation were revealed. [*Rf.* Doresse, *The Secret Books of the Egyptian Gnostics*, p. 148.]

Ampharool—an angel who was called by Solomon "king of the genii of flying." Ampharool presides over instant travel and comes to an invocant when summoned by name. [*Rf. The Book of Power.*]

Amra'il—in Arabic lore, a guardian angel invoked in rites of exorcism. [*Rf.* Hughes, *A Dictionary of Islam*, "Angels."]

Amriel [Ambriel]

Amshashpands [Amesha Spentas]

Amtiel—in hechaloth lore (*Ma'asseh Merkabah*), an angelic guard stationed at the 3rd heavenly hall.

Amudiel—an extra in the list of the 7 Electors of Hell.

Amuhael X—an angel called on in conjuring rites. [*Rf.* M. Gaster, *The Sword of Moses.*]

Amulet Angels—there were 70 of these angels and they were invoked frequently at the time of childbirth. For their names, *see* Appendix.

Amwak'il—in Arabic lore, a guardian angel invoked in rites of exorcism. [*Rf.* Hughes, *A Dictionary of Islam*, "Angels."]

Amy—once an angel of the order of angels and of the order of powers, Amy is now "a great president" in the lower realms. He "gives perfect knowledge of astrology and the liberal arts." He hopes (so he confided to King Solomon) to return to the 7th throne "in 1200 years," which, says the demonologist Wierus, "is incredible." Amy's seal is figured in *The Book of Black Magic and of Pacts*, p. 184.

Anabiel—in the cabala, an angel who, when invoked for such purposes in magical rites, is able to cure stupidity. [*Rf.* Moses Botarel's works and Enoch lore.]

Anabona—In Mathers, *The Greater Key of Solomon*, the name of a spirit or angel "by which God formed man and the whole universe." It is said that Moses heard this name (Anabona) when the Ten Commandments were given him on Mt. Sinai.

Anabotas (Arabonas)—in the *Grimorium Verum*, an angel invoked in cabalistic rites.

Anachiel—the name of one of the 4 important angels found inscribed in Hebrew characters on the 3rd pentacle of the planet Saturn, according to *The Greater Key of Solomon*. The mystical circle of evocation is reproduced on p. 54 of *The Secret Lore of Magic*. In Longfellow's *The Golden Legend* (1st American ed. 1851), Anachiel is the governing angel of the planet Saturn. In later editions Longfellow substituted Orifel for Anachiel.

Anael (Haniel, Hamiel, Onoel, Ariel, etc.)—one of the 7 angels of Creation, chief of principalities [*Cf.* Nisroc], prince of archangels, and ruler of the Friday angels. Anael exercises dominion over the planet Venus, is one of the luminaries concerned with human sexuality, and is governor of the 2nd Heaven, where he is in charge of prayer ascending from the 1st Heaven. It is Anael who proclaims "Open all ye gates" in Isaiah 26:2. In addition, he controls kingdoms and kings on earth and has dominion over the moon. Apart from variations already noted, Anael is, or appears to be, another form for Aniyel, Anaphiel (Anafiel), Aufiel. [*Rf.* Christian, *The History and Practice of Magic* II, 440.] With Uriel, Anael is combined by Shakespeare in *The Tempest* to form the sprite Ariel (see Churchill, *Shakespeare and His Betters*). In Longfellow's *The Golden Legend*, Anael is one of the angels of the 7 planets, specifically the angel of the Star of Love, (i.e., the Evening Star or Venus). In *The Book of Tobit*, Anael is the name of Tobit's brother. [*Rf.* Levi, *Transcendental Magic*; *Grimorium Verum*; de Abano, *The Heptameron*; Agrippa, *Three Books of Occult Philosophy*.]

Anafiel (Anaphiel, Anpiel, "branch of God")—chief of the 8 great angels of the Merkabah; keeper of the keys of the heavenly halls; chief seal bearer, prince of water. When, according to legend, Metatron (*q.v.*), angel of the divine face, was to be punished, Anafiel was designated by God to flog His favorite angel with 60 lashes of fire. According to *3 Enoch*, it was Anafiel (other sources credit Rasuil or Samuil) who bore Enoch to Heaven in the first place, Enoch then being transformed into Metatron. [*Rf.* Scholem, *Major Trends in Jewish Mysticism*; Schwab, *Vocabulaire de l'Angélologie*.] In *Hechaloth Rabbati*, where Anafiel is compared with the Creator, he is identified as Metatron.

Anahel—a prince of angels of the 3rd Heaven, but one who serves in the 4th Heaven (according to *The Sixth and Seventh Books of Moses*). As Anahael, he is one of numerous angelic guards of the gates of the West Wind. [*Rf. Ozar Midrashim* II, 316.]

Anahita (Anaitis)—a female angel of the highest rank in Zoroastrianism. She is the "immaculate one, genius of fertilizing water and of the fruitfulness of the earth." [*Rf.* Redfield, *Gods/A Dictionary of the Deities of All Lands*.]

Anai—a name written in Heaven "in the characters of Malachim" (angels) and invoked in powerful conjurations to command demons. [*Rf.* Mathers, *The Greater Key of Solomon*.]

Anaireton (Amereton)—one of the "high, holy angels" of God invoked in magical rites, specifically in the conjuration of Ink and Colors and the invocation or exorcism of the Salt. [*Rf.* Waite, *The Book of Ceremonial Magic; Grimorium Verum*.]

Anaitis [Anahita]

Anak—sing. for Anakim.

Anakim (-enim? "giants")—the offspring of fallen angels and mortal women, an issue touched on in Genesis 6. The anakim were so tall that, according to *The Zohar*, "the Hebrews were like grasshoppers in comparison." In the latter work, the angels Uzza and Azael are singled out as having begotten children "whom they called anakim." The original name of the anakim was nefilim. [*Rf.* Jung, *Fallen Angels in Jewish, Christian and Mohammedan Literature*; Deuteronomy 1:28; Joshua 14:12.] In Ginzberg, *The Legends of the Jews* I, 151, it is related that the anakim "touched the sun with their necks." This is consonant with the view, often expressed in rabbinic and Islamic writings, that angels reached from Heaven to earth—just as Adam did when he was first formed, and as Israfel did, or does. [*Rf. 3 Enoch.*]

Anamelech [Adramelech]

Ananchel (or Ananehel—"grace of God")—an angel sent by God to Esther to give her favor in the sight of the Persian king Ahasuerus [*Rf.* Old Testament, Esther.] Origen speaks of Ananchel in his "On Romans" (IV, 12). [*Rf. The Biblical Antiquities of Philo*, p. 73.]

Anane—one of the troop of fallen angels, as listed in *Enoch I.*

Ananehel [Ananchel]

Ananel (Anani, Hananel, Khananel)—regarded as both good and evil. As an evil angel (one of the fallen archangels), Ananel is said to have descended from Heaven on Mt. Hermon and to have brought sin to mankind. [*Rf. Enoch I*; Ambelain, *La Kabbale Pratique.*]

Anani [Ananel]

Ananiel—one of numerous angelic guards of the gates of the South Wind. [*Rf. Ozar Midrashim* II, 316.]

Anaphaxeton (Anaphazeton, Arpheton, Hipeton, Oneipheton)—one of the holy angels of God invoked in magical rites. Anaphaxeton is the name which, when pronounced, will cause the angels to summon the whole universe before the bar of justice on Judgment Day. He is also a spirit to be invoked in the exorcism of the Water. [*Rf.* Waite, *The Book of Ceremonial Magic.*]

Anaphiel [Anafiel]

Anapion—in Waite, *The Lemegeton*, an angel of the 7th hour of the night, serving under Mendrion.

Anas—"and God sent two angels, Sihail and Anas, and the four Evangelists to take hold of the fever-demons [12 of them, all female] and beat them with fiery rods." The source of the tale is a 12th-century MS in the British Museum and the tale is retold by M. Gaster in *Studies and Texts in Folklore* II, p. 1030. Gaster believes that Sihail is merely another form for Mihail (Michael) and Anas a form for St. Anne, mother of Mary, here turned into an angel.

Anataniel A'—in M. Gaster, *The Sword of Moses*, one of the angel princes of the hosts of X.

Anauel—an angel who protects commerce, bankers, commission brokers, etc. Anauel's corresponding angel is Aseij. [*Rf.* Ambelain, *La Kabbale Pratique.*]

Anayz—in de Abano, *The Heptameron*, an angel of Monday said to reside in the 1st Heaven. He is invoked from the south. Since angels are bodiless, their "residence" in any heaven, or in any place, is hypothetical. Angels are resident wherever they happen to be operating; it is only for convenience that they are given a *locus operandi*. All material descriptions of angels, (wings, size, speech, physical actions) are likewise to be taken figuratively.

Anazachia—an angel's name inscribed in Hebrew characters on the 3rd pentacle of the planet Saturn. Anazachia is one of 4 angels shown on the pentacle, the other 3 being Omeliei, Anachiel, and Aranchia. The magical circle of evocation is reproduced in Shah, *The Secret Lore of Magic*, p. 54. [*Rf.* Gollancz, *Clavicula Salomonis.*]

Anazimur—one of the 7 exalted throne angels of the 1st Heaven "which execute the commands

---

The angels ascending and descending Jacob's Ladder. A dream-incident related in Genesis 28. Reproduced from Hayley, *The Poetical Works of John Milton.*

of the potestates," according to *The Book of the Angel Raziel*. [*Rf.* de Abano, *Elementia Magica*; *The Sixth and Seventh Books of Moses*; writings of Cornelius Agrippa.]

Ancient of Days—in the cabala, a term applied to Kether, 1st of the sefiroth (*q.v.*); also to Macroposopus ("vast countenance") who is, in the cabala, "God as He is in Himself." Ancient of Days is, further, used as a term to denote the "holy ones of the highest," i.e., the most exalted and venerable of the angels. In Daniel 7:9, the expression is the prophet's title and vision of God: "I beheld till the thrones were cast down, and the Ancient of Days did sit, whose garment was white as snow, and the hair of his head like the pure wool; his throne was like the fiery flame, and his wheels as burning fire." Dionysius in *The Divine Names* defines the term Ancient of Days as "both the Eternity and the Time of all things prior to days and eternity and time." The term has also been used to apply to Israel. William Blake refers to the Ancients of Days as Urizen, the figure of Jehovah in this poet's mystical poems. It is the title of one of his famous drawings; see also Blake's "Elohim [God] Giving Life to Adam." Hymn 519 of the *Hymnal* of the Protestant Episcopal Church [Thos. Nelson, 1920] opens with "Ancient of Days, who sittest throned in glory; To thee all knees are bent."

Ancor—an angel invoked in the conjuration of the Reed. Ancor is likewise a name for God in prayers at Vestment. [*Rf.* Mathers, *The Greater Key of Solomon*; Waite, *The Book of Black Magic and of Pacts*.]

Andas—in occult writings, Andas is represented as one of the ministering angels to Varcan, a king who rules the angels of the air on Lord's Day (Sunday). In de Abano, *The Heptameron*, the magic circle for the incantation of angels for the 1st planetary hour of Sunday shows Andas at the outer perimeter.

Aneb—an angel ruler of an hour with the attribute "Dieu Clement." [*Rf.* Ambelain, *La Kabbale Pratique*; and the poem "Sagesse" by H.D. (Hilda Doolittle).]

Anepaton (Anapheneton)—"a high, holy angel of God," whose name appears in an invocation ring. Anepaton is also a name for God when conjured up by Aaron. [*Rf.* Butler, *Ritual Magic*; *Grimorium Verum*; Waite, *The Lemegeton*; *The Book of Ceremonial Magic*.]

Anereton (Anaireton)—"a high, holy angel of God" invoked in Solomonic rites. [*Rf.* Shah, *The Secret Lore of Magic*; *Grimorium Verum*.]

Anfial—one of the 64 angel wardens of the 7 celestial halls. [*Rf. Pirke Hechaloth*.]

Anfiel (Anafiel, "branch of God")—in *Pirke Hechaloth*, a guard of the 4th Heaven. See also Margouliath, *Malache Elyon* and *Bereshith Rabbah*. According to the *Jewish Encyclopedia* (p. 595), Anfiel's crown "branches out to cover the Heaven with the divine majesty." Here he is head and chief of the porters and seal-bearers of the 7 Heavens.

Angel (Hebrew, "malakh")—the word derives from *angiras* (Sanskrit), a divine spirit; from the Persian *angaros*, a courier; from the Greek *angelos*, meaning a messenger. In Arabic the word is *malak* (a Jewish loan word.) In popular usage an angel denotes, generally, a supernatural being intermediate between God and man (the Greek "daimon" being a closer approximation to our notion of angel than angelos). In early Christian and pre-Christian days, the term angel and daimon (or demon) were interchangeable, as in the writings of Paul and John. The Hebrews drew their idea of angels from the Persians and from the Babylonians during the Captivity. The 2 named angels in the Old Testament, Michael and Gabriel, were in fact lifted from Babylonian mythology. The 3rd named angel, Raphael, appears in the apocryphal *Book of Tobit*. "This whole doctrine concerning angels" (says Sales in his edition of *The Koran*, "Preliminary Discourse," p. 51) "Mohammed and his disciples borrowed from the Jews, who borrowed the names and offices of these beings from the Persians." While Enoch, in his writings dating back to earliest Christian times and even before, names many angels (and demons), these were ignored in New Testament gospels, although they began to appear in contemporaneous extracanonical works. They had a vogue in Jewish gnostic, mystic, and cabalistic tracts. Angelology came into full flower in the 11th–13th centuries when the names of literally thousands upon thousands of angels appeared, many of them created through the juggling of letters of the Hebrew alphabet, or by the simple device of adding the suffix "el" to any word which lent itself to such manipulation. An angel, though immaterial, that is, bodiless, is usually depicted as having a body or inhabiting a body, *pro tem,* and as winged and clothed. If an angel is in the service of the devil, he is a fallen angel or a demon. To Philo, in his "On Dreams," angels were incorporeal intelligences. He held that the rabbis, on the contrary, thought of angels as material beings. In Roman Catholic theology, angels were created in the earliest days of Creation, or even before Creation, *tota simul,* that is, at one and the same time. In Jewish tradition, angels are "new every morning" (Lamentations 3:23) and continue to be formed with every breath God takes (*Hagiga* 14a). In the pseudo-Dionysian scheme with its 9 heavenly choirs, angels as an order rank lowest in the scale of hierarchy, the seraphim ranking highest. The archangels show up 8th in the sequence, despite the fact that the greatest angels are often referred to as archangels. Strictly speaking, when one refers to the named angels in the Bible, it is correct to say there are only 2 or 3. But the following may be considered: Abaddon/ Apollyon, mentioned in Revelation as the "angel of the bottomless pit." Wormwood, referred to as a star (Revelation 8:11), but to be understood as an angel. And there is Satan, who in the Old Testament is a great angel, one of the most glorious, certainly not evil and with no hint of his having fallen. He goes by his title of adversary (*ha-satan*). It is only in Christian and post-Biblical Jewish writings that *ha-satan* of the Old Testament is turned into an evil spirit. A case for including Rahab among the named angels of the Bible might also be made: Talmud refers to Rahab as "the angel of the sea."

"Angel in the Forest"—the title of Marguerite Young's chronicle of the Rappites, a German religious sect that established a short-lived community on the Wabash River during the years 1815–1824. The title derives from the angel (Gabriel) whom Father Rapp, cult leader, claimed he saw in the forest—an angel "with the good taste to leave footprints behind"—for these footprints can be seen, to this day, on a stone slab in New Harmony, Indiana.

Angel of Abortion [Kasdaye]

Angel of the Abyss—usually identified as Uriel, the "angel set over the world and Tartarus." [*Cf.* Apsu, female angel of the abyss in Babylonian-Chaldean mythology; *Rf.* Charles, *Critical Commentary of the Revelation of St. John,* p. 239].

Angel of Adversity—in works like *The Zadokite Fragments* and *The Book of Jubilees,* the angel of adversity is Mastema, prince of evil, equated with Satan.

Angel of Agriculture [Risnuch]

Angel of the Air [Chasan, Casmaron, Cherub, Iahmel]

Angel of Albion—an angel "created" by Blake as a character in his "Visions of the Daughters of Albion."

Angel of Alchemy and Mineralogy—Och (*q.v.*).

Angels of the Altitudes—among the principal rulers of the 4 altitudes or chora are Barachiel, Gabriel, Gediel. [*Rf. The Almadel of Solomon.*] For the names of other rulers of this class of celestial hierarchs, *see* Appendix.

Angel of Anger—in his visit to Paradise, as reported in the apocalyptic *Revelation of Moses,* the great Lawgiver encounters the angels of anger and wrath in the 7th Heaven. He finds these angels composed "wholly of fire." Our angel of anger is Af (*q.v.*).

Angel of Annihilation—in the story relating to Esther and Ahaseurus, the angel of annihilation is Harbonah or Hasmed. [*Rf. Midrash Tehillim* on

Annunciation by Tintoretto in Scuola San Rocco, Venice. Reproduced from Régamey, *Anges.*

Psalm 7.] Both Harbonah and Hasmed are angels of punishment or of confusion.

Angel of Announcements—in ancient Persian lore, the angel of announcements is Sirushi, who ranks also as the angel of Paradise.

Angel of Annunciation—Gabriel. The Angel of Annunciation is the subject of innumerable paintings by the great masters: da Vinci, Memling, Fra Filippo Lippi, Fra Angelico, El Greco, Titian, etc. In the annunciation to Mary, as related in Matthew, the name of Gabriel does not occur; it occurs in the account by Luke (both with regard to Elizabeth and Mary).

Angel of the Apocalypse—Orifiel; also Anael (Haniel, Anafiel), Zachariel, Raphael, Samael, Michael, Gabriel, and St. Francis of Assisi. According to Cornelius Agrippa, each angel is credited with a reign of 354 years. The title "Angel of the Apocalypse" was claimed by St. Vincent Ferrer (1350–1419). [*Rf.* Levi, *Transcendental Magic.*] Malvina Hoffman, American sculptress, did a figure in gold bronze titled the "Archangel of the Apocalypse."

Angel of April—Asmodel. In ancient Persian lore, the angel was Andibehist.

Angel of Aquarius—in works of ceremonial

magic, the angel of Aquarius is Ausiel (Ausiul). Rabbi Chomer in Levi's book of magic cites the 2 governing spirits of Aquarius as Archer and Ssakmakiel (Tzakmaqiel).

Angel of Aquatic Animals [Manakel]

Angel of Aries—in ceremonial magic, the angel of Aries (the Ram) is Aiel or Machidiel, the latter being also the angel of March. In the cabala, the 2 spirits governing the sign of Aries are Sataaran and Sarahiel (Sariel).

Angel of the Ark of the Covenant—the 2 angels of the ark of the covenant are usually Zarall and Jael, both belonging to the order of cherubim. Another angel, Sandalphon, has been described as "the left-hand cherub of the Ark." Some authorities, interpreting Exodus 25, maintain that 4 angels should be represented on the ark, 2 on each side. See picturization in Schaff, *A Dictionary of the Bible*, p. 67.

Angel of Ascension—in the Acts of the Apostles (1:10) the angels of ascension are spoken of as "two men [which] stood by in white apparel." Chrysostom, Eusebius, Cyril of Jerusalem speak of angels present at the Ascension. [*Rf.* Danielou, *The Angels and Their Mission.*] In noncanonical writings there are frequent references to the angels of ascension as 2 in number, but nowhere are they named. In the "Ascension," a canvas by Mantegna (1431–1506), Christ is shown fully robed, rising to Heaven with 11 child-angels surrounding him in the ascent.

Angel of Aspirations and Dreams—according to Jewish cabala, the moon is the angel of aspirations and dreams; in occult lore, it is Gabriel. [*Rf.* Levi, *Transcendental Magic.*]

Angel of Augsburg, The—a name given to Agnes Bernauer, the lovely but low-born wife of Duke Albrecht of Würtenberg. She was drowned as a witch in 1435, at the instigation of Albrecht's father, Duke Ernest of Bavaria. The drowning is the subject of a woodcut reproduced in Paul Carus, *The History of the Devil.*

Angel of August—in Trithemius, *The Book of Secret Things*, the angel of August is Hamaliel;

he is said to have dominion over the sign of Virgo in the zodiac. Occult lore cites another angel of August, or August–September (in Hebrew, the season is *Elul*)—i.e., Morael, who is also the angel of awe or fear. In ancient Persian lore, the angel of August was Shahrivari.

Angel of Autumn—Guabarel; Tarquam. The head of the sign of August is Torquaret. [*Rf.* De Plancy, *Dictionnaire Infernal.*]

Angel of Babylon—in *Midrash Tehillim* we learn that "the angel of Babylon mounted 70 rounds [of the ladder of Jacob] and the angel of Media 52." Neither the name of the angel of Babylon nor that of Media is given.

Angel of the Balances [Soqed Hozi, Dokiel, Michael, Zehanpuryu'h]

Angel of the Baptismal Water—Raphael. But *see also* Barpharanges. It was Tertullian who declared that the baptismal water receives its healing properties from an angel (whom, however, he did not name). [*Rf.* Smith, *Man and his Gods*, p. 306.]

Angel of Barrenness [Akriel]

Angel Over (Tame) Beasts [Behemiel, Hariel]

Angel Over (Wild) Beasts [Thegri (Thuriel), Mtniel, Jehiel, Hayyal]. [*Rf. Hermes Visions; Jewish Encyclopedia* I, 595.]

Angel of Benevolence [Zadkiel, Hasdiel, Achsah]

Angel Over Birds [Arael, Anpiel]

Angel of the Bottomless Pit—same as angel of the abyss, i.e., Abaddon (which is the Hebrew form for the Greek Apollyon), as in Revelation 20. Known in post-Biblical lore as the "destroyer" and "king of the demonic locusts" or "grasshoppers." In Bunyan's *Pilgrim's Progress*, this angel is a devil, *the* devil. St. John regards the angel of the bottomless pit as apparently not evil, since it is the angel that binds Satan for 1,000 years (Revelation 20:2). As Langton makes clear in his *Satan, a Portrait* (p. 39) the angel of the abyss (i.e., the angel of the bottomless pit) "is *not* [in Revelation] identified with Satan." Dürer in his Apocalypse series (1498) executed a woodcut titled "Angel with the Key of the Bottomless Pit."

Angel of the Burning Bush—Zagzagel; Michael. A strict interpretation of the use of the term (in Exodus 3:2; Luke 20:37; Acts 7:35) would suggest that it is the Lord Himself who is the angel of the burning bush, made manifest in angelic guise. The ascription to Zagzagel is found in *Targum Yerushalmi*. Rembrandt did a well-known painting of the subject titled "Moses and the Burning Bush."

Angel of Calculations [Butator]

Angel of (the sign of) Cancer—Cael. According to Rabbi Chomer, an exegetical authority quoted by Levi in *Transcendental Magic*, the governing spirits of the sign of Cancer are Rahdar and Phakiel.

Angel of Capricorn—in ceremonial magic, the angel of Capricorn is Casujoiah. According to Rabbi Chomer, quoted by Levi, *Transcendental Magic*, the governing spirits of this zodiacal sign are Sagdalon and Semakiel (Semaqiel).

Angel of Carnal Desires [Angel of Lust]

Angel of Chance (in the sense of gambling)—Barakiel, Uriel, and Rubiel. [*Rf.* De Plancy, *Dictionnaire Infernal*.]

Angel of Chaos—Michael. Where chaos is equated with darkness, and darkness with death, then the angel of chaos is Satan. [*Rf. The Interpreter's Bible*; Ginzberg, *The Legends of the Jews* V, 16.]

Angel of the Chaste Hands [Ouestucati]

Angel of Chastisement—Amaliel. In addition, one comes upon other angels of chastisement or punishment in apocryphal and post-Biblical writings. Compare "the mail-clad lords with the flaming eyes." . . . "his eyes are as lamps of fire," in Daniel 10:6, as descriptive of one of these hierarchs. In Coptic lore, the demon of chastisement is Asmodel—who, however, in occult lore, is an angel, the angel of the month of April.

Angels (Order of)—in the pseudo-Dionysian scheme of the celestial hierarchy, the order of angels occurs last of the 9. The ruling princes of the order are usually given as Phaleg and Adnachiel (Advachiel).

Angels of Clouds—in *The Book of Jubilees* there is mention of the angels of clouds who, it is reported, were created on the 1st day of Creation. They are not named.

Angels of Cold—likewise mentioned but not named in *The Book of Jubilees*. The angels of cold are also referred to in the *Revelation of John*, a New Testament apocryphon included in the Ante-Nicene Fathers Library.

Angels of the Colonies—creation of Blake as characters in his "Visions of the Daughters of Albion."

Angel of Comets (or Meteors)—Zikiel or Ziquiel; also Akhibel.

Angel of Commission Brokers—Anauel, who also protects commerce, bankers, etc.

Angel of Commotion—Zi'iel, as noted in Odeberg, *3 Enoch*.

Angel of Compassion—Rachmiel or Raphael (*qq.v.*). The angel of compassion, symbolizing the United Nations, is interpreted in a painting by the Swiss artist Max Hunziker and done by him for the benefit of UNICEF. The Nepalese have a god of compassion called Avalokiteshvara, who renounced Nirvana in order to serve and save mankind. An image of this deity was displayed at the Asia Society headquarters in New York in 1964.

Angel of Conception [Laila(h)]

Angels of Confusion—there are 7 of these angels of confusion. They were dispatched by God to the court of Ahasuerus to put an end to this king's pleasure in the time of Queen Esther. [*Rf.* Ginzberg, *The Legends of the Jews* IV, 374.] It seems likely that the angels of confusion were also present and participated in the Tower of Babel incident. [*Rf.* Genesis 11:7.] The individual angels of confusion are described in Talmud as follows:

Mehuman—confusion; Biztha—destroyer of the house; Barbonah—annihilation; Bigtha—presser of the winepress; Abatha—another presser of the winepress; Zethar—observer of immorality; and Carcas—the knocker.

Angel of Constellations—Kakabel (Kochbiel) and Rahtiel (*qq.v.*). [*Rf.* Ginzberg, *The Legends of the Jews* I, 140.]

Angels of Corruption (or Perdition)—originally, according to Talmudic lore, there were 70 tutelary angels assigned by God to rule over the 70 nations of the earth. These angels, corrupted through national bias, became the *malache habbala* (angels of corruption). The sole angel of this group who remained uncorrupted was the tutelary or guardian angel of Israel, Michael. [*Rf.* Eisenmenger, *Traditions of the Jews* I, 18; Lea, *Materials Toward A History of Witchcraft* I, 17; Ginzberg, *The Legends of the Jews*.]

Angel of the Covenant—a title applied to Metatron, Phadiel, Michael, Elijah, the "angel of the Lord," and even to Mastema. According to *The Zohar* I, it is the angel of the covenant who is meant in such verses as Exodus 4:26, 24:1; Leviticus 1:1. In the *Vision of Paul* 14, Michael is called the "Angel of the Covenant." But Régamey

in *What Is An Angel?*, citing Malachi 3:1, says "the Angel of the Covenant must be the Lord himself." The hasidic Rabbi Elimeleckh of Lizhensk (d. 1786) refers to Elijah as the "Angel of the Covenant." [*Rf.* Buber, *Tales of the Hasidim*; *The Early Masters*, p. 257.]

Angels of Creation—there were 7 of these angels in the beginning (i.e., at the time of Creation) and they were placed in control of the 7 planets—the 7 including the sun and moon, according to the astronomical knowledge of the time of the scribes, who set down the events of the "first days." The 7 angels of creation usually given are Orifiel, Anael, Zachariel, Samael (before this angel rebelled and fell), Raphael, Gabriel, and Michael. *The Book of Enoch* reports that the angels of Creation reside in the 6th Heaven.

Angel of Darkness—also called prince of darkness and angel of death (Belial, Bernael, Haziel, Beliar, Satan, etc.). "All who practice perversity are under the domination of the angel of darkness." [*Rf. Manual of Discipline* in T. Gaster, *The Dead Sea Scriptures*, pp. 43–44.] "All men's afflictions and all of their moments of tribulation are due to this being's malevolent sway." According to Budge, *Amulets and Talismans*, quoting "the later rabbis," the angel of darkness is Kochbiel. In

Angels of the Ascension. A miniature from *The Bible of St. Paul*. Reproduced from *Lost Books of the Bible*.

ASCENDITXPS
INALTUM

Chaldean lore, and in Kramer, *From the Tablets of Sumer*, the angel is An. In Mandaean lore there were 5 primal beings of darkness: Akrun (Krun), Ashdum (Shdum), Gaf, Hagh, Zasgi-Zargana. [*Rf.* Mansoor, *The Thanksgiving Hymns*; Ginzberg, *The Legends of the Jews* V; *The Book of Jubilees*; Drower, *The Mandaeans of Iraq and Iran*, p. 251.]

Angel of Dawn—in gnosticism, applied to the dragon which, in Revelation, is a term for Satan or Lucifer. [*Rf.* Jobes, *Dictionary of Mythology Folklore and Symbols*.]

Angel of the Day (Angel of Daylight)—Shamshiel, as in *3 Enoch*. [*Rf. Amulets and Talismans*, p. 375; Ginzberg, *The Legends of the Jews* II, 314.]

Angel of Death—in rabbinic writings there are at least a dozen angels of death: Adriel, Apollyon-Abaddon, Azrael, Gabriel (as guardian of Hades), Hemah, Kafziel, Kezef, Leviathan, Malach ha-Mavet, Mashhit, Metatron, Sammael (Satan), Yehudiah (Yehudiam), Yetzer-hara. In Falasha lore the angel of death is Suriel. In Christian theology, Michael is the angel of death who "leads souls into the eternal light" at the yielding up of the ghost of all good Christians. The Arabic angel of death is Azrael. He is also Iblis, as in the Arabian Nights tale, "The Angel of Death with the Proud King." The Babylonian god of death is Mot. According to Schönblum, *Pirke Rabbenu ha-Kadosh*, there are 6 angels of death: Gabriel (over the lives of young people), Kafziel (over kings), Meshabber (over animals), Mashhit (over children), Af (over men), Hemah (over domestic animals). The angel of death is not necessarily an evil or a fallen angel. He remains at all times a legate of God and in God's service. [*Rf.* Talmud *Baba Metzia*, 86a.] In Zoroastrianism, the angel of death or the demon of death is Mairya (male or female), who offered Zoroaster the empire of the world [*Cf.* Satan tempting Jesus; see also Saltus, *Lords of the Ghostland*, chap. on Ormuzd]. In the *Apocalypse of Baruch* there is an angel of death, unnamed, who makes his first appearance in that work. [*Rf.* Smith, *Man and his Gods*.] In Ginzberg, *The Legends of the Jews* IV, 200, we read of Elijah

fighting and overcoming the angel of death. There is also a legend about Aaron seizing the angel of death and locking him in the Tabernacle "so that death ceased." The seizure must have been short-lived. (The Aaron legend may have inspired the popular Broadway play, *Death Takes a Holiday*.) This angel of death was most likely Kezef, as suggested in *Targum Yerushalmi*. The great whale or crocodile of Biblical lore, Leviathan (along with Rahab), is also identified as an angel of death, according to various rabbinic sources. In Talmud *Abodah Zarah*, 20, the angel of death, Sammael, is described as "altogether full of eyes; at the time of a sick man's departure he [the angel] takes his stand above the place of his [the sick man's] head, with his sword drawn and a drop of poison suspended on it." To Eisenmenger (*Traditions of the Jews*) the supreme angel of death is Metatron, whose subordinates are Gabriel and Sammael. In his *Book of Beliefs and Opinions*, Saadiah Gaon (10th century) says that "our teachers have informed us that the angel sent by God to separate body from soul appears to man in the form of a yellowish flame, full of eyes shining with a bluish fire, holding in his hand a drawn sword pointed at the person to whom death is coming." Saadiah then goes on to suggest a parallel or affinity with the "angel of the Lord" in I Chronicles 21:16 who stands "between the earth and the heaven, having a drawn sword in his hand stretched over Jerusalem." The angel who would qualify here, not so much in the description of him as in relation to his office, is the benevolent angel of death, Azrael (*q.v.*). Over 6 persons the angel of death has no power (says Talmud *Baba Bathra*, fol. 17), to wit: Abraham, Isaac, Jacob, Moses, Aaron, and Miriam. With regard to Jacob, it is said that "not the angel of death ended his life, but the Shekinah took his soul with a kiss"; and that Miriam also "breathed her last in this manner." A rabbi (ben Levi) outwitting the angel of death is the subject of Longfellow's poem "The Spanish Jew's Tale."

Angel of December—Haniel or Nadiel. In ancient Persian lore, the angel of December was Dai (*q.v.*).

Angel of the Deep—Tamiel, Rampel; also

Rahab. [*See* Angel of the Sea.] [*Rf.* M. Gaster, *The Sword of Moses*; Ginzberg, *The Legends of the Jews* V.]

Angel of Deliverance—in Zoharistic writings, the angel of deliverance is Pedael. [*Rf.* Abelson, *Jewish Mysticism*, p. 117.]

Angel of the Deserts—one of the unnamed "splendid, terrible and mighty angel chiefs who passed before God to extol and rejoice in the first Sabbath." [*Rf. Alphabet of Rabbi Akiba* and numerous Talmudic commentaries listed in Ginzberg, *The Legends of the Jews.*]

Angel of Destiny [Oriel or Manu]

Angels of Destruction ("malache habbalah") —Uriel, Harbonah, Azriel, Simkiel, Za'afiel, Af, Kolazonta, Hemah. Chief of the group is Kemuel, according to the *Revelation of Moses*, but, according to *3 Enoch*, the chief is Simkiel. In the latter book, the angels of destruction correspond to the angels of punishment, and these in turn may be equated with the angels of vengeance, wrath, death, ire. They may also be compared to the Avestan devas. "When executing the punishments on the world, the angels of destruction are given the 'Sword of God' to be used by them as an instrument of punishment." [*Rf. 3 Enoch*, 32:1.] According to Moses Gaster, there were 40,000 such angels but, according to a Jewish legend, there were (or still are) in Hell alone 90,000 angels of destruction. It is said that the angels of destruction helped the magicians of Egypt in Pharaoh's time; that they duplicated the miracles performed by Moses and Aaron, specifically the miracle of changing water into blood. [*Rf.* Exodus 7:20.] There is a division of opinion among rabbinic writers as to whether the angels of destruction are in the service of God or of the devil. Apparently, even when they serve the devil, it is with the permission of God. In *The Zohar* I, 63a, Rabbi Judah, discoursing on the Deluge, declared that "no doom is ever executed on the world, whether of annihilation or any other chastisement, but the destroying angel is in the midst of the visitation." In Ginzberg, *The Legends of the Jews*, it is related that when Moses visited Hell, he beheld in a region

called Titha-Yawen sinners (mainly usurers) standing "up to their navel in mud" lashed by the angels of destruction "with fiery chains, the sinners' teeth being broken with fiery stones from morning until evening." *Cf.* Dante's description of the tortures suffered by sinners in the *Inferno*. [*Rf. The Apocalypse of Baruch*; *The Book of Enoch*; Talmud *Bab-Sanhedrin*; Trachtenberg, *Jewish Magic and Superstition*; *Jewish Encyclopedia*, p. 516.]

Angel of the Disk of the Sun—Chur, in ancient Persian lore. *Cf.* Galgaliel, angel of the wheel of the sun (*q.v.*).

Angel of Divination [Eistibus]

Angel of the Divine Chariot [Rikbiel YHWH]

Angel of the Divine Presence (Angel of the Face)—Blake subtitled his engraving "The Laocoön," "The Angel of the Divine Presence."

Angel of Dominions (dominations)—Zacharael, who is usually designated prince of this hierarchic order. Dionysius, in his famous work on the celestial orders, placed the dominions or dominations first in the 2nd triad of the 9 choirs.

Angel of Doves [Alphun]

Angels (or Lords) of Dread—according to *3 Enoch*, 22, they work in unison with the Captains of Fear in surrounding the throne of Glory and "singing praise and hymns before YHWH, the God of Israel." They aggregate "thousand times thousand and ten thousand times ten thousand."

Angel of Dreams—Duma(h) and Gabriel. In the cabala, according to Levi, *Transcendental Magic*, the angel of dreams is the Moon, or Gabriel. *The Zohar* II, 183a, refers to Gabriel as the "supervisor of dreams."

Angel of the Dust [Suphlatus]

Angels of the Earth—traditionally there are 7 angels of the earth: Azriel, Admael, Arkiel (Archas), Arciciah, Ariel, Harabael or Aragael, Saragael, Yabbashael. Variants include Haldiel, Tebliel, Phorlakh, Raguel, and Samuil. The 4 angels of the earth listed in Heywood, *The*

Hierarchy of the Blessèd Angels, are actually angels of the 4 winds: Uriel (south), Michael (east), Raphael (west), Gabriel (north). In ancient Persian lore, the spirit of the earth was Isphan Darmaz. [*Rf. Enoch II; Pesikta R. Kahana* 155a.]

Angel of Earthquakes [Sui'el; Rashiel]

Angels of the East (or of the Rising Sun)—Michael, Gauriil, Ishliha, Gazardiel.

Angel of Edom—the name Edom was a designation for Rome, but the angel of Edom designated Satan. "I will ascend above the heights of the clouds, I will be like the Most High," the angel of Edom boasted. And God replied: "Though thou mount on high as the eagle, and though thy nest be set among the stars, I will bring thee down from thence." The angel of Edom was one of the angels on the ladder that Jacob saw in his dream, set between earth and Heaven. [*Rf.* Ginzberg, *The Legends of the Jews* I, V.]

Angel of Egypt—Mastema, Rahab, Duma(h), Uzza, and Sammael. On their way out of Egypt the Israelites were affrighted most "at the sight of the Angel of Egypt darting through the air as he flew to the assistance of the people under his tutelage." The identity of the angel is not given in the source quoted (Ginzberg, *The Legends of the Jews* III, 13). Some rabbinic texts say the angel was Abezi-thibod; others that it was, or might have been, Sammael, Mastema (in *The Book of Jubilees*), or Uzza. Another good guess would be Rahab (*q.v.*).

Angel of the Embryo [Sandalphon]

Angel of Esau—Sammael, with whom Jacob wrestled at Peniel.

Angel of Evil—Satan, Malach Ra, Mastema, Bernael, Beliar (Beliel), Ahriman (Persian), etc.

Angel of Evil Deeds—a holy angel in the service of God. He is pictured (but not named) as a Recording Angel in Longfellow, *The Golden Legend*.

Angels of the Face (or Angels of the Presence)—among the most frequently mentioned angels of the face in rabbinic lore are Metatron, Michael, Jehoel, Suriel, Yefehfiah, Zagzagael, Uriel. There were about 12 of them and they were also spoken of as the angels of sanctification or the angels of glory—all of them circumcised at Creation. [*See* Angels of the Presence.]

Angel of Fall (autumn)—Torquaret. [*Rf.* Shah, *Occultism, Its Theory and Practice*, p. 43.]

Angel of Fascination [Tablibik]

Angel of Fasts—Sangariah, as cited in *The Zohar* (Exodus 207a).

Angel of Fate [Manu]

Angel of Fear (Yrouel; Morael)—these are amulet angels (*q.v.*).

Angel of February (Barchiel; Barbiel)—for angels governing other months of the year, *see* Appendix. [*Rf.* De Plancy, *Dictionnaire Infernal* IV.] In ancient Persian lore, the angel of February was Isfandarmend (*q.v.*).

Angel of Fertility—in Mandaean lore, the angel of fertility is Samandiriel or Yus(h)amin. In Talmud *Pesikta Rabbati* 43:8, it is stated that "Abraham gave heed to the Angel of Fertility when the great Lawgiver, then in his 100th year, was told by God to visit Sara in her tent." Abraham heeded God's counsel. Sara was 90 at the time and barren; but, through perhaps the overshadowing of Samandiriel or Yus(h)amin, she conceived and gave birth to Isaac. Another heavenly spirit present at the union of the aged couple was the Shekinah (*q.v.*).

Angel of the Fiery Furnace—the angel of the Lord (not named) seen walking in the midst of the unconsuming fire with Sidrach, Misach, and Abednego, the 3 Judaean princes captive in Babylon who had refused to obey Nebuchadnezzar's command to worship a golden image. The angel miraculously delivered the 3 princes from death. He was later described by the Babylonian king as having a form like that of "the Son of God." [*Rf.* Daniel 3.]

Angel of the Fifth Heaven—the presiding spirit of the 5th Heaven is Michael—that is, if the 5th Heaven is Machum; but if the 5th Heaven is

Mathey, then the presiding spirit is Sammael. Assisting angels ruling the 5th Heaven include Friagne, Hyniel, Ofael, Zaliel. [*Rf.* de Abano, *The Heptameron.*] In Mohammedan lore, the 5th Heaven is the abode of the Avenging Angel "who presides over elemental fire."

Angel of Fire—Nathaniel (Nathanel), Arel, Atuniel, Jehoel, Ardarel, Gabriel, Seraph; also Uriel, "angel of the fire of the sun." Revelation 14:18 speaks of the angel of the heavenly altar "who has authority over fire." *Cf.* Agni, the Vedic god of fire and mediator (angel) between gods and men. The Zoroastrian genius of fire is Atar (*q.v.*). In the *Fourth Book of Maccabees* there is mention of an angel of fire whom Aaron overcomes; he is to be compared with the destroying spirit in Reider, *The Book of Wisdom* 18:22. When the Baal-worshipping Jair succeeded Abimelech to the throne in Israel and ordered the 7 men faithful to God to be consigned to the flames, Nathanel, "lord over fire," extinguished the flames and enabled the 7 to escape. Nathanel then burnt Jair along with 1,000 of his men. For the legend, see *Pseudo-Philo* 39; also *The Chronicles of Yerahmeel* 48:175. The Prokofieff opera *L'Ange de Feu*, composed between 1920 and 1926, is based on a novel by the Russian poet Valerie Brusoff. It was published in 1903. The chief character is Madiel, angel of fire, who returns to the heroine (a 16th-century visionary) in the form of a German knight. A concert performance of the opera was given in Venice in 1955; an American premiere occurred in New York at the City Center in September 1965. According to Kircher, *Ecstatic Voyage* (to the planets), the sun—so he reported—"is peopled with angels of fire swimming in seas of light around a volcano from which pour myriads of meteors." One of Marc Chagall's celebrated oils is his apocalyptic Angel of Fire or Flaming Angel (the canvas is titled "Descent of the Red Angel") that plunges from Heaven on a peaceful and unsuspecting world, and shatters it.

Angel of the Firmament—Hlm Hml.

Angel of the First Heaven—Sabrael, Asrulyu, Pazriel (Sidriel), Gabriel, etc.

Angel over Fish—Gagiel, Arariel, Azareel.

Angel of Flame—El Auria, a name equated with Ouriel (Uriel). [*See* Angel of Fire.]

Angel of the Flaming Sword [Angel of the Garden of Eden]

Angel of Food—Manna; the angel of nourishment is Isda.

Angel of the Footstool—in Arabic lore, the angel of the footstool (Kursi) offers arrivals to the 7th Heaven a pillar of light to support them when standing before the divine judge for interrogation. [*Rf. 3 Enoch*, 181; Nicholson, "An Early Arabic Version," etc.]

Angel of Force—Afriel, equated with Raphael.

Angel of Forests [Zuphlas]

Angel of Forgetting or Forgetfulness (or Oblivion)—usually Poteh or Purah (*q.v.*).

Angel of Fornication [Angel of Lust]

Angels of the Four Cardinal Points (or Regents of the Earth)—in Blavatsky, *The Secret Doctrine*, the "winged globe and fiery wheels," recalling Ezekiel's description of the 4 living creatures (Ezekiel I) glimpsed at the River Chebar. In Hindu lore, the 4 regents are the Chatur Maharajas, and are named Dhritar-ashtra, Virudhaka, Virupaksha, and Vaishravana. [*Rf.* Leadbeater, *The Astral Plane.*]

Angels of the Four Elements—over fire, Seraph or Nathaniel; over air, Cherub; over water, Tharsis or Tharsus; over earth, Ariel.

Angels of the Four Winds—Uriel, over the south; Michael, over the east; Raphael, over the west (serving also as governor of the south, with Uriel); Gabriel, over the north. [*Rf.* Heywood, *The Hierarchy of the Blessèd Angels*, p. 214.] Revelation 7 speaks of "four angels standing at the four corners of the earth, holding fast the four winds of the earth"—derived, supposedly, from *The Book of Enoch* (*Enoch I*). *The Book of the Angel Raziel* gives Usiel (Uzziel) as one of the 4 angels of the 4 winds.

Angels of the Fourth Heaven—Michael; Shamshiel; Shahakiel.

Angel over (Wild) Fowl—Trgiaob. [*Rf.* M. Gaster, *The Sword of Moses.*]

Angel over Free Will [Tabris]

Angels over Friday—Anael (Haniel, Anafiel); Rachiel; Sachiel.

Angel of Friendship—in ancient Persian lore, the angel of friendship was Mihr (*q.v.*). He was also the angel of love and ruled the 7th month. [*Rf.* Chateaubriand, *Genius of Christianity.*]

Angel over Fruit (or Fruit Trees)—Sofiel; Alpiel; Serakel; Ilaniel; Eirnilus.

Angel of Fury—Ksoppghiel, who is the leader of the many angels of this order. [*Cf.* Zkzoromtiel.]

Angel of the Future—Teiaiel or Isiaiel (*q.v.*). In Assyro-Babylonian mythology, the god of foresight was Adad.

Angels of the Garden of Eden—the 2 angels commonly identified as the angels of Eden are Metatron and Messiah, both of the order of cherubim. But Raphael is also regarded as the angel of the earthly paradise by virtue of his having guarded the Tree of Life. John Dryden in his *State of Innocence, or The Fall of Man* concludes his dramatic poem with Raphael hustling our first parents out of Eden (rather than Michael, as in Milton, *Paradise Lost*). [*Rf. The Zohar*; Waite, *The Secret Doctrine in Israel.*] To R. L. Gales ("The Christian Lore of Angels"), it is Jophiel who stands at the gates of the Garden of Eden with the flaming sword.

Angel of Gehenna (Gehennom, Gehinnom)—Temeluchus, Kushiel, Shaftiel, Nasargiel, Duma. In the New Testament, Gehenna is another name for Hell. [*Rf. Maseket Gan Eden and Gehinnom,* quoted in *Jewish Encyclopedia* I, 593.] In the writings of the cabalist Joseph ben Abraham Gikatilla, Gehennom is the name of the 1st lodge of the 7 lodges in Hell, with Kushiel as the presiding angel.

Angel of Gemini ("twins")—Ambriel or, in ceremonial magic, Giel. According to Rabbi Chomer (Hebrew cabalist and master of Gaffarel), the 2 governing spirits of Gemini are Sagras and Saraiel. [*Rf.* Levi, *Transcendental Magic.*]

Angel of Gethsemane—according to Gales, writing in the *National Review* on "The Christian Lore of Angels," it is the angel Chamuel (Kamuel, Haniel) who strengthened Jesus, in His agony in the Garden of Gethsemane, with the assurance of resurrection. Luke 22:43 speaks of this angel but does not name him. Some sources identify Gabriel as the angel of Gethsemane.

Angel of Glory—Sandalphon, who is also the angel of prayer and tears. See Longfellow's poem "Sandalphon." The angels of glory, as a group, are identified or equated with the angels of sanctification. They reside in the highest Heaven, Araboth, number 660,000 myriads, and "stand over against the throne of Glory and the divisions of flaming fire." [*Rf. 3 Enoch* 22; *The Book of the Angel Raziel.*]

Angel of God—Uriel, or God Himself. In the Old Testament the expression "angel of the Lord" or "angel of God" is a theophorous term. It stands for the Elohim (god or gods), as in the *Mekilta of Rabbi Ishmael.* [*Rf.* Origen, *In Joanem* quoting from the *Prayer of Joseph,* a Jewish pseudepigraphon; *see* Angel of the Lord.]

Angel of Good—so called, though unnamed, in *The Apocalypse of Abraham.*

Angel of Good Counsel—Jesus, according to Dionysius the Areopagite in *The Mystical Theology and the Celestial Hierarchies.*

Angel of Good Deeds—pictured, but not named, as a recording angel in Longfellow, *The Golden Legend.*

Angel of Grace [Ananchel]

Angel of the Grail—pictured (but not named) by the Maître de Liesborn. The painting was done or published in 1465 and is reproduced on plate III in Régamey, *Anges.* The Angel of the Grail is also shown in a frieze, "The Vision of Galahad," by

Edward A. Abbey in the Boston Public Library. [*Rf.* Baxter, *The Holy Grail.*]

Angel of the Great (or Mighty) Counsel—the Messiah, the Holy Ghost, the Head of Days. (*See* Angel of the Covenant.) "Our Lord and Savior is called an angel of great counsel because he is the announcer of His father's Will." [*Rf.* Nicetas of Remesiana (335–414 C.E.) in "The Names and Titles of our Savior" quoted in Fremantle, *A Treasury of Early Christianity.*] St. Hilary in his *On the Trinity* IV calls the son of God (i.e., Jesus) "the angel of the Great Counsel." [*Rf.* Isaiah 9:6 (Septuagint version).] Gregory Thaumaturgus in his *Panegyric Addressed to Origen* thanks "that holy angel of God who fed me from my youth ... perchance the Angel of the Mighty Counsel."

Angel of Greece—Javan or Yavan (a name for Greece). Ginzberg, *The Legends of the Jews* I, 35, quoting from various Talmudic sources, reports that "the angel of Greece mounted 180 rounds of Jacob's ladder."

Angel of Grief—depicted in the famous monument in the Protestant Cemetery in Rome. It is the work of an American sculptor and poet, W. W. Story, who, with his wife, lies buried there. A replica, at Stanford University in California, was erected to the memory of the victims of the 1906 earthquake.

Angel of Hades—Uriel, Raphael. The 1st (Uriel) is set over Tartarus; the 2nd (Raphael) is "prince of Hades." While Raphael is in charge of departed souls, the officiating angel of the newly dead was, at least originally, Uriel. [*Rf. Enoch I*, and Ginzberg, *The Legends of the Jews* V, 70, 273, 310.]

Angel of Hail (or Hailstorms)—Bardiel or Baradiel or Barchiel; also Nuriel, Yurkami, and the twin irin kaddishin.

Angel of Healing—usually Raphael; but also Suriel and Assiel.

Angel of Health—Mumiah; also Raphael.

Angel of Heavenly Baptism—Seldac (*q.v.*).

Angel of Hell—there are 7 presiding angels of Hell under the ethnarchy of Duma(h). The other 6 most commonly listed are Kshiel, Lahatiel, Shaftiel, Maccathiel, Chutriel, Pasiel. Other listings give Dalkiel, Rugziel, Nasargiel. [*Rf.* writings of Joseph ben Abraham Gikatilla; Ginzberg, *The Legends of the Jews* II.]

Angel of Herbs—in the *Alphabet of Rabbi Akiba*, the angel of herbs (unnamed) is included among the "splendid, terrible, and mighty angel chiefs" who passed before God to extol and rejoice in the 1st Sabbath.

Angel of Heroism—Narsinha, who is the "man-lion avatar" and "lord of heroism."

Angel Over Hidden Things—Satarel (Sartael), and Gethel (Ingethal).

Angel of the Hills—like the angel of herbs (*q.v.*), the angel of the hills, unnamed, was included by Rabbi Akiba among the "splendid, terrible, and mighty angel chiefs" who passed before God to extol and rejoice in the 1st Sabbath. [*Rf. Alphabet of Rabbi Akiba.*]

Angel of His Presence—usually applied to the Shekinah (*q.v.*). Cf. Isaiah 63:9: "In all their affliction he was afflicted, and the angel of his presence saved them." *See* Angels of the Face; Angel of Sanctification; Angel of Glory. In rabbinic lore there are 12 angels of this class, with Michael, Gabriel, Uriel, and Zagzagael prominent among them.

Angel of Hoarfrost—an angel mentioned but not named in *Enoch I.*

Angel of Holiness [Angel of Sanctification]

Angel of the Holy Spirit—Gabriel. In Charles, *The Ascension of Isaiah* IX, 36, Isaiah sees the angel of the holy spirit in the 7th Heaven "on the left of my Lord."

Angel of Hope—Phanuel, as designated by Jean Danielou in his *Angels and Their Missions.* Phanuel is also the angel of penance "who holds the devil in his power."

Angels of Horror—the cherubim, who surround the throne of glory and who "strike fear and terror in the hearts of all who behold them." [*See* Angels of Terror.]

Angel of Hostility (mal'akh hammastemah)—usually applied to Beliel or Beliar or Mastema. [*Rf.* Mansoor, *The Thanksgiving Hymns*; Vermes, *Discovery in the Judean Desert*, p. 184.]

Angel of Humanity—in the *Revelation of Moses*, the angel of humanity appears to Eve in Eden when she is on her knees praying for forgiveness of her sins. The angel raises her up, saying: "Arise, Eve, from thy repentance; for behold, Adam thy husband has gone forth from his body." This was the first news to Eve that Adam had died. Eve died 6 days later.

Angel of Hurricanes [Za'miel; Zaafiel]

Angel of Ice—an angel mentioned but not named in *The Book of Jubilees* and in the *Revelation of John*, the latter a New Testament apocryphon. [*See* Angel of Snow.] The Mayans have a god of ice called Iztlacoliuhqui.

Angel of (or over) Immorality—his name is Zethar and he is one of the angels of confusion. In *Targum Esther*, Zethar is the "observer of immorality." God sent him down, with 6 other angels of confusion, to put an end to King Ahasuerus' pleasure. [*Rf.* Ginzberg, *The Legends of the Jews* IV, 375.] *See* Pharzuph; Schiekron.

Angel of Iniquity—"the angel of iniquity is bitter and angry and foolish; and his works are pernicious"—from the New Testament apocryphon *Hermas II*. While the angel is not named, he may be identified as Apollyon (*q.v.*).

Angel of Insolence—Rahab, who is also the angel or demon of the primordial waters and sometimes identified as the angel of death. [*Cf.* Isaiah 51:9.]

Angel of Insomnia—Michael, who was sent by God to cause the sleeplessness of Ahasuerus (the king who, on the advice of the wicked Haman, had decreed the annihilation of all the Jews in the kingdom). The tale is told in *Targum Esther* and repeated in Ginzberg, *The Legends of the Jews*.

Angel of Intercession—an unnamed angel who intercedes "for the people of Israel, so that they may not be utterly destroyed," as the angel declared to Levi when the latter went to Heaven (in a dream). [*Rf.* the *Testament of Levi* in the *Testament of the Twelve Patriarchs*.]

Angel of Inventions—Liwet, an *uthra* (angel) in Mandaean religious lore.

Angel of Ire [Zkzoromtiel]

Angel of Irrevocable Choice [Zeffar]

Angel of Israel—Michael. Also Javan (*q.v.*) and the unnamed angel in the *Testament of Levi* and the *Testament of Dan* (in the *Testament of the Twelve Patriarchs*).

Angel of January—Gabriel. In ancient Persian lore, the angel was Bahman.

Angel of Jehovah [Angel of the Lord]

Angel of Joy [Raphael; Gabriel]

Angel of Judgment [Gabriel; Zehanpuryu; Phalgus]

Angel of July—Verchiel (Zarachiel). In ancient Persian lore, Murdad (*q.v.*).

Angel of June—Muriel (a male angel). In ancient Persian lore, Tir.

Angel of June–July [Imrief]

Angel of (the planet) Jupiter—Zachariel (Yahriel); Zadkiel; Sachiel; Adabiel; Barchiel; Zadykiel. In Longfellow's *The Golden Legend*, the angel of the planet Jupiter is Zobiachel (*q.v.*). For the names of the angels of the 7 planets, see Camfield, *A Theological Discourse of Angels*.

Angels of Justice [Tsadkiel; Azza]

Angel of Knowledge—Raphael, who is also the angel of science, health, prayer, and love.

Angel of the Last Judgment—Michael, Gabriel (also Abel, as in *The Testament of Abraham*).

Angel of the Law—where "Law" has the meaning of Torah (i.e., the Pentateuch), the angel is Dina, also known as Yefefiah, Iofiel, Zagzagael.

Angel of Lawlessness—Beliar (Beliel), Matanbuchus. [*Rf. The Martyrdom of Isaiah.*]

Angel of (the sign of) Leo—in ceremonial magic, the angel is Ol. There are also governing spirits of the sign and these are Sagham and Seratiel, according to Rabbi Chomer, the Hebrew cabalist quoted in Levi, *Transcendental Magic*. *See also* Verchiel.

Angel of Liberty—unidentified by name. In Victor Hugo's *La Fin de Satan*, it is through the angel of liberty that Satan is to be finally redeemed. [*Rf.* Papini, *The Devil.*]

Angel of Libra (the Balances)—Jael, in ceremonial magic. In *The Magus*, the angel is Zuriel. According to Rabbi Chomer the 2 governing spirits of Libra are Grasgarben and Hadakiel (Chadakiel). It was from the writings of Rabbi Chomer that Gaffarel (17th-century man of learning and librarian to Cardinal Richelieu) drew many of his predictions.

Angel of Life—in his poem "The Two Angels," Longfellow speaks of the angel of life and the angel of death (both unnamed). They are dressed in robes of white, one "crowned with amaranth as with flame," the other "with asphodels like flakes of light." Both angels, says Longfellow, are from God "on celestial embassy."

Angel of Light—Isaac, ~~Gabriel~~, Jesus, and Satan have been called angels of light, Satan only in his disguise as such (II Corinthians 11:14). In Jewish tradition, Isaac was looked upon as an angel of light because of the supernatural brightness of his countenance at birth (a birth announced by Michael). In Christian lore of the Middle Ages, Gabriel was the angel of light. [*Rf.* Christian, *The History and Practice of Magic* I, 296.] In Parsi religion, it was Mihr (Meher, Mithra); also Parvargigar (who, in Arabic, was Rab-un-naw, "lord of the species"). According to *Midrash Konen*, 300 angels of light dwell in the 3rd Heaven where they "unceasingly sing God's praises and watch over the Garden of Eden and the Tree of Life." It should be explained that there are two paradises: the terrestrial one and the heavenly one. In the cabala, the sun, included among the planets, is regarded as an angel of light.

Angel of the Light of Day—Shamshiel, who is also the prince of Paradise. [*Rf. 3 Enoch.*]

Angel of Lightning—Barkiel (Barakiel) or Uriel, according to *The Book of Jubilees*; Ginzberg, *The Legends of the Jews*; *3 Enoch*. Barkiel (*q.v.*) is also the angel of February and is customarily cited as one of the 7 archangels. In Conybeare, *The Testament of Solomon*, as in Shah, *The Secret Lore of Magic*, the angel of lightning is claimed to be the only power able to overcome the demon Envy.

Angel of Lights—in *The Zadokite Fragments* the following appears: "Moses and Aaron continued in their charge through the help of the Angel of Lights even though Beliel in his cunning had set up Jannes and his brother in opposition of them." [*Rf.* Rowley, *The Zadokite Fragments and the Dead Sea Scrolls*; Grant, *Gnosticism and Early Christianity*.] Raphael, as regent of the sun; Uriel, also called regent of the sun; and Shamshiel, "light of day," may similarly be designated angels of light.

Angel of Longevity—the angels most commonly cited in occult writings as controllers or dispensers of longevity are Seheiah, Mumiah, Rehael. The last-named is of the order of powers. For his sigil, see Ambelain, *La Kabbale Pratique*.

Angel of the Lord—a Biblical theophorism, usually identified or personified as Michael, Metatron, Malachi, Gabriel, Akatriel, Yehadriel, Homadiel, Phinehas, etc. Where the expression occurs in the Old Testament, particularly in the earlier books, it may be taken to mean, though not always, God Himself. In Numbers 22:22 the Angel of the Lord is the adversary (i.e., *ha-satan*) acting for the Lord. The apparent contradiction between similar accounts in II Samuel 24:1 (where it is the Lord who provoked David to number Israel) and I Chronicles 21:1 (where it is Satan who does the provoking) may be resolved if

(1) Satan were spelled lowercase—i.e., *satan*—to denote not the name of an angel (as it was, in fact, not meant to denote) but the designation of an office, the office of adversary; and if (2) this adversary were understood to be acting for God—that is, acting as the angel of the Lord. In Judges II, the angel of the Lord comes up from Gilgal to Bochim to remind the Israelites of the Lord's promise "which I sware unto your fathers" to lead them to the Promised land. In the New Testament, as in Acts 12:1–7 (where Peter is released from prison), the angel of the Lord is not the Lord but a heavenly messenger sent by the Lord and acting for the Lord. See Raphael's painting "The Angel Waking St. Peter." In Acts 12:23, where Herod is struck down by "the angel of the Lord," the term may be equated with, or stand for, the angel of death. Justin held that one of the 3 angels that visited Abraham (Genesis 18) was the Word (i.e., the Logos or Holy Ghost). Philo thought that the other 2 were Christ and God Himself, or (again) the angel of the Lord, the 3 constituting a prefiguring of the Trinity. The subject of Abraham "entertaining angels un-awares" was popular with painters of the early Italian school. The scene is depicted in a woodcut in the Cologne Bible (1478–1480); it also figures in one of Hans Holbein's wood engravings (where, by the way, the 3 angels are represented without wings). It was an angel of the Lord, say the rabbis, who taught Abraham Hebrew, "the language of Revelation." [*Rf. Jewish Encyclopedia*, p. 85.] The term angel of the Lord, or angel of God, or angel of Yahweh appears in connection with the story of Hagar (Genesis 16); the sacrifice of Isaac (Genesis 22); the burning bush (Exodus 3); Balaam (Numbers 22); Gideon (Judges 6); parents of Samson (Judges 13); David at the threshing-floor of Araunah (2 Samuel); Elijah (2 Kings); the smiting of the Assyrian host (2 Kings); etc.

Angel of the Lord of Hosts—on high, the angel is Michael; on earth it is the High-priest, so designated "by reason that he belongs to the side of Grace." [*Rf. The Zohar* (Numbers 145b).]

Angel of Love—Theliel, Rahmiel, Raphael, Donquel, etc. In the cabala, the Roman goddess Venus also figures as an angel of love. In rabbinic lore the angel of love (not named) approved the creation of man when God first proposed the idea to an assembly of top hierarchs (some of those who disapproved were punished—*Rf.* Ginzberg, *The Legends of the Jews*). In Talmudic, Zoharistic, and Mandaean sources we find Liwet and Anael (the latter angel of the star of love) serving as additional angels of love. In ancient Persian writings, Mihr was the angel who watched over love and friendship.

Angel of Lude—the rooftree angel of France. He is represented, though not named, in stained glass at St. Bartholomew's Protestant Episcopal Church in New York City. The bronze of the angel is by Jehan Barbet de Lyon (1475). It was intended as a weathervane for St. Chapelle in Paris. In the 19th century the statue was removed by the Marquis de Talhouet to his chateau du Lude (whence the angel's name). It was acquired by J. P. Morgan and exhibited in the United States. A reproduction is in the book *Merchants of Art*.

Angel of Lust—in Talmud *Bereshith Rabba* 85, and according to Rabbi Jochanan commenting on Genesis 38:13–26, when "Judah was about to pass by, without noticing, Tamar (Judah's daughter-in-law, squatting like a harlot at the crossroads), God caused the angel of lust to present itself to him." The angel is not named—but compare with Pharzuph (or Priapus), whom Arnobius in *Adversus Nationes* III, called "the Hellespontian god of lust." [*Cf.* also with the "spirit of whoredom" in Hosea 4:12.]

Angel of Luxury—in his commentary on Matthew, Origen says that anyone who "falls away from Michael is put into subjection to the angel of luxury, then to the angel of punishment."

Angel of Mankind—usually Metatron (*q.v.*).

Angels of the Mansions of the Moon—*see* Appendix for the names of 28 of these governing angels of the moon.

Angel of March—Machidiel (Malchidiel), Melkejal, etc. For angels governing other months

Angels of the Trinity, an icon made c. 1410–1420 by André Rublev. Here all 3 figures (Jesus, God, and the Holy Ghost) are winged and haloed. In the Tretykov Gallery, Moscow. Reproduced from Régamey, *Anges*.

of the year, *see* Angels of the Months of the Year. In ancient Persian lore, the angel of March was Favardin.

Angel of the Marriage of Contraries [Camaysar]

Angel of (the planet) Mars—Uriel, Sammael (Zamiel), Gabriel, Chamael (or Camuel, as listed in Camfield, *A Theological Discourse of Angels*). [*Rf.* Kircher, *Oedipus Aegyptiacus*; Levi, *Transcendental Magic*; Lenormant, *Chaldean Magic*.]

Angel of May—Ambriel (Amriel); also Afsi-Khof. [*Rf.* De Plancy, *Dictionnaire Infernal*.] In ancient Persian lore, the angel of May was Khurdad.

Angel of Media—the unnamed tutelary angel of the ancient land of Media who became "corrupted through national bias." According to Ginzberg, *The Legends of the Jews* I, 351, the angel of Media mounted 52 rungs of Jacob's Ladder.

Angel of Memory—Zachriel, Zadkiel, Mupiel. The angels of memory are invoked in Mosaic incantations, occult rites, etc.

Angel of (the planet) Mercury—in grimoires and goetic texts, the angels of the planet Mercury are variously given as Tiriel, Raphael, Hasdiel, Michael, Barkiel, Zadkiel. In practical cabala, the angel of Mercury is Bene (Bne) Seraphim. [*Rf.* Levi, *Transcendental Magic*; Trachtenberg, *Jewish Magic and Superstition*.]

Angel of Mercy—Rahmiel (Rhamiel), Rachmiel, Gabriel, Michael, Zehanpuryu, Zadkiel. St. Francis of Assisi has been called the angel of mercy and has been so pictured (with wings) in *The Douce Apocalypse*. (*See also The Zohar; 3 Enoch.*) As in the case of 2 other mortals (Enoch and Elijah), St. Francis, it is claimed, was transformed into an angel and now goes by the name of Rhamiel. Another angel of mercy named in Merkabah lore is Uzziel, acting under Metatron. [*Rf.* introd. *3 Enoch.*]

Angel of Meteors [Angel of Comets, *q.v.*]

Angels of Might—"from the shrines of the Egyptians, He (Christ) stole the names of the angels of might"—so claimed pagan writers, according to Arnobius in his *Adversus Nationes* I. The names of these angels of might are not given.

Angel of Mighty Counsel—the Septuagint version of the famous passage in Isaiah 9:6, which has been interpreted by Christian apologists as one of the prophecies of the advent of Christ, and as one of His appellations.

Angel of Migration—Nadiel (*q.v.*), who is the governing spirit of the month of Kislav (November–December).

Angel of Mohammed—when Mohammed, according to legend, was transported to Heaven, he saw there—as he later reported—an angel with "70,000 heads, each head having 70,000 faces, each face 70,000 mouths, each mouth 70,000 tongues, each tongue speaking 70,000 languages, and all employed in singing God's praises." Brewer in his *Dictionary of Phrase and Fable* estimates that the foregoing enumeration "would make more than 31,000 trillion languages and nearly 5 billion mouths." [*Cf.* the erelim.]

Angel of Monday—Gabriel; Arcan (king, in the nether realms); Bilet; Missabu; Abuzaha; and others.

Angels of Mons (legendary)—in Machen, *The Bowmen & Other Legends of the War*, the angels of Mons, phantom horsemen, are reported to have appeared at the battle of Mons, bringing aid to the English. The report found general acceptance among civilians as well as among many of the soldiers who fought in the battle.

Angels of the (12) Months of the Year—Gabriel (January); Barchiel (February); Malchidiel (March); Asmodel (April); Ambriel or Amriel (May); Muriel (June); Verchiel (July); Hamaliel (August); Zuriel or Uriel (September); Barbiel (October); Adnachiel or Advachiel (November); Hanael or Anael (December). In ancient Persian lore, the angels were: Bahman (January); Isfandarmend (February); Farvardin (March); Ardibehist (April); Khurdad (May); Tir (June); Murdad (July); Shahrivar (August); Mihr or Miher

(September); Aban (October); Azar (November); Dai (December). [*Rf. The Magus* II and De Plancy, *Dictionnaire Infernal.*]

Angels of the Moon—in Solomonic lore, the angels governing the moon are variously given as Yahriel, Iachadiel, Elimiel, Gabriel, Tsaphiel, Zachariel, Iaqwiel, and others. In Longfellow's *The Golden Legend*, where the 7 planetary angels are named, the angel of the moon is given as Gabriel, although in later editions of the poem Longfellow switched to the angel Onafiel. [*Rf.* Christian, *The History and Practice of Magic.*] Actually, there is no such angel as Onafiel. Longfellow coined him inadvertently through a transposition of the letters "f" and "n" in Ofaniel, who is the traditional angel of the moon.

Angel of Morals—Mehabiah, an angel who assists mortals desiring progeny. In *The Magus,* Mehabiah is cited as one of the 72 angels bearing the name of God Shemhamphorae.

Angel of Mountains [Rampel]

Angel of the Muses—Uriel, Israfel, Radueriel, Vretil (Pravuil). The 9 Etruscan gods, the Novensiles, were regarded collectively as constituting the Muses, according to Granius (on the authority of Arnobius in his *Adversus Nationes* III).

Angel of Music—in Islamic lore, the angel of music is Israfel (Israfil), who is often equated with Uriel.

Angel of the Mutations of the Moon—in ancient Persian theogony, the angel was Mah.

Angel of Mysteries—Raziel, Gabriel, Zizuph. In Christian, *The History and Practice of Magic,* Gabriel is the "genius of Mysteries."

Angel of Night [Leliel; Metatron; Lailah]

Angel of the Noonday Winds [Nariel]

Angel of the North [Oertha; Alfatha; Uriel; Chairoum]

Angels of the North Star—Abathur, Muzania, Arhum Hii, and 4 angels (*uthri*) in Mandaean lore.

Angel of the North Wind—Chairoum (*q.v.*).

Angel of Nourishment—Isda. *See* Angel of Food.

Angel of November—Adnachiel (Advachiel, Adernahael). In ancient Persian lore, the angel of November was Azar.

Angel of Obedience—Sraosha (*q.v.*) in Manicheanism.

Angel of Oblivion—Purah or Puta or Poteh. Referred to also as the angel of forgetfulness.

Angel of October—Barbiel. In ancient Persian lore, Aban.

Angel of the Odd (fictional)—in Edgar Allan Poe's short story so titled, a wingless, Dutch–English speaking angel, more like an automaton, who "presides over the contretemps of mankind." The business of this angel or genius is "to bring about the odd accidents which are continually astonishing the sceptic." [*Rf.* vol. 4 of the 10-vol. *The Works of Edgar Allan Poe.*]

Angel of Omnipotence—there are (or were) 8 angels of this class, Atuesuel, Ebuhuel, Elubatel, Tubatlu, Bualu, Tulatu, Labusi, Ublisi. In the *Citation of Leviathan,* the first 3 angels are invoked to force demons to appear and do the bidding of the invocant. [*Rf. The Sixth and Seventh Books of Moses,* p. 85.]

Angel of Oracles—Phaldor (*q.v.*).

Angel of Order—Sadriel (*q.v.*).

Angel of Orion—in the *Alphabet of Rabbi Akiba,* the angel of Orion (unnamed) is included among the "splendid, terrible and mighty angel chiefs" who passed before God to extol and rejoice in the 1st Sabbath.

Angel of Paradise—both earthly and heavenly: Shamshiel, Michael, Zephon, Zotiel, Johiel, Gabriel, etc. In Mandaean lore, the angel is Rusvon. In ancient Persian lore, the angel was Sirushi (or Surush Ashu, or Ashu). [*Rf.* Shea and Troyer, *The Dabistan,* p. 144.]

Angel of Patience—Achaiah (*q.v.*), who is also adept in discovering the secrets of nature. In

Angels Chanting the "Gloria" by Benozzo Gozzoli (1420–1498). Reproduced from Régamey, *Anges.*

the cabala, the angel of patience is one of 3, and belongs to the order of seraphim.

Angel of Peace—in Jewish legend, the angel of peace (unnamed) is reputed to have opposed the creation of man, for which opposition he was burned by God, along with the hosts under him. The angel of truth was also burned, and for the same reason. Later, it seems, they were both revived. In *Enoch I*, 40, the angel of peace leads Enoch the patriarch around Heaven and reveals to him the names of the 4 archangels of the presence—Michael, Raphael, Gabriel, Phanuel—describing their individual duties. The *Testament of Asher* speaks of "meeting the angel of peace," but does not name him. Traditionally there were 7 angels of peace. *The Zohar* translates Isaiah 33:7 as "Behold, angels cry abroad, the angels of peace weep bitterly." They weep "because they no longer know [declares Rabbi Simeon] what to make of God's promise to Abraham at the time when He brought him forth." According to tradition [*Rf. New Jewish Encyclopedia*, p. 441] "angels of peace visit every Jewish home when the holy Sabbath is being ushered in." In gnostic lore, the prince of peace is Melchisedec (*q.v.*). [*Rf.* Prince of Peace.]

Angel of Penance—Phanuel (*q.v.*). He is also the angel of hope and identified as the Shepherd of Hermas.

Angel of Persecution—according to Roman Catholic doctrine, in its prebaptismal rites, the angel of persecution is a personal devil which is in each of us (side by side with a guardian angel). *See* Angel of Perversion. [*Rf.* Corte, *Who Is the Devil?*]

Angel of Persia—Dob(b)iel or Dub(b)iel, known as the guardian angel of Persia. In Daniel 10:13, Michael contends with the prince of Persia (not identified here by name). [*Rf.* Talmud *Yoma* 77a.]

Angel of Perversion—a 2nd-century C.E. apocryphon, the *Shepherd of Hermas*, informs us that "every man has close by him 2 angels, one an angel of holiness or sanctity, the other an angel of perversion." [*Cf.* Angel of Persecution.]

Angel of Pisces—in ceremonial magic, the angel of this sign of the zodiac (Pisces, fishes) is Pasiel. According to Rabbi Chomer, quoted by Eliphas Levi, there are 2 governing spirits of Pisces and they are Rasamasa and Vocabiel (Vocatiel). Heywood, *The Hierarchy of the Blessèd Angels*, lists Varchiel as chief regent of Pisces.

Angel of the Plagues—an unnamed destroying angel who, sword in hand, appeared over Jerusalem to punish the Jews, particularly King David, for authorizing a census (the numbering of people being, apparently, an offence to God). David appeased the angel of the plagues by offering burnt sacrifices on the threshing-floor of Araunah, one of the Jebusite inhabitants of old Jerusalem. For the incident, see I Chronicles 21.

Angels of the Planets—there are commonly 7 angels of the planets which, in occult lore, include the sun and moon. The chief is Rehatiel (Rhatiel) or Rejatiel. For the name of the governing angel for each planet, his sign, the day he governs, etc., *see* Appendix. In the 1st edition of Longfellow's *The Golden Legend*, the angels of the 7 planets are given as: Raphael (Sun); Gabriel (Moon); Anael (star of love, i.e., Venus); Zobiachel (Jupiter); Michael (Mercury); Uriel (Mars); Anachiel (Saturn). In later editions, Longfellow substituted Onafiel for Gabriel and Orifel for Anachiel. Both Zobiachel and Onafiel seem to be newly coined, since they show up in no other source.

Angel of Plants—Sachluph (*q.v.*).

Angel of the Pleiades—in the *Alphabet of Rabbi Akiba*, this angel, unnamed, is included among the "splendid, terrible and mighty angel chiefs" who passed before God to extol and rejoice in the 1st Sabbath.

Angel of Poetry—Uriel, Israfel, Radueriel (Vretil), Phoenix.

Angel of (the order of) Powers—in the cabala [*Rf.* Levi, *Transcendental Magic*] the angel of the order of powers is Zacharael, or the planet Jupiter. Other sources designate Verchiel, Camael, Kafziel (Cassiel), and Sam(m)ael. The last named is given on the authority of Robert Fludd,

Baroque Angels, the work of Franz Schwanthaler (c. 1720). Made for the Heilige Maria Kirche, Dresden. From the collection of Edward R. Lubin.

16th-century alchemist. According to Gregory the Great, the powers "preside over demons." In *The Testament of Abraham*, a pseudepigraphic work, the angel of powers is Michael.

Angel of Praise—unnamed. In Ginzberg, *The Legends of the Jews* I, 16, it is related that "the third creation of the second day [of Creation] were the angel hosts, both the ministering angels and the angels of praise." Specifically, the latter would constitute the 3 orders of the 1st triad in the Dionysian scheme—seraphim, cherubim, thrones.

Angel of Prayer—in occult writings one finds usually 5 or 6 named angels of prayer: Akatriel, Gabriel, Metatron, Raphael, Sandalphon, Sizouse. But since there are "seven archangels who convey the prayers of the saints to God" (according to Oesterley in Manson, *A Companion to the Bible*, p. 337), Michael might be included among the aforementioned 6.

Angel of Precipices—Zarobi (*q.v.*).

Angels of Pregnancy—in Mosaic incantation

rites, the angels of pregnancy are Sinui and Sinsuni. These 2 luminaries are invoked to help women in labor. According to Jewish legend, God appoints an angel to make the newborn Jewish male resemble its father, in order, presumably, to preclude the charge of adultery which might be lodged against the mother where a child bears no resemblance to the male parent. [*Rf.* Ginzberg, *The Legends of the Jews* VI, 83.]

Angels of the Presence—also known as angels of the face. They are customarily 12 in number, the chiefs of the group being Michael, Metatron, Suriel, Sandalphon, Astanphaeus, Saraqael, Phanuel, Jehoel, Zagzagael, Uriel, Yefefiah, and Akatriel. The angels of the presence are also equated with the angels of sanctification and the angels of glory, 2 classes of hierarchs that were, it seems, already circumcised at the time they were created. See *The Book of Jubilees* XV, 27. In the just-named pseudepigraphon (I, 27 et seq.) the story of Creation is unfolded to Moses "by the angel of the presence," who, however, is not named. "Probably Michael," says R. H. Charles. The patriarch Judah, in the *Testament of Judah* (in the *Testament of the Twelve Patriarchs*), claims that the angel of the presence (not named) blessed him. According to *The Zohar* (I, Vayera), the angels of the presence were expelled from the divine presence when they revealed the "mystery" (i.e., God's purpose). [*Rf. A Rabbinic Anthology*, p. 162.] Blake in his poem "Milton" speaks of the "seven angels of the presence." He also has a drawing, now in the Fitzwilliam Museum, Cambridge, titled "The Angel of the Divine Presence Clothing Adam and Eve with Coats of Skins." Rabbinic tradition refers to the 70 tutelary angels as angels of the presence. According to the *Testament of Levi* (in the *Testament of the Twelve Patriarchs*), the angels of the presence dwell in the 6th Heaven. [*Rf.* Eisenmenger, *Traditions of the Jews* I; *Book of Hymns* V; *Testament of Judah* (in the *Testament of the Twelve Patriarchs*); Lea, *Materials Toward a History of Witchcraft* I, 17.]

Angel of Pride—Rahab; Satan.

Angel of Priesthoods and Sacrifices—

Sachiel-Meleck. [*Rf.* Levi, *Transcendental Magic*, p. 307.]

Angels of Principalities—the ruling princes of this order, listed 1st in the 3rd triad of the pseudo-Dionysian system of the celestial hierarchy, include Haniel, Nisroc, Cerviel, and Raguel. The order is known also as princedoms. The angels of this choir are "protectors of religion" and preside over good spirits. In Jude and in the Pauline Epistles, the principalities are regarded as both beneficent and malevolent luminaries. Nisroc is mentioned in *Paradise Lost* VI, 447 as "of Principalities the prime." This Nisroc was once an Assyrian deity (II Kings 19:37). In occult lore, he is a demon. [*Rf.* Caird, *Principalities and Powers*.]

Angel of Proclamation—Gabriel; also Ak(h)-raziel or Azkariel.

Angel of Progress—in Jewish cabala, the angel of progress is Mercury. Raphael is also referred to as the angel of progress. [*Rf.* Acts 14: 11–12; Levi, *Transcendental Magic*, p. 100.]

Angel of Prostitution—in Zoharistic cabala, the angel of prostitution is Eisheth Zenunim (mate of Sammael, prince of poison and of death). Lilith, Naamah, and Agrat bat Mahlat were 3 other mates of Sammael and, like Eisheth, angels of prostitution. [*Rf.* Masters, *Eros and Evil*.]

Angel of Punishment—there are 7 and they are named in *Maseket Gan Eden and Gehinnom*: Kushiel ("rigid one of God"); Lahatiel ("flaming one"); Shoftiel ("judge of God"); Makatiel ("plague of God"); Hutriel ("rod of God"); Pusiel or Puriel ("fire of God"); Rogziel ("wrath of God"). See *Jewish Encyclopedia* I, 593. Another angel of punishment is Amaliel (*q.v.*). The Coptic *Pistis Sophia* names Ariel as the angel in charge of punishments in Hell. *The Manual of Discipline* (plate IV) lists angels of punishment. In *Enoch II* (10:3) the angels of punishment dwell in the 3rd Heaven. *Cf.* the Levi testament in the *Testament of the Twelve Patriarchs*, where armies of punishing angels, presumably evil, dwell in the 3rd Heaven. These, says Charles in *Enoch I*, are the grigori (*q.v.*). Hell, by the way, was "in the north of the 3rd Heaven." In Coptic gnosticism, the demon of punishment is Asmodel; in occult writings, Asmodel is the angel of April. *Midrash Tehillim*, commenting on Psalm 7, lists 5 angels of punishment whom Moses encountered in Heaven, to wit: (1) Af, angel of anger; (2) Kezef, angel of wrath; (3) Hemah, angel of fury; (4) Hasmed, angel of annihilation; (5) Mashit, angel of destruction.

Angel of Purity—Tahariel. [*Rf.* Abelson, *Jewish Mysticism*.]

Angels of Quaking—the "Angels of Quaking surround the throne of glory." (*Cf.* Angels of Terror.) Moses beheld these angels during his 40-day stay in Heaven. [*Rf.* Ma'ayan ha-Hokmah 58–60 and other midrashim.]

Angel of Rage—called N'mosnikttiel in M. Gaster, *The Sword of Moses*. [*Cf.* Angels of Wrath.]

Angel of Rain—in rabbinic lore, at least 5 qualify as angels of rain: Matriel, Matarel, Matariel, Ridya (Ridia), and Zalbesael (Zelebsel). *3 Enoch* (the Hebrew Book of Enoch) vouches for "Batarrel standing for Matarel." In ancient Persian writings, the angel of rain (as also for rivers) was Dara.

Angel of Rarified Air—in Parsi angelology the angel is Ram-Khvastra; in Mandaean lore, it is Ayar Ziwa.

Angel of Repentance—according to various sources, the angel of repentance is Shepherd, Michael, Raphael, Suriel, Salathiel, Phanuel (Penuel). [*Rf. Shepherd of Hermas; Enoch I; The Interpreter's Bible (Commentary)*.]

Angel of Resurrection—the angel who rolled away the stone before Jesus' tomb. In Matthew 28 he is called the angel of the Lord. [*Cf.* Gabriel.]

Angel of Revelation—Gabriel. [See Blake's poem, "Glad Day."]

Angel of the Right—in the Valentinian (gnostic) theory of Excerpts, the Angels of the Right were those who had prior knowledge of the birth of Christ. [*Rf.* Newbold, "The Descent of Christ in the Odes of Solomon" in *Journal of Biblical Literature*, December 1912.]

Angel of Righteousness—Michael. In *The Shepherd of Hermas*, the angel (unnamed) is described as "mild, modest, gentle and quiet" and as one of 2 angels "with man," the other being an "angel of iniquity" (*q.v.*).

Angel of the River Jordan—called Silmai; also Nidbai.

Angel of Rivers—in M. Gaster, *The Sword of Moses*, the angel of rivers is Trsiel; in Persian lore the angel is Dara (*q.v.*).

Angel of Rome—usually spoken of as Sammael, who is Satan in post-Biblical lore. Edom (*q.v.*) was a designation for Rome.

Angel of Running Streams—Nahaliel (*q.v.*).

Angel of the Sabbath—named Sabbath in Jewish (rabbinic) writings, where he is represented as one of the great hierarchs in Heaven. "The angel named Sabbath who sat on a throne of glory and the chiefs of all the angels of all the heavens and the abysses danced and rejoiced before him." [*Rf.* Ginzberg, *The Legends of the Jews* I, 84.]

Angel of Sagittarius—the angel of the sign of Sagittarius in the zodiac is Ayil or Sizajasel. According to Rabbi Chomer (Levi, *Transcendental Magic*), the 2 governing spirits of the sign are Vhnori and Saritaiel (Saritiel). In Heywood, *The Hierarchy of the Blessèd Angels*, the ruler of Sagittarius is Adnachiel.

Angel of Salvation—Haurvatat, who is one of the amesha spentas (archangels) in Zoroastrianism. In noncanonical lore (Enoch and Baruch apocrypha), the angel of salvation is Uriel. [*Rf.* Graves and Patai, *Hebrew Myths*, p. 103.]

Angel of Sanctification—equated with the angel of glory and the angel of the presence. Chief among the angels of sanctification are Phanuel, Suriel, Metatron, Michael, Zagzagael. Like the angels of the presence, the angels of sanctification

were created already circumcised, a "fact" attested to in the pre-Christian *The Book of Jubilees*.

Angel of the Sanctuary—Sar ha-Kodesh. Also identified as Michael, Metatron, Yefefiah.

Angel of Saturday—Cassiel, Machatan, Uriel. In the Talismans of Paracelsus, the angel of Saturday is Orifiel. [*Rf.* Christian, *The History and Practice of Magic* I, 318.]

Angel of Saturn—Orifiel, Kafziel, Michael, Maion, Orifel, Mael, Zaphiel, Schebtaiel. In the works of Zanchy, Agrippa, and Trithemius the angel of the planet Saturn is Zapkiel. Agrippa also lists Orifiel. In Longfellow, *The Golden Legend* (1st edition, 1851), the angel governing Saturn is Anachiel. In later editions Longfellow substituted Orifel for Anachiel. [*Rf.* Camfield, *A Theological Discourse of Angels*.]

Angel of Scandal—Zahun, according to Levi, *Transcendental Magic*, p. 502. In Apollonius of Tyana, *The Nuctemeron*, Zahun is cited as one of the genii of the 1st hour.

Angel of Science—Raphael, who is also the angel of knowledge.

Angel of Scorpio—Sosol. According to Rabbi Chomer, quoted in Levi, *Transcendental Magic*, the 2 governing spirits of Scorpio are Riehol and Saissaeiel (Sartziel).

Angel of the Sea—Rahab. He is so called in Scripture and Talmud. Rahab was destroyed twice—once for refusing to divide the upper and lower waters at the time of Creation, and again for trying to save from drowning the Egyptian hosts in pursuit of the fleeing Hebrews across the Red (more correctly Reed) Sea. [*See* Tamiel; Angel of the Deep.]

Angels of the (Four) Seasons—Farlas (Winter); Telvi (Spring); Casmaran (Summer); Andarcel (Autumn). In medieval Hebrew texts the angels of the 4 seasons are Malkiel, Helemmelek, Melejal, and Narel. [*Rf.* "Angels," in *Interpreter's Dictionary of the Bible*.]

Angels of the Second Heaven—2 are usually cited: Raphael and Zachariel. But since it was in the 2nd Heaven that Moses encountered the angel Nuriel "with his retinue of 50 myriads of angels" (Ginzberg, *The Legends of the Jews* II, 306). Nuriel might be added to the rulers of this Heaven.

Angel of September—Uriel or Zuriel. The ruler of the month of Tishri (September–October) is Pahadron. However, if September is equated with the Hebrew month of Eloul, the angel is Elogium. In ancient Persian lore, the angel of September was Miher (Mihr).

Angels of Service—according to Rabbi Akiba the angels of service are "the fowl of heaven" (*Cf.* Psalm 104). *The Zohar* speaks of these angels as having 6 wings.

Angels of the Seven Days—Michael, Gabriel, Samael, Raphael, Sachiel, Anael, and Cassiel. According to Barrett, *The Magus* II (plate facing p. 105), the rulership is as follows, with the sigil of each angel reproduced in the Barrett book: Michael, lord of Sunday; Gabriel, lord of Monday; Samael, lord of Tuesday; Raphael, lord of Wednesday; Sachiel, lord of Thursday; Anael, lord of Friday; Cassiel, lord of Saturday.

Angels of the Seven Heavens—the ruling princes of the 7 Heavens are: Gabriel, 1st Heaven; Raphael, Zachariel, Galizur, 2nd Heaven; Jabniel, Rabacyel, Dalquiel, 3rd Heaven; Michael, 4th Heaven; Samael, Gadriel, 5th Heaven; Zachiel, Zebul, Sandalphon, Sabath, 6th Heaven; Cassiel (Kafziel) 7th Heaven. According to hechaloth lore, while some of the rulers reside in their respective Heavens, they are also found in other Heavens as guardians of the great halls. In Jewish legend, for example, Samael resides in the 7th Heaven (where, it is said, he is a prisoner).

Angel of the Seven Last Plagues—in Revelation 15–17 there are 7 angels of the 7 last plagues "to whom are given 7 golden vials full of the wrath of God." The angels are not named.

Angel of Showers [Zaa'fiel]

Angel of Silence [Shateiel, Duma(h)]

Angel of the Sirocco [Sikiel]

Angel of the Sixth Heaven—Zachiel, Zebul, Sabath, Sandalphon. "Here dwells the Guardian Angel of heaven and earth," according to the Muslims. The ruling prince of the 6th Heaven is Bodiel [*Rf. Hechaloth Zoterathi*].

Angel of the Sky [Sahaqiel]

Angel of Sleep—the unnamed angel who deprived King Ahasuerus of sleep in the Esther episode. [*Rf. Ozar Midrashim* I, p. 56.]

Angel over Small Birds [Tubiel]

Angels of Snow—Shalgiel, Michael. The angels of snow, unnamed, are spoken of in the apocryphal *Revelation of John*.

Angel of Solitudes—Cassiel, who is also the Angel of Tears (as is Sandalphon).

Angel of Song—Radueriel (Vretil), who is also choirmaster of the muses. In Koranic lore, the angel of song is Israfel or Uriel. In rabbinic lore, the angel is Shemiel (Shemael, Shammiel) or Metatron. The last named is called "Master of Heavenly Song."

Angels Over Sorceries—"the wizard Aod of the priests of Midian used the angels set over sorceries to make the sun shine at night," according to *The Biblical Antiquities of Philo*. [*Cf.* fallen angels, who make known secret arts to mankind, as related in *Enoch I*.]

Angel of the Sorrows of Death [Paraqlitos]

Angel of the Souls of Men [Remiel (Jeremiel)]

Angel of the South [Kerkoutha, Cedar, Raphael]

Angel of the Southwest [Naoutha]

Angel of the Spheres [Salatheel (Sealtiel); Jehudiel]

Angels of the Spring—in occult lore, there are 4: Amatiel, Caracasa, Core, Commissoros. The head of the sign of Spring is Spugliguel. The ruling angel is Milkiel.

Angel of the Star of Love [Anael]

Angel of the Stars [Kakabel, Kohabiel, Kochabiel, Kokbiel]

Angel of Sterility [Akriel]

Angel of Storm [Zakkiel, Zaamael]

Angel of Strength [Zeruch (Zeruel, Cerviel)]

Angel of Summer—Gargatel; Gaviel; Tariel. The head of the sign of summer is Tubiel.

Angels of the Summer Equinox—in this group there are 9 or more angels, with Oranir serving as chief. All are effective as amulets against the evil eye. For the names of 9 of these angels, *see* Appendix.

Angels of the Sun—in the cabala and occult lore, the angels of the sun include an array of hierarchs: Arithiel, Galgaliel, Gazardia (spelt variously), Korshid-Metatron, Michael, Och, Raphael, Uriel, Zerachiel, etc. *The Zohar* (Exodus, 188a) speaks of "the angel appointed to rule and guide the sun," declaring that at dawn this angel "steps forth with the holy letters of the supernal blessed Name inscribed upon his brow, and in the power of those letters opens all the windows of Heaven." In ancient Persian lore, the angel of the disk of the sun was Chur (*q.v.*).

Angel of Sunday—Michael (1st hour); Anael (2nd hour); Raphael (3rd hour); Gabriel (4th hour); Cassiel (5th hour); Sachiel (6th hour); Samael (7th hour); Michael (8th hour); Anael (9th hour); Raphael (10th hour); Gabriel (11th hour); Cassiel (12th hour). It will be observed that Michael, Anael, Raphael, Cassiel and Gabriel do double duty on the Sabbath day. [*Rf.* Shah, *Occultism*, pp. 55–56.]

Angel of the Sun's Rays [Schachlil]

Angel of the Supreme Mysteries [Raziel]

Angel of Sweet-Smelling Herbs [Arias]

Angel of the Sword—the chief angel of the sword is usually given as Soqed Hezi (variously spelt). But there are numerous other angels so designated, as in M. Gaster, *The Sword of Moses*.

Angel over Tame Beasts [Behemiel]

Angel over Tartarus (Hades)—Uriel; also the eponymous chief Tartaruchi.

Angel of Taurus—in ceremonial magic, the chief angel of this zodiacal sign (the Bull) is Tual, otherwise Asmodel. According to Rabbi Chomer, quoted by Levi in *Transcendental Magic*, the governing spirits of Taurus are Bagdal and Araziel.

Angel of Tears—Sandalphon and Cassiel (*qq.v.*). In Islamic lore, the Angel of Tears (not named) dwells in the 4th Heaven.

Angels of Terror—these angels are equated with the angels of quaking. They are the strongest among the hierarchs and surround the throne of glory. In Jewish mysticism, Pahadron is the chief angel of terror. He governs the month of Tishri (September–October).

Angel of the Testament—John the Baptist, according to Salkeld in *A Treatise of Angels* (1613), quoting Malachi 3:1: "and the angel of the testament whom you desire," etc. This would apply to Christ, says Lactantius in Schneweis, *Angels and Demons According to Lactantius*. The passage in Malachi is also translated as "messenger" of the covenant. [*Cf.* Matthew 2:10: "Behold, I send my messenger before thy face, which shall prepare thy way for thee."] In the view of Régamey (*What Is an Angel?*) the foregoing would denote that "Christ is to proclaim himself the angel of the testament and to cause John the Baptist to be recognized as the messenger" merely.

Angels of the Third Heaven—among the principal rulers here are Jabniel, Rabacyel, Dalquiel, Baradiel, and Shaphiel. It was in the 3rd Heaven that Moses encountered an angel "so tall, it would take a human 500 years to climb to his height; he had 70,000 heads, each head as many mouths, each mouth as many tongues, etc. Mohammed also saw such an angel in Heaven, but neither in Talmud nor in the Koran is he named. A good guess would be Erelim, eponymous head of the order of erelim; or Raziel, sometimes credited with being chief of the order. The term erelim derives from Isaiah 33:7. In de Abano, *The*

Heptameron, the angels of the 3rd Heaven include Milliel, Ucirmuel, Nelapa, Jerescue, and Babel. Some sources place the erelim in the 4th Heaven.

Angels of the Throne—the Hebrew equivalent of the order of thrones is arelim or ophanim, according to *The Book of the Angel Raziel*: "there were seven who stand before the throne." However, according to a Jewish legend, there were (or are) 70. Among the chiefs of the order the following may be mentioned: Orifiel, Ophaniel (eponymous head of the ophanim), Raziel, Zabkiel, Jophiel, Ambriel, Tychagar, Barael, Quelamia, Paschar, Boel, Raum, Murmur. A number of these hierarchs are no longer found in Heaven and are to be numbered among the fallen angels in Hell. In the Dionysian scheme, the thrones as an order are placed 3rd in the 1st triad of the celestial hierarchy. Their dominant characteristic or virtue is steadfastness.

Angel of Thunder—Ra'miel, and/or Uriel. The latter also serves as the angel of fire and lightning. In Assyro-Babylonian mythology, the god of thunder was Adad; see picturization in *Larousse Encyclopedia of Mythology*, p. 59. Another Babylonian god of thunder was Rimmon.

Angels of Thursday—Sachiel, Castiel, and Assasiel. In Paracelsus, *Talismans*, the angel of Thursday is Zachariel. [*Rf.* Christian, *The History and Practice of Magic* I, 318.]

Angel of Time—so called but not otherwise named in the Tarot (Tarot card No. 14). The angel of time "stands between earth and heaven, clothed in a white robe, with wings of flame and a golden halo around his head . . . one foot on land, the other on the sea, behind him the sun rising . . . on his brow the sign of eternity and life: the circle." In the hermetic hierarchy, says Christian, *The History and Practice of Magic*, the genius of time is Rempha.

Angel of the Torah [Yefefiah; Iofiel (or Yofiel); Zagzageal; Metatron]

Angel of Torment [Aftemelouchos]

Angel of Treasures [Parasiel]

Angel of the Treasures of the Dead [Remiel (i.e., Jeremiel)]

Angel Over Trees [Maktiel]

Angel of Trembling [Pahadron; also Angel of Quaking or Terror]

Angels of the Triplicities—in ceremonial magic, the angels who rule the zodiacal triplicities are: Michael (over the fiery triplicity); Raphael (over the airy triplicity); Gabriel (over the watery triplicity); and Uriel (over the earthy triplicity).

Angels of the Triune God—Meacheul, Lebatei, Ketuel. [*Rf.* Barrett, *The Magus*; *The Sixth and Seventh Books of Moses* (pp. 127–130).]

Angel of Truth—Amitiel; Michael; Gabriel. In Jewish legend, the angel of truth (unnamed) opposed the creation of man when God first broached the idea; for this opposition he was burned, along with the angel of peace (who also opposed the idea) and the hosts under them. Since Gabriel and Michael escaped being burned, it must have been Amitiel who was reduced to a cinder. In Muslim lore, Gabriel is the spirit of truth.

Angel of Tuesday—Samael; Satael; Amabiel; Friagne; Carmax; Arragon; and Hyniel.

Angel of Twilight [Aftiel]

Angel of Vegetables—Sealiah and Sofiel, who are also the angels over fruit.

Angels of Vengeance—the 12 angels of vengeance were among the 1st formed at Creation, although, according to Catholic doctrine, all angels were formed at one and the same time. Only 6 of these angels of vengeance are known by name—Satanel, Michael, Gabriel, Uriel, Raphael, and Nathanel (Zathael). Now, since the angels of the presence seem to be interchangeable (in Jewish lore) with the angels of vengeance, and since 12 of the former are known by name, 6 of these may be "taken over" and included in the listing of the vengeances—Suriel, Jehoel, Zagzagel, Akatriel, Metatron, and Yefefiah. The French painter Prud'hon (1758–1823) did a head of Vengeance in his painting "Divine Vengeance and Justice Pursuing Crime," which hangs in the Louvre. The head suggests that Prud'hon had the angel Uriel in mind.

Angel of (the planet) Venus—Anael (Haniel), Hasdiel, Eurabatres, Raphael, Hagiel, and Noguel.

Angel of Victory—Bahram, or Var (Adar) Bahram, who is a yazata in Parsi lore. *The Dabistan* and *The Mandaeans of Iraq and Iran* associate the angel of victory with the ascent of the soul of man.

Angel of Vindication—Douma(h) or Duma, who is also the angel of silence and the angel of the stillness of death. With Uzziel (Rahab), Douma was the governing *sar* (i.e., angel prince) of Egypt. [*Rf.* Waite, *The Holy Kabbalah*.]

Angel of Virgo (Virgin)—Voil or Voel. According to Rabbi Chomer in Levi, *Transcendental Magic*, the ruling spirits of this zodiacal sign are Iadara and Schaltiel.

Angels of (the order of) Virtues—more than a score of the angels of this order are named in G. Davidson's article, "The Celestial Virtues." Among the ruling princes of the order are Ariel, Barbiel, Haniel (Anael), Peliel, Nathanael, Atuniel.

Angel of Voyages—Susabo, who is one of the presiding genii of the 6th hour, in Apollonius of Tyana, *The Nuctemeron*.

Angel of War—Michael, Gabriel, and Gadriel. In the cabala there is Phaleg, called "the war lord" by Cornelius Agrippa.

Angel of Water (waters of the earth)—Tharsis or Tharsus; also Arariel, Talliud, Phul, Michael, Anafiel (all to be found in occult lore). In Persian lore, the angel of water is Harudha.

Angel of the Waters—in his cabalistic works, Cornelius Agrippa calls Phul (one of the 7 supreme spirits ruling the 196 provinces of Heaven) "the supreme lord of the waters." In Revelation 16:5, he is referred to but unnamed: "And I heard the angel of the waters say," etc. [*See* Arariel.]

Angel of Water Insects [Shakziel]

Angel of Weakness—Amaliel, who is also one of the angels of punishment. [*Rf.* Schwab, *Vocabulaire de l'Angélologie*, suppl.]

Angel of Wednesday [Raphael; Miel: Seraphiel]

Angel of the West—Gabriel, who is called "the guardian of the west." [*Rf.* Ambelain, *La Kabbale Pratique*.]

Angel of the Wheel of the Moon—Ofaniel, among others. [*Rf. Enoch*.]

Angel of the Wheel of the Sun [Galgaliel]

Angel of the Whirlwind—Ra'shiel or Zavael, according to *3 Enoch*. [*Rf.* Ginzberg, *The Legends of the Jews* I, 140.]

Angel of the Wild Beasts—Mtniel, Jehiel (Hayyel). [*Rf.* M. Gaster, *The Sword of Moses*; "Angelology," in *Jewish Encyclopedia*.]

Angel Over Wild Fowl and Creeping Things [Trgiaob]

Angel of the Wilderness—in Jewish cabala, and according to Levi, *Transcendental Magic*, the angel of the wilderness is the planet Saturn. The angel Orifiel has also been named a ruling spirit of the wilderness.

Angel of the Wind—in Revelation 7:1, there is mention of 4 angels of the wind. In occult works (M. Gaster, *The Sword of Moses*), in *The Book of Jubilees*, and in *3 Enoch*, the following are named as angelic rulers: Moriel, Ruhiel, Rujiel, Ben Nez, and the celestial Ephemerae. In his poem "Sandalphon" Longfellow sings of the angels of wind and of fire that "chant only one hymn and expire." Dürer engraved the 4 angels in control of the winds (see reproduction on p. 310, from Régamey's *Anges*). The cherubim were regarded as personifications of the wind. [*Rf.* Psalms 18:10.]

Angel of Winter—Amabael, Cetarari. The head of the sign of winter is Attaris (Altarib). [*Rf.* De Plancy, *Dictionnaire Infernal*; de Abano, *The Heptameron*; *The Book of Jubilees*.]

Angel of Wisdom—Zagzagel; also Metatron

(when Metatron goes under the name of Sasnigiel); also Dina (when Dina goes under the name of Yefefiah or Yofiel). According to legend, Zagzagel was ordered by God to carry Moses to a place where myriads of scholars congregated, all of them occupied with expounding the Torah. [*Rf.* Scholem, *Jewish Gnosticism, Merkabah Mysticism, and Talmudic Tradition.*]

Angel of the Womb [Armisael]

Angels of Women's Paradise—there were 9 of these female angels; they were once the mothers, wives, or daughters of the Hebrew patriarchs, and they occupied a place apart in one of the Heavens. Philo "allegorises away the wives of the Jewish patriarchs into the several Virtues" (see Philo, *About Cherubim*, chap. 13). [*Rf.* Conybeare, *Myth, Magic, and Morals*, p. 199.]

Angel (or Prince) of the World—Satan (see Pauline Epistles), Michael, Jehoel, Metatron, or Sar ha-Olam (which literally means, in Hebrew, prince of the world). Mammon is also described as "holding the throne of this world." [*Rf.* the Talmud; Bamberger, *Fallen Angels*, p. 58.]

Angels at the World's End—according to the *Revelation of Esdras* and as revealed to Esdras himself, the angels who will govern or rule "at the end of the world" are 9 in number: Michael, Gabriel, Uriel, Raphael, *Gabuthelon, *Beburos, *Zebuleon, *Aker, *Arphugitonos. Of these 9, the 5 preceded by an asterisk are found nowhere else in apocryphal or apocalyptic lore [*Rf. Ante-Nicene Fathers Library* VIII, 573]. *See* entry "Five Angels Who Lead the Souls of Men to Judgment."

Angels of Wrath—Hemah, Af, Mzpopiasaiel, Ezrael. In the *Revelation of Moses*, the Lawgiver, during his visit to Paradise, encountered the angels of anger and wrath in the 7th Heaven and found them composed "wholly of fire." [*Rf. The Zohar* I; M. Gaster, *The Sword of Moses*; Ginzberg, *The Legends of the Jews*; *Apocalypse of Peter*.] In the *Midrash Tehillim*, the angel of wrath is Kezef.

Angels of the Wrath of God—there are (or were) 7 angels of the wrath of God, as mentioned but not named in Revelation.

Angel of Yahweh—angel of the Lord, i.e., God Himself. Wherever the expression occurs in the Old Testament, it is a periphrasis. The earliest versions of the Old Testament had, in the opinion of later scribes, too many direct interventions of God in human affairs; the use of "angel of Yahweh" or "angel of the Lord" was by way of reducing His earthly appearances and the carrying out of His commands through the agency of angelic intermediaries. [*Rf.* Grant, *Gnosticism and Early Christianity*.]

Angel-Year—the angel-year, according to Cornelius Agrippa and other occultists, is either 145 years or 365 years.

Angel of Yetzirah—Sammael or Satan. [*Rf.* Fuller, *The Secret Wisdom of the Qabalah*.] The word yetzirah is Hebrew for formation. In the cabala, the world consisted of 4 great divisions, of which yetzirah was one.

Angels of the Zodiac—Malahidael (over Aries), Asmodel (over Taurus), Ambriel (over Gemini), Manuel or Muriel (over Cancer), Verchiel (over Leo), Hamaliel (over Virgo), Zuriel (over Libra), Barchiel (over Scorpio), Advachiel or Adnachiel (over Sagittarius), Hamael (over Capricorn), Cambiel (over Aquarius), Barchiel (over Pisces). [*Rf.* Barrett, *The Magus* II.] The overall ruler of the zodiac is Masleh (*q.v.*). Cornelius Agrippa, *Three Books of Occult Philosophy* III, gives additional governing angels: Acrabiel, Betuliel, Chesetiel, Dagymiel, Daliel, Geminiel, Masniel, Sartamiel, Teletiel, Tomimiel.

Angerecton (Angrecton)—in the *Grimorium Verum*, a great angel, invoked in magical rites, specifically in the invocation at fumigation. He is mentioned also in Waite, *The Book of Ceremonial Magic*.

Angromainyus—an early form of Ahriman, the Zoroastrian equivalent of the Judaeo-Christian Satan, although he is not a fallen angel and is not subject to the overlordship of God. Angromainyus was God's opposite and opponent from the beginning (in Persian lore). In the Zendavesta, Angromainyus, pregnant with death, leaps from

Heaven in the form of a serpent—a form in which he is not infrequently represented. He tries to deceive Zoroaster (Zarathustra) and to cause the latter to rebel against Ahura Mazda (the Persian equivalent of the sovereign power), but fails. [*Rf.* Jung, *Fallen Angels in Jewish, Christian and Mohammedan Literature.*]

Aniel (Haniel)—one of the numerous angelic guards of the gates of the West Wind. [*Rf. Ozar Midrashim* II, 316.]

Anihi'el—in M. Gaster, *The Sword of Moses,* one of the angel princes whom God appointed to the sword.

Animastic (the Animated)—an order of angels, "blessed souls which, by the Hebrews, is called issim, that is, nobles, lords and princes," according to Voltaire in his "Of Angels, Genii and Devils." Also, a presiding angel of the order referred to as "the soul of the Messiah, Merattron, soul of the world." Animastic is, in addition, referred to as the ruling or guardian angel of Moses. [*Rf.* Barrett, *The Magus* I, 38.]

Animated, The [Animastic]

Aniquel (Anituel)—one of the 7 great princes of the spirits, represented in the form of a serpent of paradise. He serves Aniquelis (or Antiquelis). In a Vatican Faustian manual [*Rf.* Butler, *Ritual Magic*] Aniquel—spelled also Aniquiel—is one of the 7 grand dukes of the infernal regions. See also *The Sixth and Seventh Books of Moses,* p. 111.

Anitor—a high holy angel of God, invoked in magical rites after proper investiture by the invocant. [*Rf.* Waite, *The Greater Key of Solomon; Grimorium Verum; The Book of Black Magic and of Pacts.*]

Anituel [Aniquel]

Anixiel—one of the 28 angels governing the 28 mansions of the moon. For the names of all 28 angels, *see* Appendix.

Aniyel [Anafiel]

Anmael (Chnum)—one of the leaders of the fallen angels, sometimes identified with Semyaza, for Anmael, like Semyaza, makes a bargain with a mortal woman (Istahar) in connection with the revelation of the Explicit Name (of God). [*Rf.* Jung, *Fallen Angels in Jewish, Christian and Mohammedan Literature;* and popular legends in Talmudic lore, poetic fiction, etc.]

Annael—alternate spelling (as used by H.D. in her poem "Sagesse") for Aniel or Anael (*q.v.*).

Annauel—one of the 72 angels bearing the name of God Shemhamphorae. For a list of all 72 names, *see* Appendix.

Anointed Cherub—the Prince of Tyre is so called in Ezekiel 28:14.

Anpiel (see Anfiel)—in rabbinic lore, an angel in charge of the protection of birds. He resides in the 6th Heaven, where he is a supervising chief of 70 gates. With 70 crowns, he (Anpiel) crowns all prayers that ascend to Heaven from the earth, and then transmits the prayers to the 7th Heaven for additional sanctification. [*Rf. The Zohar;* Spence, *An Encyclopaedia of Occultism.*] In Ginzberg, *The Legends of the Jews* I, 138, Anpiel conveyed Enoch to Heaven.

Anshe Shem ("men of name")—in magical incantations, the fallen angels are addressed by this term (Anshe Shem) although it should be restricted to apply to 2 angels only: Azza and Azzael. [*Rf. The Zohar;* Bamberger, *Fallen Angels.*]

Ansiel ("the constrainer")—an angel invoked in magical rites. [*Rf.* Trachtenberg, *Jewish Magic and Superstition.*]

Antichrist—usually Beliar or Belier (*q.v.*); a term applied also to Nero. For illustration, see Grillot, *A Pictorial Anthology of Witchcraft, Magic and Alchemy,* p. 48.

Antiel—an angel's name found inscribed on an oriental Hebrew charm for warding off evil. [*Rf.* Schrire, *Hebrew Amulets.*]

Antiquelis [Aniquel]

Anunna—in Akkadian theology, the anunna are "angels who are almost always terrestrial spirits." [*Rf.* Lenormant, *Chaldean Magic.*]

Anush—one of 3 ministering angels (the other 2 being Aebel and Shetel) whom God appointed to serve Adam. The celestial trio "roasted meat" for our first parent and even "cooled his wine"—according to *Yalkut Reubeni*. [*Rf. The Book of Adam and Eve*.]

Apar or **Aparsiel**—in M. Gaster, *Wisdom of the Chaldeans*, an angel in service to Sadqiel, ruler of the 5th day.

Apharoph (Apholph, Afarof)—an angel equated with Raphael and believed to be "the only true name of God." [*Rf. The Testament of Solomon; Pistis Sophia*; M. Gaster, *The Sword of Moses*.]

Aphiriza [Alphariza]

Aphredon—in gnosticism, a great celestial entity dwelling in the Pleroma with his 12 Just Ones. He is a ruler of the Indivisible.

Apollion (Appolyon, Apollyon)—the Greek form for the Hebrew Abaddon, meaning "destroyer." In Revelation 9:11 Apollion is the angel of the bottomless pit. In Revelation 20:1 he "laid hold of the dragon, that old serpent, which is the Devil, and Satan, and bound him a thousand years." According to the foregoing, Apollion is a holy (good) angel, servant and messenger of God; but in occult and, generally, in noncanonical writings, he is evil—as in the last-century *The Biblical Antiquities of Philo* and the 3rd-century *The Acts of Thomas*. The term also applied to the abode of evil spirits (Hell). In Bunyan's *Pilgrim's Progress* Apollion is the devil. Bunyan thus describes him: "clothed with scales like a fish and wings like a dragon, feet like a bear, and out of his belly came fire and smoke." He is so pictured by a 17th-century artist, the sketch reproduced in an early edition of *Pilgrim's Progress*. The exegete Volter identifies Apollion with Ahriman, the Persian devil. [*Rf.* Charles, *Critical Commentary on the Revelation of St. John*, p. 247.] In Barrett, *The Magus*, where Apollion is pictured in color, he is distinct from Abaddon (also pictured in color). The 2 are denominated "vessels of iniquity" (i.e., fallen angels or demons). Dürer did an

engraving showing the "Angel with the Key to the Abyss," reproduced on p. 3.

Apostate Angel—Satan. So named by Gregory the Great in his *Moralia* on Job, where he says: "Forasmuch then, as mankind is brought to the light of Repentance by the coming of the Redeemer, but the Apostate Angel is not recalled by any hope of pardon," etc. It was Gregory's view that man was created to replace the fallen legions of Satan.

Apparitions—according to Robert Fludd, *Utriusque cosmi majoris et minoris historia*, apparitions are one of 3 primary hierarchies (each again subdivided into 3 secondary hierarchies). [*See* Acclamations; Voices.]

Apragsin (Apragsih)—a divine messenger appointed by God to the sword, as listed in M. Gaster, *The Sword of Moses*. Apragsin is also known as Assi Asisih.

Apsinthus [Wormwood]

Apsu—in Babylonian mythology, Apsu is a female (?) angel of the abyss; "father" of the Babylonian gods as well as "wife" of Tamat. Apsu is finally slain by his (her) son Ea. [*Rf.* Lenormant, *Chaldean Magic*; Mackenzie, *Myths of Babylonia and Assyria*.]

Apudiel—one of the 7 underworld planetary rulers, called Electors by Cornelius Agrippa. The demon Ganael serves under the joint overlordship of Apudiel and Camael. [*Rf.* Conybeare, *The Testament of Solomon*.]

Aputel—an invocation angel mentioned in Mathers, *The Greater Key of Solomon*; also the name that a priest bore on his breast when entering the holy of holies. The name was reputed to have had the virtue, when pronounced, of reviving the dead; when engraved on vessels of gold or brass, it loosened every form of evil.

Aqrab—in Arabic mythology, an angel used for conjuring. [*Rf.* Shah, *Occultism, Its Theory and Practice*.]

Aquachai (or Aqua)—a holy name—one of

the *nomina barbara*—used in Solomonic conjurations to command demons. [*Rf.* Mathers, *The Greater Key of Solomon*.]

Arabonas—a spirit invoked in prayer by the Master of the Art, in Solomonic rites [*Rf. Grimorium Verum*; Waite, *The Book of Black Magic and of Pacts*.]

Araboth—the 7th Heaven, where the major experiences of Enoch occurred. Also the dwelling place of God. Here, in Araboth, dwell the seraphim, ofanim, and the angels of love, fear, grace, and dread. [*Rf. 3 Enoch*; Müller, *History of Jewish Mysticism*; Ginzberg, *The Legends of the Jews*.]

Araciel [Araqiel]

Arad—an Indo-Persian angel who protects religion and science; he is mentioned in Hyde, *Historia Religionis Veterum Persarum*.

Araebel—an angel of the 6th hour, serving under Samil. [*Rf.* Waite, *The Lemegeton*.]

Arael (Ariel)—"one of the spirits which the rabbis of the Talmud made prince over the people of the birds," according to Malchus, *The Ancient's Book of Magic*, p. 115.

Arafiel—one of the great angelic princes representing "the divine strength, majesty, and power." [*Rf. 3 Enoch* or the *Hebrew Book of Enoch*.]

Arakiba (Arakab, Aristiqifa, Artaqifa)—an evil (fallen) angel who brought sin to earth—as cited in *Enoch I*, where Arakiba is designated one of the "chiefs of ten" of the apostate troops.

Arakiel [Araqiel]

Aralim [Erelim]

Aramaiti (Armaiti)—one of the 6 amesha spentas (*q.v.*), representing holy harmony. [*Rf.* Gaynor, *Dictionary of Mysticism*.]

Araphiel ("neck of God") one of the guardians of the 2nd hall in the 7th Heaven. "When Araphiel H', the prince, sees Asrulyu, the prince, he removes the crown of glory from his head and falls on his face," in obeisance. [*3 Enoch*, 18.]

Araqael [Araqiel]

Araqiel (Araquiel, Arakiel, Araciel, Arqael, Saraquael, Arkiel, Arkas)—one of the 200 fallen angels mentioned in *Enoch I*. Araqiel taught human beings the signs of the earth. However, in the *Sibylline Oracles* (see fn. in Charles, *The Book of Enoch*, 8:3) Araqiel does not seem to be a fallen angel. He is, indeed, one of the 5 angels who lead the souls of men to judgment, the other 4 angels being Ramiel, Uriel, Samiel, Aziel. The name Araqiel denotes one who exercises dominion over the earth.

Arariel (Azareel, Uzziel?)—curer of stupidity and one of the 7 angels with dominion over the earth. Arariel is specifically an angel who presides over the waters of the earth (according to the Talmudists). He is invoked by fishermen so that they may, with luck, catch big fish [*Rf.* Spence, *An Encyclopaedia of Occultism*; *Universal Jewish Encyclopedia*; Gaynor, *Dictionary of Mysticism*].

Ararita (Araritha)—a name inscribed on a cabalistic sigil in connection with Solomonic conjurations and employed to command demons; if the name is inscribed on a gold plate, the invocant is assured he will not die a sudden death. Ararita is considered to be the "verbum inenerrabile" (the ineffable word or name) of God. [*Rf.* Barrett, *The Magus* II; Mathers, *The Greater Key of Solomon*.]

Arasbarasbiel—an angelic guard of the 6th Heaven, as listed in *Ozar Midrashim* I, 116.

Arasek—a form of Nisroc (*q.v.*) mentioned by Josephus. [*Rf.* Hayley (ed.), *The Poetical Works of John Milton*.]

Arathiel—a chief angel of the 1st hour of the night, serving under Gamiel. [*Rf.* Waite, *The Lemegeton*.]

Arathron (Aratron)—1st of the Olympian spirits governing the planet Saturn; he rules 49 of the 196 Olympic Provinces. Arathron's sigil is pictured on p. 22 of *The Secret Grimoire of Turiel*. [*Rf.* the *Arbatel of Magic*, and Girardius' arcanic book (1730.)] Arathron teaches alchemy, magic, and medicine, and is able to make a person invisible. He can also cause barren women to become fertile.

Arauchia—an angel's name found inscribed in Hebrew characters on the 3rd pentacle of the planet Saturn. [*Rf.* Shah, *The Secret Lore of Magic*; Mathers, *The Greater Key of Solomon*.]

Araxiel—in *Enoch I*, Araxiel is mentioned as one of the fallen angels.

Arayekael—one of the many angel princes appointed by God to the sword. [*Rf.* M. Gaster, *The Sword of Moses*.]

Araziel (Arazjal, Arazyal, Atriel, Esdreel, Sahariel, Seriel, Sariel, etc.,—"my moon is God") —an angel who sinned when he descended to earth to unite with mortal women. Araziel governed, with Bagdal, the sign of the Bull (Taurus). [*Rf. Enoch I*; Levi, *Transcendental Magic*; *Prince of Darkness*.]

Arbatel—a "revealing" angel, mentioned in the *Arbatel of Magic*. [*Rf.* Waite, *The Lemegeton*.]

Arbgdor—in *The Book of the Angel Raziel* (*Sefer Raziel*), an angel that governs one of the months. [*Rf.* Trachtenberg, *Jewish Magic and Superstition*, p. 99.]

Arbiel—an angel serving Anael, ruler of the 6th day. [*Rf.* M. Gaster, *Wisdom of the Chaldeans*.]

Arcade (fictional)—in Anatole France's *Revolt of the Angels*, a guardian angel, otherwise known as Abdiel (*q.v.*).

Arcan—king of the angels of the air, ruler of Monday. Arcan's ministers are Bilet, Missabu. Abuhaza. [*Rf.* Barrett, *The Magus* II.]

Archan—an angel who exercised dominion over the lower rays of the moon. May be the same as Arcan. [*Rf.* Heywood, *The Hierarchy of the Blessèd Angels*.]

Archana—an angel's name found inscribed in Hebrew characters on the 5th pentacle of the planet Saturn. [*Rf.* Mathers, *The Greater Key of Solomon*.]

Archangel of the Covenant—a term applied to Michael in the Coptic *Apocalypse of Paul*.

Archangel Ruin'd—Satan is so called by Milton in *Paradise Lost* I, 593.

Archangels—the term archangel applies generically to all angels above the grade of (the order of) angels; it also serves to designate a specific rank of angels in the celestial hierarchy. In the pseudo-Dionysian scheme of 9 orders or choirs, the order of archangel is placed 8th—that is, next to the last in rank, immediately above the order of angels. This is a bit confusing, since the greatest angels are referred to as archangels, as in the Old Testament, where Daniel calls Michael "one of the chief princes," which is taken to mean one of the archangels. In the New Testament the term archangels occurs only twice: in I Thessalonians and in Jude. In the latter only, however, is Michael specifically designated an archangel. In Revelation 8:2, John refers to the "seven angels who stand before God," and this is commonly interpreted to mean the 7 archangels. *The Book of Enoch (Enoch I)* names the 7: Uriel, Raguel, Michael, Seraqael, Gabriel, Haniel, Raphael. Later Judaism gives Phanuel as an alternate for Uriel. Other lists in apocrypha and pseudepigrapha give, as variants, such angels as Barachiel, Jehudiel, Sealtiel, Oriphiel, Zadkiel, and Anael (Haniel). The archangels, according to the *Testament of Levi*, "minister and make propitiation to the Lord for the sins of ignorance and of the righteous." The ruling prince of the order is usually given as Raphael or Michael. The Koran recognizes 4 archangels but names only 2: Gabriel (Jibril), who is the angel of revelation, and Michael, the warrior angel who fights the battle of the faithful. The 2 unnamed angels are Azrael, angel of death; and Israfel, angel of music, who will sound the trumpet (one of 3 or 4 trumpets) on the Day of Judgment. The earliest source for the names of the archangels is traced to Al-Barceloni, a writer of mystic works in the post-Talmudic period, who related them to the planets. In other writings "we meet with the conception of 12 archangels connected with the signs of the zodiac." [*Rf. The Book of the Angel Raziel* 52a, 61a; Ginzberg, *The Legends of the Jews* V, 24.] For the names of the 12 and their zodiacal signs, *see* Appendix. The cabala cites 10 archangels (actually 9) and places them in the world of Briah (2nd of the 4 created worlds), thus: Methratton, Ratziel Tzaphqiel, Tzadqiel, Khamael, Mikhale, Haniel, Raphael, Gabriel, Methrattonton. It will be noted the Methrattin, i.e., Metatron, appears twice, heading and concluding the list of 10—or rather 9. [*Rf.* Mathers, *The Kabbalah Unveiled.*] "The archangels," says Dionysius in his *Mystical Theology and the Celestial Hierarchy,* "are the messengers bearing divine decrees."

Archangels of the 10 Sefiroth—Mathers, *The Kabbalah Unveiled,* lists the archangels of the Sefiroth as follows: 1. Methattron, for Kether (crown); 2. Ratziel, for Chokmah (wisdom); 3. Tzaphqiel, for Binah (understanding); 4. Tzadqiel, for Chesed (mercy); 5. Khamael, for Geburah (strength or fortitude); 6. Mikhael, for Tiphereth (beauty); 7. Haniel, for Netzach (victory); 8. Raphael, for Hod (splendor); 9. Gabriel, for Yesod (foundation); 10. Methattron or the Shekinah, for Malkuth (kingdom).

Archarzel—an angel invoked in ritual magic by the Master of the Arts. [*Rf. Grimorium Verum.*]

Archer—a governing spirit of Aquarius. Archer shares this post with Ssakmakiel. [*Rf.* Levi, *Transcendental Magic.*]

Archistratege (Arhistratig—"chief of hosts") —when counseling Enoch, God call Michael "my intercessor, my archistratege" (*Enoch I,* 33:11). The same title is given Michael (Mihail) in the Roumanian text of *The Apocalypse of Abraham.* In this apocalypse, the tears that Michael, "herald of death," sheds over the coming demise of Abraham, "fall into a basin and turn into precious jewels." The story is found also in Ginzberg, *The Legends of the Jews* I, 300.

Archons ("rulers")—angels set over nations and identified or equated with aeons. Shamshiel or Shemuiel is "the great archon, mediator between the prayers of Israel and the princes of the 7th Heaven" [*Rf.* Scholem, *Major Trends in Jewish Mysticism*]. In occultism the archons are primordial planetary spirits. In Manicheanism they were the "Sons of Dark who swallowed the bright elements of Primal Man." Scholem uses "archon" interchangeably with "great angel." In *Major Trends* he writes that "archons and angels storm

against the traveler in his ascent [or descent] to the Merkabah." The *Papyri Graecae Magicae* names 5 of the archons: Uriel, Michael, Raphael, Gabriel, Shamuil. In the Ophitic (gnostic) system, 7 archons are designated: Jaldabaoth, Jao, Sabaoth, Adonaios, Astanphaios, Ailoaios, Oraios. In other lists other angels appear as archons: Katspiel, Erathaol, Domiel, etc. [*Rf.* Danielou, *The Angels and Their Mission;* Doresse, *The Secret Books of the Egyptian Gnostics;* Gaynor, *Dictionary of Mysticism.*]

Arciciah—an angel of earth, cited in Schwab, *Vocabulaire de l'Angélologie.*

Ardarel—in occult lore, the angel of fire. *Cf.* Gabriel, Nathanel, etc. [*Rf.* Papus, *Traité Élémentaire de Science Occulte.*]

Ardefiel or Ardesiel—one of the 28 angels ruling the 28 mansions of the moon. [*Rf.* Barrett, *The Magus.*]

Ardibehist—in ancient Persian religion, the angel of April and one of the amesha spentas. Ardibehist governed the 3rd day of the month. [*Rf. The Dabistan,* pp. 35, 136.]

Ardors—a term used in *Paradise Lost* V, 249 as an order of angels, among whom Milton counts Raphael. In de Vigny's poem "Eloa," ardors is also spoken of as an order in the celestial hierarchy.

Ardouisur (Arduisher)—in Zoroastrianism, Ardouisur is a female ized (i.e., cherub). Among the attributes of this cherub is making females prolific and giving them easy childbirth, and even supplying them with breast milk. [*Rf. The Dabistan,* p. 167.] Her title is "giver of living water," says King in *The Gnostics and Their Remains,* p. 106.

Ardour (Ardur)—an angel ruling the month of Tammuz (June–July), according to Schwab, *Vocabulaire de l'Angélologie.*

Arehanah—the name of an angel inscribed on the 3rd pentacle of the planet Saturn. [*Rf.* Mathers, *The Greater Key of Solomon.*]

Arel—an angel of fire. The name Arel is found inscribed on the 7th pentacle of the sun. In

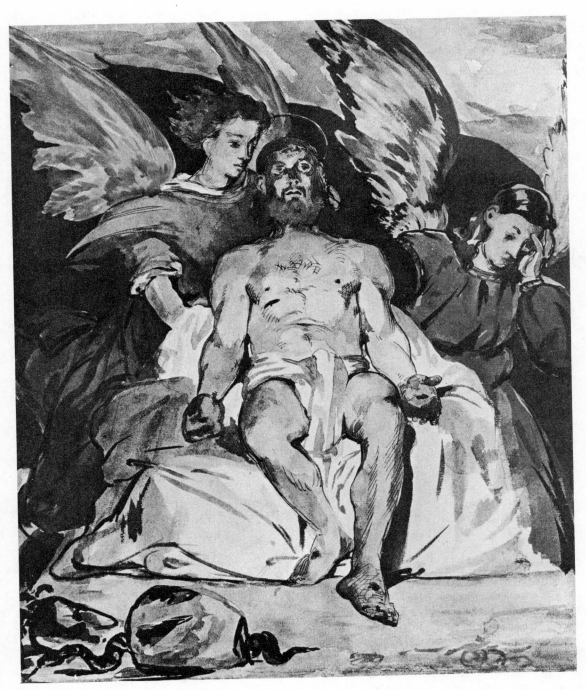

Angels at the Tomb of Christ by Edouard Manet. Reproduced from Régamey, *Anges*.

M. Gaster, *The Sword of Moses*, Arel is an angel invoked in ritual magic.

Arel(l)im [Erelim]

Arfiel—another name for the angel Raphael. In *Pirke Hechaloth*, Arfiel is an angelic guard stationed in the 2nd Heaven. [*Rf.* Schwab, *Vocabulaire del'Angélologie*, supp.]

Argeniton—an angel mentioned in Hyde, *Historia Religionis Veterum Persarum.*

Arghiel—an angel invoked in magical rites. [*Rf.* Schwab, *Vocabulaire de l'Angélologie.*]

Arhistratig [Archistratege]

Arhum Hii (Rhum)—in Mandaean lore, one of the *malki* (*uthri*, angels) of the North Star.

Arias—an angel who rules over sweet-smelling herbs. In occultism, Arias is regarded as a demon and is one of the 12 marquises of the infernal empire. [*Rf.* De Plancy, *Dictionnaire Infernal.*]

Ariel (Arael, Ariael, meaning "lion of God")—the name of an angel in the apocryphal *Ezra*; also in Mathers, *The Greater Key of Solomon*, the *Grand Grimoire*, and other tracts of magic, where he is pictured as lion-headed. Cornelius Agrippa says: "Ariel is the name of an angel, sometimes also of a demon, and of a city, whence called Ariopolis, where the idol is worshipped." In Heywood, *The Hierarchy of the Blessèd Angels*, Ariel ranks as one of 7 princes who rule the waters and is "Earth's great Lord." Jewish mystics used Ariel as a poetic name for Jerusalem. In the Bible the name denotes, variously, a man, a city (Isaiah 29), and an altar. In occult writings Ariel is the "3rd archon of the winds." Mention is also made of Ariel as an angel who assists Raphael in the cure of disease. [*Rf.* M. Gaster, *Wisdom of the Chaldeans.*] In the Coptic *Pistis Sophia*, Ariel is in charge of punishment in the lower world, corresponding with Ur of the Mandaeans (*q.v.*). In *The Testament of Solomon*, he controls demons. In gnostic lore generally he is a ruler of winds and equated with Ialdabaoth as an older name for this god. In practical cabala he is regarded as originally of the order of virtues. According to John Dee,

astrologer royal in Queen Elizabeth's day, Ariel is a conglomerate of Anael and Uriel. In *The Tempest*, Shakespeare casts Ariel as a sprite. To Milton he is a rebel angel, overcome by the seraph Abdiel in the first day of fighting in Heaven. The poet Shelley referred to himself as Ariel, and André Maurois is the author of a life of Shelley called *Ariel*. Sayce ("Athenaeum," October 1886) sees a connection between Ariel and the arelim (erelim), the valiant ones spoken of in Isaiah 33:7, an order of angels equated with the order of thrones. [*Rf. Texts of the Saviour*; Butler, *Ritual Magic*; Bonner, *Studies in Magical Amulets.*]

Ariman [Ahriman]

Arioc (Ariukh, Oriockh)—in Jewish legend, a guardian angel of the ancestors or offspring of Enoch, appointed by God to preserve the Enoch writings. In Genesis, Arioc is the name of an executioner. [*See* Arioch.]

Arioch ("fierce lion")—a demon of vengeance, a follower of Satan, a fallen angel (as in *Paradise Lost* VI, where he is overthrown by the angel Abdiel during the war in Heaven). In Nash, *Pierce Penniless*, reference is made to "the great Arioch that is termed the spirit of revenge." [*Rf.* Schwab, *Vocabulaire de l'Angélologie*; De Plancy, *Dictionnaire Infernal*, 1863 ed., where Arioch is pictured as the bat-winged demon of vengeance; *The Ancient's Book of Magic.*]

Ariukh [Oriockh]

Arkhas—from the invisible depths God summons Arkhas "firm and heavy and very red" and commands this primordial spirit to be divided. And when Arkhas divided himself, "the world came forth, very dark and great, bringing the creation of all things below." This account of the formation (not the creation) of the earth is found in *Enoch II*, 26.

Armaita (Aramaiti, Armaiti)—in Persian mythology, one of the 6 or 7 amesha spentas or archangels. She is the spirit of truth, wisdom, and goodness who became incarnate and visited the earth "to help the good." [*Rf. Grundriss der iranischen Philologie* III; Forlong, *Encyclopedia of*

Religions; Redfield, *Gods/A Dictionary of the Deities of All Lands.*]

Armaros (Armers, Pharmaros, Abaros, Arearos)—one of the fallen angels as listed in *Enoch I*. Armaros taught "the resolving of enchantments." According to R. H. Charles, the term Armaros may be a corruption of Araros.

Armas—an angel invoked in magical rites at the close of the Sabbath. [*Rf.* Trachtenberg, *Jewish Magic and Superstition*, p. 102.]

Armasa ("the great lord")—an angel in Aramaic incantations, cited in Montgomery, *Aramaic Incantation Texts from Nippur.*

Armaziel (Armisael?)—a gnostic entity mentioned in *The Secret Books of the Egyptian Gnostics*, p. 198.

Armen (Ramiel? Arakiel? Baraqel?)—one of the fallen angels listed in *Enoch I*, 69.

Armers (*see* Armaros)—the name occurs in Mark Van Doren's poem "The Prophet Enoch," where Armers is included among the fallen angels.

Armesi—an angel of the 10th hour of the day, serving under the suzerainty of the angel Oriel. [*Rf.* Waite, *The Lemegeton*, p. 68.]

Armesiel—in Waite, *The Lemegeton*, p. 69, an angel of the 4th hour of the night, serving under Jefischa.

Armiel—an angel officer of the 11th hour of the night, serving under Dardariel.

Armies—a term for one of the celestial orders, as used by Milton in *Paradise Lost*. [*Rf.* West, *Milton and the Angels*, p. 135.]

Armimas (Armimimas)—an angel invoked in magical rites at the close of the Sabbath. *Cf.* Hermes or Ormuzd. [*Rf.* Trachtenberg, *Jewish Magic and Superstition*, p. 100.]

Armisael—angel of the womb. In Talmud it is recommended that, to ease a confinement, one should recite Psalm 20 nine times, but if this does not prove efficacious, then one should try the following invocation: "I conjure you, Armisael,

angel who governs the womb, that you help this woman and the child in her body." [*Rf.* Trachtenberg, *Jewish Magic and Superstition*, p. 202.]

Armogen [Harmozei]

Armon—one of the angels of the 2nd chora or altitude invoked in magic prayer, as set forth in *The Almadel of Solomon.*

Arphugitonos—one of the 9 angels who will rule "at the end of the world," according to the *Revelation of Esdras*. [*Rf. The Ante-Nicene Fathers* 8, 573.] For the names of the other 8 angels, *see* Angels at the End of the World.

Arsyalalyur—an angel sent to Enoch with a special message from God; also to Lamech's son Noah to warn him of the impending flood, according to *The Book of Adam and Eve*. The name is a corruption or amalgamation of Israel and Uriel. [*Rf. Enoch I*, 10 (Dillman's text).]

Artakifa—an archangel mentioned in Enoch lore.

Aruru—in Sumerian mythology, a female messenger of the gods who created man from clay. She was the mother of the hero Gilgamesh.

Arvial (Avial)—one of the angels guarding the 4th Heaven. Cited in *Ozar Midrashim* I, 116.

Arzal (Arzel)—one of the 4 angels of the east who are "glorious and benevolent angels" invoked when the invocant wishes to partake of the secret wisdom of the Creator. See *Clavicula Salomonis.*

Asac(h)—an angel invoked in magical prayer. [*Rf. Grimorium Verum.*]

Asacro (Asarca)—in black magic, an angel invoked in prayer and conjuration rites.

Asael ("whom God made")—an angel under Semyaza who cohabited with the daughters of men; hence, a fallen angel. [*See* Azazel.]

Asaliah—in the cabala, an angel of the order of virtues, under the ethnarchy of Raphael. He has dominion over justice. In *The Magus* he is one of the 72 angels bearing the mystical name of God

Shemhamphorae. His sigil is shown in Ambelain, *La Kabbale Pratique*, p. 281.

Asamkis—in hechaloth lore (*Ma'asseh Merkabah*), an angelic guard stationed at the 7th heavenly hall.

Asaph (Asaf)—leader, at night, of hosts of angels in the chanting of hymns to God—just as the angel Heman leads the hosts in morning chants, and Jeduthun leads in evening chants. [*Rf. The Zohar* (Kedoshim).] Psalms 50 and 73–83 are ascribed to Asaph. In Jewish legend, Asaph was the father of medicine. Nahmanides in his *Torat ha-Adam* refers to "the Jew Asaf" and his book on healing.

Asarca [Asacro]

Asariel ("whom God has bound," i.e., by an oath)—one of the 28 angels ruling over the 28 mansions of the moon.

Asasiah—one of the many names of the angel Metatron.

Asasiel—angel of Thursday, who shares his rule with Sachiel and Cassiel. Asasiel is also one of the presiding spirits of the planet Jupiter. [*Rf.* de Abano, *The Heptameron*; Barrett, *The Magus* II; *The Secret Grimoire of Turiel*.]

Asath (Asach)—an angel invoked in Solomonic magical rites. [*Rf. Grimorium Verum*.]

Asbeel ("deserter from God")—in *Enoch I*, Asbeel is included among the fallen angels. "He imparted to the holy sons of God evil counsel and led them astray through the daughters of men."

Asbogah [Azbugay YHWH]

Ascobai—in Solomonic magical operations, an angel summoned in exorcisms of Wax. [*Rf.* Mathers, *The Greater Key of Solomon*.]

Asderel (Asredel, Asradel Shariel)—the name is a corruption of Sahariel. Asderel is an evil archangel who taught the course of the moon. [*Rf.* Charles, *Apocrypha and Pseudepigrapha of the Old Testament*.]

Asentacer—corresponding angel for the angel Lelahel.

Aseu—corresponding angel for the angel Anauel.

Asfa'el ("God adds")—in *Enoch I* and *Enoch II*, Asfa'el is a luminary of one of the months and "head of a thousand." Charles in *The Book of Enoch* refers to Asfa'el as a "chiliarch who has to do with the intercalary day under one of the 4 leaders." Asfa'el is said to be an inversion of Hilujaseph or Joseph-el.

Ashael X—an invocation angel, mentioned in M. Gaster, *The Sword of Moses*.

Ashamdon—variant for Shamdan (*q.v.*). [*Rf.* Bamberger, *Fallen Angels*, p. 171.]

Asha Vahishta—in Zoroastrian lore, one of the 6 amesha spentas (*q.v.*). An archangel of righteousness. [*Rf. Grundriss der iranischen Philologie* III.]

Ashkanizkael—in hechaloth lore (*Ma'asseh Merkabah*), an angelic guard stationed at the 7th heavenly hall.

Ashmedai (Ashmodai, Asmodée, Asmadai, Asmodeus, Chammaday, Sydonay, etc.)—in rabbinic lore, a messenger of God, hence an angel. However, being an opponent of Solomon and ruler of the south, with 66 legions of spirits under him, he is usually regarded as an evil spirit himself, some occult sources going so far as to identify him with the serpent who seduced Eve in the garden of Eden. [*Rf.* Mathers, *The Greater Key of Solomon*.] Good or evil, angel cr demon, he is not considered harmful; he has been characterized as a cherub, "prince of sheddim," and as "the great philosopher." [*Rf.* Jung, *Fallen Angels in Jewish, Christian and Mohammedan Literature*; Müller, *History of Jewish Mysticism*.]

Ashmodiel—in occultism, a zodiacal angel governing the sign of Taurus. [*Rf.* Jobes, *Dictionary of Mythology Folklore and Symbols*.]

Ashraud—"a prince over all the angels and Caesars," according to Mathers, *The Greater Key of Solomon*.

Ashriel (Azrael, Azriel, Azariel—"vow of God")—one of the 7 angels with dominion over the earth. He is the angel who separates the soul from the body at death. In the cabala, he is invoked as a curer of stupidity. See writings of Moses Botarel.

Ashrulyu (Ashrulyai, Asrulyu—"who causes to dwell")—a great angelic prince, one of the 20 names of the godhead, residing in the 1st Heaven. He is president of the institute of learning and one of the *sarim* (princes) of the Torah. *See* Yefefiah. [*Rf.* 3 *Enoch.*]

Ashu [Sirushi]

Asiel ("created of God")—in *Esdras II*, an apocryphal work, Asiel is one of 5 "men" (i.e., angels) appointed by God to transcribe the 204 books dictated by Ezra. The other 4 "men" were Dabria (Ecanus), Selemia, Selecucia, and Sarea (Sarga). Of the books, 70 were to be delivered or made available only to the wise among men; the rest of the books were for use by the general public. In *The Testament of Solomon* Asiel is a fiend who detects thieves and can reveal hidden treasure. He figures in a talisman against sudden death reproduced in Grillot, *A Pictorial Anthology of Witchcraft, Magic and Alchemy*, p. 342.

Asimon (Atimon)—an angel listed in *Malache Elyon* (*Angels on High*), where reference is made to *The Zohar*.

Asimor—in hechaloth lore, Asimor is one of 7 angelic princes of power, the other 6 being Kalmiya, Boel, Psachar, Gabriel, Sandalphon, and Uzziel. [*Rf.* Margouliath, *Malache Elyon*, p. 17.]

Asiyah [Assiah]

Asmadai—one of the 2 "potent thrones," as cited in Milton's *Paradise Lost* VI, 365. Uriel and Raphael succeed in vanquishing Asmadai (along with Adramalec), 2 powers, says Milton, "to be less than Gods/Disdain'd." (*See* Asmoday.)

Asmodal—an angel dealt with in Solomonic Wax exorcisms. [*Rf.* Mathers, *The Greater Key of Solomon.*]

Asmoday (Ashmeday, Asmodius, Sydoney)—a fallen angel "who has wings and flies about, and

has knowledge of the future," according to Budge, *Amulets and Talismans*, p. 377. Asmoday teaches mathematics and can make men invisible. He "giveth the ring of Vertues" and governs 72 legions of infernal spirits. When invoked, he manifests as a creature with 3 heads (bull, ram, man). Asmoday is a character in John Dryden's dramatic poem, *The State of Innocence*. A variant spelling of the name is Hasmoday, who is one of the demons of the moon. [*Rf.* De Plancy, *Dictionnaire Infernal*; Butler, *Ritual Magic*; Waite, *The Lemegeton*; Shah, *The Secret Lore of Magic.*]

Asmodee (*see* Ashmedai)—a French form for Asmodeus and (according to De Plancy) identical with Sammael or Satan.

Asmodel—in ceremonial magic, the angel with dominion over the month of April. He is also (as cited in Camfield, *A Theological Discourse of Angels*) ruler of the zodiacal sign of Taurus. (*See* Tual, Hamabiel.) Formerly, Asmodel was one of the chiefs of the order of cherubim. He is now a demon of punishment (as recorded in the Coptic gnostic *Pistis Sophia*). The cabala includes him among the 10 evil sefiroth (*q.v.*). [*Rf.* Barrett, *The Magus*; De Plancy, *Dictionnaire Infernal*; Ambelain, *La Kabbale Pratique.*]

Asmodeus ("creature of judgment")—the name is derived from ashma daeva (*see* Asmoday, Chammaday). Asmodeus is a Persian rather than a Jewish devil; however, incorporated into Jewish lore, he is there regarded as an evil spirit. According to Forlong, *Encyclopedia of Religions*, Asmodeus is "the talmudic Ashmedai, a demon borrowed from the Zend Aeshmadeva," a "raging fiend" (*The Book of Tobit* 3:8). It was Ashmadai (Ashmedai), says Forlong, who made Noah drunk, and who, in *Tobit*, slew the 7 bridegrooms of the young Sarah, and who, overcome by the angel Raphael, was finally "banished to upper Egypt." In demonology, Asmodeus in Hell is controller of all gaming houses. Wierus the demonographer says Asmodeus must be invoked only when the invocant is bareheaded, otherwise the demon will trick him. Barrett, *The Magus* II, pictures Asmodeus in color as one of the "Vessels of Wrath."

In Le Sage's romance *The Devil on Two Sticks* Asmodeus is the main character. In James Branch Cabell's *The Devil's Own Dear Son*, Asmodeus is the son of Adam's first wife Lilith by Samael. However, in *The Book of the Sacred Magic of Abra-Melin the Mage*, we find this report: "Some rabbins say that Asmodeus was the child of the incest of Tubal-Cain and his sister Naamah; others say he was the demon of impurity." Jewish lore charges Asmodeus with being the father-in-law of the demon Bar Shalmon [*Rf. Jewish Encyclopedia*, p. 510]. In Solomonic legends, Asmodeus also goes by the name of Saturn, Marcolf or Morolf. He is credited with being the inventor of carousels, music, dancing, drama, "and all the new French fashions." [*Rf.* Michaelis, *Admirable History of the Possession and Conversion of a Penitent Woman*; Waite, *The Book of Black Magic and of Pacts*; *Malleus Maleficarum* (p. 30); Voltaire, "Of Angels, Genii, and Devils."]

Asradel [Asderel]

Asrael—an angel in a 4-act opera of that name composed by Alberto Franchetti, with libretto by Fontana. Based on the old Flemish legend, Asrael falls in love with another angel called Nefta (female), loses her, and finally is reunited with her in Heaven. The opera had its first American performance in 1890 at the Metropolitan in New York.

Asrafil—in Arabic lore, the angel of the last judgment. A "terrible angel," says De Plancy, who includes Asrafil in his *Dictionnaire Infernal* (ed. 1863) as a demon and pictures him as such. Often mistaken for Azrael, angel of death.

Asriel X (or Asrael X—"vow of God")—chief of the 63 angel-guardians of the 7 Heavens. In hechaloth lore, Asriel X is an invocation angel. [*Rf.* M. Gaster, *The Sword of Moses*; "Angel" in *New Schaff-Herzog Encyclopedia*.]

Asron—one of numerous guards of the gates of the East Wind. [*Rf. Ozar Midrashim* II, 316.]

Assad—in Arabic lore, an angel invoked in conjuring rites. [*Rf.* Shah, *Occultism*, p. 152.]

Assafsisiel—in hechaloth lore (*Ma'asseh Merkabah*), an angelic guard stationed at the 7th heavenly hall.

Assarel—in hechaloth lore (*Ma'asseh Merkabah*), an angelic guard stationed at the 4th heavenly hall.

Asser Criel—an unutterable name (of a spirit) engraven on the breastplate of Moses and Aaron, according to the cabala. Whoever, it is said, wears the breastplate so engraved will not die a sudden death. [*Rf. The Sixth and Seventh Books of Moses.*]

Assi Asisih—a messenger of the Lord's sword sent to man. [*Rf. The Sword of Moses*, p. 30.]

Assiah (Asiyah)—in cabalistic cosmology, one of the lowest of the 4 worlds, "the world of making," or the world of action, the world of Oliphoth, that is, the world of shells or demons. It is the abode of Sammael, prince of darkness. [*Rf.* Fuller, *The Secret Wisdom of the Qabalah.*]

Assiel—angel of healing, as cited in *The Book of the Angel Raziel* and in Schwab, *Vocabulaire de l'Angélologie*, suppl. [*Cf.* Raphael.]

Assimonem—in Mathers, *The Greater Key of Solomon*, p. 45, the Assimonem are angels invoked in Solomonic conjurations to command demons to confer on the invocant the gift of invisibility.

Astachoth (Astrachios, Astroschio)—an angel invoked in the exorcism of water. [*Rf. Grimorium Verum*; Shah, *The Secret Lore of Magic.*]

Astad—in ancient Persian lore, the angel of the 26th day of each month. Astad was found at the 64th gate (of the 100 gates) of Paradise. [*Rf. The Dabistan*, p. 166.]

Astagna (Astrgna)—as listed in Barrett, *The Magus*, an angel resident in the 5th Heaven. He rules on Tuesday. When invoking this angel the invocant must face west.

Astaniel—one of the chief angel-princes appointed by God to the sword.

Astanphaeus (Astaphaeus, Astaphai, Astaphaios)—in gnostic lore, one of the 7 elohim (angels) of the presence. In the Ophitic system, he is a Hebdomad—one of the 7 potentates or archons engendered by the god Ildabaoth "in his own image." He is also lord of the 3rd gate "leading to the aeon of the archons" (according to Origen in *Contra Celsum*, who claims the name derives from the art of magic). Astanphaeus is likewise declared to be one of the 7 sons of Sydik (Melchisedec). On the other hand, the name is said to be a variant form of Satan. In Phoenician theogony, Astanphaeus is a primordial power. C. W. King, *The Gnostics and Their Remains* (pp. 214–215), declares Astanphaeus to be "the Jewish angel of the planet Mercury" and of Magian origin. King reproduces a gnostic gem (Plate VI) with the name of Astanphaeus inscribed on it. [*Rf.* "Gnosticism" in *Catholic Encyclopedia*; Grant, *Gnosticism and Early Christianity*.]

Astaribo—a name for Lilith in medieval magic.

Astaroth (Asteroth)—once a seraph, Astaroth is now, according to Waite, *The Lemegeton*, a great duke in the infernal regions. There he "discourses willingly on the fall [of the angels] but pretends that he himself was exempt from their lapse" (see Wierus, *Pseudo-Monarchia*). "In the Greek language," says Barrett in *The Magus* I, "Astaroth is called Diabolus." When Astaroth is invoked, he manifests as "a beautiful angel astride a dragon and carrying a viper in his right hand." His sigil is shown in Waite, *The Book of Black Magic and of Pacts*. Before Astaroth fell, he was (declares the *Admirable History of the Possession and Conversion of a Penitent Woman*) a prince of the order of thrones. Spence, *An Encyclopaedia of Occultism*, maintains, to the contrary, that he belonged to the order of seraphim. Voltaire finds that Astaroth was an ancient god of Syria. According to the *Grimorium Verum*, Astaroth has set up residence in America. "In the English tradition," says De Plancy, Astaroth was "one of the 7 princes of Hell who visited Faust."

Astarte (Ashteroth, Ashtoreth, Ishtar-Venus, etc.)—chief female deity of the ancient Phoenicians, Syrians, Carthaginians. Astarte was a Syrian moon goddess of fertility. As Ashteroth she was worshipped by the Jews in times when idolatry was prevalent in Palestine: "Ashtoreth, the abomination of the Zidonians" (II Kings, 23:13), the Zidonians being the Phoenicians. Jeremiah called Ashtoreth the "queen of heaven." The Greeks borrowed their Aphrodite from Astarte. Finally, Astarte shows up, in occult lore, as the demon for the month of April. In *Paradise Lost* (I, 438), Astarte is a fallen angel, equated with Astoreth. [*Rf.* Redfield, *Gods/A Dictionary of the Deities of All Lands*; De Plancy, *Dictionnaire Infernal* IV, 138; and near-Eastern mythologies.]

Astel—a spirit operating on the planet Saturn. [*Rf. The Secret Grimoire of Turiel.*]

Asteraoth—one of the 7 great planetary rulers; an angel who was able to overcome the demoness called Powers (one of the 7 demonesses summoned by King Solomon, according to legend). [*Rf. 3 Enoch*; Conybeare, *The Testament of Solomon.*]

Astiro—the corresponding angel for Mehiel (*q.v.*).

Astm (surname Kunya X)—one of the 14 conjuring angels mentioned in M. Gaster, *The Sword of Moses*. Astm is also one of the ineffable names of God.

Astoreth—in *Paradise Lost* I, 438, Astoreth is a fallen angel. She is equated with Astarte.

Astrachios (*see* Astachoth)—in Mathers, *The Greater Key of Solomon*, Astrachios is called Herachio. He is an angel invoked in the exorcism of the water. [*Rf. Grimorium Verum.*]

Astrael Iao Sabao—also known simply as Istrael or Astrael. He is an angel whose name is found inscribed on magical amulets. [*Rf.* Scholem, *Jewish Gnosticism, Merkabah Mysticism, and Talmudic Tradition*; Conybeare, *The Testament of Solomon.*]

Astrompsuchos (Etrempsuchos, also Strempsuchos)—in the Bodleian *Bruce Papyrus*, Astrompsuchos is a celestial guardian of one of the 7 Heavens. Hippolytus gives the name as one of the powers worshipped by the Peratae. [*Rf.* Legge, *Forerunners and Rivals of Christianity* I, 107 fn.]

Astrgna [Astagna]

Astrocon—an angel of the 8th hour of the night, serving under Narcoriel. [*Rf.* Waite, *The Lemegeton.*]

Astroniel—an angel of the 9th hour of the day, serving under Vadriel. [*Rf.* Waite, *The Lemegeton.*]

Asuras or **Ahuras**—angels in Aryan lore; in Hindu lore, esoterically, the azuras became evil spirits and lower gods who waged war eternally with the great deities (the suryas); they were once gods of the Secret Wisdom, and may be compared to the fallen angels of Christian doctrine. [*Rf.* Hunter, *History of India,* chap. 4; Lenormant, *Chaldean Magic,* p. 77.]

Ataf—an evil angel who is invoked to overcome an enemy, as recorded in M. Gaster, *The Sword of Moses.* He is effective in separating a husband from his wife.

Ata'il—in Arabic lore, a guardian angel invoked in rites of exorcism. [*Rf.* Hughes, *A Dictionary of Islam,* "Angels."]

Ataliel (Atliel)—one of the 28 angels who rule over the 28 Mansions of the Moon. [*Rf. The Sixth and Seventh Books of Moses.*]

Ataphiel—an angel who supports heaven with 3 fingers. [*Rf.* Barattiel in *3 Enoch.*]

Atar ("fire" in Zend and Sanskrit)—a Zoroastrian genius of fire and chief of the celestial beings called Yazatas (*q.v.*). [*Rf.* Redfield, *Gods/A Dictionary of the Deities of All Lands.*]

Atarculph—according to Voltaire in his "Of Angels, Genii, and Devils," Atarculph was one of the leaders of the fallen angels as listed in *Enoch.*

Atarniel (*see* Atrugiel).

Atarph—corresponding angel for Hahaiah (*q.v.*).

Atatiyah—a secret name for Michael or Metatron. [*Rf. Visions of Ezekiel;* Scholem, *Jewish Gnosticism, Merkabah Mysticism, and Talmudic Tradition; Sefer ha-Heshek.*]

Atbah—in gnosticism, a secret name for the dekas, who are great archons. [*Rf. Lesser Hechaloth.*]

Atbah Ah—lord of hosts, invoked by the angel Akatriel. *See* hechaloth text, Oxford MS., referred to in Scholem, *Jewish Gnosticism, Merkabah Mysticism, and Talmudic Tradition.*

Atel—in de Abano, *The Heptameron,* an angel of the 4th Heaven, an angel of the air ruling on Lord's Day, invoked from the east.

Atembui—corresponding angel for Mumiah (*q.v.*).

Aterchinis—an angel of an hour, and corresponding angel for Teiazel (*q.v.*). [*Rf.* Ambelain, *La Kabbale Pratique.*] "H. D." mentions Aterchinis in her poem "Sagesse."

Aterestin—a most holy name (of an angel or of God) invoked in the discovery of hidden treasure. [*Rf.* Waite, *The Book of Black Magic and of Pacts.*]

Athamas—an angel invoked in the conjuration of Ink and Colors. [*Rf.* Mathers, *The Greater Key of Solomon.*]

Athanatos—a conjuring spirit of the planet Mercury; a name of God used in the discovery of hidden treasure; in the cabala, a spirit invoked in the general citation of Moses, Aaron, and Solomon. [*Rf.* Scot, *Discoverie of Witchcraft.*]

Atheniel—one of the 28 angels governing the 28 Mansions of the Moon. [*Rf.* Barrett, *The Magus.*]

Athoth—in gnosticism, one of the 12 powers engendered by Iadalbaoth (*q.v.*).

Atiel—one of the chief angel-princes of the Sword; mentioned in *Malache Elyon* as equated with A'hiel. [*Rf.* M. Gaster, *The Sword of Moses.*]

Atliel [Ataliel]

Atmon—one of the many names of the angel Metatron.

Atriel [Araziel]

Atropatos—one of the many names of the angel Metatron.

Atrugiel (Atrigiel, Atarniel, Tagriel, Atrugniel)—a guardian angel of the 7th heavenly hall. (*See* Kafziel.) Atrugiel is one of the names of Metatron.

Atrugniel [Atrugiel]

Atsaftsaf and **Atshatsah**—in hechaloth lore (*Ma'asseh Merkabah*), angelic guards of the 6th heavenly hall.

Atsiluth (or Atziluth)—in cabalistic cosmogony, the world of emanation, i.e., highest of the 4 worlds, the residence of God and the superior angels.

Attarib (or Attaris)—one of the 4 angels of winter and head of the sign of winter. [*Rf.* Barrett, *The Magus*; De Plancy, *Dictionnaire Infernal*.]

At-Taum ("the twin")—in Manicheanism, the angel from whom Mani received revelations; he is identified with the Holy Ghost in Christian doctrine. [*Rf.* Doresse, *The Secret Books of Egyptian Gnostics*.]

Atuesuel—in the cabala, one of the 8 angels of omnipotence. He is invoked "to smoke out the monsters of hell" in the special citation of Leviathans, as set forth in *The Sixth and Seventh Books of Moses*.

Atufiel—in hechaloth lore (*Ma'asseh Merkabah*), an angelic guard stationed at the 6th heavenly hall.

Atuniel ("furnace")—an angel of fire in rabbinic angelology; also, one of the angels belonging to the order of virtues. Atuniel is to be compared with Nathanel (*q.v.*). [*Rf.* Ginzberg, *The Legends of the Jews* VI.]

Aub—an angel's name found inscribed on the 3rd pentacle of the moon. [*Rf.* Mathers, *The Greater Key of Solomon*, p. 81.] When Aub is invoked, versicle 13 from Psalm 40 should be recited: "Be pleased, O Lord, to deliver me."

Auel (or Amet)—an angel of the sun invoked by cabalists in conjuring rites. [*Rf. The Sixth and Seventh Books of Moses.*]

Aufiel (Auphiel)—an angel with dominion over birds. [*Rf.* Schwab, *Vocabulaire de l'Angélologie*.]

Aufniel [Ofniel]

Auphanim [Ofanim]

Aupiel (Anafiel)—a variant spelling, considered the correct one, for Anafiel, the great angel who bore Enoch to Heaven when the antediluvian patriarch was still in the flesh. Aupiel is the tallest angel in Heaven, exceeding Metatron (the next tallest) by many hundred parasangs. In Ginzberg, *The Legends of the Jews* I, 138, where the translation of Enoch to Heaven by Aupiel is recounted, he is called "the angel Anpiel."

Auriel (Oriel; Hebrew for Uriel, "light of God")—one of the 72 angels of the 72 quinaries of the degrees of the zodiac, invoked in the conjuration of the Sword. [*Rf.* Runes, *Wisdom of the Kabbala*.]

Aurkhi Be-Ram El—an angel who had sexual relations with mortal women before the Flood, according to the story in Schwab, *Vocabulaire de l'Angélologie*. Probably the same as the fallen angel Ramiel in Enoch lore.

Ausiul (Ausiel)—an angel with dominion over Aquarius (water carrier). Ausiul is invoked in ceremonial magic rites. [*Rf.* Waite, *The Lemegeton.*]

Authorities—alternate term for powers or virtues, or a distinct order of angels (pre-Dionysian) and not the equivalent of powers or virtues. In the *Constitution of the Apostles* (liturgy of the Mass called Clementina) and in John of Damascus, the orders powers (*dunamis*) and authorities (*exousia*) are considered 2 distinct orders. Enumerating the 9 Dionysian orders in *Exposition of the Orthodox Faith* (*De Fide Orthodoxa*) John of Damascus gives powers as 5th and authorities (virtues) as 6th in the sequence. In the *Testament of Levi* the authorities dwell in the 4th Heaven, where the thrones dwell also. [*Rf.* Caird, *Principalities and Powers*; Dionysius, *Celestial Hierarchy*; also Appendix, "The Orders of the Celestial Hierarchy."]

Autogenes—in gnostic lore, Autogenes is an aeon around whom stand 4 great luminaries: Harmozel (Armogen), Daveithe, Oroiael (Uriel?), Eleleth. [*Rf. Apocryphon of John*; Grant, *Gnosticism and Early Christianity*, p. 43.]

Autopator—one of the 3 powers established by the Virgin (Pistis Sophia?) of the lower world and entrusted with the hidden things reserved for the perfect. [*Rf. The Secret Books of the Egyptian Gnostics.*]

Auza (Azza, Oza)—a son of the elohim (a son of God), one of the fallen angels who had carnal knowledge of the daughters of men—an incident touched on in Genesis 6. [*Rf.* Mathers, *The Kabbalah Unveiled*, p. 249.]

Auzael [Azazel, Auza]

Auzhaya (Avzhia)—a prince of the divine countenance; one of the many names of the angel Metatron (*q.v.*). [*Rf.* hechaloth text (Oxford MS.) mentioned in Scholem, *Jewish Gnosticism, Merkabah Mysticism, and Talmudic Tradition*, p. 53.]

Avagbag—in hechaloth lore (*Ma'asseh Merkabah*), an angelic guard stationed at the 6th heavenly hall.

Avahel—a prince of angels residing in the 3rd Heaven. [*Rf. The Sixth and Seventh Books of Moses.*]

Avartiel—an angel's name found inscribed on an oriental charm (*kamea*) for warding off evil. [*Rf.* Schrire, *Hebrew Amulets.*]

Avatar—in Vedic lore, the avatar was the human or animal incarnation of a deity. There were 10 of these angelic beings, associated chiefly with the 1st avatar, Vishnu. The other 9 are usually listed as Kurmavatar (the tortoise avatar); Barah (the bear avatar); Narsinha (man-lion avatar and lord of heroism); Vamana (dwarf avatar and lord of reason); Paras u Rama (Parasuram) or Chirangivah the immortal; Ram Avatar (Rama or Ramachandra); Krisn Avatar (Krishna); Budh Avatar (Buddha); Kalki Avatar. All these are past, except Kalki the 10th avatar, who will appear in the form of a white horse with wings and come at the end of the 4 ages to destroy the earth. [*Rf. The Dabistan*, pp. 180–183.]

Avenging Angels—the 1st angels created by God, also known as the angels of destruction. The chief dwells in the 5th Heaven, according to Jewish legend. Traditionally there were 12 avenging angels. [*See* Angels of Vengeance.]

Avial—an angelic guard stationed before one of the halls (palaces) of the 7 Heavens. Avial is named in the *Pirke Hechaloth*.

Avirzahe'e—a beloved but fearsome angelprince guardian stationed at the gate leading to the 6th Heaven—according to the scholar Nachunya ben ha-Kane. [*Rf.* Margouliath, *Malache Elyon*.]

Avitue—one of the 18 names of Lilith in rabbinic lore. [*Rf.* Hanauer, *Folk-Lore of the Holy Land*, p. 325.]

Avniel—one of the chief angel-princes appointed by God to the Sword. [*Rf.* M. Gaster, *The Sword of Moses* XI.]

Avriel—in hechaloth lore (*Ma'asseh Merkabah*), an angelic guard stationed at the 7th heavenly hall.

Avtsangosh—one of the many names of the angel Metatron.

Avzhia [Auzhaya]

Awar (El Awar)—one of the sons of Eblis (*q.v.*); called the demon of lubricity.

Awel, Awitel, Awoth—angels invoked in cabalistic conjuring rites. [*Rf. The Sixth and Seventh Books of Moses.*]

Axineton—an angelic entity; by pronouncing his name God created the world. [*Rf.* Mathers, *The Greater Key of Solomon*, p. 33.]

Ayar Ziva [Ram Khastra]

Ayib—a spirit of the planet Venus whose name is found inscribed on the 4th pentacle of that planet. [*Rf.* Mathers, *The Greater Key of Solomon*, p. 73.]

Ayil—angel of Sagittarius. In ceremonial magic the angel is Sizajasel. [*Rf.* Trachtenberg, *Jewish Magic and Superstition*, p. 251.]

Ayscher—in *The Sixth and Seventh Books of Moses*, a ministering angel summoned up by cabalists in magical operations.

Aza [Azza]

Azael (Asiel, "whom God strengthens")—one of 2 fallen angels (Aza is the other) who cohabited with Naamah, Lamech's daughter, and sired the sedim, Assyrian guardian spirits. [*Rf. The Zohar.*] Azael, it is reported, is chained in a desert where he will remain until the day of judgment. [*Rf.* De Plancy, *Dictionnaire Infernal.*] In *Midrash Petirat Mosheh*, Azael is mentioned as one of 2 angels (the other being Ouza) who came down from Heaven and was corrupted. Cornelius Agrippa, in his *Occult Philosophy*, lists 4 evil angels as the opposites of the 4 holy rulers of the elements; among the evil ones Azael is included. Schwab in his *Vocabulaire de l'Angélologie* identifies Shamhazai (Semyaza) with Azael (Aziel), guardian of hidden treasures.

Azaf [Asaph]

Azar (Azur)—angel of November in ancient Persian theogony. Azar governed the 9th day of the month. [*Rf.* Hyde, *Historia Religionis Veterum Persarum.*]

Azaradel—in *The Book of Enoch* (Enoch I) Azaradel is one of the fallen angels who taught men the motions of the moon.

Azarel—an angel whose name is found inscribed on the 5th pentacle of the moon. [*Rf.* Mathers, *The Greater Key of Solomon.*]

Azargushtasp/Azarkhurdad—two of the amesha spentas (Zoroastrian archangels) who are regarded "closest to the just God," in ancient Persian religious lore. [*Rf.* Shea and Troyer, *The Dabistan*, p. 136.]

Azariah or **Azarias** ("whom God helps")—a name that the archangel Raphael assumes in *The Book of Tobit*. Later in the tale, Raphael reveals his true identity as "one of the 7 angels who stand by and enter before the glory of the Lord."

Azariel—in Talmud, Azariel is the angel governing the waters of the earth. In occult lore he is listed among the 28 angels governing the 28 mansions of the moon. [*Rf.* Barrett, *The Magus*; De Plancy, *Dictionnaire Infernal.*]

Azazel (Azael, Hazazel, "God strengthens")—in *Enoch I*, Azazel is one of the chiefs of the 200 fallen angels (Revelation speaks of one-third of the heavenly host being involved in the fall). Azazel "taught men to fashion swords and shields" while women learned from him "finery and the art of beautifying the eyelids." He is the scapegoat in rabbinic literature, Targum, and in Leviticus 16:8, although in the latter he is not actually named. In *The Zohar* (Vayeze 153a) the rider on the serpent is symbolized by "the evil Azazel." Here he is said to be chief of the order of bene elim (otherwise ischim, lower angels, "men-spirits"). Irenaeus calls Azazel "that fallen and yet mighty angel." In *The Apocalypse of Abraham* he is "lord of hell, seducer of mankind," and here his aspect, when revealed in its true form, shows him to be a demon with 7 serpent heads, 14 faces, and 12 wings. Jewish legend speaks of Azazel as the angel who refused to bow down before Adam (in the Koran the angel is Eblis or Iblis) when the 1st human was presented to God to the assembled hierarchs in Heaven. For such refusal, Azazel was thenceforth dubbed "the accursed Satan." [*Rf.* Bamberger, *Fallen Angels*, p. 278.] According to the legend in Islamic lore, when God commanded the angels to worship Adam, Azazel refused, contending "Why should a son of fire [i.e., an angel] fall down before a son of clay [i.e., a mortal]?" Whereupon God cast Azazel out of Heaven and changed his name to Eblis. Milton in *Paradise Lost* I, 534 describes Azazel as "a cherub tall," but also as a fallen angel and Satan's standard bearer.

Originally, according to Maurice Bouisson in *Magic; Its History and Principal Rites*, Azazel was an ancient Semitic god of the flocks who was later degraded to the level of a demon. [*Rf.* Trevor Ling, *The Significance of Satan in New Testament Demonology*.] Bamberger in *Fallen Angels* inclines to the notion that the first star which fell (star here having the meaning of angel) was Azazel.

Azaziel—another name for the seraph Semyaza. In Byron's poem "Heaven and Earth, a Mystery" the legend is told of a pious maiden named Anah, granddaughter of Cain, who tempts Azaziel to reveal to her the Explicit Name. In the poem, Azaziel carries Anah off, at the time of the flood, to a planet other than the earth.

Azbogah [Azbuga YHWH]

Azbuga YHWH ("strength")—one of the 8 great angel princes of the throne of judgment and of a rank superior to that of Metatron (*q.v.*). "Originally," says Gershom Scholem, "Asbogah was a secret name of God in his highest sphere." His chief duty, it appears, was to clothe with righteousness the new arrivals in Heaven—those, that is, who were deemed worthy. A late Hebrew charm contains Asbogah's name as one to be invoked for the "healing of all illness and all hurt and all evil spirit." [*Rf.* Thompson, *Semitic Magic*, p. 161; *Enoch*; and the lesser hechaloth tracts mentioned by Scholem, *Jewish Gnosticism, Merkabah Mysticism, and Talmudic Tradition*.]

Azdai—an angel in Mandaean lore. [*Rf.* Pognon, *Inscriptions Mandaïtes des Coupes de Khouabir*.]

Azer—angel of elemental fire; also the name of Zoroaster's father. [*Rf. The Ancient's Book of Magic*.]

Azfiel—in hechaloth lore (*Ma'asseh Merkabah*), an angelic guard stationed at the 1st of the 7 heavenly halls.

Azibeel—one of the 200 angels who, according to *Enoch I*, descended from Heaven to cohabit with the daughters of men, an incident touched on in Genesis 6. Azibeel thereupon became a fallen angel.

Aziel [Azael]

Aziziel—an angel in Syriac incantation rites. In *The Book of Protection*, Aziziel is grouped with Michael, Harshiel, Prukiel, and other "spellbinding angels."

Azkariel—a corruption of Ak(h)raziel (*q.v.*). [*Rf.* II *Petirat Mosheh*, pp. 376–377; Ginzberg, *The Legends of the Jews* VI, 147.]

Azkeel—one of the leaders of the 200 fallen angels, in the Enoch listings, who descended from Heaven to cohabit with the daughters of men, an incident touched on in Genesis 6.

Azliel X—an invocation angel, one of 14; also one of the ineffable names of God. [*Rf.* M. Gaster, *The Sword of Moses*.]

Azrael (Azrail, Ashriel, Azriel, Azaril, Gabriel, etc.—"whom God helps")—in Hebrew and Islamic lore, the angel of death, stationed in the 3rd Heaven. To the Moslems, Azrael is another form of Raphael. In their tradition, he has "70,000 feet and 4,000 wings, while his body is provided with as many eyes and tongues as there are men in the world." [*Rf.* Hastings, *Encyclopaedia of Religion and Ethics* IV, 617.] In Arabic tradition, Azrael is "forever writing in a large book and forever erasing what he writes; what he writes is the birth of a man, what he erases is the name of the man at death." When Michael, Gabriel, and Israfel failed to provide 7 handfuls of earth for the creation of Adam, the 4th angel on this mission, Azrael, succeeded; and because of this feat he was appointed to separate body from soul. [*Cf.* Murdad, the *angelus mortis* in ancient Persian lore.] Oriental legend has it that Azrael accomplishes his mission (i.e., bringing death first and separation afterward) by holding an apple from the Tree of Life to the nostril of the dying person. In Jewish mysticism, Azrael is the embodiment of evil. In *The Book of Protection* he is one of 3 holy angels (the other 2 being Gabriel and Michael) invoked in Syriac charms. He is the angel of death in Longfellow's poem "The Spanish Jew's Tale" and, in the popular edition of *The Complete Poetical Works of Henry Wadsworth Longfellow*, he is pictorially represented with King Solomon entertaining a "rajah of Hindostan."

Azra'il—in Arabic lore, a guardian angel invoked in rites of exorcism. [*Rf.* Hughes, *A Dictionary of Islam*, "Angels."]

Azriel—a chief angel supervisor referred to as "Azriel the Ancient," sometimes as "Mahniel" (meaning mighty camp), as in *The Zohar* (Exodus 202a). Here he commands 60 myriads of legions of spirits and is stationed on the northern side of Heaven, where he receives prayers. In *Ozar Midrashim* I, 85, Azriel is one of the chief angels of destruction. His name is found inscribed on oriental charms (*kameoth*) for warding off evil. [*Rf.* Schrire, *Hebrew Amulets*.]

Azur [Azar]

Azza (Shem-yaza, "the strong")—a fallen angel who is, according to rabbinic tradition, suspended between Heaven and earth (along with Azzael) as punishment for having had carnal knowledge of mortal women. Azza (Shemyaza, meaning "the name Azza") is said to be constantly falling, with one eye shut, the other open, so that he can see his plight and suffer the more. There is another explanation for Azza's expulsion from Heaven: it is that he objected to the high rank given Enoch when the latter was transformed from a mortal into the angel Metatron (*see* Iblis or Eblis). In Solomonic lore the story is that Azza was the angel who revealed to the Jewish king the heavenly arcana, thus making Solomon the wisest man on earth. In Talmud, the sedim (Assyrian guardian spirits) are said to have been "begotten by Azza and Azael on the body of the evil Naamah, daughter of Lamech, before the Flood." [*Rf.* Thompson, *Semitic Magic*, pp. 44–45.] In his introduction to *3 Enoch*, Odeberg remarks that, of the 2 groups of angels headed by Metatron, one group (the angels of justice) was under the rulership of Azza. At that time, evidently, Azza was not yet fallen.

Azzael (see Azza)—while Azza and Azzael, in some sources, are referred to as 2 distinct, separate angels, they seem to be one and the same in other sources. Variant spellings are Assiel, Azazel, Azzazel, etc. In the early part of *3 Enoch*, Azzael is represented as one of 3 ministering angels (Uzza and Azza being the other 2), inhabitants of the 7th Heaven; later, however, he is represented as a fallen angel and ranked with Azza as one of the *maskim* (*q.v.*). For cohabiting with the daughters of men, he was punished (with Uzza) by having his nose pierced. He taught witchcraft, by the art of which man can cause (or did cause at one time) the sun, moon and stars to descend from the sky, so as to make them closer objects of worship. [*Rf. The Alphabet of Rabbi Akiba*; Bamberger, *Fallen Angels* (p. 127); the *Midrash Petirat Mosheh*.]

The Angel of the Lord, Balaam's Ass, and Balaam (Numbers 22), by Rembrandt. Reproduced from Régamey, *Anges.*

Baabiel—in the cabala, an angel serving in the 1st Heaven. [*Rf. The Sixth and Seventh Books of Moses.*]

Baal Davar—a term for the adversary (*ha-satan*) used by chasidic Jews of the 18th century. [*Rf.* Bamberger, *Fallen Angels.*]

Baal-Peor [Belphegor]

Babel (Babiel)—in de Abano, *The Heptameron,* one of the messengers of the planet Jupiter. He is variously cited as an angel of Wednesday and/or Friday, and is to be invoked only when the invocant faces south or west. In the cabala generally, Babel is a resident of the 3rd Heaven.

Babhne'a—in Babylonian terracotta devil traps, a mighty angel whose name is inscribed in Hebrew characters and invoked for protection against evil. [*Rf.* Budge, *Amulets and Talismans,* p. 288.]

Bachanoe (or Bachanael)—in occultism, an angel of the 1st Heaven and a ruler of Monday.

Bachiel (Baciel)—one of the angels of the air serving in the 4th Heaven and invoked from the east. Bachiel is also identified as one of the spirits of the planet Saturn. In the *Ozar Midrashim* II, 316 he is one of the angelic guards of the West Wind.

Bachliel—one of the angelic guards of the South Wind.

Badariel (Batarjal)—one of the 200 fallen angels. [*Rf. Enoch I,* 69:2.]

Badpatiel—an angel's name found inscribed on an oriental Hebrew charm (*kamea*) for warding off evil. [*Rf.* Schrire, *Hebrew Amulets.*]

Bae—in *The Testament of Solomon,* an angel summoned for the exorcising of demons.

Bael (Baal—"lord" or "master")—in *The Zohar,* Bael is equated with the archangel Raphael. However, in the grimoires, and in Wierus, *Pseudo-Monarchia,* he is a great king of the underworld serving in the eastern division of Hell and attended by 60 or 70 legions of devils. He manifests, when invoked, as a creature with 3 heads (toad, man, cat).

67

Ba-En-Kekon (Bainkhookh)—an aeon-angel mentioned in *Pistis Sophia* gnosticism and referred to as "the soul of darkness." He derives from the Egyptian *Book of the Dead*.

Bagdal—in Levi, *Transcendental Magic*, a genius who, with Araziel, governs the sign of the Bull (Taurus) in the zodiac.

Bagdial (fictional)—a corpulent angel in charge of issuing cards to recent arrivals in the lower Heavens, these cards entitling the holders of them to new "bodies." Bagdial is an invention of Isaac Bashevis Singer and occurs in the latter's short story "The Warehouse," *Cavalier* (January 1966).

Baglis—a genius of measure and balance, according to Apollonius of Tyana, *The Nuctemeron*. Baglis may be invoked only in the 2nd hour of the day.

The Black Angel. In Mohammedan lore he is either Nakir or Monker. Here he is shown with features of a rackhasa (a Hindu evil spirit). Left, two lesser evil spirits. From Mohammed al Sudi's *Treatise on Astrology and Divination*, reproduced from *Larousse Encyclopedia of Mythology*.

Bagnael—one of the numerous angelic guards of the gates of the East Wind. [*Rf. Ozar Midrashim* II, 316.]

Bahaliel—one of the numerous angelic guards of the gates of the East Wind. [*Rf. Ozar Midrashim* II, 316.]

Bahman [Barman]

Bahram [Barman]

Baijel—in the cabala, Baijel is an angel serving in the 5th Heaven. [*Rf. The Sixth and Seventh Books of Moses*.]

Bainkhookh [Ba-En-Kekon]

Baktamael—one of the numerous angelic guards of the gates of the West Wind. [*Rf. Ozar Midrashim* II, 316.]

Balam (Balan)—formerly an angel of the order of dominations; now, in hell, a "terrible and powerful king, with 3 heads (bull, ram, man) and the tail of a serpent." He rides naked astride a bear (see picturization in De Plancy, *Dictionnaire Infernal*, 1863 ed.). He commands 40 legions of infernal spirits. [*Rf. Grand Grimoire*.]

Balay—in de Abano, *The Heptameron* and in Barrett, *The Magus*, a Monday angel resident in the 1st Heaven. An invocant must face north when invoking Balay.

Balberith (Berith, Beal, Elberith, Baalberith)—an ex-prince of the order of cherubim. Now in Hell, Balberith is a grand pontiff and master of ceremonies. He is usually the one to countersign or notarize the signatures on the pacts entered into between mortals and the devil. He is called "scriptor" and is so noted on documents executed in the underworld. In *The Encyclopedia of Witchcraft and Demonology*, Balberith appears to be the demon who possessed the body of Sister Madeleine at Aix-en-Provence, and who revealed to her the names of other devils. [*Rf.* Michaelis, *Admirable History of the Possession and Conversion of a Penitent Woman*; De Plancy, *Dictionnaire Infernal* (ed. 1863), where, as Berith, he is pictured with a crown on his head and astride a horse.]

Baldach—an angel called on in ritual magic, as cited in Waite, *The Greater Key of Solomon.*

Balhiel [Baliel]

Balidet—a Saturday angel of the air, ministering to Maymon (*q.v.*).

Baliel (Balhiel)—a Monday angel (*Cf.* Balay) invoked from the north. Said to reside either in the 1st or 2nd Heaven. [*Rf. The Sixth and Seventh Books of Moses.*] In *Ozar Midrashim* II, 316, as Balhiel, he is one of numerous guards of the gates of the South Wind.

Balkin—in ritual magic, a beneficent master spirit, lord and king of the northern mountains. His aide is Luridan, a domestic spirit. [*Rf.* Scot, *Discoverie of Witchcraft*; Butler, *Ritual Magic.*]

Ballaton—an angel appearing on the external circle of the pentagram of Solomon figured in Waite, *The Lemegeton.*

Baltazard—a spirit invoked in Solomonic magic for procuring a lady's garter. [*Rf. Grimorium Verum.*]

Balthial (Balthiel)—in *3 Enoch*, one of the 7 planetary angels, and the only angel who is able to overcome or thwart the machinations of the evil genius of jealousy. [*Rf. The Testament of Solomon.*]

Banech—one of the angels of the 7 planets invoked in conjuring rites. [*Rf. The Sixth and Seventh Books of Moses.*]

Baniel—an inferior spirit summoned in Solomonic magical rites. [*Rf. Grimorium Verum*; Shah, *The Secret Lore of Magic.*]

Baraborat—in occult lore, a spirit of the planet Mercury. He is a Wednesday angel, resident either in the 2nd or 3rd Heaven, and invoked from the east. [*Rf.* de Abano, *The Heptameron*; Barrett, *The Magus* II.]

Baracata—a spirit invoked in prayer by the Master of the Art in Solomonic conjurations. [*Rf.* Waite, *The Book of Black Magic and of Pacts.*]

Barach—an angel of the Seal, used for conjuring. [*Rf. The Sixth and Seventh Books of Moses.*]

Barachiel [Barakiel]

Baradiel (Yurkemo, Yurkei, Yurkemoi)—one of the 7 great archangels, a prince of the 3rd Heaven, where Baradiel shares rulership with the angel Shaphiel. Baradiel also exercises dominion over hail, with Nuriel and others. [*Rf. 3 Enoch.*]

Barael—in Jewish mysticism, one of the 7 exalted throne angels resident in the 1st Heaven. He helps "execute the commands of the potentates," according to *The Book of the Angel Raziel.* [*Rf.* Cornelius Agrippa, *Three Books of Occult Philosophy* III; de Abano, *Elementia Magica.*]

Barah—the "boar avatar," one of the 10 incarnations of divinity in Vedic lore. [*See* Avatar.]

Barakiel (Barachiel, Barbiel, Barchiel, Barkiel, Baraqiel, etc.—"lightning of God")—one of the 7 archangels, one of the 4 ruling seraphim, angel of the month of February, and prince of the 2nd Heaven as well as of the order of confessors. Barakiel has dominion over lightning and is also one of the chief angels of the 1st and 4th altitudes or chora in the *Almadel of Solomon.* In addition, he is a ruler of the planet Jupiter and the zodiacal sign of Scorpio (as cited by Camfield in *A Theological Discourse of Angels*) and Pisces. With the angels Uriel and Rubiel, Barakiel is invoked to bring success in games of chance, according to De Plancy, *Dictionnaire Infernal.* [*Rf.* Ginzberg, *The Legends of the Jews* I, 140.]

Barakon—an angel invoked in Solomonic conjuring rites. [*Rf.* Mathers, *The Greater Key of Solomon.*]

Baraqel (Barakiel)—one of the fallen angels in the Enoch listings.

Baraqijal—as noted in *The Book of Jubilees*, one of the watchers (grigori) who united with the daughters of men, an incident touched on in Genesis 6. Baraqijal, now a demon and inhabiting the nether realms, is a teacher of astrology. In *Enoch I* he is described as a leader (one of the "chiefs of ten") of a troop of fallen angels. [*Cf.* Barakiel, of which Baraqijal may be merely a variant.]

Barattiel—in *3 Enoch* 18:6, when Tagas (*q.v.*) sees Barattiel "the great angelic prince of 3 fingers" (with which, it seems, he is able to hold up the highest Heaven), he, Tagas, "removes the crown of glory from his head and falls on his face." [*See* Ataphiel, which may be another form for Barattiel.]

Barbatos—an angel formerly of the order of virtues. "This fact," reports Spence in *An Encyclopaedia of Occultism*, "was proved after infinite research." In Hell, where Barbatos now dwells, he is a great duke, ruling over 30 legions of spirits. He "giveth understanding of the song of birds, knows the past and can foretell the future." He may be invoked in magical rites, and he will appear gladly, but only when the sun is in the sign of Sagittarius. For Barbatos' sigil, see Wierus, *Pseudo-Monarchia*; Waite, *The Book of Black Magic and of Pacts* (p. 108); and *The Lemegeton*.

Barbelo—a great archon (female) "perfect in glory and next in rank to the Father-of-All." She is the consort of Cosmocrator (*q.v.*). [*Rf.* the gnostic *Gospel of Mary* and the *Apocryphon of John*.] In the *Texts of the Saviour*, Barbelo is the daughter of Pistis Sophia, procreator of the superior angels.

Barbiel (Barbuel, Baruel)—once a prince of the order of virtues and of the order of archangels. He is the angel of the month of October and one of the 28 angels of the 28 mansions of the moon. In Barrett, *The Magus*, Barbiel is equated with Barakiel (which would make Barbiel ruler also of the month of February). In the underworld, Barbiel serves as one of the 7 Electors, under the suzerainty of Zaphiel.

Barchiel [Barakiel]

Barcus—in Apollonius of Tyana, *The Nuctemeron*, Barcus is a genius (i.e., angel) of quintessence; he is also one of the genii of the 5th hour.

Bardiel (Barchiel, Baradiel)—in Jewish legend,

the angel of hail, along with Nuriel, the twin kadishin (quadisin), and others.

Baresches or **Bareschas** ("beginning")—in the grimoires, a great angel invoked to procure the woman desired by the invocant.

Barginiel—governing angel of the 7th hour of the day. [*Rf.* Waite, *The Lemegeton*.]

Bariel—ruling angel of the 11th hour of the day; also, angel of the 4th pentacle of the planet Jupiter. [*Rf.* Mathers, *The Greater Key of Solomon*, p. 64.]

Barinian—supreme beings, "exalted angels" in ancient Persian lore. They are also called Huristar. [*Rf. The Dabistan*.]

Barkaial [Baraqijal]

Barkeil—an angel in Mandaean tradition. [*Rf.* Pognon, *Inscriptions Mandaïtes Coupes de Khouabir*.]

Barkiel (Barakiel)—in *Ozar Midrashim* II, 316, one of numerous angelic guards of the gates of the East Wind.

Barku (*see* Rimmon)

Barman (Bahman, Bahram)—in ancient Persian cosmology, a great *mihr* (angel) placed over all the animals on earth except man. Barman was also chief of 30 angels appointed to preside over the 30 days of the month. [*Rf.* Hyde, *Historia Religionis Veterum Persarum*.] In *The Dabistan*, Barman is one of the amesha spentas, "the first intelligence, the first angel . . . from whom other spirits or angels proceed." He is "the mightiest of the angels whom the Muhammedans call Jabriel" (Gabriel). He was the angel of January and governor of the 2nd day of the month. Barman is usually pictured in an image of red stone, in human form, on his head a red crown. Omar Khayyam in the *Rubaiyat* sings of "Bahram, the great Hunter."

Barpharanges (Sesenges - Barharanges) — in gnosticism, Barpharanges is one of the powers in charge of the spring of the waters of life (i.e., heavenly baptism). His name appears in Coptic magical texts. *Cf.* Raphael, angel of baptismal water. [*Rf. Bruce Codex*; Doresse, *The Secret Books of the Egyptian Gnostics.*]

Barsabel (Barzabel)—in *The Magus*, one of the angels governing the planet Mars. His cabalistic number is 325.

Bartyabel—according to Paracelsus in his doctrine of Talismans, Bartyabel is a spirit of Mars, serving the angel Graphiel, who is the presiding intelligence of the planet. [*Rf.* Christian, *The History and Practice of Magic* I, 318.]

Bartzachiah (Barzachia)—found inscribed as an angel's name on the 1st pentacle of the planet Mars, along with the names of Ithuriel, Madiniel, and Eschiel, all these angels' names being set down in Hebrew characters. [*Rf.* Mathers, *The Greater Key of Solomon.*]

Baruch ("blessed")—chief guardian angel of the Tree of Life, according to the *Apocalypse of Baruch*. [*Cf.* Raphael, who is also credited with being the guardian angel of the Tree of Life.] In the Baruch *Apocalypse*, Baruch journeys through 5 Heavens, in the 1st 3 of which he sees "evil-looking monsters." In an early Ophitic (gnostic) system, Baruch was one of 3 angels sent forth by Elohim (God) "to succor the spirit in man." In witchcraft lore Baruch is one of 7 devils who possessed the body of Sister Seraphica of Loudon. [*Rf.* Mead, *Fragments of a Faith Forgotten*, p. 196.]

Baruchiachel—in *3 Enoch*, one of the 7 great planetary rulers; and the only angel able to rout the female demon named Strife [*Rf. The Testament of Solomon*].

Baryá'il—in Islamic apocalyptic writings, an angel encountered by the sufi Abu Yazid in the 7th Heaven. Baryá'il is found to be "of the tallness of the distance of a journey of 500 years." [*Cf.* equally fantastic heights of angels as measured in parasangs in ancient Persian lore.] He is head of innumerable ranks of fellow dwellers on high. As in the case of offers in the lower Heavens (by the angel Láwidh in the 2nd and by the angel Nayá'il in the 4th), Baryá'il offers the sufi "a kingdom

such as no tongue can describe," but the offer or bribe is resisted, Abu Yazid remaining throughout his *mir'aj* (heavenly ascent) singleminded in his devotion to God. [*Rf.* Nicholson, "An Early Arabic Version," etc.]

Basasael (Basasaeyal)—in *Enoch I*, an evil archangel.

Bashmallin (Hashmallim)—an order of angels equated with the dominations.

Baskabas—a variant reading for Kasbak, one of the secret names of the angel Metatron.

Basus—in hechaloth lore (*Ma'asseh Merkabah*), an angelic guard stationed at the 4th heavenly hall.

Bataliel—one of the rulers of the 12 signs of the zodiac.

Batarel (Batariel, Badariel, Batrael, Batarjal, Metarel)—one of the 200 fallen angels in the Enoch listings. He may be invoked in ceremonial magic rites. The name Batariel appears in Talisman 4 of the *Sage of the Pyramids*. [See reproduction in Waite, *The Book of Black Magic and of Pacts*, p. 95.]

Batarjal [Batarel]

Bathor—in white magic, one of the 7 olympian spirits, known as Electors or Stewards of Heaven.

Bat(h) Qol (Bath Kol—"heavenly voice" or "daughter of the voice")—a holy guardian angel said to have visited in his cell the 2nd-century sage, Simeon ben Yohai, reputed author of *The Zohar*. Bat Qol is held by many rabbis to be a form of divine pronouncement in the latter days when prophecy had ceased. She (for Bat Qol is female) is symbolized as a dove and may be compared, with the manifestation in this form, to the Holy Ghost in New Testament theophany. [*Rf. Pirke Aboth*; *The Zohar*; Newman and Spitz, *The Talmudic Anthology*; Fuller, *Secret Wisdom of the Qabalah.*] In a Syriac charm invocation (as recorded in *The Book of Protection*), Bat Qol is referred to as "the Voice which called out to Cain the murderer, 'Where is thy brother Abel?'"

Batsran—one of the many names of the angel Metatron.

Bat Zuge—a term for the evil Lilith (*q.v.*) when she is regarded as the 10th of the 10 unholy sefiroth or divine emanations issuing from the left side of God. [*Rf. The Zohar*, suppl.]

Bazathiel—one of the angelic guards of the 1st Heaven. [*Cf. Hechaloth Rabbati.*]

Bazazath (Raphael-Bazazath)—an archangel residing in the 2nd Heaven. In *The Testament of Solomon* and in magical tracts generally, Bazazath (or Bazazarath) is reported to have put to flight, among other feats, a winged dragon (female) by the name of Obizuth.

Baz Baziah—a Talmudic angel invoked to cure cutaneous disorders. [*Rf.* Talmud *Shabbath*, fol. 67.]

Bazkiel—an angelic guard of the 3rd Heaven. [*Rf. Ozar Midrashim* I, 116.]

Baztiel—in hechaloth lore (*Ma'asseh Merkabah*), an angelic guard of the 1st heavenly hall.

Bealphares—although characterized as a demon in Wierus, *Pseudo-Monarchia*, Bealphares is also declared to be "the noblest carrier that ever did serve any man upon the earth." He must therefore be called a benign spirit. Moreover, he is not listed as a demon in the rather exhaustive *Dictionnaire Infernal* or other registers of underworld hierarchs.

Bearechet—an angel of the Seal, cited in *The Sixth and Seventh Books of Moses.*

Beasts of the Field—in *The Zohar* and in cabalistic works generally, "beasts of the field" is often a designation for the higher angels.

Beatiel—an angel serving in the 4th Heaven. [*Rf. The Sixth and Seventh Books of Moses.*]

Beatrice (Portinari)—the Beatrice of Dante's *La Vita Nuova* and *The Divine Comedy* (particularly the *Paradiso*). Dante sees his beloved in Paradise as an angel; she leads him to the Empyrean, which is one of the abodes of God.

Beburos—one of the 9 angels who will rule "at the end of the world," according to *Revelation*

of Esdras. [*Rf. The Ante-Nicene Fathers Library* 8, 573.] For the names of the other 8 angels, *see* Angels at the End of the World.

Bedaliel—an angel invoked to command or exorcise demons, as cited in goetic tracts. [*Rf.* Mathers, *The Greater Key of Solomon.*]

Bedrimulael [Abedumabal]

Beelzebub (Belzebud, Belzaboul, Beelzeboul, Baalsebul, etc. "god of flies")—originally a Syrian god, Beelzebub is in II Kings 1:3, a god of Ekron in Philistia. In the cabala, he is chief of the 9 evil hierarchies of the underworld. In Matthew 10:25, Mark 3:22, and Luke 40:15, Beelzebub is chief of the demons, "prince of the devils" (as in Matthew 12:24), but he is to be distinguished from Satan (just as he is in all magic, medieval or otherwise). [*Rf.* Legge, *Forerunners and Rivals of Christianity* 9, 108.] In the *Gospel of Nicodemus*, Christ, during his 3 days in Hell, gives Beelzebub dominion over the underworld in gratitude for permitting him (Christ), over Satan's objections, to take Adam and the other "saints in prison" to Heaven. A popular title of Beelzebub was "lord of flies." Another of his titles was "lord of chaos," as given in the gnostic writings of Valentinus. Dante identifies Beelzebub with Satan, but Milton in *Paradise Lost* I, 79, ranks Beelzebub "next to Satan in power and crime;" in I, 157 Satan addresses Beelzebub as a "fallen cherub." In Hayley's edition of the *Poetical Works of John Milton* (London, 1794), there is an illustration showing "Satan conferring with Belzebuth." In Gurdjieff's *All and Everything, Beelzebub's Tales to His Grandson*, the hero is Beelzebub.

Behemiel (Hariel, Hashmal)—an angel with dominion over tame beasts. Behemiel is chief of the order of hashmallim, an order equated with that of the cherubim.

Behemoth—a male chaos-monster (whale, crocodile, hippopotamus) created on the 5th day and closely associated with the female Leviathan. [*Rf. Apocalypse of Baruch*, 29.] Also identified with Rahab, primordial angel of the sea, and with

William Blake's "Behemoth," an illustration for his *Book of Job.*

the angel of death. In Roman Catholic theology, Behemoth is the principal of darkness, although Job's (40:19) "he is the chief of the ways of God" points in an opposite direction. See picturization of Behemoth, in the form of an elephant with bear's feet, in Seligmann, *The History of Magic,* and Blake's engraving "Behemoth and Leviathan."

Beleth (Bileth, Bilet, Byleth)—once of the order of powers—an order to which he hopes to return—Beleth is a fallen angel in Hell where he rules 85 legions of demons. He is a king, rides a pale horse, and is announced by a blare of trumpets. His sigil is shown in Waite, *The Book of Black Magic and of Pacts,* p. 169, and in *The Lemegeton.* That Beleth was formerly of the order of powers "was proved after infinite research," reports Spence in *An Encyclopaedia of Occultism,* p. 119.

Belhar [Bernael]

Beli—one of the angelic guards of the gates of the North Wind. [*Rf. Ozar Midrashim* II, 316.]

Beliael—like Beli, an angelic guard of the gates of the North Wind.

Belial (Beliar or Berial)—in Jacobus de Teramo, *Das Buch Beliel,* this great fallen angel, often equated with Satan, is pictured presenting his credentials to Solomon; also as dancing before the Hebrew king. Paul, in II Corinthians 6:15, asks "What concord hath Christ with Belial?" Here, clearly, Paul regards Belial as chief of demons, or as Satan. In *Paradise Lost* I, 490–492, "Belial came last; than whom a Spirit more lewd/Fell not from Heav'n, or more gross to love/Vice it self." Later, in *Paradise Lost* II, 110–112, Milton speaks of Belial thus: "A fairer person lost not Heav'n; he seemed/For dignity compos'd and high exploit;" but hastens to add: "all was false and hollow." "Possibly an old name for Sheol," says Barton in "Origin of the Names of Angels and Demons." In *The Toilers of the Sea,* Victor Hugo, drawing on occult sources, speaks of Belial as Hell's ambassador to Turkey. [*Cf.* Mastema.] As in the case of Bileth, it was "only after infinite research," reports Spence, *An Encyclopaedia of*

Belial dancing before King Solomon, from *Das Buch Belial* by Jacobus de Teramo. Reproduced from Grillot, *Picture Museum of Sorcery, Magic and Alchemy.*

Occultism (p. 119), that Belial was "proved to have been formerly of the order of virtues."

Beliar ("worthless")—interchangeable, in most sources, with Beliel. Beliar is mentioned in Deuteronomy, Judges, and I Samuel, always as evil, its symbol or personification. In apocryphal writings Beliar is the prince of darkness, supreme adversary of God. In *The Martyrdom of Isaiah* he is the angel of lawlessness. In *The Gospel of Bartholomew*, Bartholomew asks Beliar to tell who he is, and Beliar answers: "At first I was called Satanel, which is interpreted a messenger of God, but when I rejected the image of God my name was calld Satanas, that is, an angel that keepeth Hell (Tartarus). . . . I was formed the first angel . . . Michael second, Gabriel third, Uriel fourth, Raphael fifth, Nathanael sixth. . . . These are the angels of vengeance that were first formed." [*Rf.* James, *The Apocryphal New Testament*, p. 175.] In Waite, *The Lemegeton*, Beliar is said to have been created "next after Lucifer." As a fallen angel Beliar boasts that he "fell first among the worthier sort." Milton calls him a "false-titled son of God." According to the Schoolmen, Beliar was once partly of the order of angels and partly of the order of virtues. However, Glasson, *Greek Influence in Jewish Eschatology*, argues that Beliar was never an angel and compares him with Ahriman, chief devil in Persian mythology, who was "independent of God and God's opposite equal." [*See* Ahriman.] The tradition that Beliar is Hell's primate is carried on in the work of two modern writers, Thomas Mann and Aldous Huxley, both of whom regard Beliar as the exemplar and epitome of evil.

Belphegor or **Belfagor** or **Baal-Peor** ("lord of opening" or "lord Baal of Mt. Phegor")—a Moabite god of licentiousness who was once, according to cabalists, an angel of the order of principalities. In Hell, Belphegor is the demon of discoveries and ingenious inventions. When invoked, he appears in the form of a young woman. Rufinus and Jerome identify Belphegor with Priapus (see Numbers 25:1–3). De Plancy *Dictionnaire Infernal* indicates that certain dignitaries of the infernal empire served as special

envoys or ambassadors to the nations of the earth, and that Belphegor was accredited to France. Victor Hugo in *The Toilers of the Sea* confirms De Plancy's accreditation of Belphegor to Paris. [*Rf.* Jonson, *The Devil Is an Ass*; Wilson, *Belphegor or the Marriage of the Devil* (1691).] According to Milton, Belphegor is a variant for Nisroc (*Paradise Lost* VI, 447), whom he lists as "of Principalities the prime." Masters, *Eros and Evil*, suggests that Belphegor is the counterpart of the Hindu Rutrem, who is usually represented with an erect phallus. See picturization of The Demon Belphegor in Grillot, *A Pictorial Anthology of Witchcraft, Magic and Alchemy*, p. 132.

Belsal—an angel of the 1st hour of the night under the rulership of Gamiel. [*Rf.* Waite, *The Lemegeton*.]

Bel-se-buth [Beelzebub]

Belzeboub (Beelzebub)—Dante identifies him with Satan.

Belzebuth (Beezebuth)—prince of seraphim, so titled by M. Garinet, *History of Magic in France*. In the view of De Plancy (*Dictionnaire Infernal* III and IV) Belzebuth is not an angel but a demon, and the evil genius who governs the month of July (the opposite number to the angel Verchiel, *q.v.*).

Benad Hasche ("daughters of God")—female angels worshipped by Arabs. [*Rf.* Preface to Moore, *The Loves of the Angels*.]

Ben Ani—a name written in Heaven in the characters (tongue) of angels and invoked to command demons. [*Rf.* Mathers, *The Greater Key of Solomon*, p. 33.]

Bencul—one of the 9 holy angels invoked in cabalistic rites in the general citation of Moses. [*Rf. The Sixth and Seventh Books of Moses*, p. 72.]

Bene Elim (b'ne elohim, "sons of God")—angels or archangels who unceasingly sing the praises of God; they belong to the 10th subdivision of the order of thrones, according to *The Zohar* and de Mirville, *Pneumatologie*. Chief of the order is Azazel. In *The Zohar*, the chief of the order is Hofniel. The bene elim of Genesis 6:2 are sometimes equated with the order of ischim (*q.v.*). Theologians often translate the term as meaning sons of man rather than sons of God—to avoid attributing to angels the sin of sexual involvement with mortals.

Bene ha-Elohim (lit., "children of God")—angels, same as bene elim (above). According to Rabbi Simeon ben Johai, those who translate ha-Elohim as "sons of God" are in error and should be cursed [*Rf.* Bamberger, *Fallen Angels*]. In *Targum of Onkelos and Jonathan*, the title given to the bene ha-Elohim is "Sons of the Chiefs."

Beniel—an angel invoked to command demons for conferring the gift of invisibility. [*Rf.* Mathers, *The Greater Key of Solomon*, p. 45.]

Benign Angel—in *Midrash Aggada Exodus*, the Benign Angel is Uriel; in *The Zohar* I, 93b, it is Gabriel. The Benign Angel was sent down to attack or slay Moses for neglecting to observe the covenant of circumcision with regard to the Lawgiver's son. Zipporah (Moses' wife) saved the day by performing the rite (Exodus 4:25).

Ben Nez ("hawk")—a name for the angel Rubiel or Ruhiel. Ben Nez exercises dominion over the wind. According to tradition (Talmud *Baba Bathra*, 25a), he "holds back the South Wind with his pinions lest the world be consumed." Ben Nez is referred to as a mountain as well as an angel. [*Rf.* Budge, *Amulets and Talismans*; Ginzberg, *The Legends of the Jews* I, 12 and V, 47.]

Beodonos—in Mathers, *The Greater Key of Solomon*, an angel invoked in the conjuration of the Reed.

Beratiel—one of the ruling angels of the 12th hour of the day. [*Rf.* Waite, *The Lemegeton*.]

Berekeel ("my blessing is God")—an angel of the seasons in Enoch lore (*Enoch I*, 82:17).

Berial [Belial]

Berith [Balberith]

Berka'el—in Enoch lore, Berka'el is a leading spirit of 3 months of the year, serving under Melkejal (*q.v.*).

Bernael—in Falasha lore, the angel of darkness; when he is identified or equated with Beliel, he is an angel of evil.

Beshter—the name of Michael in ancient Persian lore. He was regarded as providing sustenance for mankind, which would equate him with Metatron (*q.v.*). [*Rf.* Sale, *The Koran*, "Preliminary Discourse," p. 51.]

Bethor—one of the 7 supreme angels ruling the 196 provinces in which Heaven is divided. Bethor rules 42 Olympic regions and commands kings, princes, dukes, etc., and "governs all things that are ascribed to (the planet) Jupiter." To do Bethor's bidding there are, in addition, 29,000 legions of spirits. [*Rf.* Cornelius Agrippa, *Three Books of Occult Philosophy*, where the sigil of this angel is shown; Budge, *Amulets and Talismans*, where the sigil is reproduced.]

Bethuael ("house or man of God")—one of the 28 angels governing the 28 mansions of the moon.

Bethuel—an angel's name found inscribed on an oriental charm (*kamea*) for warding off evil. [*Rf.* Schrire, *Hebrew Amulets*.]

Betuliel—one of the governing angels of the zodiac. [*Rf.* Agrippa, *Three Books of Occult Philosophy*, III.]

Bezaliel—one of the numerous angelic guards of the gates of the North Wind. [*Rf.* Ozar Midrashim, 316.]

Bezrial—one of the angelic guards of the 3rd Heaven, as reported in the *Pirke Hechaloth*.

Bhaga—in Vedic lore, one of 7 (or 12) celestial deities, analogous to Judaeo-Christian angels. [*See* Adityas.]

Bibiyah—one of the many names of the angel Metatron.

Bifiel—in hechaloth lore (*Ma'asseh Merkabah*), an angelic guard of the 6th heavenly hall.

Bigtha (Biztha)—in Ginzberg, *The Legends of the Jews*, one of the 7 angels of confusion: also one of the 2 pressers of the winepress. In the house of Ahasuerus, Bigtha is an angel of destruction.

Bileth [Beleth]

Binah ("understanding")—the 3rd sefira (*q.v.*). In *The Book of Concealed Mystery*, Binah is called "the sea." [*Rf.* Runes, *The Wisdom of the Kabbalah*.]

Biqa (in Amharic, "good person")—the original name of the angel Kasbeel (*q.v.*). After Kasbeel's fall (he sinned by turning away from God the moment he was created), he was renamed Kazbeel, "he who lies to God."

Bird of God—a term used by Dante to denote an angel.

Bizbul (meaning, "in Zebul")—a secret name of Metatron, according to Rabbi Inyanei bar Sisson. [*Rf. The Visions of Ezekiel*.]

Black Angel—in Mohammedan demonology one comes across 2 black angels, named Monker and Nakir (*q.v.*). Another black angel, unnamed, is pictured in the *Treatise on Astrology and Divination* of Mohammed al-Sudi. This angel with the features of a rackhasa is shown with 2 other malevolent spirits in *Larousse Encyclopedia of Mythology* and reproduced on p. 68.

Blaef—in occult lore, a Friday angel of the air, ministering to Sarabotes and subject to the West Wind. [*Rf.* de Claremont, *The Ancient's Book of Magic*.]

Blautel—an angel invoked in necromancy. [*Rf.* Mathers, *The Greater Key of Solomon*.]

Bludon—one of the 7 Electors (underworld planetary spirits or rulers) in Cornelius Agrippa's listing. Bludon replaces Ganael in the planetary rulers cited by Conybeare, *The Testament of Solomon*.

Bne Seraphim—in practical cabala, the angel governing the planet Mercury. In talismanic magic he is the intelligence of the planet Venus. [*Rf.* Barrett, *The Magus* II, 147.]

Boamiel—one of the 6 angels placed over the 4 parts of Heaven, according to *The Book of the Angel Raziel*. The other 5 angels are Scamijm, Gabriel, Adrael, Dohel, Madiel. [*Rf. The Sixth and Seventh Books of Moses*.]

Bodiel—ruling prince of the 6th Heaven, according to *Hechaloth Zoterathi*, quoted in *3 Enoch* 17. The ruling angels usually designated are Sabath, Sandalphon, Zachiel, and Zebul.

Boel ("God is in him"—Boul, Booel, Bohel, Dohel)—one of 7 exalted throne angels resident in the 1st Heaven. Boel holds the 4 keys to the 4 corners of the earth; by means of these keys all the angelic hosts are able to enter the Garden of Eden—when, that is, Boel unlocks the gates and the 2 guardian cherubim permit entry. [*Rf. The Zohar* (Exodus 133b).] According to Barrett, *The Magus*, Boel resides not in the 1st Heaven but in the 7th. The star (more correctly the planet) he governs is Saturn. [*Rf.* de Abano, *The Heptameron*; *The Book of the Angel Raziel*; *The Book of Hechaloth*; *Ozar Midrashim*.]

Briel—one of the 70 childbed amulet angels. For the names of all 70, *see* Appendix.

Brieus—an angel who, it is said, is alone able to overcome the designs and machinations of the demon Rabdos. [*Rf.* Conybeare, *The Testament of Solomon*; Shah, *The Secret Lore of Magic*.]

Bualu—one of the 8 angels of omnipotence employed in conjuring rites. Among the others of this group are Atuesuel, Ebuhuel, Tabatlu, Tulatu, Labusi, Ublisi. [*Rf. The Sixth and Seventh Books of Moses*, p. 85.] The cabalistic instructions for conjuring these angels specify that they "must be called 3 times from the 4 corners of the world with a clear and powerful voice and when the name of each is pronounced 3 times, then 3 sounds must be uttered by the horn."

Buchuel—an angelic name found inscribed on an oriental charm (*kamea*) for warding off evil. [*Rf.* Schrire, *Hebrew Amulets*.]

Buddha [Budh Avatar]

Budh Avatar (Buddha)—the 9th of the 10 avatars in Vedic lore. [*See* Avatar.]

Buhair—in Mandaean lore, one of the 10 *uthri* (angels) that accompany the sun on its daily course.

Bull—in Zoroastrian mythology, the source of all light; he was created by Ormazd and destroyed by Ahriman. Out of Bull's scattered seed, according to legend, sprang the first man and woman.

Burc(h)at—in the cabala, an angel of the air serving in the 4th Heaven; he governs on Lord's Day (Sunday) and is invoked from the west. He is one of the messengers of the sun. [*Rf.* de Abano, *The Heptameron*; Barrett, *The Magus*; Malchus, *The Secret Grimoire of Turiel*.]

Burkhan—in Manicheanism, an incarnate messenger "of the God of Light to man." Zoroaster is spoken of in Manichean lore as a burkhan. [*Rf.* Legge, *Forerunners and Rivals of Christianity* II.]

Busasejal—according to *Enoch I*, one of a troop of fallen angels.

Busthariel—an angelic name found inscribed on an oriental charm (*kamea*) for warding off evil. [*Rf.* Schrire, *Hebrew Amulets*.]

Butator (or Butatar)—the genius or spirit of calculations. Butator serves in the 3rd hour of the day and may be invoked in ritual magic rites, as certified by Apollonius of Tyana in *The Nuctemeron*. [*Rf.* Levi, *Transcendental Magic*, p. 503.]

Byleth [Beleth]

Cabiel—one of the 28 angels ruling over the 28 mansions of the moon.

Cabriel (Cabrael, Kabriel)—an angel with dominion over the sign of Aquarius. He is one of 6 angels placed over the 4 parts of Heaven. [*Rf.* *The Book of the Angel Raziel*; Heywood, *The Hierarchy of the Blessèd Angels.*]

Cadat—"a most pure angel" invoked in Solomonic magic. [*Rf.* *Grimorium Verum.*]

Cadulech—a most holy angel of God invoked in the conjuration of the Sword. [*Rf.* *Grimorium Verum.*]

Cael—an angel representing, or exercising dominion over, the sign of Cancer in the zodiac. [*Rf.* Waite, *The Lemegeton.*]

Cafon [Zephon]

Cahet(h)el—one of the 8 seraphim; he rules over agricultural products and is one of the 72 angels bearing the name of God Shemhamphorae. In the cabala generally he is often invoked to increase or improve crops. His corresponding angel is Asicat. Cahethel's sigil will be found in Ambelain, *La Kabbale Pratique*, p. 260.

Cahor—genius of deception. In Apollonius of Tyana, *The Nuctemeron*, Cahor is described as a genius of the 3rd hour.

Caila—an angel invoked in Solomonic magic in the Uriel conjuration. Caila is "one of the 4 words God spoke with his mouth to his servant Moses," according to the grimoires. The other 3 words were Josta, Agla, and Ablati. [*Rf.* *Grimorium Verum.*]

Caim (Caym, Camio)—once of the order of angels, Caim is now in Hell, a great president. He manifests in the form of a thrush. As many as 30 legions of infernal spirits attend him. His seal is figured in Waite, *The Book of Black Magic and of Pacts*, p. 182. Luther had a famous encounter with Caim, according to De Plancy, *Dictionnaire Infernal* where (in the 1863 ed.) Caim is pictured as a belted bird.

Caldulech (Caldurech)—"a most pure angel," invoked in ceremonial magic rites. [*Rf.* Shah, *The Secret Lore of Magic.*]

Caliel [Calliel]

Calizantin—a "good angel" invoked in conjuring rites. [*Rf. Verus Jesuitarum Libellus.*]

Calliel (Caliel)—one of the throne angels serving in the 2nd Heaven, invoked to bring prompt help against adversity. Calliel is one of the 72 angels bearing the name of God Shemhamphorae. His corresponding angel is Tersatosoa (or Tepisatosoa). For Calliel's sigil, see Ambelain, *La Kabbale Pratique*, p. 267.

Caluel (Calvel)—a Wednesday angel residing in the 2nd or 3rd Heaven and invoked from the south. Since his corresponding angel is Tersatosoa, Caluel may be a variant for Calliel (*q.v.*).

Calvel [Caluel]

Calzas—a Tuesday angel serving in the 5th Heaven. Calzas must be invoked from the east. [*Rf.* de Abano, *The Heptameron*; Barrett, *The Magus* II.]

Camael (Camiel, Camiul, Chamuel, Kemuel, Khamael, Camniel, Cancel—"he who sees God") —chief of the order of powers and one of the sefiroth. In occult lore, Camael is of the nether regions and ranks as a Count Palatine. When invoked, he appears in the guise of a leopard crouched on a rock. In the cabala, Camael (Khamael, Kemuel) is one of the 10 (actually 9) archangels of the Briatic world. "It is a name," says Eliphas Levi in *The History of Magic*, "which personifies divine justice." In a footnote to Levi's book, Waite, the editor, in chapter 10, notes that, in Druid mythology, Camael was the god of war. This bears out the frequent citation of Camael in occultism as the ruler of the planet Mars and as among the governing angels of the 7 planets. [*Rf. Complete Book of Fortune*, p. 514, for picturization of "the Talisman of the Angels," where the name Camael occurs.] In *The Magus*, Camael is one of "seven angels which stand in the presence of God." For the legend that Moses destroyed this great angel for trying to prevent the Lawgiver from receiving the Torah at the hand of God, *see* Kemuel. Another legend speaks of Camael (Kemuel) being in charge of 12,000 angels of destruction. [*Rf. The Legends of the Jews* III.] In Clement, *Angels in Art*, Chamuel is the angel who wrestled with Jacob; also the angel (usually identified as Gabriel) who appeared to Jesus during his agony in the Garden of Gethsemane to strengthen Him.

Camal (Hebrew, "to desire God")—the name of one of the archangels in the cabala. [*Rf.* the *Book of The Sacred Magic of Abra-Melin the Mage.*]

Camaysar—in occultism, the angel "of the marriage of contraries." He is a genius of the 5th hour. [*Rf.* Apollonius of Tyana, *The Nuctemeron.*]

Cambiel—according to Trithemius, the ruler of the zodiacal sign of Aquarius, and an angel of the 9th hour.

Cambill—an angel of the 8th hour of the night, serving under Narcorial. [*Rf.* Waite, *The Lemegeton.*]

Cameron—angel of the 12th hour of the day, serving under Beratiel. He is also regarded as a demon; as such he serves in the conjuration of Beelzebuth, as well as in the conjuration of Astaroth. [*Rf. Magia Naturalis et Innaturalis*; Butler, *Ritual Magic*; Shah, *The Secret Lore of Magic.*]

Camio [Caim]

Camuel [Camael]

Caneloas—"a most holy angel" invoked in magical operations, as noted in Mathers, *The Greater Key of Solomon*.

Capabile—one of 3 angel messengers of the Sun. [*Rf.* Malchus, *The Secret Grimoire of Turiel.*]

Capabili—an angel of the 4th Heaven ruling on the Lord's Day and invoked from the west.

Caphriel—in occultism, "a strong and powerful angel," chief ruler of the 7th day (Sabbath). He is invoked in the conjuration of Saturn (the planet). [*Rf.* Barrett, *The Magus* II; de Claremont, *The Ancient's Book of Magic.*]

Capitiel—one of the angels of the 4th chora or altitude invoked in magical prayer, as set forth in *The Almadel of Solomon*.

Angel head, 15th century. From the great rose window in north transept of St. Ouens, Rouen. Reproduced from Lawrence B. Saint, *Stained Glass of the Middle Ages in England and France.* London: A. and C. Black, Ltd., 1925.

Captains of Fear [Angels of Dread]

Captain of the Host of the Lord—in Joshua 5, the man (i.e., angel) whom Joshua beheld standing over against him with drawn sword and who revealed himself as "the captain of the host of the Lord." He is usually identified as Michael.

Caracasa—in occult lore, an angel of the Spring along with the angels Core, Amatiel, and Comissoros.

Caraniel—in Mosaic mystic lore, an angel serving in the 3rd Heaven. [*Rf. The Sixth and Seventh Books of Moses.*]

Carcas—one of the 7 angels of confusion. In the legend relating to Ahasuerus, Carcas is the "knocker." [*Rf.* Ginzberg, *The Legends of the Jews* IV, 375.]

Cardiel—in ceremonial magic, an angel invoked in special rites, as in the conjuration of the Sword.

Cardinal Virtues—there are 4 cardinal virtues: justice, prudence, temperance, fortitude. The theological virtues are faith, hope, and charity. These were often personalized as angels and so represented, as in the case of fortitude, in the roundels of Lucca della Robbia in the chapel of Cardinal of Portugal, in the Church of San Miniato al Monte in Florence and reproduced on p. 114.

Caretaking Angels—Temeluch (*q.v.*) and others. "Infants of untimely birth are delivered over to Care-taking Angels," according to Clement of Alexandria, *Prophetic Eclogues,* 48. Methodius in his *Convivia,* II, 6 adds that these angels serve also the offspring of adultery.

Carmax—in occultism, a ministering angel to Samax, ruler of the Tuesday angels of the air. [*Rf.* de Abano, *The Heptameron.*] Serving with Carmax are 2 other angels: Ismoli and Paffran. [*Rf.* Shah, *Occultism, Its Theory and Practice*, p. 50.]

Carniel—an angel serving in the 3rd Heaven. [*Rf. The Sixth and Seventh Books of Moses.*]

Carnivean (Carniveau)—an ex-prince of the order of powers (*see* Carreau). Carnivean is now a demon, invoked in the litanies of the Witches' Sabbaths. [*Rf.* Michaelis, *Admirable History of the Possession and Conversion of a Penitent Woman.*]

Carreau (Carnivean)—an ex-prince of the order of powers. In Garinet, *History of Magic in France*, Carreau was one of the devils who possessed the body of Sister Seraphica of Loudun; in the absence of Baruch (another devil so named), Carreau guarded a drop of water that bewitched the sister's stomach (sic).

Carsiol—an angel of the 2nd hour, serving under Anael. [*Rf.* Waite, *The Lemegeton*, p. 67.]

Casmaron—in occult science (as in Papus, *Traité Élémentaire de Science Occulte*), an angel of the air.

Casmiros—an angel of the 11th hour of the night, serving under Dardariel.

Cass Cassiah—an angel invoked for the curing of cutaneous disorders. [*Rf.* Talmud *Shabbath*, fol. 67.]

Cassiel (Casiel, Casziel, Kafziel)—the angel of solitudes and tears who "shews forth the unity of the eternal kingdom." Cassiel is one of the rulers of the planet Saturn, also a ruling prince of the 7th Heaven and one of the *sarim* (princes) of the order of powers. Sometimes he appears as the angel of temperance. Barrett in *The Magus* speaks of Cassiel as one of the 3 angels of Saturday, serving with Machatan and Uriel. In the *Book of Spirits* as well as in *The Magus*, the sigil of Cassiel is given, along with his signature. In the latter work Cassiel Macoton (so named) is pictured in the form of a bearded jinn, astride a dragon. In Grillot, *Picture Museum of Sorcery, Magic and Al-*

The angel Cassiel, ruler of Saturday, astride a dragon. Reproduced from Francis Barrett, *The Magus.*

chemy (p. 113), there is a reproduction of a page from the *Book of Spirits* giving the conjuration of Cassiel.

Cassiel Macoton—according to Barrett, *The Magus* II, Cassiel and Macoton are 2 separate angels, both doing duty on Saturday.

Castiel—a Thursday angel mentioned in occult lore.

Casujoiah—an angel with dominion over the sign of Capricorn. [*Rf.* Waite, *The Lemegeton.*]

Catroije—in the cabala, an angel serving in the 2nd Heaven. [*Rf. The Sixth and Seventh Books of Moses.*]

Causub—a serpent-charming angel. In Apollonius of Tyana, *The Nuctemeron*, Causub is one of the genii of the 7th hour. [*Rf.* Levi, *Transcendental Magic.*]

Caym [Caim]

Cazardia—a corruption of Gazardiel (*q.v.*). [*Rf.* Régamey, *What Is An Angel?*]

Cedar—in *The Gospel of Bartholomew* (Latin version, James, *The Apocryphal New Testament*) Cedar is cited as an angel governing the south. In other versions he is called Kerkoutha (*q.v.*).

Cedrion—an angel invoked in the conjuration of the Reed, and governing the south. [*Rf.* Waite, *The Lemegeton.*]

Celestial Hierarchy—based on interpretations of Scriptural passages and as enumerated by St. Ambrose, pseudo-Dionysius, Pope Gregory, and others, the orders or choirs of the celestial hierarchy range from 7 to 10 or 11 in number; they were finally fixed at 9 in triple triads thus: seraphim, cherubim, thrones; dominations (or dominions), powers, virtues; principalities (or princedoms), archangels, angels. The 2nd triad is sometimes given as dominions, virtues, powers. Variants include orders called hosts, aeons, innocents, confessors, lordships, authorities, warriors, etc. In Mathers, *The Greater Key of Solomon*, conjurations are prescribed for "ten choirs of the Holy Angels," to wit: (1) chaioth ha-Qadesh; (2) auphanim; (3) aralim; (4) chashmalim; (5) seraphim; (6) malachim; (7) elohim; (8) beni elohim; (9) kerubim; (10) ishim; these are the 10 mentioned by Maimonides in his *Mishna Thora*. The *Berith Menucha* offers a slightly different list of 10: arellim, ishim, bene elohim, mal'achim, chashmallim, tarshishim, shina'nim, kerubim, ophannim, seraphim. [*Rf.* Charles, *The Book of the Secrets of Enoch (Enoch II)*, Chap. 20, fn.] After Aquinas "blessed" the Dionysian scheme of 9 choirs in their triple triads, the Church adhered to it. Early Protestants, however, not only disputed it but also rejected it. Some occult works such as Barrett, *The Magus*, added a 4th triad, making 12 orders. It will be recalled that Dante in his *Paradiso*, canto 28, calls Pope Gregory to account for "dissenting" from the Dionysian

setup. [*Rf. Sefer Yetzirah*; Waite, *The Holy Kabbalah*, pp. 255–256.] For variant lists by various authorities, *see* Appendix.

Celestial Pilot, The—in his poem "The Celestial Pilot," Longfellow calls the ferryman of souls "the bird of God." The poem derives from Dante's Pilot Angel in *Purgatorio* II.

Cendrion—in the grimoires, "a holy angel of God" invoked in cabalistic rites.

Cernaiul—the name of an angel of the 7th sefiroth (Netzach). [*Rf. The Sixth and Seventh Books of Moses.*]

Cerviel (Cervihel, Zeruel)—chief of the order of principalities, a post shared with Haniel, Nisroc, and others. Cerviel is the preceptor angel of David. "And God sent Cervihel, the Angel that is over strength, to help David slay Goliath," is the reference in *The Biblical Antiquities of Philo*, p. 234. [*Rf.* Barrett, *The Magus.*]

Cetarari (Ctariri, Crarari)—one of the 4 angels of winter. [*Rf.* De Plancy, *Dictionnaire Infernal.*]

Chabalym—a seraph or cherub invoked in cabalistic magic rites.

Chabril—an angel of the 2nd hour of the night, under Farris.

Chachmal (Chachmiel)—one of the 70 childbed amulet angels mentioned in *The Book of the Angel Raziel*. For the list of 70, *see* Appendix.

Chachmiel [Chachmal]

Chadakiel [Hadakiel]

Chafriel—one of the 70 childbed amulet angels.

Chahoel—in the cabala, one of the 72 angels ruling the 72 quinaries of the degrees of the zodiac.

Chaigidiel—in the world of Asaiah, the averse (opposite or left) sefira corresponding to Chochma (wisdom) in the Briatic world. [*Rf.* Waite, *The Holy Kabbalah*, p. 256.]

Chairoum—in *The Gospel of Bartholomew*, p. 176, the angel of the north. [*See* Alfatha and Gabriel, both of whom are in the same way certified as angels governing the north.] Chairoum is described as holding in his hand "a rod of fire, and restraineth the superfluity of moisture that the earth be not overmuch wet."

Chajoth [Hayyoth]

Chalkatoura—one of the 9 angels that "run together throughout the heavenly and earthly places," according to *The Gospel of Bartholomew*.

Chalkydri (Kalkydra)—archangels of the flying elements of the sun. Mentioned in *Enoch II*, where they are linked with the phoenixes and placed amidst cherubim and seraphim. The chalkydri are 12-winged. At the rising of the sun they burst into song. Their habitat is the 4th Heaven. In gnostic lore, they are demonic. In Charles' Introduction to *Enoch II*, the chalkydri are described as "monstrous serpents with the heads of crocodiles" and as "natural products of the Egyptian imagination."

Chamuel ("he who seeks God"—Kamuel, Haniel, Simiel, etc.)—one of the 7 archangels and chief of the order of dominations; also, with Nisroc and others, chief of the order of powers. Chamuel, like Gabriel, is the angel of Gethsemane: he strengthened Jesus with the assurance of resurrection. [*Rf.* Barrett, *The Magus*; *Enoch I*; R. L. Gales, "The Christian Lore of Angels," *National Review*, September 1910.]

Chamyel—one of 15 throne angels listed in *The Sixth and Seventh Books of Moses. See* Appendix.

Chaniel—one of the 70 childbed amulet angels mentioned in *The Book of the Angel Raziel* and in Budge, *Amulets and Talismans*, p. 255. In *Ozar Midrashim* II, 316, Chaniel is one of the angelic guards of the gates of the East Wind.

Chantare—in occult lore, the corresponding angel of Hahael (*q.v.*).

Charavah [Charbiel]

Charbiel (Charavah—"dryness")—an angel appointed to "draw together and dry up all the waters of the earth." It was Charbiel who dried up the waters after the Flood. [*Rf.* Genesis 8:13.] He is mentioned in the *Baraita de Ma'ase Bereshith* and in *The Book of the Angel Raziel*, ch. 11.

Charby—angel of the 5th hour serving under Abasdarhon. [*Rf.* Waite, *The Lemegeton*.]

Charciel (Charsiel)—in de Abano, *The Heptameron*, an angel resident in the 4th Heaven. He rules on Lord's Day (Sunday) and is invoked from the south.

Chardiel—in Waite, *The Lemegeton*, an angel of the 2nd hour of the day, serving under Anael.

Chardros—an angel of the 11th hour of the day, serving under Bariel.

Chariots—the angelic hosts, as in Psalms 68:17: "The chariots of God are twenty thousand, even thousands of angels; the Lord is among them, as in Sinai, in the holy place."

Chariots of God—the holy wheels (ophanim). Milton identified this class of angels with the cherubim and seraphim; they were so grouped by the Talmudists. Scholem, *The Zohar*, declares that the patriarchs were made "a holy chariot of God."

Charis ("grace")—in gnosticism, one of the great luminaries emanated from the divine will.

Charman—an angel of the 11th hour of the night, serving under Dardariel.

Charmeas—an angel of the 1st hour of the day, serving under Samael.

Charms—an angel of the 9th hour of the day, serving under Vadriel.

Charnij—an angel of the 10th hour of the day, serving under Oriel.

Charouth—one of the 9 angels that "run together throughout the heavenly and earthly places." [*See* Chalkatoura.]

Charpon—a ruling angel of the 1st hour of the day, serving under Samael.

Charsiel [Charciel]

Charuch—an angel of the 6th hour of the day, serving under Samil.

Chasan—in Mathers, *The Greater Key of Solomon*, an angel of the air; his name is inscribed on the 7th pentacle of the sun.

Chasdiel—in apocalyptic lore, a name for Metatron "when Metatron does kindness to the world." [*Rf. 3 Enoch* 43.]

Chaskiel—one of the 70 childbed amulet angels. For the names of the 70, *see* Appendix.

Chasmal [Hashmal]

Chasmodai—according to Paracelsus in his doctrine of Talismans, Chasmodai is the spirit of the moon, of which "planet" it is said that the governing intelligence is Malach Be. [*Rf.* Christian, *The History and Practice of Magic* I.]

Chassiel—one of the intelligences of the sun, as recorded in *The Secret Grimoire of Turiel*, p. 33.

Chastiser, The—Kolazonta, the destroying angel, so named in the incident involving Aaron, described in Reider, *The Book of Wisdom* 18:2.

Chaumel—one of the 72 angels ruling the 72 quinaries of the degrees of the zodiac. [*Rf.* Runes, *The Wisdom of the Kabbalah*.]

Chavakiah—in Barrett, *The Magus* II, one of the 72 angels bearing the name of God Shemhamphorae.

Chaya—sing. for Hayyoth (*q.v.*).

Chaylim—in *3 Enoch*, the chaylim are "armies of angels ruled over and led by Chayyliel."

Chaylon—a cherub or seraph invoked in ritual magic. [*Rf. The Sixth and Seventh Books of Moses*.]

Chayo—a throne angel invoked in magical conjurations. One of 15 such angels listed in *The Sixth and Seventh Books of Moses*. *See* Appendix for the names of all 15.

Chayoh [Hayyoth]

Chayyliel H' (Chayyiel, Hayyiel, Hayyal, Haileal—"army")—ruling prince of the chayyoth or hayyoth (*q.v.*). Before Chayyliel "all the children of heaven do tremble." It is said further of

this great Merkabah angel that, if he is ever so minded, he can "swallow the whole earth in one moment in a mouthful." When the ministering angels fail to chant the trisagion at the right time, Chayyliel flogs them with lashes of fire. [*Rf. 3 Enoch* 20.]

Chayyoth [Hayyoth]

Chebo—one of the 72 angels ruling the 72 quinaries of the zodiac.

Chedustaniel (Chedusitanick)—a Friday angel resident in the 3rd Heaven, invoked from the east. Chedustaniel is also one of the angelic spirits of the planet Jupiter. [*Rf.* de Abano, *The Heptameron*; Barrett, *The Magus* II.]

Chemos—equated with Peor and Nisroc. To Milton in *Paradise Lost* I, 312, 406, Chemos is a fallen angel.

Cheratiel—an angel of the 6th hour of the night, serving under Zaazonash. [*Rf.* Waite, *The Lemegeton*.]

Cheriour—a "terrible angel," charged with punishment of crime and the pursuit of criminals, according to De Plancy, *Dictionnaire Infernal*.

Chermes—angel of the 9th hour of the night, serving under Nacoriel. [*Rf.* Waite, *The Lemegeton*.]

Chermiel—a Friday angel of the 3rd Heaven invoked from the south. [*Rf.* Barrett, *The Magus* II; de Abano, *The Heptameron*.]

Cherub (sing. for cherubim)—in the cabala, Cherub is one of the angels of the air. As Kerub he is the angel "who was made the Guardian of the Terrestrial Paradise, with a Sword of Flame." [*Rf.* Mathers, *The Greater Key of Solomon*, p. 34.] "The 1st angel who sinned is called, not a seraph, but a cherub," says Aquinas in his *Summa*, vol. 1, 7th art., reply objection 1. In *The Zohar*, Cherub is chief of the order of cherubim. In Ezekiel (28:14–15) God recalls to the Prince of Tyre that he was the "anointed cherub" and was perfect in his ways "till iniquity was found" in him.

Cherubiel (Kerubiel)—eponymous chief of the order of the cherubim. [*See* Gabriel, who is also regarded as chief of the order.]

Cherubim (Kerubim)—in name as well as in concept, the cherubim are Assyrian or Akkadian in origin. The word, in Akkadian, is karibu and means "one who prays" or "one who intercedes," although Dionysius declared the word to mean knowledge. In ancient Assyrian art, the cherubim were pictured as huge, winged creatures with leonine or human faces, bodies of bulls or sphinxes, eagles, etc. They were usually placed at entrances to palaces or temples as guardian spirits. In early Canaanitish lore, the cherubim were not conceived of as angels. [*Cf.* view of Theodorus, Bishop of Heracleâa, who declared "these cherubims not to be any Angelicall powers, but rather some horrible visions of Beasts, which might terrifie Adam from

Cherubs. Italian (Neapolitan, late 18th century). Collection of Loretta Hines Howard. From *The Metropolitan Museum of Art Bulletin*, December 1965.

the entrance of paradise"—from Salkeld, *A Treatise of Angels.*] It was only later that the cherubim began to be regarded as heavenly spirits. To Philo ("On the Cherubim") they symbolized God's highest and chiefest potencies, sovereignty, and goodness. They are the 1st angels to be mentioned (and to be construed as angels) in the Old Testament (Genesis 3:22). They guarded with flaming sword the Tree of Life and Eden, hence their designation as the "flame of whirling swords." In Exodus 25:18 we find 2 cherubim "of gold," one on either side of the Ark (see picturization in Schaff, *A Dictionary of the Bible*). [*Cf.* "cherubim of glory shadowing the mercy seat" in Hebrews 9:5.] In Ezekiel (10:14) 4 cherubim, each with 4 faces and 4 wings, appear at the river Chebar where the Hebrew prophet glimpses them. In I Kings 6:23, the 2 cherubim in Solomon's temple are carved out of olive wood. In rabbinic and occult lore, the cherubim are prevailingly thought of as charioteers of God, bearers of His throne, and personifications of the winds. In Revelation (4:8) they are living creatures who render unceasing praise to their Maker. Here St. John refers to them as beasts (holy, divine beasts), 6-winged and "full of eyes within." John of Damascus in his *Exposition of the Orthodox Faith* also speaks of the cherubim as "many-eyed." In Talmud the cherubim are equated with the order ophanim (wheels or chariots) or the order hayyoth (holy beasts) and are said to reside in the 6th or 7th Heaven. In the Dionysian scheme, the cherubim rank 2nd in the 9-choir hierarchy and are guardians of the fixed stars. Chief rulers, as listed in most occult works, include Ophaniel, Rikbiel, Cherubiel, Raphael, Gabriel, Zophiel, and—before his fall—Satan, who was, as Parente says in *The Angels*, "the supreme angel in the choir of cherubim." In the early traditions of Muslim lore it is claimed that the cherubim were formed from the tears Michael shed over the sins of the faithful. [*Rf.* Hastings, *Encyclopaedia of Religion and Ethics* IV, 616, "Demons and Spirits (Muslim)."] In secular lore the cherubim have been called "black cherubim" (Dante), "young-eyed cherubim" (Shakespeare), "helmed cherubim" (Milton). Blake describes Satan as the "covering cherub" and turns

French baroque musical cherubim. Altarpiece at Champagny in Savoy. From *Horizon*, November 1960.

the Ezekiel vision of the 4 creatures into his own *Four Zoas*. The latter sound the 4 trumpets heralding the apocalypse. As angels of light, glory, and keepers of the celestial records, the cherubim excel in knowledge. [*Rf.* Lindsay, *Kerubim in Semitic Religion and Art.*] The notion of winged, multiple-headed beasts serving as guardians of temples and palaces must have been general in many near-Eastern countries, for in addition to appearing in Assyrian-Chaldean-Babylonian art and writings (where the authors of Isaiah and Ezekiel doubtlessly first came upon them), they appear, as already noted, in Canaanitish lore (with which the Israelites were, of course, familiar, and which influenced or colored the accounts in Genesis and other Old Testament books). An ivory from the collection of a king of Megiddo, circa 1200 B.C.E., reproduced on p. 45 of the *Westminster Historical Atlas to the Bible*, shows a Canaanite ruler seated on a throne, "supported by winged lions with human heads." These, say the editors of the *Atlas*, "are the imaginary, composite beings which the Israelites called cherubim." As winged beasts with human heads, 2 cherubim are shown supporting the throne of Hiram, king of ancient Byblos (see reproduction, p. 132, vol.

A–D of *Interpreter's Dictionary of the Bible*). Among works of more modern times, Rubens' "Apotheosis of James I" (hanging in the banqueting hall of Whitehall in London and filling the long side panels) shows a procession of cherubs.

Chesed ("mercy," "goodness")—the 4th sefira.

Chesetial—one of the governing angels of the zodiac. [*Rf.* Agrippa, *Three Books of Occult Philosophy* III.]

Chieftains—in the cabala, a term designating the celestial prince-guardians assigned to various nations of the earth. There were 70 of these tutelary spirits, according to *The Zohar*.

Children of Heaven—in *Enoch I*, the children of Heaven are "the sons of the holy angels who fell and violated women." The reference is to Genesis 6:2.

Chirangiyah [Parasurama]

Chismael—a spirit of Jupiter, of which planet Zophiel is the presiding intelligence, according to Paracelsus in his doctrine of Talismans. [*Rf.* Christian, *The History and Practice of Magic* I.]

Chiva [Hayyoth]

Chnum (*see* Anmael).

Chobaliel—according to Voltaire in his "Of Angels, Genii, and Devils," Chobaliel is one of the fallen angels in the Enoch listings.

Choch(k)ma (Hokhmah)—the word in Hebrew has the connotation "wisdom." Chochma is the 2nd of the holy sefiroth (divine emanations) and is equated with the personalized angel Ratziel (Raziel). According to Mathers, *The Kabbala Unveiled*, Chochma is the 1st of God's creations, the only one of the supernal abstractions which seems to have reached actual materialization or personification. [*Rf.* Guignebert, *The Jewish World in the Time of Jesus*; *Sefer Yetzirah*.]

Chochmael (Hochmael)—in Levi, *Transcendental Magic*, an angel of the sefiroth invoked in conjuration rites.

Choesed [Hoesediel]

Chofniel—chief of the angelic order of *bene elohim* (children of God), as listed in the Midrash Bereshith Menucha.

Choriel—angel of the 8th hour of the day, serving under Oscaebial. [*Rf.* Waite, *The Lemegeton*; *The Sixth and Seventh Books of Moses*.]

Chorob—angel of the 10th hour of the day, serving under Oriel.

Chosniel ("cover")—in Mosaic incantation rites, an angel invoked for the conferring of good memory and an open heart.

Chrail (Chreil)—an angel in Mandaean lore. [*Rf.* Pognon, *Inscriptions Mandaïtes des Coupes de Khouabir*.]

Chromme—corresponding angel of Nanael (*q.v.*).

Chrymos—an angel of the 5th hour of the night, serving under Abasdarhon.

Chuabotheij—in the cabala, an angel of the Seal.

Chur (Churdad)—in ancient Persian mythology, the angel in charge of the disk of the sun.

[*Rf.* Clayton, *Angelology*; Hyde, *Historia Religionis Veterum Persarum*.]

Chuscha—one of 15 throne angels listed in *The Sixth and Seventh Books of Moses*. For the names of all 15, *see* Appendix.

Chushiel—one of numerous angelic guards of the gates of the South Wind. [*Rf. Ozar Midrashim* II, 317.]

Chutriel—presiding angel of the Mire of Clay, which is 5th of the 7 lodges of Hell (arka). [*Rf.* the writings of the cabalist Joseph ben Abraham Gikatilla.]

Cochabiel (Coahabiath)—spirit of the planet Mercury, in cabala; derived from Babylonian religious lore. [*Rf.* Lenormant, *Chaldean Magic*, p. 26.] In Mosaic lore, and according to Cornelius Agrippa in *Three Books of Occult Philosophy* III, Cochabiel is one of 7 princes "who stand continually before God and to whom are given the spirit names of the planets."

Cogediel—one of the 28 angels ruling the 28 mansions of the moon.

Cohabiting Glory—a title given the Shekinah (*q.v.*) by Waite, *The Secret Doctrine in Israel*, in designating her as "the guide of man on earth and the womanhood which is part of him."

Colopatiron—in Apollonius of Tyana, *The Nuctemeron*, a genius (spirit) who sets prisons open; also one of the genii of the 9th hour.

Comadiel—an angel of the 3rd hour of the day, serving under Veguaniel.

Comary—an angel of the 9th hour of the night, serving under Nacoriel.

Comato(s)—in Gollancz, *Clavicula Salomonis*, an angel invoked in the exorcism of Wax.

Comforter—"the Comforter, which is the Holy Ghost, whom the Father will send in my name." [*Rf.* John 14:26; *see* Holy Ghost.]

Commissoros—one of the 4 angels of the Spring. [*Rf.* de Abano, *The Heptameron*; Barrett, *The Magus* II.]

Conamas—in occult magical operations, an angel invoked in the exorcism of Wax.

Confessors—one of 12 (sic) orders of the Celestial Hierarchy as enumerated in Heywood, *The Hierarchy of the Blessèd Angels.* The chief of the order of confessors is the angel Barakiel (*q.v.*).

Coniel—in the cabala, a Friday angel resident in the 3rd Heaven. He is invoked from the west. In *The Secret Grimoire of Turiel*, Coniel is listed among the messengers of the planet Jupiter.

Contemplation—a cherub (so named) in Milton's *Il Penseroso.*

Cophi—in occult lore, an angel invoked in the exorcism of Wax. [*Rf.* Gollancz, *Clavicula Salomonis.*]

Corabael—a Monday angel residing in the 1st Heaven and invoked from the west. [*Rf.* de Abano, *The Heptameron.*]

Corael—an angel petitioned in magical prayer for the fulfillment of the invocant's desires. Corael is invoked along with the angels Setchiel and Chedustaniel in *The Secret Grimoire of Turiel.*

Corat—a Friday angel of the air resident in the 3rd Heaven and invoked from the east.

Core—one of the 4 angels of the Spring. Core is mentioned as a governing spirit of this season in Barrett, *The Magus* and de Abano, *The Heptameron.*

Coriel—an angel of the 7th hour of the night, serving under Mendrion.

Corinne (fictional)—a female angel (so named) in Jonathan Daniels, *Clash of Angels.*

Corobael [Corabael]

Cosel—an angel of the 1st hour of the night, serving under Gamiel. [*Rf.* Waite, *The Book of Ceremonial Magic*, p. 69.]

Cosmagogi—in the Chaldean cosmological scheme, the 3 intellectual angelic guides of the universe. [*Rf.* Aude, *Chaldean Oracles of Zoroaster.*]

Cosmiel—the genius who accompanied the 17th-century Jesuit Athanasius Kircher on his visits to various planets. Kircher tells of this "ecstatic voyage" in his *Oedipus Egyptiacus.* [*Rf.* Christian, *The History and Practice of Magic* I, p. 73.]

Cosmocrator—in Valentinian gnosticism, Cosmocrator is ruler of the material cosmos in the guise of Diabolos (the devil). His consort is Barbelo (*q.v.*) and together "they sing praises to the Powers of the Light," which would indicate that Cosmocrator is not wholly evil. [*Rf. Pistis Sophia.*]

Covering Cherub—the covering cherub was, according to Blake, "Lucifer in his former glory." [*Rf.* Blake, *Vala.*]

Craoscha [Sraosha]

Cripon—"a holy angel of God," invoked in magical rites, specifically in the conjuration of the Reed. [*Rf.* Mathers, *The Greater Key of Solomon;* Waite, *The Lemegeton.*]

Crocell (Crokel, Procel, Pucel, Pocel)—once of the order of potestates (i.e., powers), now a great duke in Hell commanding 48 legions of infernal spirits. Crocell confided to Solomon that he expects to return to his former throne (in Heaven). Meantime he teaches geometry and the liberal arts. May be the same as Procel, in which case his sigil is shown in Waite, *The Book of Ceremonial Magic*, p. 211.

Crociel—an angel of the 7th hour of the day, serving under Barginiel.

Crowned Seraph—the devil, 6-winged, is pictured as a crowned seraph in his capacity of tempter in Eden. [See reproduction in Wall, *Devils*, p. 42.] According to Fabricius, the Devil (Lucifer) could be distinguished from all seraphs by his crown, worn by virtue of his office of light-bearer.

Cruciel—an angel of the 3rd hour of the night, serving under Sarquamich.

Ctarari—one of the 2 angels of Winter, the

other angel being Amabael. [*Rf.* de Abano, *The Heptameron.*]

Cukbiel—an angel invoked in Syrian invocation rites, as described in *The Book of Protection* and in Budge, *Amulets and Talismans.* Cukbiel figures in the "Binding [of] the Tongue of the Ruler," a special binding spell.

Cuniali—the genius (spirit) of association and one of the governing genii of the 8th hour. [*Rf.* Apollonius of Tyana, *The Nuctemeron.*]

Cupra—one of the Novensiles (*q.v.*). Cupra is the personification of light.

Curaniel—an angel of Monday, resident of the 1st Heaven, invoked from the south.

Cureton—"a holy angel of God" invoked in black magical conjurations, as described in the grimoires. [*Rf.* Waite, *The Book of Black Magic and of Pacts.*]

Curson [Purson]

Cynabal—a minister-angel serving under Varcan (king of the air ruling on the Lord's Day). [*Rf.* Barrett, *The Magus* II; de Abano, *The Heptameron*; and Shah, *Occultism, Its Theory and Practice.*]

Jacob Wrestling with the Angel by Delacroix. The angel has been variously identified as Metatron, Peniel, Sammael. Reproduced from Régamey, *Anges*.

Daath ("knowledge")—in the cabalistic system of divine emanations, Daath combines the 2nd and 3rd sefiroth (*q.v.*). [*Rf.* Runes, *The Wisdom of the Kabbalah*.]

Dabariel—variant for Radueriel. [*Rf. 3 Enoch*, chap. 27.]

Dabria—one of the 5 "men" (actually angels) who transcribed the 204 (or 94) books dictated by Ezra. The other 4 heavenly scribes were Ecanus, Sarea, Selemiah (Seleucia), Asiel. [*Rf. Revelation of Esdras IV*.]

Dabriel—the heavenly scribe, equated with Vretil (*q.v.*). Dabriel is also a Monday angel said to reside in the 1st Heaven. He is invoked from the north. [*Rf.* de Abano, *The Heptameron*.]

Daden—in gnosticism, a great celestial power dwelling in the 6th Heaven. [*Rf.* Doresse, *The Secret Books of the Egyptian Gnostics*.]

Daemon (demon)—one of 2 sets of watchers or guardian angels, according to Hesiod in his *Works and Days*. Also, "spirits of the men of the golden age." In Greek lore, daemons were benevolent spirits, familiars, or angels. Socrates had his daemon, an attending spirit. In Mead, *Thrice-Greatest Hermes*, an invocation to Hermes is addressed to "the Good Daimon Sire of all things good, and nurse of the whole world," where Daimon, as Mead suggests, stands for the "father-mother of the universe." [*Rf.* Glasson, *Greek Influence in Jewish Eschatology*, p. 69.]

Daeva (Deva)—in early Persian mythology, the daevas were evil spirits created by Ahriman; but in Hinduism they were divine and benevolent spirits. In theosophy they constitute "one of the ranks or orders of spirits who compose the hierarchy which rules the universe under the deity." [*Rf.* Spence, *An Encyclopaedia of Occultism*, p. 121.]

Daghiel [Dagiel]

Dagiel (Daghiel, Daiel)—an angel whose dominion is over fish. According to Barrett, *The Magus*, Dagiel is invoked in Friday conjuration rites. He is addressed, in such rites as "great angel, strong and powerful prince," and is supplicated in the name of the "star" Venus. [*Rf.* Trachtenberg, *Jewish Magic and Superstition*; *The Book of the Sacred*

Dagon, the national god of the Philistines, commonly represented with the body of a fish. A bas relief reproduced from Schaff, *A Dictionary of the Bible.*

Magic of Abra-Melin the Mage; and de Claremont, *The Ancient's Book of Magic.*]

Dagon—a fallen angel in *Paradise Lost* I, 457. To the ancient Phoenicians, however, Dagon was a national god, represented with the face and hands of a man and the body of a fish.

Dagymiel—a governing angel of the zodiac. [*Rf.* Cornelius Agrippa, *Three Books of Occult Philosophy* III.]

Dahak [Ahriman, the Satan of Persia]

Dahariel (Dariel)—in *Pirke Hechaloth*, a guard of the 1st Heaven, and an angel of the order of shinanim (*q.v.*). In *Hechaloth Rabbati* Dahariel is a guard of the 5th Heaven.

Dahavauron—prince of the face and one of the angelic guards of the 3rd Heaven. [*Rf. Ozar Midrashim* I, 117.]

Dahaviel (Kahaviel)—one of the 7 guards of the 1st Heaven. [*Rf. Hechaloth Rabbati.*]

Dahnay—one of the "holy angels of God" who, nevertheless, may be invoked in black-magic conjurations, as prescribed in the grimoires. [*Rf.* Waite, *The Book of Black Magic and of Pacts.*]

Dai (Dey)—in *The Sixth and Seventh Books of Moses*, an angel of the order of powers. In ancient Persian lore, Dai was the angel of December.

Daiel [Dagiel]

Daimon [Daemon]

Daksha—one of 7 shining gods of Vedic religion. [*See* Adityas.]

Dalkiel—angel of Hell, ruler of Sheol, and equated with Rugziel (*q.v.*). In *Baraita de Massachet Gehinnom*, Dalkiel operates in the 7th compartment of the underworld, "punishing 10 nations," and serving under orders of Duma(h), who is the angel of the stillness of death. [*See* writings of Joseph Gikatilla ben Abraham (1248–1305).]

Dalmai(i) (Dalmay, Damlay)—in occultism, "a holy angel of God" invoked in the exorcism of fire. [*Rf. Grimorium Verum*; *The Book of Ceremonial Magic.*]

Dalquiel—in the cabala, one of the 3 princes of the 3rd Heaven, the other 2 being Jabniel and Rabacyal. All 3 rule over fire, under the ethnarchy of Anahel. Dalquiel's special aide is the angel called Oul (*q.v.*).

Damabiah—an angel of the order of angels, with dominion over naval construction. Damabiah is one of the 72 angels bearing the name of God Shemhamphorae. His corresponding angel is Ptebiou. For the sigil of Damabiah, see Ambelain, *La Kabbale Pratique*, p. 294.

Damabiath—an angel of the order of powers, invoked in cabalistic rites. He manifests in the form of a beautiful mortal via the 5th seal. [*Rf. The Sixth and Seventh Books of Moses.*]

Dameal—a Tuesday angel resident in the 5th Heaven. He is invoked from the east. [*Rf.* de Abano, *The Heptameron*; Barrett, *The Magus* II.]

Dameb'el—one of the 72 angels ruling the 72 quinaries of the zodiac, according to Runes, *The Wisdom of the Kabbalah.*

Damiel—angel of the 5th hour, serving under the rulership of Sazquiel; or angel of the 9th hour, serving under the rulership of Vadriel. Damiel is invoked in the conjuration of the Sword. [*Rf.* Waite, *The Lemegeton*; Mathers, *The Greater Key of Solomon*.]

Damlay [Dalmai]

Daniel ("God is my judge")—an angel of the order of principalities, according to Waite, *The Lemegeton*. Daniel (as Danjal) is one of a troop of fallen angels, listed in *Enoch I*. In the lower regions he exercises authority over lawyers. His sigil is reproduced in Ambelain, *La Kabbale Pratique*, p. 289. On the other hand, according to Barrett, *The Magus*, Daniel is a high holy angel (one of 72) who bears the name of God Shemhamphorae.

Danjal [Daniel]

Dara—in Persian mythology, angel of rains and rivers. [*Rf. The Dabistan*, p. 378.]

Darbiel—an angel of the 10th hour of the day, serving under Oriel. [*Rf.* Waite, *The Lemegeton*.]

Dardael [Dardiel]

Darda'il—in Arabic lore a guardian angel invoked in rites of exorcism. [*Rf.* Hughes, *A Dictionary of Islam*, "Angels."]

Dardariel—chief ruling angel of the 11th hour of the night.

Dardiel—one of the 3 angels of the Lord's Day, the other 2 angels being Michael and Hurtapel. [*Rf.* Barrett, *The Magus* II; de Abano, *The Heptameron*.]

Daresiel—an angel of the 1st hour of the day, serving under Samael.

Dargitael—in hechaloth lore (*Ma'asseh Merkabah*), an angelic guard of the 5th heavenly hall.

Dariel [Dahariel]

Dark Angel, The—the angel-man-God who wrestled with Jacob at Peniel, an incident related in Genesis 32:30. Variously identified as Michael, Metatron, Uriel, or the Lord Himself. According to *The Zohar* (Vayishlah 170a) the angel was Samael, "chieftain of Esau." In Talmudic sources, the angel was Michael-Metatron. According to Clement of Alexandria, the angel was the Holy Ghost. [*Rf.* Clement of Alexandria *Instructor* I, 7, and, for Talmudic sources, Ginzberg, *The Legends of the Jews* V, 305.] The subject is illustrated by Rembrandt and Doré, among others.

Darkiel—one of the numerous angelic guards of the gates of the South Wind. [*Rf. Ozar Midrashim* II, 316.]

Darmosiel—an angel of the 12th hour of the night, serving under Sarindiel.

Darquiel—an angel of Monday, residing in the 1st Heaven. He is invoked from the south. [*Rf.* Barrett, *The Magus* II; de Abano, *The Heptameron*.]

Daryoel—variant form of Radueriel. [*Rf. 3 Enoch*, chap. 27.]

Dasim—one of the 5 sons of the Muslim fallen archangel Iblis or Eblis. Dasim is the demon of discord. The other 4 sons are Awar, demon of lubricity; Sut, demon of lies; Tir, demon of fatal accidents; Zalambur, demon of mercantile dishonesty.

Daveithe—in gnosticism, one of the 4 great luminaries surrounding the Self-Begotten (i.e., God).

David—one of the 7 archons in gnosticism, according to the *Catholic Encyclopedia*, "Gnosticism."

Days—in the view of Theodotus, angels are called days. See "Excerpts of Theodotus" in the *Ante-Nicene Fathers Library*.

Dealzhat—in Mosaic cabalistic lore, a mighty and secret name of God, or a great luminary whom Joshua invoked (along with the name of Baahando) to cause the sun to stand still—an incident related in Joshua 10:12-13.

Degaliel—an angel's name found inscribed on the 3rd pentacle of the planet Venus. [*Rf.* Mathers, *The Greater Key of Solomon*; Shah, *The Secret Lore of Magic*, p. 49.]

Degalim—an angelic suborder of the Song-Uttering Choirs, serving under Tagas. [*Rf. 3 Enoch*.]

Deharhiel—in hechaloth lore (*Ma'asseh Merkabah*), an angelic guard of the 5th heavenly hall.

Deheborym—in the *Pirke Hechaloth*, an angelic guard of the 1st Heaven.

Deliel—one of the angels of the 4th chora or altitude invoked in magical prayer, as set forth in *The Almadel of Solomon*. Cornelius Agrippa cites Deliel as a governing angel of the zodiac. [*Rf. Three Books of Occult Philosophy* III.]

Delukiel—one of the angelic guards of the 7th Heaven. [*Rf. Ozar Midrashim* I, 119.]

Demiurge (Demiourgos)—the gnostic writer Basilides called Demiurge the great archon (ruler). To Valentinus he was "an angel like God" and identified with the God of the Jews. Demiurge has always been identified with Mithras. A title for the Demiurge, "Architect of the Universe," denotes or suggests that it was Demiurge, not God, who formed the world, at the instance of En Soph, the Unknowable. [*Rf.* Legge, *Forerunners and Rivals of Christianity*, p. 107 fn.; Irenaeus, *Contra Haereses* I, 1.] In the cabala, says Westcott in his *The Study of the Kabalah*, the Greek Demiourgos is Metatron.

Demon [Daimon]

Demoniarch—a title for Satan. [*Rf.* Schneweis, *Angels and Demons According to Lactantius*, p. 105.]

Deputies—in his "Of Angels, Genii, and Devils" Voltaire speaks of deputies as an order of angels, "one of 10 classes in Talmud and Targum."

Deputy Angels—in Jewish magic, the deputy angels are the *memunim*, a class of spirits who appear to do the invocant's bidding when properly invoked. Usually they are regarded as evil, but Eleazar of Worms (13th-century sage) insists they are holy angels. [*Rf.* Trachtenberg, *Jewish Magic and Superstition*.]

Deramiel—an angel serving in the 3rd Heaven, as cited in *The Sixth and Seventh Books of Moses*.

Derdekea—a heavenly female power who descends to earth for the salvation of man. In the gnostic *Paraphrase of Shem*, Derdekea is referred to as the Supreme Mother. [*See* Drop.]

Destroying Angel (Angel of Destruction)—a term for the angel of death. David met and appeased the destroying angel at Mt. Moriah. In *The Book of Wisdom* (ed. Reider) the destroying angel is Kolazonta, the "chastiser." The Danites, a Christian band organized for secret assassination, were called "Destroying Angels." They were incorrectly associated with the early Mormon Church. [*Cf.* Manoah of the Danite clan in Judges 13:2; *Rf.* Jobes, *Dictionary of Mythology, Folklore and Symbols*.]

Destroying Angel of the Apocalypse—Abaddon or Apollyon, who is also called "chief of the demons of the 7th dynasty." This is according to Christian demonologists, says Grillot in *A Pictorial Anthology of Witchcraft, Magic and Alchemy*, p. 128.

Devatas—in Vedic lore, the devatas are analogous to the Judaeo-Christian angels. The term is often used interchangeably with the suryas (*q.v.*).

Devil, The [Satan]

Dey [Dai]

Diabolus or **Diabolos** [Asteroth]—to Bunyan in his *Holy War*, Diabolus is the devil. His aides in the war against Shaddai (God) include Apollyon, Python, Cerberus, Legion, Lucifer, and other "diabolonians."

Dibburiel—variant form of Radueriel. [*Rf. 3 Enoch*, chap. 27.]

Didnaor—an angel mentioned in *The Book of the Angel Raziel* (*Sefer Raziel*).

Dina—a guardian angel of the Law (Torah) and of wisdom. Dina is also known as Yefefiah and as Iofiel). He is credited with having taught 70 languages to souls created at the time of Creation. He dwells in the 7th Heaven. [*Rf. Revelation of Moses* in M. Gaster, *Studies and Texts in Folklore*.]

Diniel—an angel invoked in Syriac incantation rites. Diniel is also cited as one of the 70 childbed amulet angels. In *The Book of Protection* he is grouped with Michael, Prukiel, Zadikiel, and other "spellbinding angels" in the "binding [of] the tongue of the ruler." [*Rf.* Budge, *Amulets and Talismans*, p. 278.]

Dirachiel—one of the 28 angels ruling the 28 mansions of the moon. In the view of Barrett, *The Magus* II, Dirachiel is an "extra" among the 7 Electors of Hell.

Dirael—in hechaloth lore (*Ma'asseh Merkabah*), an angelic guard of the 6th heavenly hall.

Divine Beasts—the holy hayyoth (*q.v.*).

Divine Wisdom—in the cabala, divine wisdom or chochma is the 2nd of the holy sefiroth, and personified in the angel Raziel (*q.v.*).

Djibril (Jibril, Gabriel)—called, in the Koran, the "Faithful Spirit."

Dobiel [Dubbiel]

Dodekas—in Valentinian gnosticism, divine powers operating under the rule of Ogdoas (*q.v.*).

Dohel [Boel]

Dokiel—"the weighing angel" or, as Dokiel is called in *The Testament of Abraham* XIII, "the archangel who is like the sun, holding the balance in his hand." The name is derived from Isaiah 40:15: "by the dust [dk] in the balance."

Domedon-Doxomedon—described as the "aeon of aeons" and one of the Ogdoas (*q.v.*). [*Rf.* Doresse, *The Secret Books of the Egyptian Gnostics*, p. 178.]

Domiel (Dumiel; Abir Gahidriom)—in Merkabah mysticism, a guardian angel of the 6th hall of the 7th Heaven. Domiel is an archon, "prince of majesty, fear, and trembling." He is also a ruler of the 4 elements. [*Rf.* Barrett, *The Magus*; Schwab, *Vocabulaire de l'Angélologie*.] As the gatekeeper of Hell, says Scholem, *Major Trends in Jewish Mysticism*, p. 362, Domiel is mistakenly confused with Duma.

Dominations (dominions, lords, lordships)—in the Dionysian scheme, the dominations rank 4th in the celestial hierarchy. In Hebrew lore they are the hashmallim, according to Barrett, *The Magus*, where the chief of the order is given as Hashmal or Zadkiel. Says Dionysius: "they regulate angels' duties and are perpetually aspiring to true lordship; through them the majesty of God is manifested." The order is headed by Pi-Zeus (in horoscopy). [*Cf.* Colossians 1:16: "Dominions or principalities or powers" and *Enoch II*, 20:1: "lordships and principalities and powers."] In *The Book of Enoch*, lordships is given in lieu of dominions or dominations. Emblems of authority: sceptres, orbs.

Dominion—the name of "the oldest angel," according to Philo. [*Rf.* Mead, *Thrice-Greatest Hermes.*]

Domos—an angel invoked in magical operations; also one of the 12 names for the Evil Eye. A variation of Domol. [*Rf.* Budge, *Amulets and Talismans.*]

Donachiel—in occult lore, an angel invoked to command demons. [*Rf.* Mathers, *The Greater Key of Solomon.*]

Donahan—in the cabala, an archangel summoned in magical rites. [*Rf. The Sixth and Seventh Books of Moses.*]

Donel—one of numerous angelic guards of the gates of the South Wind. [*Rf. Ozar Midrashim* II, 316.]

Doniel—one of the 72 angel rulers of the zodiac. [*Rf.* Runes, *The Wisdom of the Kabbalah.*]

Donquel—a prince (angel) of love invoked to procure the woman of an invocant's desire. [*Rf.* Waite, *The Book of Ceremonial Magic*, p. 301.]

Doremiel—a Friday angel invoked from the north. [*Rf.* de Abano, *The Heptameron*; Barrett, *The Magus.*]

Dormiel—one of numerous angelic guards of the gates of the East Wind. [*Rf. Ozar Midrashim* II, 316.]

Doucheil—an angel in Mandaean lore. [*Rf.* Pognon, *Inscriptions Mandaïtes des Coupes de Khouabir.*]

Douth—one of the 9 angels that "run together throughout the heavenly and earthly places," as recorded in *The Gospel of Bartholomew*, p. 177, where the names of the 9 angels are revealed by Beliar to Bartholomew.

Doxomedon—one of the great luminaries cited in the gnostic *Revelations of Zostrian*.

Dracon—an angel of the 6th hour of the night, serving under Zaazonash. [*Rf.* Waite, *The Lemegeton*, p. 69.]

Dragon—in Revelation 12:9, Satan is termed "the great dragon . . . that old serpent" who was "cast out into the earth," along with the angels who followed him. In Psalms 91:13, "the saints shall trample the dragon under their feet." Michael (St. Michael) is usually represented as the slayer of the dragon. He is thus the forerunner of St. George. In classical legend, the dragon guarded the golden apples in the garden of Hesperides. In gnosticism, dragon is a term for the angel of dawn. [*Rf.* Jobes, *Dictionary of Mythology, Folklore and Symbols*.]

Dramazod—an angel of the 6th hour of the night, serving under Zaazonash.

Dramozin—an angel of the 8th hour of the night, serving under Narcoriel.

Drelmeth—an angel of the 3rd hour of the day, serving under Veguaniel.

Drial—one of the angelic guards stationed in the 5th Heaven. [*Rf. Pirke Hechaloth*.]

Drop—in the gnostic *Berlin Codex*, a female heavenly power who descends to earth for the salvation of mankind. [*See* Derdekea.]

Drsmiel—an evil angel, one of the *nomina barbara*, summoned in conjuration rites for separating a husband from his wife. [*Rf.* M. Gaster, *The Sword of Moses*.]

Dubbiel (Dubiel, Dobiel—"bear-god")—guardian angel of Persia and one of the special accusers of Israel. It is rumored that Dubbiel once officiated in Heaven for 21 days as proxy for Gabriel when the latter (over whom Dubbiel scored a victory) was in temporary disgrace. [*Rf.* Talmud *Yoma* 79a.] In the light of the legend that all 70 or 72 tutelary angels of nations (except Michael, protector of Israel) became corrupted

Vision of the ram and the he-goat (*Rf.* Daniel 8) with Daniel kneeling before the angel Gabriel. From Strachan, *Pictures from a Mediaeval Bible*. [*Note*—The ram represents the kings of Media and Persia, while the he-goat represents the king of Greece.]

Woodcut from the Cologne Bible. Left, Michael spearing the dragon (also known as the devil and Satan). Center, the beast with the 7 crowned heads. Right, a beast with horns like a lamb, and fire dropping from heaven. Illustration for Revelation 12, 7–10 and 13, 1. From Strachan, *Pictures from a Mediaeval Bible.*

through national bias, Dubbiel must be regarded corrupt and an evil angel, a demon.

Duchiel—an angel invoked in Solomonic magic for commanding demons. [*Rf.* Mathers, *The Greater Key of Solomon.*]

Duhael—an angel of non-Hebraic origin. [*Rf.* Trachtenberg, *Jewish Magic and Superstition,* p. 99.]

Duma(h) or **Douma** (Aramaic, "silence")—the angel of silence and of the stillness of death. Duma is also the tutelary angel of Egypt, prince of Hell, and angel of vindication. *The Zohar* speaks of him as having "tens of thousands of angels of destruction" under him, and as being "chief of demons in Gehinnom [i.e., Hell] with 12,000 myriads of attendants, all charged with the punishment of the souls of sinners." [*Rf.* Müller, *History of Jewish Mysticism.*] In the Babylonian legend of the descent of Istar into Hades, Duma shows up as the guardian of the 14th gate. [*Rf.* Forlong, *Encyclopedia of Religions.*] Duma is a popular figure in Yiddish folklore. I. B. Singer's *Short Friday* (1964), a collection of stories, mentions Duma(h) as a "thousand-eyed angel of death, armed with a fiery rod or flaming sword."

Dumariel—an angel of the 11th hour of the night, serving under Dardariel. [*Rf.* Waite, *The Lemegeton.*]

Dumiel [Domiel]

Dunahel [Alimiel]

Durba'il—in Arabic lore a guardian angel invoked in rites of exorcism. [*Rf.* Hughes, *A Dictionary of Islam,* "Angels."]

Duvdeviyah—one of the many names of the angel Metatron.

Dynamis (or Dunamis)—one of the 7 aeons who, as is said of Pistis Sophia, procreated the superior angels. In gnosticism, Dynamis is the chief male personification of power, just as Pistis Sophia is chief female personification of wisdom. *Cf.* Matthew 26:64: "Hereafter shall ye see the Son of man sitting on the right hand of power." [See Preisendanz, *Papyri Graecae Magicae* II.] In hechaloth lore, according to Scholem in *Jewish Gnosticism, Merkabah Mysticism, and Talmudic Tradition,* Dynamis is a secret name of Metatron. Steiner, *The Work of the Angels in Man's Astral Body,* equates Dynamis with Mights.

The Elders in the Mystic Procession by Doré. Illustration to Canto 29 of Dante's *Purgatorio*. From Dante, *The Divine Comedy*, translated by Lawrence Grant White.

Ea [Taurine Angel]

Ebed—one of the many names of the angel Metatron.

Eblis (Iblis, Haris—"despair")—in Persian and Arabic lore, Eblis is the equivalent of the Christian Satan. As an angel in good standing he was once treasurer of the heavenly Paradise, according to Ibn Abbas in Jung's *Fallen Angels in Jewish, Christian and Mohammedan Literature*. Beckford in the oriental romance *Vathek* introduces Eblis thus: "Before his fall he [Eblis] was called Azazel. When Adam was created, God commanded all the angels to worship him [Adam], but Eblis refused." *Cf.* Koran, *sura* 18; also the legend related in Ginzberg, *The Legends of the Jews* I, 63: "Me thou hast created of smokeless fire, and shall I reverence a creature made of dust?" Thereupon God turned Eblis into a *shetan* (devil) and he became the father of devils. To Augustine (*Enchiridion*, 28) and to Mohammed (in the Koran) Eblis is a jinn rather than an angel or a fallen angel. The Arabs have 3 categories of spirits: angels, jinn (good and evil), and demons. There is a tradition that the great grandson of Eblis was taught by Mohammed certain *suras* of the Koran. [*Rf. The Encyclopaedia of Islam* III, 191.]

Ebriel—the 9th of the 10 unholy sefiroth (*q.v.*). [*Rf.* Isaac ha-Cohen of Soria's texts.]

Ebuhuel—an angel of omnipotence, one of 8, as recorded in *The Sixth and Seventh Books of Moses*. Ebuhuel may be invoked in cabalistic conjurations.

Ecanus (Elkanah)—as noted in the apocalyptic *Esdras* (*IV Esdras*, 14:42) Ecanus is one of 5 "men" (i.e., angels) who, on orders from God, transcribed the 94 (or 204) books dictated to them by Ezra. The 5 "men" were, including Ecanus, Sarea, Dabria, Selemia, Asiel. Some versions give Ethan for Ecanus. Of the books, 70 were to be kept hidden, "reserved for the wise among the Jews." These contained esoteric knowledge; the rest were for public use.

Efchal (Efchiel)—another name for the angel Zophiel? [See *The Book of the Angel Raziel* I, 42b; Schwab, *Vocabulaire de l'Angélologie*; West, "Names of Milton's Angels," in *Studies in Philology* XLVII, 2 (April 1950).]

Efniel—an angel belonging to the order of cherubim. In *The Book of the Angel Raziel*, the name Efniel, which occurs there, might have been Milton's inspiration (says R. H. West, quoted in the Efchal entry) for Zephon.

Egibiel—one of the 28 angels governing the 28 mansions of the moon. [*See* Appendix for the names of all 28 angels.]

Egion—in hechaloth lore (*Ma'asseh Merkabah*), an angelic guard of the 7th heavenly hall.

Egoroi [Grigori]

Egregori [Grigori]

Egrimiel (Egrumiel)—in *Pirke Hechaloth*, an angelic guard stationed in one of the halls of the 6th Heaven.

Eheres—in occult lore, an angel invoked in the exorcism of Wax. [*Rf. Clavicula Salomonis*; Shah, *Occultism, Its Theory and Practice*, p. 25.] Lewis Spence claims that the name is "attributed to the Holy Spirit."

Eiael—an angel with dominion over occult sciences, longevity, etc. Eiael is also one of the 72 angels bearing the mystical name of God Shemhamphorae. His corresponding angel is Abiou. The sigil of Eiael is reproduced in Ambelain, *La Kabbale Pratique*, p. 294. When Eiael is conjured up, the invocant must recite the 4th verse of Psalm 36.

Eighth Heaven—this Heaven in Hebrew is called Muzaloth. *Enoch II* says it is the home of the 12 signs of the zodiac; but the 9th heaven is also given as the home of the signs.

Eirnilus—in Apollonius of Tyana, *The Nuctemeron*, a genius (angel) with dominion over fruit. He serves also as one of the genii of the 6th hour.

Eisheth Zenunim (Isheth Zenunim)—in Zoharistic cabala, an angel of whoredom or prostitution, one of the 4 mates of the evil Sammael (*q.v.*).

The other 3 angels in the profession are Lilith, Naamah, and Agrat bat Mahlah(t).

Eistibus—genius of divination, one of the genii of the 4th hour.

El (pl. elohim)—a term for God or angel. In Canaanitish epic lore, El is the angel who begot Shahar and Shalim by a mortal woman.

Eladel—one of the 72 angels ruling the zodiac, as listed in Runes, *The Wisdom of the Kabbalah*.

El-Adrel—in Shah, *The Secret Lore of Magic*, p. 248, a genius (angel) who is invoked to bring the invocant the music of his choice. El-Adrel is mentioned in the *Book of Powers*.

Elamiz—an angel of the 11th hour of the night, serving under Dardariel. [*Rf.* Waite, *The Lemegeton*, p. 70.]

Elamos—in Solomonic conjuring rites, a spirit invoked in prayer by the Master of the Art. [*Rf. Grimorium Verum*.]

El Auria—angel of flame. El Auria is equated with Ouriel or Uriel.

Elders—the Revelation of St. John speaks of 24 Elders sitting on 24 thrones around the throne of God, clothed in white garments, "having each a harp and golden bowls full of incense, which are the prayers of the saints." According to Charles, *Critical Commentary on the Revelation of St. John* (p. 130), the Elders are angels, acting as "angeli interpretes" to John. They constitute, Charles believes, "a college or order of angels," deriving originally from the 24 Babylonian star-gods, and are the angelic representatives of the 24 priestly orders. In *Enoch II* (Slavonic Enoch), the Elders are to be found in the 1st of the 7 heavens. In the pseudepigraphical *Vision of Paul* the 24 Elders are among cherubim and archangels in Heaven, "singing hymns." Dante in *Purgatorio*, canto 29, speaks of the "four and twenty elders, two-by-two, upon their brows crowns of fleurs-de-lis." Gustave Doré did an engraving for *The Divine Comedy* showing the Elders in mystic procession. Prudentius (Latin Christian poet, 4th–5th century

St. John and the Twenty-four Elders in Heaven by Dürer. From Willi Kurth, *The Complete Woodcuts of Dürer.*

C.E.) describes the Elders in a poem called "Diptychon," written to accompany paintings or mosaics for a church [*Rf.* Cockerell, *Book of the Old Testament Illustrations*].

Elect One, The—in *Enoch I* (*The Book of Enoch*), the elect one is identified as Metatron (*q.v.*) and the Son of Man, or the lord of spirits.

Electors—in Conybeare, *The Testament of Solomon*, there are 7 planetary spirits or angels of Hell, the notion deriving from the *maskim* of the Akkadians. The 7 are: Barbiel (under the rule of Zaphiel), Mephistophiel (under Zadkiel), Ganael (under Apadiel and Camael), Aciel (under Raphael), Anael (under Haniel), Ariel (under Michael), Marbuel (under Gabriel). In the *Magia Naturalis et Innaturalis*, the electors are fiends (not angels), and their names are given as: Dirachiel, Amnodiel, Adriel, Amudiel, Tagriel, Annixiel, Geliel, Eequiel. Agrippa's list of the 7 electors, which more or less agrees with the list in *The Testament of Solomon*, has Bludon and Apadiel in place of Anael and Ganael.

Eleinos—in gnostic lore, one of the powers or aeons. [*Rf.* Doresse, *The Secret Books of the Egyptian Gnostics*.]

El El—one of the angelic guards of the gates of the North Wind. Cited in *Ozar Midrashim* II, 316.

Eleleth (Heleleth)—in the *Apocryphon of John*, one of the 4 luminaries that stand around the arch-aeon Autogenes. [*Cf.* Phronesis; *see* Heleleth.]

Elemiah—one of the 8 seraphim of the Tree of Life in the *Book of Yetsirah*, and an angel (one of 72) bearing the mystical name of God Shemhamphorae. Elemiah rules over voyages and maritime expeditions. His corresponding angel is Senacher. For the sigil of Elemiah, see Ambelain, *La Kabbale Pratique*, p. 260.

Eliel (Elael)—in Montgomery's *Aramaic Incantation Texts from Nippur*, an angel "that may be invoked in ritual magic."

Elijah (Gr. Elias—"my God is Jehovah")—in the Old Testament, 2 Hebrew patriarchs were translated to Heaven while they were still in the flesh: God "took" Enoch (Genesis 5); Elijah was transported in a fiery chariot (II Kings 2:11). Enoch was transformed into the angel Metatron; Elijah into Sandalphon (although there is a legend that Elijah was an angel from the very beginning: "one of the greatest and mightiest of the fiery angel host"). Another legend relates that Elijah fought the angel of death, subdued him, and would have annihilated him but for the intervention of God (Who had, it seems, further use for the angel of death—at least, for this particular one). In Talmud there is a similar tale relating to Moses' encounter with an angel of death—in fact, with several of them. Malachi 4:5 prophesies that Elijah would be the forerunner of the Messiah. In Luke, Elijah appears with Moses on the Mount of Transfiguration, in conversation with Jesus. In Heaven, according to *Pirke Rabbi Eliezer*, Elijah is the "psychopomp whose duty is to stand at the crossways of Paradise and guide the pious to their appointed places." The hasidic Rabbi Elimelekh of Lizhensk (d. 1786) referred to Elijah after his transfiguration as the "Angel of the Covenant" (*q.v.*). In Jewish homes, at Passover festivals, the cup of Elijah is filled with wine, and a place is left vacant at the seder for him, "the expected guest." [*Rf.* Ginzberg, *The Legends of the Jews*.] The British Museum, Oriental Division, owns a manuscript (6673) showing Elijah eating the fruit of the Tree of Life in Paradise, at which he is joined by Enoch. The drawing is reproduced in Budge, *Amulets and Talismans*, p. 277. Blake, in his *Marriage of Heaven and Hell*, pictures Elijah as a composite devil and angel. "I beheld the Angel who stretched out his arms embracing the flame of fire, and he was consumed and arose as Elijah. Blake adds a note: "This Angel, who is now become a Devil, is my particular friend."

Elilaios—in gnosticism, Elilaios is one of 7 archons, resident of the 6th Heaven. [*Rf.* "Gnosticism," *Catholic Encyclopedia*; Doresse, *The Secret Books of the Egyptian Gnostics*.]

Elim ("trees"; in Hebrew, "mighty ones")—the guardian angel of Libbeus the Apostle. The term elim also denotes a high order of angels (mentioned in *3 Enoch*) along with the orders of erelim and tafsarim (*q.v.*).

Elimelech ("my God is king")—an angel of Summer, according to R. M. Grant, *Gnosticism and Early Christianity*, p. 43, who claims the name is derived from *Enoch I*, 82:13–20. Associated with the angel He'el, "leader of the heads of thousands."

Elimiel—in Jewish cabala, the angel (spirit, intelligence) of the moon.

Eliphaniasai—an angel of the 3rd chora or altitude invoked in magical prayer, as set forth in *The Almadel of Solomon*.

Elion or Elyon (Phoenician, "the most high") —an aide to Ofaniel in the 1st Heaven. Elion is an angel invoked in the conjuration of the Reed; also a ministering angel. By invoking Elion, Moses was able to bring down hail on Egypt at the time of the plagues. Elion is also the deity of Melchizedek whom Abraham is represented to have identified with Yahweh (God). Cf. Genesis 14, 18, 19, 22. [*Rf.* Forlong, *Encyclopedia of Religions.*]

Elkanah [Ecanus]

Eloa—the great (male) angel in Klopstock, *The Messiah*. In Alfred de Vigny's poem "Eloa" (1823) it is the name of a female angel born of a tear shed by Jesus.

Eloai—according to Origen, one of the 7 archons in the Ophitic (gnostic) system.

Eloeus—in Phoenician mythology, one of the 7 elohim (angels) of the presence, builders of the universe. In Ophitic (gnostic) lore, he is one of 7 potentates, rulers of the 7 Heavens, who constitute the Hebdomad. [*Rf.* Epiphanius, *Penarion.*]

Elogium—an angel who rules over the month of Elul (September), in the Hebrew calendar. [*Rf.* Schwab, *Vocabulaire de l'Angélologie.*] Ordinarily the ruling angel of September is Uriel (Zuriel).

Eloha (pl. Elohaym or Elohim)—an angel of the order of powers, as named in *The Sixth and Seventh Books of Moses*. Eloha is summoned up in conjuring rites by cabalists.

Eloheij—an angel of the Seal, as cited in *The Sixth and Seventh Books of Moses*.

Elohi—an angel invoked in the exorcism of fire. Elohi is 5th of the angelic hierarchies answering to the 10 divine names. In Solomonic conjuration rites, Elohi is invoked in prayer by the Master of the Art. [*Rf.* Spence, *An Encyclopaedia of Occultism*; Mathers, *The Greater Key of Solomon*.] According to Mathers, when the name of Elohi is pronounced "God will dry up the sea and the rivers."

Elohim—in Hebrew, elohim stands for Jehovah (YHWH) in the singular or plural. The term derives from the female singular "eloh" plus the masculine plural "im," God thus being conceived originally as androgynous. In I Samuel 28:13, where the woman (not the witch) of Endor tells Saul "I saw gods [the Hebrew here gives elohim] ascending out of the earth," the word would seem to designate spirits of the departed (from below, not from above) rather than God or gods. In *The Zohar* (Numbers 208b), Rabbi Isaac, commenting on the passage in Deuteronomy "And God [Elohim] came to Balaam," says: "What we have learnt is that Elohim in this passage designates an angel, because sometimes the angel is called by the superior name." In the Mirandola listing of the celestial hierarchy, the elohim rank 9th (where Dionysius gives the order as angels). In the *Book of Formation*, elohim is listed 7th of the 10 sefiroth and corresponds to netzach (victory). See Blake's drawing, "Elohim Giving Life to Adam."

Eloi (Eloiein)—one of the 7 angels created by Ildabaoth "in his own image." [*Rf.* King, *The Gnostics and Their Remains*, p. 15.]

Eloiein (Eloi)—one of the 7 archons (celestial powers) in gnostic cosmology. [*Rf.* "Gnosticism," *Catholic Encyclopedia*.]

Elomeel (Ilylumiel)—in Enoch lore (*Enoch I*, 82:14), one of the leaders of the angels of the seasons.

Elomnia (Elomina)—one of the 5 chief angel princes of the 3rd altitude. [*Rf. The Almadel of Solomon*.]

Elorkhaios—a mysterious entity to whom the secrets of creation were divulged, as related in the gnostic *Paraphrase of Shem*.

Elubatel—one of the 8 angels of omnipotence. Two angels of omnipotence in *The Sixth and Seventh Books of Moses* are Ebuhuel and Atuesuel. They are conjured in the citation of Leviathans. In the dismissal, each angel's name "must be called 3 times toward the 4 quarters of the earth, and 3 times must be blown with the horn."

Emekmiyahu—one of the many names of the angel Metatron.

Emial—in occultism, an angel invoked in the exorcism of the Bat. [*Rf.* Mathers, *The Greater Key of Solomon.*]

Emmanuel ("God with us")—the angel in the fiery furnace who appeared beside Sidras, Misac, and Abednego. In conjuring rites, Emmanuel is summoned up under the 3rd Seal. In de Vigny's poem "Le Déluge," Emmanuel is the name of an angel as well as the name of the son of an angel by a mortal woman. In the cabala, Emmanuel is a sefira of Malkuth (the Kingdom) in the Briatic world. [*Rf.* Ambelain, *La Kabbale Pratique.*]

Empire—an angelic order cited in lieu of virtues in White, *A History of the Warfare of Science with Theology in Christendom.*

Empyrean—in Christian angelology, the empyrean is the abode of God and the angels. To Ptolemy, it is the 5th Heaven, seat of the deity, as it is to Dante and Milton.

Enediel—one of the 28 angels governing the 28 mansions of the moon. Enediel is, specifically, a spirit of the 2nd day of the moon in its waning phase. [*Rf.* Barrett, *The Magus* II; Levi, *Transcendental Magic.*]

Eneije—in occult lore, an angel of the Seal invoked in magical rites.

Enga—one of the ineffable names of God used in Monday conjurations addressed to Lucifer. [*Rf.* Waite, *The Book of Black Magic and of Pacts.*]

Enoch-Metatron—the patriarch Enoch, on his translation to Heaven (Genesis 5:24), became Metatron, one of the greatest of the hierarchs, "king over all the angels." *Cf.* the Assyrian legend in the *Epic of Izdubar.* On earth, as a mortal, Enoch is said to have composed 366 books (the Enoch literature). Legend has it that Enoch-Metatron is twin-brother to Sandalphon (*q.v.*); that when he was glorified he was given 365,000 eyes and 36 pairs of wings. [*Rf.* Ginzberg, *The Legends of the Jews* I.] The spectacular mode of Elijah's conveyance to Heaven, as reported in II Kings 2, had, it seems, an earlier parallel in the case of Enoch, for the latter also was whisked away "in a fiery chariot drawn by fiery chargers," as related in *The Legends of the Jews* I, 130; however, a few pages farther on (p. 138) it transpires that it wasn't a horse or a team of horses, but an angel (Anpiel) who transported the antediluvian patriarch from earth to Heaven. But that may have been on a different journey. To the Arabs, Enoch was Idris (Koran, *sura* 19, 56). In the *Pirke Rabbi Eliezer* the invention of astronomy and arithmetic is laid to Enoch. Legend connects Enoch-Metatron with Behemoth. [*Rf.* Forlong, *Encyclopedia of Religions.*]

En Suf (Ain Soph—"the boundless")—in the cabala, a name for the supreme, invisible, unimaginable creator of the universe, the substance of God which became personalized in the Partsufim. *Cf.* the Zoroastrian Zervan Akarana; the writings of Cordovero and Scholem.

Entities—an order of angels in occult lore. These angels were sheathed in gold lamé. [*Rf.* Ambelain, *La Kabbale Pratique.*]

Enwo—in Mandaean lore, a spirit of one of the 7 planets; specifically he is the *uthra* (angel) of science and wisdom, to be compared wth Raphael in Judaeo-Christian angelology.

Eoluth—a cherub or seraph used for conjuring by cabalists. [*Rf. The Sixth and Seventh Books of Moses.*]

Eomiahe—in occult lore, an angel invoked in the exorcism of the Bat. [*Rf.* Mathers, *The Greater Key of Solomon.*]

Eon [Aeon]

Ephemerae—angels that lived only for a day or less, expiring right after they finished chanting the Te Deum. [*Rf.* Daniel 7:10; Talmud *Hagiga* 14a.]

Epima—the corresponding angel for Eiael (*q.v.*).

Epinoia—in Valentinian gnosticism, the 1st female manifestation of God. *Cf.* the Shekinah, also Holy Ghost (the latter being regarded in some sources as the mother of the living, Zoe, hence female). [*Rf.* Doresse, *The Secret Books of the Egyptian Gnostics*, p. 202.]

Epititiokh—a virgin aeon, mentioned in gnostic lore. [*Rf.* Doresse, *The Secret Books of the Egyptian Gnostics*, p. 178.]

Eradin—the name of an angel invoked in special ceremonial rites. [*Rf.* Waite, *The Book of Black Magic and of Pacts*.]

Erastiel—an angel serving in the 4th division of the 5th Heaven. [*Rf. The Sixth and Seventh Books of Moses*, p. 139.]

Erathaol (Erathaoth)—one of the 7 archons in gnostic theology. Origen (in *Contra Celsum* VI, 30), drawing on Ophitic sources, lists Erathaol or Erathaoth, along with Michael, Raphael, Gabriel, Onoel, Thautabaoth, and Suriel. When invoked, Erathaol manifests in the form of a dog. [*Rf.* Mead, *Thrice-Greatest Hermes* I, 294.]

Erathaoth [Erathaol]

Eregbuo—corresponding angel for the angel Daniel (*q.v.*).

Erel—the name of a holy angel or of God by which demons are commanded to appear in Solomonic conjuration rites. [*Rf.* Mathers, *The Greater Key of Solomon*.]

Erel(l)im or **Arelim** ("the valiant ones")—also called ishim; an order of angels in the celestial hierarchy equated with the order of thrones. The name is derived from Isaiah 33:7. The erelim, composed of white fire, are stationed in the 3rd (or 4th or 5th) Heaven and consist of 70,000 myriads. In Ginzberg, *The Legends of the Jews*, the erelim are said to be appointed over grass, trees, fruit, and grain. They were pointed out to

Moses by Metatron when the Lawgiver visited Paradise. [*Rf. Revelation of Moses.*] Talmud *Kathaboth* 104a speaks of the "angelic order aralim and the most distinguished of men being caught at the sacred ark," and that "the angelic order prevailed, and the sacred ark was captured." The erelim are "one of 10 classes of angels under the rulership of Michael," according to *Maseket Azilut*. [*Rf. 3 Enoch.*]

Eremiel (Jerimiel, Hierimiel, Jeremiel, Remiel, etc.)—an angel who watches over souls in the underworld. In *Apocalypse of Elias* (ed. Steindorff), Eremiel is equated with Uriel. Variants appear in *IV Esdras* and *Apocalypse of Sophonias*.

Ergedial—one of the 28 angels governing the 28 mansions of the moon. [*Rf.* Barrett, *The Magus* II.]

Erionas (Erione)—in occult lore, an angel invoked in the exorcism of Wax. [*Rf.* Gollancz, *Clavicula Salomonis*.]

Ermosiel—an angel of the 2nd hour, serving under Anael.

Ero—the corresponding angel for Haziel (*q.v.*).

Erotosi—planetary genius of Mars, invoked in talismanic magic. [*Rf. The History and Practice of Magic* (I, 68, 317; II, 475). In hermetics, Erotosi is head of the order of powers.

Ertrael—a fallen angel listed in *The Book of Enoch*.

Erygion—the name of an angel (or of God) that Joshua invoked in order to gain victory over the Moabites. [*Rf.* Mathers, *The Greater Key of Solomon*.]

Erzla—in the *Clavicula Salomonis*, a benign angel invoked in conjuring rites.

Esabiel—an angel of the order of powers; he is mentioned in Schwab, *Vocabulaire de l'Angélologie*, suppl.

Escavor—in the *Grimorium Verum*, an angel invoked in Solomonic magical rites.

Eschiel (Eshiel)—one of 4 angels whose names are inscribed on the 1st pentacle of the planet

Mars, the names of the other 3 angels being Ithuriel, Madiniel, and Bortzachiak (Barzachia).

Eschiros—in the cabala, an angel of the 7 planets invoked in conjuring rites. [*Rf. The Secret Grimoire of Turiel.*]

Eserchie/Oriston—the name of an angel (or of God) invoked by Moses when the latter brought forth frogs in Egypt as one of the plagues (frogs were also brought forth by invoking the name of Zabaoth). [*Rf.* Waite, *The Book of Black Magic and of Pacts.*] According to Barrett, *The Magus* II, the name of Eserchie/Oriston was invoked by Moses when turning the rivers of Egypt into blood.

Eshiniel—in *The Book of Protection*, an angel invoked in Syriac spellbinding charms.

Eshmadai—in rabbinic literature, a king of demons; he is compared by some with the Persian Aeshma Deva, by others with the Hebrew Shamad the Destroyer. [*Rf.* Bouisson, *Magic, Its History and Principal Rites*; see Ashmedai.]

Esor—a cherub or a seraph used by cabalists in conjuring rites. [*Rf. The Sixth and Seventh Books of Moses.*]

Esphares—the name of an angel or of God used in conjuring rites. Mentioned in *The Secret Grimoire of Turiel.*

Espiacent—an angel used in the exorcism of Wax for bringing about the successful accomplishment of one's work. Psalms must be cited after the rites of exorcism. [*Rf.* Mathers, *The Greater Key of Solomon.*]

Estael—in black-magic lore (*The Secret Grimoire of Turiel*) Estael is an intelligence of the planet Jupiter. He is usually invoked in the company of 3 other intelligences of the planet—Kadiel, Maltiel, and Huphatriel.

Estes—one of the many names of the angel Metatron.

Eth ("time")—an angelic power, a ministering angel, charged with seeing to it that "all events occur at their appointed time." [*Rf. The Zohar* (Miqez, 194a); *see also* Time.]

Ethan [Ecanus]

Ethnarchs—angels that exercise authority over nations (the tutelary angels, of which there were 70). [*See* Guardian Angels; *Rf.* Danielou, *The Angels and their Mission.*]

Etraphill—one of the Arabic angels who will sound the trumpet on the Day of Judgment. Etraphill is very likely a variant form for Israfel.

Etrempsuchos (Astrompsuchos)—one of the celestial guardians of one of the 7 Heavens. Cited in the Bodleian Library *Bruce Papyrus.*

Euchey—an angel invoked in the exorcism of evil spirits through the application of incense and fumigation. [*Rf. Grimorium Verum.*]

Eudaemon—a good spirit, a daemon. One of the Greek terms for angel.

Eurabatres—an angel of the planet Venus. [*See* Iurabatres.]

Eve [Angel of Humanity]

Eved—one of the many names of the angel Metatron.

Exael—in *Enoch I*, an angel spoken of as the "10th of the great angels that taught men how to fabricate engines of war, works in silver and gold, the uses of gems and perfume," etc. He operates supposedly from the nether regions. [*Rf.* De Plancy, *Dictionnaire Infernal.*]

Exercitus—an appellation (like Strateia, *q.v.*) for an angelic host. [*Rf. Pesikta Rabbati* XV, 69a; "Angelology," in *Jewish Encyclopedia.*]

Existon—an angel invoked in the benediction of the Salt. Existon is cited in *The Greater Key of Solomon.*

Exousia—the Greek term for the angelic order translated variously as power, authority, virtue, in the New Testament. To Steiner (*The Work of the Angels in Man's Astral Body*) the exousia are "Spirits of Form" in the angelic hierarchy.

Extabor—"one of the fair angels of God" employed in the exorcism of Wax. Extabor is mentioned in Gollancz, *Clavicula Salomonis* and in Shah, *Occultism*, p. 23.

Exterminans—the Latin name for Abaddon (*q.v.*). [*Rf.* Confraternity (Catholic) New Testament in its version of Revelation 9:11.]

Ezeqeel (Hebrew, "strength of God")—in *Enoch I*, a fallen angel who taught "augury from the clouds." [*Rf.* Ginzberg, *The Legends of the Jews* I, 125.]

Ezgadi—an angel's name used in conjuring rites for insuring the successful completion of journeys. Mentioned in *Hechaloth Rabbati*. [*Rf.* Schwab, *Vocabulaire de l'Angélologie*.]

Ezoiil—a spirit (angel?) invoked in the exorcism of the Water. [*Rf.* Mathers, *The Greater Key of Solomon*.]

Ezra—the *Apocalypse of Esdras* (IV Esdras), referring to Ezra's translation to Heaven, thereafter accounts him "the scribe of the Most High, for ever and ever." *Cf.* Vretil, Enoch, Dabriel, all of whom are also accounted celestial scribes.

Ezrael (Hebrew "help of God")—an angel of wrath, as cited in the *Apocalypse of Peter*. In *Sefer Gan Eden* an angel is introduced "whose duty it is to save those of 'middle merit' or 'the unstable' ones from the angels of destruction; that angel is Ezrael (from ezra—help)." [*Rf. 3 Enoch*, p. 182.]

Ezriel—an angel's name found inscribed in an Aramaic amulet discovered among the recent Dead Sea scrolls. Ezriel is referred to as an archangel in Montgomery's *Aramaic Incantation Texts from Nippur*. [*Rf.* Scholem, *Jewish Gnosticism, Merkabah Mysticism, and Talmudic Tradition*.]

Fallen Angels. A 12th-century French-Spanish conception, in the Bibliothèque Nationale. Reproduced from Régamey, *Anges*.

Fabriel—an angel serving in the 4th Heaven. [*Rf. The Sixth and Seventh Books of Moses.*]

Faith—one of the 3 theological virtues (with hope and charity) depicted as angels by 15th-century Florentine masters.

Fakr-Ed-Din ("poor one of faith")—one of the 7 archangels in Yezidic religion. He is invoked in prayer. For the names of the other 6 Yezidic archangels, *see* Appendix. [*Rf. Forlong, Encyclopedia of Religions.*]

Fallen Angels—the notion of fallen angels is not found in the Old Testament. In books like Job, the God-appointed adversary is *ha-satan* (meaning "the adversary" and the title of an office, not the designation or name of an angel). The possible exceptions are I Chronicles 21 and II Samuel 24, where Satan seems to emerge as a distinct personality and is identified by name; but scholars are inclined to believe that in these 2 instances the definite article was inadvertently omitted in translation and that the original read "the satan," i.e., "the adversary." In the New Testament, specifically in Revelation 12, the notion of a fallen angel and of fallen angels is spelt out: "And his [the dragon's or Satan's] tail drew the third part of the stars of heaven [angels] and did cast them to earth . . . and Satan, which deceiveth the whole world; he was cast out into the earth and his angels were cast out with him." *Enoch I* claims that 200 fell, naming about 19 (allowing for variant spellings and repetitions) and listing "chiefs of ten," the most prominent among them being Semyaza, Azazel, Sariel, Rumiel, Danjal, Turel, Kokabel. In Ginzberg, *The Legends of the Jews* I, 125, the chiefs are given as Shemhazai (Semyaza), Armaros, Barakel, Kawkabel (Kokabel), Ezekeel, Arakiel, Samsaweel, Seriel. William Auvergne, bishop of Paris (1228–1249), in his *De Universo*, held that, of the 9 orders of angels that were created, a "10th part fell," some (as Cardinal Pullus also claimed) from each order, and that in their fallen state they retained their relative rank. [*Rf. Lea, Materials Toward a History of Witchcraft* I, 89.] According to Cardinal Bishop of Tusculum (1273), reaffirmed by Alphonso de Spina (c. 1460), the one-third that fell totaled 133,306,668, those

111

that remained loyal 266,613,336. As opposed to the contention that angels fell from each of the 9 orders, an opinion backed by papal authority holds that only the angels of the 10th (sic) order fell. The question is, which of the 9 orders is the 10th. [See Moore's *The Loves of the Angels*, p. 155.] In this book, Moore quotes Tertullian (*De Habitu Mulieb*) to the effect that all the chief luxuries of female adornment and enticement—"the necklaces, armlets, rouge, and the black powder for the eye-lashes" are to be traced to the researches and discoveries of the fallen angels. After the apostate angels fell, "the rest were confirmed in the perseverance of eternal beatitude," as Isidor of Seville assures us in his *Sententiae*—although Bible references to God's finding his angels (long after the Fall) untrustworthy point to a contrary conclusion. The cause of Satan's downfall has commonly been attributed to the sin of pride or of ambition ("by that sin fell the angels"). Another explanation sometimes offered with regard to the origin of fallen angels goes back to Genesis 6, where the sons of God (angels) "saw the daughters of men . . . and took them wives" from among them. Enoch saw 7 great stars like burning mountains which (so Enoch's guide told him) were being punished because they failed to rise at the appointed time. In other early writings, fallen angels were said to be shooting stars. Aquinas identified the fallen angels with demons. The Christian writers of the later Middle Ages looked upon all heathen divinities as demons. In most sources, the leader of the apostates is Satan, but in apocryphal writings the leader has also been called Mastema, Beliar (Beliel), Azazel, Belzebub, Sammael, etc. In Mohammedan lore he is Iblis. In *Levi 3* (*Testament of the Twelve Patriarchs*) the fallen angels are "imprisoned in the 2nd Heaven." *Enoch II*, 7:1 also speaks of the fallen angels in the 2nd Heaven as "prisoners suspended [there], reserved for [and] awaiting the eternal judgment." "In most Jewish literature," says Caird in *Principalities and Powers*, "it was on account of mankind that the angels fell," and cites the *Apocalypse of Baruch* which goes so far as to say that it was "the physical nature of man which not only became a danger to his own soul, but resulted in the fall of the angels." According to legend (Budge, *Amulets and Talismans*) the rebel angels fell for 9 days.

Famiel—a Friday angel of the air. Famiel serves in the 3rd Heaven and is invoked from the south.

Fanuel (Phanuel)—one of the 4 angels of the presence, as noted in *Ezra IV*, where Fanuel is said to be "Uriel under another aspect." But *see* Phanuel, where he is equated with Raguel, Ramiel, the Shepherd of Hermes, etc.

Farris—a governing angel of the 2nd hour of the night. [*See* Praxil.]

Farun Faro Vakshur—in ancient Persian theogony, the protecting angel of mankind. *Cf.* Metatron in Judaeo-Christian occult lore, where he is often referred to as the "sustainer of mankind."

Farvardin—angel of March (in ancient Persian lore). Farvardin also governed the 19th day of each month. He is called "one of the cherubim." [*Rf. The Dabistan*, pp. 35–36.]

Favashi (Pravashi, Farohars, Ferouers, Fervers, Farchers)—in Zoroastrianism, the celestial prototype of all created beings, the guardian angels of believers. They possessed a dual character or nature: angels on the one hand and, on the other, beings with human qualities, attributes, and thoughts. They were the fravardin of the Zend-Avesta, "female genii dwelling in all things and protectors of mankind." In Jacob Wassermann's novel *Dr. Kerkhoven*, the favashi are defined as "part of the human soul yet independent of the body . . . not destructible like the conscience and the mind . . . neither are they assigned to one and the same body; they may find themselves another body, provided it belongs to the pure." [*Rf.* Gaynor, *Dictionary of Mysticism*; Heckethorn, *The Secret Societies of All Ages and Countries* I, 25; King, *The Gnostics and Their Remains*.]

Feluth [Silat]

Female Angels—in Jewish occult lore, female angels are rare (the Shekinah is one). In gnostic lore there is, pre-eminently, Pistis Sophia ("faith, knowledge"), a great female aeon or archon, or angel. In Arabic legend, female angels are not uncommon and were often objects of worship or veneration; they were called *benad hasche*, that is, daughters of God.

Ferchers [Favashi]

Fiery Angel [Angel of Fire]

Fifth Heaven—the empyrean, seat of God and the angels—according to Ptolemy. Here "crouch the gigantic fallen angels in silent and everlasting despair," says Graves in *Hebrew Myths*, p. 36. These were the grigori, who were in the "northern" regions. Elsewhere in the 5th Heaven, whither a spirit carried him, the prophet Zephaniah beheld "angels that are called lords, and each of the angels had a crown upon his head as well as a throne shining 7 times brighter than the light of the sun"—quoted by Clement of Alexandria from the lost *Apocalypse of Zephaniah*. The prince guardian of the 5th Heaven is Shatqiel (*q.v.*). In Islamic lore, the 5th Heaven is the "seat of Aaron and the Avenging Angel."

Fire-Speaking Angel—Hashmal.

First Heaven, The—in Islamic lore, the abode of the stars, "each with its angel warder." It is also the abode of Adam and Eve.

Five Angels Who Lead the Souls of Men to Judgment—Arakiel, Remiel, Uriel, Samiel, Aziel [*Rf. Sibylline Oracles* II; *see* Angels at the End of the World.]

Flaef—in the cabala, an angelic luminary concerned with human sexuality. [*Rf.* Masters, *Eros and Evil.*]

Flame of the Whirling Swords—a term applied to the cherubim who guarded Eden.

Flames—an order of angels, "one of the classes in Talmud and Targum," says Voltaire in his "Of Angels, Genii, and Devils." Chief of the order is Melha who, in Buddhist theogony, is identified with the Judaeo-Christian angel Michael. [*Cf.* chashmallim, the "scintillating flames" in Ezekiel 4.]

Flaming Angel, The [Angel of Fire]

Flauros [Hauras]

Focalor (Forcalor, Furcalor)—before he fell, Focalor was an angel of the order of thrones. This "fact" was "proved after infinite research," reports Spence in *An Encyclopaedia of Occultism*, p. 119. Focalor is a mighty duke in the infernal regions and commands 30 legions of demonic spirits. His special office or mission is to sink ships of war and slay men. After 1,000 years (or 1,500 years) he "hopes to return to the 7th Heaven," as he confided to Solomon. When invoked, Focalor manifests as a man with the wings of a griffin. Focalor is an anagram for Rofocale (*q.v.*). For Focalor's sigil, see Waite, *The Book of Black Magic and of Pacts*, p. 178.

Forcalor [Focalor]

Forcas (Foras, Forras, Furcas, Fourcas)—in occult lore it is not indicated what rank Forcas once held in the angelic hierarchy, or to what order he belonged; but he is a fallen angel; in Hell he is a renowned president or duke; and here he devotes his time to teaching rhetoric, logic, and mathematics. He can render people invisible; he knows also how to restore lost property. De Plancy, *Dictionnaire Infernal*, calls Forcas a chevalier of the infernal kingdom, with 29 legions of demons to do his bidding. His sigil is shown in Waite, *The Book of Black Magic and of Pacts*, p. 175. [*Rf.* Scot, *Discoverie of Witchcraft*; Wierus, *Pseudo-Monarchia.*] A Louis Breton engraving of Forcas is reproduced in Seligmann, *The History of Magic*, p. 230.

Forces—in the view of John of Damascus, forces constitute an angelic order sometimes identified as powers, sometimes as virtues or authorities. John of Damascus places forces 3rd in the 2nd triad of the 9 choirs. Their special duty is or was to govern earthly affairs.

Forerunner Angel, The [John the Baptist; Metatron; Shekinah]

Forfax (Morax, Marax)—in Scot's *Discoverie of Witchcraft*, a great earl and president of the underworld in command of 36 legions of spirits; he gives skill in astronomy and liberal arts. He is also called Foraii (by Weirus). Manifests in the form of a heifer. His sign is reproduced in Shah, *The Secret Lore of Magic*.

Forneus—before he fell, Forneus was of the order of thrones and partly also of the order of angels. In the underworld he is a great marquis, with 29 legions of infernal spirits ready to carry out his commands. In addition to teaching art, rhetoric, and all languages, he causes men to be loved by their enemies. The sigil of Forneus is shown in Waite, *The Book of Black Magic and of Pacts*, p. 174. It is said that, when he is invoked, Forneus manifests in the form of a sea monster.

Fortitude—one of the cardinal virtues, depicted by the 15th-century Florentine masters as an angel.

Four Angels—Revelation 7 speaks of the 4 angels "standing on the 4 corners of the earth,

The Angel Fortitude. Enameled terracotta roundel by Luca della Robbia in the Church of San Miniato al Monte, Florence, 1461–1466. From *The Metropolitan Museum of Art Bulletin*, December 1961.

holding the 4 winds of the earth." The angels are not named. [*See* Angels of the Four Winds.]

Four Angels of the East—in the *Clavicula Salomonis*, the 4 angels of the east are Urzla, Zlar, Larzod, and Arzal. They are "benevolent and glorious angels" and are invoked "so that the invocant may partake of some of the secret wisdom of the Creator."

Four Archangels—as listed in *Enoch I*, the 4 archangels are Michael, Raphael, Gabriel, Phanuel. In the *Universal Standard Encyclopaedia* the 4 are given as Michael, Gabriel, Uriel, and Suriel (the last name being equated with Raphael). According to Arabic traditional lore, the 4 are: Gabriel, angel of revelation; Michael, who fights the battle of faith; Azrael, angel of death; and Israfel, who will sound the trumpet at the Resurrection.

Fourcas [Forcas]

Four Spirits of the Heaven—angels in the guise of black, white, grizzled, and bay horses "which go forth from standing before the Lord of all the earth" (Zechariah 6). The horses, harnessed to chariots, were shown to the Old Testament prophet by an angel (unnamed). In rabbinic lore, Zechariah, 300 years before Daniel, had already graded angels according to rank, but did not name them. It is said, further, that Zechariah drew his inspiration for the "seven eyes of the Lord" (Zechariah 4) from the Parsee archangels, the amesha spentas.

Fourth Angel, The—John, in Revelation 8, speaks of the 4th angel as one of the 7 angels of wrath who sound trumpets. When the trumpet of the 4th angel is sounded, a 3rd part of the sun is smitten, and a 3rd part of the moon, and a 3rd part of the stars.

Fourth Heaven—the abode of Shamshiel, Sapiel, Zagzagel, and Michael. According to Talmud *Hagiga* 12, it contained the heavenly Jerusalem, the temple, and the altar. Here, too, dwelt Sandalphon, angel of tears. [*Rf.* Brewer, *Dictionary of Phrase and Fable*, p. 537.] It was in the 4th Heaven that Mohammed encountered Enoch. [*Rf.* Hughes, *A Dictionary of Islam*, "Angels."]

Fowl of Heaven [Angels of Service]

Fraciel—a Tuesday angel of the 5th Heaven, invoked from the north. [*Rf.* de Abano, *The Heptameron*; Barrett, *The Magus* II.]

Framoch—in Waite, *The Lemegeton*, an angel of the 7th hour of the night, under Mandrion.

Francis, St. [Rhamiel; *see also* St. Francis]

Fravardin [Favashi]

Fravashi [Favashi]

Fravishi [Favashi]

Fremiel—in de Abano, *The Heptameron* and Waite, *The Lemegeton*, an angel of the 4th hour of the night, serving under Jefischa.

Friagne—in occult texts generally, a Tuesday angel serving in the 5th Heaven and invoked from the east.

Fromezin—an angel of the 2nd hour of the night under the command of Farris. [*Rf.* Waite, *The Lemegeton.*]

Fromzon—an angel of the 3rd hour of the night, serving under Sarquamich.

Fuleriel—angel of the 6th hour of the night, serving under Zaazonash.

Furiel—an angel of the 3rd hour of the day, serving under Veguaniel.

Furlac (Phorlakh)—in occult science, an angel of the earth. [*Rf.* Papus, *Traité Élémentaire de Science Occulte.*]

Furmiel—an angel of the 11th hour of the day, serving under Bariel.

Fustiel—an angel of the 5th hour of the day, serving under Sazquiel.

Futiniel—an angel of the 5th hour of the day, serving under Sazquiel.

Gabriel pictured in the "Annunciation" by Melozzo Da Forli (1438–1494). Reproduced from Régamey, *Anges.*

Gaap (Tap)—once of the order of potentates (powers), now a fallen angel, Gaap serves, in Hell, as a "great president and a mighty prince." As king of the south, he rules 66 legions of infernal spirits. His sigil is reproduced in *The Book of Black Magic and of Pacts*, p. 176. [See also *The Book of Ceremonial Magic* and the *Lesser Key of Solomon* (the latter known also as *The Lemegeton*).] Gaap is pictured in De Plancy, *Dictionnaire Infernal*, 1863 ed., in the form of a human being with huge bat's wings.

Gabamiah—in Solomonic goetic rites, a great angel invoked by the use of the incantatory power of the name of the angel Uriel. [*Rf. Grimorium Verum.*]

Gabriel ("God is my strength")—one of the 2 highest-ranking angels in Judaeo-Christian and Mohammedan religious lore. He is the angel of annunciation, resurrection, mercy, vengeance, death, revelation. Apart from Michael, he is the only angel mentioned by name in the Old Testament—unless we include among the Old Testament books the *Book of Tobit*, usually considered

apocryphal, in which case Raphael, who appears there, becomes the 3rd-named angel in Scripture (but see Gustav Davidson's article "The Named Angels in Scripture," wherein no less than 7 angels are named). Gabriel presides over Paradise, and although he is the ruling prince of the 1st Heaven, he is said to sit on the left-hand side of God (whose dwelling is popularly believed to be the 7th Heaven, or the 10th Heaven). Mohammed claimed it was Gabriel (Jibril in Islamic) of the "140 pairs of wings" who dictated to him the Koran, *sura* by *sura*. To the Mohammedans, Gabriel is the spirit of truth. In Jewish legend it was Gabriel who dealt death and destruction to the sinful cities of the plain (Sodom and Gommorah among them). And it was Gabriel who, according to Talmud *Sanhedrin* 95b, smote Sennacherib's hosts "with a sharpened scythe which had been ready since Creation." Elsewhere in Talmud it is Gabriel who, it is said, prevented Queen Vashti from appearing naked before King Ahasuerus and his guests in order to bring about the election of Esther in her place. In Daniel 8, Daniel falls on his face before Gabriel to learn the meaning of the encounter

117

Leonardo da Vinci's conception of Gabriel, a detail from the *Annunciation*, in the Uffizi Gallery, Florence. Reproduced from Régamey, *Anges*.

between the ram and the he-goat. The incident is pictured in a woodcut in the famous Cologne Bible. Cabalists identify Gabriel as "the man clothed in linen" (Exekiel 9, 10 ff.). In Daniel 10–11 this man clothed in linen is helped by Michael. In rabbinic literature, Gabriel is the prince of justice [*Rf.* Cordovero, *Palm Tree of Deborah,* p. 56.] Origen in *De Principiis* I, 81, calls Gabriel the angel of war. Jerome equates Gabriel with Hamon (*q.v.*). According to Milton (*Paradise Lost* IV, 549) Gabriel is chief of the angelic guards placed over Paradise. As for the incident of the 3 holy men (Hananiah, Mishael, Azariah) who were rescued from the furnace, it was Gabriel, according to Jewish legend, who performed this miracle. Other sources credit Michael. Gabriel is likewise identified as the man-God-angel who wrestled with Jacob at Peniel, although Michael, Uriel, Metatron, Samael, and Chamuel have also been put forward as "the dark antagonist." Rembrandt did a canvas of the celebrated encounter. A Mohammedan legend, growing out of the Koran, *sura* 20, 88, relates that when the dust from the hoofprints of Gabriel's horse was thrown into the mouth of the Golden Calf, the Calf at once became animated. According to the *Encyclopaedia of Islam* I, 502, Mohammed confused Gabriel with the Holy Ghost—a confusion understandable or explainable by virtue of the conflicting accounts in Matthew 1:20 and Luke 1:26 where, in the 1st instance, it is the Holy Ghost that begets Mary with Child and, in the 2nd instance, it is Gabriel who "came in unto her," and also then informs her that she "had found favor with the Lord" and "would conceive in her womb." In Bamberger's *Fallen Angels,* p. 109, quoting a Babylonian legend, Gabriel once fell into disgrace "for not obeying a command exactly as given, and remained for a while outside the heavenly Curtain." During this period the guardian angel of Persia, Dobiel, acted as Gabriel's proxy. The name Gabriel is of Chaldean origin and was unknown to the Jews prior to the Captivity. In the original listing of 119 angels of the Parsees, Gabriel's name is missing. Gabriel is the preceptor angel of Joseph. In Midrash *Eleh Ezkerah,* Gabriel figures in the tale of the legendary 10 Martyrs (Jewish sages). One of these 10, Rabbi Ishmael ascends to Heaven and asks Gabriel why they merit death. Gabriel replies that they are atoning for the sin of the 10 sons of Jacob who sold Joseph into slavery. According to the court testimony of Joan of Arc, it was Gabriel who inspired her to go to the succor of the King of France. In more recent times, Gabriel figures as the angel who visited Father George Rapp, leader of the 2nd Advent community in New Harmony, Indiana, and left his footprint on a limestone slab preserved in the yard of the Maclure-Owen residence in that city. Longfellow's *The Golden Legend* makes Gabriel the angel of the moon who brings man the gift of hope. There are innumerable paintings by the masters of the Annunciation with Gabriel pictured as the angel who brings the glad tidings to Mary. Word-pictures of the event, in rhyme, are rare. One of these is by the 17th-century English poet, Richard Crashaw. The quatrain is from *Steps to the Temple*: "Heavens Golden-winged Herald, late hee saw/To a poor Galilean virgin sent./How low the Bright Youth bow'd, and with what awe/Immortall flowers to her faire hand present."

Gabuthelon—an angel whose name was revealed to Esdras as among the 9 who will govern "at the end of the world." Apart from Gabuthelon, the others are: Michael, Gabriel, Uriel, Raphael, and Aker, Arphugitonos, Beburos, Zebuleon. [See *Revelation of Esdras* in the *Ante-Nicene Fathers Library* VIII, 573.]

Gadal—an angel invoked in magic rites, according to Waite, *The Book of Ceremonial Magic,* p. 155.

Gadamel [Hagiel]

Gader—in hechaloth lore (*Ma'asseh Merkabah*), an angelic guard stationed at the 4th heavenly hall.

Gadiel—a "most holy angel" invoked in goetic operations, as directed in Mathers, *The Greater Key of Solomon.* Gadiel is a resident of the 5th Heaven. [*Rf. The Sixth and Seventh Books of Moses.*] In *Ozar Midrashim* II, 316, Gadiel is one of numerous angelic guards of the gates of the

South Wind. The fact that Gadiel's name is found inscribed on an oriental charm (*kamea*) suggests that he must have been regarded as a power to protect the wearer against evil. [*Rf.* Schrire, *Hebrew Amulets.*]

Gadreel (Gadriel—Aramaic, "God is my helper")—one of the fallen angels in Enoch lore. It was Gadreel who, reputedly, led Eve astray—which, if true, would make Gadreel rather than Satan the talking serpent and seducer in the Garden of Eden. Like Azazel, Gadreel made man familiar with the weapons of war (*Enoch I*, 69, 6). The *IV Book of Maccabees* refers to the seduction of Eve, but speaks of her as protesting that "no false beguiling serpent" sullied "the purity of my maidenhood." Gadreel is not mentioned by name in this source.

Gadriel—chief ruling angel of the 5th Heaven in charge of wars among nations. [*See* Gadreel.] When a prayer ascends to Heaven, Gadriel crowns it, then accompanies it to the 6th Heaven. [*Rf. The Zohar* (Exodus 202a).] Sandalphon, another great angel, is also said to crown prayers for transmission—not, however, from heaven to heaven, but direct from man to God.

Ga'ga—in hechaloth lore (*Ma'asseh Merkabah*), an angelic guard stationed at the 7th heavenly hall.

Gaghiel—an angelic guard of the 6th Heaven. [*Rf. Ozar Midrashim* I, 116.]

Galdel—a Tuesday angel resident of the 5th Heaven; he is to be invoked from the south. [*Rf.* de Abano, *The Heptameron*; Barrett, *The Magus* II.]

Galearii ("army servants")—according to the *Jewish Encyclopedia*, "Angelology," the galearii are angels of the lowest rank. [*Rf.* Friedmann, *Pesikta Rabbati* V, 45b and XV, 69a.]

Gale Raziya—one of the many names of the angel Metatron.

Galgaliel (Galgliel)—with Raphael, Galgaliel serves as a chief angel of the sun. He is also credited with being the angel governing the wheel of the sun, and as the eponymous head of the order of galgallim.

Galgal(l)im ("spheres")—a superior order of angels of a rank equal to the seraphim. The galgallim are called "the wheels of the Merkabah" (i.e., chariots of God) and are equated with the ophanim (*q.v.*). There are 8 ruling angels in the order, with Galgaliel or Rikbiel generally designated as chief. [*Rf. Pirke Hechaloth*; Odeberg, *3 Enoch.*] The galgallim share with the other Merkabah angels in the performance of the Celestial Song.

Galgliel [Galgaliel]

Galiel—one of the many names of the angel Metatron.

Galizur (Hebrew, "revealer of the rock"—Gallitzur, Gallizur, Raziel, Raguil, Akrasiel)—one of the great angels in Talmudic lore whom Moses encountered in Heaven, as related by Simon ben Lakish. It was Galizur, "surnamed Raziel," who is reputed to have given Adam *The Book of the Angel Raziel* (but *see* Rahab). He is a ruling prince of the 2nd Heaven and an expounder of the Torah's divine wisdom. "He spreads his wings over the hayyoth lest their fiery breath consume the ministering angels." (The hayyoth are the holy beasts who "uphold the universe.") [*Rf. Pirke Rabbi Eliezer*; *Pesikta Rabbati.*]

Gallizur [Galizur]

Galmon—in hechaloth lore (*Ma'asseh Merkabah*), an angelic guard stationed at the 4th heavenly hall.

Gamaliel (Hebrew, "recompense of God")—in the cabala and gnostic writings, one of the great aeons or luminaries, a beneficent spirit associated with Gabriel, Abraxas, Mikhar, and Samlo. However, Levi in his *Philosophie Occulte* rates Gamaliel as evil, "an adversary of the cherubim" serving under Lilith (who is the demon of debauchery). In the *Revelation of Adam to His Son Seth* (a Coptic apocalypse), Gamaliel is one of the high, holy, celestial powers whose mission is "to draw the elect up to Heaven."

Gambiel—ruler of the zodiacal sign of Aquarius, as cited in Camfield, *A Theological Discourse of Angels*. He is mentioned also in *The Sixth and Seventh Books of Moses* as a zodiacal angel.

Gambriel—one of the guardian angels of the 5th Heaven. [*Rf. Pirke Hechaloth*.]

Gamerin—in ceremonial magical rites, an angel called in for special service, according to Waite, *The Book of Ceremonial Magic*, p. 160, quoting from the *Grimorium Verum*. The name Gamerin should be engraved on the Sword of the Art, before the start of the conjuring rite.

Gamidoi—a "most holy angel" invoked in magical operations, as directed in Mathers, *The Greater Key of Solomon*.

Gamiel—supreme ruling angel of the 1st hour of the night, according to Waite, *The Lemegeton*.

Gamorin Debabim (Gamerin)—an angel invoked in the conjuration of the Sword. [*Rf.* Mathers, *The Greater Key of Solomon*.]

Gamrial—one of the 64 angel wardens of the 7 celestial halls. [*Rf. Pirke Hechaloth*.]

Gamsiel—angel of the 8th hour of the night, serving under Narcoriel.

Ganael—one of the 7 planetary rulers (Electors) serving under the joint rule of the angels Apudiel and Camael. [*Rf.* Conybeare, *The Testament of Solomon*.]

Gardon—an angel invoked in the benediction of the Salt, according to Mathers, *The Greater Key of Solomon*.

Garfial (Garfiel)—one of the guardians of the 5th Heaven. [*Rf. Pirke Hechaloth*.]

Gargatel—one of the 3 angels of the summer; he acts in association with Tariel and Gaviel. [*Rf.* de Abano, *The Heptameron*; Barrett, *The Magus* II.]

Gariel—an angel of the order of shinanim, according to Hayim Haziz, "The Seraph," *The Literary Review*, Spring 1958. In *Hechaloth Rabbati*, Gariel is an angelic guard of the 5th Heaven.

Garshanel—an angelic name found inscribed on an oriental charm (*kamea*) for warding off evil. [*Rf.* Schrire, *Hebrew Amulets*.]

Garthiel—chief officer angel of the 1st hour of the night, serving under Gamiel. [*Rf.* Waite, *The Lemegeton*.]

Garzanal—an angel's name found inscribed on an oriental charm (*kamea*) for warding off evil. [*Rf.* Schrire, *Hebrew Amulets*.]

Gaspard—a spirit invoked in Solomonic magical rites to procure to the invocant a lady's garter. [*Rf. Grimorium Verum*; Shah, *The Secret Lore of Magic*.]

Gastrion—an angel of the 8th hour of the night, serving under Narcoriel.

Gat(h)iel—one of the angelic guards of the 5th Heaven. [*Rf. Ozar Midrashim* I, 116.]

Gauriil Ishliha—a Talmudic angel who presides over the east. [*Cf.* Gazardiel.] His duty is to see to it that the sun rises every morning at the right

A Syriac amulet. Gabriel on a white horse spearing the body of the devil-woman (evil eye). British Museum Ms. Orient, No. 6673. Reproduced from Budge, *Amulets and Talismans*.

time. Gauriil also appears in Mandaean lore and corresponds to the Zoroastrian Sraosha or to the Hebrew Gabriel.

Gaviel—with Gargatel and Tariel, Gaviel serves as one of the 3 angels of the summer. [*Rf.* Barrett, *The Magus* II; de Abano, *The Heptameron.*]

Gavreel (Gavriel)—a variant for Gabriel used by the Ethiopian Hebrew Rabbinical College of the Black Jews of Harlem (New York). To this sect there are 4 cardinal angels (of whom Gavreel is one) and they are to be invoked for the curing of disease, the restoring of sight, turning enemies into friends, and "keeping the invocant from going crazy in the night." The other 3 cardinal angels are Micharel (for Michael), Owreel (for Uriel), and Rafarel (for Raphael). [*Rf.* Brotz, *The Black Jews of Harlem*, pp. 32–33.] In *Ozar Midrashim* Gavreel is one of numerous angelic guards of the gates of the East Wind. In hechaloth lore (*Ma'asseh Merkabah*), he is an angelic guard stationed either at the 2nd or 4th heavenly hall.

Gazardiel (Casardia, Gazardiya)—chief angelic supervisor of the east. Gazardiel "kisses the prayers of the faithful and conveys them to the supernal firmament," as related in *The Zohar*. Hyde mentions Gazardiel in *Historia Religionis Veterum Persarum*. In De Plancy, *Dictionnaire Infernal*, Gazardiel is a Talmudic angel charged with the rising and setting of the sun. Régamey in *What Is An Angel?*, speaking of "later Judaism teaching the names of the angels of the elements," refers to Casardia (i.e., Gazardiel) as having to "see to it that the sun rose every day at the right time and set at the right time."

Gazarniel—an angel of "flame of fire" who sought to oppose and wound Moses at the time that the Lawgiver visited Heaven. Moses routed Gazarniel, we are told, "by pronouncing the Holy Name consisting of 12 letters." (*Note*: the only reference so far come upon to Gazarniel is in Raskin, *Kabbalah, Book of Creation, Zohar*. Mr. Raskin may have intended Hadraniel, and 72 letters rather than 12.)

Gazriel—one of 70 childbed amulet angels. [*See* Appendix.]

Gdiel [Gediel]

Geal—in hechaloth lore (*Ma'asseh Merkabah*), an angelic guard stationed at the 5th heavenly hall.

Gebiel—an angel of the 4th altitude. [*Rf.* Waite, *The Almadel of Solomon.*]

Gebril—an angel invoked in conjuring rites. [*Rf. The Sixth and Seventh Books of Moses.*]

Geburael (Geburah)—a sefira of the Briatic world who figures frequently in cabalistic conjuring operations. In *The Ancient's Book of Magic*, Geburah or Geburael (meaning strength) is equated with Gamaliel and it is said that the influence of Elohi (God) "penetrates the angel Geburah (or Gamaliel) and descends through the sphere of [the planet] Mars." For additional facts about this angel, *see* Geburah.

Geburah or **Geburael** ("divine power or strength")—an angel who is the upholder of the left hand of God. In occult works, Geburah is usually listed as 5th of the 10 holy sefiroth (divine emanations). He is also of the order of seraphim. Identified variously as Gemaliel, Khamael (Camael) and, in Isaac ha-Cohen of Soria's text, as Geviririon.

Geburathiel—the angel of geburah. In *3 Enoch* (the Hebrew Enoch), Geburat(h)iel is one of the great angel princes representing "the divine strength, might, and power." He is the chief steward of the 4th hall in the 7th Heaven.

Gedael (Giadaiyal, "fortune of God")—in *Enoch I* Gedael is an angel of one of the seasons. Cornelius Agrippa cites Gedael (Gediel) as a governing angel of the zodiac. [*Rf.* Cornelius Agrippa, *Three Books of Occult Philosophy* III.]

Gedariah—a supervising chief *sar* (angel) of the 3rd Heaven, as noted in *The Zohar*. Gedariah ministers 3 times a day; he bows to prayers ascending from the 2nd Heaven, crowns such prayers, then transmits them for further ascent.

Gedemel—a spirit of Venus, of which planet the angel Hagiel is the presiding intelligence, according to Paracelsus in his doctrine of Talis-

Musical angels by Hans Memling (c. 1490). Reproduced from E. H. Gombrich, *The Story of Art*. New York: Oxford University Press, 1951.

mans. [*Rf.* Christian, *The History and Practice of Magic* I, 315.]

Gediel (Gdiel)—in *The Almadel of Solomon*, Gediel is one of the chief princes in the 4th chora or altitude. In *The Book of the Angel Raziel*, Gediel figures as one of the 70 childbed amulet angels; he is also, in occult lore, an angel of the zodiac.

Gedobonai—an angel of the 3rd chora or altitude invoked in magical prayer, as set forth in *The Almadel of Solomon*.

Gedudiel—in hechaloth lore (*Ma'asseh Merkabah*), an angelic guard stationed at the 7th heavenly hall.

Gedudim—a class of angels of the Song-Uttering Choirs under the leadership of Tagas. [*Rf. 3 Enoch*.]

Gedulael—one of the sefiroth (divine emanations) invoked in cabalistic rites. [*Rf.* Levi, *Transcendental Magic*.]

Gehatsitsa—in hechaloth lore (*Ma'asseh Merkabah*), an angelic guard stationed at the 5th heavenly hall.

Gehegiel—an angelic guard of the 6th Heaven. [*Rf. Pirke Hechaloth*.]

Gehirael—in hechaloth lore (*Ma'asseh Merkabah*), an angelic guard stationed at the 7th heavenly hall.

Gehorey—in hechaloth lore (*Ma'asseh Merkabah*), an angelic guard stationed at the 7th heavenly hall.

Gehoriel—in hechaloth lore (*Ma'asseh Merkabah*), an angelic guard stationed at the 1st heavenly hall.

Gehuel—in hechaloth lore (*Ma'asseh . Merkabah*), an angelic guard stationed at the 6th heavenly hall.

Geliel—one of the 28 angels who govern the 28 mansions of the moon.

Gelomiros—an angel of the 3rd chora or altitude invoked in magical prayer, as set forth in *The Almadel of Solomon*.

Geminiel—one of the governing angels of the zodiac. [*Rf.* Cornelius Agrippa, *Three Books of Occult Philosophy*, III.]

Gemmut—in *Pistis Sophia*, a Coptic work, Gemmut is an archon who serves under the rulership of Kalapatauroth (who causes all aeons and all destinies to revolve).

Genaritzod—a chief officer-angel of the 7th hour of the night, serving under Mendrion. [*Rf.* Waite, *The Lemegeton*, 69.]

Genii of Fire—in occultism, there are 3 genii of fire: Anael, king of astral light; Michael, king of the sun; and Sammael, king of volcanoes. [*Rf.* Jobes, *Dictionary of Mythology, Folklore and Symbols*.]

Genius (pl. genii)—another name for angel or spirit or intelligence. [*Cf.* Blake: "the forms of all things are derived from their Genius, which by the Ancients was call'd an Angel & Spirit &

Demon"; *Rf.* Blake, *All Religions Are One,
First Principle.*] Paul Christian in *The History
and Practice of Magic* I, 303, says: "the genii of the
orient [were] the originals of the Christian angels."
Athanasius Kircher, 17th-century Jesuit, in his
voyage to the planets, accompanied by the genius
Cosmiel, finds the genii (whom he dubs "sinister")
inhabiting the planet Saturn. According to
Kircher, the genii "administer divine justice to the
wicked, and suffering to the righteous."

Genius of Bestial Love [Schiekron]

Genius of the Contretemps [Angel of the
Odd]

Geno—an angel of the order of powers. [*Rf.
The Sixth and Seventh Books of Moses.*]

Genon—an angel of the 2nd chora or altitude
invoked in magical prayer. [*Rf. The Almadel of
Solomon.*]

Gereimon—like Genon, an angel of the 2nd
chora.

Gergot—in hechaloth lore (*Ma'asseh Merkabah*), an angelic guard stationed at the 6th
heavenly hall.

Germael ("majesty of God")—an angel sent
by God to create Adam from the dust—a mission
also ascribed to Gabriel. [*Rf. Falasha Anthology.*]

Geron—like Genon and Gereimon (*q.v.*), one
of the angels of the 2nd chora or altitude invoked
in magical prayer.

Geroskesufael—in hechaloth lore (*Ma'asseh
Merkabah*), an angelic guard stationed at the 7th
heavenly hall.

Gerviel (Cerviel)—in Jewish cabala, the preceptor angel of King David. [*Rf. Clayton,
Angelology.*] As Cerviel, this angel is chief of the
order of principalities (elohim), sharing the post
with Haniel, Nisroc, and others.

Gethel (Ingethel)—an angel set over hidden
things. According to *The Biblical Antiquities of
Philo*, Gethel was the angel who smote the Amorites with blindness in their battle with Cenez.

Gethel was assisted by Zeruel, another angel sent
by God against the Amorites.

Geviririon—an angel symbolizing or personi-
fying geburah (fear or strength). Geviririon ranks
5th of the 10 holy sefiroth.

Geviriyah—one of the many names of the
angel Metatron.

Gezardiya [Gazardiel]

Gezuriya—in *Malache Elyon*, an angel of the
order of powers; he is a guard of one of the celestial halls (hechaloth) and ruler over 6 other angels,
among them the angel of the sun, Gazardiya.

Gheoriah—an angel's name inscribed on the 3rd
pentacle of the planet Mercury. [*Rf. Mathers,
The Greater Key of Solomon.*]

Giant Angels—the great demons are so called
by Milton in *Paradise Lost* VII, 605.

Giatiyah—one of the many names of the angel
Metatron.

Gibborim ("mighty ones")—an order of angels
of the Song-Uttering Choirs under the leadership
of Tagas. "They are the mighty ones . . . men of
name" (Genesis 6). According to *The Zohar* I,
25a–b, the gibborim "erect synagogues and col-
leges, and place in them scrolls of the law with
rich ornaments, but only to make themselves a
name." If that is so, then the gibborim must be
regarded as evil, and they usually are so regarded.

Gidaijal (Gedael—"fortune of God")—a luminary of the seasons, as listed in *Enoch I*. He is
among the leaders of "heads of thousands."

Giel—in ceremonial magic, the angel with
dominion over the zodiacal sign of Gemini
(the Twins).

Gippuyel—one of the many names of the angel
Metatron. [*Rf. 3 Enoch, chap. 48.*]

Glaras—an angel of the 1st hour of the night,
serving under Gamiel.

Glauron or **Glaura**—a beneficent spirit of the
air, invoked from the north. He is mentioned in
Scot, *Discoverie of Witchcraft*.

Glmarij—an angel of the 3rd hour of the day, serving under Veguaniel.

Glorious Ones—a term for the highest order of archangels. [*Rf. Enoch II; Slavonic Encyclopedia.*]

Glory of God—according to the 11th-12th century Jewish poet and sage Judah ha-Levi, "glory of God" is a term which "denotes the whole class of angels, together with their spiritual instruments—the thrones, chariots, firmament, ophanim, and the spheres (galgalim)." [*Rf.* Abelson, *Jewish Mysticism*, p. 64.]

Gmial—one of the 64 angel wardens of the 7 celestial halls. [*Rf. Pirke Hechaloth.*]

Goap—formerly an angel of the order of powers; now fallen and in Hell. Goap is one of the infernal regions' 11 presidents. He is also known as Gaap and Tap. [*Rf.* Scot, *Discoverie of Witchcraft*; Waite, *The Lemegeton.*] That Goap was once of the order of powers "was proved after infinite research," reports Spence, *An Encyclopaedia of Occultism.* According to demonologists, Goap was "prince of the west."

God of this Age (or God of This World)—see II Corinthians 4, "in whom the god of this world hath blinded the minds of them which believe not," etc. Here Paul has in mind Satan, chief of the fallen angels.

Gog and **Magog**—in the grimoires of Honorius III, ineffable names of God used to command spirits. "The unexpected appearance of Gog and Magog amongst the other holy names of God must be put down," says Butler, *Ritual Magic*, "to the ignorance of Honorius." The Koran (*sura* 18, 95) mentions Gog and Magog as "spoiling the land."

Golab ("incendiaries")—one of the adversaries of the seraphim, one of the 10 unholy sefiroth "whose cortex is Usiel." Golab has also been denoted a spirit of wrath and sedition, operating under his chief, "Sammael the Black." [*Rf.* Levi, *Philosophie Occulte*; Waite, *The Holy Kabbalah*, p. 237.]

Golandes—an angel invoked in the exorcism of Wax, according to Mathers, *The Greater Key of Solomon.*

Gonael—one of numerous guards of the gates of the North Wind. [*Rf. Ozar Midrashim* II, 316.]

Gonfalons—an order of angels in the celestial hierarchy, according to Milton, *Paradise Lost* V, 590–591. In the latter book, the angel Raphael speaks of "Standards and Gonfalons" who "for the distinction serve/Of hierarchies, of Orders, and Degrees."

Good Daimon—the "aeon of the aeons," a term applied to Thoth in Hermetic theology. [*Rf. Thrice-Greatest Hermes* I, 280.]

Gorfiniel—an angelic guard of the 7th Heaven, as listed in *Ozar Midrashim* I, 119.

Gorson or **Gorsou** [Gurson]

Governments—in the *Apocalypse of the Holy Mother of God*, governments is an order of angels mentioned along with thrones, lordships, authorities, archangels, etc.

Gradhiel [Gradiel]

Gradiel (Gradhiel, Graphiel—"might of God") —the intelligence (angel) of the planet Mars when this luminary enters the signs of the Ram and Scorpio. Gradiel's corresponding angel (for Mars) is Bartyabel (*q.v.*).

Graniel—an angel of the 2nd hour, serving under Anael.

Granozin—an angel of the 2nd hour of the night, serving under Farris.

Graphathas—"one of the 9 angels that run together throughout the heavenly and earthly places," as certified in the *Gospel of Bartholomew*, p. 177, where the names of the 9 angels are revealed by Beliar to Bartholomew.

Graphiel (Gradiel)—a spirit in cabalistic enumerations answering to Gabriel, according to Forlong, *Encyclopedia of Religions.*

Grasgarben—with Hadakiel, Grasgarben governs the sign of Libra. [*Rf.* Levi, *Transcendental Magic.*]

Great and Wonderful—when Michael came

"Guardian Angels" by Georges Rouault. Reproduced from Régamey, *Anges*.

. to announce to Mary her impending death, the
Virgin is said to have asked the archangel who he
was, and that he answered, "My name is Great and
Wonderful." The legend is retold in Clement,
Angels in Art, where there is a reproduction of Fra
Filippo Lippi's painting, depicting the scene.

Grial (Griel)—a guardian angel of the 5th

Heaven; also one of the 70 childbed amulet angels.
[*Rf. Pirke Hechaloth.*]

Griel [*see* Grial]

Grigori (egoroi, egregori, "watchers")—in
Jewish legendary lore, the grigori are a superior
order of angels in both the 2nd and 5th Heavens
(depending on whether they are the holy or

unholy ones). They resemble men in appearance, but are taller than giants, and are eternally silent. Ruling prince of the order is Salamiel "who rejected the Lord" (*Enoch II*). [*Rf. Testament of Levi* (in the *Testament of the Twelve Patriarchs*); Talmud *Hagiga*.]

Guabarel—angel of autumn. In addition to Guabarel, another angel cited in occult lore as governing autumn is Tarquam (*q.v.*).

Guael (Guel)—an angel of the 5th Heaven ruling on Tuesday. Guael is invoked from the east.

Guardian Angels of Adam and Eve—our 1st parents had 2 guardian angels, according to *The Book of Adam and Eve*, and these were of the order of virtues, says Ginzberg. [*Rf.* Charles, *Apocrypha and Pseudepigrapha of the Old Testament*, p. 142.]

Guardian Angel of Barcelona—an unnamed angel who visited St. Vincent Ferrer. The angel never actually protected the city since it was frequently captured. There is a statue of this guardian angel in Barcelona. [*Rf.* Brewer, *A Dictionary of Miracles*, p. 504.]

Guardian Angel of the Earth—originally Satan, according to Irenaeus, Athenagoras, Methodius of Philippi, and other early Church Fathers.

Guardian Angel of France [Hakamiah]

Guardian Angel of Heaven and Earth—in the Islamic scheme of 7 Heavens, the Guardian Angel of Heaven and Earth dwells in the 6th Heaven. He has not been identified by name but is described as being composed of snow and fire.

Guardian Angels—of a class with national (tutelary) or ministering angels. In the cabala, there are 4 ruling princes of the order: Uriel, Raphael Gabriel, Michael. There are also 70 guardian angels of nations, one in charge of each state. [*Rf. Ecclesiasticus.*] This was the doctrine of St. Basil of Caesarea and other doctors of the Church. According to Buber, in the glossary to his *Tales of the Hasidim Early Masters*, these 70 tutelary princes

"The Angel Gabriel Appearing to Mohammed." From the Ms. of Jami'al-Tawarikh, at the University of Edinburgh.

of nations "are either angels or demons." It would be more conformable to rabbinic tradition to say that the 70 started out as angels, but became corrupted through national bias and are now demons—with the sole exception of Michael, *sar* of Israel, whose bias was excusable or even justified, since he espoused the cause of the "chosen people." It is said that every human being is assigned at birth to one or more guardian angels. Talmud indeed speaks of every Jew being attended throughout his life by 11,000 guardian angels; also that "every blade of grass has over it an angel saying 'grow.'" That every child has its protecting spirit is adduced from Matthew 18:10 where Jesus bids his disciples not to despise the little ones and speaks of their "angels in heaven." According to Charles, *Apocrypha and Pseudepigrapha of the Old Testament*, the earliest reference to a belief in guardian angels, in noncanonical lore, is to be found in *The Book of Jubilees*, 35:17. Another early source might be cited: *The Biblical Antiquities of Philo*, the writing of which is said to date back to the 1st century C.E. In Athanasius Kircher's account of his voyage to the planets, "the guardian angels of all the virtues" are found inhabiting "the Elysian shores of the planet Jupiter." [*Rf.* Kircher, *Oedipus Aegyptiacus.*] The liturgical feast of the Holy Guardian Angels, in Catholic observances, occurs on October 2. [*Note:* Of the 70 tutelary angels, only those of 4 nations are named in rabbinic writings: Dobiel for Persia; Samael for Rome (Edom); Rahab, Uzza, Duma, and/or Semyaza for Egypt; and Michael for Israel.]

Guards—an order of the celestial hierarchy mentioned in *Paradise Lost* IV, 550; XII, 590, where the guards, earlier referred to as powers and equated likewise with the cherubim, are under the command of Michael. Alfred de Vigny mentions the order of guards in his poem "Eloa." [*Rf.* West, *Milton and the Angels.*]

Guel (Guael)—an angel of the 5th Heaven ruling on Tuesday and invoked from the east.

No doubt the same as Guael. [*Rf.* Barrett, *The Magus* II, 119.]

Gulacoc—an angel of the Seal, used for conjuring. [*Rf. The Sixth and Seventh Books of Moses.*]

Gulhab—5th of the 10 unholy sefiroth, as noted in Moses de Burgos' text. For a list of the sefiroth, *see* Appendix.

Gurid—a summer equinox angel, effective when invoked as an amulet against the evil eye. [*Rf.* Trachtenberg, *Jewish Magic and Superstition.*]

Guriel ("whelp of God")—one of the angels ruling the zodiacal sign of Leo. [*Rf.* Trachtenberg, *Jewish Magic and Superstition.*]

Gurson (Gorson or Gorsou)—one of the routed forces under Lucifer, now serving in the nether regions as king of the south. [*Rf.* Spence, *An Encyclopaedia of Occultism*, p. 119.]

Guth—one of the angelic ..iers of the planet Jupiter. [*Rf.* Heywood, *The Hierarchy of the Blessèd Angels*, p. 215.]

Gutrix—in occultism, a Thursday angel of the air, ministering to Suth, chief of these angels, all of whom are subject in turn to the South Wind. Acting with Gutrix is Maguth, who likewise ministers to Suth. [*Rf. The Ancient's Book of Magic*; de Abano, *The Heptameron*; Barrett, *The Magus* II, 122; Shah, *Occultism*, 52.]

Guziel—in M. Gaster, *The Sword of Moses*, an evil angel summoned in incantation rites against an enemy.

Gvurtial—an angelic guard of one of the great halls (or palaces) of the 4th Heaven. [*Rf. Pirke Hechaloth.*]

Gzrel—in Trachtenberg, *Jewish Magic and Superstition*, an angel invoked to countermand evil decrees. The word Gzrel is part of a 42-letter name for God.

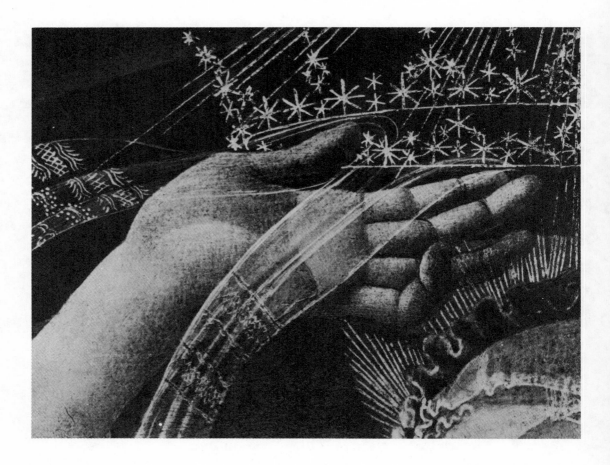

Hand of an angel by Botticelli. Detail from the *Magnificat*, in the Uffizi Gallery, Florence. Reproduced from Régamey, *Anges*.

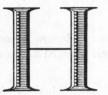

Haael—one of the 72 angels of the zodiac.

Haaiah—an angel of the order of dominations. Haaiah rules over diplomacy and ambassadors, and is one of the 72 angels bearing the name of God Shemhamphorae. Haaiah's sigil is reproduced in Ambelain, *La Kabbale Pratique*, p. 273.

Haamiah—an angel of the order of powers. Haamiah dominates religious cults and "protects all those who seek the truth." His corresponding angel (in the cabala) is Serucuth. For Haamiah's sigil, see Ambelain, *La Kabbale Pratique*, p. 281.

Haarez—an angel of the Seal, as noted in *The Sixth and Seventh Books of Moses*.

Haatan—a genius who conceals treasures, according to Apollonius of Tyana, *The Nuctemeron*.

Habbiel (Habiel)—a Monday angel of the 1st Heaven, invoked in love charms. [*Rf.* de Abano, *The Heptameron*; M. Gaster, *The Sword of Moses*.]

Haborym [Raum]

Habriel—an angel of the order of powers, summoned in conjuring rites. [*Rf. The Sixth and Seventh Books of Moses*.]

Habudiel—in occultism, an angel of the Lord's Day, resident of the 4th Heaven. He is invoked from the south. [*Rf.* de Abano, *The Heptameron*.]

Habu(h)iah—an angel who exercises dominion over agriculture and fecundity. Habuhiah is one of the 72 angels bearing the name of God Shemhamphorae.

Hachashel—one of the 72 angels of the zodiac. [*Rf.* Runes, *The Wisdom of the Kabbalah*, p. 87.]

Hadakiel (Chadakiel)—with Grasgarben, another genius, Hadakiel governs the sign of Libra (the Balance) in the zodiac. [*Rf. Prince of Darkness (A Witchcraft Anthology)*, pp. 177–178.]

Hadar—"the superior Benignity" conceived of by cabalists as a sefira. [*Rf.* Runes, *The Wisdom of the Kabbalah*.]

Hadariel [Hadraniel]

Hadariron—an archon named in lesser hechaloth lore and in the *Alphabet of Rabbi Akiba*. [*Rf.*

131

Scholem, *Jewish Gnosticism, Merkabah Mysticism, and Talmudic Tradition*, p. 63.]

Hadarmiel—a holy angel named in Mathers, *The Greater Key of Solomon.*

Hadarniel [Hadraniel]

Hadasdagedoy—in hechaloth lore (*Ma'asseh Merkabah*), an angelic guard of the 6th heavenly hall.

Hadiririon—"the beloved angel of God," who may be invoked in ritual magic rites. [*Rf.* M. Gaster, *The Sword of Moses.*]

Hadraniel (Hadarniel, Hadariel, Hadriel— "majesty of God")—a porter angel stationed at the 2nd gate in Heaven (according to one view). He is taller than Kemuel (*q.v.*) "by 60 myriads of parasangs" but shorter than Sandalphon "by a 500 years' journey." On seeing Hadraniel in Heaven, Moses was "struck dumb with awe"; but when Moses uttered the Supreme Name, Hadraniel in turn trembled. Legend speaks of Adam visiting Heaven some 2,000 years before Moses did. On that occasion, Hadraniel spoke to Adam about the latter's possession of *The Book of the Angel Raziel*, a holy tome reputed to have contained secrets and knowledge unknown even to the angels [*Rf. The Zohar* I, 55b]. The precious book came finally into the possession of Solomon, via Noah and Abraham. According to a Zoharic legend (*The Zohar* III), "when Hadraniel proclaims the will of the Lord, his voice penetrates through 200,000 firmaments," and "with every word from his mouth go forth 12,000 flashes of lightning" (the latter, according to the *Revelation of Moses*). In gnosticism Hadraniel, great as he is, is "only one of 7 subordinates to Jehuel, prince of fire." [*Rf.* King, *The Gnostics and Their Remains*, p. 15.] As Hadriel, he serves among the numerous angelic guards of the gates of the East Wind. In *Sefer ha-Heshek*, Hadraniel is one of the more than 72 names (actually more than 100) of Metatron. In *3 Enoch*, Odeberg holds that it is possible for Hadraniel to be identified with Metatron and that he has indeed been so identified in apocalyptic literature.

Hadriel (Hadraniel)—equated with Pusiel in the *Revelation of Rabbi Joshua Ben Levi.*

Hadrion—a variant form of Hadariron (*q.v.*).

Haduriel—in hechaloth lore (*Ma'asseh Merkabah*), an angelic guard stationed at the 6th heavenly hall.

Hafaza—in Muslim lore, a term denoting angels. The hafaza constitute a special class, are 4 in number, and "protect man from jinn, men, and Satans." On these 4 angels devolves the duty of writing down the actions of mortals. [*Rf.* Hastings, *Encyclopaedia of Religion and Ethics* IV, 617.]

Hafkiel—in Montgomery, *Aramaic Incantation Texts from Nippur*, an angel invoked in the exorcism of demons.

Hagai—in hechaloth lore (*Ma'asseh Merkabah*), an angelic guard stationed at the 5th heavenly hall.

Hagedola—an angel of the Seal, invoked in ceremonial rites. [*Rf. The Sixth and Seventh Books of Moses.*]

Haggai—a minor Hebrew prophet called "God's messenger or angel." See book of Haggai in the Old Testament.

Haggo—an angel of the Seal who could be summoned in conjuring rites, like Hagedola (*q.v.*). [*Rf. The Sixth and Seventh Books of Moses.*]

Hagiel—the intelligence of Venus when that planet enters the signs of Taurus and Libra. Hagiel's cabalistic number is 49. His corresponding angel, the spirit ruler of Venus, is Gadamel (*q.v.*). [*Rf.* Barrett, *The Magus*; Budge, *Amulets and Talismans*; Lenormant, *Chaldean Magic.*]

Hagios—the name of a great angel, or one of the secret names of God, used in invocation rites. [*Rf.* Malchus, *The Secret Grimoire of Turiel.*]

Hagith—ruler of the planet Venus and one of the 7 Olympian spirits. Hagith is governor of 21 or 35 of the 196 Olympian provinces. His day is Friday. According to Cornelius Agrippa, Hagith commands 4,000 legions of spirits; he has the power of transmuting metals. For a reproduction of Hagith's sigil, *see* Budge, *Amulets and Talismans*, p. 389. In white magic, Hagith is one of the 7 stewards of Heaven.

Haglon—angel of the 3rd hour of the night, serving under Sarquamich. [*Rf.* Waite, *The Lemegeton*.]

Hahael (Hahahel)—an angel of the order of virtues. Hahael protects Christian missionaries and all disciples of Christ; he is also one of the 72 angels that bear the name of God Shemhamphorae. His corresponding angel (in occult lore) is Chantaré. The sigil of Hahael is shown in Ambelain, *La Kabbale Pratique*, p. 281.

Hahahel [Hahael]

Hahaiah—an angel of the order of cherubim. He influences thoughts and reveals hidden mysteries to mortals. His corresponding angel is Atarph. The sigil of Hahaiah is shown in Ambelain, *La Kabbale Pratique*, p. 260.

Hahayel (Chayyliel)—in *3 Enoch*, Hahayel is prince of ministering angels when these angels sit in at the divine judgment councils.

Hahaziah—one of the 72 angels bearing the name of God Shemhamphorae, according to Barrett, *The Magus* II.

Hahiniah—in the cabala, one of the throne angels. [*Rf.* Ambelain, *La Kabbale Pratique*.]

Hahlii—in occult lore, an angel invoked in the conjuration of Ink and Colors. [*Rf.* Mathers, *The Greater Key of Solomon*.]

Hahowel—in *The Sixth and Seventh Books of Moses*, a ministering angel.

Hahuiah—one of 72 angels bearing the name of God Shemhamphorae.

Haiaiel (Hahahel)—one of the 72 angels of the zodiac and one of the 72 angels bearing the name of God Shemhamphorae. The sigil of Haiaiel is shown in Ambelain, *La Kabbale Pratique*, p. 294.

Hailael (Hayael)—chief angel of the order of hayyoth ("holy beasts").

Haim—an angel who exercises dominion over the zodiacal sign of Virgo. [*Rf.* Heywood, *The Hierarchy of the Blessèd Angels*.]

Hajoth Hakados—a species of angels inhabiting one of the hierarchies named "Jehovah," according to Spencer, *An Encyclopaedia of Occultism*, p. 199. Hajoth Hakados is also referred to as one of the spheres of the angels.

Hakael—one of the 7 leaders of the apostate angels, "the seventh Satan." [*Rf.* Charles, *The Book of Enoch*, p. 138 fn.; Schmidt, *The Apocalypse of Noah and the Parables of Enoch*.]

Hakamiah—one of the cherubim (invoked against traitors) and guardian angel of France. His corresponding angel is Verasua. His sigil is shown in Ambelain, *La Kabbale Pratique*, p. 267.

Hakem—in hechaloth lore (*Ma'asseh Merkabah*), an angelic guard stationed at the 4th heavenly hall.

Hakha—in *The Sixth and Seventh Books of Moses* an angel of the Seal.

Hakham—one of the many names of the angel Metatron.

Halacho—genius of sympathies; also one of the genii of the 11th hour. [*Rf.* Apollonius of Tyana, *The Nuctemeron*.]

Halahel—a spirit, partly good and partly evil, under the rule of Bael. His seal is shown in Waite, *The Lemegeton*, Fig. 175.

Halelviel—in hechaloth lore (*Ma'asseh Merkabah*), an angelic guard stationed at the 7th heavenly hall.

Halliza—the name of an angel appearing on the external circle of the pentagram of Solomon (Fig. 156). [*Rf.* Waite, *The Lemegeton*.]

Halqim—one of the numerous angelic guards of the gates of the North Wind. [*Rf.* Ozar Midrashim II, 316.]

Haludiel—an angel of the 4th Heaven invoked on Lord's Day, with the invocant facing south. Haludiel is also an intelligence of the sun. [*Rf.* Malchus, *The Secret Grimoire of Turiel*.]

Halwaya—a secret name of the angel Metatron, as revealed in *The Visions of Ezekiel*.

Hamabiel—in Heywood, *The Hierarchy of the Blessèd Angels*, an angel that exercises dominion over the zodiacal sign of Taurus. In ceremonial magic, however, the angel over Taurus is Tual. Asmodel is also credited with dominion over this zodiacal sign.

Hamal (Hmnal)—an angel with dominion over water. Also one of the 7 angels worshipped by Balaam. Hamal is invoked in Arabic incantation rites. [*Rf.* M. Gaster, *The Asatir*.]

Hamaliel—angel of the month of August, one of the rulers of the order of virtues, and governor of the zodiacal sign of Virgo—all the foregoing according to Trithemius. In ceremonial magic, the governor of Virgo is Voil or Voel. [*Rf.* Barrett, *The Magus*; De Plancy, *Dictionnaire Infernal*; *The Sixth and Seventh Books of Moses*; Camfield, *A Theological Discourse of Angels*.]

Hamarytzod—in Waite, *The Lemegeton*, an angel of the 11th hour, serving under Dardariel.

Hamatiel—in occultism, a zodiacal angel governing Virgo. [*Rf.* Jobes, *Dictionary of Mythology Folklore and Symbols*.]

Hamaya—a ministering angel, mentioned in *The Sixth and Seventh Books of Moses*.

Hamayzod—angel of the 4th hour of the night serving under Jefischa. [*Rf.* Waite, *The Lemegeton*.]

Hameriel—angel of the 5th hour of the night, serving under Abasdarhon.

Hamiel [Haniel]

Ham Meyuchad—an angel of the order of cherubim. Ham Meyuchad is sometimes equated with the great angel Akatriel. [*Rf. 3 Enoch*.]

Hamneijs—an angel of the Seal, mentioned in *The Sixth and Seventh Books of Moses*.

Hamon—according to Jerome, commenting on Isaiah 10:13, Hamon is another name for the angel Gabriel. [*Rf. 3 Enoch*; Ginzberg, *The Legends of the Jews* VI.] In *Ozar Midrashim* (II, 316) Hamon is one of numerous angelic guards of the gates of the South Wind. In *3 Enoch* (chap. 18) Hamon is a "great prince, fearful and honored, pleasant and terrible, who maketh all the children of heaven to tremble when the time draweth nigh for the singing of the Thrice Holy."

Hamshalim (Hashmallim)—one of the 10 angelic hierarchic orders as listed in *The Zohar*; in this cabalistic work the hamshalim are under the ministry of Samael.

Hamwak'il—in Arabic lore, a guardian angel invoked in rites of exorcism. [*Rf.* Hughes, *A Dictionary of Islam*, "Angels."]

Hanaeb—one of the 12 angels of the zodiac. [*Rf. The Sixth and Seventh Books of Moses*.]

Hanael [Haniel]

Hananel—one of the fallen angels in *Enoch I*.

Hananiel ("graciously given of God")—an archangel whose name appears inscribed on a pentagram, i.e., a Hebrew amulet of cabalistic origin. See reproduction of pentagram in Budge, *Amulets and Talismans*, p. 233.

Hanhl—the angel who ordered Balaam to build the first 7 altars. [*Rf.* M. Gaster, *The Asatir*.]

Haniel (Aniel, Hamiel, Onoel, Hanael— "glory or grace of God" or "he who sees God")— angel of the month of December, chief of the order of principalities, virtues (tarshishim), and innocents, according to Barrett, *The Magus*. Haniel is also governor of the sign of Capricorn (as cited by Camfield in *A Theological Discourse of Angels*), and of Venus. He figures in the list of the 7 (or 10) archangels and the 10 holy sefiroth. Variants of the name occur: Hamiel, Simiel, Onoel, Anael, etc. In occult writings Haniel is credited with the feat (usually ascribed to Anafiel) of transporting Enoch to Heaven. Haniel has been compared to the Chaldean Ishtar (who ruled Venus) and is invoked as an amulet against evil. [*Rf.* Heywood, *The Hierarchy of the Blessèd Angels*; Trachtenberg, *Jewish Magic and Superstition*; Ambelain, *La Kabbale Pratique*; Barrett, *The Magus*.]

Hanniniel—in Aramaic incantation rites, an angel appealed to in love charms. [*Rf.* Montgomery, *Aramaic Incantation Texts from Nippur.*]

Hannuel—an angel who exercises dominion over the zodiacal sign of Capricorn. [*Rf.* Heywood, *The Hierarchy of the Blessèd Angels.*]

Hanoziz—an angel of the 8th hour of the night, serving under Narcoriel, as cited in Waite, *The Lemegeton.*

Hanozoz—an angel of the 9th hour of the night, serving under Nacoriel.

Hantiel—an angel of the 3rd hour of the day, serving under Veguaniel.

Hanum (Hanun)—a Monday angel residing in the 1st Heaven and invoked from the south. [*Rf.* de Abano, *The Heptameron*; Barrett, *The Magus* II.] de Claremont, *The Ancient's Book of Magic*, claims that Hanum must be invoked from the north.

Ha-Qadosch Berakha—in Mathers, *The Greater Key of Solomon*, a name for the "Holy and Blessed One" called on in Solomonic conjurations.

Haqemel—one of the 72 angels of the zodiac, as listed in Runes, *The Wisdom of the Kabbalah.*

Harabael (Harabiel)—an angel with dominion over the earth.

Harab-Serapel ("ravens of death")—an averse sefira to Netzach, whose cortices are Theuniel and Baal Chanan. Harab-Serapel is 7th of the 10 demons in the Asiatic world; he is also a leader in the infernal regions. *Cf.* "adversaries of the Elohim or the Gods, and their chief is Baal" in Levi, *Philosophie Occulte*, where Harab-Serapel is regarded as plural. [*Rf.* chart in Ambelain, *La Kabbale Pratique*, facing p. 80.]

Harahel—in the cabala, an angel in charge of archives, libraries, and rare cabinets; also one of the 72 angels bearing the name of God Shemhamphorae. [*Rf.* sigil of Harahel in Ambelain, *La Kabbale Pratique*, p. 289.]

Harariel—an angel's name found inscribed on an oriental charm (*kamea*) for warding off evil. [*Rf.* Schrire, *Hebrew Amulets.*]

Harbonah ("ass driver")—one of the 7 angels of confusion, as cited in Ginzberg, *The Legends of the Jews*. In the story relating to Ahasuerus and Esther, Harbonah is the angel of annihilation.

Harchiel—in black magic rites, an angel invoked to command the demons that confer the gift of invisibility. [*Rf.* Mathers, *The Greater Key of Solomon*, p. 45.]

Harhaziel (Harhazial)—one of the guardian angels of one of the halls or palaces of the 3rd Heaven. [*Rf. Pirke Hechaloth.*]

Hariel (Harael, Behemial)—angel with dominion over tame beasts. Hariel is invoked against impieties. He rules science and the arts and is of the order of cherubim. [*Rf.* Barrett, *The Magus* II.] Hariel's sigil is in Ambelain, *La Kabbale Pratique*, p. 267.

Hariph—another name for the angel Raphael in Maria Brooks' book-length poem *Zophiel (q.v.)*.

Haris—another name for Iblis, chief of the jinn and leader of the fallen angels in Arabic lore.

Hariton (fictional)—an archangel who figures in Gurdjieff's cosmic myth, *All and Everything, Beelzebub's Tales to His Grandson*. Hariton devises a new type of ship for navigating interplanetary space.

Harmozey (Harmozel, Armogen)—in gnostic lore, one of the 4 great luminaries that "surround the self-begotten, the savior, or God." [*Rf. Apocryphon of John*; Irenaeus, *Contra Haereses*; Grant, *Gnosticism and Early Christianity*.] The 3 other luminaries that surround the self-begotten are usually listed as Oroiael, Daveitha, and Eleleth.

Harshael [Harshiel]

Harshiel—an angel invoked in Syriac conjuring ceremonies. In *The Book of Protection*, Harshiel, as a spellbinding power, is cited (especially for the binding of sorcerers) along with Michael, Gabriel, Sarphiel, Azrael, and others.

Harta'il—in Arabic lore, a guardian angel invoked in rites of exorcism. [*Rf.* Hughes, *A Dictionary of Islam*, "Angels."]

Harudha—in Persian mythology, the angel who rules the element of water. In Mandaean lore, Harudha is equated with the female Haurvatat, who is the spirit of health and vegetation, as well as ruler of water.

Harut (Haroth, Haurvatati, Haroot)—usually linked with Maroth in Islamic legend. Harut was sent down from Heaven (with Maroth) to teach mortals the art of government (see the Koran, *sura* 2, 102). In Persian lore, Harut and Maroth were angels of the highest rank, claimed to be 2 of the amesha spentas, and in possession of the secret name of God; this name unhappily they revealed to Zobra or Zuhrah, a mortal woman, with whom they both fell in love. A footnote to Ode 14 of Hafiz (in the English rendering by Richard Le Gallienne) states that, by the power of the Explicit Name, Zuhrah ascended to the planet Venus "with which she became identified in Mohammedan mythology"; and goes on to say that the fallen angels (Marut and Harut) "were punished by being confined, head down, in a pit near Babylon, where they were supposed to teach magic and sorcery." In Hastings, *Encyclopaedia of Religion and Ethics* IV, 615, the pair are characterized as "fallen angels with a Satanic role."

Harviel—in hechaloth lore (*Ma'asseh Merkabah*), an angelic guard stationed at the 2nd heavenly hall.

Hasdiel—an angel of the planet Venus; also the angel of benevolence, as recorded in a German-type mezuza. In his duties as angel of benevolence, Hasdiel shares the office with Zadkiel (*q.v.*). [*Rf. The Book of the Angel Raziel.*] In *The Zohar* (Numbers 154b), Hasdiel is one of 2 chieftains (the other being Shamshiel) that accompanied Uriel when the latter bore his standard in battle.

Haseha—one of 15 throne angels listed in *The Sixth and Seventh Books of Moses.* For the names of all 15, *see* Appendix.

Hashesiyah—one of the many names of the angel Metatron.

Hashmal (Chasmal, Hayyah)—chief angel of the order of hashmallim (dominations). According to *The Zohar*, the term denotes "an inner, supernal sphere, hidden and veiled, in which the mysteries of the celestial letters of the Holy Name are suspended." [*Rf.* Ezekiel 1:4; *Cf.* Talmud *Hagiga* 13.] In Ginzberg, *The Legends of the Jews* I, 18, it is said that "Hashmal surrounds the throne of God." He is the "fire-speaking angel." Joseph Albo in *Sefer ha-'Ikkarim* (Book of Principles) I, 14, reports that the rabbis, when speaking of Hashmal, mean "the hayyot of fire-speaking." In *Hagiga*, it is related that "once upon a time a young man was studying the vision of Ezekiel and was dwelling upon the angel Chashmal when fire proceeded from Chashmal and consumed him." The moral of this is not explained.

Hashmallim (the "hayyot," living creatures)—a high order of angels, equated with the dominations. The hashmallim are ranked with the cherubim and seraphim. While the eponymous chief is Hashmal, Zadkiel or Zacharael is also designated head of the order. In the cabala, the hashmallim belong to the yetziratic world, the world of foundation, the abode of angels presided over by the angel Metatron. [*Rf.* Abelson, *Jewish Mysticism*, p. 38.] It is said (*Bereshith Rabba*) that the river Dinur ("fiery river") was created "out of the sweat of those animals [the hashmallim] who sweat because they carry the throne of the Holy and Blessed God."

Hashul—one of the chiefs of the order of the hashmallim, as reported in *Maseket Azilut*. [*Rf. Ozar Midrashim* I, 67.]

Hasmed—the angel of annihilation, and one of the five angels of punishment that Moses encountered in Heaven. [*Rf. Midrash Tehillim* on Psalm 7.]

Hasmiyah—one of the many names of the angel Metatron.

Hasmodai—a spirit of the moon, invoked in talismanic magic. [*Rf.* Barrett, *The Magus* II, 147.]

Hasriel—an angel's name found inscribed on an oriental charm (*kamea*) for warding off evil. [*Rf.* Schrire, *Hebrew Amulets.*]

"Hastening Angel"—a term applied by Milton (*Paradise Lost* XII, 637) to Michael as the angel who "caught/Our lingring Parents" and led them out of Eden. Dryden in his *State of Innocence* informs us that it was Raphael, not Michael, who expelled the ill-fated pair. [*Rf.* Angels of the Garden of Eden.]

Hatach—an angel invoked in medieval Jewish incantation rites. The name derives from the initials of the words of the incantation. [*Rf.* Trachtenberg, *Jewish Magic and Superstition*, p. 165.]

Hatiphas—genius of finery, mentioned in Apollonius of Tyana, *The Nuctemeron.*

Hatspatsiel—one of the many names of the angel Metatron.

Hauras (Haures, Havres, Flauros)—one of the 72 spirits that Solomon, according to legend, shut up in a brass vessel and cast into a deep lake (or into the sea). Formerly, as he confided to Solomon, Hauras was a mighty celestial power (but to which order he belonged he did not say). He converses gladly about the creation of the world and the fall of the angels. In Hell, where he is a great duke, he appears in the form of a leopard but, on command of an exorcist, will manifest in human shape. He gives true answers concerning the past and the future. Under his sway, and ready to do his bidding, are 36 legions of the damned. His sigil is shown in Waite, *The Book of Black Magic and of Pacts*, p. 186. In De Plancy, *Dictionnaire Infernal* (1863 ed.) he is pictured in the shape of a man-leopard.

Haurvatat ("wholeness")—in Zoroastrianism, one of the 6 amesha spentas (archangels). Haurvatat is female and the personification of salvation. She is also a spirit of the waters. In Mandaean lore she is known as Harudha, or equated with Harudha, since the latter is male. [*Rf. Grundriss der iranischen Philologie* III.] Some scholars see a derivation of the Koranic fallen angel Harut from this Persian archangel. [*Rf.* Jung, *Fallen Angels in Jewish, Christian and Mohammedan Literature*, p. 131.]

Haurvatati (Haurvatat)—an angel in Arabic lore derived from the amesha spentas; also called Chordad.

Haven—in Levi, *Transcendental Magic* (p. 503), one of the 12 genii who preside over the 12 hours of the day. Haven is the genius of dignity.

Havhaviyah, Haviyahu, Hayat—3 of the many names of the angel Metatron.

Hayya—singular for hayyoth.

Hayyael [Hayyel]

Hayyel (Hashmal, Chayyiel, Hayyliel, Johiel, Yayael)—chief angel of the hayyoth (*q.v.*). He has dominion over wild beasts, according to *3 Enoch*, but shares the dominion with Thegri (Thuriel), Mtniel, and Jehiel.

Hayyliel [Hayyel]

Hayyoth ("holy, heavenly beasts"—Chayoh, chayyoth, Chiva)—a class of Merkabah angels equated or ranked with the cherubim, residing in the 7th Heaven. Angels of fire, they support the throne of Glory (*see* hashmallim). As reported in *3 Enoch*, they each have "4 faces, 4 wings, 2,000 thrones, and are placed next to the wheels of the Merkabah." Ezekiel saw the hayyoth (cherubim) by the river Chebar (Ezekiel 20). According to *The Zohar* (Vayigash 211a) there are 36 hayyoth—although, in *3 Enoch*, they number only 4. They constitute the "camp of the Shekinah." They receive the holy effluence from above and disseminate it to the hayyoth, who are the "movers of the wheels." [See Abelson, *Jewish Mysticism*.] According to *The Zohar* (Noah, 71b) the hayyoth uphold the universe; when they spread their wings, they break forth at the same moment into songs of praise "as the voice of the Almighty." [*Cf.* Ezekiel 1:24; 6:3.] The prophet's vision of the hayyoth and the post-Biblical lore on these holy beasts strongly influenced, it is claimed, the work of the contemporary painter, Marc Chagall.

Haziel ("vision of God")—a cherub invoked to obtain the pity of God. Haziel is one of 72 angels bearing the mystical name of God Shemhamphorae (*see* Appendix). When equated with

Bernael (*q.v.*), he is an angel of darkness. For Haziel's sigil, see Ambelain, *La Kabbale Pratique*, p. 260. [*Rf. Falasha Anthology*.] In I Chronicles 23:9 Haziel is a mortal, an offspring of the Gershonites. The cabalists very likely drew the name from this source.

Heavenly Academy—the trial body of angels that assemble to judge human beings when the latter appear in Heaven for judgment. If a mortal proves worthy, he is "crowned with many radiant crowns," but if he proves unworthy, he is "thrust outside, and stands within the pillar until he is taken to his punishment." [*Rf. The Zohar* (Balak 185b).]

Heavenly Host—a term denoting the angels of Heaven as a whole. Job conceived the heavenly host as morning stars singing together and shouting for joy. In Dante's *Paradiso*, canto 27, the heavenly host intone the "Gloria in Excelsis." For this and the succeeding canto, Doré provided wood engravings. Blake saw the innumerable company (the heavenly host) crying "Holy, Holy, Holy, is the Lord God Almighty."

Heavenly Scribe—Michael, Enoch, Vretil, Metatron, Radueriel, Soferiel. The heavenly scribe is associated with the "man clothed in linen," an image found in Ezekiel 9:2 and in Daniel 10.

Hebdomad—a term in Ophitic (gnostic) lore for the 7 angels or potentates, rulers of the 7 Heavens, the 7 being Iadalbaoth, Jao, Sabaoth, Adoneus (Adonai), Eloeus, Horeus (Oreus), Astaphaeus. Origen, in *Contra Celsum* VI, spells out equivalent names of these 7, to wit: Michael (in the form of a lion); Suriel (in the form of an ox); Raphael (in the form of a dragon); Gabriel (in the form of an eagle); Thautabaoth (in the form of a bear); Erataoth (in the form of a dog); Onoel (in the form of an ass). [*Rf.* Mead, *Thrice-Greatest Hermes* III, p. 294.]

Hechaloth (hekhaloth)—the hechaloth are the 7 female emanations of God, the counterpart of the 10 male sefiroth (*q.v.*). *The Zohar* (Exodus 128a), translates the word to mean beautiful virgins. The term "hechaloth" also denotes the

heavenly halls or palaces guarded over by the great warden angels. It should be pointed out that these emanations are from the right side of the Creator. There are also unholy emanations (the unholy sefiroth, the averse ones) and these issue from His left side (the dark or evil side). For a listing of both choirs, *see* Appendix. The *Book of Hechaloth*, originally published by Jellinek, was reissued by Odeberg as *3 Enoch* or *The Hebrew Book of Enoch*. *See* Hechaloth for an angel so named.

He'el ("life of God")—an angel leader of the "heads of thousands." He'el is ruler of one of the seasons of the year, as noted in *Enoch I*. In the Apocrypha, He'el is associated with the angel Elimelech (*q.v.*).

Heiglot—in transcendental magic, a genius or angel of snowstorms. He is also a ruler of the 1st hour. In Apollonius of Tyana's *The Nuctemeron* the 12 hours, analogous to the 12 zodiacal signs, are presided over by 12 genii or angels, of whom Heiglot is one.

Heikhali—in hechaloth lore (*Ma'asseh Merkabah*), an angelic guard stationed at the 7th heavenly hall.

Hekaloth (hechaloth)—an angel in the heavenly Paradise mentioned in the treatise *Hekaloth* and in *The Zohar* I, 141 fn.

Hel—according to Scot, *Discoverie of Witchcraft*, a name for God (or of an angel of God) invoked in conjuring rites.

Helayaseph (Jiluyaseph, Hilujaseph)—an angel governing one of the seasons. In *Enoch I* Helayaseph is "head of a thousand" angels of the seasons. [*Rf.* Charles, *The Book of Enoch*, p. 177.]

Helech [Abelech]

Helel—in Canaanitish mythology, a fallen angel, son of Sahar or Sharer, a winged deity. Helel sought to usurp the throne of the chief god and, as punishment, was cast down into the abyss. *Cf.* the Lucifer legend. The 1st star to fall from Heaven (*Enoch I*, 86:1) was Satan-Helel. This is an interpretation offered by Morgenstern, "The Mythological Background of Psalm 82" (*Hebrew Union College–Jewish Institute of Religion*

The sparkling circle of the heavenly host by Doré. Illustration to Canto 27 of Dante's *Paradiso*.
From Dante, *The Divine Comedy*, translated by Lawrence Grant White.

Annual XIV, pp. 29–126). However, in his *Fallen Angels*, Bamberger argues: "The more natural explanation is that the 1st star [that fell] was Azazel." Helel was head or leader of the nephilim (*q.v.*). Generally speaking, angels can have no off-spring, since they are pure spirits; but when angels sin, when they "put on the corruptibility of the flesh" and cohabit with mortal women, they are capable of producing progeny. A case in point is the incident in Genesis 6. In the cabala and rabbinic lore there are numerous instances of such heteroclitish productivity. [*Rf.* Graves and Patai, *Hebrew Myths.*]

Heleleth (Eleleth)—in gnostic lore, a great luminary, described thus in the *Hypostasis of the Archons*: "the great Heleleth descends from before the holy spirit; his aspect is like gold, his vesture like snow." [*Rf.* Doresse, *The Secret Books of the Egyptian Gnostics*, p. 178.]

Helemmelek—in *Enoch I*, an angel governing one of the seasons. The name is said to be an inversion of Milkiel.

Helias the Prophet—a name for the forerunner angel. *See* John the Baptist.

Hel(l)ison—one of the 5 angels of the 1st altitude, the other 4 being Alimiel, Gabriel, Barachiel, Lebes. When invoked, Helison appears carrying a banner adorned with a crimson cross, crowned with roses. [*Rf. The Almadel of Solomon.*]

Hemah—angel of wrath, with dominion over the death of domestic animals; also an angel of destruction. According to *The Zohar* I, Hemah, with the help of a brother angel named Af, well-nigh swallowed Moses, and would have succeeded in doing so, but for the timely intervention of God. When the Lawgiver was disgorged, he turned around and slew Hemah—one of the rare instances where a mortal was able to do away with an immortal, an angel. Like Af, Hemah was 500 parasangs tall, and was "forged out of chains of black and red fire," as described in Ginzberg, *The Legends of the Jews* II, 308.

Heman ("trust")—according to Rabbi Judah in *The Zohar* (Kedoshim) and according to *3 Enoch*,

Heman is a leader of one of the heavenly choirs. Heman and the angels under him sing hosannas in the morning hours, just as those under Jeduthun sing hosannas in the evening hours, and those under Asaph sing at night. Psalm 88 is headed: "To the chief Musician upon Mahalath Leannoth, Maschil of Heman the Ezrahite." In the course of time, it seems that the 3 psalmists (Heman, Asaph, and Jeduthun) were transformed into maestro-angels in order to perform, in Heaven, services for which they showed special skill on earth.

Herachio [Astrachios]

Herald Angel—identified as Raziel or Akra-ziel; also Michael. Said to have announced Jesus' resurrection. The term was made popular by Wesley's "Hark! The Herald Angels Sing!" When pictured with right hand raised in benedic-tion and wings outspread, the herald angel is the symbol of the Nativity.

Herald of Hell—the angel Zophiel. [*Rf.* Klopstock, *The Messiah.*]

Hermes—the agathosdaimon, the "bringer of good, the angel standing by the side of Tyche." [*Rf.* Harrison, *Epilegomena to the Study of Greek Religion*, pp. 294ff.] Hermes is the psychopompos (*q.v.*), god of the underworld, daimon of rein-carnation. He is also the god of flocks and herds. He received his art of divination and golden wand from Apollo, his winged sandals from Perseus. In Homer it is Hermes who leads the ghosts of slain suitors to Hades. He was given the name Trismegistus—"thrice-greatest Intelligencer"—be-cause, so it is said, he was the 1st intelligence to communicate celestial knowledge to man. It is also said that the cabala was shown to Hermes by God on Mt. Sinai and that, in fact, he was none other than the Hebrew lawgiver Moses [*Rf.* Barrett, *The Magus*, "Biographia Antiqua," p. 150.] This identification, however, is disputed by N. Wieder in his article "Idea of a Second Coming of Moses" (*Jewish Quarterly Review*, April 1956), declaring "Nowhere in rabbinic literature does one meet with this designation [i.e., Hermes]. And this is only natural: the rabbis must have regarded it as most objectionable to attach to Moses the name of a heathen deity." The last poem Longfellow wrote (1882) was titled "Hermes Trismegistus."

Hermesiel—a leader of the heavenly choir, sharing this post with Metatron, Radueriel, Tagas, and other celestial masters of song. Hermesiel is an angel "created" from Hermes, the Greek divinity. Says T. Gaster in *The Holy and the Profane*: "Hermes, inventor of the lyre, was transmogrified into the angel Hermesiel"—a suffix device by which sundry pagan material and sources were made to serve the uses of early Jewish angelologists. In time, Prof. Gaster adds, Hermesiel was identified with David, "sweet singer of Israel."

Heroes of Heaven—a term for good angels, as in Mansoor, *The Thanksgiving Hymns*.

Hetabor—an angel invoked in the exorcism of Wax. Found in works of practical cabala, originally in Gollancz, *Clavicula Salomonis*.

Heziel—an angel of the zodiac.

Hhml Haml—angel of the firmament, one of the 7 angels worshipped by Balaam. The name was created through permutations of the letters of the Hebrew alphabet. [*Rf.* M. Gaster, *The Asatir.*]

Hibel-Ziwa—in Mandaean lore, an angel equated with Gabriel. *See* Hiwel-Ziwa.

Hiel—an angel's name found inscribed on an oriental charm (*kamea*) for warding off evil. [*Rf.* Schrire, *Hebrew Amulets*.]

Hierarchy [Celestial Hierarchy]

Hierimiel [Jeremiel]

Hilofatei and **Hilofei**—in hechaloth lore (*Ma'asseh Merkabah*), angelic guards stationed in the 4th heavenly hall.

Hiniel—an angel invoked in Syriac incantation rites, along with Michael, Gabriel, Sarphiel, and other "spellbinding angels," as cited in *The Book of Protection*.

Hipeton (Anaphaxeton)—a spirit or angel of the planet Jupiter, sharing rulership with the angel Johphiel (i.e., Jophiel). [*Rf.* Barrett, *The Magus*.]

Hiphkadiel—an angel's name found inscribed on an oriental charm (*kamea*) for warding off evil. [*Rf.* Schrire, *Hebrew Amulets*.]

Hismael—the spirit of the planet Jupiter. [*Rf.* Barrett, *The Magus* II, 146.]

Hivvah—one of 2 sons of the fallen angel Semyaza. *See* Hiyyah.

Hiwel-Ziwa (Hibel-Ziwa)—in Mandaean lore, one of the 360 divine beings, created by Alaha, the Supreme Being. Hiwel in turn is said to have created this world.

Hiyyah—a son of the fallen angel Semyaza. [*See* Hivvah.] According to legend, Hiyyah and his brother together consumed daily 1,000 camels, 1,000 horses, and 1,000 oxen.

Hizarbin—a genius of the sea and one of the genii of the 2nd hour. [*Rf.* Levi, *Transcendental Magic*, quoting *The Nuctemeron* of Apollonius of Tyana.]

Hizkiel—with Kafziel, Hizkiel serves as chief aide to Gabriel when the latter bears his standard in battle. [*Rf. The Zohar*, Numbers 155a.] In *Ozar Midrashim* II, 316, Hizkiel (or Hizqiel) is one of numerous guards of the gates of the North Wind.

Hlin Hntr—one of the "nomina barbara," Hlin Hntr is an angel of winds and among the 7 angels worshipped by Balaam, as noted in M. Gaster, *The Asatir*.

Hlk Lil Hlk Lib—one of the "nomina barbara," an angel of holiness, and one of the 7 worshipped by Balaam.

Hlm Hml [Hhml Haml]

Hngel—an angel of the summer equinox, effective as an amulet against the evil eye.

Hochmel (Hocroel, Hochmal, Hokmael, Hochmael—"wisdom of God")—the angel who is reputed to have inspired the 7-volume *Grimoire of Pope Honorius III*. Hochmel is one of the 10 sefiroth.

Hocus Pocus—in Jewish magical rites of the Middle Ages, Hocus Pocus manifests as "a prince [angel] on high"—in fact, as two princes. The term derives, it is said, from "hoc est corpus meum." [*Rf.* Grant, *Gnosticism and Early Christianity*, p. 45.]

Hod [Hodiriron]

Hodiel ("victory of God")—an angel of the Briatic world (the world of Creation), according to cabalists. [*See* Hodiriron.] In Moses Botarel's work on the efficacy of amulets, Hodiel is mentioned as an angel who might profitably be invoked, along with Kabniel, Tarpiel, and other invocation spirits.

Hodiriron (from "hod," meaning splendor)—9th of the 10 holy sefiroth (*q.v.*), as listed in the text of Isaac ha-Cohen of Soria, and in the works of other cabalists.

Hodniel—an angel reputed to have the power of curing stupidity in man.

Hoesediel ("mercy of God"—*choesed*)—like Hodiel, Hoesediel is an angel of the Briatic world (one of the 4 archetypal worlds). See chart facing p. 60, Ambelain, *La Kabbale Pratique*, where Hoesediel is listed along with Zadkiel as belonging to the order of hashmalim or dominations. Hoesediel is also ranked as one of the 10 sefiras.

Hofniel ("fighter for God")—chief of the *bene elohim* ("sons of God"), an order among the 10 hierarchies in the cabala. [*Rf. Jewish Encyclopedia*, "Angelology."]

Hokmael [Hochmel]

Holy Beasts—in Talmud the holy beasts are the cherubim. In *Hagiga* "the holy beasts are numbered with the ophanim [wheels, thrones] and the seraphim, and the ministering angels." *See* hashmallim and hayyoth.

Holy Ghost (or Holy Spirit)—another name for the Comforter (*q.v.*), the 3rd person in the Trinity, sometimes regarded as female. The apocryphal *The Gospel According to the Hebrews* makes the Lord speak of "my mother the Holy Ghost" who "took me by one of my hairs and carried me to the great mountain Tabor" (traditionally the mountain of the Transfiguration). The "mother" reference here is explained by the fact that in Aramaic, which Jesus spoke, as also in Hebrew, the word *spirit* or *ghost* is of the feminine gender. Origen *On John* II, 12, quotes the cited passage from *The Gospel According to the Hebrews*. [*Rf.* Harnack, *History of Dogma* IV, 308; Hervieux, *The New Testament Apocrypha* (p. 132); Hastings, *Dictionary of the Bible*, "Tabor."] The *Commentary on the Apocalypse of the Blessed John* suggests that "by the angel flying through the midst of Heaven is signified the Holy Spirit."

Holy Ones—another term for archangels.

Homadiel—identified as the "Angel of the Lord." [*Rf.* introduction to Mathers, *The Greater Key of Solomon*.]

Horaios (Oreus, Horeus)—one of the 7 archons in the Ophitic (gnostic) system and ruler of one of the 7 Heavens "leading to the aeon of the archons." See Invocation to Horaios reproduced in Legge, *Forerunners and Rivals of Christianity* II, 74. Origen in *Contra Celsum* also mentions Horaios.

Hormuz—in ancient Persian lore, the angel in charge of the 1st day of the month. [*Rf. The Dabistan*, p. 35.]

Horses—a term for angels, as in Zechariah 6:2–5: "These [red, black, white, and grizzled horses] are the four spirits of the heaven which go forth to stand before the Lord of all the earth." For a similar use of the term, see the Book of Revelation.

Hosampsich—one of the leaders of the fallen angels in Enoch writings. [*Rf.* Voltaire, "Of Angels, Genii, and Devils."]

Hosts—a term for angels; also a designation for one of the 10 angelic orders (before Dionysius fixed the orders at 9 and omitted hosts). [*Rf. Apostolic Constitutions*; Parente, *The Angels*.]

Hosts of the High Ones or **Hosts of the Height**—a term for angels, as in Isaiah 24:21, where God threatens dire punishment on his servitors, mortal and divine: "And it shall come to pass in that day that the Lord shall punish the host of the high ones that are on high and the kings of the earth upon the earth." [*Cf.* God's dissatisfaction with the angels in Job 4:18: "Behold, he put no trust in his servants, and his angels he charged with folly."]

Hosts of the Lord—according to the *Mekilta of Rabbi Ishmael*, the Hosts of the Lord are the ministering angels led by Michael.

Household of the Upper World—in hechaloth literature, the Household of the Upper World constitutes one of the highest angelic groups—called, in Hebrew, "pamelia shel ma'alah." [*Rf.* Müller, *History of Jewish Mysticism*, p. 152.]

Hout—an angel invoked in Arabic conjuring rites. [*Rf.* Shah, *Occultism*, p. 152.]

Hoveh Hayah—one of the many names of the angel Metatron.

Hshahshiel—a Syrian "spellbinding" angel mentioned in *The Book of Protection*. [*Rf.* Budge, *Amulets and Talismans*, p. 273.]

Hsprh Hsmim—one of the 7 angelic creatures worshiped by Balaam. [*Rf.* M. Gaster, *The Asatir*, p. 263.]

Hubaiel—an angel serving in the 1st Heaven, according to a listing in *The Sixth and Seventh Books of Moses*.

Hubaril—an angelic messenger of the planet Saturn. [*Rf.* Malchus, *The Secret Grimoire of Turiel*, p. 33.]

Hufaltiel (Huphaltiel)—an angel serving in the 3rd Heaven. He officiates on Friday and is to be invoked from the west. [*Rf.* Barrett, *The Magus*; de Abano, *The Heptameron*; Shah, *Occultism*; *The Sixth and Seventh Books of Moses*.]

Hugron Kunya—one of the 14 great conjuring angels named in M. Gaster, *The Sword of Moses*.

Huha—a name for God or of an angel mentioned by the Essenes in their *Covenant of the Community* (a scroll recently discovered among the Dead Sea Scrolls). [*Rf.* Potter, *The Last Years of Jesus Revealed*.]

Hukiel—in hechaloth lore (*Ma'asseh Merkabah*), an angelic guard stationed at the 7th heavenly hall.

Hula'il—in Arabic lore, a guardian angel invoked in rites of exorcism. [*Rf.* Hughes, *A Dictionary of Islam*, "Angels."]

Humastrav (Humastraw)—a Monday angel invoked from the north. Humastrav is said to reside in the 1st Heaven. [*Rf.* de Abano, *The Heptameron*.]

Humiel—in occultism, a zodiacal angel governing Capricorn. [*Rf.* Jobes, *Dictionary of Mythology Folklore and Symbols*.]

Huphaltiel [Hufaltiel]

Huphatriel—one of the angelic intelligences of the planet Jupiter. [*Rf.* Malchus, *The Secret Grimoire of Turiel*.]

Huristar [Barinian]

Hurmin—another name for Satan.

Hurmiz—one of the daughters of Lilith (*q.v.*). Hurmiz is mentioned in Talmud *Sabbath* 151b. [*Rf.* Thompson, *Semitic Magic*, p. 71.]

Hurtapal—one of 3 angels of Lord's Day (Sunday), the other 2 angels being Michael and Dardael. [*Rf.* de Abano, *The Heptameron*.]

Husael—an angel serving in the 3rd Heaven. [*Rf. The Sixth and Seventh Books of Moses*.]

Hushmael—an angel's name found inscribed on an oriental Hebrew charm (*kamea*) for warding off evil. [*Rf.* Schrire, *Hebrew Amulets*.]

Hutriel ("rod of God")—one of the 7 angels of punishment, equated with Oniel (*q.v.*). Hutriel lodges in the 5th camp of Hell, and helps in the "punishment of the 10 nations." [*Rf. Maseket Gan Eden and Gehinnom*; Jellinek, *Beth ha-Midrasch*; *see also* the *Jewish Encyclopedia* I, 593.]

Huzia—one of the 64 angel wardens of the 7 celestial halls. [*Rf. Pirke Hechaloth*.]

Huznoth—a spirit invoked in the exorcism of the water. [*Rf.* Mathers, *The Greater Key of Solomon*, p. 93.]

Hydra(s)—compare with the Chalkydri (*q.v.*).

Hyniel—one of the angels ruling on Tuesday and subject to the East Wind. Hyniel is to be invoked from the north. [*Rf.* Barrett, *The Magus* II.]

Hyoskiel Jhvhh—one of the angelic princes of the hosts of X. [*Rf.* M. Gaster, *The Sword of Moses* XI.]

Hyperachii—in Chaldean theogony, a group of archangels who guide the universe. [*Rf.* Aude, *Chaldean Oracles of Zoroaster.*]

Hypezokos ("flower of fire")—one of the "effable, essential and elemental orders" in the Chaldean cosmological scheme.

Israfel, the Arabic angel of resurrection and song, by Hugo Steiner-Prag. From *The Poems of Edgar Allan Poe.* New York: Limited Editions Club, 1943.

I

Iabiel—an evil angel invoked in ceremonial magic for separating a husband from his wife. Iabiel is mentioned in *The Sword of Moses.*

Iachadiel—an angel whose name is found inscribed on the 5th pentacle of the moon. [*Rf.* Mathers, *The Greater Key of Solomon,* p. 80.] He "serveth unto destruction and loss ... thou mayest call upon him against all Phantoms of the night and to summon the souls of the departed from Hades."

Iadalbaoth (Ialdabaoth, Jaldabaoth, Ildabaoth, etc.)—the 1st archon of darkness. In Hebrew cabala and gnostic lore, Iadalbaoth is the demiourgos, occupying a position immediately below the "unknown Father." In Phoenician mythology, he is one of the 7 elohim, creators of the visible universe. In Ophitic gnosticism, Iadalbaoth is said to have generated the 7 elohim (angels) in "his own image," the 7 being: Iao, Sabaoth, Adonai, Ouraios, Eloi, Astaphaios, and Iadalbaoth's own mother, Achamoth! Origen, who also refers to Iadalbaoth as one of the 7, or as the creator of the 7, speaks of him as "Michael's second name." In

Enoch I, Iadalbaoth is equated with Sammael as the fallen angel and as the supreme hierarch of the order of thrones.

Iadara—in association with another spirit named Schaltiel, Iadara governs the sign of the virgin (Virgo) in the zodiac.

Iadiel ("hand of God")—an angel listed in Schwab, *Vocabulaire de l'Angélologie.*

Iaeo—an angel invoked to exorcise demons. [*Rf.* Conybeare, *The Testament of Solomon*; Butler, *Ritual Magic.*] Iaeo is able, with the aid of other angels, to frustrate the machinations of the demon Saphathorael.

Iahhel—in the cabala, an archangel who has dominion over philosophers and those who wish to withdraw from worldly concerns. Iahhel is also one of the 72 angels bearing the mystical name of God Shemhamphorae. [See Ambelain, *La Kabbale Pratique* for Iahhel's sigil, p. 294.]

Iahmel—an angel who has dominion over the air. [*Rf. The Book of the Angel Raziel.*]

147

Iaho (Jehovah)—the name of a divine spirit pronounced by Moses on Pharaoh Necho, causing the Egyptian king to die on the spot. [*Rf.* Voltaire, "Of Angels, Genii, and Devils," quoting Clement of Alexandria's *Stromatei*, 5.]

Ialcoajul—angel of the 11th hour of the night, serving under Dardariel. [*Rf.* Waite, *The Lemegeton*, p. 70.]

Ialdabaoth [Iadalbaoth]

Iamariel—angel of the 9th hour of the night, serving under Nacoriel.

Iameth—an angel encountered in occult and apocryphal writings. He is the only beneficent spirit who is able to overcome the machinations of Kunospaston, demon of the sea. [*Rf.* Odeberg, *3 Enoch*; Conybeare, *The Testament of Solomon*; Shah, *The Secret Lore of Magic*.]

Iao the Great—1st of the 7 archons constituting the Hebdomad in the gnostic system of primordial powers. [*Rf. Pistis Sophia*.] According to Doresse, *The Secret Books of the Egyptian Gnostics*, Iao the Great is the demiurge, master of the 7 Heavens. In *3 Enoch*, Iao's assistant, Little Iao, is actually Metatron under one of his many agnomina. [*Cf.* Jeu.]

Iaoth—in *The Testament of Solomon*, one of the 7 archangels. By the power of Iaoth's name, the demon Kurteel (who causes bowel pains) can be overcome. [*Rf.* Shah, *The Secret Lore of Magic*.]

Iaqwiel—an angel of the moon, cited in Schwab, *Vocabulaire de l'Angélologie*.

Iax—an angel capable of thwarting the demon Roeled (who causes stomach trouble) and the demon Envy. [*Rf.* Conybeare, *The Testament of Solomon*.]

Iblis [Eblis]

Iboriel—in hechaloth lore (*Ma'asseh Merkabah*), an angelic guard of the 7th heavenly hall.

Iciriel—one of the 28 angels ruling the 28 mansions of the moon.

Idedi—in Akkadian theology, angels who have their dwelling in Heaven. [*Rf.* Lenormant, *Chaldean Magic*, p. 148.]

Idrael—in hechaloth lore (*Ma'asseh Merkabah*), an angelic guard of the 5th heavenly hall.

Idris—a name for Enoch in Koranic lore. [*Rf. 3 Enoch*.]

Iealo—an angel invoked to exorcise demons. [*Rf.* Butler, *Ritual Magic*, p. 32; Conybeare, *The Testament of Solomon*.] Probably a variant of Iaeo (*q.v.*).

Iedidiel—an angel summoned up in ritual invocation. [*Rf.* Schwab, *Vocabulaire de l'Angélologie*.]

Iehuiah—an angel of the order of thrones or of powers, a protector of princes, and one of the 72 angels bearing the mystical name of God Shemhamphorae. For Iehuiah's sigil, *see* Ambelain, *La Kabbale Pratique*, p. 273.

Ieiaiel—angel of the future, sharing the office with Teiaiel (*q.v.*). Ieiaiel is also one of the 72 angels bearing the name of God Shemhamphorae.

Ieilael—one of the 72 angels bearing the name of God Shemhamphorae.

Ielahiah—formerly an angel of the order of virtues, Ielahiah protects magistrates, and renders decisions in legal suits. He is also one of the 72 angels bearing the name of God Shemhamphorae. His corresponding angel is Sentacer. [*Rf.* Ambelain, *La Kabbale Pratique*.]

Ieliel—one of the 72 angels bearing the name of God Shemhamphorae.

Ierahlem—in Mathers, *The Greater Key of Solomon*, an angel invoked in ceremonial magic.

Ierathel (Terather)—an angel of the order of dominations, according to Barrett, *The Magus* II.

Ierimiel (Hierimiel)—a form of Jeremiel (*q.v.*).

Iesaia—one of the many names of the angel Metatron.

Ietuqiel—in occult lore, an angel invoked by women at childbirth. Ietuqiel is said to be the primitive name of Moses. [*Rf.* Schwab, *Vocabulaire de l'Angélologie.*]

'Ifafi—in hechaloth lore (*Ma'asseh Merkabah*), an angelic guard of the 7th heavenly hall.

Iggereth bath Mahalath—a variant spelling in *The Zohar* (Leviticus 114a) for Agrat bat Mahlat (*q.v.*).

Ihiazel—one of the 72 angels bearing the name of God Shemhamphorae.

Iibamiah—one of the 72 angels bearing the name of God Shemhamphorae.

Ijasusael—in Enoch lore, one of the leaders of the angels of the seasons.

Ikkar Sof—the angelic ruler of the month of Schebat (January–February). [*Rf.* Schwab, *Vocabulaire de l'Angélologie.*]

Ilaniel—in Jewish legend, an angel with dominion over fruit-bearing trees. [*See* Sofiel.]

Ili-Abrat (Ilabrat)—a winged angel, Babylonian chief messenger of the god Anu. He carries a staff or wand in his right hand. Also called Papukkal.

Im—Akkadian name for Rimmon (*q.v.*).

Imachedel—according to listing in Mathers, *The Greater Key of Solomon*, an angel, in ceremonial magic, invoked by the Master of the Art.

Images—"one of the 10 orders of angels in Talmud and Targum," according to Voltaire in his essay "Of Angels, Genii, and Devils."

Imamiah—in the cabala, an angel of the order of principalities, or rather an ex-angel of that order, since he is fallen. In Hell he supervises and controls voyages, and destroys and humiliates enemies, when he is invoked to do so, or is so disposed. He was once one of the 72 angels that bore the name of God Shemhamphorae. His sigil is pictured in Ambelain, *La Kabbale Pratique*, p. 289.

'Immiel—in hechaloth lore, an angel who assists

Metatron (*q.v.*) in reciting the *Shema*. [*Rf. 3 Enoch.*]

Imriaf—in Schwab, *Vocabulaire de l'Angélologie*, the angelic ruler of the month of Tamouz (June–July).

Imriel ("eloquence of God")—the angelic ruler of the month of Siwan (May–June). [*Rf.* Schwab, *Vocabulaire de l'Angélologie.*]

Incubi—Justin Martyr, Clement, and Tertullian believe the incubi are "corporeal angels who allowed themselves to fall into the sin of lewdness with women." [*Rf.* Sinistrari, *Demoniality; or Incubi and Succubi.*]

Indri—in Vedic lore, one of the celestial deities analogous to the Judaeo-Christian angels. [*See* Adityas.]

Informer—a designation for Satan in *The Zohar.*

Ingethal or **Ingethel** [Gethel]

In Hii—in Mandaean mythology, one of the 4 *malki* or *uthri* (i.e., angels) of the North Star. [*Rf.* Drower, *The Mandaeans of Iraq and Iran.*]

Inias—one of the 7 angels reprobated at the church council in Rome (745 C.E.). The other reprobated angels were Uriel (sic), Raguel, Simiel (Semibel), Tubuel, Tubuas, and Saboac.

Innocents—according to Barrett, *The Magus*, the innocents rank 10th of the 12 orders in the celestial hierarchy, with the angel Hanael as ruler. In the pseudo-Dionysian scheme there are only 9 orders.

Innon—in Mathers, *The Greater Key of Solomon*, the holy name of an angel by which demons are commanded to appear in Solomonic conjuration rites.

Intelligences—the neo-Platonic equivalent of the Judaeo-Christian angels or sefiroth. Usually 10 in number. They are mentioned in the *Enchiridion of Pope Leo the Third* (Rome, 1523), where they are called planetary intelligences. [*Rf.* Jung, *Fallen Angels in Jewish, Christian and Mohammedan Literature.*]

Infant angels by Raphael. Reproduced from Régamey, *Anges*.

Iobel—in gnostic lore, one of the 12 powers engendered by the god Ialdabaoth. [*Rf.* Doresse, *The Secret Books of the Egyptian Gnostics*.]

Ioelet—according to *The Testament of Solomon*, an angel invoked to exorcise demons. [*Rf.* Butler, *Ritual Magic*.] With the help of other angels, Ioelet is able to frustrate the designs of the demon Saphathorael.

Iofiel ("beauty of God"—Iophiel, Zophiel, Jofiel, Jophiel)—a companion angel of Metatron; a prince of the Law (Torah), usually included among the 7 archangels and equated with Yefefiah (*q.v.*). According to Cornelius Agrippa, Iofiel is ruler of the planet Saturn, alternating with Zaphchiel (Zaphkiel). In his doctrine of Talismans, Paracelsus cites Iofiel as the intelligence of the planet Jupiter. [*Rf.* Christian, *The History and Practice of Magic* I, 318.] According to de Bles, *How to Distinguish Saints in Art*, it is Iofiel (Jophiel) who drove Adam and Eve out of Eden. This is also the view of the Rev. R. L. Gales in "The Christian Lore of Angels." In a work called *Angels in Art* by C. E. Clement, Iofiel is cited as the preceptor angel of the sons of Noah (Shem, Ham, and Japhet).

Iomuel—an angel who had sexual relations with women before the Flood, according to Schwab, *Vocabulaire de l'Angélologie*. Iomuel is to be included with the fallen angels.

Ioniel—in Solomonic lore, one of the 2 princes ruling the universe, the other angel being Sefoniel. He (Ioniel) may be invoked under the proper auspices and according to the proper magical rites.

Iophiel [Iofiel]

Irel—in occultism, an angel resident of the 5th Heaven. He rules Tuesday and is invoked from the west.

Irin ("watchers" or irin qaddisin, "holy watchers")—twin angels resident in the 6th Heaven (the 7th according to *3 Enoch*). The irin constitute, together with the twin qaddisin (*q.v.*), the supreme judgment council of the heavenly court. They are among the 8 exalted hierarchs that enjoy a rank superior to that of Metatron (who is considered, in occult and apocalyptic lore, one of the greatest angels serving God). According to Daniel 4:17, the irin are the watchers or grigori (*q.v.*). In *3 Enoch* it is said that each of the irin "is equal to the rest of the angels and princes together." Hyde in *Historia Religionis Veterum Persarum* states that the irin are of Persian origin. In the *Revelation of Moses*, Metatron points out the irin to Moses in the 6th Heaven, at the time the Lawgiver visited Paradise while still in the flesh.

Isaac (Hebrew, Ishak, "he laughed")—called "angel of light" because, at birth, Isaac had a supernatural brightness about him. His birth was announced by the angel Michael; and the fact that Abraham was too old at the time to be the begetter of offspring (Genesis 21) lent color to the legend that Isaac was of divine origin. "Jewish tradition," says Forlong in *Encyclopedia of Religions*, "makes Isaac an angel of light, created before the world, and afterwards incarnate as one of the sinless patriarchs over whom death had no power."

Isda—an angel who provides nourishment to human beings. [*Rf.* Schwab, *Vocabulaire de l'Angélologie*.]

Isfandarmend (Isphan Darmaz)—in Persian mythology, the angel of February; also ruler of the 5th day of each month. [*Rf.* Hyde, *Historia Religionis Veterum Persarum.*]

Isheth Zenunim [Eisheth Zenunim]

Is(c)him (Aishim, Izachim)—angels composed of snow and fire, resident of the 5th Heaven (*Cf.* Psalms 104:4) where Moses encountered them. [*Rf.* Ginzberg, *The Legends of the Jews* II, 308; also V, 124.] In the cabala the ishim are "the beautiful souls of just men (the saints). In *The Zohar*, they are interchangeable with the bene elim, who are of the order of thrones or angels, with Azazel chief of the order. In the scheme of Mirandola, the ishim rank 9th in the hierarchic system (Dionysius does not mention them). Their duty, since Creation, has been to extol the Lord. Among the angelic hosts the ishim represent the 9th sefiroth (Eliphas Levi says the 10th). In this connection, see works of de Mirville, 19th-century pneumatologist. In *The Zohar*, Zephaniah (Zephemiah) is listed as chief of the order. Maimonides speaks of the ishim in his *Mishna Thora* as a high order of angels.

Ishliah—one of the angels governing the east. [*See* Gauriil Ishliha.]

Isiael—in de Abano, *The Heptameron*, and Barrett, *The Magus*, one of the Tuesday angels resident in the 5th Heaven.

Isis—in *Paradise Lost* I, 478, Milton places this Egyptian deity among the fallen angels. The Phoenicians confused Isis with Ashteroth who, in goetic lore, was once a seraph but is now a great duke serving in the nether regions.

Isma'il—in Arabic tradition, a guardian angel invoked in rites of exorcism. [*Rf.* Hughes, *A Dictionary of Islam*, "Angels."] Also, an angel in the 1st Heaven in charge of a group of angels (in the guise of cows) engaged in worshipping Allah. [*Rf.* Hastings, *Encyclopaedia of Religion and Ethics* IV, 619.]

Ismoli—in occultism, the ministering angel to Samax, the latter ruler of the angels of the air operating on Monday. [*Rf.* de Abano, *The*

Heptameron; Barrett, *The Magus* II; de Claremont, *The Ancient's Book of Magic.*]

Isphan Darmaz (Isphendarmoz, Spendarmoz) —in ancient Persian lore, the tutelary spirit of the earth and the angel who presided over the month of February. He also served as the genius (i.e., angel) for virtuous women. [*Rf.* Clayton, *Angelology*; Hyde, *Historia Religionis Veterum Persarum.*]

Israel ("striver with God")—an angel of the order of hayyoth, a distinguished class of angels surrounding God's throne and to be compared with the cherubim and seraphim. In *The Book of the Angel Raziel*, Israel is ranked 6th of the throne angels. In the *Prayer of Joseph*, an Alexandrian gnostic apocryphon, commented on by Origen and Eusebius, there occurs this passage: "He who speaks to you, I, Jacob and Israel, am an angel of God and a principal (archikon) spirit." And elsewhere in the same: "I am Israel the archangel of the power of the Lord and the chief tribune among the sons of God." Further along, Jacob-Israel identifies himself as the angel Uriel. In this apocryphon, the patriarch Jacob is an archangel (angelic name: Israel) who has entered earthly life from a pre-existent state. [*Rf.* introd. *3 Enoch.*] The mystics of the geonic period (7th–11th centuries) speak of a heavenly being named Israel; the function of this angel is to "call the hosts of angels to chant God's praise." He addresses them with these words: "Bless ye the Lord who is to be blessed." Philo identifies Israel with the Logos. In Ginzberg, *The Legends of the Jews* V, 307, Israel is designated "Jacob's countenance in the throne of Glory." [*Rf. Hekaloth*, 4:29; *The Book of the Angel Raziel*, 6b.]

Israfel (Israfil, Isrephel, Sarafiel, etc.)—in Arabic folklore, "the burning one," the angel of resurrection and song, who will blow the trumpet on Judgment Day. He is described as 4-winged and "while his feet are under the 7th earth, his head reaches to the pillars of the divine throne." Also "3 times a day and 3 times during the night he looks down into Hell and is so convulsed with grief that his tears would inundate the earth if Allah did not stop their flow." It is further "revealed" that for 3 years Israfel served as companion to Mohammed, whom he initiated in the work of a prophet, and that then Gabriel came and took over. [*Rf. Shorter Encyclopaedia of Islam,* "Israfil."] Another tradition in Islamic folklore speaks of Israfel, Gabriel, Michael, and Azrael being sent by Allah to the 4 corners of the earth to fetch 7 handfuls of dust for the creation of Adam—a variant of the Genesis account in which God Himself creates Adam out of the dust on the ground; or, according to Jewish lore (Ginzberg, *The Legends of the Jews* I, 55), "from a spoonful of dust taken from the spot where, in time, the altar of atonement would stand in Jerusalem." On this mission only Azrael, angel of death, succeeded. Israfel, further, is one of the same 4 angels to be destroyed in the universal conflagration at the end of the world, of which the Koran speaks and which will occur at the sounding of the 3rd and final blast. However, there is a strong feeling that God or Allah will revive them, just as he has revived less deserving spirits (Rahab, for instance). [*Rf.* Hastings, *Encyclopaedia of Religion and Ethics* IV, 615.] Attention should be called here to the fact that Israfel is not mentioned by name in the Koran. It would be incorrect therefore to identify him as a Koranic angel—which, however, is what Poe has done in a footnote to his poem ("And the angel Israfel, whose heart strings are a lute, and who has the sweetest voice of all God's creatures—Koran"). Poe must have derived his quotation and description from a source or sources other than the Koran, for nothing of the kind can be found in it. (The matter has been made the subject of an article by the compiler of this Dictionary.) Israfel figures as a character in C. E. S. Wood's satire, *Heavenly Discourse,* Chapter 14, called "Preparedness in Heaven," in which God orders Israfel to "mobilize the Old Body Guard." In the Limited Editions Club *The Poems of Edgar Allan Poe* is a lithograph by Hugo Steiner-Prag, reproduced on p. 146. See Hervey Allen's biography of Poe called *Israfel,* and Edwin Markham's poem "Our Israfel."

Itatiyah—one of the many names of the angel Metatron (*q.v.*).

Ithoth—in Conybeare, *The Testament of Solomon,* an angel who, with the aid of other angels, is able to subvert the designs of the demon Saphathoreal.

Ithuriel ("discovery of God")—one of the 3 deputy *sarim* (princes) of the holy sefiroth serving under the ethnarchy of the angel Sephuriron. The name Ithuriel occurs in the 16th-century tracts of Isaac ha-Cohen of Soria, where the term is interpreted as denoting "a great golden crown"; and in Cordovero's *Pardes Rimmonim* (Orchard of Pomegranates). Earlier sources may yet come to light. The name appears also in the grimoires, as in the 1st pentacle of the planet Mars, figured in Mathers, *The Greater Key of Solomon,* p. 63. In *Paradise Lost* IV, 788, Milton refers to Ithuriel as a cherub ("mistakenly," says Gershom Scholem) who, along with Zephon, is dispatched by Gabriel to locate Satan. The "grieslie King" is discovered in the Garden of Eden "squat like a Toad close at the ear of Eve." By touching Satan with his spear, Ithuriel causes the Tempter to resume his proper likeness. The incident is illustrated in Hayley's edition of Milton's works (London, 1794). In Dryden, *The State of Innocence,* Ithuriel figures in the cast of characters as one of 4 angels. *Note:* It is clear from the sources cited that Milton did not coin Ithuriel (or Abdiel or Zophiel, as certain Milton scholars claim) but found him ready at hand. [*Rf.* West, "The Names of Milton's Angels" in *Studies in Philology* (April 1950).]

Itmon—one of the many names of the angel Metatron (*q.v.*).

Itqal—an angel of affection, invoked in cases of dissension among human beings. [*Rf.* Schwab, *Vocabulaire de l'Angélologie.*]

Itra'il—in Arabic lore, a guardian angel invoked in rites of exorcism. [*Rf.* Hughes, *A Dictionary of Islam,* "Angels."]

Iurabatres—in Heywood, *The Hierarchy of the Blessèd Angels,* an angel with dominion over the planet Venus. Other angels credited with governing Venus include Anael, Hasdiel, Raphael, Hagiel, and Noguel. Variant form, Eurabatres.

Michelangelo's "Kneeling Angel with Candlestick." From *The Sculptures of Michelangelo.*
New York: Oxford University Press, 1939.

Iuvart—an ex-prince of the order of angels, now serving in Hell. He is mentioned in Michaelis, *Admirable History of the Possession and Conversion of a Penitent Woman.*

Iyar—a Talmudic angel said to have been derived from Babylonian sources, just as Gabriel and Michael were. Iyar is cited in Hyde, *Historia Religionis Veterum Persarum* and in Voltaire, "Of Angels, Genii, and Devils."

Iyasusael [Ijasusael]

Izachel—in *The Greater Key of Solomon*, an angel invoked in ritual magic, specifically in prayer by the Master of the Art. [*Rf.* Waite, *The Book of Black Magic and of Pacts*, p. 204.]

Izads (Izeds)—in Zoroastrianism, heavenly hosts, the 2nd series of emanations after the amesha spentas. The izads are sometimes equated with the cherubim. There are 27 or 28 in the order. Their duty consists in watching over the "innocence, happiness, and preservation of the world," of which they are the protecting genii and guardians. The most powerful and chief of these "spirits of light" is (or was) Mithras. [*Rf.* King, *The Gnostics and Their Remains*; Saltus, *Lords of the Ghostland*, p. 42.]

Iz'iel—in hechaloth lore (*Ma'asseh Merkabah*), an angelic guard of the 6th heavenly hall.

Izrael—one of 4 angels who will be exempt from the terrifying blast of the 1st Trumpet on Judgment Day (the other 3 angels being Gabriel, Michael, and Israfel). According to Islamic lore, there will be 3 blasts in all, the final one the blast of the Resurrection. [*Rf.* Sale, *The Koran*, "Preliminary Discourse," p. 59.] There will be, it seems, a 40-year (or 40-day) interval between each blast. At the very end, at Allah's command, "the dry and rotten bones and dispersed parts of the bodies of all human creatures, even to the very hairs, will be called to judgment."

Izrafel [Israfel]

Izschim [Ischim]

The Last Judgment. From a Persian miniature of the 8th century, reproduced from *The Lost Books of the Bible.*

Jabniel ("Jehovah causes to be built")—one of the ruling angels of the 3rd Heaven, as listed in *The Sixth and Seventh Books of Moses.*

Jabriel [Jibril]

Jachniel—one of numerous angelic guards of the gates of the South Wind. [*Rf. Ozar Midrashim* II, 316.]

Jacob [Israel]

Jael (Joel)—one of the twin cherubim on the Mercy Seat of the Ark of the Covenant, the other cherub being Zarall. In occult lore, Jael is an angel governing the zodiacal sign of Libra.

Jahoel [Jehoel]

Jaluha—in the gnostic work *Texts of the Savior,* Jaluha is the "receiver of Sabaoth Adamas." To sinners who are being judged or purged, Jaluha bears the cup of oblivion so that the soul "may drink therein and forget all the places which it has passed through." [*Rf.* Legge, *Forerunners and Rivals of Christianity* X, 187.]

Janax—a Monday angel of the 1st Heaven invoked from the east. [*Rf.* Barrett, *The Magus* II, 118.]

Janiel—angel of the 5th Heaven ruling on Tuesday and subject to the East Wind. [*Rf.* Barrett, *The Magus* II.]

Jareahel [Jevanael]

Jareriel [Jazeriel]

Jariel—an angel of the divine face or presence. A variant form of Suriel, Sariel, Raziel.

Javan (Yavan; Greek, for Greece)—a guardian angel whose special sovereignty is (or was) Greece. In Jewish legend, Javan exercises dominion also over Israel, although, traditionally, it is Michael who serves as tutelary guardian of the chosen people. [*Rf.* Ginzberg, *The Legends of the Jews* VI, 434.]

Jazar—a genius who "compels love." Jazar is one of the genii of the 7th hour, according to *The Nuctemeron* of Apollonius of Tyana.

Jazeriel (Jareriel)—one of the 28 angels ruling over the 28 mansions of the moon.

"When the morning stars sang together," by William Blake, illustrating Job 38:7. Frontispiece in Jastrow, *The Book of Job.*

Jeduthun ("praising" or "judgment")—in the cabala, lord of the evening choirs in Heaven. As "Master of Howling" he leads myriads of angels in chanting hymns of praise to God at the close of each day. Psalms 39, 62, 77 are inscribed "To the chief Musician, even Jeduthun." Here, clearly, Jeduthun is a mortal (a Levite), one of the directors of music at the temple; but in the early Middle Ages the Zoharists transformed Jeduthun into an angel and assigned him in Heaven a post similar to the one he invested on earth. [*See* Asaph; Heman.]

Jehoel (Jehuel, Jaoel, Yahoel, Shemuel, Kemuel, Metatron)—mediator of the ineffable name and one of the princes of the presence. In Jewish legend, Jehoel is "the angel who holds the Leviathan in check." He is chief of the order of seraphim (although it is Seraphiel who is commonly invested with this rank). According to *The Apocalypse of Abraham*, Jehoel (otherwise Metatron-Yahoel) is the heavenly choirmaster, "singer of the eternal" and "heavenly Son of Man" who accompanied Abraham on his visit to Paradise and revealed to him the course of human history. In his *Jewish Gnosticism, Merkabah Mysticism, and Talmudic Tradition*, Scholem suggests that Jehoel is an earlier name of Metatron. In the cabalistic *Berith Menuha* 57a, Jaoel (Jehoel) is the principal angel over fire. King, *The Gnostics and Their Remains* (p. 15), lists 7 subordinates of Jehuel—Seraphiel, Gabriel, Nuriel, Temmael, Shimshael, Hadarniel, and Sarmiel.

Jehovah-Angel—the angel in Genesis 48:16 is so termed (i.e., angel of the Lord) by Gregory Thaumaturgus in his "Panegyric Addressed to Origen."

Jehudiam—in *The Zohar* (Exodus 129a), Jehudiam is an angel "who keeps the accounts of the righteous." In addition, he "carries the 70 keys of all the treasures of the Lord."

Jehudiel—ruler of the movements of the celestial spheres. *Cf.* Metatron, "who doth the Primum Mobile guide." Jehudiel is sometimes included in the list of the 7 archangels. [*See* Salatheel.]

Jehuel [Jehoel]

Jekusiel—in *Pirke Hechaloth*, Jekusiel is an angelic guard stationed in one of the halls of the 1st Heaven.

Jekut(h)iel—an amulet spirit, invoked by women at childbirth. [*Rf.* Schwab, *Vocabulaire de l'Angélologie.*] Moses was christened Jekuthiel, says *Pirke Rabbi Eliezer*, because "his form was like that of an angel."

Jeliel—a seraph whose name is inscribed on the Tree of Life in the world of Yetzirah (Formation). In the cabala, Jeliel is the heavenly prince-ruler of Turkey. He controls the destiny of kings and other high dignitaries and gives the palm of victory to those who are unjustly attacked or invaded. In addition, he inspires passion between the sexes and insures marital fidelity. His sigil is reproduced in Ambelain, *La Kabbale Pratique*, p. 260.

Jeou—in gnostic lore, a great heavenly power who shackles the god Ialdabaoth to a sphere of fate. Jeou deprives the god of his rank and elevates in his place Ialdabaoth's son, Ibraoth (or Sabaoth). [*Rf.* Doresse, *The Secret Books of the Egyptian Gnostics*, p. 176.]

Jeqon (Yeqon, Yikon, "inciter")—a ringleader of the fallen angels, as listed in *Enoch I*. Of Jeqon it is said that, with the help of Asbeel, another apostate (*q.v.*), he led astray the sons of God (i.e., other angels) by tempting them with the sight of mortal women; and that it was with these women that these sons of God later had sexual relations. [*Rf.* Bamberger, *Fallen Angels*.]

Jerazol—an angel of power mentioned in cabalistic works. He is invoked in conjuring rites. [*Rf. The Sixth and Seventh Books of Moses*.]

Jeremiel ("mercy of God" or "whom God sets up")—in *Enoch I* and *II Esdras*, Jeremiel is equated with Remiel; also with Uriel. He is one of the 7 archangels in the original or earliest listings. He has been described as the "lord of souls awaiting resurrection." [*Rf.* various editions of the Apocrypha by Goodspeed, Metzger, and Komroff.] In *II Esdras* 4:36, Jeremiel is referred to as an archangel. In *The Masque of Angels*, a one-act opera produced in February 1966 at St. George's Church in New York, Jeremiel was cast as a principality.

Jerescue (Jeruscue)—a Wednesday angel, residing in the 3rd Heaven; he is invoked from the west—according to de Abano, *The Heptameron*; but, according to Barrett, *The Magus* II, Jerescue is a resident of the 2nd Heaven (which may make a difference as to the direction from which he is to be invoked).

Jesodoth—in rabbinic tradition, an angel who receives wisdom and knowledge direct from God for transmission to man. He is 10th in the hierarchy

of the elohim. [*Rf.* Spence, *An Encyclopaedia of Occultism*, p. 238.] Cornelius Agrippa, *Three Books of Occult Philosophy*, speaks of Jesodoth receiving beneficence from the 10th of the divine essences, elohim.

Jesubilin—according to the *Grimorium Verum*, a "holy angel of God" invoked in gnostic rites. The name is a variant form of Serabilin.

Jesus—regarded by Philo, Justin Martyr, and early Christian writers as "a leading angel" or archangel; also identified as the Logos or Word, and as such is said to have been one of the 3 angels that visited Abraham under the oak of Mamre. [*Rf.* Conybeare, *Myth, Magic, and Morals*, p. 226.]

Jetrel—one of 200 fallen angels in the Enoch listings.

Jeu—in gnostic lore, specifically in *Pistis Sophia*, Jeu is a great angel, "overseer of light, arranger of the Cosmos." He is one of the 3 great powers on high, occupying the place on God's right, with Propator on God's left. [*Rf.* works of Valentinus.]

Jevanael (Jareahel)—in Mosaic lore, one of the 7 princes that stand continually before God and to whom are given the spirit-names of the planets. [*Rf.* Cornelius Agrippa, *Three Books of Occult Philosophy* III.]

Jibril (Jabriel, Jabril, Jibra'il, Jabriyel, Abruel)—the name of Gabriel in Koranic Scripture. As Jibra'il in Arabic rites of exorcism, he is regarded as a guardian angel. [*Rf.* Hughes, *A Dictionary of Islam*, "Angels."] In Persian lore, Jibril is Bahram, "the mightiest of all the angels"; also "Serosh, the message-bringer." [*Rf. The Dabistan*, pp. 127, 379.]

Jinn—in Moslem theology, the jinn were created 2,000 years before Adam. They were originally of a high estate, equal to the angels, with Eblis chief among them. When, on the creation of Adam, Eblis refused to worship the earthling, Eblis was degraded and cast out of Heaven along with the jinn, who thenceforth became demons. Five sons of Eblis (*q.v.*) were among the evil jinn. In Hughes, *A Dictionary of*

Angels bewailing the death of Jesus, a detail from a fresco by Giotto in the Arena Chapel, Padua. Reproduced from Régamey, *Anges.*

Islam, "Genii," we find the following quotation: "The most noble and honorable among the angels are called the Ginn, because they are veiled from the eyes of the other angels on account of their superiority."

Jinniyeh (fem. for jinn).

Joel (Jael, Jehoel, Yahoel, Jah-el, etc.)—in *The Book of Adam and Eve,* a pseudepigraphic work, Joel is the archangel who allotted our first parents a 7th part of the earthly paradise. Joel is also credited with being the angel who bade Adam name all things, an incident related in Genesis 2:19–20 (where it is God Himself who appoints Adam to the task). Joel (or Yahoel) is the 1st of Metatron's names. In Conybeare, *The Testament of Solomon,* the female demon Onoskelis, on being

interrogated by Solomon, declared she was subject to Joel.

Jofiel [Iofiel]

Johiel—angel of Paradise, although Shamshiel, Zephon, Zotiel, Michael, and Gabriel, among others, have been called angels of Paradise. There are actually two paradises, the one heavenly, the other earthly (Eden).

John the Baptist—the "forerunner angel," as in Exodus 23:20; Malachi 3:1; Matthew 11:10. "Behold, I send an angel before thee, to keep thee in the way and to bring thee into the place I have prepared." In *The Zohar* (Vayehi, 232a), Rabbi Judah declared: "This angel, this deliverer of the world, is sometimes male, sometimes female.

When he procures blessings for the world, he is male, resembling the male who provides blessings for the female. But when he comes to bring chastisement on the world, he is female, being, as it were, pregnant with the judgment." [*See* Metatron; Shekinah; Helias the Prophet.] In the Coptic *Book of John the Evangelist*, Jesus speaks of "Helias the prophet" (meaning John the Baptist) and refers to the latter as an angel sent by Satan (sic) to baptize with water. [*Rf.* James, *The Apocryphal New Testament*, p. 191.] "In the icons of the Eastern Church he (John the Baptist) is always depicted with wings, to indicate his office as messenger [i.e., angel] sent before the face of Christ"—from Gales, "The Christian Lore of Angels."

Jomiael [Jomjael]

Jomjael (Yomyael, "day of God")—one of the fallen angels cast out of Heaven, along with Semyaza, Satan, etc. [*Rf. Enoch I.*]

Jophiel [Iofiel]

Jorkemo [Yurkemi]

Josata (Josta)—an angel invoked in Solomonic magic rites in the Uriel conjuration. Josata is one of the 4 magical words or names spoken by God ("with his mouth, to his servant Moses"), the other 3 names being Ablati, Abla, and Caila. [*Rf. Grimorium Verum.*]

Josephel [Asfa'el]

Joth—a secret name of God which "Jacob learned from the angel in the night of his wrestling, and by which he was delivered from the hands of his brother Esau." [*Rf.* Malchus, *The Secret Grimoire of Turiel*; Waite, *The Book of Black Magic and of Pacts.*]

Joustriel—in Waite, *The Lemegeton*, an angel of the 6th hour of the day, serving under Samil.

Jove—a fallen angel in *Paradise Lost* I, 512. Milton derived him from Greek mythology, where he is Zeus, lord of heaven; or from Roman mythology, where he is Jupiter or Jove.

Jukar—"a prince over all the angels and all the Caesars," according to Mathers, *The Greater Key of Solomon.*

Junier—an ex-prince of the order of angels. [*Rf.* Garinet, *The History of Magic in France*; De Plancy, *Dictionnaire Infernal* III, p. 459.]

Jusguarin—a ruling angel of the 10th hour of the night. Jusguarin has 10 chief angelic officers under him, as well as 100 lesser officers. [*Rf.* Waite, *The Book of Ceremonial Magic*, p. 70.]

Uriel descending from heaven on a sunbeam to join Gabriel, Ithuriel, and Zephon in the Garden of Eden, where they come upon Adam and Eve in embrace (lower right) and Satan in the form of a toad "squat at the ear of Eve." From *Paradise Lost*. London: Richard Bently, 1688.

Kabchiel—an angel in Mandaean religious lore. [*Rf.* Pognon, *Inscriptions Mandaïtes des Coupes de Khouabir.*]

Kabiri—there are 7 kabiri; in Phoenician mythology, they are the creators of the world. They may be compared to the 7 angels of the presence in gnostic and rabbinic lore.

Kabniel—in the cabala, an angel invoked to cure stupidity. [*Rf.* Moses Botarel, *Mayan Hahochmah.*]

Kabriel [Cabriel]

Kabshiel—in Jewish mysticism, an angel who, when conjured up and agreeable to the invocant, confers grace and power. The name "Kabshiel" is found engraved on amulets. [*Rf.* Trachtenberg, *Jewish Magic and Superstition.*]

Kadal—one of the 70 childbed amulet angels.

Kadashiel—one of numerous angelic guards of the gates of the South Wind. [*Rf. Ozar Midrashim* II, 3, 7.]

Kadashim [Kadishim]

Kadi(el)—a Friday angel serving in the 3rd Heaven and invoked from the west. [*Rf.* Barrett, *The Magus* II; de Abano, *The Heptameron.*]

Kadir-Rahman ("power of mercy")—one of the 7 archangels in Yezidic devil-worship, invoked in prayer. For the names of all 7 of these "powers of mercy," *see* Appendix.

Kadishim (Kadashim or Qaddisin—"holy ones")—angels of a rank higher than the Merkabah angels, and resident in the 6th or 7th Heaven. They praise God in unceasing hymns of adoration. With the irin (*q.v.*), they constitute the angelic *beth din*, i.e., seat of judgment. The chief of the order "was made of hail, and he was so tall, it would take 500 years to walk a distance to his height," according to rabbinic legend. Moses encountered these angels in the company of the irin during the Lawgiver's visit to Paradise. [*Rf. 3 Enoch*; Ginzberg, *The Legends of the Jews* II, 308.]

163

Amulet from *The Book of the Angel Raziel.* Outside the concentric circles are the names of the four rivers of paradise; within is the hexagram (shield of Solomon) with groups of three letters. Between the circles are the names of Adam, Eve, Lilith, Khasdiel, Senoi, Sansenoi, Samangeloph, and the words "He hath given his angels charge concerning thee, that they may keep thee in all thy ways."

Kadkadael—in hechaloth lore (*Ma'asseh Merkabah*), an angelic guard stationed at the 6th heavenly hall.

Kadmiel ("before God")—one of the 70 angels to be invoked at the time of childbirth, as recommended in *The Book of the Angel Raziel.*

Kadosh—in hechaloth lore (*Ma'asseh Merkabah*), an angelic guard stationed at the 4th heavenly hall.

Kadriel—in *The Zohar* (Balak 201b), one of 3 "mouths" created by God at the start of Creation. Another "mouth" created at the same time was (or is) the angel Yahadriel. The term very likely denotes the voice of prophecy. And in this connection, the "start of Creation" would mean the eve of the first Sabbath.

Kafkefoni—one of the 7 enduring unholy sefiroth. Kafkefoni is king of the *mazzikin* and husband of the "little leprous one." [*Rf.* Bamberger, *Fallen Angels,* p. 174.]

Kafziel (Cassiel, "speed of God")—the angel governing the death of kings. In geonic tradition, one of the 7 archangels with dominion over the planet Saturn. As Qaphsiel, a variant spelling, he is controller of the moon. [*Rf. Jewish Magic and Superstition.*] In *The Zohar* (Numbers 155a) Kafziel serves with Hizkiel as chief aide to Gabriel when the latter bears his standard in battle.

Kahaviel [Dahaviel]

Kakabel (Kochbiel, Kokbiel, Kabaiel, Kochab—"star of God")—a great angelic prince who exercises dominion over the stars and constellations. In *The Book of the Angel Raziel,* Kakabel is a high, holy angel; but in apocryphal lore generally, as in *Enoch I,* he is evil (a fallen angel) and a resident of the nether realms. Whether in Heaven or in Hell, Kakabel commands 365,000 surrogate spirits who do his bidding. Among other duties he instructs his fellows in astrology. [*See* Rathiel.]

Kal—the guardian angel of Nebuchadnezzar. [*Rf.* Ginzberg, *The Legends of the Jews* VI, 424.]

Kalka'il—in Islamic tradition, a guardian angel invoked in rites of exorcism. [*Rf.* Hughes, *A Dictionary of Islam,* "Angels."] Also, an angel in the 5th Heaven in charge of a group of angels in the guise of houris (black-eyed celestial nymphs) engaged in worshipping Allah. [*Rf.* Hastings, *Encyclopaedia of Religion and Ethics* IV, 619.]

Kalkelmiyah—one of the many names of the angel Metatron.

Kalki Avatar—the 10th of the 10 avatars in Vedic lore. [*See* Avatar.]

Kalkydri [Chalkydri]

Kalmiya—one of the 7 angelic princes of power, guards of the veil or curtain of the 7th Heaven. The other 6 angels are usually given as Boel, Asimor, Psachar (Paschar), Gabriel, Sandalphon, and Uzziel. [*Rf.* Margouliath, *Malache Elyon,* p. 17; *Ozar Midrashim* I, p. 110.]

Kamuel [Camael]

Kandile—one of the 9 holy angels invoked by cabalists, according to *The Sixth and Seventh Books of Moses.*

Kaniel—one of the 70 childbed amulet angels. For the names of all 70, *see* Appendix.

Kaphkaphiel—an angel's name found inscribed on an oriental charm (*kamea*) for warding off evil. [*Rf.* Schrire, *Hebrew Amulets.*]

Karkiel—one of the 70 childbed amulet angels.

Karmiel—one of the numerous angelic guards of the gates of the East Wind. [*Rf. Ozar Midrashim* II, 316.]

Karniel—an angelic guard of the gates of the West Wind. [*Rf. Ozar Midrashim* II, 316.]

Karoz—in rabbinic lore, the Karoz are "reporter angels." [*Rf. The Thanksgiving Hymns.*]

Kartion—in hechaloth lore (*Ma'asseh Merkabah*), an angelic guard stationed at the 7th heavenly hall.

Kasbak (Baskabas)—a secret name of the angel Metatron. [*Rf. The Vision of Ezekiel.*]

Kasbeel (Kazbiel, Kaspiel—"sorcery")—a "sinful" angel, referred to as "chief of the oath," whose original name was Biqa, meaning "good person." [*Cf.* Akae.] But Kasbeel fell, and after his fall he was renamed Kazbiel, meaning "he who lies to God." He once asked Michael for the hidden name of the Lord, which Michael of course refused to divulge. For the story, see *Enoch I,* 69:13. For comment, see Bamberger, *Fallen Angels,* p. 264.

Kasdaye (Kesdeya, Kasdeja)—a fallen angel who teaches "a variety of demonic practices, including abortion." Kasdaye is one of 7 angels reputed to have led the apostate angels, according to *The Book of Enoch (Enoch I),* p. 69.

Kashiel—one of numerous angelic guards of the gates of the South Wind. [*Rf. Ozar Midrashim* II, 316.]

Kashriel (Tophnar)—one of the 7 angelic guards of the 1st Heaven, serving (or identified with) Zevudiel. [*Rf. Hechaloth Rabbati.*]

Kaspiel [Kasbeel]

Katchiel—one of the 70 childbed amulet angels.

Katzfiel—an angelic prince of the Sword, and guard of the 6th Heaven. It is said that Katzfiel's sword emits lightning. [*Rf. Ozar Midrashim* I, p. 118.]

Katzmiel—one of the angelic guards stationed in the 6th Heaven. [*Rf. Pirke Hechaloth.*]

Kautel [Ketuel]

Kavod—in chasidic lore, a term meaning the glory of God, i.e., that aspect of the godhead which God reveals to man. Identical with the demiurge, holy spirit, the "great radiance called Shekinah." Kavod also is a term to describe "the cherub on the throne of God." [*Rf.* Scholem, *Major Trends in Jewish Mysticism,* p. 110ff.]

Kavzakiel—one of the angel-princes of the Sword, as listed in M. Gaster, *The Sword of Moses.*

Kawkabel [Kakabel]

Kazbiel [Kasbeel]

Kazpiel [Kasbeel]

Kazviel—an angelic guard of the 4th Heaven. [*Rf. Ozar Midrashim* I, 116.]

Kedemel—in talismanic magic, the spirit of the planet Venus. [*Rf.* Barrett, *The Magus* II, 147.]

Keel ("like God")—angel of a season; one of the "leaders of heads of thousands," as cited in *Enoch I.*

Kelail—in Islamic traditional lore, the governor of the 5th Heaven. [*Rf.* Clayton, *Angelology.*]

Keliel—one of the 72 angels of the 72 quinaries of the degrees of the zodiac. [*Rf.* Runes, *The Wisdom of the Kabbalah.*]

Kelkhea and **Kelkheak**—as described in the *Paraphrase of Shem,* Kelkhea and Kelkheak are 2 mysterious entities (angels) to whom the secrets of Creation were revealed.

Kemos [Kimos]

Kemuel (Shemuel, Camael, Seraphiel—"helper" or "assembly of God")—the great archon who stands at the windows of Heaven as mediator between the prayers of Israel and the princes of the 7th Heaven. Kemuel is chief of seraphim and one of the 10 holy sefiroth. Legend tells of Moses destroying Kemuel (Camael) when this great hierarch tried to prevent the Lawgiver from receiving the Torah at the hand of God. [*Rf.* Ginzberg, *The Legends of the Jews*.] Kemuel, according to the *Revelation of Moses*, is (or was) leader of the 12,000 angels of destruction.

Kenunit—one of the 70 childbed amulet angels. [*Rf. The Book of the Angel Raziel*.]

Kered—an angel of the Seal in Mosaic magical conjurations.

Kerkoutha—in the *Gospel of Bartholomew*, an angel with rulership over the south.

Kerubiel—eponymous head of the order of cherubim. According to *3 Enoch* Kerubiel's body is "full of burning coals ... there is a crown of holiness on his head . . . and the bow of the Shekinah is between his shoulders."

Ketheriel ("crown of God")—an angel of the sefiroth invoked in cabalistic rites. [*Rf.* Levi, *Transcendental Magic*.] [*See* Akatriel.]

Ketuel (Kautel)—one of the 3 angels constituting the Triune God, the other 2 angels being Meachuel and Lebatei. [*Rf. The Sixth and Seventh Books of Moses*.]

Keveqel—one of the 72 angels of the zodiac, as cited in Runes, *The Wisdom of the Kabbalah*.

Kezef—in Jewish legend, an angel of death and one of the 5 angels of destruction (along with Af, Hemah, Mashhit, and Haron-Peor). Kezef fought against Moses in Horeb; and it was Kezef, as the angel of death, whom Aaron seized and imprisoned in the Holy Tabernacle. [*Rf.* Ginzberg, *The Legends of the Jews* III, 306.] In the *Midrash Tehillim*, Kezef is the angel of wrath.

Kfial—one of the 64 angel wardens of the 7 celestial halls. [*Rf. Pirke Hechaloth*.]

Khabiel—one of the supervising guards of the 1st Heaven. He is named in the *Pirke Hechaloth*.

Khamael [Camael]

Kharael—in *The Testament of Solomon*, an angel who, when his name is pronounced, is able to exorcise the demon Belbel, as Belbel himself concedes. [*Rf. The Secret Books of the Egyptian Gnostics*, p. 203.]

Kharura'il—in Arabic lore, a guardian angel invoked in rites of exorcism. [*Rf.* Hughes, *A Dictionary of Islam*, "Angels."]

Khasdiel—the name of an angel inscribed on a Hebrew amulet, and pictured in *The Book of the Angel Raziel*. Khasdiel appears here along with the names of the angels Senoi, Sansenoi, and Samangeloph, as well as the names of Adam, Eve, and Lilith. See Budge, *Amulets and Talismans*, p. 227; reproduction on p. 164.

Khurdad—the angel of May in ancient Persian lore. Khurdad also governed the 6th day of the month. He is one of the amesha spentas, and is prayed to at the 56th gate of Paradise as an intercessor. [*Rf. The Dabistan*, p. 164.]

Kidumiel—one of 70 childbed amulet angels. *The Book of the Angel Raziel* contains the names of all 70 of these spirits invoked to protect the newborn child and its mother against calamity and disease.

Kimos (Kemos)—a secret name for Michael or Metatron, as vouched for in *The Visions of Ezekiel*. [*Rf.* Scholem, *Jewish Gnosticism, Merkabah Mysticism, and Talmudic Tradition*.]

Kinor—one of 3 angels stationed at the upper gates of Hell.

Kipod—an angel like Kinor (*q.v.*). The other 2 angels are given as Nagrasagiel (or Nasragiel) and Nairyo Sangha, the latter a messenger of Ahura Mazda. It was Kipod who conducted Rabbi Joshua to the gates of Hell and showed him the compartments into which the underworld is

"Angels Transporting St. Paul to Heaven" by Poussin. Reproduced from Régamey, *Anges*.

divided. [*Rf. Revelation of Rabbi Joshua ben Levi; Midrash Konen.*]

Kiramu 'l-katibin—the name of 2 recording angels in Arabic lore. [*See* Recording Angel.]

Kirtabus—genius of languages and one of the genii of the 9th hour. [*Rf. Apollonius of Tyana, The Nuctemeron.*]

Kisael—in hechaloth lore (*Ma'asseh Merkabah*), an angelic guard stationed at the 5th heavenly hall.

Kitreal (Kitriel)—a form of Akatriel (*q.v.*). [*Rf. Schwab, Vocabulaire de l'Angélologie.*]

Klaha—one of numerous angelic guards of the gates of the South Wind. [*Rf. Ozar Midrashim* II, 316.]

Kmiel—in Jewish mysticism, an angel of the summer equinox, effective as an amulet against the evil eye. [*Rf. Trachtenberg, Jewish Magic and Superstition.*]

Kokabiel [Kakabel]

Kokaviel—the name of an angel found inscribed on the 3rd pentacle of the planet Mercury.

Kokhabriel [Kakabel]

Kolazonta (Greek, "the chastiser")—the destroying angel who figures in the Aaron incident related in Reider, *The Book of Wisdom*, 18:22. Kolazonta is the "personification of the destroying spirit" who in IV Maccabees 7:11 is called an angel.

Komm—mentioned in the *Revelation of Rabbi Joshua ben Levi*. Komm is the angel who refused, when summoned, to give Rabbi Joshua a description of Hell. [*Rf. M. Gaster, Studies and Texts of Folklore.*]

Korniel—one of numerous angelic guards of the South Wind. Named in *Ozar Midrashim* II, 316.

Korshid—a Mandaean—also a Mazdean—archspirit, comparable to Metatron in Jewish cabala. [*Rf. de Mirville, Pneumatologie.*]

Kotecha—in *The Sixth and Seventh Books of Moses* an angel of the Seal, conjured in ceremonial magic.

Koustiel—an angel's name found engraved on a carnelian in the British Museum (56013). "May be a blunder for Uriel," says Bonner, in *Studies in Magical Amulets*, p. 170.

Krishna [Krisn Avatar]

Krisn Avatar (Krishna)—8th of the 10 avatars in Vedic lore. [*See* Avatar.]

Kshathra Vairya—one of the 6 amesha spentas (*q.v.*).

Kshiel [Kushiel]

Kso'ppghiel—a leader of the angels of fury, one of the *nomina barbara* listed in M. Gaster, *The Sword of Moses*. [*Cf.* Angels of ire.]

Kunospaston—in occultism, the demon of the sea. [*Cf.* Rahab.] He is a hoar-fish and delights in destroying ships. He is also greedy for gold. [*Rf. Conybeare, The Testament of Solomon.*]

Kuriel [Kyriel]

Kurmavatar—the "tortoise avatar," one of 10.

Kurzi [Angel of the Footstool]

Kushiel ("rigid one of God")—one of 7 angels of punishment and a "presiding angel of Hell." According to *Midrash Konen*, Kushiel "punishes the nations with a whip of fire." [*Rf. Jewish Encyclopedia* I, 593; Jellinek, *Beth ha-Midrasch.*]

Kutiel—an angel invoked in connection with the use of divining rods. [*Rf. Trachtenberg, Jewish Magic and Superstition.*]

Kyniel—an angel serving in the 3rd Heaven. [*Rf. The Sixth and Seventh Books of Moses.*]

Kyriel (Kuriel)—one of 28 angels governing the 28 mansions of the moon. [*Rf. Barrett, The Magus* II.] As Kuriel, he is one of numerous angelic guards of the gates of the West Wind. [*Rf. Ozar Midrashim* II, 316.]

Kyriotates—in his *Karmic Relationships*, Rudolf Steiner speaks of 3 celestial hierarchies, the kyriotates being an order of the 2nd. The triad here consists of exusiai (virtues or authorities), kyriotates (dominations?) and dynamis (powers).

Kzuial—an angelic guard stationed in the 4th Heaven. [*Rf. Pirke Hechaloth.*]

L

Labarfiel—one of the angelic guards of the 7th Heaven. [*Rf. Ozar Midrashim* I, 119.]

Labbiel—original name of the angel Raphael. The name was changed when, according to Jewish legend, Labbiel complied with God's command concerning the creation of man. It should be noted here that 2 groups of angels (the angels of truth and the angels of peace), not complying with the divine command, were burned. [*Rf.* Ginzberg, *The Legends of the Jews* I, 52ff.]

Labezerin—in talismanic magic, the genius (spirit) of success. Labezerin serves in the 2nd hour of the day. [*Rf.* Apollonius of Tyana, *The Nuctemeron.*]

Labusi—one of the 5 angels of omnipotence, the other 4 being Tubatlu, Bualu, Tulatu, Ublisi. [*Rf. The Sixth and Seventh Books of Moses*, p. 85.]

Lad (Hebrew, "tender age")—one of the many names of the angel Metatron.

Lahabiel—an angel who assists Raphael in the rulership of the 1st day (Samael ruling the 3rd day and Anael the 6th). Along with Phaniel, Rahabiel, Ariel, and others, Lahabiel used to be invoked as an amulet against evil spirits (and perhaps still is), as indicated in a late Hebrew charm. [*Rf.* Thompson, *Semitic Magic*, p. 161.]

Lahariel—one of the 70 childbed amulet angels. Lahariel assists Michael in the rulership of the 2nd day. [*Rf. The Book of the Angel Raziel*; Budge, *Amulets and Talismans*; M. Gaster, *Wisdom of the Chaldeans*, pp. 338ff.]

Lahash—in rabbinic lore, a great angel who, with the aid of Zakun, led 184 myriads of spirits to snatch away the prayer of Moses before it could reach God. For this attempt at interference with the divine will, the 2 angels were punished with "60 blows [lashes] of fire." [*Rf.* Ginzberg, *The Legends of the Jews* III, 434.] Bamberger, *Fallen Angels*, p. 138, cites another form of the same legend wherein it is Sammael who metes out the punishment on Lahash by "binding him with fiery chains, flogging him with 70 stripes of fire, and expelling him from the divine presence."

Lahatiel ("the flaming one")—one of the 7 angels of punishment, as listed in *Maseket Gan*

Eden and *Gehinnom*. [*Rf. Jewish Encyclopedia* I, 593.] In the writings of the cabalist Joseph ben Abraham Gikatilla, Lahatiel is the presiding angel of the gates of death, which is the designation for the 2nd lodge of the 7 lodges in which Hell (arka) is divided. According to the *Revelation of Rabbi Joshua ben Levi*, Lahatiel is one of the angels in Hell who punishes nations "for cause." [*Rf.* M. Gaster, *Studies and Texts in Folklore*.]

Laila(h) (Leliel, Lailahel, Layla)—the name is said to derive from a rabbinic exegesis of the word "lailah" (meaning night) in Job 3:3. According to *The Zohar* (Exodus) Lailah is "an angel appointed to guard the spirits at their birth." In Jewish legendary lore, Lailah is a demonic angel of night, the "prince of conception," to be compared with Lilith, demoness of conception. However, in *Genesis Rabba* 417 and in *Sanhedrin* 96a [*Rf. Jewish Encyclopedia* I, 588] the story is that Lailah fought for Abraham when the patriarch battled kings—which would make Lailah a good, rather than a wicked, angel.

Lama—in de Abano, *The Heptameron*, Lama (or La Ma) is an angel of the air, ruler of Tuesday, and a resident of the 5th Heaven. He is invoked from the west.

Lamach—an angel who exercises dominion over the planet Mars. [*Rf.* Heywood, *The Hierarchy of the Blessèd Angels*, p. 215.]

Lamas (*see* Nirgal)—one of the 4 principal

Lamenting angel, from an ancient Greek pietà. Reproduced from Jameson, *Legends of the Madonna*.

classes of protecting genii in Chaldean lore, usually represented with the body of a lion and the head of a man. *Cf.* cherubim. [*Rf.* Lenormant, *Chaldean Magic*, p. 121.]

Lamassu—in Assyrian lore, a kindly spirit appealed to at the end of invocations for the exorcism of evil spirits. [*Rf.* Thompson, *Semitic Magic*, p. 45.] According to Trachtenberg, *Jewish Magic and Superstition*, p. 156, Lamassu is a Babylonian spirit.

Lamechalal (Lamechiel)—a planetary ruler cited in *3 Enoch* (Hebrew Enoch). Lamechalal was the only angel who, as the reader is assured in Conybeare, *The Testament of Solomon*, could overcome the female demon called Deceit.

Lamechiel [Lamechalal]

Lameck (Lamideck)—a pure angel, invoked in black-magic rites, specifically in the conjuration of the Sword. [*Rf. Grimorium Verum*; Shah, *The Secret Lore of Magic*.]

Lamediel—an angel of the 4th hour of the night, serving under Jefischa. [*Rf.* Waite, *The Lemegeton*.]

Lamedk—an angel like Lameck (but not to be confused with him) who is invoked in the conjuration of the Sword.

Lamideck [Lameck]

Larzod—one of the "glorious and benevolent angels" invoked in Solomonic conjuring rites for imparting to the invocant some of the secret wisdom of the Creator. [*Rf.* Gollancz, *Clavicula Salomonis*.]

Lauday—an angel invoked in the benediction of the Salt, as cited in the *Grimorium Verum*.

Lau(v)iah—in the cabala, an angel of the order of thrones; also of the order of cherubim. More correctly, he formerly belonged to these orders. Lauviah influences savants and great personages. For his sigil, see Ambelain, *La Kabbale Pratique*, pp. 260, 267.

Láwidh—in Islamic apocalyptic lore, a "chief of angels." The sufi Abu Yazid in his *mir'aj* (ascent) to the 7 Heavens comes upon Láwidh in the 2nd Heaven and is there offered "a kingdom such as no tongue can describe," but Abu Yazid resists the offer (actually a bribe), knowing it to be only a test of his single-minded devotion to God. [*Rf.* Nicholson, "An Early Arabic Version," etc.]

Layla [Lailah]

Lazai (Lazay)—a "holy angel of God" invoked in the exorcism of fire. [*Rf. Grimorium Verum*; Mathers, *The Greater Key of Solomon.*]

Lebes—one of the chief angels of the 1st chora or altitude. [*Rf. The Almadel of Solomon.*] When invoked, Lebes appears carrying a banner with a red cross on it. Of the 1st altitude there are 5 chief rulers or governors, the other 4 (apart from Lebes) being Alimiel, Barachiel, Gabriel, and Hel(l)ison.

Lecabel—an angel in control of vegetation and agriculture, and one of the 72 angels bearing the mystical name of God Shemhamphorae. [For Lecabel's sigil, see Ambelain, *La Kabbale Pratique*, p. 273; *Rf.* Barrett, *The Magus.*]

Lecahel—an angel belonging to the order of dominations (dominions). [*Rf.* Ambelain, *La Kabbale Pratique*, p. 88.]

Ledrion—an angel invoked in the exorcism of spirits through application of incense and fumigations. [*Rf. Grimorium Verum.*]

Lehachel—one of the rulers of the 72 quinaries of the degrees of the zodiac. [*Rf.* Runes, *The Wisdom of the Kabbalah.*]

Lehahel—one of the 8 seraphim in the cabala. [*Rf.* Ambelain, *La Kabbale Pratique*, p. 88.]

Lehahiah—once of the order of powers (potentates), Lehahiah protects crowned heads and makes subjects obedient to their superiors. He is (or was, depending on his current status as a holy or evil angel) one of the 72 hierarchs bearing the mystical name of God Shemhamphorae. [For Lehahiah's sigil, see Ambelain, *La Kabbale Pratique*, p. 273.]

Lehavah—in hechaloth lore (*Ma'asseh Merkabah*), an angelic guard stationed at the 7th heavenly hall.

Lelahel—an angel of the zodiac exercising dominion over love, art, science, and fortune. His corresponding angel, in cabalistic lore, is Asentacer. [For Lelahel's sigil, see Ambelain, *La Kabbale Pratique*, p. 260.]

Lelahiah—one of the 72 angels bearing the mystical name of God Shemhamphorae.

Leliel—one of the angelic rulers of the night. [*See* Lailah.]

Lemanael—in the cabala, the spirit of the moon. His corresponding angel is Elimiel (*q.v.*). [*Rf.* Lenormant, *Chaldean Magic*, p. 26.]

Lepha—an angel of the Seal. Lepha is cited in *The Sixth and Seventh Books of Moses* as one of the invocation spirits in special conjuring rites.

Leuuiah (Leviah)—one of the 72 angels bearing the mystical name of God Shemhamphorae.

Levanael (Iaraehel)—the spirit of the Moon, according to Cornelius Agrippa, *Three Books of Occult Philosophy* III.

Leviah [Leuuiah]

Leviathan (Hebrew, "that which gathers itself together in folds")—in the Enoch parables, Leviathan is the primitive female sea-dragon and monster of evil; in rabbinic writings, she (or he) is identified with Rahab, angel of the primordial deep, and associated with Behemoth (*q.v.*). Both Leviathan and Behemoth are said to have been created on the 5th day (see *Greek Apocalypse of Baruch*). In the system of Justinus, Leviathan is "a bad angel." [*Rf.* Ginzberg, *The Legends of the Jews* V, 46; *The Apocalypse of Abraham* 10.] In the view of George Barton in the *Journal of Biblical Literature* (December 1912), p. 161, Leviathan is "a Hebrew name for the Babylonian Tiamat." In Biblical lore (Job 41:1) Leviathan is the great whale. In Psalm 74:14 he is the hippopotamus or crocodile, or is so intended. [*Cf.* Isaiah 27:1 where Leviathan is called "that crooked serpent," an epithet which recalls Revelation 12:9, where Satan is dubbed "that old serpent."] In Mandaean lore, the final end for all but the purified souls is to be swallowed up by Leviathan.

Signature of the demon Asmodee (Asmodeus) to a deed dated May 29, 1629, and executed in the Church of the Holy Cross, in which Asmodee attests to quitting the body of a possessed nun. The deed mentions other demons: Gresil, Amand, Beheria, Leviatam (sic), etc. From De Givry, *Picture Museum of Sorcery, Magic and Alchemy*.

Libanel—the angelic guide of Philip, according to Klopstock, *The Messiah*.

Liberating Angel—the Shekinah (*q.v.*) who "delivers the world in all ages" has been referred to as the Liberating Angel. She is always close to man and "never separated from the just." The Exodus 23:20 passage ("Behold I send an angel before thee") has been applied to the Liberating Angel, although it is more commonly applied to John the Baptist. [*Rf.* Waite, *The Holy Kabbalah*, p. 344.]

Librabis—genius of hidden gold and one of the genii of the 7th hour. [*Rf.* Apollonius of Tyana, *The Nuctemeron*.]

Lifton—in hechaloth lore (*Ma'asseh Merkabah*), an angelic guard stationed at the 7th heavenly hall.

Lights—angels, luminaries. [*Rf. The Sacred Book of the Great Invisible Spirit* (one of the finds at Nag-Hammadi) and Grant, *Gnosticism and Early Christianity*, p. 44.]

Lilith—in Jewish tradition, where she originated, Lilith is a female demon, enemy of infants, bride of the evil angel Sammael (Satan). She predated Eve, had marital relations with Adam, and must thus be regarded as our first parent's 1st wife. According to Rabbi Eliezer (*The Book of Adam and Eve*), Lilith bore Adam every day 100 children. *The Zohar* (Leviticus 19a) describes Lilith as "a hot fiery female who at first cohabited with man" but, when Eve was created, "flew to the cities of the sea coast," where she is "still trying to ensnare mankind." She has been identified (incorrectly) with the screech owl in Isaiah 34:14. In the cabala she is the demon of Friday and is represented as a naked woman whose body terminates in a serpent's tail. While commonly regarded as the creation of the rabbis of the early Middle Ages (the first traceable mention of Lilith occurs in a 10th-century folktale called the *Alphabet of Ben Sira*), Lilith is in fact drawn from the *lili*, female demonic spirits in Mesopotamian demonology, and known as *ardat lili*. The rabbis read Lilith into Scripture as the 1st temptress, as Adam's demon wife, and as the mother of Cain. [*Rf.* Thompson,

Semitic Magic; Christian, *The History and Practice of Magic*.] In Talmudic lore, as also in the cabala (*The Zohar*), most demons are mortal, but Lilith and two other notorious female spirits of evil (Naamah and Agrat bat Mahlat) will "continue to exist and plague man until the Messianic day, when God will finally extirpate uncleanliness and evil from the face of the earth." In Scholem's article on one of the medieval writers in the magazine *Mada'e ha Yahadut* (II, 164ff.), Lilith and Sammael are said to have "emanated from beneath the throne of Divine Glory, the legs of which were somewhat shaken by their [joint] activity." It is known, of course, that Sammael (Satan) was once a familiar figure in Heaven, but not that Lilith was up there also, assisting him. Lilith went by a score of names, 17 of which she revealed to Elijah when she was forced to do so by the Old Testament prophet. For a list of Lilith's names, *see* Appendix.

Lithargoel—a great angel whose name appears in the Coptic *The Investiture of the Archangel Gabriel*; also in the *Acts of Peter*. [*Rf*. Doresse, *The Secret Books of the Egyptian Gnostics*, pp. 235–236.]

Little Iao—one of the many names of the angel Metatron. [*Rf. 3 Enoch*.]

Liwet—in Mandaean lore, the angel of love and invention; also one of the 7 planetary spirits. [*Rf*. Drower, *The Mandaeans of Iraq and Iran*.]

Lobkir—one of numerous angelic guards of the gates of the West Wind. [*Rf. Ozar Midrashim* II, 316.]

Lobquin—one of the angels of the 5th Heaven ruling on Tuesday in the west. Lobquin is subject to the East Wind. [*Rf*. Barrett, *The Magus* II.]

Loel—one of numerous angelic guards of the gates of the South Wind. [*Rf. Ozar Midrashim* II, 316.]

Logoi—a designation for angels by Philo in his "On Dreams." It is also the plural form for Logos, the "Word" (or Reason). [*Rf*. Müller, *History of Jewish Mysticism*.]

Logos (Greek, the "Word")—according to Philo, Logos is "the angel that appeared to Hagar, the cloud at the Red Sea, one of the 3 angels that appeared to Abraham (at Mamre, as Justin Martyr also taught), the divine form that changed the name of Jacob to Israel at Peniel." In rabbinic mysticism, Metatron is the personified Logos. Michael and the Messiah have also been identified with the concept, as has the Holy Ghost. [*Rf*. Müller, *History of Jewish Mysticism*.] Philo calls Logos (reason) "the image of God, His Angel"; also, "the Oldest Angel, who is as though it were the Angel-chief of many names; for he is called Dominion, and Name of God." [*Rf*. Mead, *Thrice-Greatest Hermes* I, pp. 161–162.]

Loquel—an angel serving in the 1st Heaven. [*Rf. The Sixth and Seventh Books of Moses*.]

Lords (or lordships)—a celestial order of angels mentioned, along with cherubim, powers, thrones, in the *Apocalypse of the Holy Mother of God* (in the *Ante-Nicene Fathers Library*) and in the *Arkhangelike of Moses*. In *Enoch II* 20:1, lordships is given in lieu of dominions (Ephesians 1:21; I Colossians 1:16). Lords may also be equated with principalities and virtues. Clement of Alexandria quotes from the lost *Apocalypse of Zephaniah*: "And the spirit took me up and carried me into the fifth Heaven and I saw angels called Lords and their diadem was lying in the Holy Spirit, and for each of them there was a throne seven times as bright as the light of the sun." [*Rf*. Caird, *Principalities and Powers*; Doresse, *The Sacred Books of the Egyptian Gnostics*.]

Lord of Hosts—Sabaoth, Akatriel, God. On his return from a visit to Heaven, Rabbi Ismael ben Elisha reported: "I once entered into the innermost part [of the sanctuary] to offer incense, and saw Akathriel Jah, the Lord of Hosts, seated upon a high and exalted throne." [*Rf*. Berakoth 30 (Soncino Talmud).]

Lord of Lightning [Angel of Lightning]

Lords of Shouting—also called masters of howling (*q.v.*). The lords of shouting consist of 1,550 myriads of angels, "all singing glory to the Lord." They are led by the angel Jeduthun (*q.v.*). [*Rf*. Scholem, *The Zohar*.] It is said that, at dawn, because of the chanting of the lords of shouting, "judgment is lightened and the world is blessed."

Lords of the Sword—the 14 conjuring angels as listed in M. Gaster, *The Sword of Moses*. They are Aziel, Arel, Ta'Aniel, Tafel, Yofiel, Mittron (Metatron), Yadiel, Ra'asiel (Raziel), Haniel (Anael), Asrael (later repeated), Yisriel, A'shael, Amuhael, Asrael. [*Rf.* Butler, *Ritual Magic*, p. 41.]

Lord Zebaot—in Jewish legendary lore, the lord of hosts; it is the name that God went by when he battled sinners. [*Rf.* Ginzberg, *The Legends of the Jews.*]

Los (Lucifer?)—the agent of divine providence, "the laborer of ages." Since his fall (he is one of the fallen angels), he has spent 6,000 years trying to give form to the world: "I am that shadowy Prophet who, 6,000 years ago/Fell from my station in the Eternal bosom." [*Rf.* Blake, *Vala (The Four Zoas)* and *Jerusalem*.]

Lucifer ("light giver")—erroneously equated with the fallen angel (Satan) due to a misreading of Isaiah 14:12: "How art thou fallen from heaven, O Lucifer, son of the morning," an apostrophe which applied to Nebuchadnezzar, king of Babylon (but *see* under Satan). It should be pointed out that the authors of the books of the Old Testament knew nothing of fallen or evil angels, and do not mention them, although, at times, as in Job 4:18, the Lord "put no trust" in his angels and "charged them with folly," which

would indicate that angels were not all that they should be. The name Lucifer was applied to Satan by St. Jerome and other Church Fathers. Milton in *Paradise Lost* applied the name to the demon of sinful pride. Lucifer is the title and principal character of the epic poem by the Dutch Shakespeare, Vondel (who uses Lucifer in lieu of Satan), and a principal character in the mystery play by Imre Madach, *The Tragedy of Man.* Blake pictured Lucifer in his illustrations to Dante. George Meredith's sonnet "Lucifer in Starlight" addresses the "fiend" as Prince Lucifer. Actually, Lucifer connotes star, and applies (or originally meant to apply) to the morning or evening star (Venus). To Spenser in "An Hymne of Heavenly Love," Lucifer is "the brightest angel, even the Child of Light."

Luel—in 15th-century Jewish magical lore, an angel invoked in connection with the use of divining rods. [*Rf.* Trachtenberg, *Jewish Magic and Superstition*, p. 225.]

Luma'il—in Arabic lore a guardian angel invoked in rites of exorcism. [*Rf.* Hughes, *A Dictionary of Islam*, "Angels."]

Lumazi—in Assyrian cosmology there were 7 lumazi, creators of the universe. They may be compared with the 7 (otherwise 12) angels of the presence (rabbinic), the 7 prajapati (Hindu), and the Middoth (of which, however, there were only 2) in Talmudic writings.

Michael. A terracotta lunette (c. 1475) by Andrea della Robbia. From *The Metropolitan Museum of Art Bulletin*, December 1961.

Maadim—one of 2 big stars (i.e., angels) that Metatron pointed out to Moses in the 4th Heaven. Maadim "stands near the moon in order to warm the world from the cold," according to the *Revelation of Moses.*

Mach—an angel called up in Solomonic conjuring rites for rendering the invocant invisible.

Machal—an angel invoked in the exorcism of the Bat. [*Rf.* Mathers, *The Greater Key of Solomon.*]

Machasiel—in both Barrett, *The Magus* II, and de Abano, *The Heptameron*, one of the angels invoked from the south. He resides in the 4th Heaven and rules on Lord's Day. He is listed among the intelligences of the sun. [*Rf.* Malchus, *The Secret Grimoire of Turiel.*]

Machatan (Machator, Macoton)—a Saturday angel and one of the powers of the spirits of the air, sharing rulership with Uriel, Cassiel, and Seraquiel, according to Barrett, *The Magus*; *The Ancient's Book of Magic*; and other occult sources.

Machidiel ("fulness of God"—Malchidiel, Malahidael, Malchedael, Melkeial, Melkejal, etc.)

—governing angel of the month of March; also ruler of the zodiacal sign of Aries. [*Rf.* Camfield, *A Theological Discourse of Angels*, p. 67.] In *Enoch I* Machidiel is called Melkejal: he "rises and rules in the beginning of the year" and exercises dominion "for 91 days, from spring to summer." In cabalistic writings, Machidiel (as Melchulael) is one of 4 angelic personifications of the holy sefira Malkut, the other 3 personifications being Sandalphon, Messiah, and Emmanuel. In grimoire conjurations, Prince Machidiel (as he is referred to) may be commanded to send the invocant the maiden of his desire; and if the invocant will fix the time and place, "the maiden invoked will not fail to appear."

Mach(k)iel—one of the angelic guards of the 6th Heaven, according to listing in *Pirke Hechaloth.* Machiel's pentacle is shown in Shah, *Occultism*, p. 77.

Machmay—in Waite, *The Lemegeton*, an angel of the 7th hour of the night, serving under Mendrion.

Machnia (Machniel)—one of the 70 childbed

179

amulet angels. As Machniel he is an angelic guard of the gates of the South Wind, according to listing in *Ozar Midrashim.*

Macoton [Machatan]

Macroprosopus—in the cabala, the 1st of the holy sefiroth; he is the "God of concealed form." [*Cf.* Microprosopus.]

Madagabiel—one of numerous angelic guards of the gates of the North Wind. [*Rf. Ozar Midrashim* II, 316.]

Madan—an angel that exercises dominion over the planet Mercury, as cited in Heywood, *The Hierarchy of the Blessèd Angels.*

Madiel—in occult lore, a governing archangel of the watery triplicity. He is a resident of the 1st Heaven and is invoked from the east. [*Rf.* de Abano, *The Heptameron*; Waite, *The Lemegeton.*] Madiel is the angel in Prokofieff's opera *L'Ange de feu.* [*See* Angel of Fire.]

Madimiel (Madiniel, Madamiel)—one of 4 angels' names found inscribed on the 1st pentacle of the planet Mars, the other 3 being Ithuriel, Bartzachiah, and Eschiel. [*Rf.* Mathers, *The Greater Key of Solomon.*] In Mosaic lore, Madimiel is one of 7 princes "who stand continually before God and to whom are given the spirit-names of the planets." [*Rf.* Cornelius Agrippa, *Three Books of Occult Philosophy* III.]

Mador—in hechaloth lore (*Ma'asseh Merkabah*), an angelic guard stationed at the 4th heavenly hall.

Madriel—an angel of the 9th hour of the day, serving under Vadriel. [*Rf.* Waite, *The Lemegeton.*]

Mael—in occult lore, a ruling archangel of the water triplicity (*cf.* Madiel). He is also one of the intelligences of the planet Saturn. As a Monday angel of the 1st Heaven, he may be invoked from the north.

Magog [Gog and Magog]

Magirkon—one of the many names of the angel Metatron.

Maguth—an angel of the air operating on Thursday. Maguth is a minister to Suth, chief of the air angels, all of whom are, in turn, subject to the South Wind. [*Rf. The Ancient's Book of Magic*; de Abano, *The Heptameron*; Barrett, *The Magus* II.]

Mah—in ancient Persian lore, the angel overseer of the mutations of the moon. [*Rf.* Clayton, *Angelology.*]

Mahadeo (Mahesh)—in Vedic lore, Mahadeo (Siva) is one of 11 angels "with matted locks and 3 eyes" that represent symbolically the sun, moon, and fire. Mahadeo also has (or had) 5 heads. [*Rf. The Dabistan*, p. 189.]

Mahalel and **Mahalkiel**—angels' names found inscribed on an oriental charm (*kamea*) for·warding off evil. [*Rf.* Schrire, *Hebrew Amulets.*]

Mahanaim ("double host")—when Jacob departed from Haran, he was accompanied by a double host ("Mahanaim") of angels, each host numbering 600,000. The incident is told in Genesis 32. [*Rf.* Ginzberg, *The Legends of the Jews* I, 377.]

Mahananel—one of the numerous angelic guards of the gates of the North Wind, as listed in *Ozar Midrashim* II, 316.

Mahariel ("swift")—an angel of Paradise stationed at the 1st portal; he provides new souls for the purified ones. [*Rf. Ozar Midrashim* I, 85.]

Mahashel—in the cabala, one of 72 angels ruling the 72 quinaries of the degrees of the zodiac. [*Rf.* Runes, *The Wisdom of the Kabbalah.*]

Mahasiah—one of 72 angels bearing the mystical name of God Shemhamphorae. [*Rf.* Barrett, *The Magus* II.]

Mahish (Mahash)—in the *Bhagavad Gita*, a mighty angel who, with Brahma ·and Vishna, sprang from one of the primary properties. [*Rf. The Dabistan*, p. 178.]

Mahka'il—in Arabic lore, a guardian angel invoked in rites of exorcism. [*Rf.* Hughes, *A Dictionary of Islam*, "Angels."]

Mahniel ("mighty camp")—another name for "Azriel the Ancient." According to *The Zohar*

(Exodus 202a), Mahniel is an angel who commands "60 myriads of legions, all winged, some full of eyes, some full of ears."

Mahonin (m)—in the exorcism at Auch (1618), the devil, possessing a noblewoman, gave his name as "Mahonin of the 3rd hierarchy and the 2nd order of archangels," claiming further that his adversary in Heaven was "St. Mark the Evangelist." [*Rf.* Robbins, *The Encyclopedia of Witchcraft and Demonology*, pp. 128 and 185.]

Mahzeil—an angel in Mandaean lore. [*Rf.* Pognon, *Inscriptions Mandaïtes des Coupes de Khouabir.*]

Mahzian—in Mandaean lore, a spirit who bestows sight. [*Rf.* Drower, *Canonical Prayerbook of the Mandaeans.*]

Maianiel—an angel serving in the 5th Heaven; he is named and listed in *The Sixth and Seventh Books of Moses.*

Maion—an angel who exercises dominion over the planet Saturn, and is so described in Heywood, *The Hierarchy of the Blessèd Angels.*

Maiphiat—an angel invoked in the exorcism of the Bat. [*Rf.* Mathers, *The Greater Key of Solomon.*]

Majesties—an order of angels mentioned by Tyndale and Cranmer, who give majesties in lieu of thrones. [*Rf. The Thanksgiving Hymns* V, where God is addressed as "prince of gods, king of majesties."] Vermes, *Discovery in the Judean Desert*, interprets the term as "probably some class of angels" and refers his readers to Jude 8.

Makatiel ("plague of God")—one of the 7 angels of punishment, as cited in *Maseket Gan Eden and Gehinnom.* [*Rf. Jewish Encyclopedia* I, 593; Jellinek, *Beth ha-Midrasch.*]

Makiel—an angel invoked in Syriac incantation rites. Makiel is grouped with Michael, Gabriel, Harshiel, and other spellbinding angels. [*Rf. The Book of Protection*; Budge, *Amulets and Talismans.*]

Maktiel—an angel with dominion over trees.

The name is found in M. Gaster, *The Sword of Moses.* In the *Baraita de Massechet Gehinnom*, Maktiel (or Matniel) is one of the angels of punishment over 10 nations. He lodges in the 4th compartment of Hell.

Malach ha-Mavet—in rabbinic literature as in Koranic lore, the angel of death, identified usually as Sammael or Azrael.

Malach ha-Sopher—an aide to Duma, angel of the silence of death. With Malach Memune (*q.v.*), ha-Sopher computed the span of a man's life. [*Rf. Ozar Midrashim* I, 92.]

Malachi or **Malachy** ("angel of God")—the angel of Jehovah. *See* Esdras 4, where we find: "Malachy, which is called also an angel of the Lord." [*Rf.* Talmud *Hagiga.*] The final book in the Old Testament is called Malachi.

Malach Memune ("the appointed one")—an aide to Duma. With Malach ha-Sopher he computed the span of a man's life.

Malach Ra—an angel of evil (in the causative sense), not necessarily himself evil. (Good angels, under orders from God, often perform missions or acts commonly regarded as unjust, wicked, etc.) [*Cf.* Angels of Destruction or Angels of Punishment.]

Malakim ("kings")—an order of angels equated with the virtues. The ruling prince is variously designated Peliel, Uriel, Uzziel, Raphael.

Malaku 'l-Maut—in the Koran, *sura* 32, 11, the angel of death. He may be equated with or identified as Izrael or Azrael.

Malashiel—in Jewish cabala, the preceptor angel of Elijah. [*Cf.* Maltiel.]

Malbushiel (fictional, from "malbush," clothing)—in I. B. Singer's story "The Warehouse" (*Cavalier*, January 1966), 2nd cousin to the angel Bagdial. Malbushiel serves as quartermaster in one of the "lower heavens."

Malchedael [Machidiel]

Malchiel [Malkiel]

Malchira [Malkira]

Malik (Malec)—in Arabic mythology, a terrible angel who guards Hell. He is assisted by 19 sbires (zabaniya) or guardians. In the Koran, *sura* 43, 77, Malik tells the wicked who appeal to him that they must remain in Hell forever because "they abhorred the truth when the truth was brought to them." [*Rf.* Hughes, *A Dictionary of Islam; Jewish Encyclopedia,* "Angelology"; Hastings, *Encyclopaedia of Religion and Ethics* IV, 618.]

Malkiel (Malchiel—"God's king")—one of 3 angelic princes serving under Sephuriron, who is last in rank of the 10 holy sefiroth. The other 2 princes are Ithuriel and Nashriel. In *Ozar Midrashim,* Malchiel is one of numerous angelic guards of the gates of the South Wind.

Malkira ("king of the wicked")—the surname for Sammael in *The Martyrdom of Isaiah.* [*Rf.* Box, introd. to Charles, *The Ascension of Isaiah.*]

Malkiyyah—an angel who "serves the blood." The name is found inscribed on amulets as a protection against hemorrhages; it is mentioned in an unpublished Hebrew manuscript referred to by Bonner, *Studies in Magical Amulets.* The name occurs also in Ezra 10:31 as Melchiah.

Malkuth (Melkout, Malchut)—the 10th sefira, the En Soph, the Shekinah, soul of the Messiah, or Metatron. According to *The Zohar,* Ezekiel saw Malkuth "under the God of Israel by the river Chebar." [*Rf.* Ezekiel 1:3, 15; 10:15.] Here the creatures sighted by the Old Testament prophet were the cherubim.

Malmeliyah—one of the many names of the angel Metatron.

Malthidrelis—in Heywood, *The Hierarchy of the Blessèd Angels,* an angel who exercises dominion over the sign of Aries (the Ram) in the zodiac.

Maltiel—in the cabala, a Friday angel resident in the 3rd Heaven and invoked from the west. He is also one of the intelligences of the planet Jupiter. In Ginzberg, *The Legends of the Jews,* Maltiel is the preceptor angel of Elijah (but *see*

Malashiel). In *Ozar Midrashim* II, 316, Maltiel serves as one of the numerous guards of the West Wind.

Maluzim—a holy angel of God invoked in goetic rites. [*Rf. Verus Jesuitarum Libellus* and Waite, *The Book of Black Magic and of Pacts.*]

Mambe'a—a mighty angel whose name appears inscribed on a terra cotta devil trap (amulet) in Hebrew characters dated circa 1st–2nd centuries B.C.E. Mambe'a was invoked as a protective spirit (Babylonian) against sorceries. [*Rf.* Budge, *Amulets and Talismans,* p. 288.] A companion angel to Mambe'a was Babhne'a.

Mameroijud—in *The Pauline Art,* chief angel-officer of the 10th hour of the night, serving under Jusguarin. [*Rf.* Waite, *The Book of Ceremonial Magic,* p. 70.]

Mamiel—one of the chief angel-officers of the 7th hour of the day, serving under the ruler Barginiel.

Mamlaketi—in *3 Enoch* (Hebrew Book of Enoch), Mamlaketi is an angel whose other name is Uzza (*q.v.*).

Mammon (Aramaic, "riches")—in occult lore, a fallen angel now ruling in Hell as one of the arch-demons and prince of tempters. In De Plancy, *Dictionnaire Infernal,* Mammon is certified as Hell's ambassador to England. He is equated with Lucifer, Satan, Beelzebub, and even with Nebuchadnezzar. Mammon is the demon of avarice. He "holds the throne of this world," as St. Francesca observed in one of her 93 visions. The medieval notion was that Mammon was a Syrian god. Gregory of Nyssa took Mammon to be a name for Beelzebub. Matthew 6:24 and Luke 16:13 speak of Mammon as a power hostile to God. He is pictured in Barrett, *The Magus,* and mentioned in *Paradise Lost* I, 678–681: "Mammon led them on/Mammon, the least erected Spirit that fell/from heav'n, e'en in heav'n his looks and thoughts were always Downward bent."

Manah—in Arabic lore, a goddess-angel of fertility. Her idol, the oldest known to the Arabs, was destroyed on Mohammed's orders. [*Rf.* Jobes, *Dictionary of Mythology Folklore and Symbols.*]

Manakel (Menakel, Menaqel)—according to Ambelain, *La Kabbale Pratique*, an angel with dominion over aquatic animals. In Runes, *The Wisdom of the Kabbalah*, Menakel is one of the 72 angels of the zodiac.

Man Clothed in Linen—applied to Gabriel; the expression occurs several times in Ezekiel (9:10); also in Daniel (10 and 12). The man clothed in linen with a writer's inkhorn by his side is associated with the heavenly scribe, and this heavenly scribe has been identified as Enoch, Michael, and Vretil. [*Rf.* Charles, *The Book of Enoch*, p. 28; *The Zohar* (Exodus 231a).] In his *Critical Commentary on the Revelation of St. John*, p. 266, Charles asserts that the man clothed in linen is not to be identified with Gabriel or Michael, but should rather be identified as the nameless Angel of Peace (*q.v.*), the same Angel of Peace mentioned in the *Testament of Asher* (in the *Testament of the Twelve Patriarchs*).

Maneij—a chief officer-angel of the 4th hour of the night, serving under Jefischa. [*Rf.* Waite, *The Lemegeton.*]

Maniel—an angel invoked in Syriac spellbinding charms. [*Rf. The Book of Protection*; Budge, *Amulets and Talismans.*]

Manna (Hebrew, "what is this?")—Justin thought manna was the regular food of angels. [*Cf.* Psalm 78:24: "they ate the food of angels" in the descent.] Elijah, as we know, was nourished during his 40 days in the wilderness (I Kings 19) by angel food fed to him by ravens. [*Rf.* Schneweiss, *Angels and Demons According to Lactantius*, p. 40.] Hughes, *A Dictionary of Islam*, quotes Ibn Majah as holding that the food of angels consists in "the celebrating of God's glory"; and that the drink of angels is "the proclaiming of His holiness."

Man of Macedonia—in Acts 16:10 Paul has the vision of "the man of Macedonia" as an angel. Danielou, *The Angels and Their Mission*, refers to this vision of St. Paul's, and quotes Origen.

Mansemat—another name for Mastema (Satan) as used in *Acts of Philip*. [*Rf.* James, *The Apocryphal New Testament*, p. 440.]

Mantus—in Etruscan religion, one of the 9 Novensiles, supreme spirits worshipped by this ancient people.

Manu—in Assyro-Babylonian mythology, "Manu the Great" was a spirit who presided over fate. [*Rf.* Lenormant, *Chaldean Magic.*]

Manuel—an angel governing the zodiacal sign of Cancer. Mentioned in Heywood, *The Hierarchy of the Blessèd Angels.*

Many-Eyed Ones—the ofanim (wheels), a high order of angels equated with the thrones. Enoch speaks of the "ofanim of fiery coals." All patriarchs became angels of this order on arriving in Heaven, as claimed in rabbinic writings. [*Rf.* Talmud *Bereshith Rabba* 82:6.] Raphael is usually designated chief. Ezekiel 10:20 describes the living creatures at the river Chebar as "full of eyes round about" and speaks of the "fire that was between the cherubim." Accordingly, but perhaps incorrectly, the "many-eyed ones" have been equated with the cherubim. [*Cf. Enoch II*, 19–20, "the watchfulness of many eyes" as describing the fiery hosts of great archangels.]

Mara—the Satan of Buddhist mythology. Arnold in *The Light of Asia* (VI, 19) speaks of Mara's mighty ones,/Angels of evil," of whom, says Arnold, there were 10—"ten chief Sins."

Marax [Forfax]

Marchosias (Marchocias)—an angel who, before he fell, belonged to the order of dominations. In Hell, where he now serves, Marchosias is a mighty marquis. When invoked, he manifests in the form of a wolf or an ox, with griffin wings and serpent's tail, as he is pictured in De Plancy, *Dictionnaire Infernal* (1863 ed.). He confided to Solomon that he "hopes to return to the 7th throne after 1,200 years." For the sigil of this spirit, see Waite, *The Book of Black Magic and of Pacts*, p. 176.

Marfiel—an angel of the 4th hour of the day,

serving under Vachmiel, as noted in Waite, *The Lemegeton.*

Margash—one of the many names of the angel Metatron.

Margesiel—one of the many names of the angel Metatron.

Margiviel—prince of the face and one of the angelic guards of the 4th Heaven. [*Rf. Ozar Midrashim* I, 117.]

Mariel—in *The Book of Protection*, an angel who is conjured up in Syriac spellbinding charms. [*Rf.* Budge, *Amulets and Talismans.*]

Marifiel—a chief officer-angel of the 8th hour of the night, serving under Narcoriel. [*Rf.* Waite, *The Lemegeton.*]

Marioc(h) or **Mariuk**—in Ginzberg, *The Legends of the Jews*, the angel who watched over the writings of Enoch. With another angel (Ariuk), Marioc was placed by God as guardian over the immediate descendants of Enoch to see to it that his books were preserved. [*Rf. Enoch II*, 33.]

Marmarao—a spirit invoked to overcome or cure bladder trouble caused by the demon Anoster (one of the 36 decani, demons of disease). [*Rf.* Shah, *The Secret Lore of Magic*, 224.]

Marmarath (Marmaraoth)—in Conybeare, *The Testament of Solomon*, Marmarath is one of the 7 planetary angels, and the only angel capable of overcoming the female jinn of war, Klothod.

Marniel—an angel's name found inscribed on an oriental charm (*kamea*) for warding off evil. [*Rf.* Schrire, *Hebrew Amulets.*]

Marnuel—an angel mentioned in the writings of Rabbi Akiba. [*Rf.* Bamberger, *Fallen Angels.*]

Marnuthiel—an angel mentioned in the writings of Rabbi Akiba.

Maroch—Waite, *The Lemegeton*, cites Maroch as an angel of the 5th hour of the day, serving under Sazquiel.

Maron—a holy name (of a spirit or an angel) by which demons are commanded in Solomonic conjurations. [*Rf.* Mathers, *The Greater Key of Solomon.*]

Maroth (Hebrew, "bitterness"—Maroot, Marout)—with another angel Haroth, Maroth was sent down by God "with full commission to exercise government over all mankind, and to tutor and instruct them." [*Rf.* Heywood, *The Hierarchy of the Blessèd Angels*, p. 289.] Maroth is a character in Eastern lore (Persian) taken over by the Jews. The Koran also speaks of Maroth as an angel.

Marou—once a cherub, now a demon. In the trial of Urbain Grandier, Marou was cited as one of 6 demons who possessed the body of Elizabeth Blanchard. [*Rf.* De Plancy, *Dictionnaire Infernal.*]

Martyrs—according to Barrett, *The Magus*, the martyrs are 11th in the 12 orders of the blessed spirits, with Gabriel as ruler of the order.

Mary—the Virgin Mary is spoken of as an angel in the *Book of John the Evangelist*. According to James, *The Apocryphal New Testament*, p. 191, Mary is the angel sent by God to receive the Lord, who enters her "through the ear," and who "comes forth by the ear." In the Litany of Loretto, Mary is "queen of angels."

Masgabriel—in de Abano, *The Heptameron*, an angel resident in the 4th Heaven and invoked from the north. Masgabriel rules on Lord's Day (Sunday).

Mashit(h) ("destroyer")—an angel appointed over the death of children. [*Rf.* Ginzberg, *The Legends of the Jews.*] In *The Zohar* he is one of 3 demons in gehinnom (Hell) who punish those who sin by idolatry, murder, and incest. The other 2 demons are Af and Hemah (*q.v.*). In *Midrash Tehillim* (commentary on Psalms), Mashit is one of 5 angels of punishment whom Moses encounters in Heaven.

Masim—one of numerous angelic guards of the gates of the East Wind. [*Rf. Ozar Midrashim* II, 316.]

Maskelli (Maskelli-Maskello). [Zarazaz]

Maskiel—an angelic guard of the 1st Heaven. [*Rf. Pirke Hechaloth.*]

A woodcut from the Cologne Bible. Left, the Scarlet Woman seated on seven-headed dragon and worshipped by minor kings of the earth. Center (top), angel drops great millstone into the sea. Right, angel with key to bottomless pit about to consign to it the devil. Extreme right, closing scene of Revelation 14, showing harvest of the world and vintage of the grapes of wrath. From *Pictures from a Mediaeval Bible.*

Maskim—in Akkadian religion the maskim are the 7 great princes of Hell, otherwise known as the 7 spirits of the abyss, of whom it was said that "although their seat is in the depths of the earth, yet their voice resounds on the heights," and that they "reside at will in the immensity of space." Mephistopheles is one of the 7. [*Rf.* Lenormant, *Chaldean Magic;* Agrippa's Electors; and Conybeare's listing of the underworld planetary rulers in *The Testament of Solomon.*]

Masleh—in occultism, the angel who "actuated the chaos and produced the 4 elements." In Jewish legendary lore, Masleh is the ruler of the zodiac. In *The Ancient's Book of Magic,* "the power and influence of Logos descends through the angel Masleh into the sphere of the zodiac."

Masniel—a governing angel of the zodiac. [*Rf.* Cornelius Agrippa, *Three Books of Occult Philosophy* III.]

Maspiel—an angelic guard stationed in the 2nd Heaven. He is named in *Pirke Hechaloth.*

Mass Massiah—in Talmud *Shabbath,* an angel invoked for the curing of cutaneous disorders.

Mastema (Mansemat)—the accusing angel; like Satan, he works for God as tempter and executioner; he is prince of evil, injustice, and condemnation. *Cf. The Book of Jubilees* and *The Zadokite Fragments and the Dead Sea Scrolls,* where Mastema is the angel of adversity, "father of all evil, yet subservient to God." It was Mastema who tried to kill Moses (in the incident mentioned in Exodus 4:24ff.) and who hardened Pharaoh's heart (although, according to *Midrash Abkir,* it was Uzza who did this). There is a legend that Mastema appealed to God to spare some of the demons so that he (Mastema) might execute the power of his will on the sons of man. God apparently thought this was a good idea and permitted 1/10th of the demons to remain at large, in the service of Mastema. It is also claimed that Mastema helped the Egyptian sorcerers when Moses and Aaron appeared before Pharaoh to perform their magical tricks. [*Cf.* Beliel; Satan.] In *The Damascus Document,* quoted by Vermes in

Discovery in the Judean Desert, an angel of hostility is spoken of, and this is applied to Mastema.

Master of Howling—the angel Jeduthun. [*See* Lord(s) of Shouting.]

Mastho—in Levi, *Transcendental Magic*, Mastho is called the "genius of delusive appearances." He is one of the spirits of the 10th hour, according to a listing in Apollonius of Tyana, *The Nuctemeron.*

Mastinim—a term characterizing the accusing angels, of whom Sammael (*q.v.*) is chief. In Bamberger, *Fallen Angels*, the mastinim are called "the greatest angels of the nations." In Ginzberg, *The Legends of the Jews* III, 17, mention is made of Uzza, tutelary angel of Egypt, as an accusing angel. Elijah is characterized as an accusing angel of Israel—when, that is, he accuses in behalf of the Chosen People.

Matafiel—as noted in *Hechaloth Rabbati*, one of the 7 angelic guards of the 2nd Heaven.

Matanbuchus (Mechembechus, Meterbuchus, Beliar, Mastema)—in *The Martyrdom of Isaiah*, *Testament of Job*, and in the Introduction to *The Ascension of Isaiah*, Matanbuchus is referred to as the angel of lawlessness, and identified with Beliar: "Beliar, whose name is Matanbuchus." The name is believed to be composed of 2 Hebrew words: *mattan buka*, meaning "worthless gift"; or, better, a form of the Hebrew *mithdabek*, "one who attaches himself," i.e., an evil spirit.

Mataqiel ("sweet")—one of the 7 angel guards of the 1st Heaven, as noted in *Hechaloth Rabbati*.

Matarel (Matariel)—in rabbinic and pseudepigraphic lore, the angel of rain. Others so designated include Ridya (Ridia), Zalbesael, and Batarrel. In *3 Enoch*, Matarel is one of the rulers of the world.

Matariel [Matarel]

Mathiel—in de Abano, *The Heptameron*, Barrett, *The Magus*, and other occult works, Mathiel is an angel serving in the 5th Heaven. He is ruler of Tuesday, invoked from the north.

Mathlai—one of the spirits of the planet Mercury, angel of Wednesday, resident of the 3rd Heaven—according to de Abano, *The Heptameron*; but, according to Barrett, *The Magus*, Mathlai is a resident of the 2nd Heaven, and invoked from the east.

Matmoniel—a "holy minister of God" who may be summoned up in Solomonic conjurations for procuring to the invocant a magic carpet. [*Rf.* Mathers, *The Greater Key of Solomon.*]

Matniel [Maktiel]

Matrona—the Shekinah (*q.v.*) called "angel of the Lord" in *The Zohar*.

Matsmetsiyah—one of the many names of the angel Metatron.

Mavet—angel of death. [*See* Malach ha-Mavet.]

Mavkiel—an angel's name found inscribed on an oriental charm (*kamea*) for warding off evil. [*Rf.* Schrire, *Hebrew Amulets.*]

Maymon—chief angel of the air, ruler of Saturday, and subject to the South Wind. Three angels minister to Maymon: Abumalith, Assaibi, and Belidet. In de Abano's works, Maymon is "king of the Saturday angels of the air."

Mbriel—an angel who rules over winds, according to M. Gasster, *The Sword of Moses.*

McWilliams, Sandy (fictional)—a baldheaded angel in Mark Twain's *Captain Stormfield's Visit to Heaven.*

Meachuel—in occult works, specifically in *The Sixth and Seventh Books of Moses*, Meachuel is one of the 3 angels of the Triune God used for conjuring, the other 2 being Lebatei and Ketuel.

Mebabel—one of the 72 angels of the 72 quinaries of the degrees of the zodiac. Mebabel is invoked by those who seek to usurp the fortune of others. He is known to protect the innocent. His corresponding angel is Thesogar. [*See* Barrett, *The Magus*; Ambelain, *La Kabbale Pratique*; Runes, *The Wisdom of the Kabbalah.*]

Mebahel—one of the 72 angels bearing the name of God Shemhamphorae.

Mebahiah—in the cabala, an angel who exercises dominion over morals and religion; also one who helps those desiring offspring. Mebahiah is one of the 72 angels bearing the name of God Shemhamphorae. His corresponding angel is Smat. Mebahiah's sigil is shown in Ambelain, *La Kabbale Pratique*, p. 289.

Mechiel—one of the 72 angels of the zodiac, according to listing in Runes, *The Wisdom of the Kabbalah*.

Mediat (Modiat)—king of the angels ruling Wednesday; also one of the intelligences of the planet Mercury. [*Rf.* de Abano, *The Heptameron*; Malchus, *The Secret Grimoire of Turiel*.]

Medorin—an angel in the heavenly Paradise. [*Rf. The Zohar* (Bereshith 39b, fn.).]

Medussusiel—as mentioned in Waite, *The Lemegeton*, an angel of the 6th hour of the day, serving under Samil.

Meetatron [Metatron]

Mefathiel—"an opener of doors," hence, according to Trachtenberg, *Jewish Magic and Superstition*, Mefathiel is an angel favored of thieves and other miscreants.

Megiddon—a seraph, in Klopstock, *The Messiah*.

Mehahel—an angel belonging to the order of cherubim and cited in Ambelain, *La Kabbale Pratique*.

Mehaiah—an angel of the order of principalities, as listed in the "L'Arbre de Vie en Iesirah" chart reproduced in Ambelain, *La Kabbale Pratique*, facing p. 88.

Mehalalel—in *The Book of Protection*, an angel invoked in Syriac spellbinding charms. [*Rf.* Budge, *Amulets and Talismans*.]

Mehekiel—one of the 72 angels bearing the mystical name of God Shemhamphorae. [*Rf.* Barrett, *The Magus*.]

Meher (Mithra)—in Mandaean religious lore, the yazata or angel presiding over light and justice. [*Rf.* Drower, *The Mandaeans of Iraq and Iran*.]

Mehiel—in the cabala, an angel who protects university professors, orators, and authors. His corresponding angel is Astiro. [*Rf.* Ambelain, *La Kabbale Pratique*.]

Mehriel—one of the archangels in the cabala.

Mehuman ("true, faithful")—one of the 7 angels of confusion. Mehuman figures in the story relating to Esther and Ahasuerus, as told in Ginzberg, *The Legends of the Jews*.

Meil—a Wednesday angel (one of 3) invoked in ceremonial magic rites. [*Rf.* Barrett, *The Magus* II.]

Meimeiriron—in Isaac ha-Cohen's text, "Emanations of the Left Side," Meimeiriron is the 4th of the 10 holy sefiroth, the "personalized Hesed." The "less authentic angel" of this sefira is Zadkiel.

Mekhapperyah—one of the many names of the angel Metatron. [*Rf. 3 Enoch*.]

Melahel—one of the 72 angels bearing the mystical name of God Shemhamphorae, according to Barrett, *The Magus* II.

Melchi(d)ael—in Waite, *The Book of Black Magic and of Pacts*, and in *Grimorium Verum*, Melchiael is an angelic prince conjured up in Solomonic black magic rites. He is efficacious in providing the invocant with the woman of his desires.

Melchisedec (or Melchizedek or Melch-Zadok—"the god Zedek is my king")—king of righteousness whom pseudo-Dionysius called "the hierarch most beloved of God." Epiphanius in his *Adversus Heareses* calls Melchisedec an angel of the order of virtues. According to pseudo-Tertullian, Melchisedec is a "celestial virtue of great grace who does for heavenly angels and virtues what Christ does for man." [*Rf.* Legge, *Forerunners and Rivals of Christianity* II, p. 148.] In the Bible (Genesis 14), Melchisedec is the fabled priest-king of Salem, ancient name for Jerusalem. It was to Melchisedec that Abraham gave tithes. In Phoenician mythology Melchisedec, called Sydik, is the father of the 7 elohim or angels of the divine presence. In the gnostic *Book of the Great Logos*, Melchisedec is Zorokothera. Hippolytus refers

Melchisedec, Abraham, and Moses, from the porch of the northern transept of Chartres Cathedral (late 12th century). From E. H. Gombrich, *The Story of Art*. New York: Oxford University Press, 1951.

to a sect, followers of one Theodotus (probably the 3rd-century heretics known as the Melchisedans), who claimed that there was "a great power named Melchizedek who was greater than Christ." In certain occult sources, Melchisedec is identified as the Holy Ghost. In the *Book of Mormon* (Alma) he is referred to as "the prince of peace." His symbol is a chalice and a loaf of bread. R. H. Charles appends to his edition of *Enoch II* a fragment ("a new form of the Melchizedek myth, the work of an early Christian"), wherein Melchisedec figures as the supernatural offspring of Noah's brother Nir, who is preserved in infancy by Michael, and who becomes, after the Flood, a great high priest, the "Word of God," and king of Salem, with "power to work great and glorious marvels that have never been." The term "word of God" very likely stems from St. John's "in the beginning was the Word, and the Word was with God, and the Word was God." In *Midrash Tehillim*, commenting on Psalm 76, Melchisedec is identified as Shem, one of Noah's sons. This source also contains the legend of Melchisedec feeding the beasts in Noah's ark. The meeting of Abraham and Melchisedec (Genesis 14:17–24) is pictured in a woodcut in the great Cologne Bible (1478–1480) and in Rubens' famous painting, "The Meeting of Abraham and Melchizedec"; also in the painting by Dierik Bouts (c. 1415–1475).

Melech—an angel of the order of powers invoked in conjuration rites. [*Rf. The Sixth and Seventh Books of Moses*.]

Melek-I-Taus (Taus-Melek)—the peacock angel in Yezidic devil-worshipping religion. The name is a paraphrase for the devil in Buddhist lore. [*Rf.* Wall, *Devils*.] According to Forlong, *Encyclopedia of Religions*, "the Melek-Tawus was once an angel or demiurge who created Eve from the body of Adam." [*See* Taus-Melek.]

Meleyal or **Melejal** ("fulness of God")—in Enoch writings, an angel of autumn, ruling 3 months of the year. [*Rf. Enoch I*.]

Melha—chief of the order of flames, and Buddhist counterpart of the seraphim. [*Rf.* Blavatsky, *The Secret Doctrine* II.]

Melioth—one of 9 angels "that run together throughout heavenly and earthly places." The 9 angels are named by Beliar and revealed to Bartholomew in the *Gospel of Bartholomew*, p. 177.

Melkejal (Machidiel)—angelic ruler of March. "In the beginning of the year," says *Enoch I*, "Melkejal rises first and rules."

Melkharadonin—in gnostic lore, one of 12 powers engendered by Ialdabaoth. [*Rf.* Doresse, *The Secret Books of the Egyptian Gnostics*.]

Melki—in Mandaean religion, the *melki* or *malki* are semidivinities (like the *uthri*) who carry out the Will of the Great Life. All are "subordinate to the Creator, whose first manifestations they were." A Mandaean legend tells of 2 *melki*, Zutheyr and Zahrun, conjured down from Heaven to aid believers in baptismal rites. [*Rf.* Drower, *The Mandaeans of Iraq and Iran*, p. 328.]

Melkiel—one of the angels of the 4 seasons, serving with Helemmelek, Melejal, and Narel.

Melkoutael—the sefira of Malkuth in the Briatic world. [*Rf.* Ambelain, *La Kabbale Pratique*.]

Membra (logos)—the Word of God; an hypostasis of God; an intermediary (i.e., an angel) of God. In Jewish cabala, Membra denotes the divine name. [*Rf. The Jewish World in the Time of Jesus*; Lenormant, *Chaldean Magic*.]

Memeon—an angel invoked in the benediction of the Salt. [*Rf.* Mathers, *The Greater Key of Solomon*.]

Memsiel—a chief officer-angel of the 7th hour of the night, serving under Mendrion. [*Rf.* Waite, *The Lemegeton*.]

Memuneh ("appointed one")—a deputy angel, a dispenser of dreams. Through Memuneh, it is said, the universe operates. The plural form is memunim. These memunim are the defenders in Heaven of their earthly charges. In Jewish ceremonial magic, the memunim were regarded as demons, although Eleazor of Worms insisted they were angels. *3 Enoch* speaks of the memunim as belonging to the class of angels of the Song-Uttering Choirs.

Memunim (plural for Memuneh)—appointed ones, a class of angels. [*Rf. 3 Enoch*.]

Menadel—an angel of the order of powers,

according to Ambelain; also one of the 72 angels of the zodiac, according to Runes, *The Wisdom of the Kabbalah.* Menadel keeps exiles faithful or loyal to their native land. His corresponding angel, in the cabala, is Aphut. For the sigil of Menadel, see Ambelain, *La Kabbale Pratique,* p. 273.

Menafiel—in Waite, *The Lemegeton,* an angel of the 11th hour of the day, serving under Bariel.

Menakel [Manakel]

Menaqel [Manakel]

Mendrion—in the cabala [*Rf.* Waite, *The Lemegeton*] the supreme ruling angel of the 7th hour of the night.

Menerva (Menvra)—one of the Novensiles, the 9 supreme spirits or gods of the Etruscans.

Meniel—one of the 72 angels bearing the name of God Shemhamphorae. [*Rf.* Barrett, *The Magus* II.]

Menor—an angel conjured in the exorcism of Wax in Solomonic magical operations. [*Rf.* Mathers, *The Greater Key of Solomon.*]

Mentor—an angel invoked in the exorcism of Wax. Mentioned in the *Clavicula Salomonis.* [*See* Menor.]

Menvra [Menerva]

Mephistopheles (Mephistophiel, "he who loves not the light")—the name, originally Hebrew, is derived from "mephiz" meaning destroyer, and "tophel" meaning liar. Mephistopheles is a fallen archangel, one of 7 great princes of Hell (one of the maskim, *q.v.*). According to Cornelius Agrippa, Mephistopheles "stands under the planet Jupiter, his regent is named Zadkiel, who is an enthroned angel of the holy Jehovah." [*Rf. Dr. Faust's Höllenzwang,* a book of magic.] In Seligmann, *The History of Magic,* Mephistopheles is "a subordinate demon, a fallen angel too, and sometimes admitted to the presence of God, but he is not the devil." In secular literature, Mephistopheles is either a minion of Satan or a stand-in for Satan. In Marlowe's *Dr. Faustus,* he is a leading character, along with Lucifer, Beelzebub,

and other devils (the angels in the play, good or evil, are not named). In Goethe's *Faust* it is Mephistopheles who, acting for his overlord Satan, seals the pact with Faust. Mephistopheles is also a character is Busoni's uncompleted opera *Doktor Faust,* which was heard for the 1st time in America in 1964. Hegel the philosopher saw in Mephistopheles the symbol of "the negative principle."

Merasin [Meresin]

Merattron [Metatron]

Merciless Angel, The [Temeluch]

Mercury (Greek, Hermes)—in the cabala, the angel of progress, also a designation for Raphael. [*Rf.* Acts 14 :11–12; Levi, *Transcendental Magic.*]

Meresijm—angel of the 1st hour of the day, serving under Sammael. [*Rf.* Waite, *The Lemegeton.*]

Meresin (Merasin, Meris, Metiris, Merihim, Meririm)—a fallen angel, chief of the aerial powers, as in *Paradise Lost.* In Camfield, *A Theological Discourse of Angels,* Meresin (spelt *Miririm*) is one of the 4 angels of revelation—which would make him a holy angel; however, in Heywood, *The Hierarchy of the Blessèd Angels,* he is lord of thunder and lightning in Hell—which, presumably, would make him one of the damned.

Meriarijm—a chief officer-angel of the night, serving under Sarquamish.

Meririm (Meresin)—in Barrett, *The Magus* I, Meririm is identified as the evil power whom Paul in Ephesians calls "the prince of the power of the air" (i.e., Satan). Barrett claims that Meririm is prince over the angels of whom Revelation speaks and "to whom is given to hurt the earth and the sea . . . he is the meridian devil, a boiling spirit, a devil ranging in the south."

Merkabah—angel of the chariot (the cherubim).

Merkabah Angels—6 classes of angels [*Rf. 3 Enoch*] closest to, or guardian of, the throne of Glory. They include the galgallim, the hayyoth, the ofanim, the seraphim.

Merkaboth ("carriage")—there were (or are) 7 merkaboth, corresponding to the 7 Heavens or "the actual vision of the divine might." They are to be compared with the middoth or the sefiroth (*q.v.*), and are regarded as personifications of the divine attributes, serving before the throne of Glory. [*Rf.* Scholem, *Major Trends in Jewish Mysticism*; Müller, *History of Jewish Mysticism*; Zechariah 6.]

Merloy—an "inferior" spirit invoked in Solomonic magical rites. [*Rf. Grimorium Verum*; Waite, *The Book of Ceremonial Magic*, p. 239; Shah, *The Secret Lore of Magic*, p. 98.]

Mermeoth—one of the 9 angels that "run together throughout heavenly and earthly places," as cited in the *Gospel of Bartholomew* in James, *The Apocryphal New Testament*.

Merod—"a most holy angel" invoked in magical operations, as set forth in Waite, *The Greater Key of Solomon*.

Merof—in occult lore (*The Sixth and Seventh Books of Moses*), an angel of the Seal, summoned in magical rites.

Meros—an angel of the 9th hour of the day, serving under Vadriel. [*Rf.* Waite, *The Lemegeton*.]

Merroe—"a most pure angel" invoked in Solomonic black magic operations, specifically in the conjuration of the Sword. [*Rf. Grimorium Verum*; Shah, *The Secret Lore of Magic*.]

Mesarepim (Mesharethim)—an order of angels of the Song-Uttering Choirs, serving under the leadership of the angel Tagas. [*Rf. 3 Enoch.*]

Meserach [Nisroc]

Meshabber—in rabbinic legendary lore, the angel in charge of the death of animals. [*Rf.* Ginzberg, *The Legends of the Jews* V, p. 57.]

Mesharethim [Mesarepim]

Mesharim—the name of Joseph Caro's angel, through whom Caro received visions and after whom he titled his *Maggid Mesharim*, a book which contains a description of these visions. The angel served as a personified Mishnah. Caro (1488–1575)

was doyen of the 15th-century cabalistic Safed community in Upper Galilee (Palestine). [*Rf.* Müller, *History of Jewish Mysticism*, p. 120.]

Meshulhiel—10th of the averse (unholy) sefiroth, as set forth in Isaac ha-Cohen's text. For a list of the 10 sefiroth, both holy and unholy, *see* Appendix.

Mesriel—an angel of the 10th hour of the day, serving under Oriel. [*Rf.* Waite, *The Lemegeton*.]

Messenger of the Covenant [Angel of the Testament]

Messiach—an angel invoked in magical operations. Messiach is named in Mathers, *The Greater Key of Solomon*, p. 107, in connection with the invocation "of the water and of the hyssop." The invocant is advised to recite, at the time of the operations, versicles out of Psalms 6, 67, 64, and 102.

Messiah—equated with Soter, Christ, Savior, God. With Metatron, Messiah is designated a cherub and guardian angel of Eden armed with a flaming sword. He is also the angel of the Great Council, angel of the Lord, a sefira in the Briatic world (one of the 4 worlds of creation) and analogous to the Logos or Holy Ghost. Paul in Colossians 1:16 and Ephesians 1:21 has Messiah in mind when he speaks of the angel "raised above all principalities and powers, virtues, dominations." So too Enoch, when he speaks of the "head of days." [For cabalistic references, see Ambelain, *La Kabbale Pratique*.]

Mesukiel—one of the 10 holy sefiras (3rd of the 10). He is to be compared or equated with Machut or Malkuth (*q.v.*); also with En Soph and the Shekinah. However, according to Isaac ha-Cohen of Soria, in his "Emanations of the Left Side," worlds of horror and destructive imaginings spring from Mesukiel, resulting in a double emanation, with 7 successive groups of pure angels (the holy sefiroth) on one side and 7 camps of dark spirits (the evil sefiroth) on the other. [*Rf.* Bamberger, *Fallen Angels*, p. 173.]

Metathiax—in Conybeare, *The Testament of Solomon*, one of the 36 decani (i.e., spirits of the zodiac who are demons of disease). Metathiax causes trouble of the reins, and only the holy angel Adonael (*q.v.*) is able to thwart or undo his evil work. [*Rf.* Shah, *The Secret Lore of Magic,* p. 222.]

Metatron (Metratton, Mittron, Metaraon, Merraton, etc.)—in noncanonical writings, Metatron is perhaps the greatest of all the heavenly hierarchs, the 1st (as also the last) of the 10 archangels of the Briatic world. He has been called king of angels, prince of the divine face or presence, chancellor of Heaven, angel of the covenant, chief of the ministering angels, and the lesser YHWH (the tetragrammaton). He is charged with the sustenance of mankind. In Talmud and Targum, Metatron is the link between the human and divine. In his earthly incarnation he was the patriarch Enoch—although *Tanhuna Genesis* [*Rf. Jewish Encyclopedia* I, 94] claims he was originally Michael. Talmudic authorities for the most part shy away from identifying Enoch with Metatron; on the contrary, the tendency is to play down the relationship and even to suppress it. In a curious tale of the marriage of God and Earth (Elohim and Edem), told in the *Alphabet of Ben Sira,* God

Metatron (El Shaddai). Reproduced from Mathers, *The Greater Key of Solomon.*

demands from Earth the "loan" of Adam for 1,000 years. Upon Earth agreeing to the loan, God writes out a formal receipt, and this is witnessed by the archangels Michael and Gabriel. The receipt, so the story goes, is on deposit "to this day" in the archives of Metatron, the heavenly scribe. Metatron has been variously identified as the dark angel who wrestled with Jacob at Peniel (Genesis 32); as the watchman is "Watchman, what of the night?" (Isaiah 21); as the Logos; as Uriel; and even as the evil Sammael. It is said that Exodus 23:20 refers to Metatron: "Behold, I send an angel before thee, to keep thee in the way and to bring thee unto the place which I have prepared" (usually applied to John the Baptist), and Exodus 23:22: "My name is in him." In addition, Metatron has been identified as the Liberating Angel and the Shekinah (who is regarded in some sources as Metatron in his female aspect); in Trachtenberg, *Jewish Magic and Superstition* (p. 76), he is the "demiurge of classical Jewish mysticism." According to the cabala, Metatron is the angel who led the children of Israel through the wilderness after the Exodus; in other occult writings he is described as the twin brother or half-brother of the angel Sandalphon (*cf.* the twin brothers Ormuzd and Ahriman in Zoroastrian lore). With the possible exception of Anafiel (*q.v.*), Metatron is the tallest angel in Heaven, and the greatest, apart from the "eight great princes, the honored and revered ones, who are called YHWH by the name of their king." This is according to *3 Enoch.* Jewish legend relates that upon Metatron (while still Enoch, a mortal) arriving in Heaven, he was transformed into a spirit of fire and equipped with 36 pairs of wings as well as innumerable eyes. The meaning of the name Metatron has never been satisfactorily explained. Eleazor of Worms thought it derived from the Latin *metator,* a guide or measurer. Hugo Odeberg advanced the hypothesis (*3 Enoch,* append. 2) that the name Metatron originated in Jewish circles and "should be regarded as a pure Jewish invention, viz., a metonym for the term 'little YHWH.'" Odeberg is inclined to interpret the name as meaning "one who occupies the throne next to the divine throne." Accordingly Metatron is said to reside in the 7th Heaven (the dwelling place of God). He appears, when invoked, "as a pillar of fire, his face more dazzling than the sun." Gershom Scholem, on the basis of *The Apocalypse of Abraham*, believes the name might be a "vox mystica" for Yahoel (i.e., God). Metatron has also been identified as Isaiah's suffering servant, the Messiah of Christian theology; but see Orlinsky, "The So-Called 'Suffering Servant' in Isaiah 53." The 72 names of God find a match in the 72 (and more) names of Metatron—Surya, Tatriel, Sasnigiel, Lad, Yofiel, to mention a few. Metatron has also been credited with the authorship of Psalms 37:25 according to Talmud *Yebamoth* 16b; and the authorship, in part, of Isaiah 24:16. In *The Zohar* I, Metatron is spoken of as Moses' rod, "from one side of which comes life and from the other, death." In Eisenmenger, *Traditions of the Jews* II, 408, Metatron is indeed the supreme angel of death, to whom God daily gives orders as to the souls to be "taken" that day. These orders Metatron transmits to his subordinates Gabriel and Sammael. That Metatron was considered, at least in some sources, mightier than either Michael or Gabriel is the view expressed in the *Chronicles of Jerahmeel*. Here the story goes that whereas neither of the two great Biblical angels was able to eject Jannes and Jambres, the Egyptian wizards, from Heaven (whither they managed, it seems, to ascend by witchcraft), Metatron was able to accomplish their expulsion. In *Yalkut Hadash*, also, Metatron is said to be "appointed over Michael and Gabriel." As for the size or height of Metatron, *The Zohar* computes it to be "equal to the breadth of the whole world." In rabbinic lore, this was the size of Adam before he sinned. One of Metatron's secret names is Bizbul (according to the *Visions of Ezekiel* where, however, the meaning of this name is not given). King, *The Gnostics and Their Remains*, p. 15, says of Metatron: "This is the Persian Mithra." Many other sources, supporting this identification, are cited by Odeberg, *3 Enoch*. In Jewish angelology, Metatron is "the angel who caused another angel to announce, before the Flood, that God would destroy the world." [*Rf. Jewish Encyclopedia*, "Metatron," vol. 8.] Among numerous other missions or deeds credited to Metatron is the staying of Abraham's hand on the point of sacrificing Isaac. But this 11th-hour intercession has also been imputed to Michael, Zadkiel, Tadhiel, and of course to the "angel of the Lord," who is the one designated in Genesis 22. Finally, according to Talmud *Abodah Zarah* 3b, Metatron is the "teacher of prematurely dead children in Paradise."

Metrator—"a most holy angel" invoked in magical operations. The specific conjuration is the one "concerning the Needle and other Iron Instruments," during which the invocant is advised to recite versicles from Psalms 31, 42. [*Rf.* Mathers, *The Greater Key of Solomon*, p. 118.]

Miahel—one of the 72 angels of the 72 quinaries of the degrees of the zodiac. [*Rf.* Runes, *The Wisdom of the Kabbalah*.]

Mibi—a ministering angel invoked in cabalistic rites. [*Rf. The Sixth and Seventh Books of Moses*.]

Michael ("who is as God")—in Biblical and post-Biblical lore, Michael ranks as the greatest of all angels, whether in Jewish, Christian, or Islamic writings, secular or religious. He derives originally from the Chaldeans by whom he was worshipped as something of a god. He is chief of the order of virtues, chief of archangels, prince of the presence, angel of repentance, righteousness, mercy, and sanctification; also ruler of the 4th Heaven, tutelary *sar* (angelic prince) of Israel, guardian of Jacob, conqueror of Satan (bearing in mind, however, that Satan is still very much around and unvanquished), etc. His mystery name is Sabbathiel. In Islamic writings he is called Mika'il. As the deliverer of the faithful he accords, in the Avesta, with Saosyhant the Redeemer. *Midrash Rabba* (Exodus 18) credits Michael with being the author of the whole of Psalm 85. In addition, he has been identified with the angel who destroyed the hosts of Sennacherib (a feat also ascribed to the prowess of Uriel, Gabriel, Ramiel) and as the angel who stayed the hand of Abraham when the latter was on the point of sacrificing his son Isaac (a feat also ascribed to Tadhiel, Metatron, and other angels). In Jewish lore (Ginzberg, *The Legends of the Jews* II, 303) "the fire that Moses saw in the burning

Michael announces to the Virgin her approaching death. A predella by Fra Filippo Lippi. From Jameson, *Legends of the Madonna*.

bush had the appearance of Michael, who had descended from Heaven as the forerunner of the Shekinah." Zagzagel (*q.v.*) is usually denominated the angel of the burning bush. According to Talmud *Berakot* 35, where the comment is on Genesis 18:1–10, Michael is recognized by Sarah as one of 3 "men" whom Abraham entertained unawares. Legend speaks of Michael having assisted 4 other great angels—Gabriel, Uriel, Raphael, Metatron—in the burial of Moses, Michael disputing with Satan for possession of the body [*Rf.* Jude 9.] In mystic and occult writings, Michael has often been equated with the Holy Ghost, the Logos, God, Metatron, etc. In *Baruch III*, Michael "holds the keys of the kingdom of Heaven"—which, traditionally, and in the popular image, applies more aptly to St. Peter. In Hastings, *Encyclopaedia of Religion and Ethics* IV, 616, the article "Demons and Spirits" speaks of the earliest traditions in Muslim lore as locating Michael in the 7th Heaven "on the borders of the Full Sea, crowded with an innumerable array of angels"; and after describing Michael's wings as "of the color of green emerald," goes on to say that he "is covered with saffron hairs, each of them containing a million faces and mouths and as many tongues

which, in a million dialects, implore the pardon of Allah." In ancient Persian lore, Michael was called Beshter, "one who provides sustenance for mankind," which would equate him with Metatron. [*Rf.* Sale, *The Koran*, "Preliminary Discourse."] Here it is revealed that the cherubim were formed from the tears Michael shed over the sins of the faithful. Christians invoke Michael as St. Michael, the benevolent angel of death, in the sense of deliverance and immortality, and for leading the souls of the faithful "into the eternal light." To the Jews, according to Régamey, *What Is an Angel?*, Michael is the "viceroy of Heaven" (a title applied to the great adversary *ha-Satan*, before the latter fell). With Gabriel, Michael is the most commonly pictured angel in the work of the classic masters. He is depicted most often as winged, with unsheathed sword, the warrior of God and slayer of the Dragon (a role later apportioned to St. George). As the angel of the final reckoning and the weigher of souls (an office he shares with Dokiel, Zehanpuryu, and others) he holds in his hand the scales of justice. Fra Filippo Lippi, in a sketch reproduced on p. 436 in Jameson, *Legends of the Madonna*, shows Michael kneeling and offering a taper, as the angel who announces to Mary her approaching death (it was Gabriel who announced the birth of the Virgin's God-child). On p. 433 of the same book an oriental legend is recalled which tells of Michael having cut off the hands of "a wicked Jewish high priest" who had attempted to overturn the bier of the just-deceased Virgin; however, the hands of the "audacious Jew" were reunited to his body at the intercession of St. Peter. Among the recently discovered Dead Sea scrolls there is one titled the *War of the Sons of Light Against the Sons of Darkness*. Here Michael is called the "Prince of Light." He leads the angels of light in battle against the legions of the angels of darkness, the latter under the command of the demon Belial. In Ginzberg, *The Legends of the Jews*, Michael is regarded as the forerunner of the Shekinah (*q.v.*); as the angel who brought Asenath from Palestine as a wife to Joseph; as the one who saved Daniel's companions from the fire; as the intermediary between Mordecai and Esther; as the destroyer of Babylon, etc.,

etc. He is also said to have informed the fallen angels of the Deluge. When he wept, his tears changed into precious stones. In Longfellow's *The Golden Legend*, Michael is the spirit of the planet Mercury and "brings the gift of patience." In secular writings, notably in Dante and Milton, Michael figures prominently. In contemporary fiction, he serves as archdeacon to Bishop Brougham in Robert Nathan's *The Bishop's Wife*. To Yeats, in the latter's poem "The Rose of Peace," Michael is styled "leader of God's host." The latest news on Michael is that Pope Pius XII declared him to be (in 1950) the patron of policemen.

Michar [Mikhar]

Micheu—in gnostic lore, a power (with Mikhar) "set over the waters of life." [*Rf.* the *Bruce Papyrus.*]

Microprosopus—"the left side" of the operative good in cabalistic cosmogony; he was formed, it is claimed, out of the 4th, 5th, 6th, 7th, 8th, and 9th sefiroth. [*Rf.* Runes, *The Wisdom of the Kabbalah.*]

Midael—"a chief and captain" in the celestial army. Cited in *The Magus* as an angel of the order of warriors. *Cf.* Psalms 34–35. Reference to Midael is found also in Mathers, *The Greater Key of Solomon.*

Middoth—in the view of Rabbi Nathan (*Abot*), the middoth are the 7 personifications of the divine attributes or emanations; they are to be compared with the sefiroth (*q.v.*). Two of the middoth—the angels of mercy and of justice—are reputed to have been the principal agents in the creation of the world, according to rabbinic legend. The other 5 middoth are personifications of wisdom, right, love, truth, peace.

Midrash—one of the many names of the angel Metatron.

Miel—the angel of Wednesday. [*Rf.* de Abano, *The Heptameron.*] In Shah's *The Secret Lore of Magic* (p. 294), Miel is cited as one of 3 angels of the planet Mercury, the other 2 angels being Raphael and Seraphiel.

Michael. A 6th-century Byzantine mosaic. Reproduced from Régamey, *Anges.*

Mights—another term for the order of virtues (q.v.), as used by Benjamin Camfield in his *Theological Discourse of Angels*. Steiner in his *The Work of the Angels in Man's Astral Body* equates Mights with Dynamis (q.v.).

Migon—one of the many names of the angel Metatron enumerated in *3 Enoch*.

Mihael—in the cabala, an angel in control of conjugal fidelity and fertility. Ambelain, *La Kabbale Pratique*, lists Mihael as belonging to the order of virtues. According to *The Magus*, he is of the 72 angels bearing the name of God Shemhamphorae.

Miha'il—in Muslim lore, an angel of the 2nd Heaven in charge of a group of angels (in the guise of eagles) engaged in worshipping Allah. [*Rf.* Hastings, *Encyclopaedia of Religion and Ethics* IV, 619.]

Mihr (Mihir, Miher, Mithra)—in ancient Persian lore, the angel presiding over the 7th month (September) and over the 16th day of that month. Mihr watched over friendship and love. [*Rf.* Hyde, *Historia Religionis Veterum Persarum.*] The magi held that, on Judgment Day, 2 angels would stand on the bridge called *al Sirat* (which is finer than a hair and sharper than the edge of a sword) to examine every person crossing. Mihr would be one of those angels, Sorush the other. Mihr, representing divine mercy, and holding a balance in his hand, would weigh the person's actions performed during his lifetime. If found worthy, the person would be permitted to pass on to Paradise. If he was found unworthy, then Sorush, representing divine justice, would hurl him into Hell. [*Rf.* Sale, *The Koran*, "Preliminary Discourse," p. 64.]

Mijcol (Mijkol)—an angel of the Seal, used in conjuring. [*Rf. The Sixth and Seventh Books of Moses.*]

Mikael—an angel who influences the decisions of monarchs, nobles, and governors; also useful in uncovering conspiracies against states. His corresponding angel is Arpien. [*Rf.* Ambelain, *La Kabbale Pratique*, p. 277.]

Mikail or **Mikhael** (Michael)—in Arabic lore, Mika'il is a guardian angel invoked in rites of exorcism. [*Rf.* Hughes, *A Dictionary of Islam*, "Angels."]

Mikhar (Mikheus)—in gnosticism, one of the celestial powers with dominion over the springs of the waters of life (heavenly baptism). [*Rf.* Doresse, *The Secret Books of Egyptian Gnosticism*, p. 85 and 182; *cf.* Micheu.]

Mikheus [Mikhar]

Mikiel—one of the 72 angels in charge of the zodiac. [*Rf.* Runes, *The Wisdom of the Kabbalah.*]

Milkiel (Melkeyal, Tamaano—"my kingdom is God")—in *The Zohar* an angel who rules over spring. The name Milkiel, according to Charles, *The Book of Enoch*, is an "inversion" of Helemmelek (q.v.). According to Barton, *Origin of the Names of Angels*, Milkiel rules one of the summer months and goes also under the names of Tamaani and Sun. [*Rf. Enoch I*, 82:15.]

Milliel—a Wednesday angel residing in the 3rd Heaven, as cited in de Abano, *The Heptameron*. However, according to Barrett, *The Magus*, Milliel resides in the 2nd Heaven. But whatever Heaven Milliel resides in, he must be invoked from the south.

Miniel—in occult lore, one of the great luminaries whose chief virtue is that he can, when invoked, induce love in an otherwise cold and reluctant maid; but for the best results, the invocant must be sure he is facing south. [*Rf.* Barrett, *The Magus.*] Miniel is also invoked in spells for the manufacture and use of magic carpets. One such spell is given in Shah, *Occultism* (p. 167), and is reproduced in the Appendix.

Ministering Angels (Hebrew, *malache hashareth*)—in the judgment of some Talmudists, the ministering angels constitute the highest order in the celestial hierarchy, and are the "hosts of the Lord," as in the *Mekilta of Rabbi Ishmael*; in the view of others, the ministering angels are of an inferior order or rank and, since they are so numerous, the most expendable. In Talmud *Sanhedrin* it is reported that "the ministering angels roasted meat and cooled wine for Adam" during the brief while that our 1st parents dwelt in Eden. In *Yalkut Reubeni* and *The Book of Adam and Eve*, 3 of the ministering angels who thus served Adam are named: Aebel, Anush, and Shetel. The *Testament of Naphtali* (in the *Testament of the Twelve Patriarchs*) speaks of God "bringing down from his highest Heaven 70 ministering angels (with Michael at their head) to teach languages to the 70 children that sprang from the loins of Noah." [*Cf.* Guardian Angels.] In Talmud *Hagiga* we learn that "the ministering angels are daily created out of the river Dinur ... they sing a Hymn and thenceforth perish, as it is said, 'Each morning they are new.' "

Ministers—a term for angels, as in Hebrews 1:7: "He maketh the winds his angels, and the flaming fires his ministers."

Mirael—a "captain and chief" of the celestial armies, invoked in Solomonic magical rites. [*Rf.* Mathers, *The Greater Key of Solomon*, p. 112, and Psalms 34–35.]

Miri—angel of an hour, mentioned and invoked by H.D. (Hilda Doolittle) in her poem "Sagesse." Miri is listed in Ambelain, *La Kabbale Pratique*, a source from which the American poet drew many of the names of angels found in her work.

Miriael—an angel of the order of warriors. According to Barrett, *The Magus* II, 58, the name Miriael derives from Psalms 34 and 35, where the expression "angel of the Lord" occurs.

Misran—genius of persecution and one of the genii of the 12th hour, as noted in Apollonius of Tyana, *The Nuctemeron*.

Missabu—in occultism, a ministering angel to Arcan, king of the angels of the air serving on Monday. [*Rf.* de Abano, *The Heptameron*; Shah, *Occultism*, p. 49.]

Missaln—one of the angels of the Moon, serving on Monday, and responsive to invocations in magical rites. [*Rf.* Shah, *The Secret Lore of Magic*, p. 296.]

Mitatron (Metatron?)—as described in de Abano, *The Heptameron*, a Wednesday angel resident of the 3rd Heaven and invoked from the west.

Mithghiiel A'—one of the angel princes of the Hosts of X, as cited in M. Gaster, *The Sword of Moses* XI.

Mithra (Mitra, Mihir, Mihr, Ized, etc.)—in Vedic cosmology, one of the shining gods, analogous to the Judaean-Christian angels. King in *The Gnostics and Their Remains* equates Mithra with Metatron (*q.v.*). In Persian theology, Mithra or Mihr is one of the 28 izeds (spirits) that surround the great god Ahura-Mazda. He "rises from a paradise in the east, has 1,000 ears and 10,000 eyes." Among Aryans, he is a god of light. In Heaven, he assigns places to the souls of the just. [*Rf. The Dabistan*, p. 145; Lenormant, *Chaldean Magic*.]

Mitmon—an angel called on in goetic conjurations. [*Rf.* Mathers, *The Greater Key of Solomon*.]

Miton—one of the many names of the angel Metatron.

Mitox(t)—a Zoroastrian daeva of the "falsely spoken word;" a servant of Ahriman, Persian prince of demons. [*Rf. Grundriss der iranischen Philologie* III; Seligmann, *History of Magic*, p. 39.]

Mitspad—one of the many names of the angel Metatron.

Mitzrael (Mizrael)—one of the archangels in cabalistic lore. Mitzrael induces obedience on the part of inferiors toward superiors. He is one of 72 angels bearing the name of God Shemhamphorae. His corresponding angel is Homoth. For the sigil of Mitzrael, see Ambelain, *La Kabbale Pratique*, p. 289.

Mitzraim (Hebrew name for Egypt)—the guardian angel of Egypt (but *see* Uzza; also Rahab). [*Rf.* Bamberger, *Fallen Angels*.]

Mivon—one of the many names of the angel Metatron.

Mizabu—a spirit of the 4 quarters of the Universal Mansions, called on in Monday invocations. [*Rf. The Secret Grimoire of Turiel.*]

Mizan—an angel invoked in Arabic incantation rites. [*Rf.* Shah, *Occultism.*]

Mizgitari—genius of eagles and one of the genii of the 7th hour, as noted in Apollonius of Tyana, *The Nuctemeron.*

Mizkun—genius of amulets and one of the genii of the 1st hour. Noted in Apollonius of Tyana, *The Nuctemeron.*

Mizumah—in ancient Persian lore, the angel who "attended the servants of God and promoted the better faith." [*Rf. The Dabistan,* p. 126.]

Mnesinous—in the *Revelation of Adam to His Son Seth,* one of the great celestial powers "who are to draw the elect up to Heaven." [*Rf.* Doresse, *The Secret Books of the Egyptian Gnostics,* p. 182.]

Moak(k)ibat—in Muslim lore, the recording angel, just as Pravuil or Radueriel is in Judaeo-Christian lore, or as Nebo or Nabu is in Babylonian lore. The term "al Moakkibat" stands for 2 guardian angels who, in Arabic legend, write down men's activities. The angels succeed each other daily. [*Rf.* Sale, *The Koran,* "Preliminary Discourse," IV.]

Modiel—one of the numerous angelic guards of the gates of the East Wind, according to listing in the *Ozar Midrashim* II, 316.

Modiniel—in Jewish cabala, one of the spirits of the planet Mars. His corresponding intelligence is Graphael. [See Lenormant, *Chaldean Magic: Its Origin and Development.*]

Moloc(h) (Molech)—a fallen angel in *Paradise Lost* II, 4, where he is described as "the fiercest Spirit/That fought in Heav'n; now fiercer by despair." In Hebrew lore, he is a Canaanitish god of fire to whom children were sacrificed. Solomon built a temple to him [*Rf.* I Kings II, 7.]

Monadel—one of the 72 angels bearing the mystical name of God Shemhamphorae.

Monker (Munkar)—one of 2 blue-eyed black angels (the other being Nakir) in Arabic demonology. Monker's special job is to examine the souls of the recently deceased so as to determine whether they are worthy of a place in Paradise. See "A Mandaean Hymn of the Soul" by Schulim Ochser, mentioned in Thompson, *Semitic Magic.* [*Rf.* Hughes, *A Dictionary of Islam,* "Azabu'l-Qabr."]

Morael (Moriel)—in geonic lore, the angel of awe or fear. He rules over the month of Elul (August–September). He has the power of making everything in the world invisible—according to Waite, *The Book of Black Magic and of Pacts,* where, on p. 161, Morael's sigil is reproduced.

Morax [Forfax]

Mordad—the angel of death in ancient Persian lore. [*Rf.* Sale, *The Koran,* "Preliminary Discourse," p. 51.]

Moroni—the Mormon angel of God, son of "Mormon, the last great leader of the Nephites." A statue of Moroni tops the 40-foot monument at Hill Cumorah, 4 miles south of Palmyra, New York, where Joseph Smith claimed he received, from the hand of this angel, the gold plates containing "the gospel of a new revelation." [*Rf.* the *Book of Mormon.*]

Moses—in tannaitic sources, Moses is not infrequently referred to as an angel, or as a patriarch-prophet who enjoys a status above an angel. He is one of 3 humans who "ascended to Heaven to perform service" (Enoch, Elijah, Moses); but while we know the angelic names of Enoch and Elijah (Metatron and Sandalphon) we have no angelic name for Moses. True, there is a legend (*Midrash Tannaim* relates it) that, on occasion, Michael assumed the form of Moses.

Mqttro—an angel (one of the *nomina barbara*) "that ministers to the son of man." [*Rf.* M. Gaster, *The Sword of Moses.*]

Mrgioial—an invocation angel (one of the *nomina barbara*), and among the 4 angels appointed by God to the Sword who communicated th-divine name to Moses. [*Rf.* M. Gaster, *The Sword of Moses.*]

Mtniel—an angel who exercises dominion over wild beasts, just as Behemiel (*q.v.*) exercises dominion over tame beasts. Mtniel shares his office with 2 other angels, Jehiel and Hayyel.

Mufgar—in *Pirke Hechaloth* an angelic guard serving in the 1st Heaven.

Mufliel—in hechaloth lore (*Ma'asseh Merkabah*), an angelic guard stationed at the 7th heavenly hall.

Mulciber—in *Paradise Lost* I, 740ff., Mulciber once "built in Heav'n high Towers." [*Cf.* Vulcan.]

Mumiah—in the cabala, an angel who controls the science of physics and medicine and is in charge of health and longevity. His corresponding angel is Atembui. For Mumiah's sigil, see Ambelain, *La Kabbale Pratique*, p. 294.

Mumol—an angel invoked with Mutuol (*q.v.*) in the consecration of Pen and Ink.

Munkar [Monker]

Mupiel ("out of the mouth of God")—in Mosaic incantation rites, an angel invoked for the obtaining of a good memory and an open heart.

Murdad—in ancient Persian lore, the angel of July; also the angel governing the 7th day of the month. [*Rf.* Hyde, *Historia Religionis Veterum Persarum.*] Where Murdad is equated with Azrael, he is the angel who separates the body from the soul, at death.

Muriel (Murriel, from the Greek "myrrh")—angel of the month of June and ruler of the sign of Cancer (crab), as cited in Camfield, *A Theological Discourse of Angels*, p. 67. Muriel is also one of the rulers of the order of dominations. He is invoked from the south and is able to procure for the invocant a magic carpet. In addition, he serves under Veguaniel as one of the chief angelic officers of the 3rd hour of the day.

Murmur (Murmus)—before he turned into a fallen angel, Murmur was partly of the order of thrones and partly of the order of angels. This "fact was proved after infinite research," reports Spence in *An Encyclopaedia of Occultism*, p. 119. In Hell, Murmur is a great duke with 30 legions

A woodcut from the Cologne Bible showing the burial of Moses. On left, God, interring the Lawgiver. Assisting angels are Michael and Gabriel (or Zagzagel). From *Pictures from a Mediaeval Bible*.

of infernal spirits attending him. He manifests in the form of a warrior astride a gryphon, with a ducal crown upon his head. He teaches philosophy and constrains the souls of the dead to appear before him for the answering of questions. His sigil is shown in Waite, *The Book of Black Magic and of Pacts*, p. 182.

Musanios—in gnostic lore, an aeon of the lower ranks; yet he serves as a ruler of the realm of the invisible. [*Rf.* Doresse, *The Secret Books of the Egyptian Gnostics.*]

Mutuol—in *The Grand Grimoire*, an angel invoked in the consecration of Pen and Ink, a powerful device for the binding of evil spirits, or of exorcising them. [*Rf.* Shah, *Occultism*, p. 20.]

Mzpopiasaiel—a leader of the angels of wrath. He is so designated in M. Gaster, *The Sword of Moses*.

Angel of Eden expelling Adam and Eve.
Identified as Michael by Milton in *Paradise Lost*, but as Raphael by Dryden in *State of Innocence*. Reproduced from Hayley, *The Poetical Works of John Milton*.

Naadame—a "prince over all the angels and Caesars." [*Rf.* Mathers, *The Greater Key of Solomon*.]

Naamah ("pleasing")—in the cabala, one of 4 angels of prostitution, all mates of Sammael, the other 3 being Lilith, Eisheth Zenunim, and Agrat (Iggereth) bat Mahlat. According to Rabbi Isaac, the sons of God, specifically Uzza and Azael, were corrupted by Naamah. Rabbi Simeon called her mother of demons, and Rabbi Hiya believed she was the "great seducer not only of men but of spirits and demons," and that, with Lilith, she "brought epilepsy to children." [*Rf. The Zohar* I, 55a.] In *The Legends of the Jews* I, 150, Naamah is the mother of the devil Asmodeus by the angel-demon Shamdan. In Genesis 4:22, Naamah is a mortal, the sister of Tubal-cain.

Naar (Hebrew, "lad")—one of the many names of the angel Metatron.

Naaririel (variant of Naar)—an angelic guard of the 7th Heaven.

Nabu (Nebo, "prophet, proclaimer")—the Babylonian prototype of the Judaeo-Christian archangel. Nabu was the son and minister of the god Marduk and in Sumerian theosophy was known as "the angel of the Lord." As the scribe of the book of fate, his emblem is the lamp. He was also regarded as one of the recording angels. In Akkadian myth, Nabu was the god of the planet Mercury. Relating the Eastern divinity to Enoch-Metatron, Ginzberg, in *The Legends of the Jews* V, 163, says: "The Babylonian Nebo, heavenly scribe, gave Enoch to the Palestinian, Metatron to the Babylonian Jews, and nothing could be more natural than the final combination of Enoch-Metatron." [*Rf. Catholic Encyclopedia* I, "Angel."]

Nachiel (Nakiel, Nakhiel)—in the cabala, the intelligence of the sun, when the sun enters the sign of Leo. Nachiel's cabalistic number is 111. His corresponding spirit is Sorath (*q.v.*), according to Paracelsus' doctrine of Talismans. [*Rf.* Christian, *The History and Practice of Magic* I, 318.]

Nachmiel—an angelic guard of the gates of the South Wind. [*Rf. Ozar Midrashim* II, 317.]

Nacoriel—an angel of the 9th hour of the night. [*See* Hanozoz.]

Nadiel—in Schwab, *Vocabulaire de l'Angélologie*, the angel of migration; also ruler of December (Kislav). [*See* Haniel.]

Nafriel—an angelic guard of the gates of the South Wind. [*Rf. Ozar Midrashim* II, 317.]

Nagrasagiel (Nasragiel, Nagdasgiel, Nagazdiel) —prince of gehinnom (Hell) who showed Moses around when the Lawgiver toured the underworld. [*Rf. Midrash Konen* and *The Legends of the Jews* II, 310.] *Cf.* Sargiel; also the Sumerian-Chaldean Nergal.

Nahaliel ("valley of God")—an angel presiding over running streams. [*Rf. Jewish Magic and Superstition.*] In Numbers 21:19 Nahaliel is the name of a town.

Nahoriel [Nahuriel]

Nahuriel—one of 7 angelic guards of the 1st Heaven, as listed in *Pirke Hechaloth.*

Nairyo Sangha (Persian)—one of 3 angel princes of the 3 upper gates of the nether world, a messenger of Ahura-Mazda. [*Rf. Midrash Konen*; *Jewish Encyclopedia* I, 593.] "To Nairyo Sangha the souls of the righteous are entrusted."

Nakhiel [Nachiel]

Nakiel [Nachiel]

Nakir—a black angel in Mohammedan lore. [*See* Monker.]

Nakriel—one of numerous angelic guards of the gates of the South Wind. [*Rf. Ozar Midrashim* II, 316.]

Nanael—in practical cabala, one of the principalities; also one of the 72 angels bearing the mystical name of God Shemhamphorae. Nanael exercises dominion over the great sciences, influences philosophers and ecclesiastics. His corresponding angel is Chomme. [*Rf.* Barrett, *The Magus*; Ambelain, *La Kabbale Pratique.*]

Naoutha—the *Gospel of Bartholomew*, p. 176, speaks of Naoutha as an angel with dominion over the southwest. He is described as having "a rod of snow in his hand" which he "putteth into his mouth," and as quenching the fire "that cometh out of his mouth."

Narcoriel—an angel of the 8th hour of the night. [*See* Hanoziz.]

Narel—in Enoch lore, the angel of winter.

Nariel—according to Barrett, *The Magus*, Nariel governs the South Wind. He is also ruler of the noonday winds. "By some called Ariel," says *The Magus.*

Naromiel—in occult lore, one of the intelligences of the moon, and ruler of Lord's Day (Sunday). He resides in the 4th Heaven and is invoked from the south. [*Rf.* de Abano, *The Heptameron*; Lenormant, *Chaldean Magic*; Barrett, *The Magus.*]

Narsinha—the "man-lion" avatar, one of the 10 divine incarnations in Vedic lore. He is "lord of heroism." [*See* Avatar.]

Narudi—an Akkadian spirit, "lord of the great gods," whose image was placed in houses to ward off wicked people. [*Rf.* Lenormant, *Chaldean Magic*, p. 48.]

Nasarach (Nisroch)—another form for Nisroc (*q.v.*) used in Isaiah and in II Kings 19:37.

Nasargiel (Nagrasagiel, Nasragiel)—a great, holy, lion-headed angel who, with Kipod and Nairyo Sangha, exercised dominion over Hell. He is to be compared with the Sumerian-Chaldean Nergal. Nasargiel showed Moses around the nether realms on orders from God. [*Rf.* Ginzberg, *The Legends of the Jews* II, 310.]

Nasharon—an angel prince "over all the angels and Caesars." [*Rf.* Mathers, *The Greater Key of Solomon.*]

Nashriel—in the text of Isaac ha-Cohen, Nashriel is one of 3 *sarim* (angelic princes) under the suzerainty of Sephuriron, the latter ranking as 10th of the 10 holy sefiroth. The other 2 *sarim* are Ithuriel and Malkiel.

Nasragiel [Nasargiel]

Nasr-ed-Din ("help of faith")—one of the 7 archangels in Yezidic devil-worshipping religion. For the names of the other 6 archangels, *see* Appendix.

Nathanael ("gift of God"—Xathaniel, Zathael, etc.)—in Jewish legendary lore, Nathanael is the 6th created angel and one of the 12 angels of vengeance. He is lord over the element of fire. He is the angel (*The Biblical Antiquities of Philo*) who "burned the servants of Jair" in the contest between God and Baal, saving from fire the 7 men who would not sacrifice to the pagan deity. In Waite, *The Lemegeton*, Nathanael is an angel of the 6th hour, serving under Samil. He is also one of 3 angels (with Ingethal and Zeruch) set over hidden things. Ferrar, *The Uncanonical Jewish Books*, mentions the legend of Nathanael being sent down from Heaven by God to help the warrior Cerez defeat the Amorites.

Natiel—an angel's name found inscribed on an oriental Hebrew charm (*kamea*) for warding off evil. [*Rf.* Schrire, *Hebrew Amulets*.]

Nattig—in Chaldean lore, one of the 4 principal classes of protecting genii; to be compared with the kerubs of Babylonian myth.

Natzhiriron—in Isaac ha-Cohen's text, one of the 10 holy sefiroth, the personalized angel of Netzach. In the cabala, the personalized angel is Haniel or Anael.

Nayá'il—in Islamic apocalyptic lore, an angel encountered by the sufi Abu Yazid in the 4th Heaven during the sufi's *mir'aj* (ascent) to all 7 Heavens. The angel Nayá'il offers Abu Yazid "a kingdom such as no tongue can describe," but, knowing the offer (actually a bribe) to be only a test of his single-minded devotion to God, Abu Yazid "pays no heed to it." [*Rf.* Nicholson, "An Early Arabic Version," etc.]

Nbat—a Mandaean "light-being" (angel). [*Rf.* Drower, *The Mandaeans of Iraq and Iran*.]

Ndmh—angel of the summer equinox invoked as an amulet against the evil eye. [*Rf.* Trachtenberg, *Jewish Magic and Superstition*.]

Nebo [Nabu]

Neciel—one of the 28 angels governing the 28 mansions of the moon.

Nectaire (fictional)—in Anatole France, *Revolt of the Angels*, the wondrous flutist. In Heaven, according to France, Nectaire was of the order of dominations and known as Alaciel.

Nefilim [Nephilim]

Nefta (fictional)—an angel (female) loved by Asrael in the opera by Francetti. [*See* Asrael.]

Negarsanel (Nasargiel)—prince of Hell, "der Fürst des Gehinnom," as Negarsanel is called in the *Alphabet of Rabbi Akiba* (German translation).

Negef—a holy angel of destruction invoked in ritual magic at the close of the Sabbath. [*Rf.* Trachtenberg, *Jewish Magic and Superstition*.]

Nehinah—an angel invoked in necromantic operations. [*Rf.* Trachtenberg, *Jewish Magic and Superstition*.]

Neithel—Runes, *The Wisdom of the Kabbalah*, cites Neithel as one of the 72 angels ruling over the 72 quinaries of the degrees of the zodiac.

Nekir—in Arabic lore (drawn from the Talmud, according to De Plancy), Nekir is an angel who, with Monker and Munkir, interrogates the dead in order to discover what god they worshipped when alive. Both Nekir and Monker are said to have hideous aspects and frightening voices.

Nelapa—in Barrett, *The Magus*, a Wednesday angel who resides in the 2nd Heaven and is invoked from the south in theurgic operations.

Nelchael—an angel belonging to the order of thrones and one of the 72 angels bearing the mystical name of God Shemhamphorae, according to Barrett, *The Magus*, and Ambelain, *La Kabbale Pratique*. However, he appears to be not a holy angel but a fallen one who, in Hell, teaches astronomy, mathematics, and geography to his fellow demons. His corresponding spirit is known as Sith.

Nergal, one of the four principal protecting genii (guardian angels) in Chaldean cosmology. From Schaff, *A Dictionary of the Bible.*

Nemamiah—in the cabala, an archangel, guardian of admirals, generals, and all who engage in just causes. He is also one of the 72 bearing the mystical name of God Shemhamphorae. [*Rf.* Ambelain, *La Kabbale Pratique*, p. 289, where Nemamiah's sigil is reproduced.]

Nememel—one of the 72 angels ruling over the 72 quinaries of the degrees of the zodiac. [*Rf.* Runes, *The Wisdom of the Kabbalah.*]

Nephilim (Nephelin, Nefilim)—in Hebrew lore, the nephilim stood for giants of primeval times; also as fallen angels, or their offspring (the "sons of God" who cohabited with the daughters of men, as in Genesis 6). Closely related were the emim ("terrors"), the rephaim ("weakeners"), the gibborium ("giants"), the zamzummim ("achievers"), etc. [*Rf. Enoch I*; De Plancy, *Dictionnaire Infernal*; Ginzberg, *The Legends of the Jews*; Numbers 13:33.] Head of the nephilim was Helel (*q.v.*). According to the 9th-century writer Hiwi al Balkhi, the nephilim were the builders of the Tower of Babel. [*Rf.* Saadiah, *Polemic against Hiwi al Balkhi*, pp. 54–56.]

Nephonos—one of the 9 angels that "run together throughout the heavenly and earthly places." The 9 angels are named by Beliar and revealed to Bartholomew in the *Gospel of Bartholomew*, p. 177.

Neqael (Nuqael)—an evil (i.e., fallen) archangel included in the Enoch listings. The name is actually a corruption or variant of Ezeeqael.

Nergal ("great hero," "great king," "king death")—in Babylonian mythology, Nergal (or Nirgal or Nirgali) is a planetary ruler of the week. To the Akkadians he was a lion-headed god; to the Chaldeans, one of 4 principal protecting genii (guardian angels). He was also the god of Kutha, as in II Kings 17:30, and answered to Baal as a deity of Hades. [*Rf.* Forlong, *Encyclopedia of Religions.*] In Sumerian-Chaldean-Palestinian lore, Nergal is ruler of the summer sun. In gnosticism he is king of Hades (as in Scripture). In occultism he is chief of secret police in the nether regions. He is also credited with being a god of pestilence, war, fever, as well as the spirit of the planet Mars and one of the governors of the 12 signs of the zodiac. In Le Clercq's collection, Nergal is figured on a bronze medallion: obverse, lion-headed; verso, wings and clawed feet. In De Plancy, *Dictionnaire Infernal*, he is "an honorary spy in the service of Belzebuth." See picturization from Schaff, *A Dictionary of the Bible.*

Neria(h) ("lamp of God")—one of the 70 childbed amulet angels.

Neriel—probably the same as Neria. In *The Sixth and Seventh Books of Moses*, Neriel is listed among the 28 angels who govern the 28 mansions of the moon.

Nesanel—in Mosaic incantation rites, Nesanel, along with the angels Meachuel and Gabril, is summoned to free or purge the invocant of all sin.

Nestoriel—an angel of the 1st hour of the day, serving Sammael. [*Rf.* Waite, *The Lemegeton.*]

Nestozoz—chief officiating angel of the 3rd hour of the night, serving Sarquamich.

Nethahel—in Runes, *The Wisdom of the Kabbalah*, one of the 72 angels ruling over the 72 quinaries of the degrees of the zodiac.

Netoniel—in black magic, an angelic name found inscribed in Hebrew characters on the 1st pentacle of the planet Jupiter. [*Rf.* Shah, *The*

Secret Lore of Magic; Mathers, *The Greater Key of Solomon*.]

Netzach ("victory, firmness")—the 7th of the 10 holy sefiroth (emanations of God). The personalized angel of Netzach is Haniel (Anael) of the order of elohim.

Netzael [Netzach]

Nibra Ha-Rishon—one of the emanations of God (i.e., a sefira). According to Müller, *History of Jewish Mysticism*, Nibra Ha-Rishon must be ranked among the highest angelic beings and to be compared with Makon, Logos, Sophia, Metatron.

Nichbadiel—one of numerous angelic guards of the gates of the South Wind. [See *Ozar Midrashim* II, 317.]

Nidbai—in Mandaean mythology, one of 2 guardian *uthri* (angels) of the River Jordan; the other guardian angel is Silmai or Shilmai. [*Rf.* Drower, *The Canonical Prayerbook of the Mandaeans*, and *The Mandaeans of Iraq and Iran*.]

Nilaihah (or Nith-haiah)—Ambelain, *La Kabbale Pratique*, lists Nilaihah as a poet-angel of the order of dominations. He is invoked by pronouncing any of the divine names along with the 1st verse of Psalm 9. He is in charge of occult sciences, delivers prophecies in rhyme, and exercises influence over wise men who love peace and solitude. His sigil is figured on p. 273 of Ambelain's work.

Nine Angels That Rule the Nine Hierarchies in Heaven—1. Merattron or Metatron (over the seraphim); 2. Ophaniel (over the cherubim); 3. Zaphkiel (over thrones); 4. Zadkiel (over dominations); 5. Camael (over powers); 6. Raphael (over virtues); 7. Haniel (over principalities); 8. Michael (over archangels); 9. Gabriel (over angels). [*Rf.* Barrett, *The Magus*.]

Ninety-nine Sheep—comprising the world of the angels. Methodius of Philippi, *Convivia* 3, 6, writes: "We must see in the 99 sheep a representation of the powers and the principalities and the dominations." Origen, Cyril of Jerusalem, and Gregory of Nyssa wrote to the same effect.

Ninip—in Babylonian theosophy, chief of the angels (i.e., chief of the igigi). [*Rf. Catholic Encyclopedia*, "Angels"; Mackenzie, *Myths of Babylonia and Assyria*.]

Ninth Heaven—the home of the 12 signs of the zodiac, according to *Enoch II*; but *see* Eighth Heaven. In Hebrew, the 9th Heaven is called *kukhavim*.

Nirgal (Nirgali)—one of the 4 principal classes of protecting genii (i.e., guardian angels) in Chaldean lore. Usually represented as spirits in the form of lions with men's heads. [*Rf.* Lenormant, *Chaldean Magic*, p. 121.] *See* Nergal.

Nisah [Netzach]

Nisan—a Talmudic angel mentioned in Hyde, *Historia Religionis Veterum Persarum*.

Nisroc(h) ("the great eagle")—originally an Assyrian deity, worshipped by Sennacherib (II Kings 19:37). But, according to Milton (*Paradise Lost* VI, 447), Nisroc is a ruling angel of the order of principalities. In occult lore, he is regarded as a demon, serving as chief of cuisine in the House of Princes (in Hell). See illustration from Schaff, *A Dictionary of the Bible*. Nisroc is equated with Chemos, Baal-Peor, Meserach and Arasek.

Nisroch, an Assyrian deity worshipped by Sennacherib (II Kings 19, 37). From Schaff, *A Dictionary of the Bible*.

The nine orders of the celestial hierarchy. A 14th-century conception. From Hans Werner Hegemann, *Der Engel in der deutschen Kunst.* Munich: R. Piper, 1950.

Nithael—in the cabala, an angel formerly of the order of principalities. Barrett, *The Magus*, claims that Nithael is, despite his fall, still one of the 72 angels bearing the name of God Shemhamphorae. The prevailing belief is that Nithael joined Satan during the rebellion in Heaven and that now, in Hell, he governs emperors and kings, also civil and ecclesiastical personages of the highest rank. For Nithael's sigil, see Ambelain, *La Kabbale Pratique*, p. 289.

Nithaiah (Nith-Haiah) [Nilaihah]

Nitibus—a genius of the stars, cited in Levi, *Transcendental Magic*. In Apollonius of Tyana, *The Nuclemeron*, Nitibus is an angel of the 2nd hour.

Nitika—a genius of precious stones; he presides over the 6th hour. [*Rf.* Apollonius of Tyana, *The Nuctemeron*; Levi, *Transcendental Magic*.]

N'Mosnikttiel—a leader of the angels of rage. Cited in Jewish mysticism tracts. [*Rf.* M. Gaster, *The Sword of Moses*.]

Noaphiel—an angel whose name is inscribed in Hebrew characters on the 5th pentacle of the planet Saturn. In conjuring Noaphiel, the invocant is advised (for best results) to recite a versicle from Deuteronomy 10.

Nogah—one of 2 big stars (i.e., angels) that Metatron pointed out to Moses in the 4th Heaven. Nogah "stands above the sun in summer to cool the earth." [*Rf. Revelation of Moses*.]

Nogahel—one of the princes "who stand continually before God and to whom are given the spirit names of the planets." [*Rf.* Cornelius Agrippa, *Three Books of Occult Philosophy* III.]

Noguel—in the cabala, a spirit of the planet Venus. His corresponding intelligence is Hagiel. [*Rf.* Lenormant, *Chaldean Magic*, p. 26.]

Nohariel—an angelic guard of the East Wind. [*Rf. Ozar Midrashim* II, 316.]

Noriel ("fire of God")—in *The Zohar* (Exodus 147a), one of angels symbolized by special colors; in the case of Noriel, "by the gold of brass, lit with orange." [*Rf. Divine Pymander of Hermes Trismegistus*.] In *Ozar Midrashim* (II, 316), Noriel is one of the angelic guards of the gates of the East Wind.

Novensiles—the 9 great deities of the Etruscans who controlled thunderbolts. Their names were Tina, Cupra, Menrva (Menerva), Summanus, Vejovis (Vedius), Sethlans, Mars, Mantus, Ercle (Hercle). In his *The Case Against the Pagans* (*Adversus Nationes*), Arnobius reports that, according to Granius, the Novensiles are the Muses; according to Cornificius, they watch over the renewing of things; according to Manilius, they are the gods to whom alone Jupiter gave power to wield his thunderbolts.

Nudriel—in hechaloth lore (*Ma'asseh Merkabah*), an angelic guard stationed at the 3rd heavenly hall.

Nukha'il and **Nura'il**—in Arabic lore, guardian angels invoked in rites of exorcism. [*Rf.* Hughes, *A Dictionary of Islam*, "Angels."]

Nuriel ("fire")—angel of hailstorms in Jewish legend. Moses encountered Nuriel in the 2nd Heaven. When he issues from the side of Hesed (kindness), Nuriel manifests in the form of an eagle, an eagle that, when issuing from the side of Geburah (force), is Uriel. In *The Book of Protection*, Nuriel is characterized as a "spellbinding power" and is grouped with Michael, Shamshiel, Seraphiel, and other great angels. According to *The Zohar* I, Nuriel governs Virgo. He is 300 parasangs tall and has a retinue of 50 myriads of angels "all fashioned out of water and fire." The height of Nuriel is exceeded only by the erelim; by the watchers; by Af and Hemah; and of course by Metatron, who is the tallest hierarch in heaven—excepting, perhaps, Hadraniel and Anafiel. In gnostic lore, Nuriel is one of 7 subordinates to Jehuel, prince of fire. [*Rf.* King, *The Gnostics and Their Remains*, p. 15; Ginzberg, *The Legends of the Jews* II, 306 and V, 418.] As a charm for warding off evil, Nuriel is also effective. His name is found engraved on oriental amulets, as noted by Schrire, *Hebrew Amulets*.

N'Zuriel Yhwh—one of the 8 highest ranking angel princes of the Merkabah, all of whom, it seems, occupy stations superior to Metatron.]*Rf. 3 Enoch*.]

Michael ☉ ♌  Och

Machen

Gabriel ☽ Phul

Shamain

Samael ♀ ♈ ♏ Phaleg

Machon

Raphael ☿ ♊ ♍ Ophiel

Raquie

Sachiel ♃ ♐ ♓ Bethor

Zebul

Anael ♀ ♉ ♎ Hagith

Sagun

Cassiel ♄ ♑ ♒ Aratron

The Olympic spirits and angels of the seven planets along with their sigils and other signs. From Waite, *The Book of Ceremonial Magic*.

Obaddon—another form for Abaddon. In Klopstock, *The Messiah*, Obaddon is a seraph and companion to Ithuriel (*q.v.*). In canto VII of Klopstock's work, Obaddon is titled the "minister of death." [*Cf.* this with Abaddon (Apollyon), called in Revelation 9:10 the "angel of the bottomless pit."]

Obizuth—a winged female dragon who is put to flight by the archangel Bazazath (*q.v.*).

Och—in occultism, the angel who governs the sun (but *see* entry "Angel of the Sun" for other hierarchs designated as rulers of this "planet"). Och gives 600 years of perfect health (if, that is, the invocant lives that long). Och is also ruler of 28 of the 196 Olympian provinces in which Heaven is divided. He is cited as a mineralogist and "prince of alchemy." For Och's sigil, see Budge, *Amulets and Talismans*, p. 389. In this work one finds Och credited with ruling 36,536 legions of spirits. For additional mention of Och, see the works of Cornelius Agrippa.

Octinomon (Octinomos)—a "most holy angel of God" invoked in the conjuration of the Reed.

Oertha—angel of the north. "He hath a torch of fire and putteth it to his sides, and they warm the great coldness of him [so] that he freeze not the world." [*Rf. Gospel of Bartholomew*, p. 176.]

Oethra—one of the 9 angels that "run together throughout heavenly and earthly places." Beliar names these 9 angels to Bartholomew on the latter's inquiry as to their identity. [*Rf. Gospel of Bartholomew*, p. 177.]

Ofael—a Tuesday angel of the 5th Heaven, invoked from the south. [*Rf.* de Abano, *The Heptameron*.]

Ofaniel or **Ofan** (Ofniel, Ophan, Ophaniel, Yahriel)—eponymous chief of the order of ofanim (thrones). Ofaniel is said to exercise dominion over the moon and is sometimes referred to as "the angel of the wheel of the moon." In *3 Enoch*, he has 16 faces, 100 pairs of wings, and 8,466 eyes. He is "one of the 7 exalted throne angels who carry out the commands of the powers." [*Rf. Almadel of Solomon*; *The Sixth and Seventh Books of Moses*.] "By the ancient sages," says Rashi, commenting on Ezekiel 1:20, "Ophan, prince of this order, is

211

regarded as identical with Sandalphon." [*Rf.* glossary to C. D. Ginsburg, *The Essenes and The Kabbalah*.]

Ofanim (Ophanim, literally "wheels," "many-eyed ones")—in Merkabah lore, the ofanim (later called galgallim) are equivalent to the order of thrones. Enoch speaks of the "ofanim of the fiery coals." In *The Zohar*, the ofanim rank higher than the seraphim. In Mirandola's scheme, they are placed 6th in the 9-choir hierarchic order. While Ofaniel is the eponymous head, Rikbiel and Raphael are also denoted chief. The sefira Wisdom is represented, among the angelic hosts, by the ofanim, says Ginsburg, *The Essenes and The Kabbalah*, p. 90. Milton associates the ofanim with the cherubim. [*Rf.* West, *Milton and the Angels*.]

Ofiel—one of the 70 childbed amulet angels. [*Rf. The Book of the Angel Raziel*; Budge, *Amulets and Talismans*, p. 225.]

Ofniel [Ofaniel]

Og—a descendant of the fallen angels; the son of Ahijah, the grandson of Semyaza, and the brother of Sihon. In Jewish tradition, Og was an Amorite giant slain in the ankle by Moses. In Numbers 21:33, Og is king of Bashan who is delivered into the hands of Israel by God. However, there is a legend that Og was in the Flood and was saved from it by climbing to the roof of the ark. Palit (*q.v.*) is another name for Og. [*See* Gog and Magog.]

Ogdoas—in gnosticism, the ogdoas constitute a group of the highest heavenly powers. In the view of Basilides, a noted gnostic writer, the ogdoas compose "the world of the great archons." In Hellenic lore, the 8th Heaven is called ogdoas, and is the dwelling place of divine wisdom.

Ohazia—a prince of the face and one of the angelic guards of the 3rd Heaven. [*Rf. Ozar Midrashim* I, 117.]

Oirin—in Chaldean cosmology, angelic watchers over the kingdoms of the earth. (*Cf.* irin.) [*Rf. The Book of the Sacred Magic of Abra-Melin, The Mage*, p. 208.]

Ol—one of the angels of the 12 signs of the zodiac. Ol represents the sign of Leo and is in control of it. He is also regarded as one of the fiery triplicities. [*Rf.* Waite, *The Lemegeton*.]

Oldest Angel—the Logos (Reason or the Word) is called by Philo the "oldest Angel, Dominion, God's likeness." [*Rf.* Mead, *Thrice-Greatest Hermes* I, 137, 161–162.]

Olivier—an ex-prince of the order of archangels, as noted in Michaelis, *Admirable History of the Possession and Conversion of a Penitent Woman.* [*Rf.* Garinet, *History of Magic in France*; De Plancy, *Dictionnaire Infernal* III.]

Olympian Spirits—in the *Arbatel of Magic*, a ritual magic work of the 16th century, the Olympian spirits dwell in the air and in interplanetary space, each spirit governing a number of the 196 provinces in which the universe is divided. There are (or were) 7 of these great hierarchs: Araton or Aratron, Bethor, Phaleg, Och, Hagith, Ophiel (or Orifiel), Phul. [*Rf.* Gaynor, *Dictionary of Mysticism*.] The Olympian spirits were also known as the Stewards of Heaven.

Omael—an angel who multiplies species, perpetuates races, influences chemists, etc. Omael is (or was) of the order of dominations and is among the 72 angels bearing the mystical name of God Shemhamphorae. Whether Omael is fallen or still upright is difficult to determine from the data available. He seems to operate in both domains (Heaven and Hell). [*Rf.* Ambelain, *La Kabbale Pratique*.]

Omeliel (Omeliei)—one of the 4 angelic names inscribed in Hebrew characters on the 3rd pentacle of Saturn. The circle of evocation (where the name Omeliel occurs) is reproduced in Shah, *The Secret Lore of Magic*, p. 54.

Omiel—an angel who "mixed" with mortals before the Deluge, as noted in Schwab, *Vocabulaire de l'Angélologie*.

Omophorus—in Manicheanism, a "world-supporting angel." He carries the earth on his shoulders, like another Atlas. [*See* Splenditenes.]

On—in Mathers, *The Greater Key of Solomon,* an angel or a divine name invoked in the conjuration of the Reed. In *The Book of Black Magic and of Pacts,* On is a demon invoked in Monday conjurations addressed to Lucifer.

Onafiel—an angel governing the moon, according to Longfellow, *The Golden Legend* (late editions). In earlier editions of this work, the angel governing the moon is given by Longfellow as Gabriel. Onafiel appears to be a coinage of Longfellow's, through his inadvertent transposition of the letters *f* and *n*, in setting down Ofaniel.

Onayepheton (Oneipheton)—the name of a spirit by which God will summon the dead and raise them to life again. [*Rf.* Mathers, *The Greater Key of Solomon.*]

Oniel—perhaps the same as Onoel. Equated with Hutriel (*q.v.*). Oniel is supervisor of the 5th division of Hell, where Ahab dwells, Ahab being one of the few "who have no portion in the world to come." [*Rf. Midrash Konen;* Ginzberg, *The Legends of the Jews* IV, 188; *Revelation of Rabbi Joshua ben Levi.*]

Onoel (Oniel, Hamiel, Haniel, Anael)—in gnostic lore, Onoel is one of the 7 archons. Origen cites him as hostile, a demon, who manifests in the form of an ass. In the list given by Origen, however, Gabriel and Michael are included among the 7 archons. [*Rf.* Conybeare, *The Testament of Solomon;* Grant, *Gnosticism and Early Christianity;* Mead, *Thrice-Greatest Hermes* (I, 294); Origen, *Contra Celsum.*]

Onomatath—one of 9 angels that "run together throughout the heavenly and earthly places," as cited in the *Gospel of Bartholomew,* p. 117, where the names of the 9 angels are named by Beliar and revealed to Bartholomew.

Onzo—"a fair angel of God" invoked in the exorcism of Wax. [*Rf. Clavicula Salomonis.*]

Ophan—identified by the ancient sages as the angel Sandalphon (*q.v.*).

Ophaniel [Ofaniel]

Ophanim (ofan(n)im)—a term in Hebrew for the order of cherubim (*q.v.*).

Ophiel—one of the 7 Olympian spirits (or one of 14 such spirits). Ophiel rules the planet Mercury. As an angel of the order of powers, he can be invoked. As many as 100,000 legions of lesser spirits are under his command. In Cornelius Agrippa's works, Ophiel's sigil is shown; his name appears also on the Necromantic Bell of Girardius, which is rung to summon the dead. [*Rf.* Grillot, *Witchcraft, Magic and Alchemy,* fig. 144; the *Arbatel of Magic.*]

Ophiomorphus—in Ophitic (gnostic) lore, the serpent Ophiomorphus is a name for the Hebrew devil Sammael. [*Rf.* Legge, *Forerunners and Rivals of Christianity* II, p. 52.]

Ophis ("serpent")—"head of the rebellious angels"—so described by the Assyrian author Phercies and quoted by Barrett in *The Magus;* also referred to in Butler, *Ritual Magic.* Ophis was revered by the ophites as a symbol of divine wisdom who, in the form of a serpent, befriended Adam and Eve in Eden, persuading them to eat of the forbidden fruit (as a service to man). In Barrett, *The Magus* II (opposite p. 46), Ophis is pictured as a demon.

Opiel—an angel invoked in love charms, according to Montgomery, *Aramaic Incantation Texts from Nippur.*

Or—a great angel invoked in exorcism rites, specifically in the invocation at fumigation, as noted in *Grimorium Verum.*

Orael—one of the intelligences of the planet Saturn.

Oraios (Oreus)—in gnosticism, one of the 7 archons that figure in the Ophitic system. [*Rf. Catholic Encyclopedia,* "Gnosticism."]

Oranir—chief prince of the 9 angels of the summer equinox, and effective as an amulet against the evil eye. [*Rf.* Trachtenberg, *Jewish Magic and Superstition.*]

Ore'a—in hechaloth lore (*Ma'asseh Merkabah*), an angelic guard stationed at the 4th heavenly hall.

Toome's conception of an angel of the order of cherubim. From Heywood, *The Hierarchy of the Blessèd Angels*.

Oreus (Oraios, Horaios)—in Phoencian mythology, one of the 7 elohim (angels) of the divine presence, creators of the universe. According to Irenaeus, Oreus is one of the 7 archons in the Ophitic system. Origen, *Contra Celsum*, believes that the name Oreus derives from the art of magic.

Oriares (Narel)—an angel governing the season of winter.

Oribel—variant for Uriel as one of the angels reprobated by Pope Zachary in 745 C.E. [*Rf.* Hugo, *The Toilers of the Sea*; Heywood, *The Hierarchy of the Blessèd Angels*.]

Oriel (Auriel, "light of God")—one of the 70 childbed amulet angels; also one of the angelic rulers of the 10th hour during daylight. In *Malache Elyon*, Oriel is called the angel of destiny. [*Rf. The Book of the Angel Raziel*; Budge, *Amulets and Talismans*.]

Orifel [Orifiel]

Orifiel (Oriphiel, Orifel, Orfiel, Orphiel)—in Pope Gregory's listing, Orifiel is one of the 7 archangels. Elsewhere he is cited a prince of the order of thrones and (in Cornelius Agrippa, *The Third Book of Philosophy*) an angel with dominion over the planet Saturn. In Hebrew cabala, according to Eliphas Levi, Orifiel, like Saturn, is the angel of the wilderness. In Waite, *The Lemegeton*, Orphiel (so spelt) is one of the 7 regents of the world and an angel of the 2nd hour of the day serving under Anael. In Paracelsus' doctrine of Talismans, Orifiel is a chief Talisman and replaces one of the planetary genii of Egypt. Orifiel is also cited here as an angel of Saturday. In secular lore, Longfellow, *The Golden Legend*, gives Orfiel as the angel governing the planet Saturn, although, in the 1st edition of this work, the angel is given as Anachiel. Orifiel appears as a character in Remy de Gourmont's play *Lilith*. In Cabell, *The Devil's Own Dear Son*, he is a "time-serving archangel." [*Rf.* Christian, *The History and Practice of Magic* I, 317.]

Origin of Angels—angels were conceived of as existing before the creation of the world (Job 38:7; Ambrose in "Ministrations and Communion with Angels"; Origen; *Ketab Tamin* 59; *Yalkut Hadash* 11b). In later Judaism, angels are said to have been created on the 1st day of Creation (*The Book of Jubilees* 2:1; *Enoch II*, 29:3; *Baruch III*, 21; Augustine); on the 2nd day of Creation (*Bereshith Rabba* 1:5; *Pirke Rabbi Eliezer*, 3; *Enoch II*; *Targum Yerushalmi*; Rabbi Jochanan; Isaac of Corbeil); on the 4th day of Creation (Ibn Anas); and on the 5th day of Creation (*Genesis Rabbah*, Rabbi Haninah). No authorities have thus far come to light favoring the 3rd day of Creation.

Oriockh (Ariukh)—in *Enoch II*, God instructs his 2 angels, Oriockh and Mariockh, to guard the books authored by Enoch. The name Orioc is found in Genesis 14:1 and 9; also in Daniel 2:14, but not as the name of an angel.

Orion—in Klopstock, *The Messiah*, Orion is St. Peter's guardian angel. Eliphas Levi finds an identity between Orion and Michael. [*Rf.* Semyaza for a symbolic connection between that fallen seraph and the constellation called Orion (the hunter) by the Greeks.]

Oriphiel [Orifiel]

Ormael—an angel of the 4th hour of the night, serving under Jefischa. [*Rf.* Waite, *The Lemegeton*.]

Ormary—an angel of the 11th hour of the day, serving under Bariel.

Ormas—an angel of the 10th hour of the day, serving under Uriel.

Ormazd (Ormuzd)—in Zoroastrian lore, the supreme power of good, the prince of light and twin brother of Ahriman, the latter being prince of darkness and evil; both are supreme, each in his own realm. This dualism was rejected by Jews and Christians alike in their espousal of monotheism, where evil exists only on the sufferance of God. Ormazd is sometimes represented as a bearded man attended by angels.

Ormijel—angel of the 4th hour of the day, serving under Vachmiel.

Ormisiel—angel of the 2nd hour of the night, serving under Farris.

Oroiael—in gnostic lore, one of 4 great luminaries identified with Uriel or Raguel by Irenaeus. [Rf. *Apocryphon of John*.]

Oromasim—one of the 3 princes of the world, the other 2 being Araminem and Mitrim, according to *The Sixth and Seventh Books of Moses*.

Orphaniel—in occult lore, "a great, precious and honorable angel, ruler of the 1st legion." His star is Luna. He is invoked in Monday conjurations. [Rf. *The Ancient's Book of Magic*; *The Secret Grimoire of Turiel*.]

Orphiel [Orifiel]

Orus (or Horus)—a fallen angel in Milton's *Paradise Lost* I, 478.

Osael—a Tuesday angel resident of the 5th Heaven. He is invoked from the south. [Rf. Barrett, *The Magus* II.]

Oseny—in *The Sixth and Seventh Books of Moses*, a cherub (also called a seraph) summoned in ceremonial magic.

Osgaebial—an angelic ruler of the 8th hour of the day; he commands "a great cloud of attending spirits." [Rf. Waite, *The Lemegeton*.]

Osiris—a fallen angel in *Paradise Lost* I, 478. Milton derived him from Egyptian mythology, where Osiris, a great divinity and husband of Isis, is slain by his brother Typhon.

Otheos—"a most holy name invoked for discovering treasure," according to Waite, *The Book of Black Magic and of Pacts*. In *The Sixth and Seventh Books of Moses*, Otheos is a spirit of the earth used by cabalists in conjuring rites.

Othriel—a spirit invoked in magical operations. [Rf. Schwab, *Vocabulaire de l'Angélologie*.]

Otmon—in Merkabah lore, a name for Metatron "when he seals the guilty in Israel." [Rf. *3 Enoch*, 43.]

Ou—variant for Uriel. The angel Ou appears in *The War Between the Sons of Light and the Sons of Darkness*, a copy of which was found among the recently discovered Dead Sea scrolls.

Ouestucati—a female angel of an hour who comes from the Hesperides and brings the sea wind. She is called "the lady of the chaste hands" by H.D. (Hilda Doolittle) in the latter's poem "Sagesse." In the cabala, Ouestucati is the corresponding angel of Iehuiah (q.v.).

Oul—a special aide to the angel Dalquiel in the 3rd Heaven. [Rf. Schwab, *Vocabulaire de l'Angélologie*.]

Oumriel—angel of service residing in the 4th Heaven. [Rf. Schwab, *Vocabulaire de l'Angélologie*.]

Ourpahil (Ourpail)—an angel in Mandaean tradition. [Rf. Pognon, *Inscriptions Mandaïtes des Coupes de Khouabir*.]

Ouza (Uzza)—in the *Midrash Petirat Mosheh*, which contains a dialogue between God and the soul of Moses, God is reminded that "the angels Ouza and Azael came down from Heaven and were corrupted [through cohabiting with the daughters of men], but that Moses was not corrupted," the reason for Moses remaining pure was that, after God had revealed Himself to the Lawgiver, the latter abstained from intimacy with his wife. In Exodus 19:15, it will be recalled, husbands were exhorted to "come not at your wives" so as to keep themselves clean preparatory to meeting with their Lord on the mount. All this seems inconsistent with the traditional and prevailing belief among Jews that conjugal union, far from being a contaminating act, is a holy one, blessed by the Shekinah herself.

Overseer of Light—the angel Jeu (q.v.).

Overshadowing Cherub—the king Nebuchadnezzar or the Prince of Tyre was called the "overshadowing cherub" (Ezekiel 28:16). He is slain by God. [Rf. "Select Demonstrations of Aphrahat" in *Nicene and Post-Nicene Fathers*, vol. 13, p. 355.]

Ozah (Uzah)—one of the many names of the angel Metatron in *Sefer ha-Heshek* listing.

Christopher Beeston's conception of an angle of the order of powers. From Heywood, *The Hierarchy of the Blessèd Angels.*

P

Pa'aziel—in *3 Enoch*, a name for the angel Metatron.

Pabael—one of the spirit messengers of the moon. Probably the same as Pabel.

Pabel—an angel of the 4th Heaven ruling on Lord's Day. Pabel must be invoked when the invocant faces west. [*Rf.* de Abano, *The Heptameron*.]

Pachdiel ("fear")—chief angelic guard of the 4th Heaven, according to a listing in *Pirke Hechaloth*.

Pachriel—one of the 7 great angels appointed over the 7 Heavens, as cited in *3 Enoch*, 17. Every one of these angels, including Pachriel, "is accompanied by 496,000 myriads of ministering angels."

Padael (Phadihel)—one of numerous angelic guards of the gates of the West Wind, as cited in *Ozar Midrashim* II, 316.

Padiel (Phadihel)—one of the 70 childbed amulet angels named in *The Book of the Angel Raziel*. Padiel is the angel who appeared to Samson's parents (see *Jewish Quarterly Review*, 1898, p. 328). [*Rf.* Judges 13.]

Paffran—in occultism, a Tuesday angel of the air, serving under the rule of Samax.

Pagiel—an angel petitioned in ritual prayer for fulfilment of the invocant's desires. Pagiel is cited, along with other "great and glorious spirits," in Malchus, *The Secret Grimoire of Turiel.*

Pahadiel—in hechaloth lore (*Ma'asseh Merkabah*), an angelic guard stationed in the 7th heavenly hall.

Pahadron—in Jewish mysticism, the chief angel of terror. Pahadron governs the month of Tishri (September-October). [*Rf.* Trachtenberg, *Jewish Magic and Superstition*, p. 99.]

Pahaliah—an angel invoked to convert heathens to Christianity. He rules theology and morals and is one of the angels bearing the mystical name of God Shemhamphorae. Pahaliah's corresponding angel is Sothis. [*Rf.* Ambelain, *La Kabbale Pratique*, p. 264.]

Paimon (Paymon, "tinkling sound")—before he fell, Paimon was an angel of the order of dominations. In Hell he is a great king, obedient only to Lucifer. Under Paimon are 200 legions of spirits "part of them of the order of angels, part potentates [powers]." When invoked he appears in the form of a young woman mounted on a dromedary, with a crown upon his head, as he is pictured in *Dictionnaire Infernal* (1863 ed.), p. 521. On special invocations he is accompanied by 2 great princes of the underworld, Bebal and Abalam, according to Wierus, *Pseudo-Monarchia.* For Paimon's sigil, see Waite, *The Book of Black Magic and of Pacts,* p. 168.

Palalael—to be distinguished from Palaliel, both serving as angelic guards of the gate of the West Wind. [*Rf. Ozar Midrashim* II, 316.]

Palatinates—a term for one of the 9 hierarchic orders; a variant for the order of powers, as given in a spell or conjuration in *The Greater Key of Solomon* for conferring the gift of invisibility on the conjuror. [*Rf.* Shah, *Occultism,* p. 161.]

Palit ("the escaped")—in Jewish legend, Palit is a name for Michael when Michael escaped from the grip of Sammael (Satan) at the time the latter was hurled from Heaven. [*Rf.* Ginzberg, *The Legends of the Jews* I, 231.] The *Midrash Tehillim* gives Og as another name for Palit. Still another form, Praklit, appears in *Rabbinic Philosophy and Ethics.*

Palpeltiyah—one of the many names of Metatron.

Paltellon—an angel invoked in the benediction of the Salt. [*Rf.* Mathers, *The Greater Key of Solomon,* p. 94.]

Paltriel—an angelic guard of the 5th Heaven, as listed in *Pirke Hechaloth.*

Pammon—angel of the 6th hour of the night, serving under Zaazonash. [*Rf.* Waite, *The Lemegeton,* p. 69.]

Panael—one of the angelic guards of the North Wind. He is to be distinguished from Paniel, another angel in the same service. [*Rf. Ozar Midrashim* II, 316.]

Panaion—in the view of Scholem, *Jewish Gnosticism, Merkabah Mysticism, and Talmudic Tradition* (p. 63), Panaion is "possibly another name for Metatron." Rabbi Ishmael in *Lesser Hechaloth* speaks of seeing "Panaion the Archon, one of the highest servants, and he stands before the throne of glory."

Pancia—a "most pure angel" invoked in ceremonial magic, specifically in the conjuration of the Sword. [*Rf. Grimorium Verum.*]

Paniel—an angel's name found engraved on a charm (*kamea*) for warding off evil. A guard of the North Wind. [*Rf.* Schrire, *Hebrew Amulets.*]

Papsukul—in Chaldean lore, an angelic messenger of the greater gods. [*Rf.* Lenormant, *Chaldean Magic,* p. 120.] Possibly a variant for Papukkal.

Paradise—in his *Adversus haereses* I, i, Irenaeus quotes the gnostic Valentinians: "They say that Paradise, which is above the 3rd Heaven [i.e., in the 4th Heaven] is virtually a 4th angel." The *Apocalypse of Moses* locates Paradise in the 3rd Heaven, as does *Enoch II.* [*Rf.* Newbold, "The Descent of Christ in the Odes of Solomon," *Journal of Biblical Literature,* December 1912.]

Paraqlitos (Paraclete)—in the *Falasha Anthology,* the guardian angel of the sorrows of death.

Parasiel—an angelic name inscribed in Hebrew characters on the 1st pentacle of the planet Jupiter. Parasiel is lord and master of treasures. [*Rf.* Shah, *The Secret Lore of Magic,* p. 56.]

Parasim (Parashim)—an order of angels or celestial horsemen [*Cf.* Pegasus] of the Song-Uttering Choirs, under the leadership of Tagas or Radueriel. [*Rf. 3 Enoch.*] "When, it is said, the time comes for the recital of the divine song—the qedusha—the parashim 'do rage' in the general commotion and excitement of the occasion."

Parasurama—the 6th of the 10 avatars (divine incarnations) in Vedic theosophy. Parasurama was known also as Chirangivah the Immortal.

Pariel—an angel's name inscribed on an oriental

Hebrew charm (*kamea*) for warding off evil. [*Rf.* Schrire, *Hebrew Amulets.*]

Pariukh (Mariokh)—one of 2 angels (the other is Ariukh) appointed by God to serve as guardian of the Enoch literature. [*Rf. Enoch II* and *3 Enoch.*]

Parmiel—angel of the 3rd hour of the day, serving under Veguaniel. [*Rf.* Waite, *The Lemegeton*, p. 67.]

Parshiyah—one of the many names of the angel Metatron.

Partashah—one of the many names of Lilith. [*Rf.* Hanauer, *Folk-Lore of the Holy Land*, p. 325.]

Partsuf (pl. partsufim or parzupheim, "the godhead")—in cabalistic lore, Partsuf is the countenance of God inherent in the sefiroth. The 5 chief partsufim who "dwell in the world of aziluth" are: 1. Ariukh Anpin (long face or long suffering) or Attika Kaddisha (holy ancient one); 2. Abba (the partsuf of Hochma or Wisdom); 3. Imma (the partsuf of Binah or Understanding), who is a feminine manifestation; 4. Zeir Anpin (the Impatient, the Holy One); 5. Shekinah (another female, counterpart of God). [*Rf.* King, *The Gnostics and Their Remains*; Scholem, *Major Trends in Jewish Mysticism.*]

Parvardigar—angel of light in ancient Persian theogony. [*Rf. The Dabistan*, p. 15.] In Arabic lore, the angel of light was Rab-un-maw.

Parymel—in *The Sixth and Seventh Books of Moses*, an angel of the throne invoked in conjuring rites. He is one of 15 such angels. For their names, *see* Appendix.

Parziel—an angelic guard of the 6th Heaven, according to a listing in *Pirke Hechaloth*.

Paschar (Psachar)—one of the 7 exalted throne angels "which execute the commands of the potentates," as reported in *The Book of the Angel Raziel*. Also cited in de Abano, *The Heptameron*; *The Sixth and Seventh Books of Moses*; and Cornelius Agrippa's works. In the *Pirke Hechaloth*, Paschar is one of the 7 angelic guards of the curtain or veil of the 7th Heaven. [*Rf. Ozar Midrashim* I, 110.]

Pasiel—in ceremonial magic, the angel that exercises dominion over the zodiacal sign of Pisces (the fishes). In Jewish cabala, Pasiel is the angel of Hell (arka)—that is, he is ruler over Abaddon, the 6th lodge of the 7 divisions into which Hell is divided, according to Joseph ben Abraham Gikatilla.

Pasisiel—in hechaloth lore (*Ma'asseh Merkabah*), an angelic guard stationed at the 7th heavenly hall.

Paspassim—in hechaloth lore, an angel who assists Metatron (*q.v.*) in reciting the *Shema*. [*Rf. 3 Enoch*, introd.]

Pastor—an angel petitioned in magic conjurations for the fulfilment of the invocant's desires. [*Rf.* Malchus, *The Secret Grimoire of Turiel.*]

Pasuy—in hechaloth lore (*Ma'asseh Merkabah*), an angelic guard stationed at the 4th heavenly hall.

Patha (Pathiel)—an angel invoked at the close of the Sabbath. [*Rf.* Trachtenberg, *Jewish Magic and Superstition.*]

Pathatumon (Pathtumon, Patheon, Pathumaton)—in Solomonic invocations, a name for God; a name Moses invoked to cause darkness to fall over Egypt; a name Solomon used to bind demons. [*Rf.* Waite, *The Book of Black Magic and of Pacts*; Mathers, *The Greater Key of Solomon.*]

Patheon [Pathatumon]

Pathiel ("the opener"; *see* Patha)—In *Ozar Midrashim* (I, 106), Pathiel is one of the angels that bear the mystical name of God Shemhamphorae.

Patriarchs—in the glossary to Vol. 2 of the 5-vol. 1956 Soncino *Zohar*, it is said that all Jewish patriarchs are transformed into great angels on their arrival in Paradise (as was specifically the case of Enoch and Elijah) and constitute one of the 3 highest grades in the celestial hierarchy. Not so, says *Universal Jewish Encyclopedia* (I, 314), which claims that such a belief was never part of Jewish thought.

Patrozin—an angel of the 5th hour of the night, under the rule of Abasdarhon. [*Rf.* Waite, *The Lemegeton.*]

Patspetsiyah—one of the many names of the angel Metatron.

Patteny—a ministering angel summoned in cabalistic rites. [*Rf. The Sixth and Seventh Books of Moses.*]

Paula (fictional)—a female angel mentioned in Daniels, *Clash of Angels.*

Pazriel (Sidriel)—in *3 Enoch*, one of the great archangels and prince of the 1st Heaven, sharing the post with Gabriel, Sabrael, Asrulyu, and others.

Peacock Angel, The [Taus-Melek]

Pedael ("whom God delivers")—in Jewish mysticism, the angel of deliverance. [*Rf.* Abelson, *Jewish Mysticism,* p. 127.]

Pedenij—an angel of the Seal, as recorded in *The Sixth and Seventh Books of Moses.*

Peliel—chief of the order of virtues and the preceptor angel of Jacob. Peliel alternates with Zekuniel as 2nd of the 10 holy sefiroth (*q.v.*). [*Rf.* Barrett, *The Magus*; also the tracts of Isaac ha-Cohen of Soria.]

Penac—an angel serving in the 3rd Heaven, as cited in *The Sixth and Seventh Books of Moses.*

Penael—in de Abano's occultism, a Friday angel residing in the 3rd Heaven and invoked from the north. He is also one of the messengers of the planet Venus. [*Rf.* Barrett, *The Magus* II; Malchus, *The Secret Grimoire of Turiel.*]

Penarys—angel of the 3rd hour of the night, serving under Sarquamich. [*Rf.* Waite, *The Lemegeton.*]

Penat—a Friday angel residing in the 3rd Heaven (like Penael) and one of the intelligences of the planet Venus.

Penatiel—an angel of the 12th hour of the day, serving under Beratiel.

Pendroz—an angel of the 7th hour of the night, serving under Mendrion.

Peneal—an angel serving in the 3rd Heaven.

Peneme [Penemue]

Penemue ("the inside")—in Enoch lore, one of the fallen angels who "taught mankind the art of writing with ink and paper," an art which was condemned as evil and corrupting. Penemue also taught "the children of men the bitter and the sweet and the secrets of their wisdom." He is one of the curers of stupidity in man, and is mentioned in *Bereshith Rabba.* Variants: Penemuel, Tamuel, Tamel, Tumael.

Peniel ("face of God"; *see* Penuel, Fanuel)—in the writings of Moses Botarel, de Abano, Barrett, etc., Peniel is the angel Jehovah, the dark antagonist, the one who wrestled with Jacob [*Rf.* Genesis 32.] It should be noted that *The Zohar* identifies the antagonist as Sammael. In the cabala generally, Peniel is a Friday angel, resident of the 3rd Heaven, and (like Penemue) a curer of human stupidity. In Genesis, Peniel is a place—the hallowed place where God revealed himself to Jacob face to face.

Penitent Angel, The [Abbadona]

Penpalabim—a "most holy angel" invoked in the conjuration for hidden treasure. [*Rf. Verum Jesuitarum Libellus*; Waite, *The Book of Black Magic and of Pacts.*]

Penuel [Peniel]

Peor [Chemos]

Peri—in Arabic lore, the Peri are fallen angels under the sovereignty of Eblis. In Persian myth, they are beautiful but malevolent spirits, also fairylike beings begotten by fallen angels and excluded from Paradise until penance is accomplished. Mohammed, it is said, sought to convert them. [*Rf.* Gaynor, *Dictionary of Mysticism.*]

Periel—a name for Metatron in the enumeration of more than 100 of his names listed in *3 Enoch,* 43.

Permaz—an angel of the 2nd hour of the night, serving under Farris. [*Rf.* Waite, *The Lemegeton.*]

Permiel—an angel of the 4th hour of the day, serving under Vachmiel.

Perrier—an ex-prince of the order of princi-

A peri (Persian angel) of the 16th century. Miniature, from *Horizon*, November 1960.

palities. [*Rf.* Garinet, *History of Magic in France*; De Plancy, *Dictionnaire Infernal* III.]

Pesagniyah—in *The Zohar* (Exodus 201b), a supervisory angel of the south in charge of the keys of the ethereal spaces. When prayers of persons in deep sorrow ascend, Pesagniyah kisses such prayers and accompanies them to a higher region.

Pesak—in hechaloth lore (*Ma'asseh Merkabah*), an angelic guard stationed at the 5th heavenly hall.

Peshtvogner—in Gurdjieff, *All and Everything, Beelzebub's Tales to his Grandson*, Peshtvogner is an arch-cherub whose title or other name is "All-Quarters-Maintainer." He decrees the sprouting of horns on the head of Beelzebub.

Petahel—a "most holy angel" invoked in magical rites at the close of the Sabbath. [*Rf. Jewish Encyclopedia*, p. 520; Trachtenberg, *Jewish Magic and Superstition*.]

Petahyah—in *The Zohar* (Exodus 201b), the chief in charge of the northernly region of Heaven, "appointed over that side to which prayers offered for deliverance from enemies ascend." If such prayers are found worthy, "Petahyah kisses them."

Phadahel [Phadihel]

Phadihel (Padael)—in Jewish legend, the angel sent to Manoah's wife (who conceived and bore Samson). [*Rf. The Biblical Antiquities of Philo*.] He is also said to be the angel that appeared to Abraham, Jacob, and Gideon (Genesis 32:29; Judges 13:3–18; Luke 13:34).

Phaiar—an angel invoked in the conjuration of the Reed. [*Rf.* Mathers, *The Greater Key of Solomon*.]

Phakiel—with another genius named Rahdar, Phakiel controls the sign of the Crab in the zodiac. [*Rf.* Levi, *Transcendental Magic*; *Prince of Darkness*, p. 177.]

Phaldor—genius of oracles. [*Rf.* Apollonius of Tyana, *The Nuctemeron*.]

Phalec (Phaleg)—ruling prince of the order of angels. Phalec is also the governing spirit of the planet Mars (and hence often referred to, as he is by Cornelius Agrippa, as the war lord). Of the 106 Olympic Provinces, Phalec has dominion over 35. His day, for invocation, is Tuesday. According to Agrippa, Heaven has 196 provinces, with 7 supreme angels governing them, of whom Phalec is one. The sigil of Phalec is given in Budge,

Amulets and Talismans, p. 389. In white magic, Phaleg is one of the 7 stewards of Heaven.

Phalgus—as noted in Levi, *Transcendental Magic*, Phalgus is the genius of judgment. In Apollonius of Tyana, *The Nuctemeron*, he is the genius of the 4th hour of the day.

Phamael (Phanuel)—this "corrupt" spelling of Phanuel occurs in *Baruch III*.

Phanuel (Uriel, Raguel, Fanuel, Ramiel, etc.—"face of God")—the archangel of penance and one of the 4 angels of the presence, the other 3, as usually given, being Michael, Gabriel, and Raphael. In *Enoch I* Phanuel "fends off the Satans" and forbids them "to come before the Lord of spirits to accuse them who dwell on earth." Phanuel is also identified as the Shepherd in the *Shepherd of Hermas*. In *Enoch I* (40) Phanuel is equated with Uriel. Says Charles: "In the later Judaism we find Uriel instead of Phanuel," that is, as one of the 4 angels of the presence. In *IV Ezra*, Phanuel is equated with Ramiel (Jeremiel) or Hieremihel, or Eremiel (the last named in the *Apocalypse of Sophonias*). In the *Sibylline Oracles* he is "one of the 5 angels who know all the evils that men have wrought." As Phaniel, our angel is invoked, in an early Hebrew amulet, against evil spirits. [*Rf.* Thompson, *Semitic Magic*, p. 161; *Baruch III*.] In Müller, *History of Jewish Mysticism*, we find Phanuel identified with Uriel. Ethiopians celebrate a holy day of the "archangel Fanuel" on the 3rd day of Taxsas. [*Rf. Falasha Anthology*.]

Pharmaros [Armaros]

Pharniel—an angel of the 12th hour of the day, serving under Beratiel.

Pharzuph—genius of fornication, angel of lust. The meaning of the word in Hebrew is "two-faced" or "hypocritical." See Apollonius of Tyana, *The Nuctemeron*, where Pharzuph is one of the genii of the 4th hour. In *Bereshith Rabba* it is the "angel of lust" (not named) that presents itself to Judah at the crossroads in order to entice the patriarch to "observe" his daughter-in-law Tamar and to mate with her (Genesis 38). [*See* Angel of Lust; Schiekron.]

Phatiel—angel of the 5th hour of the night, serving under Abasdarhon.

Phenex (Phenix, Phoenix, Pheynix)—an angel now serving in Hell who "hopes to return to the 7th throne after 1,200 years," as he confided to King Solomon. [*Rf.* Waite, *The Lemegeton*.] In the nether regions Phenex is a great marquis, a poet, and commands 20 legions of spirits. Spence, *Encyclopaedia of Occultism*, reports that Phenex was formerly of the order of thrones and that this "was proved after infinite research." In *Baruch III*, 6, the phoenix is the bird that circles before the sun to receive the rays on its outspread wings so as to preserve living things from being consumed. It is the same bird that awakens from slumber all the cocks on earth. A parallel may be cited (in Indian lore) in the bird Gadura "who carried Aruna on its back and placed him in front of the sun where he acted as charioteer and screened the world from the sun's consuming rays."

Phinehas—in Judges 2:1, "the angel of the Lord [who] came up from Gilgal" and whose countenance "when the Holy Ghost rested upon it, glowed like a torch." [*Rf. Midrash Leviticus Rabba* I, et seq.]

Phoenixes—in Enoch lore, the Phoenixes and the Chalkydri are angels of a high order, classed with the seraphim and cherubim. They are described as "elements of the sun" and as attending the chariot of that "planet" (in early occult and apocryphal writings the sun was classed as a planet, one of 7). The Phoenixes, like the Chalkydri, dwelt in the 4th or 6th Heaven, and were 12-winged. *Enoch II*, 19, speaks of 7 phoenixes sighted in the 6th Heaven, where their song, with which they greeted the rising of the sun, was celebrated for its sweetness. Their color, according to Pliny, was purple. "To such creatures in literature," writes Charles in his note to chapter 12 of *Enoch II*, "this seems to be the only reference"—i.e., the only reference to these creatures jointly as angels. Dr. K. Kohler in "The pre-Talmudic Haggada" (*Jewish Quarterly Review*, 1893, pp. 399–419), quoting from an old mishna, *Massecheth Derech Eretz*, calls to mind a legend that the phoenixes

"The Pillared Angel" by Dürer illustrating Revelation 10:1-5, "And I saw another mighty angel come down from heaven, clothed with a cloud . . . and his feet as pillars of fire." From Willi Kurth, *The Complete Woodcuts of Albrecht Dürer*. New York: Dover Publications, 1963.

referred to, in Enoch, were of a class of birds that went alive into Paradise. [*Cf.* sun birds in *Baruch III.*]

Phorlakh (Furlac)—angel of earth. The name Phorlakh is found inscribed on the 7th pentacle of the sun. [*Rf.* Mathers, *The Greater Key of Solomon.*]

Phorsiel—angel of the 4th hour of the night, serving under Jefischa.

Phronesis ("prudence")—in gnosticism, one of 4 luminaries emanated from the divine will. [*Rf.* Eleleth.]

Phul (Phuel)—lord of the moon and ruler of 7 of the Olympian Provinces. As a Monday angel, Phul is to be invoked only on Monday. In the cabalistic works of Cornelius Agrippa, Phul's sigil is given. There he is called "lord of the powers of the moon and supreme lord of the waters." [*Rf.* Budge, *Amulets and Talismans,* p. 389, for Phul's sigil.]

Pi-Hermes—equated with the angel Raphael. In hermetics, Pi-Hermes is the genius of Mercury and head of the order of archangels. [*Rf.* Christian, *The History and Practice of Magic* I, 68.]

Pihon—a name for the angel Metatron "when opening the doors through which the prayers of men are admitted into the celestial abode." Metatron is called Sigron when he shuts the doors. [*Rf.* introd., *3 Enoch.*]

Pi-Joh (Pi-Ioh)—equated with Gabriel. In hermetics, Pi-Joh is the genius of the moon and head of the order of angels.

Pilalael—one of numerous angels guarding the gates of the West Wind. [*Rf. Ozar Midrashim* II, 316.]

Pillared Angel—the angel "clothed with a cloud" (Revelation 9). He has one foot on the sea, the other on land; with his right hand he supports Heaven, swearing "time shall be no more." The passage is illustrated in a woodcut in the Cologne Bible.

Pilot Angel—in the *Purgatorio,* an unnamed angel called by Dante "God's angel" ferries souls destined for Purgatory from the south of the Tiber. It is this angel who greets Dante and Virgil at the start of their journey.

Pi-Ré—equated with Michael. In hermetics, one of the 7 planetary genii (archangels) and head of the order of virtues.

Pisqon—one of the many names of the angel Metatron. [*See* Appendix.]

Pistis Sophia ("faith," "wisdom")—a female aeon, one of the greatest in gnostic lore. She is said to have procreated "the superior angels." It was Pistis Sophia who sent the serpent to entice Adam and Eve. [*Rf.* Mead, *Pistis Sophia.*] According to the *Texts of the Saviour,* she is the daughter of Barbelo (*q.v.*).

Pi-Zeus—genius of Jupiter and head of the order of dominations. [*See* Zachariel.]

Plague of Evil Angels—according to Rabbi Eliezer, of the plagues visited on the ancient Egyptians, one was the "Plague of Evil Angels." Rabbi Akiba also spoke of this plague and called it "the fifth plague." [*Rf. Form of Services for the First Two Nights of Passover,* Hebrew Publishing Co., New York, 1921.]

Plesithea—in gnosticism, the "mother of angels," a virgin pictured with 4 breasts. [*Rf.* Doresse, *The Secret Books of the Egyptian Gnostics.*]

Pniel—in geonic lore, an angel who exercises rulership over one of the months of the year. [*Rf.* Trachtenberg, *Jewish Magic and Superstition,* p. 99.]

Poiel—an angel of the order of principalities. He rules over fortune and philosophy; he is also one of the 72 angels of the zodiac. His corresponding angel is Themeso. Barrett, *The Magus* II, lists Poiel as one of the 72 angels bearing the mystical name of God Shemhamphorae. His sigil is reproduced in Ambelain, *La Kabbale Pratique,* p. 289.

Porna—a Friday angel serving in the 3rd Heaven and invoked from the south. [*Rf.* de Abano, *The Heptameron*; *The Sixth and Seventh Books of Moses.*]

Poro—an angel of the order of powers, invoked in conjuring rites. [*Rf. The Sixth and Seventh Books of Moses.*]

Porosa—a Friday angel of the 3rd Heaven, like Porna, invoked from the south. [*Rf.* Barrett, *The Magus* II.]

Posriel (Hadriel?)—an angel in charge of the 6th division of Hell. It is in this division of the underworld that the prophet Micah may be found. [*Rf.* Ginzberg, *The Legends of the Jews* IV, 53, and VI, 214.]

Poteh (Purah)—the prince (*sar*, angel) of forgetting. Poteh is invoked in necromantic rites by Jews at the close of the Sabbath. [*Rf.* Trachtenberg, *Jewish Magic and Superstition.*]

Potentates—an alternate term for the order of powers. In *Paradise Lost* V, Milton speaks of "Seraphim and Potentates and Thrones."

Powers (potentates, authorities, dynamis)—the Septuagint first applied the term powers (*dynamis*) to an angelic order, equivalent to the Greek concept of the Lord's Hosts. [*Rf.* Caird, *Principalities and Powers*, p. 11.] Dionysius placed the powers 3rd in the 2nd triad of the celestial hierarchy; he equated the powers (incorrectly) with the seraphim. [*Rf.* Barrett, *The Magus.*] According to Fludd, Sammael is chief of the order of powers, although Camael is commonly so designated. In hermetics, the chief is Ertosi. The principal task of the powers is to see to it that order is imposed on the heavenly pathways. "The powers," says Dionysius, "stop the efforts of demons who would overthrow the world." In Pope Gregory's view, the powers preside over demons. Philo Judaeus classified the 6 highest powers in the following manner: divine logos, creative power, sovereign power, mercy, legislation, and punitive power. St. Paul's references in the various Epistles denote that, to this Apostle to the Gentiles, the powers are (or could be) evil. In *Excerpts of Theodotus*, the powers are said to be "the first of created angels." Milton in *Paradise Lost* XI, 221, uses the term as the equivalent of the order of guards (XII, 590).

Powers of Glory—a term for angels in *The Testament of the Twelve Patriarchs* (Judah 25), where it is equated with the angel of the presence, the sun, moon, and stars, as one of the heavenly luminaries.

Prajapati—to be compared with the Rishis who are, it is said, the 7 or 10 Vedic spirits from whom all mankind is descended. They are also to be compared with the 7 angels of the presence and the 7 (or 6) amesha spentas in Zoroastrian lore.

Praklit [Palit]

Pralimiel—an angel of the 11th hour of the day serving under Bariel. [*Rf.* Waite, *The Lemegeton.*]

Pravuil (Vretil)—designated as the "scribe of the knowledge of the Most High" and as "keeper of the heavenly books and records." [*See* Radueriel.] According to *Enoch II*, 22:11, Pravuil is "quicker in wisdom than the other archangels." He is mentioned only once in the Enoch writings.

Praxil—an officer angel of the 2nd hour of the night, serving under Farris (*q.v.*). [*Rf.* Waite, *The Lemegeton.*]

Preceptor Angels—in Jewish cabala, each of the great patriarchs had his special angelic counselor and guide, viz.: Adam: Raziel; Shem: Jophiel (Yophiel); Noah: Zaphkiel; Abraham: Zidekiel (Zadkiel); Isaac: Raphael (also preceptor angel of Toby the Younger); Joseph, Joshua, and Daniel: Gabriel; Jacob: Peliel (Pehel); Moses: Metatron; Elijah: Malashiel or Maltiel (Elijah himself became an angel: Sandalphon); Samson: Camael (Gamael); David: Cerviel (Gerviel, Gernaiul); Solomon: Michael.

Preil—an angel (called "le grand") in Mandaean lore. [*Rf.* Pognon, *Inscriptions Mandaïtes des Coupes de Khouabir.*]

Prenostix—angel of the 6th hour of the night, serving under Zaazonash.

Primeumaton—a spirit invoked in the exorcism of water. [*Rf.* Mathers, *The Greater Key of Solomon.*] "By this name [Primeumaton] Moses caused hail in Egypt" and "swallowed Corah,

Dathan and Abiram." [*Rf.* Numbers 16:16; Barrett, *The Magus* II.]

Prince of Alchemy [Och]

Prince of Angels—usually Christ, as in "princeps angelorum," an expression used by Lactantius.

Prince of Cherubim—Cherubiel and/or Gabriel; but also, originally, Satan. [*Rf.* Parente, *The Angels*, p. 47.]

Prince of Conception [Lailah]

Prince of Darkness—in Jewish legendary lore, the prince of darkness is the prince (angel) of death, who is Satan. He is also Belial (*q.v.*).

Prince of Death—in the infernal regions the prince of death is (in occult writings) Euronymous, bearer of the Grand Cross of the Order of the Fly; but the prince of death is, first and foremost, Satan. [*Rf.* Hebrews 2:14–15.]

Princedoms—another term for the order of principalities. [*Cf.* Milton's *Paradise Lost* V: "Thrones, Dominations, Princedoms," etc.]

Prince of the Face—otherwise prince of the presence. Among the great hierarchs answering to this title are Michael, Akatriel, Fanuel (Phanuel), Raziel, Uriel, Metatron, Yefefiah, Suriel, Sandalphon, etc.

Prince of Fire—Nathanel, called "lord of fire." [*Rf.* King, *The Gnostics and Their Remains*, p. 15.] Jehuel is also referred to as prince of fire. In the infernal empire, the prince of fire is Pluto. [*See* also Atuniel; *Grimorium Verum*, and other goetic tracts.]

Prince of Hades (or Prince of Hell)—Raphael, so called in *The Book of Enoch*, 22. As "presider over Tartarus," Uriel would qualify here. [*See* also Negarsanel; *Rf.* Ginzberg, *The Legends of the Jews* V, 71.]

Prince of Heavenly Hosts [Michael]

Prince of Light—Michael, so characterized in the Dead Sea scroll, *War of the Sons of Light against the Sons of Darkness. The Manual of Discipline* speaks of the prince of light who, in man,

contends constantly with the angel of darkness (i.e., the spirit of perversion). He is Uriel, according to Ginzberg, *The Legends of the Jews.*

Prince of Peace (Angel of Peace)—the title is usually associated with Jesus; but it has also been applied to Melchisedec (*q.v.*).

Prince of Persia—Dubbiel, who was worsted in battle with Michael [*Rf.* Daniel 10:13].

Prince of the Power of the Air—according to Paul, Ephesians 1, the title applies to Satan; but it applies also to Wormwood, Meririm, and other spirits of comparable stature.

Prince of the Presence [Angel of the Presence]

Prince of the Time of Iniquity—Satan is so characterized in the *Epistle of Barnabas.*

Prince of the World—a designation for Metatron (*q.v.*).

Prince of this World—in the Fourth Gospel, Jesus calls Satan the "prince of this world" (John 12:31). Loisy, *The Birth of the Christian Religion*, speaks of the prince of this world as having "the function of the principalities and powers spoken of in the Epistles; but [that] his character is perceptibly different." In his *Kabbalistic Conclusions*, Mirandola wrote: "The letters of the name of the evil demon who is the prince of this world are the same as those of the name of God Tetragrammaton—and he who knows how to effect their transposition can extract one from the other."

Principalities (or Princedoms)—one of the 9 orders of the celestial hierarchy and usually ranked 1st in the 3rd triad. The principalities are protectors of religion; they also, as Dionysius declares, "watch over the leaders of people" and presumably inspire them to make right decisions. According to Barrett, *The Magus*, the principalities "are called by the Hebrews elohim"—which is a doubtful equivalent. The chief ruling angels of the order include Requel, Anael, (Haniel), Cerviel, Nisroc. The last-named is characterized by Milton in *Paradise Lost* VI, 447 as "of principalities the prime." In Egyptian hermetics, the head of the order of principalities is Suroth. [*Rf.* Christian,

The History and Practice of Magic, vol. I, p. 68.] As far back as the 2nd century C.E., St. Ignatius Martyr (d. 107), touching on the ranks of angels in "Epistle to the Trallians," spoke of the "hierarchy of principalities."

Principals—in the gnostic *Paraphrase of Shem,* 3 principals (or primordial powers) are listed: Light, Darkness, and "An Intermediary Spirit." [*Rf.* Doresse, *The Secret Books of the Egyptian Gnostics,* p. 151.]

Prion—a "high, holy angel of God" invoked in magical rites, specifically in the conjuration of the Reed. [*Rf.* Waite, *The Book of Ceremonial Magic,* p. 175; Mathers, *The Greater Key of Solomon.* p. 116.]

Procel [Crocell]

Progenie of Light—a term used for angels, as in Milton's *Paradise Lost* V, 600.

Pronoia—in gnosticism, a great archon or power who, according to legend, assisted God in fashioning Adam. Pronoia provided the nerve tissue. [*Rf. Apocryphon of John*; Doresse, *The Secret Books of the Egyptian Gnostics,* pp. 204–205.] The Arabic legend of God sending 4 great angels to fetch 7 handfuls of earth for the creation of Adam has been referred to in the entry under Israfel. The Iranians believed that each of the planets (and here Pronoia is regarded as one of these planets) had a hand in fashioning our first parent. Bar-Khonia affirms that "this myth had been borrowed from the Chaldeans." [*See* Pthahil.]

Propator—an aeon who remains motionless on the constellation of the chariot (the Merkabah). Propator is master of the Pole and is surrounded by his decans and myriads of angels. He is designated pro-Father and the aeon who dwells in the zenith of Heaven with the aeon Sophia beside him. [*Rf.* Doresse, *The Secret Books of the Egyptian Gnostics.*]

Protoctist Angels—the first "operating angels" responsible for delivering the Torah to man through the lesser angels. [*Rf.* Clement of Alexandria, *Prophetic Eclogues*; Danielou, *The Angels and Their Mission.*]

Pruel—an angelic guard of the gates of the South Wind. [*Rf. Ozar Midrashim* II, 316.]

Pruflas—a fallen angel, formerly of the order of thrones and partly also of the order of angels. [*Rf.* Wierus, *Pseudo-Monarchia Daemonium.*]

Prukiel—an angel invoked in Syriac charms, along with Michael, Gabriel, Harshiel, and other spellbinding angels, as cited in *The Book of Protection.*

Prunicos—in Ophitic (gnostic) lore, the supreme celestial power, by some called Sophia. [*Rf.* Doresse, *The Secret Books of the Egyptian Gnostics,* p. 212.]

Prziel—an evil angel employed in conjuring rites against an enemy. [*Rf.* M. Gaster, *The Sword of Moses.*]

Psachar (Paschar)—one of 7 angelic princes of power, the others being Kalmiya, Boel, Asimor, Gabriel, Sandalphon, Uzziel. [*Rf. Pirke Hechaloth.*]

Psdiel—an evil angel employed in conjuring rites against an enemy. [*Rf.* M. Gaster, *The Sword of Moses.*]

Psisya—in *The Book of the Angel Raziel,* one of the 70 childbed amulet angels.

Psuker—an angel of the 6th Heaven who has Uzziel under him as officiating, ministering angel. [*Rf.* Schwab, *Vocabulaire de l'Angélologie*; West, "The Names of Milton's Angels," *Studies in Philology* XLVII (April 1950), p. 220.]

Psyche—in gnosticism, the name of Valentinus' demiurge (*q.v.*).

Psychopomp(us)—Elijah (Sandalphon) in Paradise is the psychopomp who leads the pious to their appointed places. [*Rf.* Ginzberg, *The Legends of the Jews,* p. 589; *cf.* Hermes Psychopompus in Greek mythology.]

Psychopompoi—soul-escorting angels (with Elijah-Sandalphon at their head) who accompany the souls after bodily death toward their heavenly abode. Michael is also regarded as a guide of the psychopompoi.

Pthahil—the Mandaean demiourgos; an angel ruling the lesser stars; said to have been an "assistant to the Lord of Life at Creation." Pthahil created Adam's body but could not give it life. He is also denoted a prince of evil, seeking support from planets and demons. [*See* Pronoia.]

Pucel [Crocell]

Purah (Puta, Poteh)—an angel invoked in magical rites at the close of the Sabbath. Isaac Luria associates Purah with Esau-Samuel. In Jewish legendary lore, Purah is the lord of oblivion, the angel of forgetfulness. In Isaac Bashevis Singer's "Jachid and Jechidah," one of the tales in his *Short Friday* (1964), Purah is described as an angel "who dissipates God's light."

Puriel [Puruel]

Purson (Pursan, Curson)—before he fell, Purson was an angel of the order of virtues and partly also of the order of thrones. This fact, reports Spence in *Encyclopaedia of Occultism* (p. 119), "was proved after infinite research." Be that as it may, Purson is now a king in the nether regions with 22 legions of spirits to do his bidding. His appearance is that of "a man with a lion's face, carrying a viper in his hand and astride a bear." He knows the past and future, and can discover hidden treasure. The seal of Purson is figured in Waite, *The Book of Ceremonial Magic*, p. 201.

Puruel (Pusiel, "fire")—the "fiery and pitiless" angel who "probes the soul," as described in the apocalyptic *Testament of Abraham*. G. H. Box in his edition of this work believes that Puruel is a Graecized form of the angel Uriel.

Purusha—the cosmic spirit in Sanskrit lore. He is the 1st cause, itself being uncaused. Compare with the cabalistic En Sof, the "unimaginable creator of the universe." [*Rf.* Gaynor, *Dictionary of Mysticism.*]

Pusiel (Puruel)—one of the 7 angels of punishment, as listed in *Maseket Gan Edem and Gehinnom*. In the *Revelation of Rabbi Joshua ben Levi*, Pusiel is equated with Hadriel, and dwells in the 6th compartment of Hell.

Puziel—an evil angel cited in M. Gaster, *The Sword of Moses*. He is employed in conjuring rites against an enemy.

Pymander—the nous of the supreme God, the Logos, the Word made manifest, the ideal archetype of all mankind. [*Rf. The Divine Pymander of Hermes Trismegistus.*]

Python—the 2nd of the 9 archangels or archdemons in the evil hierarchy. Python is "prince of the lying spirits." [*Rf.* Camfield, *A Theological Discourse of Angels.*] In Greek mythology, Python is the monster serpent, hatched from the mud of Deucalion's deluge, that lurked in a deep cleft of Parnassus; he was wounded and finally killed by the arrows of the sun god Apollo. [*Rf. Encyclopaedia Britannica*, "Dragon"; Summers, *The History of Witchcraft and Demonology*; Redfield, *Gods/A Dictionary of the Deities of All Lands.*]

The saintly throng in the form of a rose by Doré. Illustrations to Canto 31 of Dante's *Paradiso*. From Dante, *The Divine Comedy*, translated by Lawrence Grant White.

Qaddis (pl. qaddisin, "holy ones")—one of 2 angels who, with the twin irin, constitute the judgment council of God.

Qaddisin—in Merkabah lore, the 2 qaddisin are ranked, along with the twin irin, higher than the seraphim. The 4 of these judgment angels are—to quote from *3 Enoch*—"greater than all the children of Heaven, and none their equal among all the servants [of God]. For each one of them is equal to all the rest together."

Qadosch—an angel invoked in the conjuration of Ink and Colors. [*Rf.* Mathers, *The Greater Key of Solomon.*]

Qafsiel (Qaspiel, Qaphsiel, Quaphsiel)—an angel with dominion over the moon. In *3 Enoch* Qafsiel is guardian of the 7th heavenly hall. (*Cf.* Atrugiel). In ancient Hebrew charms, Qafsiel is invoked to drive away enemies by tying the charm, written in bird's blood, to the foot or wing of a dove and then bidding the dove to fly away. If it flies away, that is a sign that the enemy is in flight also. [*Rf.* Thompson, *Semitic Magic*, p. 817.]

Qalbam—one of the numerous angelic guards of the gates of the South Wind. [*Rf. Ozar Midrashim* II, 316.]

Qamamir Ziwa—in Mandaean lore, an angel of light. [*Cf.* Raphael.]

Qamiel—an angelic guard of the South Wind.

Qaphsiel [Qafsiel]

Qangiel Yah—a name of Metatron, cited in *3 Enoch*.

Qaniel—one of numerous angelic guards of the gates of the South Wind. [*Rf. Ozar Midrashim* II, 316.]

Qaus—an angel invoked in Arabic conjuring rites. [*Rf.* Shah, *Occultism*, p. 152.]

Qemuel (Kemuel, Camael)—an angel who was destroyed by God (in Jewish legendary lore, he is destroyed by Moses) when he tried to prevent the Lawgiver from receiving the Torah at the time God promulgated it. On that occasion Qemuel led angels in opposition to the number of 12,000. [*Rf.* Schwab, *Vocabulaire de l'Angélologie*; Ginzberg, *The Legends of the Jews.*]

Enthroned Madonna (Queen of the angels) flanked by four archangels (presumably Michael, Gabriel, Raphael, Uriel). Ancient mosaic in Sant-Apollinare-Novo at Ravenna. From Jameson, *Legends of the Madonna.*

Quaphsiel [Qafsiel]

Queen of Angels—in Catholicism, the queen of angels ("regina angelium") is the Virgin Mary. In the cabala, it is the Shekinah; in gnosticism, it is Pistis Sophia. [*Rf.* Voragine, *The Golden Legend.*]

Quelamia—one of the 7 exalted throne angels residing in the 1st Heaven "which execute the commands of the potentates" (according to *The Book of the Angel Raziel*). [*Rf.* de Abano, *The Heptameron*; Cornelius Agrippa, *Three Books of Occult Philosophy* III.]

Quoriel—an "inferior spirit" serving Vachmiel, ruler of the 4th hour of the day. Quoriel is invoked in ritual magic of the Pauline Art. [*Rf.* Waite, *The Book of Ceremonial Magic*, p. 67.]

"Angel of Eden" (Raphael or Michael) by Dürer, expelling Adam and Eve from their earthly paradise. From Willi Kurth, *The Complete Woodcuts of Albrecht Dürer*. New York: Dover Publications, 1963.

Raahel—one of the 72 angels ruling over the 72 quinaries of the degrees of the zodiac. [*Rf.* Runes, *The Wisdom of the Kabbalah*.]

Raamiel ("trembling before God")—an angel with dominion over thunder. In some occult sources, Raamiel is referred to as a fallen angel. [*See* Ramiel.]

Ra'asiel X (Rashiel; Sui'el)—in M. Gaster, *The Sword of Moses*, Ra'asiel X is an angel invoked in ritual magic.

Rabacyel—one of the 3 ruling princes of the 3rd Heaven. [Rf. *The Sixth and Seventh Books of Moses*.]

Rabdos ("staff")—a mighty luminary who is able to stop the stars in their courses; now a demon who throttles people. Rabdos can be subdued only by the power of the angel Brieus. [*Rf.* Conybeare, *The Testament of Solomon*; Shah, *The Secret Lore of Magic*.]

Rabia—one of the 10 *uthri* (angels) in Mandaean lore; the *uthri* accompany the sun on its daily course.

Rab-un-Naw—an angel of light in Arabic lore, equated with the Persian Parvardigar (*q.v.*).

Rachab [Rahab]

Rachel ("a ewe")—in the cabala, the Shekinah when "re-organized" as the Celestial Bride on her way to reunification with God. She is one of the 4 matriarchs, rulers of a province in Heaven reserved for the daughters, wives, and sisters of the great Hebrew patriarchs. [*Rf.* Scholem, *Major Trends in Jewish Mysticism*; Ginzberg, *The Legends of the Jews* V, 33.]

Rachiel—in the cabala, one of the angelic luminaries concerned with human sexuality (Masters, *Eros and Evil*). In Barrett, *The Magus* II, Rachiel is one of the 3 angels of Friday (the other 2 being Anael and Sachiel). Also, one of the presiding spirits of the planet Venus—according to *The Secret Grimoire of Turiel*. In *Ozar Midrashim* I, 86, Rachiel is an angel of the order of ophanim (*q.v.*).

Rachmiah—one of the 70 childbed amulet angels. [*Rf. The Book of the Angel Raziel*; Budge, *Amulets and Talismans*.]

Rachmiel ("mercy")—in rabbinic tradition, the angel of mercy (*cf.* Gabriel). He is also one of the 70 childbed amulet angels and an administering angel invoked in ceremonial rites. [*Rf. Universal Jewish Encyclopedia*, p. 314; *The Book of the Angel Raziel.*] In *Ozar Midrashim* II, 316, Rachmiel is included among the angelic guards of the gates of the East Wind.

Rachsiel—one of the 70 childbed amulet angels.

Rad'adael—in hechaloth lore (*Ma'asseh Merkabah*), an angelic guard stationed at the 6th heavenly hall.

Radueriel (Radwriel H')—identified or equated with Dabriel, Vretil, Pravuil, etc., as the heavenly register and recording angel. Radueriel is included occasionally among the 8 great judgment princes of the throne whose rank is superior to Metatron's. He is the angel of poetry, master of the muses. Of Radueriel it was said, "out of every word that goeth forth from his mouth a song-uttering angel is born." [*Rf.* Talmud *Hagiga*, 13a.] *Note*: since God alone is credited with the creation of angels, this power and privilege to do likewise makes Radueriel unique among his fellow hierarchs—except for Pistis Sophia, who is claimed to be, in *3 Enoch*, the "procreator of the superior angels." Another exception is Dynamis (*q.v.*).

Rael—in occultism, a Wednesday angel residing in the 3rd Heaven. He is also one of the intelligences of the planet Venus. When conjuring up Rael, the invocant must face north. [*Rf.* de Abano, *The Heptameron*; *The Secret Grimoire of Turiel.*]

Raftma'il—in Arabic lore, a guardian angel invoked in rites of exorcism. [*Rf.* Hughes, *A Dictionary of Islam*, "Angels."]

Ragat—in *The Sixth and Seventh Books of Moses*, an angel (cherub or seraph) summoned in cabalistic conjuring rites.

Ragiel [Raguel]

Raguel (Raguil, Rasuil, Rufael, Suryan, Akrasiel—"friend of God")—one of the 7 archangels listed in the Enoch writings. Raguel is an angel of earth, a guard of the 2nd (or 4th) Heaven. He "takes vengeance on the world of luminaries," which is interpreted to mean that, for cause, he brings other angels to account. Great as Raguel is, he was reprobated at a church council in Rome in 745 C.E., along with other high-ranking angels, Uriel among them. In Hugo, *The Toilers of the Sea*, Raguhel (so spelt) is a demon who "passed himself off as a saint" whom Pope Zachary in 745 C.E. "unearthed and turned out of the saintly calendar, along with two other demons called Oribel and Tobiel." [*See* Tubuas.] In *The Revelation of John*, Tischendorf, who edits this New Testament apocryphon, gives an extract from the termination of MS. E: "Then shall He send the angel Raguel, saying: Go and sound the trumpet for the angels of cold and snow and ice, and bring together every kind of wrath upon them that stand on the left." This would occur after the separation of the sheep from the goats. In gnosticism, Raguel is equated with Thelesis, another great angel (*q.v.*). According to *Enoch II*, Raguel (as Raguil or Rasuil or Samuil) is the angel who transported Enoch to Heaven while the antediluvian patriarch was still in the flesh—an incident alluded to in Genesis 5:24. The feat of transporting Enoch is also credited to Anafiel (*q.v.*). In *The Masque of Angels* (one-act opera produced in February 1966 at St. George's Church in New York), Raguel was cast as one of the principalities.

Raguhel [Raguel]

Rahab ("violence"; in Hebrew *sar shel yam*, "prince of the primordial sea.")—In Job 26:12; Psalms 37:4, Rahab designates Egypt as an earthly power of evil; also as "an angel of insolence and pride" (Isaiah 51:9). In the Talmudic *Baba Batra* 74b, Rahab is called the "angel of the sea." (In occult lore the demon of the sea is Kupospaston.) [See Conybeare, *The Testament of Solomon*, where Kupospaston is a hore-fish and delights in overwhelming ships.] According to legend (Ginzberg, *The Legends of the Jews* V, 26), Rahab was destroyed by God for refusing to separate the upper and lower waters at the time of Creation; and was destroyed again for trying to hinder the Hebrews from escaping the pursuing hosts of Pharaoh at the time of the crossing of the Red (Reed) Sea. Another legend relates that Rahab restored to Adam the mystical *Sefer Raziel* (*The Book of the Angel Raziel*) after it had been cast into the sea by envious angels. [*Cf.* legend of the sacred book, containing all knowledge, that Raphael is said to have given Noah.] The Babylonian Talmud regards Rahab, Leviathan, Behemoth, and the Angel of Death as identical or interchangeable. [*Rf.* Midrash *Genesis Rabba* 283; Talmud *Sanhedrin* 108b.] In Blake's *Jerusalem*, Rahab emerges as the Great Whore, triple goddess (sic) of Heaven, earth, and Hell. In Blake's *Vala* or *The Four Zoas* (Night the 8th), Rahab, as "representative of Urizen's mysteries unclothed, sits among the judges at the trial of Jesus." This Rahab is not to be confused with the Rahab of Joshua 2, the harlot of Jericho, grandmother of David and, it might be said, ancestress of all future quislings, whom Dante nevertheless, in his *Paradiso*, canto 9, places in Heaven among the elect.

Rahabiel—an angel invoked in a late Hebrew charm, along with Phaniel, Ariel, Lahabiel, Raphael. [*Rf.* M. Gaster, *Proceedings of the Society of Biblical Archeology*, p. 339.]

Rahatiel [Rahtiel]

Rahaviel—in hechaloth lore (*Ma'asseh Merkabah*), an angelic guard stationed at the 2nd heavenly hall.

Rahdar—with the aid of a brother genius called Phakiel, Rahdar governs the sign of the Crab in the zodiac. [*Rf.* Levi, *Transcendental Magic*, p. 413.]

Rahmiel (Rachmiel, Rahamael)—angel of mercy; also, one of the angels of love. For other angels of love, *see* Zadkiel, Zehanpuryu, Theliel, Anael (Haniel). Rahmiel may be invoked as an amulet against the evil eye. As Rhamiel, he is St. Francis Assisi who, like Enoch and Elijah, was transformed into an angel upon his arrival in Paradise. [*Rf.* Montgomery, *Aramaic Incantation Texts from Nippur*, p. 97; *The Douce Apocalypse*; Trachtenberg, *Jewish Magic and Superstition*, pp. 99, 140; Schrire, *Hebrew Amulets*.]

Rahtiel (Rahatiel—"to run")—in Jewish legendary lore, the angel of constellations, like Kakabel. He is the angel who, after Metatron names the stars to Rabbi Ishmael, "enters them in counted order," as related in *3 Enoch*, 46. [*See* also Ginzberg, *The Legends of the Jews* I, 140.]

Rahzeil—an angel in Mandaean theosophy. [*Rf.* Pognon, *Inscriptions Mandaïtes des Coupes de Khouabir*.]

Rakhaniel—an angel whose name appears in Hebrew characters on the 5th pentacle of the planet Saturn. When conjuring Rakhaniel, the invocant should recite a versicle from Deuteronomy (preferably 10:17).

Ramael [Ramiel]

Ramal—one of the 70 childbed amulet angels.

Ramamel—one of numerous angelic guards of the gates of the East Wind. [*Rf.* *Ozar Midrashim* II, 316.]

Ram Avatar (Rama or Ramachandra)—the 7th of the 10 avatars in Vedic Lore. [*See* Avatar.]

Ramiel (Remiel, Phanuel, Uriel, Yerahmeel, Jeremiel, etc.)—in the Syriac *Apocalypse of Baruch* (3rd section) Ramiel is the angel who, as presider over true visions, provides Baruch with an interpretation of the vision Baruch saw and speaks of. In this vision, Ramiel appears as the angel who destroys Sennacherib's hosts—a feat credited also to Uriel, Michael, Gabriel, and other redoubtable hierarchs. Ramiel is chief of thunder (as is Uriel); and he has charge of the souls that come up for judgment on the last day (as has Zehanpuryu). In the Enoch writings, Ramiel or Remiel is both a holy angel and a fallen one (*Enoch I*, 6, and *I*, 20). In verse 20, Ramiel is a leader of the apostates; in verse 6, he is one of the 7 archangels standing before God's throne. In *Paradise Lost* VI, Ramiel, along with Ariel and Arioc, is overcome by Abdiel in the 1st day of fighting in Heaven. To Milton, therefore, Ramiel, being on the side of Satan, is evil. In the *Sibylline Oracles* II, 2, 5, Ramiel is "one of 5 angels who lead the souls of men to judgment," the 5 angels cited being Arakiel, Ramiel, Uriel, Samiel, and Aziel. A number of Milton scholars (Keightley and Baldwin among them) have long believed that Milton coined Ramiel as well as Ithuriel, Zophiel, and Zephon. The names of these angels, however, have come to light in early apocryphal, apocalyptic, Talmudic sources; hence, Milton (who was familiar with such sources) had no need to invent these angels.

Ram Izad—in ancient Persian lore, an angel to whom services were paid. [*Rf. The Dabistan*, p. 156.]

Ram Khastra (Ram Khvastra)—the Parsi equivalent of the Mandaean *uthri* (angel) Ayar Ziwa, who "brings the sounds" or "stirs the air." [*Rf.* Drower, *The Mandaeans of Iraq and Iran*.]

Rampel—an angel exercising dominion over deep waters and mountain ranges. [*Rf.* M. Gaster's *The Sword of Moses*.] In *The Alphabet of Rabbi Akiba* the angel of mountains (unnamed) is included among the "splendid, terrible, and mighty angel chiefs" who passed before God to rejoice in the 1st Sabbath.

Raphael ("God has healed")—of Chaldean origin, originally called Labbiel. Raphael is one of 3 great angels in post-Biblical lore. He first appears in *The Book of Tobit* (a work external to the Hebrew canon, apocryphal in Protestant Scripture, canonical in Catholic). In *The Book of Tobit*, Raphael acts as companion and guide to Tobit's son Tobias who journeys to Media from Nineveh. It is only at the end of the journey that Raphael reveals himself by name as "one of the 7 holy angels" that attend the throne of God. [See woodcut in the Cologne Bible (1478–1480), picturing various incidents in the story.] In *Enoch I*, 20, Raphael is declared to be "one of the watchers" (*q.v.*). In *Enoch I*, 22, Raphael is a guide in sheol (i.e., the underworld). In *Enoch I*, 40, he is "one of the 4 presences, set over all the diseases and all the wounds of the children of men." [*Cf.* Rabbi Abba in *The Zohar* I: "Raphael is charged to heal the earth, and through him . . . the earth furnishes an abode for man, whom also he heals of his maladies."] According to gamatria (cabala) and *Yoma* 37a, Raphael is one of the 3 angels that

visited Abraham (Genesis 18), the other 2 angels identified usually as Gabriel and Michael. Raphael is credited also with healing Abraham of the pain of circumcision, the patriarch having neglected to observe this rite earlier in life. In *The Legends of the Jews* I, 385, Raphael is the angel sent by God to cure Jacob of the injury to his thigh when Jacob wrestled with his dark adversary at Peniel (the adversary having been identified variously as Michael, Metatron, Uriel, Sammael or God Himself.) Another legend (*Sefer Noah*) claims it was Raphael who handed Noah, after the flood, a "medical book," which may have been the famous *Sefer Raziel* (*The Book of the Angel Raziel*). Among other high offices, Raphael is the regent of the sun (Longfellow refers to him as the angel of the sun), chief of the order of virtues, governor of the south, guardian of the west, ruling prince of the 2nd Heaven, overseer of the evening winds, guardian of the Tree of Life in the Garden of Eden, one of the 6 angels of repentance, angel of prayer, love, joy, and light. Above all, he is, as his name denotes, the angel of healing (*cf.* Aslepios, ancient Greek god of healing). He is also the angel of science and knowledge, and the preceptor angel of Isaac. [*Rf.* Barrett, *The Magus* II.] Raphael belongs to at least 4 of the celestial orders: seraphim, cherubim, dominions (or dominations), powers. According to Trithemius of Spanheim, the 15th-century occultist, Raphael is one of the 7 angels of the Apocalypse. He is also numbered among the 10 holy sefiroth. And while he is not specifically named as the angel who troubled the waters at the pool in ancient Bethesda (John 5), he is generally so credited. [*Rf.* Summers, *The Vampire in Europe*.] Curiously enough (because, perhaps, Raphael has been called a guide in Hell) an ophite diagram represents Raphael as a terrestrial daemon with a beastlike form (!) and is associated with 3 other angels: Michael, Suriel, and Gabriel in the same guise. [*Rf.* Legge, *Forerunners and Rivals of Christianity* II, p. 70.] In the canvases of such masters as Botticini, Lorrain, Pollajuolo, Ghirlandaio, Titian, and Rembrandt, Raphael is variously pictured holding a pilgrim's staff and a fish (*Tobit*); as a winged saint supping with Adam and Eve; as the "sociable archangel" (*Paradise*

Raphael descending to earth. An illustration for *Paradise Lost*. From Hayley, *The Poetical Works of John Milton*.

Lost V); as a "six-winged seraph"; and as one of the 7 angels of the presence. Reference to these 7 angels of the presence is made by Blake in his "Milton." In the off-Broadway play *Tobias and the Angel*, Raphael is represented as a scoffing and jesting angel "knocking sense into the head of Tobias." The file on Raphael is inexhaustible, but one additional legend may be worth repeating here: it is taken from Conybeare, *The Testament of Solomon*. When Solomon prayed to God for help in the building of the Temple, God answered with the gift of a magic ring brought to the Hebrew king personally by Raphael. The ring, engraved with the pentalpha (5-pointed star), had the power to subdue all demons. And it was with the "slave labor" of demons that Solomon was able to complete the building of the Temple.

Rapid, The—an order of angels, "one of the 10 classes in Talmud and Targum," according to Voltaire in "Of Angels, Genii, and Devils."

Raquiel—one of the numerous angelic guards of the gates of the West Wind. [*Rf. Ozar Midrashim* II, 316.]

Rasamasa—with Vocabiel, a brother spirit, Rasamasa controls the sign of Pisces in the zodiac. [*Rf.* Levi, *Transcendental Magic.*]

Rasesiyah—one of the many names of the angel Metatron.

Rash (Rashin Rast)—the angel minister of justice in the service of Mithra. [*Rf. The Dabistan*, p. 145.]

Rashiel (Zavael)—an angel who exercises dominion over whirlwinds and earthquakes. [*Cf.* Su'iel.]

Rashin Rast [Rash]

Rasuil [Raguel]

Rathanael—an angel "who sits in the 3rd Heaven." *The Testament of Solomon* is authority for the fact that Rathanael is the only angel who is able to frustrate the machinations of the female demon Enepsigos. [*Rf. 3 Enoch* 17.]

Ratsitsiel—in hechaloth lore (*Ma'asseh Merk-*

abah), an angelic guard stationed at the 1st of the 6 heavenly halls.

Ratziel [Raziel]

Ratzuziel—an angelic guard of the 3rd Heaven. [*Rf. Ozar Midrashim* I, 116.]

Raum (Raym)—before he fell, Raum was of the order of thrones. In Hell, he is a great earl and manifests in the form of a crow. His mission or office is to destroy cities and subvert the dignities of men. He commands 30 legions of infernal spirits. His sigil is figured in Waite, *The Book of Black Magic and of Pacts*, p. 178. Raum also answers to the name of Haborym and is pictured in De Plancy, *Dictionnaire Infernal* (1863 ed.) with 3 heads—man, cat, viper.

Ravadlediel—in hechaloth lore (*Ma'asseh Merkabah*), an angelic guard stationed at the 5th heavenly hall.

Raziel ("secret of God," "angel of mysteries" —Ratziel, Akrasiel, Gallizur, Saraqael, Suriel, etc.) —the "angel of the secret regions and chief of the Supreme Mysteries." [*Rf.* M. Gaster, *The Sword of Moses.*] In the cabala, Raziel is the personification of Cochma (divine wisdom), 2nd of the 10 holy sefiroth. In rabbinic lore, Raziel is the legendary author of *The Book of the Angel Raziel (Sefer Raziel)*, "wherein all celestial and earthly knowledge is set down." The true author is unknown but he has been commonly identified as Eleazer of Worms or Isaac the Blind, medieval writers. Legend has it that the angel Raziel handed his book to Adam, and that the other angels, out of envy, purloined the precious grimoire and cast it into the sea, whereat God ordered Rahab, primordial angel/demon of the deep, to fish it out and restore it to Adam—which Rahab obediently did, although it should be pointed out that before this, Rahab had been destroyed. *The Book of the Angel Raziel* finally came into possession of, first, Enoch (who, it is said, gave it out as his own work i.e., *The Book of Enoch*); then of Noah; then of Solomon, the latter deriving from it, according to demonographers, his great knowledge and power in magic. [*Rf.* De Plancy, *Dictionnaire Infernal.*] From a midrash (Ginzberg, *The Legends of the*

Jews I, 154–157) it develops that Noah learned how to go about building the Ark by poring over the Raziel tome. [*Rf.* Jastrow, *Hebrew and Babylonian Traditions*.] In Targum Ecclesiastes 10, 20, it is reported that "each day the angel Raziel, standing on Mount Horeb, proclaims the secrets of men to all mankind." Searching further in the cabala, one learns that Raziel is one of 10 (actually one of 9) archangels in the Briatic world, which is the 2nd of the 4 worlds of creation. In this Briatic world each sefira is allotted an archangel to govern it, the chief being Metatron, the others being, apart from Raziel, Tzaphkiel, Tzadquiel, Kamael, Michael, Haniel, Raphael, Gabriel, and Sandalphon—as we find in a listing by Macgregor Mathers. [*Rf.* Westcott, *The Study of the Kabalah*, pp. 54–55.] According to Maimonides in his *Mishna Thora*, Raziel is chief of the order of erelim (*q.v.*); also, the herald of deity and preceptor angel of Adam. In further connection with *The Book of the Angel Raziel*, *The Zohar* I, 55a, reports that in the middle of the book there occurs a secret writing "explaining the 1,500 keys [to the mystery of the world] which were not revealed even to the holy angels." The noted 13th-century cabalist Abraham ben Samuel Abulafia wrote under the name of Raziel (also under the name of Zechariah).

Razvan—in Arabic lore, the "treasurer of Paradise," and the "porter of Heaven." [*Rf. The Dabistan*, p. 385.]

Razziel—an angel of the 7th hour of the night, serving under Mendrion. [*Rf.* Waite, *The Lemegeton*.]

Reapers—a designation for angels in Matthew 13:29: "and the reapers are the angels." Henry Vaughan, the English poet, concludes his poem "The Seed Growing Secretly" with the line "Till the white winged Reapers come." In Longfellow's poem "The Reaper and the Flowers" the Reaper is the angel of death, Azrael.

Recabustira—a prayer addressed to Recabustira (for providing the invocant with a magic carpet) is made by gradually reducing the name thus: Cabustira, Bustira, Stira, Ira, etc. [*Rf.* Mathers, *The Greater Key of Solomon*.]

Recording Angel—Pravuil, Vretil, Radueriel, Dabriel (the same angel under different forms). In Arabic tradition, the recording angel is Moakkibat. But there is the tradition of 2 recording angels called Kiramu 'l-katibin who attend every believer, one recording the good deeds, the other the evil deeds. When the believer dies, his record is conveyed by the recording angels to Azrael, angel of death. In Babylonian lore, the recording angel is Nabu or Nebo. "To marry is to domesticate the Recording Angel," says R. L. Stevenson in *Virginibus Puerisque*. [*Rf.* Hughes, *A Dictionary of Islam*, "Angels."]

Rectacon—an angel invoked in the benediction of the Salt. Rectacon is mentioned in the grimoires and tracts of Solomonic magic.

Rectores Mundorum—in Chaldean mythology, the divine regents or powers that order the world below. [*Rf.* Aude, *Chaldean Oracles of Zoroaster*.]

Red Angel, The—an angel so named in Marc Chagall's celebrated canvas titled "Descent of the Red Angel." [*See* Angel of Fire.]

Regent—in *Paradise Lost* V, 698, a fallen angel under Satan's command, He is either head of, or one of, the regent powers that fought in the Great Revolt.

Regents—an order of angels mentioned in *Paradise Regained* I, 117.

Region—an angel invoked for special uses in ceremonial magic, specifically in the conjuration of the Sword. [*Rf.* Waite, *The Lemegeton*; Mathers, *The Greater Key of Solomon*.]

Rehael—an angel of the order of powers. He rules over health and longevity, and inspires respect for one's parents. Rehael is one of the 72 angels bearing the mystical name of God Shemhamphorae. His corresponding angel is Ptechout. [*Rf.* Barrett, *The Magus* II; Ambelain, *La Kabbale Pratique*.]

Rehauel—in Runes, *The Wisdom of the Kabbalah*, one of the 72 angels of the zodiac.

Round of the Angels by Fra Angelico, detail from *The Last Judgment*. Reproduced from Régamey, *Anges*.

Rehel—an angel who battles against the enemies of religion. His corresponding angel is Phupe. [*Rf.* Ambelain, *La Kabbale Pratique.*]

Reiiel—an angel of the order of dominations. Reiiel is also one of the 72 angels bearing the mystical name of God Shemhamphorae.

Reivtip (Rirvtip)—in Mosaic incantation rites, an angel who serves the angel-prince Alimon (*q.v.*).

Rekhodiah—one of the 4 angel names found inscribed on the 2nd pentacle of the sun. [*Rf.* Mathers, *The Greater Key of Solomon.*]

Relail—in Arabic lore, governor of the 5th Heaven. [*Rf.* Moore, *The Loves of the Angels.*]

Remiel (Ramiel, Rumael, etc.)—one of the 7 archangels who attend the throne of God, as stated in *Enoch I*, 20. He is called Jeremiel or Uriel in various translations of *IV Esdras*, and described as "one of the holy angels whom God has set over those who rise" (from the dead). He is the same angel (given as Ramiel) who, in *The Apocalypse of Baruch*, destroys the army of Sennacherib. See *Enoch II*, and Geffcken, *Sibylline Oracles* II, 215.

Rempha—in Egyptian theogony, chief of the order of thrones and genius of time. In hermetics, Rempha is one of the 7 planetary genii and the genius (archangel) of Saturn. [*Rf.* Christian, *The History and Practice of Magic* I, 317; II, 475; *see* Orifiel.]

Reno—the corresponding angel for the angel Vehuel (*q.v.*).

Reprobated Angels—at a church council in Rome, 745 C.E., under Pope Zachary, 7 high angels were reprobated: Uriel, Raguel, Inias, Adimus, Simiel (Semibel), Tubuael (Tubuas), and Sabaothe (Saboac). The bishops Clement and Adalbert, who taught the veneration of these angels, were convicted of heresy. It was the rash of newly coined angels that prompted the Church at that time to forbid invoking or venerating angels other than those named in the Bible (Michael, Gabriel, Raphael). The trouble, however, dated earlier than the 8th century, for in the 4th–5th centuries, Eusebius and Theodoret tried, without success, to put a stop to the practice. [*Rf.* Régamey, *What Is an Angel?* p. 119.]

Requel—in *The Sixth and Seventh Books of Moses*, a ruling prince of the order of principalities. In other sources the ruling prince of the order is given as Nisroc (*Paradise Lost*), Anael, Cerviel, etc.

Requiel—one of the 28 angels governing the 28 mansions of the moon. [*Rf.* Barrett, *The Magus.*]

Reschith Hajalalim (Rashith ha-Galgalim)—in Jewish cabala, Reschith is a ministering spirit through whom "the essence of divinity flows." He guides the *primum mobile*, a task or office usually linked with Metatron. [*Rf.* Heywood, *The Hierarchy of the Blessèd Angels.*]

Resh (Rash?)—an Indo-Persian angel mentioned in Hyde, *Historia Religionis Veterum Persarum.*

Retsutsiel [Rezoziel]

Revealing Angel, The—in the Koran, *sura* 51, 50, the revealing angel is spoken of as "a plain warner from Him," but is not identified by name.

Rezoziel—an angelic guard of the 3rd Heaven mentioned in *Pirke Hechaloth.*

Rhamiel (Rahmiel)—the angelic name of St. Francis of Assisi as the angel of mercy. St. Francis has also been referred to as the angel of the apocalypse. As such he warns the winds not to complete the destruction of the world "until the elect should be gathered." [*Rf. The Douce Apocalypse.*]

Rhaumel—a Friday angel resident in the 5th Heaven and invoked from the north [*Rf.* Barrett, *The Magus*].

Ribbotaim—angels used as chariots by God. These would be the cherubim (*q.v.*). [*Rf. 3 Enoch.*]

Richol—an angel of the order of powers, summoned in conjuring rites. [*Rf. The Sixth and Seventh Books of Moses.*]

Riddia (Ridya, Ridjah, Mathariel—"the irrigator")—prince of rain in command of the element of water. Riddia is said to reside between 2 abysses. In Hebrew lore, he is described as an angel who, when invoked, shows himself in the form of a 3-year-old heifer with cleft lips. [*Rf.* Talmud, *Yoma* 21a.]

Ridwan—in Islamic tradition, an angel placed at the entrance to the earthly paradise. [*Rf.* Hastings, *Encyclopaedia of Religion and Ethics* IV, 618.] It is in this role, as the archangelic guardian of the Garden of Eden, that Ridwan appears in Remy de Gourmont's play, *Lilith*.

Ridya [Riddia]

Riehol—in the cabala, governor of the zodiacal sign of Scorpio; in this office Riehol is assisted by Saissaiel. [*Rf.* Levi, *Transcendental Magic.*]

Riff (fictional)—a cherub in Daniels, *Clash of Angels*.

Rifion—in hechaloth lore (*Ma'asseh Merkabah*), an angelic guard stationed at the 5th heavenly hall.

Rigal—one of the 70 childbed amulet angels. For a list of all 70, *see* Appendix.

Rigziel—in Isaac ha-Cohen's text, "Emanations of the Left Side," Rigziel is 8th of the 10 holy sefiroth.

Rikbiel YHWH—an angel appointed over the divine chariot (i.e., Merkabah) or wheels; also chief of the order of galgallim, of which there are 6 other ruling angels. In Enoch lore, Rikbiel ranks higher than Metatron, which would make him one of the great crown princes of heavenly judgment (there being 8 such, according to Ginzberg, *The Legends of the Jews* I, 139.)

Rimezin—an angel of the 4th hour of the night, serving under Jefischa. [*Rf.* Waite, *The Lemegeton.*]

Rimmon (Hebrew, "roarer" or "exalted")—a fallen archangel, now an "inferior demon." Rimmon was originally an Aramaean deity worshipped at Damascus; also an idol of Syria. In occultism he is the devil's ambassador to Russia.

In Bates' *The Bible Designed to Be Read as Living Literature* (p. 1262, glossary) "Elisha allowed Naaman the Syrian to bow down with his master in the house of Rimmon." Thus, to bow down in the house of Rimmon implies "to conform to a reprehensible custom to save one's life." To the Semites, Rimmon was the god of storms, the Akkadian name being Im (Forlong, *Encyclopedia of Religions*). His emblem is the pomegranate. The Assyrians called him Barku (lightning) and the Kassites named him Tessub. In Babylonian myth, Rimmon was the thunder god, pictured with a trident.

Rishis—to be compared with the Prajapati (*q.v.*). The Rishis are the 7 or 10 Vedic spirits from whom it is claimed all mankind is descended. They may also be compared with the 7 angels of the presence and the 7 (or 6) amesha spentas in Zoroastrian lore.

Risnuch—genius of agriculture, according to Levi, *Transcendental Magic*. In Apollonius of Tyana, *The Nuctemeron*, Risnuch is one of the genii of the 9th hour.

Riswan (Rusvon)—in the *Odes* of Hafiz (Ode 586), the gatekeeper of Heaven. Hafiz' reference is to "dread Riswan's throne."

Riyiel—in the cabala, one of the 72 angels of the zodiac.

Rochel—an angel who finds lost objects. Rochel's corresponding angel is Chontaré. Rochel also figures among the 72 angels bearing the mystical name of God Shemhamphorae.

Roelhaiphar—an angel whose name is found inscribed on the 5th pentacle of Saturn. When Roelhaiphar is invoked, the invocant should, for the best results, recite a versicle from Deuteronomy 10:17. [*Rf.* Mathers, *The Greater Key of Solomon.*]

Rofael [Raphael]

Rofocale—more usually called Lucifuge Rofocale, prime minister in the infernal regions, according to the *Grand Grimoire*. Rofocale has control over all the wealth and treasures of the world. His subordinate is Baal (a king, ruling in the east). Two other subordinates are Agares (one of the dukes in Hell and formerly of the angelic order of virtues) and Marbas.

Rogziel ("wrath of God")—one of the 7 angels of punishment, as listed in *Maseket Gan Edem and Gehinnom*. [*Rf. Jewish Encyclopedia*, 593.]

Rombomare—corresponding angel for Lauviah.

Romiel—in geonic (Middle Ages) lore, an angel assigned to rulership over one of the months of the year. [*Rf.* Trachtenberg, *Jewish Magic and Superstition*.]

Rorex—in Conybeare, *The Testament of Solomon*, a spirit (angel) invoked to counteract the power of Alath (demon of disease, one of the infernal decani).

Rosabis—genius of metals and one of the genii of the 11th hour. [*Rf.* Apollonius of Tyana, *The Nuctemeron*.]

Rosier—a former lesser-rank angel of the order of dominations, now officiating in Hell. [*Rf.* Michaelis, *Admirable History of the Possession and Conversion of a Penitent Woman*.]

Roupa'il—an angel in Mandaean lore. [*Rf.* Pognon, *Inscriptions Mandaïtes des Coupes de Khouabir*.]

Rsassiel—one of the 70 childbed amulet angels.

Ruah Piskonit—one of the many names of the angel Metatron.

Ruba'il—in Islamic lore, an angel of the 7th Heaven in charge of a group of angels (in the guise of men) engaged in worshipping Allah. [*Rf.* Hastings, *Encyclopaedia of Religion and Ethics* IV, 619.]

Rubi (fictional)—the 2nd angel, a cherub, in Moore's *The Loves of the Angels*.

Rubiel—as cited in De Plancy, *Dictionnaire Infernal*, an angel (along with Uriel and Barachiel) invoked in games of chance. For good results, the name Rubiel, when prayed to, must be inscribed on virgin parchment.

Ruchiel—an angel appointed over the wind. [*Rf. 3 Enoch*, 14.]

Rudiel—in hechaloth lore (*Ma'asseh Merkabah*), an angelic guard stationed at the 3rd heavenly hall.

Rudosor—an angel of the 6th hour of the night, serving under Zaazonash. [*Rf.* Waite, *The Lemegeton*.]

Rufael—another form of the angel Raphael, or a corruption of Raguel (*q.v.*). According to *Enoch I*, 68:4, Rufael spoke with Michael concerning the fallen angels.

Rugziel (Dalkiel)—an angel who operates in the 7th compartment of Hell in the "punishment of 10 nations." [*Rf. Baraita de Massechet Gehinnom*.]

Ruhiel—in Jewish legendary lore, the angel governing the wind. He is mentioned as one of the great luminaries in Heaven who, "when they encounter Metatron, tremble before him and prostrate themselves." [*Rf.* Ginzberg, *The Legends of the Jews* I, 140.]

Rumael (Ramiel)—one of the fallen angels in the Enoch listings.

Ruined Archangel—an epithet used by Milton in *Paradise Lost* I, 593, to describe Satan in his fallen state: "his form had yet not lost/All her Original brightness, nor appear'd/Less than Arch Angel ruin'd."

Rulers—in the Septuagint, the term is used to denote an order of the celestial hierarchy. Usually equated with the order of dominations. Caird in *Principalities and Powers*, p. 11, uses rulers as a translation of the Greek "ἄρχονες." John of Damascus, in *Exposition of the Orthodox Faith* II, lists rulers (where customarily "principalities" appears) as 1st of the last triad in the 9-fold division of the celestial hierarchy.

Ruman—in Islamic lore, a special angel of the lower regions who requires of all the deceased that come before him to write down the evil deeds they performed on earth and for which they were consigned to Hell. Ruman then delivers the deceased to the angels Munkar and Nakir (*q.q.v.*)

for punishment. [*Rf. Jewish Encyclopedia*; Hastings, *Encyclopaedia of Religion and Ethics* IV, 617.]

Rumiel—an angelic guard of the 6th Heaven; also one of the 70 childbed amulet angels. [*Rf. Pirke Hechaloth*; *The Book of the Angel Raziel*; Budge, *Amulets and Talismans*, p. 225.]

Rumjal (Rumael?)—an evil, fallen archangel, one of the original 200 that were seduced by Satan into rebellion, according to *Enoch I.*

Rusvon (Riswan)—an angel who holds the keys to the Muslim earthly paradise. [See De Plancy, *Dictionnaire Infernal*; *Cf.* Ridwan.]

Ruwano—a ministering angel invoked in conjuring rites. [*Rf. The Sixth and Seventh Books of Moses.*]

Ruya'il—in Arabic lore, a guardian angel invoked in rites of exorcism. [*Rf.* Hughes, *A Dictionary of Islam*, "Angels."]

"Prince of the Power of the Air" (Satan) by Doré. Reproduced from Langton, *Satan, A Portrait.*

Sa'adiya'il—in Islamic religious lore, an angel of the 3rd Heaven in charge of a group of angels (in the guise of vultures) engaged in worshipping Allah. [*Rf.* Hastings, *Encyclopaedia of Religion and Ethics* IV, 619.]

Saaphiel—angel of hurricanes, mentioned in *Sefer Yetzirah* (*The Book of Formation*).

Saaqael (Sarakiel, Suriel?)—in *Enoch I*, an angel of the presence.

Sabaoc—one of the 7 reprobated angels at the trial which took place in a church council in Rome, 745 C.E. Other angels reprobated at the same trial included Uriel, Raguel, Simiel. [*Rf.* Heywood, *The Hierarchy of the Blessèd Angels; see* Reprobated Angels.]

Sabaoth (Tsabaoth, Ibraoth, "hosts")—one of the 7 angels of the presence; one of the divine names in gnostic and cabalistic lore. In the Ophitic (gnostic) system, Sabaoth is one of the 7 archons, creators of the universe.

Sabaoth Adamas—in the *Texts of the Saviour*, Sabaoth Adamas is an evil power, ruler of the wicked aeons; he is mentioned also in the Coptic *Pistis Sophia.*

Sabathiel (Sabbathi)—in Jewish cabala, a spirit (intelligence) of the planet Saturn. He receives the divine light of the holy spirit and communicates it to the dwellers in his kingdom. In Mosaic lore, Sabathiel is one of 7 princes "who stand continually before God, and to whom are given the spirit-names of the planets." [*Rf.* Cornelius Agrippa, *Three Books of Occult Philosophy* III.]

Sabbath—an angel (so named) who sits on a throne of glory in Heaven, the chiefs of orders of angels doing him honor. He is the lord of the Sabbath.

Sabbathi [Sabbathiel]

Sabiel—the 1st of the personalized angels of the 10 holy sefiroth. In Montgomery, *Aramaic Incantation Texts from Nippur*, Sabiel is an angel who is invoked in ritual rites.

Sablil—according to Levi, *Transcendental Magic*, a genius who runs down thieves. Levi's authority is Apollonius of Tyana, *The Nuctemeron.* In the latter work, Sablil is one of the spirits or genii of the 9th hour.

Sabrael (Sabriel)—one of the 7 archangels, as noted in Conybeare, *The Testament of Solomon*, and in *3 Enoch*. Sabrael is chief of the order of tarshishim ("the brilliant ones," equated with the order of virtues), sharing the post with Tarshiel—according to *Maseket Azilut*. Sabrael is also guard of the 1st Heaven. [*Rf. Jewish Encyclopedia*, "Angelology."] In occultism, Sabrael is the only angel who can overcome the demon of disease, Sphendonael.

Sabtabiel—in the cabala, an angel invoked in necromantic rites. [*Rf.* Levi, *Transcendental Magic*, p. 281.]

Sachiel ("covering of God")—an angel of the order of hashmallim (cherubim). Sachiel is resident of the 1st Heaven (in some sources, the 6th Heaven). He is a Monday (or Thursday or Friday) angel, invoked from the south (also from the west). In addition, he is a presiding spirit of the planet Jupiter. In goetic lore, he is called a servitor of the 4 sub-princes of the infernal empire. His sigil is shown facing p. 105 of Barrett, *The Magus* II.

Sachiel-Melek—in the cabala, a king of the underworld hierarchy governing priesthoods and sacrifices. [*Rf.* Levi, *Transcendental Magic*, p. 307.]

Sachluph—a genius in control of plants and one of the genii of the 2nd hour, as listed by Apollonius of Tyana, *The Nuctemeron.*

Sacriel—in occult lore (Barrett, *The Magus* II, etc.) an angel serving in the 5th Heaven. He rules on Tuesday and is invoked from the south.

Sadayel—one of 3 archangels (the other 2 being Tiriel and Raphael) whose name is found inscribed in a pentagram on a ring amulet. [*Rf.* Budge, *Amulets and Talismans.*]

Sadial (Sadiel)—in Islamic lore, an angel governing the 3rd Heaven. [*Rf.* De Plancy, *Dictionnaire Infernal*; Clayton, *Angelology.*]

Saditel—an angel of the 3rd Heaven in the listing of Cornelius Agrippa, *Three Books of Occult Philosophy* III. [*Rf. The Sixth and Seventh Books of Moses*, p. 139.]

Sadqiel—in M. Gaster, *Wisdom of the Chaldeans*, a ruling angel of the 5th day.

Sadriel—an angel of order. [*Rf.* Charles, *Apocrypha and Pseudepigrapha of the Old Testament.*] In the *Masque of Angels*, a one-act opera produced in New York in February, 1966 at St. George's Church, Sadriel was cast as the company clerk.

Saelel—in the cabala, one of the 72 angels in control of the zodiac.

Saeliah [Seeliah]

Safkas—one of the many names of the angel Metatron.

Safriel—an angelic guard of the 5th Heaven. *Rf. Ozar Midrashim* II, 116.] He is said to be effective as a charm (*kamea*) for warding off the evil eye. [*Rf.* Schrire, *Hebrew Amulets.*]

Sagansagel [Sagnessagiel]

Sagdalon—governor, with Semakiel, of the sign of Capricorn in the zodiac.

Sagham—according to Levi, *Transcendental Magic*, Sagham is ruler with Seratiel of the sign of Leo in the zodiac.

Sagiel—an angel of the 7th hour of the day, serving under Barginiel. [*Rf.* Waite, *The Lemegeton.*]

Sagmagigrin—one of the many names of the angel Metatron.

Sagnessagiel (Sasniel, Sagansagel, Sasnigiel, etc.)—prince of wisdom and chief of the angelic guards of the 4th hall of the 7th Heaven. Sagnessagiel is one of the many names of Metatron, as listed in *3 Enoch*. In the *Baraita de Massechet Gehinnom*, Sagansagel (so written), during a talk with Rabbi Ishmael in Heaven, showed the latter the holy books wherein the decrees for Israel are spelt out.

Sagras—with another angel named Saraiel,

Head of a sorrowing angel by Filippino Lippi (1457–1504). Reproduced from Régamey, *Anges.*

Sagras governs the sign of the Bull (Taurus) in the zodiac.

Sagsagel [Zagzagel]

Sahaqiel—angelic ruler of the sky, according to *3 Enoch.*

Sahariel (Asderel)—an angel invoked in Syriac spellbinding charms. Sahariel governs the sign of Aries (Ram) in the zodiac. [*Rf. Prince of Darkness* (a witchcraft anthology), p. 177; *The Book of Protection*; Budge, *Amulets and Talismans.*]

Sahiviel—angelic guard of the 3rd Heaven, mentioned along with numerous other such guards in *Ozar Midrashim* I, 116.

Sahon—in the cabala, one of the angels of the Seal; also a planetary angel.

Sahriel—one of the 64 angel wardens of the 7 celestial halls. [*Rf. Pirke Hechaloth.*]

Sahtail (Sahteil)—an angel in Mandaean lore. [*Rf.* Pognon, *Inscriptions Mandaïtes des Coupes de Khouabir.*]

Saint Francis—pictured as an angel of mercy (with wings) as well as the angel of the Apocalypse. [*Rf.* Bonaventura, *Life of Saint Francis.*] In his role of angel of the Apocalypse, Saint Francis warns the winds not to complete the destruction of the world—not until "the elect should be gathered." [*See* Rhamiel.]

Saints—an order of angels in Jewish Talmud and Targum, according to Voltaire, "Of Angels, Genii, and Devils." A term for angels, as in the Authorized Version of Psalms 89:7, where "council of the holy ones" is translated into "assembly of saints."

Saissaiel—with Riehol (a brother genius), Saissaiel governs the sign of Scorpio. [*Rf.* Levi, *Transcendental Magic*, p. 413.]

Sakniel—one of numerous angelic guards of the gates of the West Wind, as cited in *Ozar Midrashim* II, 316.

Sakriel (Samriel)—a porter angel of the 2nd Heaven. [*Rf. Pirke Hechaloth.*]

Saktas—one of the many names of the angel Metatron.

Salamiel (Satanail, Satomail)—a great angel, prince of the grigori (*q.v.*). Though the grigori dwell in Heaven, a certain number of them are malign. A legend has it that Salamiel rejected the Lord and is now a fallen angel. [*Rf.* Ginzberg, *The Legends of the Jews* I, 133.]

Salatheel (Sealtiel, Sealthiel, Salathiel—"I have asked God")—one of the 7 great ministering archangels, rulers of the movements of the spheres. With Suriel (Suriyel), Salatheel conducted Adam and Eve from the top of a high mountain, where Satan had lured them, to the cave of treasures (as reported in *The Book of Adam and Eve*). Ezra IV refers to him as Salathiel. In secular writings, there is a romance by the Rev. George Croly (published in 1829, again in 1900, under the title *Tarry Thou Till I Come*) in which the Wandering Jew is the name of a 16th-century Venetian called Salathiel ben Sadi. [*Rf.* Levi, *Transcendental Magic*; Barnhart, *The New Century Handbook of English Literature*, p. 960.]

Salbabiel—an angel invoked in Aramaic love charms. [*Rf.* Montgomery, *Aramaic Incantation Texts from Nippur.*]

Salem—the guardian angel of St. John; probably Melchizedec, who was the legendary king of Salem (i.e., Jerusalem). [*Rf.* Klopstock, *The Messiah*, notes to canto vii.]

Salemia—in *Esdras II*, one of the 5 "men" (angels) who transcribed the 204 books dictated by Ezra.

Salilus—in magical arts [*Rf.* Levi, *Transcendental Magic*] a genius who opens sealed doors. In Apollonius of Tyana, *The Nuctemeron*, Salilus is a genius of the 7th hour.

Sallisim—in *3 Enoch*, an order of angels within the order of the Song-Uttering Choirs, the latter being under the direction of Tagas (*q.v.*).

Salmael (Samael)—a prince of one of the angelic orders. Salmael used to accuse Israel on Yom

Kippur, calling for the annihilation of the Jews (forerunner of a genocide like Hitler?). Salmael is equated with Samael and Azazel. He has also been identified as Jacob's dark antagonist at Peniel, as have other angels. [Rf. Bamberger, *Fallen Angels*, pp. 284–285.]

Salmay (Zalmaii, Samaey)—in the *Grimorium Verum*, one of the "holy angels of God" invoked in ceremonial magic rites, specifically in the benediction of the Salt. [Rf. Waite, *The Book of Ceremonial Magic*, p. 175.]

Salmia—an angel petitioned in ritual prayer, along with other "great and glorious spirits" for the fulfilment of the invocant's desires. [Rf. Malchus, *The Secret Grimoire of Turiel*.]

Salmon—an angel of the 6th hour of the night, serving under Zaazonash. [Rf. Waite, *The Lemegeton*, p. 69.]

Salpsan—a son of Satan, according to the *Gospel of Bartholomew*, in James, *The Apocryphal New Testament*.

Salun—an angel petitioned in ritual prayer. [Rf. Malchus, *The Secret Grimoire of Turiel*, p. 36.]

Samaey [Salmay]

Sam(m)ael (Satanil, Samil, Satan, Seir, Salmael, etc.)—a combination of "sam" meaning poison and "el" meaning angel. In rabbinic literature, Samael is chief of the Satans and the angel of death. In the *Secrets of Enoch* (*Enoch II*) he is the prince of demons and a magician. Samael has been regarded both as evil and good; as one of the greatest and as one of the foulest spirits operating in Heaven, on earth, and in Hell. On the one hand he is said to be chief ruler of the 5th Heaven (in Jewish legendary lore his residence is usually placed in the 7th Heaven), one of the 7 regents of the world served by 2 million angels; on the other hand, he is "that great serpent with 12 wings that draws after him, in his fall, the solar system." [Cf. Revelation 12.] Samael is also the angel of death (one of a number of such angels) whom God sent to fetch the soul of Moses when the Lawgiver's days on earth had come to an end. Talmud

Yalkut I, 110, speaks of Samael as Esau's guardian angel. *Sotah* 10b speaks of Samael as Edom's *sar* (angelic prince guardian). In the *Sayings of Rabbi Eliezer*, Samael is charged with being the one (in the guise of a serpent) who tempted Eve, seduced her, and became by her the father of Cain. In *The Zohar* (Vayishlah 170b), Samael is the dark angel who wrestled with Jacob at Peniel, although Michael, Uriel, Metatron, and others have been identified as this antagonist. Samael is also equated with the satan (i.e., the adversary) who tempted David to number Israel [Rf. I Chronicles 21]. *Targum Jonathan to the Prophets* renders Genesis 3:6 as: "And the woman saw Samael the angel of death." This verse is translated in the *Paraphrase of Job*, 28:7, as: "the path of the Tree of Life which Samael, who flies like a bird, did not know, and which the eye of Eve did not perceive." In Waite, *The Holy Kabbalah*, p. 255, Samael is characterized as the "severity of God" and is listed as 5th of the archangels of the world of Briah. Here he corresponds to the sefira Geburah. Cornelius Agrippa, *Three Books of Occult Philosophy*, equates Samael with the Greek god Typhon. *Baruch III*, 4, mentions "the angel Sammael." In Charles, *The Ascension of Isaiah* IV, 7, occurs this passage: "And we ascended to the firmament, I and he [i.e., Isaiah and his escorting angel, a very glorious one, not named—but compare with the angel that Abraham encounters in the *Apocalypse of Abraham*], and there I saw Sammael and his hosts, and there was great fighting therein and the angels of Satan were envying one another." It is clear here that Sammael and Satan are interchangeable. In Longfellow's extensive poem, *The Golden Legend*, when the rabbi asks Judas Iscariot why the dogs howl at night, the answer is: *In the Rabbinical book it sayeth/The dogs howl when, with icy breath,/Great Sammael, the Angel of Death,/Takes through the town his flight.* In fiction, "Red Samael the Seducer," father of the hero, is a character in Cabell, *The Devil's Own Dear Son*. Cabell calls Samael the "youngest and most virile of the 72 princes of Hell, a red-headed rogue who had made his reputation some centuries ago with both Eve and Lilith." To Cabell, Samael belongs to the order of seraphim and is "first of the art critics."

Samaha'il—in Muslim tradition, an angel in the 6th Heaven in charge of a group of angels (in the guise of boys) engaged in worshipping Allah. [*Rf.* Hastings, *Encyclopaedia of Religion and Ethics* IV, 619.]

Samandiriel (Smandriel)—in Mandaean lore, a spirit of fertility who receives prayers; and who keeps such prayers until the time comes when he believes they should be acted on. *See* Yus(h)amin. [*Rf.* Drower, *The Canonical Prayerbook of the Mandaeans*, p. 272.]

Samangaluf (Smnglf, Samangeloph)—according to pseudo-Sirach, one of the 3 angels who brought Lilith back to Adam in the pre-Eve days, after a long separation. A Hebrew amulet, showing the seal of Samangaluf and taken from *The Book of the Angel Raziel*, is reproduced in Budge, *Amulets and Talismans*, p. 225.

Samas—a master spirit in Babylonian and Chaldean occultism. Samas figures as one of the signs (the sun) of the zodiac. [*Rf.* Lenormant, *Chaldean Magic*; Seligmann, *The History of Magic*.]

Samax—chief of the angels of the air and ruling angel of Tuesday. His ministering angels are Carmax, Ismoli, and Paffran. [*Rf.* de Abano, *The Heptameron*; Barrett, *The Magus* II.]

Samax Rex—as recorded in a book of Elizabethan black magic, a spirit of evil. [*Rf.* Butler, *Ritual Magic*, p. 256.]

Sambula—in Arabic lore, an angel invoked in conjuring rites. [*Rf.* Shah, *Occultism*.]

Samchia (Samchiel)—one of the 70 childbed amulet angels. For a list of all 70, *see* Appendix.

Samchiel [Samchia]

Sameon—in Waite, *The Lemegeton*, an angel of the 6th hour of the day, serving under Samil.

Sameron—an angel of the 12th hour of the day, serving under Beratiel.

Sameveel—one of the fallen angels, listed in *Enoch I*.

Samhiel—in the cabala, an angel invoked to cure stupidity. [*Rf.* Botarel, *Mayan Hahochmah*; *Enoch I*.]

Sam Hii (Shom Hii)—in Mandaean lore, one of the 4 *malki* (*uthri* or angels) of the North Star. The name means "creation of life."

Samiaza(z) [Semyaza]

Samiel—in the *Apocalypse of Peter* (also in James, *The Apocryphal New Testament*) Samiel is an "immortal angel of God." In *The Book of Protection*, he is grouped with Michael, Gabriel, and other spellbinding angels. However, according to Voltaire in his "Of Angels, Genii, and Devils," Samiel is one of the leaders of the fallen angels, and hence evil. To Voltaire, apparently, Samiel was another form for Samael, prince of evil. In Bar-Khonai, *The Book of Scholia*, Samiel is described as "blind, malformed, and evil."

Samil—an angel ruler of the 6th hour, with a vast concourse of serving spirits under him. [*Rf.* Waite, *The Lemegeton*.]

Samjaza [Semyaza]

Samlo—in gnosticism, one of the great luminaries or aeons who "are to draw the elect up to Heaven." [*Rf.* Doresse, *The Secret Books of the Egyptian Gnostics*.]

Sammael [Samael]

Sammangaloph [Samangaluf]

Samoel (Samoy?)—a spirit invoked in prayer to the Master of the Art in Solomonic ritual operations. [*Rf.* Mathers, *The Greater Key of Solomon*.]

Samohayl—a ministering archangel evoked in cabalistic conjuring rites. [*Rf. The Sixth and Seventh Books of Moses*.]

Samoy—in the *Grimorium Verum*, an angel conjured up in black magic operations. He may be the same as Samoel.

Samriel [Sakriel]

Samsapeel (Samsaveel, Shamshiel)—an evil archangel listed among the apostates in *Enoch I*. He was one of 200 who descended from Heaven to cohabit with the daughters of men.

Samsaveel [Samsapeel]

Samuil (Semil, "heard of God")—in Jewish legendary lore, an angel of the earth—that is, one who exercises dominion over the earth. In *Enoch II*, 33, he is the angel who not only transported Enoch to Heaven (while Enoch was still in the flesh) but, as commanded by God, returned him to earth—although this mission and feat are also ascribed to other angels, among them Rasuil and Anafiel.

Samyaza [Semyaza]

Sanasiel—in Mandaean angelology, a spirit who stands at the gate of life and prays for souls. [*Rf.* Drower, *The Canonical Prayerbook of the Mandaeans.*]

Sanctities—a term for one of the celestial orders, as employed by Milton in *Paradise Lost* III, 60. [*Rf.* West, *Milton and his Angels*, p. 135.]

Sandalphon (Sandolphon, Sandolfon—Greek, "co-brother")—originally the prophet Elias (Elijah). In rabbinic lore, Sandalphon is one of the great *sarim* (angelic princes), twin brother of Metatron, master (*hazzan*) of heavenly song. Exceeding Hadraniel in height by a 500-year foot journey, he is regarded as one of the tallest hierarchs in the celestial realms—Moses, sighting him in the 3rd Heaven, called him "the tall angel." Talmud *Hagiga* 13b says his head reaches Heaven (which was said also of Israfel and of the Greek giant Typhon). In Mathers, *The Greater Key of Solomon*, Sandalphon is designated "the left-hand feminine cherub of the ark." In the liturgy for the Feast of Tabernacles, he is credited with gathering the prayers of the faithful, making a garland of such prayers, and then "adjuring them to ascend as an orb to the supreme King of Kings." In *3 Enoch*, Sandalphon is described as ruler of the 6th Heaven (*makon*) but, in *The Zohar* (Exodus 202b), he is "chief of the 7th Heaven." According to Islamic lore, he dwells in the 4th Heaven. As is reported of Michael, he carries on ceaseless combat with the apparently indestructible Samael (Satan), prince of evil. In popular etymology, Sandalphon

is a fancier of sandals (soft shoes) when he stands in the presence of his Maker, but leather shoegear when he appears before the Shekinah (see *The Zohar*). The ancient sages identified Sandalphon with Ophan (*q.v.*). He is said also, by cabalists, to be instrumental in bringing about the differentiation of sex in the embryo—a good thing to bring to the attention of expectant mothers. [*Rf. Yalkut Reubeni.*] In Longfellow's "Sandalphon," he is the "Angel of Glory, Angel of Prayer," Longfellow's inspiration for the poem deriving from J. P. Stehelin, *Traditions of the Jews.*

Sandolfon [Sandolphon]

Sangariah—angel of fasts, whose chief office is accusing those who fail to observe the Sabbath. [*Rf. The Zohar* (Exodus 207a).]

Sangariel—an angel who guards the portals of Heaven. [*Rf.* Mathers, *The Greater Key of Solomon.*]

Sanigron Kunya—in M. Gaster, *The Sword of Moses*, one of the 14 great angels who may be invoked in special ceremonial rites.

Sannul (Sanul)—an angel of the order of powers; in occultism, he is summoned up in ritual magic rites. [*Rf. The Sixth and Seventh Books of Moses.*]

Sansanui (Sansanvi, Sanvi, Sansennoi, Snvi, Sanzanuy)—one of the 3 angels credited with bringing Lilith back to Adam after their separation (in the pre-Eve days). The other 2 angels who assisted in the reconciliation were Sanuy (or Sennoi) and Samangaluf. Sansanui is now a potent prophylactic against the deprivations of Lilith and her minions. [*Rf.* Trachtenberg, *Jewish Magic and Superstition.*]

Santanael—a Friday angel, resident of the 3rd Heaven. Summoned up, Santanael will appear only when the invocant faces south. [*Rf.* de Abano, *The Heptameron*; Barrett, *The Magus* II.]

Santriel—the sole reference to Santriel occurs in *The Zohar* (Exodus 151a), where his function is clearly described: "And a certain angel named Santriel goes away to fetch the body of such a sinner [i.e., such a one who kept not the Sabbath] from the grave and brings it to Gehenna, holding it up before the eyes of all the [other] sinners, that they may see how it bred worms."

Saphar—in the *Sefer Yetzirah* (*Book of Foundation*) it is said that Saphar is "one of the 3 seraphim through whom the world was made," the other 2 being Sepher and Sipur.

Sapiel (Saphiel)—an angel of the 4th Heaven and ruler of the Lord's Day. Sapiel is a guardian angel and is to be invoked from the north.

Sar (pl., *sarim*)—a Hebrew term for an angel prince. There are 70 *sarim*, one for each nation. The *sarim* are also identified as the 70 Shepherds, as in the *Shepherd of Hermas*.

Saraiel (Sariel)—governor of the sign of the Twins in the zodiac, at which post Saraiel is assisted by another genius (i.e., angel) named Sagras. [*Rf. The Prince of Darkness*, p. 177.]

Sarafiel—in Islamic mythology, an angel equated with Israfil or Israfel. [*Rf. Jewish Encyclopedia*, "Angelology."]

Sarafsion—in hechaloth lore (*Ma'asseh Merkabah*), an angelic guard stationed at the 7th heavenly hall.

Sarahiel—one of the 7 angelic guards of the 2nd Heaven, according to *Hechaloth Rabbati*. [*Rf. Ozar Midrashim* I, 116.]

Sarakiel (Saraquael)—the prince of ministering angels, officiating when these angels convene at judgment councils. Sarakiel is "one of the 7 holy angels set over the children of men whose spirits have sinned." [*Rf. The Book of Enoch.*] With another angel, Sataaran, Sarakiel governs the sign of the Ram.

Sarakika'il—in Arabic lore, a guardian angel invoked in rites of exorcism. [*Rf. Hughes, A Dictionary of Islam*, "Angels."]

Saraknyal (Sarakuyal)—one of the 200 angels under the leadership of Semyaza who descended to earth to cohabit with the daughters of men, an incident touched on in Genesis 6. The American poet Mark Van Doren mentions Saraknyal in his poem "The Prophet Enoch." The variant form Sarakuyal is provided by Levi, *The History of Magic*, when listing the leaders of the 200 apostates.

Saranana—in *The Almadel of Solomon*, an angel of the 3rd altitude.

Saraquael [Sarakiel]

Sarasael (Sarea, Sarga, Saraqael)—a seraph; one of the 5 "men" who wrote down the 204 books dictated by Ezra. He is one of the holy angels "set over the spirits of those who sin in the spirit." As recorded in *Baruch III*, Sarasael is the angel God sent to Noah to advise the latter in the matter of replanting the Tree (in Eden) "which led Adam astray."

Saratan—in Arabic lore, an angel invoked in incantation rites.

Sarea (Sarga)—in Duff, *II Esdras*, one of 5 "men" referred to under Sarasael. Of the 204 books dictated by Ezra, 70 were to be delivered only to the wise; the others were to be published openly.

Sarfiel—an ancient amulet angel whose name is recorded in a Palestinian mezuzah, along with the names of 6 other angels. In occultism, Sarfiel is an angel of the 8th hour of the day, serving under Osgaebial. In *Ozar Midrashim* II, 316, he is one of the numerous guards of the gates of the East Wind.

Sarga (Sarasael)—one of the 5 heavenly scribes appointed by God to transcribe the 204 books dictated by Ezra. The other 4 scribes are Dabria, Seleucia, Ethan (or Ecanus), and Asiel. Here, clearly, Sarga is considered another form for Sarea and Sarasael.

Sargiel (Nasargiel)—an angel who fills Hell with the souls of the wicked.

Sar ha-Kodesh—the angelic prince of the sanctuary, or of holiness. Sar ha-Kodesh has been identified with Metatron and Yefefiah (*q.q.v.*).

Sar ha-Olam—literally "prince of the world"

Satan and Belzebuth (fallen angels) in consultation on battle strategy. An illustration for *Paradise Lost* I, after a sculpture by Darodes. Reproduced from Hayley, *The Poetical Works of John Milton.*

and the equivalent of Sar ha-Panim, "prince of the face." Identified as Michael, Jehoel, Metatron, and—by St. Paul—as Satan. Talmud calls Sar ha-Olam an angel who "bears God's name within him," referring to Exodus 23:21. [*Rf.* Talmud *Yebamoth* 16b; *Hullin* 60a; *Sanhedrin* 94a.] Sar ha-Olam, like Metatron, is credited with composing Psalms 37:25 and Isaiah 24:16.

Sar ha-Panim—literally "prince of the face" and equated with the prince of the presence; also with Sar ha-Olam.

Sar ha-Torah—literally "prince of the Torah" (Law), who is Yefefiah (*q.v.*).

Sarhma'il—in Arabic lore, a guardian angel invoked in rites of exorcism. [*Rf.* Hughes, *A Dictionary of Islam*, "Angels."]

Sariel (Suriel, Zerachiel, Sarakiel, Uriel, etc.)—one of the 7 archangels originally listed in the Enoch books as Saraqel and differentiated from Uriel, although Sariel is identified as Uriel in T. Gaster, *Dead Sea Scriptures*. Sariel is cited both as a holy angel and a fallen one. In occultism he is one of the 9 angels of the summer equinox and is effective as an amulet against the evil eye. He governs the zodiacal sign of the Ram (Aries). In addition, he teaches the course of the moon (which was regarded at one time as forbidden knowledge). [*Rf.* Glasson, *Greek Influence in Jewish Eschatology*.] In the recently discovered Dead Sea scrolls, one of the books, *The War of the Sons of Light Against the Sons of Darkness*, speaks of the angel Sariel as a name that appears on the shields of the "third Tower," the term Tower having the meaning of a fighting unit. There were 4 Towers in all.

Sarim (Hebrew plural for *sar*, "prince")—an angelic order of the Song-Uttering Choirs under the leadership of Tagas (*q.v.*). [*Rf. 3 Enoch.*]

Saritaiel (Saritiel)—with a brother genius called Vhnori, Saritaiel governs the zodiacal sign of Sagittarius.

Saritiel [Saritaiel]

Sarmiel—a subordinate of Jehoel, prince of fire (*q.v.*). [*Rf.* King, *The Gnostics and Their Remains*, p. 15.]

Sarospa—"the angel who executes the commands of Ahura-Mazda." [*Rf.* Forlong, *Encyclopedia of Religions*.]

Sarphiel—an angel invoked in Syriac incantation charms. In *The Book of Protection*, Sarphiel is grouped with Michael, Shamshiel, and Nuriel as "a spellbinding power."

Sarquamich—a ruling angel of the 3rd hour of the night. [*See* Haglow.]

Sar Shel Yam ("prince of the sea")—Rahab (*q.v.*). [*Rf. Midrash Rabbah.*]

Sartael ("God's side")—also called Satarel. An evil archangel, in control of hidden things. Mentioned in Talmud *Berakoth* 57b.

Sartamiel—one of the governing angels of the zodiac. [*Rf.* Cornelius Agrippa, *Three Books of Occult Philosophy* III.]

Sartziel (Saissaiel)—according to Lèvi, *Transcendental Magic*, the genius governing the zodiacal sign of Scorpio. [*Rf. Prince of Darkness.*]

Sarush [Sirushi, Sraosha]

Sasa'il—in Muslim tradition, an angel of the 4th Heaven in charge of a group of angels (all in the guise of horses) engaged in worshipping Allah. [*Rf.* Hastings, *Encyclopaedia of Religion and Ethics* IV, 619.]

Sasgabiel—an angel invoked in rites of exorcism. [*Rf.* Montgomery, *Aramaic Incantation Texts from Nippur*.]

Sasniel [Sasnigiel]

Sasnigiel (Sasniel, Sagansagel, Sasnesagiel)—in *3 Enoch*, the angelic prince of wisdom, prince of the world, and prince of the presence (or face); also one of the seraphim "appointed over peace." Sasnigiel is one of the many names of the angel Metatron.

Sastashiel Jhvhh—one of the angelic princes of the hosts of X. [*Rf.* M. Gaster, *The Sword of Moses*.]

Sataaran—the genius in control of the zodiacal sign of the Ram (Aries). Sataaran shares this post with another genius, Sarahiel (Sariel). [*Rf.* Levi, *Transcendental Magic*, p. 413.]

Satael—one of the Tuesday angels of the air invoked in magic rites. Satael serves also as a presiding spirit of the planet Mars. [*Rf.* de Abano, *The Heptameron*; Barrett, *The Magus*.]

Satan—the Hebrew meaning of the word is "adversary." In Numbers 22:22 the angel of the Lord stands against Balaam "for an adversary" (satan). In other Old Testament books (Job, I Chronicles, Psalms, Zechariah) the term likewise designates an office; and the angel investing that office is not apostate or fallen. He becomes such starting in early New Testament times and writings, when he emerges as Satan (capital S), the prince of evil and enemy of God, and is characterized by such titles as "prince of this world" (John 16:11) and "prince of the power of the air" (Ephesians 2:2). When Peter was rebuked by Jesus, he was called Satan (Luke 4:8). Reading back into Genesis, medieval writers like Peter Lombard (c. 1100–1160) saw Satan in the guise of the serpent tempting Eve, although other writers, like the 9th-century Bishop Agobard, held that Satan tempted Eve *through* the serpent. As Langton says in *Satan, A Portrait*: "In the later Jewish literature, Satan and the serpent are either identified, or one is made the vehicle of the other." Originally, Satan (as *ha-satan*) was a great angel, chief of the seraphim, head of the order of virtues. While seraphim were usually pictured as 6-winged, Satan was shown as 12-winged. Gregory the Great in his *Moralia*, after listing the 9 hierarchic orders, pays this tribute to Satan: "he wore all of them [all the angels] as a garment, transcending all in glory and knowledge." Talmud claims that Satan was created on the 6th day of Creation (*Bereshith Rabba*, 17). Through a misreading of Isaiah 14:12, he has been identified with Lucifer. To Aquinas, Satan, as "the first angel who sinned" is not a seraph but a cherub, the argument being that "cherubim is [sic] derived from knowledge, which is compatible with mortal sin; but seraphim is [sic] derived from the heat of charity, which is incompatible with mortal sin" (*Summa* 1, 7th art., reply obj. 1). In time, according to Jerome,

Gregory of Nyssa, Origen, Ambrosiaster, and others, Satan will be reinstated in his "pristine splendor and original rank." This is also cabalistic doctrine. In secular lore, Satan figures in many works, notably in Milton's *Paradise Lost*, where he is chief of rebels and the "Arch Angel ruin'd" (I, 593) and in *Paradise Regained*, where he is the "Thief of Paradise" (IV, 604). Also in Vondel's *Lucifer*; in Dryden's *The State of Innocence*; and in Goethe's *Faust* (where he is represented by Mephistopheles). Other names for Satan include Mastema, Beliar or Beliel, Duma, Gadreel, Azazel, Sammael, angel of Edom. In rabbinic lore he has a nickname "the ugly one" (Ginzberg, *The Legends of the Jews* V, 123). In *Midrash Tehillim* Satan appears to David (when the latter was out hunting) in the form of a gazelle. Compare with figure of Mutabilitie (as conceived by Spenser in "Two Cantos of Mutabilitie" in *The Fairie*

Satan bound for a thousand years by the angel of the abyss (Appollyon/Abaddon), a 17th-century illustration of I Revelation 20. Reproduced from Langton, *Satan, A Portrait*.

Queene), the Greek Titaness who challenges Jove's sovereignty and who, like Satan, aspired to and attempted "the empire of the Heavens hight."

Satanail—"his name [Satan's] was formerly Satanail." [*Rf. Enoch II* (the Slavonic Enoch), chap. 31, Morfill edition.]

Satarel [Sartael]

Sathariel ("concealment of God")—the "averse" sefira (*q.v.*) "who hides the face of mercy." In *The Zohar* (supplement), Sathariel is called Sheiriel. [*Rf.* Waite, *The Holy Kabbalah*, p. 257.]

Satrapies—a term Milton uses in his "The Reason of Church-Government Urged against Prelaty" to denote an order in the angelic hierarchy not mentioned by pseudo-Dionysius or any other angelologist, as in "Their celestial princedoms and satrapies."

Saturn—in Persian religious lore, an angel, lord of the 7th Heaven. In the cabala, Saturn is the angel of the wilderness. In Chaldean mythology, he was Adar, one of the ruling gods of the 5 planets. Milton refers to Saturn as a fallen angel (*Paradise Lost* I, 512.)

Saulasau—a power of the upper world. [*Rf.* Doresse, *The Secret Books of the Egyptian Gnostics*.]

Sauriel (Sauriil, Suriel, Sowrill)—an angel of death, so designated in Drower, *The Canonical Prayerbook of the Mandaeans*, where Sauriel is referred to as "Sauriel the Releaser."

Savaliel—angelic guard of the 3rd Heaven. Mentioned among numerous other guards in *Ozar Midrashim* I, 116.

Savaniah—an angel's name found inscribed on the 3rd pentacle of the planet Mercury. [*Rf.* Mathers, *The Greater Key of Solomon*.]

Savatri (Savitri, Savitar)—one of the 7 or 12 adityas or "infinite ones" (angels) in Vedic lore. He (or she) is a sun god or goddess, and is described as having "a golden hand, golden eyes" and "drawn by luminous brown steeds with white feet." In Vedic hymns Savatri is identified with

Prajapati, the Creator. "Upon that excellent glory/of the god Savitar may we meditate;/May he stimulate our prayers." [*Rf.* Forlong, *Encyclopedia of Religions*; Gaynor, *Dictionary of Mysticism*; Redfield, *Gods/A Dictionary of the Deities of All Lands*.]

Savitar [Savatri]

Savitri [Savatri]

Savliel—in *Pirke Hechaloth*, an angelic porter or guard of the 3rd Heaven.

Savsa—in hechaloth lore (*Ma'asseh Merkabah*), an angelic guard stationed at the 6th heavenly hall.

Savuriel—an angelic guard of the 3rd Heaven. [*Rf. Ozar Midrashim* I, 116.]

Sawael—in the *Book of Formation* (a cabalistic work), the angel of the whirlwind. [*Rf.* Budge, *Amulets and Talismans*, p. 375.]

Sazquiel—angelic ruler of the 5th hour, with 10 chiefs and 100 lesser officers serving under him, each with his own attendants. [*Rf.* Waite, *The Lemegeton*.]

Scamijm—an angel serving in the 1st Heaven, according to *The Sixth and Seventh Books of Moses*.

Schabtaiel [Schebtaiel]

Schachlil—in transcendental magic, the genius governing the sun's rays; also the governor of the 9th hour, as cited in Apollonius of Tyana, *The Nuctemeron*.

Schachniel—one of the 70 childbed amulet angels.

Schaddyl—a throne angel, one of 15, listed in *The Sixth and Seventh Books of Moses*.

Schaltiel—a spirit who, with the help of Iadara (*q.v.*), governs the sign of the Virgin in the zodiac. [*Rf. The Prince of Darkness*, p. 177.]

Scharial—in occult lore, an angel who is said to have come out of Sodom for the purpose of curing painful boils. [*Rf. The Sixth and Seventh Books of Moses*.]

Schawayt—one of 15 throne angels. [*Rf. The Sixth and Seventh Books of Moses*.]

Schebtaiel (Sabbathi)—in the cabala, the lord of the planet Saturn. The term derives from *schebtai*, Hebrew for Saturn. In Notes to his translation of Dante's *Paradiso*, quoting Stehelin, *Rabbinical Literature*, Longfellow refers to Schebtaiel as the intelligence of Saturn. In the earliest manuscript version of *The Golden Legend*, Longfellow favored Anachiel, and then Schebtaiel, as lord of Saturn. Subsequently, however, he discarded both these angels in favor of Orifel.

Schekinah [Shekinah]

Scheliel—one of the 28 angels governing the 28 mansions of the moon.

Schiekron—in Apollonius of Tyana, *The Nuctemeron*, the genius of bestial love, and one of the genii of the 4th hour. [*Cf.* Pharzuph.]

Schimuel—one of 15 throne angels listed in *The Sixth and Seventh Books of Moses*.

Schioel—an angel whose name is found inscribed on the 1st pentacle of the moon. [*Rf.* Mathers, *The Greater Key of Solomon*.]

Schrewniel ("convert")—in Mosaic incantation rites, an angel to be invoked for obtaining a good memory and an open heart.

Scigin—an angel invoked in goetic rites and mentioned in the grimoires.

Scourging Angels (Hebrew, *malache habbala*)—angels "pitiless of mind" whom Abraham encountered during his visit to Paradise. [*Rf. The Testament of Abraham*.]

Scribe of the Knowledge of the Most High —any of the following 9 answer to the title: Vretil, Enoch, Dabriel, Ezra, Pravuil, Uriel, Radueriel, Soferiel Memith, and Soferiel Mehayye.

Scribe of Righteousness—identified as Enoch in the *Vision of Paul* XX. In this Vision, Paul sees Enoch as an angel "at the interior of Paradise."

Scribes—in *3 Enoch*, the scribes constitute a high order of angels; they register the deeds of all men and read aloud the books of judgment at the convening of the sessions of the celestial court.

Sealiah (Seeliah)—in the cabala, an angel who governs or controls vegetation on earth. He is also one of the 72 angels bearing the mystical name of God Shemhamphorae. For Sealiah's sigil *see* Ambelain, *La Kabbale Pratique*, p. 281.

Sealtiel (Hebrew, "request of God")—an archangel cited in Jobes, *Dictionary of Mythology Folklore and Symbols*.

Seats—an order of angels mentioned by Augustine in his *City of God* as *sedes*, and referred to by John Salkeld in the latter's *A Treatise of Angels* (1613), p. 303. The term "seats" may be equated with thrones. Edmund Spenser indicates such use in his "An Hymne of Heavenly Beautie."

Seba'im—a class of angels spoken of in *3 Enoch*, chap. 19: "When the time draws nigh for the recital of the heavenly song, all the hosts (the *seba'im*) are afrighted."

Sebalim—an order of angels comprised in the Song-Uttering Choirs, operating under the leadership of Tagas (*q.v.*). [*Rf. 3 Enoch*.]

Sebhael (Sebhil)—a spirit in Arabic lore who is in charge of the books wherein are recorded the good and evil actions of man. [*Rf.* De Plancy, *Dictionnaire Infernal*, 1863 ed.]

Second Angel—in *Enoch II*, 30:12, Adam is called "a second angel."

Second Heaven, The—in Islamic lore, the abode of Jesus and John the Baptist. Here (in Jewish lore) the fallen angels are imprisoned and the planets fastened. It was in this Heaven that Moses, during his visit to Paradise, encountered the angel Nuriel, "standing 300 parasangs high, with a retinue of 50 myriads of angels all fashioned out of water and fire." [*Rf. The Legends of the Jews* I, 131, and II, 306.]

Seconds (fictional)—the name of an angel in Charles Angoff's short story "God Repents." [*See* Time.]

Sedekiah—a "treasure-finding angel" whose name figures on the pentacle of the planet Jupiter. Sedekiah may be invoked in Solomonic magical operations.

Sedim (sing. *sedu*)—in Talmud *Abot(h)* the *sedim* are guardian spirits, invoked in the exorcism of evil spirits.

Sedu [sing. for *sedim*]

Seehiah (Seheiah)—in the cabala, one of the 72 angels bearing the mystical name of God Shemhamphorae. In Ambelain, *La Kabbale Pratique*, chart of *L'Arbre de Vie* (facing p. 88), Seehiah is listed as one of 9 angels of the order of dominations, led by Zadkiel. He is credited with the power of bestowing long life and improving the health of those who invoke him. [*Rf.* Barrett, *The Magus* II, chart facing p. 62.]

Seeliah (Saeliah)—in the cabala, a fallen angel once of the order of virtues. He has (or had) dominion over vegetables. When invoking him, and for the best results, it is advisable to recite a verse from Psalm 93. Seeliah is mentioned in Ambelain, *La Kabbale Pratique*, p. 278.

Sefira (sephira; pl. sefiroth or sephiroth)—a divine emanation through which God manifested His existence in the creation of the universe. In the cabala, there are 10 holy and 10 unholy successive sefiroth, the holy ones issuing from the right side of God, the unholy ones from His left. The 10 holy ones are usually given as: 1. Kether (crown), 2. Chokmah (wisdom), 3. Binah (understanding), 4. Chesed (mercy), 5. Geburah (strength), 6. Tiphereth (beauty), 7. Netzach (victory), 8. Hod (splendor), 9. Jesod (foundation), 10. Malkuth (kingdom). The sefiroth may be compared with the Platonic powers or intelligences, or with the gnostic aeons. In the cabala, the great sefiroth in the form of personalized angels are: Metatron, archangel of the hayyoth hakodesh; Raziel, archangel of the arelim or erelim; Zadkiel, archangel of the hashmalim; Kamael, archangel of the seraphim; Michael, archangel of the shinanim; Haniel, archangel of the tarshishim; Raphael, archangel of the bene elohim; Gabriel, archangel of the kerubim. In the *Book of Formation* is this description of the 10 "ineffable" sefiroth: "They are without limits; the infinity of the Beginning and the infinity of the End; the infinity of the Good and the infinity of the Evil; the infinity of the Height and the infinity of the Depth . . . their appearance is like that of a flash of lightning, their goal is infinite. His [God's] word is in them when they emanate and when they return . . . and before His throne they prostrate themselves." In the opinion of the 16th-century commentator Isaac ha-Cohen of Soria, of the 10 evil emanations, only 7 were permitted to endure, and of these 7 only 5 have been "authenticated"—Ashmedai, Kafkefoni, Taninniver (blind dragon), Sammael, and Sammael's mate Lilith.

Sefoniel—in Mathers, *The Greater Key of Solomon*, one of two princes ruling the universe, the other being Ioniel. Sefoniel may be invoked in magical operations.

Sefriel—an angelic guard of the 5th Heaven, as listed in *Pirke Hechaloth*.

Segef—an angel of destruction invoked at the close of the Sabbath. [*Rf.* Trachtenberg, *Jewish Magic and Superstition*.] It should be pointed out that the angels of destruction are not by nature evil; only so in a causative sense. They were among the 1st angels to be created. There is no mention of them as among the one-third of the hosts that defected at the time of the great rebellion in Heaven.

Segsuhiel YHWH—one of the angel princes of the hosts of X (i.e., God), as listed in M. Gaster, *The Sword of Moses*. [*Rf.* Levi, *Transcendental Magic*.]

Sehaltiel—an angel to be invoked when one wishes to drive away the archfiend Moloch. [*Rf.* Levi, *Transcendental Magic*.]

Seheiah—in the cabala, an angel who provides protection against fire, sickness, etc., and governs longevity. His corresponding angel is Sethacer. For Seheiah's sigil, see Ambelain, *La Kabbale Pratique*, p. 269.

Sehibiel—an angelic guard of the 2nd Heaven, as listed in *Pirke Hechaloth*.

Seimelkhe—a celestial being in gnostic lore, commonly referred to as a power or an aeon. [*Rf.* Doresse, *The Secret Books of the Egyptian Gnostics*.]

Seir—another name for Samael, according to Nahmanides. [*Rf.* Bamberger, *Fallen Angels*, p. 154.]

Seket—in the cabala, a female angel who dwells in Egypt; she is the angel of part of an hour and appears when properly invoked. The poet H.D. sings of Seket in her poem "Sagesse." Seket is also mentioned in Ambelain, *La Kabbale Pratique.*

Seldac (Sellao, Esaldaio, Sacla)—in gnosticism, one of the angels of the order of powers, in charge of heavenly baptism. [*Rf.* Doresse, *The Secret Books of the Egyptian Gnostics.*]

Selemia (Shelemiah, Seleucia)—one of the 5 "men" (i.e., angels) who wrote down the 94 (or 204) books dictated by Ezra, according to popular legend. The other angelic scribes are usually listed as Asiel, Dabria, Ecanus, and Sarae (Sarga). [*Rf.* the apocryphal work *Esdras II*; Charles, *Apocrypha and Pseudepigrapha of the Old Testament.*]

Selith—in Klopstock, *The Messiah*, a seraph, one of the 2 guardian angels of the Virgin Mary and St. John the Divine.

Semakiel (Semaqiel)—with another genius called Sagdalon, Semakiel rules the zodiacal sign of Capricorn. [*Rf.* Levi, *Transcendental Magic.*]

Semalion—in Talmud *Sotah* 13b, the angel who announced the death of Moses with the words "The great scribe is dead!" [*Rf.* Ginzberg, *The Legends of the Jews* V, 6.] *Note*: since Sammael was the one sent from heaven to fetch Moses' soul, Semalion may be a variant spelling for Sammael. The name occurs also in Talmud *Sanhedrin* 38b and *Hagiga* 13b.

Semanglaf (Samangaluf)—an angel who is to be invoked for help when a woman becomes pregnant; also one of 3 angels who brought Lilith back to Adam.

Semaqiel [Samakiel]

Semeliel (Semishial)—one of the 7 princes "who stand continually before God, and to whom are given the spirit-names of the planets,"according to Cornelius Agrippa. [*Rf. The Sixth and Seventh Book of Moses.*] In Cornelius Agrippa's view, as recorded in his *Three Books of Occult Philosophy* III, Semeliel (Semeshiah) is the spirit of the Sun.

Semeschiah [Semeliel]

Semiaxas [Semyaza]

Semiazaz [Semyaza]

Semibel (Simiel)—one of the 7 angels reprobated at the church council in Rome in 743 C.E. Uriel was one of the 7 reprobated. [*Rf.* Heywood, *The Hierarchy of the Blessèd Angels.*]

Semil [Samuil]

Semishia [Semeliel]

Semjaza [Semyaza]

Semyaza (Semiaza, Shemhazai, Shamazya, Amezyarak, etc.)—probably a running together of Shem (meaning name) and Azza (the angel Azza, or Uzza). He was the leader of the evil angels who fell, or one of the leaders. In legend, he is the seraph tempted by the maiden Ishtahar to reveal to her the Explicit Name (of God.) It is said that he now hangs between heaven and earth, head down, and is the constellation Orion. [*Rf.* Graves, *Hebrew Myths.*] Levi, *Transcendental Magic*, suggests that Orion "would be identical with the angel Michael doing battle with the dragon, and the appearance of this sign in the sky would be, for the cabalist, a portent of victory and happiness." According to *The Zohar* (Genesis) Semyaza's sons, Hiwa and Hiya, by one of Eve's daughters, were so mighty that they ate daily 1,000 camels, 1,000 horses, and 1,000 oxen. In Byron's version of the legend ("Heaven and Earth, a Mystery"), Semyaza is transformed into Azaziel, and the female Ishtahar into Aholibamah. A recently unearthed version of *Enoch* (Qumram collection) contains a letter from Enoch addressed to Semyaza (Shemazya) and his companions. [*Rf.* Allegro, *The Dead Sea Scrolls*, p. 119.] Schwab, *Vocabulaire de l'Angélologie*, identifies Semyaza with Azael.

Senacher—the corresponding angel for Elemiah (*q.v.*).

Senciner—corresponding angel for Michael;

An 18th-century conception of Adam and Eve after the Fall, with Sin and Death in the background. Having failed to prevent the entrance of Satan into the Garden of Eden, the guardian angels are shown returning to heaven. Reproduced from Langton, *Satan, A Portrait.*

also an angel of the order of powers. Senciner watched over Aedipus Aegyptiacus, as noted in Ambelain, *La Kabbale Pratique.* In H.D.'s poem "Sagesse," Senciner is an angel of a quarter of an hour.

Senegorin—advocate angels who form the suite of the chief advocate Metatron. They are 1,800 in number. [*Rf. 3 Enoch.*]

Sennoi (Sinui, Senoi, Sanuy)—with Sansennoi and Sammangeloph, Sennoi was dispatched by God to bring Lilith back to Adam after a falling out between the pair in the pre-Eve days. Lilith was evil, but an amulet bearing the name Sennoi was sufficient, when Lilith beheld it, to deter her from harming anyone, particularly infants (in, that is, the post-Eden days). For the sigil of Sennoi see *The Book of the Angel Raziel* and Budge, *Amulets and Talismans,* 225. [*Rf.* Ausable, *A Treasury of Jewish Folklore;* Hyde, *Historia Religionis Veterum Persarum.*]

Sensenoi [Sennoi]

Sensenya—one of the 70 childbed amulet angels.

Sentacer [Ielahiah]

Seclam—an angel of the order of powers, summoned in ceremonial rites [*Rf. The Sixth and Seventh Books of Moses.*]

Sephar [Vepar]

Sepharon—in Waite, *The Lemegeton,* a chief officer-angel of the 1st hour of the night, serving under Gamiel.

Sepher—one of the 3 seraphim "through whom the world was created," the other 2 being Saphar and Sipur. [*Rf. Sefer Yetzirah.*]

Sepheriel—a great luminary, on the pronouncement of whose name "God will come to Universal Judgment." [*Rf.* Mathers, *The Greater Key of Solomon.*]

Sephira [Sefira]

Sephiroth (Sefiroth)—in *The Sixth and Seventh Books of Moses,* a power angel of the 5th Seal. He is invoked in cabalistic conjuring rites. [*See* Sefira.]

Sephuriron—the 10th of the 10 holy sefiroth. He has 3 deputy *sarim* (angelic princes) answerable to him. They are Malkiel, Ithuriel, and Nashriel. Note that, in *Paradise Lost* IV, 800, Ithuriel is the angel dispatched to locate Satan. [*Rf.* Isaac ha-Cohen of Soria's "Emanations of the Left."]

Serabilin [Jesubilin]

Serael—an angel serving in the 5th Heaven. [*Rf. The Sixth and Seventh Books of Moses.*]

Serakel—an angel who exercises dominion over fruit-bearing trees. [*Rf. Jewish Encyclopedia,* "Angelology."]

Seralif—an anagram for Israfel. An angel who participates in a dialogue with Gabriel, Michael, Raphael, and a chorus of angels in the poem "Virginalia" by Thomas Holley Chivers. For a while Chivers (American poet, 1809–1858) was associated with Poe, whose biography he wrote.

Seraph ("fiery serpent," sing. for seraphim)—an angel by that name of the order of seraphim. In Ginzberg, *The Legends of the Jews* IV, 263, it is Seraph who touches Isaiah's lips with a live coal, an incident related in Isaiah 6:6. Seraph is also named one of the angels with dominion over the element of fire, of which there are quite a number. See Heywood, *The Hierarchy of the Blessèd Angels.*

Seraphiel—eponymous chief of the order of seraphim, although Jehoel and others are also designated chief. Seraphiel ranks highest of the princes of the Merkabah as one of the judgment throne angels (of which there are commonly 8). In occult lore, Seraphiel is a presiding spirit of the planet Mercury, ruling on Tuesday and invoked from the north. [*Rf. Barrett, The Magus* II, 119; *The Secret Grimoire of Turiel,* p. 35; *The Sixth and Seventh Books of Moses.*]

Seraphim (pl. for seraph)—the highest order of angels in the pseudo-Dionysian hierarchic scheme and generally also in Jewish lore. The seraphim surround the throne of Glory and unceasingly intone the trisagion ("holy, holy, holy"). They are the angels of love, of light, and of fire. How many are there? The answer (in *3 Enoch*) is 4, "corresponding to the 4 winds of the world." In rabbinic writings they are equated with the hayyoth (*q.v.*). According to *Enoch II,* the seraphim have 4 faces and 6 wings, as in Isaiah 6. It is to be noted that the Isaiah mention is the only one to seraphim in the Old Testament, unless the expression "fiery serpents" (Numbers 21:6) may be taken to denote them. There is no mention of seraphim in the New Testament, except by implication (Revelation 4:8). The ruling prince of the order has been given variously as Seraphiel, Jehoel, Metatron, Michael, and originally as Satan (before he fell). Some of the order defected at the time of the great rebellion. In his "On the Morning of Christ's Nativity," Milton speaks of the "sworded seraphim." The *Revelation of Moses* speaks of "one of the 6-winged seraphim hurrying Adam to the Acherusian lake and washing him in the presence of God." In this book the seraphim are said to "roar like lions." Mathias Gruenewald (1470–1529) painted seraphim playing on the viola d'amour. [*Rf.* reproductions in Régamey, *Anges.*]

Serapiel—an angel of the 5th hour of the day, serving under Sazquiel, as cited in Solomonic magical lore. [*Rf. Waite, The Lemegeton.*]

Seraquiel—a "strong and powerful angel" who is invoked on Saturday. [*Rf. Barrett, The Magus* II, p. 126.]

Seratiel—with Sagham (another genius or angel), Seratiel is said to govern the sign of Leo. [*Rf. Levi, Transcendental Magic,* p. 413; *Prince of Darkness: A Witchcraft Anthology,* p. 177.]

Sereda (fictional)—in Cabell's *Jurgen,* Mother Sereda has dominion over Wednesday. She is the one who "washes away all the colors in the world." She is the sister of Pandelis.

Seref—an angel who transported to Heaven the bodies of deceased Egyptian kings. [*Rf. Langton, Essentials of Demonology,* p. 39.]

Seriel (Sariel)—a fallen angel who taught men the signs of the moon. However, as Sariel, he is one of the 7 archangels who stand around the throne of God. He is sometimes equated with Uriel. [*Rf. Enoch I*; Ginzberg, *The Legends of the Jews.*]

Serosh [Sraosha]

Serpanim ("prince of the face")—an angelic power in the world of Briah (one of the 4 worlds of Creation). [*Rf. Ambelain, La Kabbale Pratique.*]

Seruf (or Seruph)—an angel prince set over the element of fire. He is a seraph, as his name denotes, and is another name for Nathaniel. [*Rf. The Sixth* *and Seventh Books of Moses.*] Seruf is also credited with being, in occult works, an angel of the order of force (i.e., virtues) and of the order of seraphim.

Servant of God—the angel Abdiel (*q.v.*). "Servant of God" is the literal meaning of Abdiel, who is so addressed in *Paradise Lost* VI, 29.

Servants (*'ebed*)—a term for God's serving angels in hechaloth and Merkabah lore. [*Rf. 3 Enoch.*]

Serviel—an angel of the 3rd hour of the day, serving under Vaguaniel.

Sesenges(n)-Barpharanges — the term or name of a group of angels, according to the Coptic Christians. [*Rf.* Scholem, *Jewish Gnosticism, Merkabah Mysticism, and Talmudic Tradition,* p. 100.] Also the name of a powerful demonic spirit.

Setchiel—an angel who is served by Turiel in magical conjurations. [*Rf.* Malchus, *The Secret Grimoire of Turiel,* p. 36.]

Seth—one of the 7 archons in the gnostic system. [*Rf. Catholic Encyclopedia,* "Gnosticism."]

Setheus—one of the great celestial powers dwelling in the 6th Heaven. [*Rf.* Malinine, *Revelations of Zostrian;* Doresse, *The Secret Books of the Egyptian Gnostics.*]

Sethlans—one of the Novensiles (who are the 9 great gods of the Etruscans). For a list of the Novensiles, *see* Appendix.

Setphael—in hechaloth lore (*Ma'asseh Merkabah*), an angelic guard of the 1st of the 7 heavenly halls.

Seven Archangels—known as the 7 holy ones who stand around the throne of God and attend Him (Revelation 8:2; *Book of Tobit* 12:15). In Ezra IV and *Enoch I,* the 7 are named: 1. Uriel, 2. Raphael, 3. Raguel, 4. Michael, 5. Sariel or Seraqel, 6. Gabriel, 7. Remiel or Jeremiel. Other lists give Anael, Samael, Zadkiel, Orifiel (in addition to the others already named). *See* also Ezekiel 9:2 for the 6 "men" (i.e., angels) and a 7th, the "man clothed with linen" (Christ) carrying a writer's inkhorn. In horoscopy and hermetics, the

7 great planetary genii (archangels) are: 1. Rampha, genius of Saturn; 2. Pi-Zeus, genius of Jupiter; 3. Ertosi, genius of Mars; 4. Pi-Re, genius of the Sun; 5. Suroth, genius of Venus; 6. Pi-Hermes, genius of Mercury; 7. Pi-Joh, genius of the Moon. [*Rf.* Christian, *The History and Practice of Magic* II, 475.] Camfield, *A Theological Discourse of Angels,* gives the "7 spirits who always stand in the presence of God" (i.e., the angels of the presence) as rulers of the 7 planets, to wit: 1. Zapkiel, over Saturn; 2. Zadkiel, over Jupiter; 3. Camuel, over Mars; 4. Raphael, over the Sun; 5. Haniel, over Venus; 6. Michael, over Mercury; 7. Gabriel, over the Moon. But *see* entry, Seven Olympic Spirits, for the names of others as rulers of these "planets." The 7 Akkadian elemental spirits or deities, which may have been the prototype of the 7 rulers or creators in the cosmology of later cultures, are given as: An (Heaven), Gula (earth), Ud (sun), Im (storm), Istar (moon), Ea or Dara (ocean), En-lil (Hell). In "Angelology and Demonology in Early Judaism" (Manson, *A Companion to the Bible*) W. O. E. Oesterley expresses the belief that "the prototype of the 7 archangels were the 7 planets, all of them Babylonian Deities."

Seven Heavens—in Hebrew terms and lore, the 7 Heavens are designated as follows, along with their governing angels: 1. Shamayim, ruled over by Gabriel; 2. Raqia, ruled over by Zachariel and Raphael; 3. Shehaqim, ruled over by Anahel and three subordinate *sarim*: Jagniel, Rabacyel, and Dalquiel; 4. Machonon, ruled over by Michael; 5. Mathey, ruled over by Sandalphon; 6. Zebul, ruled over by Zachiel, assisted by Zebul (by day) and Sabath (by night); 7. Araboth, ruled over by Cassiel. In *Enoch II,* 8, the Garden of Eden and the Tree of Life are both found in the 3rd Heaven (see in this connection II Corinthians 12:2–3, which speaks of Paul being caught up in the 3rd Heaven). *The Zohar* mentions 390 Heavens and 70,000 worlds. The gnostic Basilides vouched for 365 Heavens; Jellinek (in *Beth Ha-Midrasch*) recalls a legend which tells of 955 Heavens. In *Enoch II* the Heavens number 10. Here the 8th Heaven is called Muzaloth. This Heaven, according to *Hagiga* 12b, is really the 7th Heaven. The 9th Heaven, home of the 12 signs of the zodiac, is called Kukhavim. The 10th, where Enoch saw the "vision of the face of the Lord," is called Aravoth (Hebrew term for the 12 signs of the zodiac). The confusion of the Heavens is clear here from the fact that the signs of the zodiac do not lodge in the Heavens named after them. [*Rf. The Book of the Angel Raziel*; de Abano, *The Heptameron*; Agrippa, *Three Books of Occult Philosophy*.] The notion of 7 Heavens appears in *The Testament of the Twelve Patriarchs* and other Jewish apocrypha, and was familiar to the ancient Persians and Babylonians. The Persians pictured the Almighty in the highest of the 7 Heavens, "seated on a great white throne, surrounded by winged cherubim." The Koran (*sura* 23) also speaks of 7 Heavens.

Seven Holy Ones [Seven Archangels]

Seven Olympic Spirits—according to the grimoires, the 7 Olympic Spirits are: 1. Aratron, who governs the planet Saturn; 2. Bethor, who governs the planet Jupiter; 3. Hagith, who governs the planet Venus; 4. Och, who governs the Sun; 5. Ophiel, who governs the planet Mercury; 6. Phaleg, who governs the planet Mars; 7. Phul, who governs the Moon. [*Rf. The Secret Grimoire of Turiel.*]

Seven Stewards of Heaven—another term for the seven Olympic Spirits (*q.v.*).

Seven Supreme Angels—in the cabala, rulers of the 196 provinces into which Heaven is divided. The sigils of these angels are shown in Cornelius Agrippa's philosophical works and are reproduced in Budge, *Amulets and Talismans*.

Seventh Heaven—the abode of human souls waiting to be born. It is also the seat of God; of Zagzagel, prince of the Torah; and the dwelling place of the seraphim, hayyoth, etc. [*Rf.* Talmud *Hagiga* 12b; *Enoch II*; *The Legends of the Jews* II, 309.] It is in the 7th Heaven, according to the apocalyptic *The Ascension of Isaiah*, that Isaiah has a glimpse of God and the Christ and "hears the Most High dictating the program of his [Christ's] earthly manifestation and return."

Seventh Satan [Hakael]

Seventy-two Names of God—cited in the *Grimoire of Pope Honorius the Great*. Many of these names are identifiable with the names of angels. [*Rf.* Waite, *The Book of Black Magic and of Pacts*, p. 240; Shah, *The Secret Lore of Magic*, p. 261.]

Sgrdtsih—an angel (one of the *nomina barbara*) who "ministers to the son of man," according to M. Gaster, *The Sword of Moses*.

Shabni (or Shabti)—an angel invoked in ceremonial magic rites, as noted in Mathers, *The Greater Key of Solomon*.

Shachmiel—an angel's name found inscribed on an oriental Hebrew charm (*kamea*) for warding off evil. [*Rf.* Schrire, *Hebrew Amulets*.]

Shadfiel—one of the numerous angelic guards of the gates of the North Wind. [*Rf. Ozar Midrashim* II, 316.]

Shaftiel—an angel who rules in Hell. He is lord of the shadow of death and his special province is in the 3rd lodge of the 7 divisions in which the underworld is divided. He punishes 10 nations "for cause." [*Rf. Baraita de Massechet Gehinnom*; *Midrash Konen*; *Brewer's Dictionary of Phrase and Fable*, "Hell."]

Shaftiyah—one of the many names of the angel Metatron.

Shahakiel (Shachaqiel)—an angelic prince resident in the 4th Heaven. According to *3 Enoch*, Shahakiel is one of the 7 archangels as well as eponymous head of the order of Shahakim. [*Rf.* Charles, *Apocrypha and Pseudepigrapha of the Old Testament*.]

Shahakim—in rabbinic lore, an order of angels in the celestial hierarchy. [*Rf. Jewish Encyclopedia*.]

Shahariel—an angelic guard of the 2nd Heaven, as listed in *Pirke Hechaloth*.

Shahiel—an angel's name found inscribed on an oriental charm (*kamea*) for warding off evil. [*Rf.* Schrire, *Hebrew Amulets*.]

Shahrivar(i)—the angel of August in ancient Persian lore. Shahrivar also governed the 4th day of the month. [*Rf.* Hyde, *Historia Religionis Veterum Persarum.*]

Shaitan (Satan)—one of the fallen angels in Arabic lore. Shaitan is a cognate term for Iblis (*q.v.*). In the Koran, *sura* 27, 24, Shaitan (Satan) induces the Queen of Sheba and her people to adore the sun instead of Allah.

Shaitans (shedeem, sheytans, shedim, mazikeen)—evil spirits in Hebrew and Arabic mythology; they have cock's feet. In rabbinic lore, the shaitans are male demons, the female being known as lilin. [*Rf.* Talmud *Berachoth*; Langton, *Essentials of Demonology*; Oesterley's article in Manson, *A Companion to the Bible.*]

Shakti—in Vedic lore the bride of Shiva. Shakti is the prototype of the Shekinah (*q.v.*).

Shakziel—an angel with dominion over water insects. [*Rf. The Book of Enoch.*]

Shalgiel—an angel with dominion over snow. [*Rf.* Ginzberg, *The Legends of the Jews* I, 140.]

Shalhevita—in hechaloth lore (*Ma'asseh Merkabah*), an angelic guard stationed at the 7th heavenly hall.

Shalkiel and **Shalmiel**—angels whose names are found inscribed on an oriental charm (*kamea*) for warding off evil. [*Rf.* Schrire, *Hebrew Amulets.*]

Shaltiel—an angel's name inscribed (along with the names of Michael, Raphael, Uriel) on earthen bowls found in the Euphrates Valley and invoked as a charm. [*Rf.* Boswell, "The Evolution of Angels and Demons."]

Shamain (Shamayim)—a name for the 1st Heaven, of which the chief ruler is the angel Mikael (Michael) or Qemuel (Kemuel).

Shamchazai, Shamhazai, Shamiazaz [Semyaza]

Shamdan (Ashamdon)—the angel-demon who mated with Naamah, "lovely sister of Tubal-cain, who led the angels astray with her beauty." The fruit of the union of Shamdan and Naamah was Asmodeus (*q.v.*). [*Rf. The Legends of the Jews* I, 150–151.] According to *Bereshith Rabba*, 36:3,

A benevolent genie (in Assyro-Babylonian mythology) holding in his hand the pail of lustral water and the pine cone with which he sprinkles the water to keep off evil spirits. This genie was the guardian of the gate of Sargon's palace. A work of the 8th century B.C.E., now in the Louvre. From *Larousse Encyclopedia of Mythology.*

Shamdan was Noah's partner in planting a vineyard, which led to Noah's drinking, and being "uncovered within his tent," an incident related in Genesis 9:20–22.

Sham(m)iel (Shamael)—master of heavenly song and divine herald. (In Jewish legend, Metatron and Radueriel are likewise denoted masters of heavenly song.) Shamiel is invoked in Syriac spellbinding charms, along with Michael, Harshiel, Nuriel, and other angels of similar rank. [*Rf. The Book of Protection.*] In the *Ozar Midrashim*, Shamiel (as distinguished from Shamael) is listed among the angelic guards of the gates of the South Wind.

Shamlon—a "prince over all the angels and the Caesars," according to *The Greater Key of Solomon.*

Shamriel—in occultism, designated a guardian angel who may be invoked as a charm against the evil eye. [*Rf.* Schrire, *Hebrew Amulets*; Trachtenberg, *Jewish Magic and Superstition.*]

Shams-ed-Din ("sun of the faith")—one of the 7 Yezidic archangels invoked in prayer by the devil worshippers. For the names of the 6 other archangels, *see* Appendix.

Shamsha—like Shamlon, a "prince over all the angels and the Caesars."

Shams(h)iel ("light of day," "mighty sun of God")—a ruler of the 4th Heaven and prince of Paradise; also guardian angel of Eden (Eden being the earthly paradise). It was Shamshiel who conducted Moses around the heavenly Paradise when the Lawgiver, according to legend, visited the upper regions while he was still in the flesh. It was to Shamshiel that the treasures of David and Solomon were turned over by the scribe Hilkiah. In *The Zohar*, Shamshiel is head of 365 legions of spirits (angels). He crowns prayers, just as other great angels do, and accompanies them to the 5th Heaven. In *The Book of Protection*, Shamshiel is grouped with Michael, Nuriel, and Sarphiel as a spellbinding power. In *The Book of Jubilees* he is one of the watchers or grigori (*q.v.*), and is equated with Samsapeel. In *Enoch I* he rates as a fallen angel who "taught the signs of the sun." According to *The Zohar* (Numbers 154b) he served as one of the 2 chief aides to Uriel (the other aide being Hasdiel) when Uriel bore his standard in battle.

Shaphiel—a ruling prince of the 3rd Heaven sharing the post with Baradiel (*q.v.*).

Shariel [Asderel]

Sharka'il—in Arabic lore, a guardian angel invoked in rites of exorcism. [*Rf.* Hughes, *A Dictionary of Islam,* "Angels."]

Sharlaii—in the Talmud, an angel invoked for the curing of cutaneous disorders. [*Rf.* Talmud *Shabbath,* fol. 67.]

Sharshiyah—one of the many names of the angel Metatron.

Shashmasrihiel Jhvhh—an angel prince of the hosts of X (one of the *nomina barbara*) cited in M. Gaster, *The Sword of Moses.*

Shastaniel—one of the numerous angelic guards of the gates of the South Wind. [*Rf.* *Ozar Midrashim* II, 316.]

Shateiel—angel of silence, to be compared with Duma (*q.v.*). Shateiel probably inspired the creation of the Greek God Sigalion (if, indeed, it was not the other way around). *Cf.* also Tacita, Roman goddess of silence, and Harpocratos, son of Isis, who was a god of silence. [*Rf.* Woodcock, *Short Dictionary of Mythology.*]

Shathniel—an angel's name found inscribed on an oriental charm (*kamea*) for warding off evil. [*Rf.* Schrire, *Hebrew Amulets.*]

Shatqiel—in *3 Enoch* (Hebrew Book of Enoch) Shatqiel figures among the 7 great archangels, and as a guardian prince of the 5th Heaven. In *Hechaloth Rabbati,* he is a guard of the 4th Heaven. [*Rf.* *Ozar Midrashim* I, 116.]

Shaviel—one of the 7 angelic guards of the 1st Heaven, as noted in *Hechaloth Rabbati.*

Shavzriel—in hechaloth lore (*Ma'asseh Merkabah*), an angelic guard stationed at the 2nd heavenly hall.

Shebniel—one of the 70 childbed amulet angels. [*Rf.* *The Book of the Angel Raziel.*]

Sheburiel—chief porter of the 3rd Heaven, as designated in *Pirke Hechaloth.*

Shedu—a Babylonian protecting household spirit, invoked in conjuring rites. [*Rf.* Mackenzie, *Myths of Babylonia and Assyria*; Trachtenberg, *Jewish Magic and Superstition,* p. 156.]

Shegatsiel—an angelic prince of the hosts of X (i.e., God). [*Rf.* M. Gaster, *The Sword of Moses.*]

Sheikh Bakra and **Sheikh Ism**—two of the 7 archangels in Yezidic religion invoked in prayer by the devil worshippers. [*See* Appendix for the names of the other 5 Yezidic archangels.]

Sheireil [Sathariel]

Shekinah (Hebrew, *shachan*, meaning "to reside"—Schechinah, Matrona, etc.)—the female manifestation of God in man, the divine *inwohnung* (indwelling). Also, the "bride of the Lord," compatible with the shakti of Shiva. The expression "the Shekinah rests" is used as a paraphrase for "God dwells." In Genesis 48:16 "the Angel which redeemed me from all evil," uttered by Israel (Jacob), applies to the Shekinah, according to *The Zohar* (Balak 187a). In the New Testament sense, the Shekinah is the glory emanating from God, His effulgence. The passage in Matthew 18:20 is translated by C. W. Emmet (in Hastings, *Dictionary of the Bible*) to read: "when two sit together and are occupied with the word of the Law, the Shekinah is with him." As interpreted by Rabbi Johanan (*Midrash Rabba*; Exodus), Michael is the glory of the Shekinah. The Shekinah is the liberating Angel, manifesting in her male aspect as Metatron. In the cabala, she is the 10th sefira Malkuth, otherwise the Queen. The creation of the world was, according to *The Zohar* (suppl.), the work of the Shekinah. Here, too, the Shekinah is spoken of as "abiding in the 12 holy chariots and the 12 supernal hayyoth." Elsewhere in *The Zohar* (Balak-Numbers 187a) she is mentioned as a messenger from on high who, when she first appeared to Moses, was called an angel, just as she was called by Jacob. In *The Zohar* (Exodus 51a) she is "the way of the Tree of Life" and the "angel of the Lord." Maimonides in *Moreh Nebuchim* regarded the Shekinah as an intermediary between God and the world, or as a periphrasis for God. [*Rf. Universal Jewish Encyclopaedia*, vol. 9, p. 501.] The Shekinah has been identified with the Holy Ghost and the Epinoia of the gnostic Valentinus. Of her it has been said (Waite, *The Holy Kabbalah*) "Behold, I send an angel before thee, to keep thee in the way" (Exodus 23:20), which has also been applied to Metatron and John the Baptist, "the forerunner angel." According to legend (Ginz-berg, *The Legends of the Jews* II, 148 and 200), Aaron died by a kiss from the Shekinah. In the same source (II, 260) it is related that Abraham caused the Shekinah to come down from the 2nd Heaven. And Talmud tells us that when God drove Adam out of the earthly paradise, the Shekinah remained behind "enthroned above a cherub under the Tree of Life, her splendor being 65,000 times brighter than the sun," and that this radiance "made all upon whom it fell exempt from disease"; and, further, that then "neither insects nor demons could come nigh unto such to do them harm." An account somewhat at variance with the foregoing is given in Scholem's two works: *Major Trends in Jewish Mysticism* and *Jewish Gnosticism, Merkabah Mysticism, and Talmudic Tradition*, where it is reported that the Shekinah was sent into exile on Adam's fall and that "to lead the Shekinah back to God and to unite her with Him is the true purpose of the Torah." A reference to the dwelling place of the Shekinah occurs in *Canticles Rabba* 6: "The original abode of the Shekinah was among the tahtonim [that is, among the lower ones: human beings, earth]. When Adam sinned, it [the abode] ascended to the 1st Heaven. With Cain's sin, it ascended to the 2nd Heaven. With Enoch's, to the 3rd. With the generation of the Flood, to the 4th. With the generation of the Tower of Babel, to the 5th. With the Sodomites, to the 6th. With the sin of the Egyptians in the days of Abraham, to the 7th." Corresponding to these, there arose 7 righteous men who brought the Shekinah back to earth again. They were Abraham, Isaac, Jacob, Levi, Kehath (Levi's son and Moses' grandfather), Amram, and Moses. A haggadah about the Shekinah is that she hovers over all conjugal unions between Jewish husbands and wives and blesses such unions with her presence. [*See* Talmud *Shabbath* 55b; *Bereshith Rabba* 98, 4, etc. In this reference, *cf.* the Roman goddess Pertunda, presider over the marriage couch.]

Shekiniel—angelic guard of the 4th Heaven. [*Rf. Ozar Midrashim* I, 116.]

Shelemial—angelic guard of the 3rd Heaven. [*Rf. Pirke Hechaloth.*]

Shelviel—angel of the order of tarshishim. [*Rf. Ozar Midrashim* I, 67.]

Shem ("name") (Melchizedec)—in Manichaean lore, "one of the great envoys of Heaven to whom the angels revealed the divine wisdom." In Mandaean theology, Shem is Shum-Kushta. [*Rf.* Mandaean *Book of John the Baptist*; Doresse, *The Secret Books of the Egyptian Gnostics*, p. 155.]

Shemael (Kemuel, Camael, Shemuiel—"name of God")—the mighty angel who stands at the windows of Heaven listening for the songs of praise ascending from synagogues and houses of study of the Jews. He is the archon in Sholem, *Major Trends in Jewish Mysticism*. The name derives from the 1st word of the Hebrew song of praise.

Shemhazai [Semyaza]

Shemmiel [Shemael]

Shepherd—one of the 6 angels of repentance, equated with Phanuel (*q.v.*). It was Shepherd who dictated the vision to Hermas. [*Rf. The Shepherd of Hermas* II and III.] In the work just referred to, however, another Shepherd is spoken of: "a cruel and implacable Shepherd" and "one of the holy angels appointed for the punishment of sinners." He is not named. Moses was known in later Jewish literature as "the faithful shepherd" and Jesus applied the title "good shepherd" to himself in John 10:11. [*Rf.* T. Gaster, *The Dead Sea Scriptures*, p. 321.] *Note*: *The Shepherd of Hermas* was at one time quoted as sacred Scripture by Origen, Irenaeus, pseudo-Cyprian, etc.

Shepherd of Hermas [Phanuel]

Shetel—one of 3 ministering angels (the other 2 being Aebel and Anush), whom God appointed to serve Adam. According to *Yalkut Reubeni* and *The Book of Adam and Eve*, the 3 angels not only "roasted meat" for Adam, but also "cooled his wine."

Sheviel (Shaviel)—an angelic porter at the 1st Heaven, cited in *Pirke Hechaloth*.

Sheziem—an angel invoked in cabalistic rites. [*Rf. The Sixth and Seventh Books of Moses*.]

Shimshiel—an angelic guard of the gates of the East Wind.

Shinanin (Shin'an)—a high class of angels, "the shinanin of the fire," adduced from Psalms 68:18 and referred to in *3 Enoch*. Myriads of these shinanin descended from Heaven to be present at the revelation on Sinai. [*Rf. Pesikta Rabba*.] According to *The Zohar* (1:18b) "myriads of thousands of shin'an are on the chariot of God." Chief of the order is Zadkiel or Sidquiel. Compare with the ofanim. [*Rf.* Psalms 68:18; Scholem, *Major Trends in Jewish Mysticism*; Mathers, *The Kabbalah Unveiled*, p. 26.] "The 6th sefira, tifereth (tiphereth) is represented among the angels of the shinanim," says C. D. Ginsburg, in *The Essenes and The Kabbalah*.

Shinial—one of the 64 angel wardens of the 7 celestial halls. [*Rf. Pirke Hechaloth*.]

Shitimichum (Shitinichus Kitagnifai)—in M. Gaster, *The Sword of Moses*, Shitimichum (one of the *nomina barbara*) is among the 13 angel chiefs appointed by God to the sword.

Shlasiel A' (Shlotiel A' and other variants)—an angel prince of the hosts of X (God), cited in M. Gaster, *The Sword of Moses*.

Shlomiel—an angelic guard of the 3rd Heaven. [*Rf. Ozar Midrashim* I, 116.]

Shmuiel (Samael)—"chief of all the angels and all the 10 classes who spoke to Solomon and gave him the key to the mysteries," according to a citation in Gollancz, *Clavicula Salomonis*.

Shoel—one of the 64 angel wardens of the 7 celestial halls. [*Rf. Pirke Hechaloth*.]

Shoftiel ("judge of God")—one of the 7 angels of punishment. [*Rf.* Jellinek, *Beth ha-Midrasch*; *Maseket Gan Edem and Gehinnom*; *Jewish Encyclopedia*, I, 593.]

Shokad—one of the 64 angel wardens of the 7 celestial halls. [*Rf. Pirke Hechaloth*.]

Shomrom (Shunaron)—"a prince over all the angels and Caesars," according to Mathers, *The Greater Key of Solomon*.

Shosoriyah—one of the many names of the angel Metatron.

Shriniel—an angelic guard of the 4th Heaven. [*Rf. Pirke Hechaloth.*]

Shtukial—one of the 64 angel wardens of the 7 celestial halls. [*Rf. Pirke Hechaloth.*]

Shufiel—an angel invoked in Syriac conjuring rites. Grouped with Gabriel, Michael, Harshiel, and other spellbinding angels. [*Rf. The Book of Protection*; Budge, *Amulets and Talismans.*]

Shunaron—"a prince over all the angels and Caesars," so Shunaron is ranked in Mathers, *The Greater Key of Solomon.*

Sialul—the genius of prosperity. In de Abano, *The Heptameron*, Sialul is included among the spirits of the 7th hour, and may be invoked during that hour.

Sidqiel—in *3 Enoch*, governor of the planet Venus and prince of the order of ofanim or shinanim (the ofanim being the Hebrew equivalent of the order of thrones, and the shinanim of an order close to the seraphim in rank).

Sidriel (Pazriel)—prince of the 1st Heaven and one of the 7 archangels in the Enoch listings.

Sieme—in the cabala, an angel of part of an hour, specifically 3:20 p.m. He is of the order of virtues and is called "ange du Seigneur" in H.D.'s (Hilda Doolittle's) poem "Sagesse." Sieme's corresponding angel is Asaliah.

Sigron—in hechaloth lore, a name for Metatron "when he shuts the doors of prayers (doors through which a man's prayers are let into Heaven). When the doors are opened, Metatron is then called Pihon." [*Rf. 3 Enoch*, 48.]

Sihail—"and God sent 2 angels, Sihail and Anas, and 4 Evangelists to take hold of the 12 fever demons [all female] and beat them with fiery rods." The tale is told in a 12th-century Ms. in the British Museum and is retold by M. Gaster, *Studies and Texts in Folklore* II, 1030. Gaster believes that Sihail is merely another form for Michail (Michael) and Anas is St. Anne, here turned into an angel.

Sihon—grandson of the fallen angel Semyaza and brother of Og (*q.v.*). [*Rf.* Jung, *Fallen Angels in Jewish, Christian and Mohammedan Literature.*]

Sij-ed-Din ("power of mercy")—one of the 7 archangels in Yezidic religious lore, invoked in prayer.

Sikiel—an angel of the sirocco. Sikiel is cited in the *Sefer Yetzirah* (*Book of Formation*). [*Rf.* Budge, *Amulets and Talismans.*] In *Ozar Midrashim* II, 316, Sikiel is a guardian angel of the gates of the West Wind.

Sila—an angel of power; also the angel of an hour invoked in cabalistic rites. [*Rf.* H.D.'s (Hilda Doolittle's) poem "Sagesse"; Ambelain, *La Kabbale Pratique.*]

Silat (Tilath, Feluth)—in the *Grimorium Verum*, an angel invoked in goetic ritual. In Mohammedan lore, Silat is a female demon. [*Rf. Jewish Encyclopedia*, p. 521.]

Silmai (Shelmai)—in Mandaean religious lore, one of two guardian spirits (*uthri*) of the river Jordan; the other *uthra* is Nidbai.

Simapesiel—one of the fallen angels in Enoch listings.

Simiel (Chamuel, Semibel)—one of the 7 archangels. However, at a Church Council in Rome, 745 C.E., Simiel was reprobated (along with Uriel, Raguel, and other high-ranking angels) as a false or evil spirit and not to be venerated. [*Rf.* Heywood, *The Hierarchy of the Blessèd Angels.*] At the Council of Laodicia (343–381? C.E.), to name angels was expressly forbidden (canon 35). Josephus mentions, as among the religious rites of the Essenes, the taking of oaths not to reveal the names of angels. [*Rf.* Trachtenberg, *Jewish Magic and Superstition*, p. 89.]

Simkiel—chief of the angels of destruction appointed by God to deal with the wicked on earth. [*See* Za'arfiel.] According to *3 Enoch*, Simkiel has the function not only of executing judgment on man but also of purifying him.

Simulator—in Solomonic magic, an angel invoked in the conjuration of Ink and Colors.

Sinui—an amulet angel invoked in Mosaic incantation rites when a woman is pregnant. [*See* Sennoi.*]*

Siona—a seraph in Klopstock, *The Messiah.*

Sipur—one of the 3 seraphim (the other 2 being Sepher and Saphar) through whom the world is said to have been created. [*Rf.* Waite, *Book of Formation.*]

Sirbiel—one of the angelic princes of the Merkabah, as noted in *3 Enoch* and *Hechaloth Rabbati.*

Sirushi (Surush Ashu, Sarush, Sraosha, Ashu)—the angel of Paradise in ancient Persian lore; also the "master of announcements." [*Rf. The Dabistan,* p. 144.]

Sisera—genius of desire; one of the genii to be invoked during the 2nd hour, according to Apollonius of Tyana, *The Nuctemeron.* In the Old Testament (Judges 4), Sisera is a general slain by Jael "with the aid of the stars and the angels."

Sislau—genius of poisons and one of the genii of the 4th hour. [*Rf.* Apollonius of Tyana, *The Nuctemeron.*]

Sitael—a seraph invoked to overcome adversity. He rules the nobility and is one of the 72 angels of the zodiac; also one of the 72 angels that bear the name of God Shemhamphorae. See H.D.'s poem "Sagesse" and Ambelain, *La Kabbale Pratique,* p. 260, where Sitael's sigil is shown.

Sith—angel of an hour (6 to 7 o'clock); a regent ruling a planet. Sith's corresponding angel is Nelchael. [*Rf.* H.D.'s poem "Sagesse"; Ambelain, *La Kabbale Pratique.*]

Sithacer—corresponding angel for Seheiah (*q.v.*).

Sithriel—a name by which Metatron is called "when he hides the children of the world under his wings to preserve them from the angels of destruction." [*Rf. 3 Enoch,* 48.]

Sitiel [Sitael]

Sitra Kadisha—in the *Tosefta* ii, 69b, a holy spirit. He is contrasted with Sitra Ahara (unclean spirit). [*Rf. The Talmudic Anthology,* p. 115.]

Sitriel—in the listing of Moses of Burgos, Sitriel is 3rd of the 10 unholy sefiroth.

Sittacibor—an angel conjured up in Wax exorcisms. [*Rf.* Mathers, *The Greater Key of Solomon.*]

Sittiah—like Sittacibor, an angel conjured up in Wax exorcism. [*Rf.* de Abano, *The Heptameron;* Mathers, *The Greater Key of Solomon.*]

Six Highest Angelic (or Philonic) Powers —these 6 highest angelic powers correspond to, or are derived from, the 6 amesha spentas that surround the throne of God (in Zoroastrianism, God being Ahura-Mazda). In *Baruch III* the 6 highest angelic powers are: 1. divine logos (identified by Philo as Michael); 2. creative power; 3. sovereign power; 4. mercy; 5. legislation; 6. punitive power.

Sixth Angel, The—in Revelation, the 6th angel (not named) is one of the 7 angels of wrath that "loosed the 4 angels which were bound in the great river Euphrates" and that were "prepared to slay the 3rd part of men."

Sixth Heaven, The—in Islamic lore, the abode of the guardian angel of Heaven and earth, "half snow, half fire." The angel is not identified by name.

Sizajasel—in ceremonial magic, an angel representing or governing the sign of Sagittarius in the zodiac. [*Rf.* Waite, *The Lemegeton.*]

Sizouze—in ancient Persian mythology, the angel who presided over prayers. [*Cf.* Akatriel; Metatron; Sandalphon.]

Skd Huzi [Soqed Hozi]

Sktm—one of 14 conjuring angels of the Sword as cited in M. Gaster, *The Sword of Moses.* Sktm is also one of the ineffable names of God.

Slattery (fictional)—an angel referred to in the Introduction by Dixon Wecter to Mark Twain's *Report from Paradise.* It is in an unprinted fragment of Twain's Stormfield cycle that Slattery appears. In that fragment, Slattery is reported to have witnessed the creation of Man.

Smal (Sammael)—angel of death and of poison, whose wife, Eisheth Zenunim, is the woman of whoredom. The 2 together, united, are known as the beast Chioa. [*Rf.* Mathers, *The Kabbalah Unveiled.*]

Smandriel [Samandiriel]

Smat—corresponding angel for Mebahiah (*q.v.*). In the cabala, Smat shares with Mebahiah in exercising dominion over morals and religion.

Smeliel—in Lenormant, *Chaldean Magic*, the spirit of the sun. His corresponding intelligence is Nagiel.

Smnglf [Samangaluf]

Smoel [Sammael]

Sngotiqtel—an angel that ministers to the son of man [*Rf.* M. Gaster, *The Sword of Moses*].

Sniel—one of the 70 childbed amulet angels. [*Rf. The Book of the Angel Raziel*; Budge, *Amulets and Talismans.*]

Sochiel—one of the ruling archangels of the earthly triplicities governing the 360 degrees of the zodiac, as reported in Waite, *The Lemegeton.*

Sociable Spirit, The—the angel Raphael is so referred to by Milton in *Paradise Lost* V.

Socodiah (Socohiah)—an angel's name inscribed on the 1st pentacle of the planet Venus. [*Rf.* Shah, *The Secret Lore of Magic.*]

Sodiel—in *3 Enoch*, 17, a ruling prince of the 3rd Heaven.

Sodyah—in hechaloth lore, an angel who assists Metatron (*q.v.*) in reciting the *Shema.* [*Rf.* introd., *3 Enoch.*]

Sofiel—an angel who ministers to garden fruit and vegetables. [*Rf.* M. Gaster, *The Sword of Moses.*]

Sofriel (Sopher, Sopheriel)—an angelic bookkeeper appointed over the records of the living and the dead. There are two Sofriels: Sofriel Memith and Sofriel Mehayye. They are bearers of God's name (YHWH). [*Rf. The Zohar; 3 Enoch.*]

Hebrew amulet inscribed with the hexagon of Solomon and Shaddai (a name for God). From Budge, *Amulets and Talismans.*

Sohemne—an angel of the Seal. [*Rf. The Sixth and Seventh Books of Moses.*]

Sokath—a spirit of the sun, of which "planet" the angel Nakhiel is the presiding intelligence, according to Paracelsus in his doctrine of Talismans. Sokath apparently shares the post with Nakhiel or alternates with him. [*Rf.* Christian, *The History and Practice of Magic* I.]

Solmis—a great celestial luminary cited in the gnostic *Revelations of Zostrian.*

Soluzen—the name of an angel inscribed (in green) on the pentagon of Solomon, Fig. 156, in Waite, *The Lemegeton.*

Somcham—one of the numerous angelic guards of the gates of the West Wind.

Soncas (Soneas)—an angel of the 5th Heaven, ruler of Tuesday. He is to be invoked from the west. [*Rf.* Abano, *The Heptameron*; Barrett, *The Magus.*]

Song-Uttering Choirs—a class of singing angels under the direction of Tagas. The Sallisim (*q.v.*) were a part of these choirs and inhabited the 5th Heaven (Maon). [*Rf.* Talmud *Hagiga.*] When the Song-Uttering Choirs failed to perform the Qedussa (trisagion) at the right time, they were consumed by fire.

Sonitas—an angel serving in the 5th Heaven. [*Rf. The Sixth and Seventh Books of Moses.*]

Sonneillon (Sonnillon)—an angel, now fallen,

once of the order of thrones. He is cited as one of 3 "devils" that possessed the body of the notorious 16th-century nun, Sister Louise Capeau (or Capelle). [*Rf.* Michaelis, *Admirable History of the Possession and Conversion of a Penitent Woman.*]

Son of God—an angel so called in *II Esdras* (*IV* Esdras). The title is commonly applied to Jesus.

Sons of God—a term in Genesis 6 commonly interpreted to mean angels. The Sons of God, having consorted with mortal women, became fallen angels. This was the view of Josephus, a view that has persisted for many centuries, even down to our own times, although other interpretations have not been wanting. Milton thought (*Paradise Regained* II) that these "false-titled sons of God were fallen angels." *Cf.* Job 38:7, "When the morning stars sang together and the sons of God shouted for joy." In the cabala, the term stands for "a distinctive order of celestial beings (the *bene elohim*), answering to the 8th sephira [Hod]," says C. D. Ginsburg in *The Essenes/The Kabbalah*, p. 92. Apropos of what has just been said of "other interpretations," it should be noted that Simeon ben Yohai, alleged author of *The Zohar*, cursed anyone, particularly his disciples, who interpreted Genesis 6 as representing the sons of God "having sexual organs and committing fornication with the daughters of men." [*Rf. The New Schaff-Herzog Encyclopedia of Religious Knowledge*, "Angels."]

Sons of Heaven—angels, according to *The Manual of Discipline*, who sit at the divine council deliberations. In Mansoor *The Thanksgiving Hymns*, the term connotes simply good angels.

Sons of Princes—an order of angels, "one of 10 classes in Talmud and Targum," says Voltaire in his "Of Angels, Genii, and Devils." Literally speaking, there can be no "sons of princes" (sons used here in the sense of offspring and princes in the sense of angels), since angels, unlike demons and earthly creatures, do not reproduce their kind.

Sophar (fictional)—in Anatole France, *Revolt of the Angels*, a fallen angel who once kept the treasures in Heaven for the god Ialdabaoth. In his

earthly guise, Sophar is Max Everdingen, a banker.

Sopher, Sopheriel [Sofriel]

Sopheriel Yhwh Mehayye and **Sopheriel Yhwh Memith** [Sofriel]

Sophia [Pistis Sophia]

Sophiel—angel of the 4th pentacle of the moon. In Jewish cabala, Sophiel is the intelligence of Jupiter (the corresponding angel here being Zadykiel). [*Rf.* Lenormant, *Chaldean Magic*, p. 26.]

Soqed Hozi (Shoqed Chozi, Skd Huzi, etc.)—an angel prince of the Merkabah, keeper of the divine balances, and one of the 4 angels appointed by God to the Sword. [*Rf. 3 Enoch*; M. Gaster, *The Sword of Moses*.]

Sorath—an evil power, bearer of the mysterious number 666, which is also applied cabalistically to the Emperor Nero. [*Rf. Apocalypse of John*.] In talismanic magic, Sorath is the spirit of the sun. See *The Magus* II, 147.

Sorush—to the ancient Persians, Gabriel, "giver of souls." The Magi held that, on Judgment Day, 2 angels, Sorush and Mihr, will stand on the bridge called *al Sirat* (which is finer than a hair and sharper than the edge of a sword) and examine every person crossing. Mihr, representing divine mercy and holding a balance in his hand, will weigh the actions performed during the person's lifetime. If found worthy, the person will be permitted to pass on to Paradise. Otherwise he will be handed over to Sorush, representing divine justice, who will hurl him into Hell. [*Rf.* Sale, *The Koran*, "Preliminary Discourse," p. 64.]

Sosol—an angel invoked in ceremonial magic rites. He represents or governs the sign of Scorpio in the zodiac. [*Rf.* Waite, *The Lemegeton*.]

Sother or **Sother As(h)iel**—prosecuting angel prince, serving the throne of divine judgment; a great hierarch of the Merkabah. Sother is 7,000 parasangs tall. In the cabala he marries Sophia in a heavenly union. In gnostic lore he is another name for God. According to *3 Enoch*, "Every angelprince who goes out or enters before the Shekinah, does so only by Sother's permission." He has been equated with the luminary Armogen. The name has the meaning of "who stirs up the fire of God."

Sothis (Sotis)—angel of an hour. [*Rf.* H.D.'s poem "Sagesse"; Ambelain, *La Kabbale Pratique*.]

Sovereignty—one of the angelic orders, according to an interpretation of I Corinthians 15:24 where Paul speaks of Christ's doing away with "all sovereignty, authority and power" (in the Confraternity edition of The New Testament). The King James version gives "rule" in lieu of sovereignty.

Sparks—referring to sparks, Voltaire in "Of Angels, Genii, and Devils" says they are "an order of angels in Talmud and Targum." The sparks are sometimes included among the 9 (or 10 or 12) orders when equated with the tarshishim (i.e., "brilliant ones") or with the splendors (*q.v.*).

Spendarmoz [Ishpan Darmaz]

Sphener—in occultism, the name of a celestial power invoked to combat Mardero, a demon of disease. [*Rf.* Shah, *The Secret Lore of Magic*, p. 223.]

Spheres [Galgallim]

Sphinxes—in Mathers, *The Kabbalah Unveiled*, where the reference is to the *Apocalypse of John*, the sphinxes are mentioned as an alternate term for the kerubim of Ezekiel's vision (Ezekiel I, 10ff.).

Spirit—any angel or demon is a spirit, and a pure one. Man is an impure spirit. God is divine spirit. [*See* Introduction.]

Spirit of Discord—in Judges 9:23 we learn that "God sent a spirit of discord between Abimelech and the men of Schechem." Such a spirit (called "an evil spirit" in some versions of Judges 9) is evil only in the causative sense. Since he serves God, the spirit of discord is without taint.

Spirit of Fornication (Angel of Lust)—*See* Pharzuph.

Spirit of Ill-Will—an angel and envoy of God, as in I Kings 18:10–11, where it is reported that

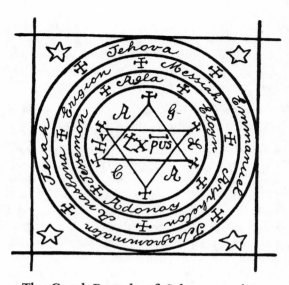

The Grand Pentacle of Solomon used in evoking and dismissing spirits. From Waite, *The Book of Ceremonial Magic*.

this spirit from God "came upon Saul and he prophesied in the midst of his house. And David played . . . as at other times. And Saul held a spear in his hand. And threw it, thinking to nail David to the wall."

Spirit of Jealousy—an angel and envoy of God, as in Numbers 5:14: "If the spirit of jealousy stir up the husband against his wife," etc.

Spirit of Knowledge—a term used in Mansoor, *The Thanksgiving Hymns*, to denote an angel, presumably of the order of cherubim.

Spirit of Lying—an angel and envoy of God, as in I Kings 22:22: "And I will be a lying spirit in the mouth of all his prophets."

Spirit of Perversion [Angel of Darkness]

Spirit of Whoredom—mentioned in Hosea 4, 12. [*See* Angel of Lust.]

Spiritus Dei—"the breath of God," an expression used by Lanctantius to denote an angel. [*Rf.* Schneweis, *Angels and Demons According to Lactantius*.]

Splenditenes—in Manicheanism, a "world-supporting angel." He supports the heavens on his back. [*See* Omophorus.] Augustine mentions Splenditenes in his *Contra Faustum* XV, and describes him as bearing 6 faces and mouths "and glittering with light." Bar-Khonai in the *Book of Scholia* calls Splenditenes the "ornament of Splendor." He appears in Mithraic monuments and is believed to be the prototype of the Greek Atlas. [*Rf.* Manichean *Hymn of the Soul*.]

Splendors—another name for the tarshishim (*q.v.*). Equated with the virtues. Alfred de Vigny in his poem "Eloa" mentions splendors (along with ardors and guards) as an order in the celestial hierarchy.

Spugliguel—an angel who serves as the head of the sign of Spring. [*Rf.* de Abano, *The Heptameron*; Barrett, *The Magus* II.]

Sraosha (Srosh, Sirush, Serosh, etc.)—a Persian angel who, it is claimed, set the world in motion. Sraosha is one of the amesha spentas (the 7th), otherwise one of the yazatas. In Zoroastrianism, he is the angel who bears the soul aloft on death. The red chrysanthemum is his emblem. [*Rf. Vendidad*, 18, in *The Sacred Books of the East*.] In Manichean lore, Sraosha is the "angel of obedience," the "fiend-smiter," who judges the dead. As Sirushi he is the angel of Paradise and "master of announcements." [*Rf.* Legge, *Forerunners and Rivals of Christianity* II, p. 327.]

Sro—corresponding angel for Nemamiah (*q.v.*).

Ssakmakiel—with another spirit called Archer, Ssakmakiel governs the sign of the Water Bearer (Aquarius) in the zodiac. [*Rf.* Levi, *Transcendental Magic*.]

Ssnialiah—in M. Gaster, *The Sword of Moses*, one of the 14 great conjuring angels.

Sstiel YHWH—one of the 8 great angel princes of the Merkabah. In *3 Enoch*, Sstiel outranks in eminence the angel Metatron, who must dismount whenever he encounters Sstiel on the crystal highways. In Ginzberg, *The Legends of the Jews* I, where a herald proclaims Metatron as chief of princes, the exception is made of "eight august and exalted princes that bear My [i.e., His] name." Sstiel is one of these 8. Others would

be Anafiel (Aufiel, Anpiel), N'Zuriel, Akatriel, Gallisur, the two Sofriels, and Radueriel.

Stalwarts—another term for one of the angelic orders. [*Rf. Book of Hymns* III, referred to by T. Gaster in *The Dead Sea Scriptures*, p. 341.]

Standards—a term for an angelic order employed by Milton in *Paradise Lost* V, 590, where the angel Raphael speaks of "Standards, and Gonfalons [that] . . . for distinction serve/Of Hierarchies, of Orders."

Stars—in Biblical lore, stars and planets were regarded as messengers, angels, in the service of God. [*Rf.* Judges 5:20; Job 38:7: "when the morning stars sang together, and all the sons of God shouted for joy."] Caird, *Principalities and Powers*, observes that the stars "were included in Yahweh's angelic retinue."

Stimulator—an angel invoked in the exorcism of Ink. [*Rf. Grimorium Verum*.]

Strateia—an angelic host, as mentioned in

A **talisman** reputed to have the power of causing the stars to fall from heaven. From Waite, *The Book of Ceremonial Magic*.

Pesikta Rabbati. [*Rf. Jewish Encyclopedia*, "Angelology," p. 585.]

Strempsuchos [Astrompsuchos]

Striel—an angelic guard stationed in one of the 7 great heavenly halls. [*Rf. Pirke Hechaloth*.]

Strong, The—an order of angels, "one of the 10 classes in Talmud and Targum," according to Voltaire, "Of Angels, Genii, and Devils."

Strophaeos—in the gnostic *Paraphrase of Shem*, a mysterious entity to whom the secrets of Creation were revealed.

Sturbiel—an angel of the 4th hour of the day, serving under Vachmiel. [*Rf.* Waite, *The Book of Ceremonial Magic*, p. 67.]

Sturi(el)—one of the 70 childbed amulet angels.

Suceratos—an angel serving in the 4th Heaven; he rules on Lord's Day and is invoked from the west. [*Rf.* de Abano, *The Heptameron*; Shah, *Occultism*.]

Sui'el (Raashiel)—an angel with dominion over earthquakes. [*Rf.* Waite, *Book of Formation*; Ginzberg, *The Legends of the Jews* I.]

Sukalli (Sukallin)—angels in Sumerian-Babylonian theosophy. [*Rf. Catholic Encyclopedia*, "Angelology."]

Sumiel—in Voltaire, "Of Angels, Genii, and Devils," one of the leaders of the fallen angels. Voltaire quotes Enoch as his source, but no close equivalent for Sumiel can be found in the Enoch books, unless Voltaire had in mind Sammael or Simapesiel (*q.v.*). The name Sumiel is found inscribed on an oriental charm (*kamea*) for warding off evil. [*Rf.* Schrire, *Hebrew Amulets*.]

Summanus—one of the 9 Novensiles, the supreme divinities in Etruscan religion. [*Rf.* Redfield, *Gods/A Dictionary of the Deities of All Lands*.]

Sun—in the cabala, the sun is a "planet" and, also, an angel of light. [*Rf.* Levi, *Transcendental Magic*.]

Suna—a cherub or seraph used in conjuring rites. [*Rf. The Sixth and Seventh Books of Moses*.]

Suphlatus—genius of dust. [*Rf.* Apollonius of Tyana, *The Nuctemeron*.]

Suria (Suryah, Suriya)—in *Pirke Hechaloth*, one of the throne angels or one of the angels of the presence. He is also warden of the 1st hall (palace) of the 1st Heaven. According to *The Zohar*, Suria is the "high angelic being who takes up all the holy words that are uttered at a table [at which, and when, words from the Torah are spoken] and sets the form of them before the Holy One; and all the words, and the table also, are crowned before the Holy King."

Suriel (Sariel, Sauriel, Suriyel, Surya—"God's command")—identified with Uriel, Metatron, Ariel, Saraqael, etc. Like Metatron, Suriel is a prince of the presence and like Raphael, an angel of healing. He is likewise the angel of death (one of a number), and as such Suriel was sent to Mt. Sinai or Mt. Nebo to fetch the soul of Moses. In *Enoch I* Suriel is one of the 4 great archangels. In the *Falasha Anthology* he is dubbed "Suriel the Trumpeter" and "Suriel, angel of Death." It is said that Moses received all his knowledge from Suriel (although Zagzagel is likewise credited with being the source of Moses' knowledge.) According to Talmud *Berachoth* 51a, it was Suriel who instructed Rabbi Ishmael ben Elisha in the laws of hygiene. On gnostic amulets, Suriel's name appears beside those of Raguel, Peniel, Uriel, and Raphael. Origen, *Contra Celsum* VI, 30, lists Suriel as one of the 7 angels in the Ophitic Hebdomad system of primordial powers. Here, when invoked, Suriel makes his appearance in the form of an ox. In the cabala he is one of the 7 angels that rule the earth. In King, *The Gnostics and Their Remains*, p. 88, Suriel, along with Erataoth and Thautabaoth, is called "a Jewish angel of Magian origin" and as one whose name is found among those of genii presiding over the fixed stars." [*Rf.* Mead, *Thrice-Greatest Hermes* I; Budge, *Amulets and Talismans*, pp. 203, 375.]

Suriya [Suria]

Suriyah (Suriel)—an angel who revealed to

Rabbi Ishmael [*see* Suriel] the secrets of chiromancy and physiognomy. [*Rf.* Scholem, *Major Trends in Jewish Mysticism.*]

Suriyel (Suriel)—an angel who, with Salathiel, brought Adam and Eve from the top of the high mountain (where Satan had lured them) to the cave of treasures—a Garden of Eden incident touched on in *The Book of Adam and Eve (q.v.).*

Suroth—in Paracelsus' doctrine of Talismans, Suroth is a planetary genius of Egypt, replaced by the angel Anael. In Waite, "The Occult Sciences" (in his *The Secret Doctrine in Israel*), Suroth is the planetary genius of Venus. In hermetics he is head of the order of principalities. "He presides over the harmonies of vegetable nature." [*Rf.* Christian, *The History and Practice of Magic* I, 68.]

Surtaq—in hechaloth lore, an angel who assists Metatron (*q.v.*) in reciting the *Shema*. [*Rf.* introd. *3 Enoch.*]

Suruph ("strength of God")—an angel cited in Hyde, *Historia Religionis Veterum Persarum.*

Surush Ashu [Sirushi]

Surya (pl. suryas)—one of the 7 (or 12) shining gods of Vedic religion. [*See* Adityas.] In *3 Enoch* Surya is one of the many names of the angel Metatron.

Suryan—a "corruption" of Raphael, according to Barton, *Journal of Biblical Literature,* vol. 31.

Suryas (sing. surya)—in Vedic lore, the suryas (later the asuryas) are deities analogous to the Judaeo-Christian angels. The asuryas (*q.v.*) are the fallen ones, i.e., the demons or devils.

Susabo—genius of voyages and one of the genii of the 6th hour. [*Rf.* Apollonius of Tyana, *The Nuctemeron.*]

Susniel—an angel invoked in Syriac invocation charms. As a "spellbinding power," Susniel is grouped with Michael, Azriel, Shamshiel, and other angels. [*Rf. The Book of Protection.*]

Sut—one of the 5 sons of the Moslem fallen archangel Iblis. Sut is the demon of lies. The other 4 sons are: Awar, demon of lubricity; Dasim, demon of discord; Tir, demon of fatal accidents; Zalambur, demon of mercantile dishonesty.

Sutuel (Suryal)—in Falasha lore, the angel who conveyed Baruch to the holy Jerusalem. [*Rf.* Charles, *Apocalypse of Baruch* VI, 3, where, however, Sutuel is not specifically named.]

Symnay—an angel of the order of powers used for conjuring in cabalistic rites. From the extant records, it is not clear whether Symnay joined Satan in the revolt or remained loyal. [*Rf. The Sixth and Seventh Books of Moses.*]

Synesis ("understanding")—in gnosticism, one of the 4 great luminaries emanated from the Divine Will. [*Rf.* Mead, *Fragments of a Faith Forgotten.*]

Synoches—in Chaldean cosmology, one of the 3 intelligences of the Empyrean. [*Rf. Chaldean Oracles of Zoroaster.*]

Syth—angel of an hour, whose corresponding angel is Teiaiel. [*Rf.* H.D. (Hilda Doolittle), "Sagesse"; Ambelain, *La Kabbale Pratique.*]

Sywaro—a ministering archangel conjured up by cabalists in magical rites. [*Rf. The Sixth and Seventh Books of Moses.*]

The **Abraham-and-Isaac sacrifice episode** with the angel (identified as Tadhiel) holding back the knife. From Strachan, *Pictures from a Mediaeval Bible.*

Ta'aniel—in M. Gaster, *The Sword of Moses*, an angel summoned up in magical rites.

Tabkiel—one of the more than 100 names of the angel Metatron, as enumerated in *3 Enoch*, chap. 48.

Tablibik—a spirit of fascination and one of the genii of the 5th hour. [*Rf.* Apollonius of Tyana, *The Nuctemeron.*]

Tabris—in occult lore, the angel or genius of free will, and one of the genii of the 6th hour. [*Rf.* Apollonius of Tyana, *The Nuctemeron.*]

T'achnu—an angel whose name is found in *The Book of the Angel Raziel.* [*Rf.* Trachtenberg, *Jewish Magic and Superstition*, where T'achnu is believed to be a name "concocted" through manipulation of the letters of the Hebrew alphabet.]

Tacouin—in Islamic lore, a species of fay; "beautiful, winged, minor angels who secure man against the wiles of demons, and reveal the future." [*Rf.* De Plancy, *Dictionnaire Infernal* IV, 464.]

Tadhiel ("righteousness of God")—an angel credited with preventing the sacrifice of Isaac, according to Follansbee, *Heavenly History.* Other sources credit Metatron, Zadkiel, and the angel of the Lord (the last, in Genesis).

Tafel X—an angel invoked in magical rites. [*Rf.* M. Gaster, *The Sword of Moses.*]

Tafsarim—a class of Merkabah angels grouped with the elim and erelim (*q.v.*). In *3 Enoch*, the tafsarim are ranked "greater than all the ministering angels who minister before the throne of glory."

Taftefiah—one of the many names of the angel Metatron.

Taftian (Taphi)—in the cabala, a wonder-working angel, servant of Alimon (*q.v.*). He was invoked by the renowned Raf Anram. [*Rf. The Sixth and Seventh Books of Moses.*]

Tagas—a great angelic prince, conductor of the Song-Uttering Choirs (*q.v.*). [*Rf. 3 Enoch.*]

Tagriel (Tagried, Thigra)—chief of the angelic guards of the 2nd or 7th Heaven, and one of the

28 angels ruling the 28 mansions of the moon. [*Rf. Pirke Hechaloth*; *Ozar Midrashim* I, 111.]

Tahariel—angel of purity and one of the 70 childbed amulet angels. [*Rf. The Book of the Angel Raziel*; Budge, *Amulets and Talismans*.]

Tahsasiyah—one of the many names of the angel Metatron.

Takifiel—an angel invoked in Syrian magical rites; grouped with Michael, Gabriel, Sahariel, and other "spellbinding angels" in *The Book of Protection*.

Talia—in Mandaean lore, one of the 10 *uthri* (angels) that accompany the sun on its daily course.

Taliahad (Talliud)—angel of water. The name Taliahad is found inscribed on the 7th pentacle of the sun. [*Rf.* Papus, *Traité Elémentaire de Science Occulte*, p. 222; Mathers, *The Greater Key of Solomon*, p. 72.]

Tall Angel, The—in the 3rd Heaven, Moses, with Metatron acting as his guide, encounters a "tall angel" with 70,000 heads, assumed to be Sandalphon (although Sandalphon is said to reside in the 6th or 7th Heaven). In Wertheimer, *Bate Midrashot* IV, the angel is declared to have been Nuriel; but this identification, says Ginzberg, *The Legends of the Jews* V, 416, is due to a scribal error—a reasonable deduction, since Nuriel is a resident of the 2nd Heaven, where Moses encounters him, and, as far as we know, has only one head. The tallest angel of all is either Metatron or Hadraniel, or Anafiel.

Talmai—an angel invoked in the conjuration of the Reed, according to Mathers. In *The Zohar* (Numbers 159a) Talmai is an evil spirit, "a descendant of the giants whom God cast down to earth and who coupled with the daughters of men."

Tamael—in occult lore, a Friday angel of the 3rd Heaven. He is invoked from the east.

Tamaii—an angel invoked in the conjuration of Ink and Colors. [*Rf.* Mathers, *The Greater Key of Solomon*.]

Tamarid—a chief officer angel of the 2nd hour of the night, serving under the rule of Farris. [*Rf.* Waite, *The Lemegeton*, p. 69.]

Tamiel (Tamel, Temel, Tamuel—"perfection of God")—angel of the deep. In *Enoch I*, Tamiel is listed among the fallen angels. [*Rf. The New Schaff-Herzog Encyclopedia*, "Angels."]

Tamtemiyah—one of the many names of the angel Metatron.

Tandal—one of the 64 angel wardens of the 7 celestial halls. [*Rf. Pirke Hechaloth*.]

Tandariel—an angel mentioned in Hyde, *Historia Religionis Veterum Persarum*; mentioned also by Voltaire in "Of Angels, Genii, and Devils."

Taninivver—one of the 7 surviving evil emanations of God. The future extermination of this being is predicted in Isaiah 27:1, says Bamberger in *Fallen Angels*, p. 175. [*Rf.* Isaac B'ne Rabbi Jacob ha-Cohen in *Mada'e ha-Yahadut* II.]

Tankf'il—in Arabic lore, a guardian angel invoked in rites of exorcism. [*Rf.* Hughes, *A Dictionary of Islam*, "Angels."]

Tap [Gaap]

Taptharthareth [Tophtharthareth]

Tar—in Mandaean lore, one of the 10 *uthri* (angels) that accompany the sun on its daily course.

Tara—an angel with the attribute "Dieu, fontaine de Sagesse" mentioned in H.D.'s (Hilda Doolittle's) poem "Sagesse" and listed among the angels in Ambelain, *La Kabbale Pratique*.

Taranava—in *The Almadel of Solomon* (comprised in *The Lemegeton*), Taranava is one of the chief angelic powers of the 3rd altitude.

Tarfaniel—one of the many angelic guards of the gates of the West Wind. [*Rf. Ozar Midrashim* II, 316.]

Tarfiel ("God nourishes")—in the cabala, an angel invoked to cure stupidity. [*Rf.* Botarel, *Mayan Hahochmah*, and other works on the efficacy of amulets; as in Schwab, *Vocabulaire de* *l'Angélologie.*] In *Ozar Midrashim* (II, 316), Tarfiel is one of the guards of the gates of the East Wind.

Tariel—one of the 3 angels of summer. Tariel figures in Syriac incantation charms. He is invoked, along with other spellbinding angels, in the "Binding [of] the Tongue of the Ruler." [*Rf. The Book of Protection.*]

Tarniel—a Wednesday angel resident in the 3rd Heaven and invoked from the east. Tarniel is one of the spirits of the planet Mercury. In *Ozar Midrashim* (II, 316), he is one of the guards of the gates of the East Wind.

Tarpiel [Tarfiel]

Tarquam—in occult lore, one of 2 angels governing autumn, the other angel being Guabarel, according to de Abano, *The Heptameron*. [*Rf.* Shah, *Occultism*, pp. 43–44.]

Tarshish (Hebrew, "pearl")—in *The Zohar*, the eponymous chief of the order of tarshishim (i.e., virtues). Other chiefs of the order include Haniel and Sabriel. [*See* Tarshishim.]

Tarshishim ("brilliant ones")—an angelic order in Jewish lore, the term said to derive from Daniel 16:6 and, in the cabala, answering to the 7th sefira (firmness). In de Vigny's poem "Eloa," the order is called splendors.

Tarsisim [Tarshishim]

Tartaruch—in the *Vision of Paul*, 16, "the angel Tartaruch is set over punishments."

Tartaruchi—angels set over the torments of Hell.

Tartaruchian Angels—"observed by the fiery river, the tartaruchian angels have in their hands iron rods with 3 hooks with which they pierce the bowels of sinners"—*Vision of Paul*, 34.

Tartaruchus ("keeper of Hell") [*see* Temeluch]—chief of the angels set over the torments of Hell. Tartaruchus alternates with Uriel at this office, Uriel being "chief of the spirits who preside over Tartarus." [*Rf. Apocalypse of Paul*; James, *The Apocryphal New Testament.*]

Tartarus—the angel who presides over Hell (or a term for Hell itself). The angel, usually Uriel or Tartaruchus, is in charge of the torments of the nether regions, as already noted. For the names of other angels of these regions, *see* Angels of Hell. *See* particularly entry of Duma(h), who is "prince of Hell" and "angel of the stillness of death."

Tarwan—in Mandaean lore, one of the 10 *uthri* (angels) that accompany the sun on its daily course.

Tashriel—an angelic guard of one of the halls in the 1st Heaven. [*Rf. Pirke Hechaloth.*]

Tata'il—in Arabic lore, a guardian angel invoked in rites of exorcism. [*Rf.* Hughes, *A Dictionary of Islam*, "Angels."]

Tatirokos [Tartaruchus]

Tatonon—an angel invoked in the benediction of the Salt. [*Rf.* Mathers, *The Greater Key of Solomon.*]

Tatriel—one of the many names of the angel Metatron.

Tatrusia—one of the 70 childbed amulet angels. For a list of all 70, *see* Appendix.

Tau—a luminary, by the pronouncing of whose name "God brought on the Deluge," according to Mathers, *The Greater Key of Solomon*.

Tauriel—in Mandaean prayer books, a spirit (*uthra*) invoked through the fingering of phylacteries. He is known as a "call-spirit." Agrippa, *Three Books of Occult Philosophy* III, lists Tauriel as a governing angel of the zodiac.

Taurine Angel—in Ginzberg, *The Legends of the Jews* V, 39, there is mention of the "roaring of the taurine angel," which is said to be a recast of the Babylonian belief about the god Ea. The full name of the angel is "the taurine angel of the abyss" and his roar is heard when he "causes the water from the lower abyss to be poured into the upper abyss." [*Rf.* Talmud *Ta'anit* 25b; also *Bereshith Rabba* 10.] It will be recalled that Rahab, angel of the deep, was destroyed by God when he refused to separate the upper from the lower waters at Creation.

Tausa (*see* Taus-Melek)—according to Drower, *The Mandaeans of Iraq and Iran*, Tausa is the name given to a *malka* (angel) who bewails having sinned against the Great Life by allowing his pride to have led him into rebellion.

Taus-Melek (Malek Tawûs, Melek-I-Taus)—the peacock angel worshipped by the Yezidis as the devil-god and benefactor of mankind. Taus-Melek is a Buddhist paraphrase for the devil (Satan). To the Yezidis, a Kurdish Moslem sect inhabiting the mountains of Upper Mesopotamia (Iraq), Taus-Melek "is a fallen archangel, now pardoned, to whom God has committed the government of the world and the management of the transmigration of souls." [*Rf.* Louis Massignon, "The Yezidis of Mount Sindjar" in the symposium, *Satan.*] *See* also Wall, *Devils.*

Tavtavel—one of the many names of the angel Metatron.

Tazbun—in *The Book of the Angel Raziel*, an angel who exercises dominion over one of the months of the year.

Teba'at—one of the 7 leaders of the apostate angels. [*Rf.* Schmidt, *The Apocalypse of Noah and the Parables of Enoch.*]

Tebliel—one of the 7 angels with dominion over the earth. [*See* Angels of the Earth.]

Techial—chief of the angelic guards of the 5th Heaven. [*Rf. Pirke Hechaloth.*]

Tehom—a throne angel, or an administering angel, invoked in ritual magic rites. He is one of 15 listed in *The Sixth and Seventh Books of Moses.*

Tehoriel—one of numerous angelic guards of the gates of the South Wind. [*Rf. Ozar Midrashim* II, 316.]

Teiaiel (Isiaiel)—in the cabala, an angel that can foretell the future. He is a throne angel and controls maritime expeditions and commercial ventures. His sigil is reproduced in Ambelain, *La Kabbale Pratique*, p. 267. His corresponding angel is Syth.

Teiazel (Ieiazel)—an angel of the order of powers. Teiazel influences men of letters, artists, and librarians. His corresponding angel is Aterchinis. His sigil is reproduced in Ambelain, *La Kabbale Pratique*, p. 281.

Telantes—an angel invoked in Solomonic Wax magical operations. [*Rf.* Mathers, *The Greater Key of Solomon*, p. 117.]

Teletarchae—in the Chaldean cosmological scheme, the teletarchae are celestial intelligences or luminaries. [*Rf. Chaldean Oracles of Zoroaster.*]

Teletiel—a governing angel of the zodiac. [*Rf.* Cornelius Agrippa, *Three Books of Occult Philosophy* III.]

Temel [Tamiel]

Temeluch (Temeluchus, Abtelmoluchos, Tartaruchus, Temleyakos)—a caretaking angel, protector of children at birth and in infancy; also an angel of Gehenna (Hell) and the "merciless angel, all fire" in charge of torments, to whom souls are delivered at the death of the body. [*Rf. Revelation of Paul*; *Apocalypse of Peter*; James, *The Apocryphal New Testament.*]

Temlakos [Temeluch]

Temleyakos [Temeluch]

Tempast—an angel of the 1st hour of the night, serving under Gamiel.

Temperance—in cabalistic lore, "an angel with the sign of the sun on his forehead, on his breast the square and triangle of the septenary, pouring from one chalice into another the two essences which compose the elixir of life." [*Rf. The Divine Pymander.*]

Tempha—a planetary genius of Saturn invoked in talismanic magic. [*Rf.* Waite, "The Occult Sciences" in *The Secret Doctrine in Israel.*]

Tenaciel—a Friday angel of the 3rd hour invoked from the east. [*Rf.* de Abano, *The Heptameron*; Barrett, *The Magus*; Mathers, *The Greater Key of Solomon.*]

Tendac—an angel invoked in the exorcism of the Bat. [*Rf.* Mathers, *The Greater Key of Solomon.*]

Tephros (Tephras)—as revealed in *The Testament of Solomon*, an evil spirit who brings on darkness and sets fires to fields; he is also a demon of ashes conjured up by Beelzeboul (Beelzebub) at the behest of Solomon. But Tephros is not wholly evil, since he cures fever through the power or aid of Azael. He can be invoked in the names of Bultala, Thallel, and Melchal. [*Rf.* Butler, *Ritual Magic*; Shah, *The Secret Lore of Magic*; Ginzberg, *The Legends of the Jews* IV, 151.]

Tepiseuth—angel of part of an hour, as in H.D.'s (Hilda Doolittle's) poem "Sagesse." [*Rf.* Ambelain, *La Kabbale Pratique*.]

Terafniel—an angel of prey, mentioned in Schwab, *Vocabulaire de l'Angélologie*.

Teraphim ("obscenity")—according to Jewish cabalists of the Middle Ages, the teraphim were male and female idols, their power deriving from wizardry; they correspond to the serpent imagery, the seraphim, which, in turn, are said to derive from the Kabeiri, Assyrian divinities. [*Rf.* Judges 17–18; Ezekiel 21, 21; II Kings; *The Zohar*.]

Terathel (Ierathel)—an angel of the order of dominations (dominions). He "propagates light, civilization, and liberty." Terathel's corresponding angel is Hepe, according to Ambelain, *La Kabbale*

Teraphim. Small idols or superstitious figures used as talismans and sometimes worshipped. From *A Dictionary of the Holy Bible*, 1859.

Pratique, where Terathel's sigil is reproduced on p. 273.

Teriapel—one of the intelligences of the planet Venus. [*Rf. The Secret Grimoire of Turiel*.]

Terly (Erly, Irix)—in the *Grimorium Verum*, a congenial and obliging spirit who, in Solomonic conjurations, will procure for the invocant (when the conditions are right) the garter of a loved one. [*Rf.* Shah, *The Secret Lore of Magic*.]

Tessub [Rimmon]

Tetra—an angel invoked in ritual magic prayer for the fulfilment of an invocant's desires. Tetra is cited, along with other "great and glorious spirits," in *The Secret Grimoire of Turiel*.

Tetrasiyah—one of the many names of the angel Metatron.

Teumiel—the 7th sefira of the 10 unholy sefiroth (*q.v.*).

Tezalel (Icabel)—an angel who regulates marital fidelity. His corresponding angel is Theosolk. Tezalel's sigil is reproduced in Ambelain, *La Kabbale Pratique*, p. 267.

Thagrinus—one of the genii of confusion; also one of the genii of the 4th hour in Apollonius of Tyana, *The Nuctemeron*.

Thammuz—a fallen angel in Milton's *Paradise Lost* I, 446. "Whose annual wound in Lebanon allur'd/The Syrian Damsels to lament his fate/In amorous ditties." The reference is to Ezekiel 8:14. Thammuz is the Phoenician equivalent of the Greek Adonis.

Thamy—an angel of the order of powers, summoned in cabalistic conjuring rites. [*Rf. The Sixth and Seventh Books of Moses*.]

Thaphabaoth (Thartharoth, Thautabaoth, Onoel)—drawing on Ophitic sources, Origen, in his *Contra Celsum*, lists Thaphabaoth, along with Michael and Gabriel, as an angel (or demon) hostile to man. In gnostic lore, Thaphabaoth is an archontic demon, one of 7 rulers of the lower realms. When invoked, he manifests in the form of a bear Thaphabaoth is the Hebraized form of the Greek Tartarus. [*Rf.* Thorndike, *The History of Magic and Experimental Sciences*; Grant, *Gnosticism and Early Christianity*; Mead, *Thrice-Greatest Hermes* I, 294.]

Thaq—an angel in Mandaean lore. [*Rf.* Pognon, *Inscriptions Mandaïtes des Coupes de Khouabir.*]

Tharshishim [Tarshishim]

Tharsis (Tharsus)—in rabbinical literature, an angel governing the element of water. [*Rf.* Heywood, *The Hierarchy of the Blessèd Angels.*]

Thaumiel—an "averse" (i.e., unholy) sefira, corresponding to, or opposite to, Kether ("crown"). Thaumiel's cortex is Cathariel. [*Rf.* Waite, *The Holy Kabbalah.*]

Thaur—an angel summoned in Arabic incantation rites. [*Rf.* Shah, *Occultism.*]

Thausael—one of the leaders of the fallen angels mentioned in the Enoch books. See also Voltaire, "Of Angels, Genii, and Devils."

Thauthabaoth [Thaphabaoth]

Thegri (Thuriel, "bull-god")—the angel who has dominion over beasts. [*Rf.* the *Hermas Visions.*]

Thelesis (Aisthesis, "free will")—in gnostic lore, one of the 4 great luminaries or aeons emanated from the Divine Will. Raguel is sometimes identified with Thelesis. [*Rf.* Mead, *Fragments of a Faith Forgotten.*]

Theliel—in occultism, the angelic prince of love, invoked in ceremonial magic to procure the woman desired by the invocant. [*Rf.* Waite, *The Book of Black Magic and of Pacts.*]

Theodonias (Theodomai)—a holy name (of God or of an angel) called on in prayer at vesting ceremonies and in Solomonic conjuring rites. [*Rf.* Waite, *The Book of Black Magic and of Pacts.*]

Theodoniel—probably the same as Theodonias.

Theophile (fictional)—in Anatole France, *The Revolt of the Angels*, Theophile is one of the heavenly apostates.

Theoska—a ministering archangel invoked in ritual magic. [*Rf. The Sixth and Seventh Books of Moses.*]

Thief of Paradise—Satan is so called by Milton in *Paradise Regained* IV, 604.

Thiel—an angel serving in the 2nd Heaven, but said also to serve in the 3rd Heaven. Thiel is a ruling prince of Wednesday, invoked from the north. He is ranked as one of the intelligences of the planet Venus. [*Rf.* de Abano, *Heptameron*; Malchus, *The Secret Grimoire of Turiel.*]

Thigra [Tagriel]

Third Angel, The—mentioned in Revelation 8 as one of 7 angels that sound trumpets. When the 3rd angel sounds his, a great star Wormwood (regarded also as an angel) falls from Heaven. *See* Wormwood.

Third Heaven, The (Angels of the 3rd Heaven)—seat of the upper Paradise where manna is stored or produced by angels "according to a widespread view" (*The Legends of the Jews* V, 374). The honey (manna) in the Asenath-Joseph 2nd-century romance was supposedly brought from this 3rd Heaven by "divine bees" at the behest of Michael, who figures in the tale. The 3rd Heaven is the dwelling place of John the Baptist, as cited in the apocryphal *Apocalypse* attributed to James (Jesus' brother); however, in Islamic lore, the dwelling place of John the Baptist is the 2nd Heaven. The Mohammedans also place Azrael, angel of death, in the 3rd Heaven. It is in this Heaven, it will be recalled, that Paul was caught up and "heard unspeakable words which it is not lawful for a man to utter" (II Corinthians 12:2–4). [*Rf.* James, *The Apocryphal New Testament*, p. 37.] To the author of *Enoch II*, the 3rd Heaven accommodates both Paradise and Hell, with Hell located simply "on the northern side."

Thirteen Angels, The—in his apocalyptic poem "America," plate 12, Blake visions, in addition to the "Angels of Albion" and "Boston's Angels," 13 other angels who, Blake says, "Rent off their robes to the hungry wind, and threw their golden scepters/Down on the land of

America; indignant they descended/Headlong from out their heav'nly heights, descending swift as fires/Over the land."

Thomax—an angel of the 8th hour of the night, serving under Narcoriel. [*Rf.* Waite, *The Lemegeton.*]

Thopitus—in the cabala, an angel invoked in ritual incantation rites. His corresponding angel is Lehahiah. Thopitus figures in H.D.'s (Hilda Doolittle's) poem "Sagesse" and in Ambelain, *La Kabbale Pratique.*

Thoth—in hermetics, the head of the order of archangels. Thoth (or Pi-Hermes) is characterized as the "aeon of the aeons" and identified as the Good Daimon.

Three Angels of Abraham—the 3 "men" whom Abraham "entertained unawares" at Mamre (Genesis 18) have been identified variously as God, Michael, and Gabriel; as the Logos, Michael, and Raphael; and as the Holy Ghost, God, and Jesus. [See Mathers, *The Kabbalah Unveiled* and Conybeare, *Origins of Christianity,* p. 226.] The promise of one of the 3 angels to the 90-year-old Sarah of a son was fulfilled in the birth of Isaac. It might not be out of place to recall here a Greek parallel preserved by Ovid: 3 of the chief Olympians (Zeux, Poseidon, Hermes) were guests of Hyrieus, an old man of Tanagra; bidden by the gods to express a wish, the old man, being childless, asked for a son. The wish was granted; the son was Orion.

Thrgar—an angel of the month, cited in *The Book of the Angel Raziel.* Thrgar is also mentioned in Trachtenberg, *Jewish Magic and Superstition.*

Throne Bearers—a class of angels in Islamic lore. It is said that there are now only 4 angels in this class, but that the number will be increased to 8 on the day of resurrection. [*Rf.* The Koran, *suras* 40 and 69; Thompson, *Semitic Magic.*]

Thrones—in the pseudo-Dionysian scheme, the thrones rank 3rd in the 1st triad of the celestial hierarchy. They reside in the 4th Heaven. The ruling prince of this angelic order is variously given as Oriphiel, Zabkiel, Zaphkiel (*see* Angels of the Thrones; Many-Eyed Ones). In *Paradise Lost* VI, 199, Milton speaks of "the Rebel Thrones." It is through the thrones, says Dionysius, that "God brings his justice to bear upon us." The *Testament of Levi* (in *Testament of the Twelve Patriarchs*) mentions thrones as an order in the celestial hierarchy.

Thronus—one of the 15 throne angels listed in *The Sixth and Seventh Books of Moses.*

Thummim [Urim]

Tiel—one of the angelic guards of the gates of the North Wind.

Tifereth [Tiphereth]

Tif(th)eriel (Tiphtheriel)—a sefira of Tiphereth (Beauty) in the Briatic world of the cabala. [*Rf.* Waite, *The Holy Kabbalah.*]

Tijmneik—an angel of the Seal (one of the *nomina barbara*) listed in *The Sixth and Seventh Books of Moses.*

Tikarathin (Thikarathin, Thikarthin)—lord of hosts, invoked in ritual magic rites; also a secret name of God. [*Rf.* Scholem, *Jewish Gnosticism, Merkabah Mysticism, and Talmudic Tradition*, p. 53.]

Tilath (Silat)—a spirit invoked in prayer by the Master of the Art in Solomonic conjuration rites. [*Rf.* Mathers, *The Greater Key of Solomon.*]

Tileion—an angel invoked in the benediction of the Salt.

Tilli—in occultism, a seraph or cherub addressed in conjurations.

Tilonas—an angel invoked in the conjuration of Ink and Colors. [*Rf.* Mathers, *The Greater Key of Solomon.*]

Time—an angel, so named, in the Tarot card No. 14. He is winged, the sign of the sun on his forehead, the square and triangle of the septenary on his breast. He pours the essence of life from one chalice to another. He is also called Temperance (*q.v.*). According to *The Zohar* (Miqez 195b), the 'eth in Ecclesiastes 9, 12, which is a term for time, "refers to the ministering angel who presides over

Angel holding a star. A woodcut done in Nuremberg, 1505. From the Museum of Fine Arts, Boston.

each act a man performs." Angoff's story "God Repents" (*Adventures in Heaven*) relates that once, when the Creator contemplated destroying the world, He called in His angels for consultation, and that among the angels were 3 named Time, Minutes, and Seconds.

Time Spirit, The—a designation above the rank of archangel for Michael, as in Steiner, *The Mission of the Archangel Michael*. In this book the Swiss occultist contends that Michael is now on earth helping human souls "fight counterstriving spirits" here, so as to "enable us to acquire spiritualized concepts." The descent of Michael to earth is said to have occurred in the middle of the 19th century.

Tiphereth—the 6th sefira.

Tiphtheriel [Tiftheriel]

Tipperah (Zipporah)—the wife of the lawgiver Moses; she is now a virtue in the woman's division of Paradise.

Tir—the angel of June in ancient Persian lore; also the angel governing the 13th day of the month. Tir was regent of the planet Mercury and has been represented as having the body of a fish, with a boar's face. His one arm is black, the other

white; on his head rests a crown. In Muslim lore, Tir is the demon of fatal accidents and one of the 5 sons of the fallen archangel Iblis.

Tiriel—an archangel, the intelligence of the planet Mercury, with the cabalistic number 260. Tiriel's name (joined with those of Raphael and Sadayel) was discovered on a ring amulet. [*Rf.* Budge, *Amulets and Talismans*; Barrett, *The Magus* II.]

Tiril—in his "Of Angels, Genii, and Devils," Voltaire calls Tiril one of the leaders of the fallen angels.

Tirtael—a guard, one of many, of the gates of the East Wind. [*Rf. Ozar Midrashim* II, 316.]

Tishbash—one of the many names of Metatron.

Tishgash—one of the many names of Metatron.

Titmon—one of the more than 100 names of the angel Metatron as enumerated in *3 Enoch*.

Tixmion—an angel invoked in the benediction of the Salt.

Tmsmael—an evil angel used in conjuring rites for separating a husband from his wife. [*Rf.* M. Gaster, *The Sword of Moses.*]

Tobiel—a variant for Tubuel in Hugo, *The Toilers of the Sea.*

Todatamael—one of the angelic guards of the gates of the East Wind. [*Rf. Ozar Midrashim* II, 316.]

Tomimiel—a governing angel of the zodiac. [*Rf.* Cornelius Agrippa, *Three Books of Occult Philosophy* III.]

Tophiel—as noted in *Hechaloth Rabbati*, one of 7 angelic guards of the 1st Heaven.

Tophnar (Tophrag)—like Tophiel, one of the 7 angelic guards of the 1st Heaven. He serves, or is identified with, Zevudiel and Kashriel.

Tophrag [Tophnar]

Tophtharthareth (Taptharthareth)—according to Paracelsus in his doctrine of Talismans, a spirit of the planet Mercury of which the presiding intelligence is Tiriel. [*Rf.* Christian, *The History and Practice of Magic* I.]

Torquaret—an angel who heads the sign of autumn. [*Rf.* de Abano, *The Heptameron*; Barrett, *The Magus* II.]

Totraviel—in *Hechaloth Rabbati*, a seal holder and angelic guard of the 5th Heaven. He serves with Zahaftirii (*q.v.*).

Totrisi—one of the 4 angels appointed by God to the Sword. [*Rf.* M. Gaster, *The Sword of Moses.*]

Touriel [Turel]

Tractatu—an angel who had a book named after him, according to Cornelius Agrippa. [*Cf.* Raziel.]

Transin—in Mathers, *The Greater Key of Solomon*, a name written in Heaven in the character (i.e., tongue) of angels and invoked to command demons.

Trgiaob—one of the *nomina barbara*. Trgiaob is an angel who exercises dominion over wild fowl and creeping things. [*Rf.* M. Gaster, *The Sword of Moses.*]

Trotrosi X (Totrisi)—an invocation spirit who communicated to Moses the divine name.

Trsiel—in Merkabah mysticism, an angel who exercises dominion over rivers.

Tsadi'ael—in hechaloth lore (*Ma'asseh Merkabah*), an angelic guard stationed at the 6th heavenly hall.

Tsadkiel (Tzadkiel, Azza)—angel of justice, as is Azza (*q.v.*). In *The Zohar*, Tsadkiel is 4th of the 10 archangels of the Briatic world. In *Ozar Midrashim* II, 316, he is called Tzadkiel, or Kaddisha "the holy one," and is listed among the angelic guards of the gates of the East Wind. [*See* Zadkiel.] In the cabala, Tsadkiel is the intelligence or angel of the planet Jupiter; also the protecting angel of Abraham. In an early version of *The Golden Legend*, Longfellow cited Tsadkiel as the governor of Jupiter, but later substituted Zobiachel.

Tsaftsefiah, Tsaftsefiel, Tsahtsehiyah, Tsaltselim, Tsaltseliyah—variant names of Metatron.

Tsaphiel—in occult science, an angel of the moon. [*Rf.* Papus, *Traité Élémentaire de Science Occulte.*] Angels governing the moon include Yahriel, Yachadiel, Zachariel, Gabriel.

Tsaphkiel [Tzaphquiel]

Tsavniyah, Tsavtsiyah—variant names of the angel Metatron.

Tse'an—in hechaloth lore (*Ma'asseh Merkabah*), an angelic guard stationed at the 6th heavenly hall.

Tsedeck—the Hebrew for Jupiter and root-source for the angel Tsadkiel or Zadkiel (*q.q.v.*).

Tshndrnis—as recorded in *The Book of the Angel Raziel*, Tshndrnis (one of the *nomina barbara*) is an angel ruling over one of the months of the year.

Tsirya—one of the 70 childbed amulet angels.

Tsuria—one of the 70 childbed amulet angels.

Tsuriel—a variant of Zuriel (*q.v.*) as the zodiacal angel governing Libra. [*Rf.* Jobes, *Dictionary of Mythology, Folklore and Symbols.*]

Tual—in ceremonial magic, one of the angels of the 12 signs of the zodiac, representing Taurus (the Bull). In mystic lore, another angel representing this sign is Asmodel.

Tubatlu—in *The Sixth and Seventh Books of Moses*, one of the 8 angels of omnipotence. [*See* Tulatu.]

Tubiel—an angel invoked for the return of small birds to their owners. Tubiel is head of the sign of summer. [*Rf.* de Abano, *The Heptameron*; Barrett, *The Magus*; Schwab, *Vocabulaire de l'Angélologie.*]

Tubuas—one of the 6 or 7 angels reprobated at a Church Council in Rome, 745 C.E., the other reprobated angels including Uriel, Raguel, Tubuel, Inias, Sabaoc, Simiel. They were invoked by the bishops Adelbert and Clement. [*Rf.* Heywood, *The Hierarchy of the Blessèd Angels*, p. 261.]

Tobi (from *The Book of Tobit*) and three archangels—presumably Raphael (center), Michael, and Gabriel. The painter, Giovanni Botticini (1446–1497), was evidently unfamiliar with the details of the apocryphal tale, for nowhere in it is there mention of any angel other than Raphael. Reproduced from Régamey, *Anges*.

Tubuel [Tubuas]

Tufiel—an angelic guard of the 1st Heaven. [*Rf. Pirke Hechaloth.*]

Tufriel—an angelic guard of the 6th Heaven.

Tuiel—an angel mentioned in *The Book of the Angel Raziel* and incorrectly equated with Milton's Ithuriel. [*Rf.* West, "The Names of Milton's Angels."]

Tulatu—in *The Sixth and Seventh Books of Moses*, one of the 8 angels of omnipotence. May be a different form for Tublatu.

Tumael (Tumiel, Tuniel, Tamiel)—one of the fallen angels in the Enoch listings.

Tummim [Urim]

Tumoriel—an angel of the 11th hour of the night, serving under Dardariel. [*Rf.* Waite, *The Lemegeton.*]

Turel ("rock of God"—Turiel, Turael)—one of 200 angels listed in *The Book of Enoch* who followed Semyaza in the descent from Heaven to cohabit with the daughters of men, an incident touched on in Genesis 6. The sigil of the fallen Turel is pictured in *The Secret Grimoire of Turiel*, p. 39. As Turiel, Turel is a messenger of the spirits of the planet Jupiter; also, a messenger for the angel Sachiel or Setchiel (*q.q.v.*).

Turlos—an angel invoked in the conjuration of the Reed. [*Rf.* Mathers, *The Greater Key of Solomon.*]

Turmiel—one of numerous angelic guards of the gates of the West Wind. [*Rf. Ozar Midrashim* II, 316.]

Tusmas—an angel of the 7th hour of the day, serving under Barginiel. [*Rf.* Waite, *The Lemegeton*, p. 67.]

Tutelary Angels [Guardian Angels]

Tutiel—a "mysterious" spirit invoked in conjuring rites. [*Rf.* Schwab, *Vocabulaire de l'Angélologie.*]

Tutrbebial—the last of the 64 angel wardens of the 7 celestial halls. [*Rf. Pirke Hechaloth.*]

Tutresiel (Stutrayah—"piercing God")—a great angel prince in *3 Enoch*. Here it is related of the angel Hamon that when he sees Tutresiel, he removes the crown of glory from his head and falls on his face—in obeisance. In turn, Tutresiel does the same when he sees Atrugiel, and Atrugiel does the same when he sees Na'aririel. The baffling thing is that all these names of angels are actually variant names of Metatron!

Tutrusa'i (Tutrachiel, Tuphgar, Tzurtag, etc.) —an angelic guard of the 1st Heaven. [*Rf. Pirke Hechaloth.*]

Tuwahel—a ministering angel invoked in ritual magic. [*Rf. The Sixth and Seventh Books of Moses.*]

Twelve Spirits of the Zodiacal Cycle—as given by Eliphas Levi, the list consists of Sarahiel for Aries; Saraiel for Gemini; Seratiel for Leo; Chadakiel for Libra; Araziel for Taurus; Phakiel for Cancer; Schaltiel for Virgo; Sartzeil for Scorpio; Saritiel for Sagittarius; Semaqiel for Capricorn; Tzakmaqiel for Aquarius; Vocatiel for Pisces. The list given by Camfield, *A Theological Discourse of Angels* (p. 67), differs considerably from that supplied by Levi, and runs as follows: Malchedael for Aries; Ambriel for Gemini; Verchiel for Leo; Zuriel for Libra; Asmodel for Taurus; Muriel for Cancer; Hamaliel for Virgo; Barchiel for Scorpio; Adnachiel for Sagittarius; Haniel for Capricorn; Gambiel for Aquarius; Barchiel for Pisces.

Twenty-Four Elders [Elders]

Tychagara—one of the 7 exalted throne angels "which execute the commands of potentates," the other 6 angels including Ophaniel and Barael. [*Rf. The Book of the Angel Raziel*; Cornelius Agrippa, *Three Books of Occult Philosophy* III.] It should be pointed out that, in the usual schematic arrangement of the hierarchic orders, the thrones are of the 1st triad while the potentates (powers) are of the 2nd triad, so that commands ought properly to emanate from the thrones to the potentates, not the other way around.

Typhon—the Hebrew Sephon, meaning

"dark" or "northern"; in Aramaic he is Tuphon, identified by the Greeks with Set, god of darkness. In Cornelius Agrippa, *Three Books of Occult Philosophy*, Typhon of classic mythology is identified with the cabalistic angel Sammael (*q.v.*).

Tzadiqel—the archangel who rules the planet Jupiter on Thursday. [*Rf.* Mathers, *The Greater Key of Solomon*, Table of Planetary Hours.]

Tzadkiel [Tsadkiel]

Tzadqiel [Tsadkiel]

Tzakmaqiel (Ssakmakiel)—a spirit governing Aquarius. [*Rf. Prince of Darkness*, p. 178.]

Tzaphniel—when an invocant wishes to procure a magic carpet, it is Tzaphniel, "holy minister of God," who must be appealed to—as recommended in works like Barrett, *The Magus*; Mathers, *The Greater Key of Solomon*.

Tzaphq(u)iel (Tzaphkiel, "contemplation of God")—in *The Zohar*, Tzaphqiel is 3rd of the 10 holy sefiras, or 3rd of the 10 archangels. [*Rf.*

Mathers, *The Kabbalah Unveiled*.] In the tables provided in Mathers, *The Greater Key of Solomon*, Tzaphqiel rules the planet Saturn on Saturday.

Tzarmiel—one of the numerous angelic guards of the gates of the North Wind. [*Rf. Ozar Midrashim* II, 316.]

Tzartak (Tzortaq)—one of the 70 childbed amulet angels. [*Rf. The Book of the Angel Raziel*; Budge, *Amulets and Talismans*, p. 225.] As Tzortaq, in *Ozar Midrashim* II, 316, he is one of numerous angelic guards of the gates of the West Wind.

Tzedeqiah—an angel's name inscribed in Hebrew characters on the 1st pentacle of the planet Jupiter. [*Rf.* Mathers, *The Greater Key of Solomon*.]

Tzephon [Zephon]

Tzortaq [Tzartak]

Tzurel—one of the numerous angelic guards of the gates of the South Wind. [*Rf. Ozar Midrashim* II, 316.]

Uriel, "gliding through the Ev'n/On a Sun beam," illustrating *Paradise Lost* IV. From Hayley, *The Poetical Works of John Milton.*

U

Ubaviel—an angel with dominion over the zodiacal sign of Capricorn. [*Rf.* Trachtenberg, *Jewish Magic and Superstition.*]

Ublisi—in occult lore, one of 8 angels of omnipotence invoked in magical conjuring rites.

Ucimiel [Ucirmiel]

Ucirmiel (Ucirnuel)—a Wednesday angel residing in the 2nd or 3rd Heaven. When invoking Ucirmiel, the invocant must look north. [*Rf.* de Abano, *The Heptameron*; Barrett, *The Magus* II.]

Udrgazyia—one of the 70 childbed amulet angels. [*Rf. The Book of the Angel Raziel*; Budge, *Amulets and Talismans.*]

Udriel—a childbed amulet angel, found in the same sources as for Udrgazyia.

Ugiel—2nd of the 10 unholy sefiroth in Moses of Burgos' listing.

Uini—a ministering angel invoked in conjuring rites. [*Rf. The Sixth and Seventh Books of Moses.*]

Umabel—in the cabala, Umabel is said to have dominion over physics and astronomy. He is also one of the 72 angels bearing the name of God Shemhamphorae. [*Rf.* Barrett, *The Magus* II.] Umabel's corresponding angel is Ptiau. His sigil is figured in *La Kabbale Pratique*, p. 294.

Umahel—one of the archangels. Ambelain, *La Kabbale Pratique*, does not say what the mission of this archangel is. Umahel is listed as one of 9 of the order in a chart facing p. 88 of the Ambelain book.

Umeroz—angel of the 2nd hour of the night, serving under Farris. [*Rf.* Waite, *The Lemegeton.*]

Umiel—an angel invoked in Syriac spellbinding charms. [*Rf. The Book of Protection.*]

Umikol—in Jewish mysticism, one of the angels of the Seal.

Unael—an angel serving in the 1st Heaven. [*Rf. The Sixth and Seventh Books of Moses.*] The name Unael (Unhael) is found inscribed on an oriental charm (*kamea*) for warding off evil. [*Rf.* Schrire, *Hebrew Amulets.*]

Ur (Hebrew, Aur, meaning "fire" or "light")—in Mandaean lore, the king of the nether world. [*Rf. Jewish Encyclopedia,* "Angelology."]

Urakabarameel—a run-together of Arakib and Ramiel. Urakabarameel was one of the leaders of the fallen angels (see *Enoch I*). He is mentioned in Thomas Moore's book-length poem *The Loves of the Angels.*

Urfiel—chief of the angelic order of malachim or malakim (*q.v.*) [*Rf. Berith Menucha.*]

Urian (Uryan)—a form of Uriel, as in *Enoch I,* 9:1. In low German folklore, Sir Urian is a sobriquet for Satan.

Uriel ("fire of God")—one of the leading angels in noncanonical lore, and ranked variously as a seraph, cherub, regent of the sun, flame of God, angel of the presence, presider over Tartarus (Hades), archangel of salvation (as in II Esdras), etc. In the latter work he acts as heavenly interpreter of Ezra's visions. In *Enoch I,* he is the angel who "watches over thunder and terror." In *The Book of Adam and Eve* he presides over repentance. Uriel "is supposed to be," says Abbot Anscar Vonier in *The Teaching of the Catholic Church,* "the spirit who stood at the gate of the lost Eden with the fiery sword." *The Book of Adam and Eve* designates him as this spirit, i.e., one of the "cherubims" of Genesis 3. He is invoked in some of the ancient litanies. He has been identified as one of the angels who helped bury Adam and Abel in Paradise (Hastings, *Dictionary of the Bible*); as the dark angel who wrestled with Jacob at Peniel; as the destroyer of the hosts of Sennacherib (II Kings 19:35; *II Maccabees* 15:22); as the messenger sent by God to Noah to warn him of the impending deluge (*Enoch I,* 10:1–3), all of which feats or missions have been credited to other angels, as elsewhere noted. In the view of Louis Ginzberg, the "prince of lights" in *The Manual of Discipline* refers to Uriel. In addition, Uriel is said to have disclosed the mysteries of the heavenly arcana to Ezra; interpreted prophecies, and led Abraham out of Ur. In later Judaism, says R. H. Charles (*The Book of Enoch*), "we find Uriel instead of Phanuel" as one of the 4 angels of the presence. Uriel is also the angel of the month of September and may be invoked ritually by those born in that month. *The Magus* claims that alchemy "which is of divine origin" was brought down to earth by Uriel, and that it was Uriel who gave the cabala to man, although this "key to the mystical interpretation of Scripture" is also said to have been the gift of Metatron. Milton describes Uriel as "Regent of the Sun" and the "sharpest sighted spirit of all in Heaven" (*Paradise Lost* III). Dryden, *The State of Innocence,* pictures Uriel as descending from heaven in a chariot drawn by white horses. Despite his eminence, Uriel was reprobated at a Church Council in Rome, 745 C.E. Now, however, he is Saint Uriel, and his symbol is an open hand holding a flame. Burne-Jones' painting of Uriel is reproduced as a frontispiece in Duff, *First and Second Books of Esdras.* The name Uriel derives, it is claimed, from Uriah the prophet. In apocryphal and occult works Uriel has been equated or identified with Nuriel, Uryan, Jeremiel, Vretil, Suriel, Puruel, Phanuel, Jehoel, Israfel, and the angel Jacob-Israel. See the pseudepigraphic *Prayer of Joseph,* quoted in part in Ginzberg, *The Legends of the Jews* V, 310. In this work Jacob says: "When I was coming from Mesopotamia of Syria [sic], Uriel, the angel of God, came forth and spoke: 'I have come down to the earth to make my dwelling among men, and I am called Jacob by name.'" The meaning of the foregoing is puzzling, unless Uriel turned into Jacob after wrestling with the patriarch at Peniel; but the incident as related in Genesis 32 suggests a different interpretation. A commentary on Exodus 4:25 speaks of a "benign angel" attacking Moses for neglecting to observe the covenantal rite of circumcision with regard to the latter's son Gershom, the benign angel being identified as Uriel in *Midrash Aggada Exodus,* and as Gabriel in *The Zohar* I, 93b. The latter source reports that Gabriel "came down in a flame of fire, having the appearance of a burning serpent," with the express purpose of destroying Moses "because of his sin." In *The Legends of the Jews* II, 328, the angel here is neither Uriel nor Gabriel but 2 angels, the wicked Hemah and Af. Uriel is said to be the angel of vengeance that Prud'hon pictured in his "Divine Vengeance and Justice," a canvas to be found in the Louvre. Uriel, "gliding through the Ev'n/On a Sun beam" (*Paradise Lost* IV, 555) is reproduced on p. 296 from Hayley, *The Poetical Works of John Milton*. The Uriel in Percy MacKaye's *Uriel and Other Poems* is not our angel but William Vaughn Moody, American poet and playwright (1869–1910), to whom the title poem is addressed in memory. The most recent appraisal of Uriel is the one offered by Walter Clyde Curry in *Milton's Ontology Cosmology and Physics*, where, on p. 93, Professor Curry says of Uriel that he "seems to be largely a pious but not too perceptive physicist with inclinations towards atomistic philosophy." To illustrate in what high esteem Uriel was held, we find him described in the 2nd book of the *Sibylline Oracles* as one of the "immortal angels of the undying God" who, on the day of judgment, will "break the monstrous bars framed of unyielding and unbroken adamant of the brazen gates of Hades, and cast them down straightway, and bring forth to judgment all the sorrowful forms, yea, of the ghosts of the ancient Titans and of the giants, and all whom the flood overtook . . . and all these shall he bring to the judgment seat . . . and set before God's seat."

Urim ("illumination")—a cherub in Klopstock's poetic drama *Der Messias* (The Messiah). The Bible meaning of the term is a "household idol" and it is almost always used in association with tummin (or thummim), meaning "perfection" and signifying oracles for ascertaining the will of God. The urim and tummin derive from the Babylonian-Chaldean tablets of destiny ("owned" by Tiamat, female monster and reputed source of all evil), which were credited with possessing the virtue of casting the fate of men. Aaron, it will be recalled, bore the urim and tummin engraved on his breastplate as the insignia of his office of high priest (*see* Asser Criel). In Talmud *Yoma*, the urim and tummin are listed among the 5 holy things found in the First Temple and absent from the Second Temple. *The Zohar* (Exodus 234b) thus defines and distinguishes the 2 terms: "Urim signifies the luminous speculum,

which consisted of the engravure of the Divine Name composed of 42 letters by which the world was created; whereas the Thummim consisted of the nonluminous speculum made of the Divine Name as manifested in the 22 letters. The combination of the 2 is thus called Urim and Thummim." Milton, *Paradise Regained* III, 14, refers to the urim and thummim as "those oraculous gems/ On Aaron's breast." The seal of Yale University incorporates the 2 names in Hebrew characters. [*Rf.* Exodus 28:30; Leviticus 8:8; Ezra 2:63; Nehemiah 7:65; Driver, *Canaanite Myths and Legends*, p. 103; Budge, *Amulets and Talismans*, p. 407; and Ginzberg, *The Legends of the Jews* II, 329.]

Urion [Orion]

Uriron—an angel invoked as an amulet against sorcery and sudden death. [*Rf.* Trachtenberg, *Jewish Magic and Superstition*, p. 140.]

Urizen—in Blake's *Book of Urizen*, the angel of England, alternating with Orc. He is one of the Four Zoas and the embodiment of the god of reason. Urizen's son is the angel that Blake meets in *The Marriage of Heaven and Hell*.

Urjan (Uryan)—variant form of Uriel.

Urpaniel—an angel's name found inscribed on an oriental charm (*kamea*) for warding off evil. [*Rf.* Schrire, *Hebrew Amulets*.]

Uryan [Urjan]

Urzla—in the cabala, an angel of the east, summoned in conjuring rites; he is a "glorious and benevolent angel and is asked to share with the invocant the secret wisdom of the Creator." [*Rf.* Gollancz, *Clavicula Salomonis*.]

Usera—an angel serving in the 1st Heaven. [*Rf. The Sixth and Seventh Books of Moses*.]

Usiel (Uziel, Uzziel, "strength of God")—in the cabala generally, as in *Targum Onkeles and Jonathan*, Usiel is an angel that fell, and is therefore evil; he was among those who wedded human wives and begat giants. Of the 10 unholy sefiroth, Usiel is listed 5th. In *The Book of the Angel Raziel*, Usiel (Uzziel) is among the 7 angels before the

The archangel Uriel shown with the falling Satan, illustrating *Paradise Lost* III. From Hayley, *The Poetical Works of John Milton.*

throne of God and among 9 set over the 4 winds. [*Rf.* Bischoff, *Die Elemente der Kabbalah.*] Usiel replaces Uriel in the reprint English translation of *Verus Jesuitarum Libellus* ("True Magical Work of the Jesuits"). [*Rf.* Waite, *The Book of Ceremonial Magic,* p. 110.] The *Key to Faust's Threefold Harrowing of Hell* (otherwise known as a *Key to the Black Raven*) contains a general conjuration to Usiel and a list of his adjutant princes. [*Rf.* Butler, *Ritual Magic,* p. 190.] Finally, according to Milton, Usiel is a good angel, of the order of virtues, a lieutenant of Gabriel's in the fighting in Heaven at the time of Satan's defection.

Uslael—an angel serving in the 4th Heaven. [*Rf. The Sixth and Seventh Books of Moses.*]

Ustael—in Barrett, *The Magus,* and in de Abano, *The Heptameron,* an angel of the 4th Heaven and a ruler on Lord's Day. He is invoked from the west. He is also one of 3 angelic messengers of the moon.

Ustur—in Chaldean lore, one of 4 chief classes of protecting genii, limned after the human likeness. *Cf.* the Ezekiel cherubim. [*Rf.* Lenormant, *Chaldean Magic.*]

Uthra (pl. *uthri*)—in Mandaean mythology, an angel or spirit of life, one of 10, that accompany the sun on its daily course. The 10 are Zuhair, Zahrun, Buhair Bahrun, Sar, Sarwan, Tar, Tarwan, Rabia, Talia. A list of 20 *uthri* is given in Drower, *The Mandaeans of Iraq and Iran,* with the names Pthahil, Zaharill, Adam, Qin, Ram, Rud, Shurbai, Sharhabiil, Shumbar Nu, Nuraitha, Yahya Yuhana, Qinta, Anhar, Eve, Abathur, Bahrat, Yushamin, Dnuth Hiia, Habshaba, Kana d Zidqa.

Uthri [*Uthra*]

Uvabriel—an angel of the 3rd hour of the night, serving under Sarquamich.

Uvael—an angel of Monday, resident of the 1st Heaven, and invoked from the north. [*Rf.* Barrett, *The Magus* II.]

Uvall (Vual, Voval)—before he fell, an angel of the order of powers. Now, in Hell, Uvall is a great duke with 37 legions of infernal spirits ready to do his bidding. His office is to procure the love of women at the behest of invocants. He speaks Egyptian "but not perfectly," according to Waite, *The Lemegeton.* Nowadays, it appears, Uvall converses in colloquial Coptic. His sigil is figured in Waite, *The Book of Black Magic and of Pacts,* p. 180.

Uvayah—one of the many names of the angel Metatron.

Uvmiel—in hechaloth lore (*Ma'asseh Merkabah*), an angelic guard stationed at the 2nd heavenly hall.

Uwula—a ministering angel invoked at an eclipse of the sun or moon. [*Rf. The Sixth and Seventh Books of Moses.*]

Uzah, Usiah (Uzza)—as Ozah or Uzah, one of the names of Metatron, as listed in *Sefer ha-Heshek.*

Uzbazbiel—in hechaloth lore (*Ma'asseh Merkabah*), an angelic guard stationed at the 1st of the 7 heavenly halls.

Uziel—5th of the 10 unholy sefiroth. [*Rf. Pirke Hechaloth.*]

Uziphiel—in hechaloth lore (*Ma'asseh Merkabah*), an angelic guard stationed at the 1st of the 7 heavenly halls.

Uzoh [Uzza]

Uzza (Uzzah, Ouza—"strength")—a name changed to Semyaza (*q.v.*). Like Rahab, Uzza is the tutelary angel of the Egyptians. [*Rf.* Ginzberg, *The Legends of the Jews* III, 17.]

Uzziel (Usiel, Azareel?—"strength of God")—one of the principal angels in rabbinic angelology; of the order of cherubim, also of the order of virtues (i.e., malachim), of which Uzziel is sometimes ranked as chief. According to *The Book of the Angel Raziel,* Uzziel (Usiel) is among the 7 angels who stand before the throne of Glory, and among the 9 set over the 4 winds. In Milton, *Paradise Lost* IV, Uzziel is commanded by Gabriel to "coast the south with strictest watch." In Merkabah lore, he is an angel of mercy under the rulership of Metatron. [*Rf.* introd. *3 Enoch.*]

Heads of Evil
Dæmons.
Nº 2.

Vessels of Wrath

Theutus

Asmodeus

The Incubus

Vessels of wrath (demons or fallen angels): Theutus, Asmodeus, and Incubus. From Barrett, *The Magus.*

Vacabiel (Vacatiel)—in joint rule with Rasamasa (another genius), Vacabiel controls the sign of Fishes (Pisces) in the zodiac. [*Rf. Prince of Darkness*, p. 178.]

Vacatiel [Vacabiel]

Vachmiel—an angel governing the 4th hour of the day. Vachmiel is served by 10 chief officers and 100 inferior spirits. [*Rf.* Waite, *The Lemegeton.*]

Vadriel—ruling angel of the 9th hour of the day. Vadriel, like Vachmiel, is served by 10 chief officers and 100 lesser spirits. The chief officers include Astroniel, Damiel, Madriel. [*Rf.* Waite, *The Lemegeton.*]

Vahoel—one of the 72 angels in control of the 12 signs of the zodiac.

Vaij—in Jewish mysticism, one of the angels of the Seal. [*Rf. The Sixth and Seventh Book of Moses.*]

Valiants (of the Heavens; *see* Warriors)—A term for angels, as in Isaiah 33:7, and *Psalms of Thanksgiving of the New Covenant.* [*Rf.* Dupont-Sommer, *The Dead Sea Scrolls.*]

Valnum—in occult lore, a Monday angel resident of the 1st Heaven and invoked from the north. He is also one of the 3 intelligences of the planet Saturn.

Vametel—in Runes, *The Wisdom of the Kabbalah*, one of the 72 angels of the zodiac.

Vamona(h)—the "dwarf avatar" in Vedic lore. He is "lord of reason." Of the 10 avatars, Vamona is 5th and Vishnu 1st.

Vanand Yezad—the only angel allowed by the Magians to preside over all the 7 Hells. [*Rf.* Sale, *The Koran*, "Preliminary Discourse," p. 67.]

Vaol—an angel whose name appears on the 1st pentacle of the moon. [*Rf.* Mathers, *The Greater Key of Solomon.*]

Vaphoron—an angel invoked in the benediction of the Salt. Vaphoron is mentioned in Solomonic (black magic) tracts.

Varcan—according to Heywood, *The Hierarchy of the Blessèd Angels*, an angel with dominion over the sun. (For others exercising such dominion, *see* Angels of the Sun.) In de Abano, *The Hepta-meron*, Varcan is referred to as "king of angels of the air ruling on Lord's Day."

Varchiel—an angel with dominion over one of the zodiacal signs, variously given as Leo, Pisces, Corona. [*Rf.* Heywood, *The Hierachy of the Blessèd Angels*, p. 215.]

Variel—one of the 70 childbed amulet angels.

Varuna—chief of the 7 Vedic divinities (i.e., suryas), analogous to the Judaeo-Christian angels. [*See* Suryas.]

Vasariah—in the cabala, an angel of the order of dominations. He is also one of the 72 angels bearing the name of God Shemhamphorae.

Vashyash—"a prince over all the angels and Caesars." [*Rf.* Mathers, *The Greater Key of Solomon*.]

Vasiariah—in the cabala, an angel who rules over justice, nobility, magistrates, and lawyers. His sigil is reproduced in Ambelain, *La Kabbale Pratique*, p. 271.

Vassago—in the grimoires, a "good spirit" invoked to discover a woman's deepest secret.

[*Rf.* Christian, *The History and Practice of Magic* II, 402.] In Waite, *The Lemegeton*, Vassago is a prince of the nether realms where he busies himself finding lost possessions and foretelling the future. His sigil is shown in Shah, *The Secret Lore of Magic*, p. 210.

Vatale—like Vashyash, Vatale is described as "a prince over all the angels and Caesars."

Veguaniel—an angel ruler of the 3rd hour of the day.

Vehiel—an angel whose name is inscribed on the 1st pentacle of the moon.

Vehofnehu—one of the many names of the angel Metatron.

Vehuel—an angel of the order of principalities; also a zodiac angel and one of the 72 bearing the name of God Shemhamphorae. His sigil is shown in Ambelain, *La Kabbale Pratique*, p. 289.

Vehuiah—in the cabala, one of the 8 seraphim, invoked to fulfill prayers. He governs the first rays of the sun. His sigil is shown in Ambelain, *La Kabbale Pratique*, p. 260.

Infant angels by Velazquez. Detail from the *Coronation of the Virgin*. From Régamey, *Anges*.

Veischax—in Mosaic magic lore, an angel of the Seal.

Vel—a Wednesday angel, resident of the 3rd Heaven, invoked from the south.

Vel Aquiel—an angel ruler on Lord's Day (Sunday) and a resident of the 4th Heaven. For good results, he must be invoked from the north.

Velel—in de Abano, *The Heptameron*, and in Barrett, *The Magus*, a Wednesday angel resident in the 2nd or 3rd Heaven. Since he is invoked from the north, he cannot be identified with Vel (with whom, however, he seems to have much in common).

Veloas (Velous)—"a most pure angel of God" invoked in Solomonic black magic rites, specifically in the conjuration of the Sword. Veloas is a familiar figure in the grimoires.

Venahel (Venoel)—a Wednesday angel residing in the 2nd or 3rd Heaven, and invoked from the north.

Venibbeth—an angel invoked in the conjuration of Invisibility, operating under Almiras, Master of Invisibility. [*Rf. The Greater Key of Solomon.*]

Verchiel (Zerachiel)—angel of the month of July and ruler of the sign of Leo in the zodiac. [*Rf.* Camfield, *A Theological Discourse of Angels,* p. 67.] Verchiel is also one of the rulers of the order of powers. Budge, *Amulets and Talismans,* equates Verchiel with Nakiel. According to Papus in *Traité Élémentaire de Science Occulte,* Verchiel (here called Zerachiel) is governor of the sun.

Vertues—Milton's spelling (with lowercase "v") for the order of virtues in *Paradise Lost*.

Veruah—one of the many names of the angel Metatron.

Vetuel—a Monday angel resident of the 1st Heaven and invoked from the south. [*Rf.* de Abano, *The Heptameron*; Barrett, *The Magus*.]

Veualiah—one of the 9 virtues, according to a chart of "L'Arbre de Vie en Iesirah" facing p. 88 in Ambelain, *La Kabbale Pratique.* Veualiah presides over prosperity of empires and strengthens the power of kings. His corresponding angel (for purposes of invocation) is Stochene. For Veualiah's sigil, see p. 281 of Ambelain's work.

Vevalel—one of the 72 angels of the zodiac. [*Rf.* Runes, *The Wisdom of the Kabbalah.*]

Vevaliah—one of the 72 angels bearing the name of God Shemhamphorae. [*Rf.* Barrett, *The Magus* II.]

Vevaphel—an angel's name found inscribed on the 3rd pentacle of the moon. [*Rf.* Mathers, *The Greater Key of Solomon.*]

Veyothiel—an angel's name in a North Italy manuscript containing, among other cabalistic items, the *Habdalah shel Rabbi Akiba* (the *Alphabet of Rabbi Akiba*).

Vhdrziolo—one of the *nomina barbara* given in M. Gaster, *The Sword of Moses,* where Vhdrziolo is spoken of as among the 4 great angels appointed by God to the Sword.

Vhnori—one of 2 governing spirits of the sign of Sagittarius. Vhnori shares the rulership with Saritaiel [*Rf.* Levi, *Transcendental Magic,* p. 413.]

Vianuel (Vianiel)—an angel of the 5th Heaven ruling on Tuesday, and invoked from the south. [*Rf. The Magus* II; Agrippa, *Three Books of Occult Philosophy* III; *The Sixth and Seventh Books of Moses.*]

Victor—an angel so called in Hyde, *A Literary History of Ireland.* Victor appears to St. Patrick and asks him to return to Ireland for the purpose of converting the pagans to Christianity.

Victor Angels—a group of luminaries so designated in *Paradise Lost* VI, where Milton speaks of them as "in Arms they stood/of Golden Panoplie, refulgent host."

Vionatraba (Vianathraba)—in occultism, an angel of the 4th Heaven ruling on Lord's Day. He is invoked from the east. He serves also as one of 3 spirits of the sun. [*Rf.* de Abano, *The Heptameron*; Barrett, *The Magus* II.]

Annunciation group in glazed terracotta by Andrea Della Robbia, showing (top) God the Father symbolized also by a dove; (left) the Virgin Mary, and (right) the angel of annunciation, Gabriel. Now in the Oratorio della Anima del Purgatorio, a chapel near the church of San Nicolo, Florence. Reproduced from *Italian Masters*. New York: Museum of Modern Art, 1940.

Virgin Mary—to Roman Catholics, the Virgin Mary is queen of the angels.

Virgin of Light—in Manichaean lore, a great angel of the order of virtues, dwelling in the moon. In *Pistis Sophia*, the Virgin of Light replaces Sophia as judge of souls and a distributor of holy seals. She has, as her aides, 7 other Virgins of Light. [*Rf.* Legge, *Forerunners and Rivals of Christianity* II, 150.] In Coptic texts the Virgin of Light is the one who "chooses the bodies into which the souls of men shall be put at conception," in discharge of which duty "she sends the soul of Elijah into the body of John the Baptist."

Virgins—an order of angels mentioned in the Coptic *Book of the Resurrection of Christ by Bartholomew the Apostle*. [*Rf.* James, *The Apocryphal New Testament*, p. 183.] "Virgins" is very likely another term for virtues.

Virtues—a high order of angels placed usually 2nd or 3rd in the 2nd triad of the 9 choirs in the Dionysian scheme. In Hebrew lore the virtues are equated with the malakim or the tarshishim (*q.q.v.*). The principal duty of the virtues is to work miracles on earth. They are said to be the chief bestowers of grace and valor. Among the ruling princes of the order are Michael, Raphael, Barbiel, Uzziel, Peliel, and (originally) Satan. In the planetary scheme of the Egyptians, and in hermetics, the chief of virtues was Pi-Rhé (Pi-Ré, *q.v.*). More than a score of virtues are cited by name in Gustav Davidson's monograph "The Celestial Virtues." In the pseudepigraphic *Book of Adam and Eve*, 2 virtues, accompanied by 12 other angels, prepared Eve for the birth of Cain. In the just-mentioned work, its translator, L. S. A. Wells, believes that these 2 virtues "are the guardian angels of which our Lord speaks in Matthew 18:10." The 2 angels of the ascension are traditionally regarded as belonging to the order of virtues. *Cf.* Eusebius: "The Virtues of heaven, seeing Him rise, surrounded Him to form His escort." [*Rf.* Danielou, *The Angels and Their Mission*, p. 35.] When enumerating the 9 orders, Camfield, *A Theological Discourse of Angels*, uses mights in lieu of virtues. In *Larousse Illustrated Encyclopedia of Byzantine and Medieval Art*, fig. 815, the virtues are pictorially represented in a group.

Virtues of the Camps—in the *Testament of the Twelve Patriarchs*, Levi is carried to the 2nd Heaven; there he finds the "Virtues of the Camps, ready for the Day of Judgment."

Vishna—in the *Bhagavad Gita*, a mighty angel who, with Brahma and Mahish, sprang into existence from one of the primary properties. [*Rf. The Dabistan*, p. 178.]

Vishnu—the first avatar (incarnation), to whom, according to the *Bhagavad Gita*, was confided the preservation of all that Brahma created. The legend is that Vishnu, by assuming the form of a fish, recovered the Anant-Ved (source of the 4 Vedas) from Rakshas, a demon also known as Samak Azur, who had fled with it into the deep waters. Vishnu performed other miraculous feats.

Vngsursh—an angel of the summer equinox, invoked as an effective amulet against the evil eye. [*Rf.* Trachtenberg, *Jewish Magic and Superstition*, p. 139.]

Vocasiel (Vocatiel)—one of two governing spirits of the zodiacal sign of Pisces (fish), the other spirit being Rasamasa.

Vocatiel [Vocasiel]

Voel (Voil)—one of the angels of the zodiac. Voel represents or governs the sign of Virgo (the Virgin). [*Rf.* Waite, *The Lemegeton.*]

Vohal—an angel of power invoked in conjuring rites. [*Rf. The Sixth and Seventh Books of Moses.*]

Vohu Manah (Vohu Mano, "good thought")—one of the 6 amesha spentas (archangels) in Zoroastrianism. Vohu Manah is the personification of good thought. In the Avesta, Vohu is the 1st of the amesha spentas. He receives the faithful soul at death. [*Rf. Apocalypse of Salathiel* (embodied in Duff, *IV Esdras*).]

Voices, The—is gnostic mysticism, the voices are angelic entities inhabiting the Treasury of Light. It appears that there are 7 voices. [*Rf. Bruce Codex* (British Museum).] In Fludd, *Utriusque cosmi majoris et minoris historia*, the hierarchies are divided into 3 primary choirs called (by Fludd) voices, acclamations, apparitions.

Voil [Voel]

Voizia—an angel of the 12th hour of the day, serving under Beratiel. [*Rf.* Waite, *The Lemegeton.*]

Voval [Uvall]

Vraniel—an angel of the 10th hour of the night, serving under Jusguarin. [*Rf.* Waite, *The Lemegeton.*]

Vretil (Pravuil, Radueriel, etc.)—the archangelic keeper of the treasury of the Sacred Books, said to be "more wise than the other archangels." Vretil is frequently referred to, in *Enoch II* and Ezra lore, as "the scribe of the knowledge of the Most High." "The idea of a heavenly scribe," says Charles, *The Book of Enoch* (p. 28), is "derived in the main from the Babylonian Nebu." Vretil is equated with Dabriel, Uriel, Enoch, Radueriel, and Pravuil, and is associated or identified with "the man clothed in linen." (Ezekiel 9:2 et seq.).

In *Enoch II*, 23:3ff., Vretil dictates, while Enoch writes, "366 books in 30 days and 30 nights."

Vrihaspati—guardian of hymns and prayers in Vedic mythology; also "instructor of the gods" and "first-born in the highest Heaven of supreme light." Otherwise known as Vachaspati and Brihaspati. [*Rf.* Redfield, *Gods/A Dictionary of the Deities of All Lands.*]

Vual [Uvall]

Vulamahi—an angel invoked in the exorcism of the Bat. [*Rf.* Mathers, *The Greater Key of Solomon.*]

Vvael—a Monday angel resident of the 1st Heaven, invoked from the north.

Wall—an angel formerly of the order of powers, now a grand duke in Hell. When invoked he manifests in the form of a dromedary, and he is so shown in De Plancy, *Dictionnaire Infernal* (1863 edition). Under Wall's command are 36 legions of infernal spirits.

Wallim—an angel serving in the 1st Heaven. [*Rf. The Sixth and Seventh Books of Moses.*]

Warrior Angel, The [Michael]

Warriors—a term for one of the celestial orders of angels. So used in Milton, *Paradise Lost* I, 315, and by Zanchy, *Opera Omnia Theologica.* [*Rf.* Valiants (of the Heavens).]

Watchers—a high order of angels called also the grigori. They never sleep—which is said likewise of the irin (*q.v.*). Originally, according to *The Book of Jubilees*, the watchers were sent by God to instruct the children of men, but they fell after they descended to earth and started cohabiting with mortal women [*Cf.* the "sons of God" in Genesis 6.] In *Enoch I* there is mention of 7 watchers, and here the story is that they fell because they failed to appear on time for certain tasks apportioned to them. Some versions in rabbinic and cabalistic lore speak of good and evil watchers, with the good watchers still dwelling in the 5th Heaven, the evil ones in the 3rd Heaven (a kind of Hell-in-Heaven realm). Chief among the good watchers are Uriel, Raphael, Raguel, Michael, Zerachiel, Gabriel, Remiel; the evil ones include Azazel, Semyaza, Shamshiel, Kokabel, Sariel, Satanil. In the recently discovered *A Genesis Apocryphon*, Lamech suspects his wife, Bat-Enosh, of having had relations with one of the watchers (called "holy ones or fallen angels") and that Noah is the seed of such a union. Bat-Enosh swears "by the King of the worlds" that the fruit is his (Lamech's). The cause of Lamech's suspicion is the fact that when Noah was born, he immediately started conversing with "the Lord of righteousness" and that his likeness was "in the likeness of the angels of Heaven." Lamech hastens to his father Methuselah for enlightenment. Methuselah in turn appeals to Enoch for the truth. Since the *Apocryphon* breaks off here, we shall probably never know what Enoch told Methuselah. In Daniel 4:13, 17, the Hebrew prophet speaks of a

The Weigher of Souls, St. Michael. A 15th-century fresco in St. Agnes, Rome. From Wall, *Devils.*

watcher whom he saw in a vision coming down from Heaven with "a decree of the watchers." [*Rf.* Müllers, *History of Jewish Mysticism,* p. 52.]

Weatta—an angel of the Seal. [*Rf. The Sixth and Seventh Books of Moses.*]

Weighing Angel [Dokiel]

Wezynna—a ministering angel summoned in cabalistic rites. [*Rf. The Sixth and Seventh Books of Moses.*]

Wheels—the "many-eyed ones" or the ofanim (*q.v.*). The wheels are grouped with the cherubim and the seraphim by Talmudists as a high order of angels (thrones being the closest approximation). The angel Rikbiel is chief of the order. Cornelius Agrippa (as does Milton) identifies or associates the ofanim (wheels) with the cherubim. *The Zohar* (Exodus 233b) in a footnote ranks wheels as an angelic order *"above* that of seraphim."

Winds—Hebrews 1:7, in a passage often cited and here given, would indicate that "winds" (at least in this usage) denote angels: "He maketh the winds his angels, and flaming fires his ministers."

Wisdom (*Pistis Sophia*)—in *Enoch II,* 33, wisdom is hypostatized. God orders wisdom, on the 6th day of Creation, "to make man of 7 substances." In Reider, *The Book of Wisdom,* wisdom is the "assessor on God's throne," the instrument or divine agent (i.e., angel) "by which all things were created." [*Cf.* the Logos of Philo.] According to the *Catholic Encyclopedia,* "Angel," the term "angel of the Lord" finds a "counterpart in the personification of wisdom in the Sapiential books, and in at least one passage (Zachariah 3:1) it seems to stand for that son of Man whom Daniel (Daniel 7:13) saw brought before the Ancient of Days."

Woman Clothed with the Sun—"And there appeared a great wonder in heaven; a woman clothed with the sun, and the moon under her feet, and upon her head a crown of 12 stars. And she being with child cried, travailing in birth, and pained to be delivered" (Revelation 12:1–2). This is perhaps the only instance in angelology where a heavenly creature is pregnant. From the text, she is the celestial prototype or counterpart of the Virgin Mary, mother of the son of God. According to Heckethorn, *The Secret Societies of All Ages and Countries* (I, 108), the Woman Clothed with the Sun stems from the Egyptian Isis.

World-Supporting Angels [Omophorus; Splenditenes]

Wormwood—in Revelation 8:11, Wormwood is the name of a star that fell from Heaven at the blast of the 3rd angel. According to *A Dictionary of the Holy Bible* (American Tract Society, 1859), Wormwood "denotes a mighty prince or power of the air, the instrument of sore judgments on large numbers of the wicked." In St. Paul's view, Wormwood would be the equivalent of Satan, whom Paul refers to as the "prince of the power of the air." Marie Corelli, the English romantic novelist, is the author of a novel called *Wormwood.* In another piece of fiction—*The Screwtape Letters* by C. S. Lewis—Wormwood (to whom the Letters are addressed) is a "junior devil on earth" and a nephew of Screwtape (the latter being, according to Lewis, "an important official in His Satanic Majesty's 'Lowerarchy.'" The reader's attention is called here to *Hamlet* III, ii, where the Player Queen's "None wed the second [husband] but who kill'd the first" draws from Hamlet the aside "Wormwood, wormwood." It is unlikely, however, that Shakespeare had our Revelation angel in mind, rather that he used the word as an expression of distaste or bitterness, a meaning that the word has, derived from the Latin *absinthium*.

Xaphan (Zephon) and Ithuriel confront Satan, transformed into his proper shape, after discovering him "squat like a toad at the ear of Eve." By J. Martin, illustrating *Paradise Lost* IV. From Hayley, *The Poetical Works of John Milton.*

Xaphan (Zephon)—one of the apostate angels, now a demon of the 2nd rank. When Satan and his angels rebelled, Xaphan joined them. Warmly welcomed because of his inventive mind, he suggested to the rebels that they set fire to Heaven; but, before the idea could be carried out, Xaphan and his colleagues were hurled to the bottom of the abyss, where Xaphan is (and presumably will be) forever engaged in fanning the embers in the furnaces. His emblem is a pair of bellows. For a likeness of Xaphan see De Plancy, *Dictionnaire Infernal,* 1863 ed.

Xathanael (Nathanael)—According to the Jerusalem manuscript of the *Gospel of Bartholomew,* and according to the testimony of Beliar the devil (which, of course, is not always to be taken at face value), Xathanael was the 6th angel created by God—a notion that does not sit well with the *tota simul* doctrine of angels professed by Roman Catholics and others, which holds that all angels were created at one and the same time.

Xexor—in occultism, a benevolent spirit invoked in conjuring rites. [*Rf. The Sixth and Seventh Books of Moses.*]

Xomoy—a benevolent spirit, like Xexor, invoked in conjuring rites.

Xonor—a benevolent spirit, like Xexor and Xomoy, invoked in conjuring rites.

The angel Yahoel (Metatron) leading the patriarch Abraham to heaven on the wings of eagles. From *The Apocalypse of Abraham*, a Slavonic Church Ms. published in St. Petersburg in 1891, reproduced from a 14th-century text.

Yaasriel—an angel in Jewish legend who is in charge of the "70 holy pencils." With these pencils Yaasriel constantly engraves anew on shards the Ineffable Name. [*Rf.* Ginzberg, *The Legends of the Jews* III, 99.]

Yabbashael—one of the 7 angels who exercise dominion over the earth. Derived from Yabbashah, the meaning of which is "the mainland." [*Rf.* Ginzberg, *The Legends of the Jews* I, 10.] Yabbashael is cited in Schwab, *Vocabulaire de l'Angélologie*. For the names of the other 6 angels with dominion over the earth, *see* Angels of the Earth.

Yadiel (Yadael)—in *The Sword of Moses*, an angel who is called on to assist an invocant in ceremonial rites. In *Ozar Midrashim* II, 316, Yadiel is listed among the angelic guards of the gates of the North Wind.

Yael (Yale, Yehel; in Hebrew "mountain goat")—a throne angel invoked in magical rites at the close of the Sabbath. [*Rf.* Trachtenberg, *Jewish Magic and Superstition*, p. 102.]

Yahadriel—according to *The Zohar* (Numbers 201b), one of the "mouths" created on the eve of the 1st Sabbath. Yahadriel is the "mouth of the well." The other 2 are "the mouth of the ass" (Kadriel) and "the mouth of the Lord."

Yahala—one of the numerous angelic guards of the gates of the West Wind. [*Rf. Ozar Midrashim* II, 316.]

Yahanaq Rabba—one of the numerous angelic guards of the gates of the East Wind. [*Rf. Ozar Midrashim* II, 316.]

Yahel (Yael)—an angel whose name is inscribed on the 4th pentacle of the moon. [*Rf.* Mathers, *The Greater Key of Solomon*.] Yahel is also one of the 15 throne angels listed in *The Sixth and Seventh Books of Moses*.

Yahoel (Yaho, Jehoel, Jaoel)—an angel equated with Metatron (Yahoel is, in fact, the 1st of Metatron's many names). He taught Abraham the Torah and was the patriarch's guide on earth as well as in Paradise. [*Rf. The Testament of Abraham*.] In *The Apocalypse of Abraham*, another pseudepigraphic work, Yahoel says to Abraham: "I am called Yahoel . . . a power by virtue of the ineffable name dwelling in me." As Jehoel, he is the heavenly choirmaster, or one of them.

Yahrameel—in occult lore, a great angel. His name appears in Schwab, *Vocabulaire de l'Angélologie* as Iofi El ("beauty of God"), which would equate Yahrameel with Yahoel. Robert Fludd, 17th-century alchemist, mentions Yahrameel in his *Cosmology of the Microcosm.*

Yahriel (Yehra, Yarheil, Zachariel—Hebrew, *yerah*, moon)—an angel with dominion over the moon. [*Rf.* Levi, *The History of Magic,* p. 147; Trachtenberg, *Jewish Magic and Superstition,* p. 261.]

Yahsiyah—one of the many names of the angel Metatron.

Yakriel—angelic guard of the 7th Heaven. [*Rf. Ozar Midrashim* I, 119.]

Yalda Bahut (Ialdabaoth, "child of chaos")—in the Ophitic (gnostic) system, one of the 7 archons; named also Ariel. As the demiourgos, he occupies a position immediately below the "unknown Father." *See* Iadalbaoth. [*Rf. Jewish Encyclopedia* I, 595.]

Yamenton—in the cabala, an angel invoked in the benediction of the Salt. [*Rf. Grimorium Verum.*]

Yaqroun—an angel in Mandaean lore. [*Rf.* Pognon, *Inscriptions Mandaïtes des Coupes de Khouabir.*]

Yarashiel—one of numerous angelic guards of the gates of the East Wind. [*Rf. Ozar Midrashim* II 316.]

Yarhiel [Yahriel]

Yaron—in Mathers, *The Greater Key of Solomon,* a cherub or seraph invoked in the benediction of the Salt.

Yashiel—an angel whose name is found inscribed on the 1st pentacle of the moon. [*Rf.* Mathers, *The Greater Key of Solomon.*]

Yazatas (yezids, "worshipful ones")—in Zoroastrianism, the Yazatas are celestial beings, genii of the elements, angels in the Persian hierarchy.

They guard the interests of mankind under the aegis of the amesha spentas (archangels). Chief of the order is Mithra (*q.v.*), the personification of light and truth.

Yazroun—an angel in Mandaean lore. [*Rf.* Pognon, *Inscriptions Mandaïtes des Coupes de Khouabir.*]

Yebemel—one of the 72 angels in control of the signs of the zodiac. [*Rf.* Runes, *The Wisdom of the Kabbalah.*]

Yechoel—an angel of the zodiac, an associate of Yebemel.

Yedideron—the 6th of the personalized angels of the 10 holy sefiroth. In Isaac ha-Cohen of Soria's text, the less "authoritative" personalized angel is Raphael or Michael or Pehel or Tzephon.

Yefe(h)fiah (Jefefiyah, Iofiel, Yofiel—"divine beauty")—the angelic prince of the Torah. Yefefiah taught Moses the mystery of the cabala. In Aramaic incantation texts, Yefefiah figures as one of the 6 (or 7) great archangels. In Mandaean lore, he is known as Yfin-Yufafin. He may be compared or identified with Metatron. *See* also Dina, which is another name for Yefefiah, according to the *Revelation of Moses.* Yefefiah is a variant spelling. [*Rf.* Drower, *Canonical Prayerbook of the Mandaeans* (p. 84); Ginzberg, *The Legends of the Jews* III, 114; VI, 47.]

Yehadriel [Akathriel]

Yehemiel—an angel's name found inscribed on an oriental charm (*kamea*) for warding off evil. [*Rf.* Schrire, *Hebrew Amulets.*]

Yehoel—a name for the angel Metatron. [*Rf. 3 Enoch,* p. 23.]

Yehovah Vehayah—one of the many names of Metatron.

Yehudiah (Yehudiam)—in *The Zohar,* one of the chief angelic envoys. He descends with myriads of attending angels for the purpose of bearing aloft the souls of persons about to die, or who have just died. He is a beneficent angel of death. [*Cf.* Yahriel; Michael.]

Yekahel—in the cabala, one of the spirits of the

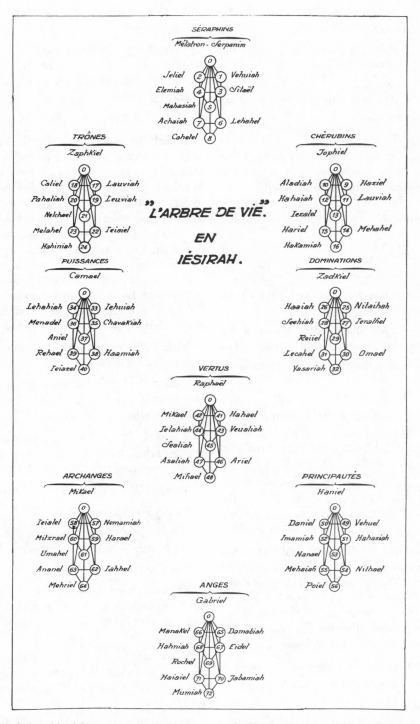

In Yetsirah (world of formation), the tree of life, showing the nine celestial orders and the chief angels governing each. From Ambelain, *La Kabbale Pratique*.

planet Mercury. His name is inscribed on the 1st pentacle of the planet.

Yeliel—an angelic guard of the gates of the South Wind. [*Rf. Ozar Midrashim* II, 316.]

Yephiel—an angel's name found inscribed on an oriental charm (*kamea*) for warding off evil. [*Rf.* Schrire, *Hebrew Amulets.*]

Yeqon [Jeqon]

Yerachmiel—in the cabala, one of 7 angels that rule the earth. These 7, says Budge in *Amulets and Talismans*, "appear to be identified with the 7 planets of the Babylonians." The 7 are Uriel, Raphael, Raguel, Michael, Suriel, Gabriel, and Yerachmiel.

Yerathel [Terathel]

Yeruel—one of 70 childbed amulet angels.

Yeruiel—according to Isaac ha-Cohen's text, Yeruiel is 3rd of the 10 holy sefiroth.

Yeshamiel—in Jewish legendary lore, an angel with dominion over the sign of Libra in the zodiac.

Yeshayah—one of the many names of the angel Metatron.

Yesod (or Yesodiel—"foundation")—ranked in the cabala as 9th of the 10 holy sefiroth. Moses invoked this name (Yesod) to bring death to the first-born of men and animals in Egypt at the time of the plagues.

Yetsirah ("formation")—the world of formation (i.e., the world of angels formed from the emanations of God). In Jewish mysticism, yetsirah (or yetzirah) is the chief domain of the angels.

Yetzer Hara (Yetzer Ra)—the evil inclination in man. In Jewish tradition, and in the view of some rabbis, the Yetzer Hara is the evil spirit itself, i.e., Satan. This is how Rabbi Simeon ben Lakish, 3rd-century scholar, expressed it: "The Yetzer Ra, Satan, and the angel of death are one and the same." [*Rf. Universal Jewish Encyclopedia* I, 303.]

Yezriel—one of the 70 childbed amulet angels.

Ygal—one of the 70 childbed amulet angels.

Yikon [Jeqon]

Yisrael ("princehood and strength")—in *The Zohar* (Vayishlah 171a), Yisrael is a variant for Israel.

Yizriel X ("princehood")—in M. Gaster, *The Sword of Moses*, one of the 14 invocation angels; also an ineffable name for God.

Ylrng—an angel (one of the *nomina barbara*) mentioned in *The Book of the Angel Raziel.*

Yofiel (Iofiel, Youfiel, Jofiel, Yefefiah)—the angel preceptor of Shem; prince of the Torah, according to an aggada of an early century. [*Rf.* Scholem, *Jewish Gnosticism, Merkabah Mysticism, and Talmudic Tradition.*] In *The Zohar*, Yofiel is a great angelic chief with 53 legions of lesser hierarchs serving him; the latter superintend the reading of the Torah in congregations at the Sabbath. In the cabala, Yofiel is the spirit of the planet Jupiter (when Jupiter enters the signs of Pisces and Sagittarius). He is also invoked as an amulet angel. "To Yofiel, the king of the mazzikin, Kafzefoni, must submit," quotes Bamberger in *Fallen Angels.*

Yofiel Mittron X—an angel cited in M. Gaster, *The Sword of Moses.*

Yofim (Yofafin)—an angel in Mandaean lore. [*Rf.* Brandt, *Die Mandaische Religion*, pp. 26, 198; *Jewish Encyclopedia*, "Angelology."]

Yomael (Yomiel)—in *3 Enoch*, an angelic prince of the 7th Heaven; also, an angel invoked in Syriac conjuring rites. [*Rf. The Book of Protection.*]

Yomiel [Yomael]

Yomyael [Jomjael]

Yonel—one of the angelic guards of the gates of the North Wind. [*Rf. Ozar Midrashim* II, 316.]

Yourba [Yurba]

Yrouel—angel of fear. The name Yrouel is found inscribed on amulets worn by women during pregnancy. [*Rf.* Schwab, *Vocabulaire de l'Angélologie.*]

Yura—in Mandaean lore, a spirit of light and of rain. He is called "the great mystic Yura." [*Rf.* Drower, *The Canonical Prayerbook of the Mandaeans*, p. 304.]

Yurba (Yourba)—in Mandaean lore, chief of

From the "Triumph of Death," ascribed to Francesco Traini, in the Campo Santo, Pisa. Angels and devils are shown withdrawing the souls of the dead or dying (left) while in the air seraphim and devils are bearing away the souls of the blessed and/or damned, or fighting for possession of one or the other. Right, a group of happy persons whom Death, with a scythe, is about to cut down. From de Bles, *Saints in Art*. New York: Art Culture Publications, 1925.

the evil genii, or chief of the powers of darkness, but acting as the servant of the, powers of light. It is said that the great Buhram (*q.v.*) derived his power from Yurba. [*Rf.* Drower, *The Mandaeans of Iraq and Iran*.]

Yurkemi—(Yorkami, Baradiel)—angel of hail. In Jewish legend Yurkemi offered to extinguish the fire consuming the 3 men in the fiery furnace, but Gabriel would not have it, contending that Yurkemi's help would not suffice. [*Rf. Sefer Yetzirah; Midrash Tehillim* on Psalm 117; Talmud *Pesahim* 118a.]

Yus(h)amin—in Mandaean lore, Yusamin or Yushamin is a spirit of fertility dwelling in the wellsprings of light; he is one of the 3 supreme *uthri* (angels). [*See* Samandiriel.]

"**Zophiel**, of Cherubim the swiftest wind,/
Came flying, and in mid-air aloud thus cried."
By Singleton, illustrating *Paradise Lost* VI. From
Hayley, *The Poetical Works of John Milton*.

Za'afiel (Za'aphiel, "wrath of God")—a holy
angel with dominion over storm-winds, i.e.,
hurricanes; an angel of destruction appointed by
God to deal with the wicked on earth. Za'afiel is
5th of the unholy sefiroth, as listed in Isaac
ha-Cohen's text. He is mentioned also in *3 Enoch*.
As in other instances, Za'afiel, because of his
missions, is regarded in some sources as a good
angel, in others as evil.

Zaamael (Za'amiel)—an angel with dominion
over storms, as listed in *3 Enoch*. In Isaac ha-
Cohen's text, "Emanations of the Left Side,"
Zaamael is 6th of the unholy sefiroth.

Zabaniyah—in Arabic lore, the name of subordinate angels (guards) serving Malik (*q.v.*).

Zabdiel—an angel with the surname Kunya.
According to M. Gaster, *The Sword of Moses*,
Zabdiel Kunya is one of the 14 ineffable names of
God.

Zabesael—an angel of the seasons associated
with Milkiel (*q.v.*). [*Rf.* Grant, *Gnosticism and
Early Christianity*.]

Zabkiel—one of the angelic rulers of the order
of thrones, an order equated with the arelim.
[*Rf.* Fludd, *Mosaicall Philosophy*.]

Zacharael (Yahriel, "remembrance of God")
—in geonic lore, one of the 7 archangels; also,
prince of the order of dominations and ruler of
the 2nd Heaven. In the cabala [*Rf.* Levi, *Transcendental Magic*, p. 100] he is an angel of the order
of powers, as is the planet Jupiter. In Paracelsus'
doctrine of Talismans, Zacharael replaces Pi-Zeus,
one of the planetary genii of Egypt, and is the angel of Thursday. [*Rf.* Christian, *The History and
Practice of Magic* I, 317.]

Zacharel—an angel of the 7th hour of the
night, serving under Mendrion. [*Rf.* Waite, *The
Lemegeton*.]

Zachariel [Zacharael]

Zachiel (Zadkiel)—overall ruler of the 6th
Heaven. [*Rf.* Trachtenberg, *Jewish Magic and
Superstition*.]

Zachriel—an angel who rules over memory.
[*Rf.* Trachtenberg, *Jewish Magic and Superstition*.]

Zaciel Parmar—one of the leaders of the fallen angels in the Enoch listings, according to Voltaire, "Of Angels, Genii and Devils."

Zacrath—an angel invoked in the exorcism of the Bat. [*Rf.* Mathers, *The Greater Key of Solomon.*]

Zada—a ministering angel used for conjuring. [*Rf. The Sixth and Seventh Books of Moses.*]

Zadakiel (Zadkiel)—spirit of the planet Jupiter. [*Rf.* Lenormant, *Chaldean Magic*, p. 26.]

Zaday—one of the angels of the 7 planets. [*Rf. The Sixth and Seventh Books of Moses.*]

Zades—in occult lore (*Clavicula Salomonis*), an angel invoked in the exorcism of Wax. [*Rf.* Mathers, *The Greater Key of Solomon.*]

Zadikiel—an angel invoked in Syriac conjuration rites. [*Rf. The Book of Protection*; Budge, *Amulets and Talismans.*]

Zadkiel (Tzadkiel, Zidekiel, Zadakiel, Zedekiel—"righteousness of God")—in rabbinic writings, the angel of benevolence, mercy, memory, and chief of the order of dominations (equated with hashmallim). In *Maseket Azilut*, with its 10 hierarchic orders, Zadkiel (or Zedekiel) is listed as co-chief with Gabriel of the order of shinanim. He is also one of the 9 rulers of Heaven and one of the 7 archangels that stand in the presence of God. In *The Zohar* (Numbers 154a) Zadkiel is represented as one of 2 chieftains, the other being Zophiel, who assists Michael when the great archangel bears his standard in battle. In the magical book *Höllenzwang of Dr. Faust*, Zadkiel (called "an enthroned angel of the holy Jehovah") is the regent of Mephistopheles. [*Rf.* Christian, *The History and Practice of Magic*, II.] According to Trachtenberg, *Jewish Magic and Superstition*, Zadkiel is another form of Sachiel. Camfield, in *A Theological Discourse of Angels*, titles Zadkiel ruler of the zodiacal sign of the planet Jupiter—although the angel of Jupiter has been identified as Zachariel, Abadiel, Zobiachel, Barchiel, and others. To Zadkiel (as also to Michael, Tadhiel, and others) is ascribed, by some writers, the act of holding back Abraham's arm when the patriarch

was about to sacrifice his son Isaac. [*Rf.* de Bles, *How to Distinguish the Saints in Art*, p. 52.]

Zadykiel (Zadkiel)—in Lenormant, *Chaldean Magic*, Zadykiel (so spelt) is the angel of the planet Jupiter.

Zafiel—in Jewish legendary lore, the angel in control of rain showers. [*Rf.* Ginzberg, *The Legends of the Jews* I, 140.]

Zafniel—the angel who in geonic lore exercises rulership over one of the months of the year. [*Rf.* Trachtenberg, *Jewish Magic and Superstition.*]

Zafrire—morning spirits. [*Rf. Jewish Encyclopedia*, 516.]

Zagiel—an evil archangel, mentioned in *Enoch I*.

Zagin—a ministering angel, mentioned in *The Sixth and Seventh Books of Moses.*

Zagnzaqiel [Zagzagel]

Zagveron—an angel invoked in the benediction of the Salt. [*Rf.* Mathers, *The Greater Key of Solomon.*]

Zagzagel (Zagzagael, Zagnzagiel, Zamzagiel—"divine splendor")—prince of the Torah and of Wisdom (but *see* Yefefiah, Iofiel, Metatron). Zagzagel instructed Moses in the knowledge of the Ineffable Name. He is the angel of the burning bush (but *see* Michael) and chief guard of the 4th Heaven, although he is said to reside in the 7th Heaven, the abode of God. A prince of the presence, Zagzagel is a teacher of angels and speaks 70 languages (*cf.* Metatron). [*Rf. 3 Enoch*; Ginzberg, *The Legends of the Jews.*] In the latter source, Zagzagel is described as the "angel with the horns of glory." In *Midrash Petirat Mosheh*, Zagzagel joined 2 other ministering angels, Michael and Gabriel, in accompanying God when the Holy One descended from Heaven to take the soul of Moses (and to assist in burying him). [*Rf. Post-Biblical Hebrew Literature*, p. 42.]

Zahabriel—in the *Pirke Hechaloth*, an angelic guard of the 1st Heaven.

Zahaftirii—in *Hechaloth Rabbati*, a prince of

the face (presence) and, with Totraviel, a seal holder at the 5th gate in Heaven.

Zahariel ("brightness")—a great angel mentioned in the works of Jewish mystic writers, specifically *The Apocalypse of Abraham*. In Levi, *Transcendental Magic*, Zahariel is an angel invoked to resist the temptations or the person of the archfiend Moloch.

Zahari'il—in Mandaean lore, a genius of generation and childbirth, a kindly spirit of light, also a "beneficent Lilith" (which would make Zahari'il female).

Zahbuk—an evil angel supplicated in conjurations for the separation of a husband from his wife. [*Rf.* M. Gaster, *The Sword of Moses.*]

Zahrun—a *malki* (angel) in Mandaean lore whom Milka d Anhura, the Giver of Life, sent down from Heaven to help in baptismal rites. For the legend, *see* Drower, *The Mandaeans of Iraq and Iran*, p. 328. There were 2 *malki* sent on this mission, the other being Zuheyr (*q.v.*).

Zahun—angel of scandal and one of the genii of the 1st hour. [*Rf.* Levi, *Transcendental Magic*; Apollonius of Tyana, *The Nuctemeron*.]

Zahzahiel (Zagzagel)—an angel of the order of shinanim. [*Rf.* Hazaz, "The Seraph."]

Zainon—in occult lore, an angel invoked in the conjuration of the Reed.

Zakiel—an angel invoked in Syriac charms, along with Michael, Gabriel, Sarphiel, and other spellbinding angels. Zakiel figures in the "binding [of] the tongue of the ruler." [*Rf. The Book of Protection.*]

Zakkiel—the angel governing storms; one of the great hierarchs present when God exalted Enoch in Heaven, transforming the O.T. patriarch from a mortal into Metatron. [*Rf.* Ginzberg *The Legends of the Jews* I, 140.]

Zakun—a great angel who, with Lahash, led 184 myriad angels to snatch away Moses' prayer (against dying) before it could reach God. (Lahash had a change of heart; brought before

God, he received 60 blows of fire and was expelled from the inner chamber.) What Zakun's punishment was, the legend (in *Midrash Petirat Mosheh*) does not say.

Zakzakiel ("merit-God") the prince appointed to write down the merits of Israel on the throne of Glory. (*Cf.* Talmud *Hagiga* 15a on Metatron.) In *3 Enoch*, when the great angel Gallisur sees Zakzakiel, he (Gallisur) removes the crown of glory from his head and falls on his face, in obeisance.

Zalbesael ("heart of God")—an angel who has dominion over the rainy season. Variant spellings: Zehlebhsheel, Zalebsel, etc.

Zalburis—in Apollonius of Tyana, *The Nuctemeron*, the genius of therapeutics, and one of the genii of the 8th hour.

Zaliel—a Tuesday angel, resident of the 5th Heaven. He is invoked from the south.

Zamael [Sammael]

Zamarchad—an angel's name found inscribed on an oriental Hebrew charm (*kamea*) for warding off evil. [*Rf.* Schrire, *Hebrew Amulets*.]

Zamiyad—to the care of this angel the Persian Magi assign the black-eyed houri or nymphs of Paradise. [*Rf.* Sale, *The Koran*, "Preliminary Discourse," p. 72.]

Zaniel—an angel with dominion over the sign of Libra in the zodiac. Zaniel is a Monday angel serving in the 1st Heaven and invoked from the west.

Zanzagiel [Zagzagel]

Zanziel—one of the numerous angelic guards of the gates of the West Wind, as listed in *Ozar Midrashim* II, 316.

Zaphiel (Zophiel, Iofiel, etc.)—a ruler of the order of cherubim, and prince of the planet Saturn. Zaphiel is also the preceptor angel of Noah. Milton (*Paradise Lost* VI, 535) calls Zaphiel (Zophiel) "of cherubim the swiftest wing." A "likeness" of Zophiel appears in Hayley, *The*

Poetical Works of John Milton. According to Ambelain, *La Kabbale Pratique*, Zaphiel is also "chief of (the order of) thrones."

Zaphkiel (Zaphchial, Zaphiel, Zophiel, etc.— "knowledge of God")—chief of the order of thrones and one of the 9 angels that rule Heaven; also one of the 7 archangels. Zaphkiel is a governor of the planet Saturn (sharing this post, it should be noted, with such other luminaries as Iophiel and Orifiel). According to Fludd, Zaphkiel, as Zophiel, is the ruler of the order of cherubim (the rabbinic ophanim). [See references in the works of Agrippa, Camfield, Heywood, and Milton.] In Klopstock, *The Messiah*, Zophiel is the "herald of Hell." But there is still some question as to whether Zophiel can properly be equated with Zaphkiel.

Zaqen—one of the angel Metatron's many names.

Zarall—one of the twin cherubim that occupied the Mercy Seat of the Ark of the Covenant; the other cherub was Jael.

Zaraph (fictional)—the 3rd angel, a seraph, in Moore's *The Loves of the Angels*.

Zarazaz (Maskelli)—in *Pistis Sophia* (p. 370), the name of an angel "called by the demons after a strong demon of their own place Maskelli." [*Rf.* Legge, *Forerunners and Rivals of Christianity* II, pp. 75, 148.] Zarazaz is the guard of the veil of the celestial treasure house.

Zaren—in Apollonius of Tyana, *The Nuctemeron*, an avenging genius.

Zarobi—in occultism, the spirit (genius) of precipices. In Apollonius of Tyana, *The Nuctemeron*, he is one of the rulers of the 3rd hour.

Zaron—in Solomonic magic, an angel invoked in the conjuration of the Reed. [*Rf.* Mathers, *The Greater Key of Solomon*, p. 115.]

Zaroteij—an angel of the Seal. [*Rf. The Sixth and Seventh Books of Moses.*]

Zarzakiel (Zagzagel?)—the angelic prince "appointed by God to write down the merits of Israel on the throne of glory." Zarzakiel is compared or identified with Sopheriel the Lifegiver. [*Rf. 3 Enoch*; Müller, *History of Jewish Mysticism.*]

Zathael—one of the 12 angels of vengeance, the 1st angels formed by God at Creation (*see* Nathanael). The names of only 6 of these angels of vengeance are known: apart from Zathael, Satanael, Michael, Gabriel, Uriel, Raphael, Nathanael. In some sources (Jewish legend) the angels of vengeance are equated with the angels of the presence, who were also 12 in number.

Zatriel—an angel invoked in Syriac ritual magic. Zatriel is grouped with Michael, Gabriel, Shamshiel, and other "spellbinding angels" in *The Book of Protection.* [*Rf.* Budge, *Amulets and Talismans*, p. 278.]

Zauir Aphin or **Zauir Aupin**—identified with Microprosopus, the "Lesser Countenance" (of God), a cabalistic concept.

Zaurva(n)—a daeva in Zoroastrian lore. Zaurva is referred to as the demon of decrepitude. [*Rf.* Geiger and Kuhn, *Grundriss der iranischen Philologie* III; Seligmann, *History of Magic.*]

Zavael (Rashiel)—an angel who controls and has dominion over whirlwinds, as noted in *3 Enoch.* Another angel credited with having such dominion and control is Rashiel.

Zavebe—one of the 200 angels who, under the leadership of Semyaza, descended to earth and cohabited with the daughters of men, an incident touched on in Genesis 6. While Enoch speaks of only 200 angels that fell, John in Revelation speaks of one third of the heavenly host that defected; and they defected, it seems, from each of the 9 orders. [*See* Fallen Angels.] There is a reference to Zavebe in Mark Van Doren's poem "The Prophet Enoch."

Zawar—a throne angel, one of 15, used in cabalistic conjuring rites. [*Rf. The Sixth and Seventh Books of Moses.*]

Zazahiel—angelic guard of the 3rd Heaven. Mentioned, with numerous others, in *Ozar Midrashim* I, 116.

Zazaii (or Zazay)—in the grimoires, a "high holy angel of God" who can be invoked in ritual rites for the exorcism of evil spirits through the application of incense and fumigations [*Rf. Grimorium Verum.*]

Zazay [Zazaii]

Zazean—an angel invoked in the exorcism of the Bat. [*Rf.* Mathers, *The Greater Key of Solomon,* p. 113.]

Zazel—a great angel invoked in Solomonic magic, particularly effective in love conjurations. He is the spirit of Saturn, with the cabalistic number 45. [*Rf. Grimorium Verum;* Barrett, *The Magus* II, 146.] Zazel figures, along with Asiel, in a talisman against sudden death, reproduced in Grillot, *A Pictorial Anthology of Witchcraft, Magic and Alchemy,* p. 342.

Zazriel ("strength of God")—in *3 Enoch,* an angelic prince representing the "divine strength, might, and power." When, in Heaven, Zazriel sees Geburatiel the prince, "he [Zazriel] removes the crown of glory from his head and falls on his face," in obeisance. *Note:* the angels of the Merkabah are all, it seems, on horseback and must dismount every time one of them runs into a brother angel of higher rank.

Zeasar—regarded by the Naassenes (a gnostic sect) as "one of the great powers of the higher world, and related to [the rulership of] the river Jordan flowing upstream." [*Rf.* Doresse, *The Secret Books of the Egyptian Gnostics,* p. 49.]

Zeba'marom—a term for angels used in Isaiah 24:21, where it denotes "hosts of the heights."

Zeba'shamaim—a term for angels used in Deuteronomy 17:3, where it denotes "hosts of Heaven."

Zebul ("habitation," "temple")—an angel who shares the rule of the 6th Heaven with Sabath—Zebul ruling by night, Sabath by day. However, Zebul is also a designation for the 3rd Heaven (as in *Visions of Ezekiel*) and a designation for the 4th Heaven (as in *3 Enoch* and Talmud *Hagiga* 12b.)

Zebuleon—one of the 9 angels who will rule or judge "at the end of the world," according to *Revelation of Esdras.* For the names of the 8 other angels, *see* Angels at the End of the World.

Zebuliel—in *The Zohar* (Exodus 201b) the chief angel of the west in the 1st Heaven, ruling only when the moon appears. He presides also over numerous chieftains who stand sentry over 9 doors. It is said that Zebuliel, in addition, accompanies prayers to the 2nd Heaven.

Zeburial—in *Pirke Hechaloth,* an angelic guard of one of the halls of the 7th Heaven.

Zechariel ("Jehovah remembers")—one of the 7 regents of the world; according to Cornelius Agrippa, Zechariel governs the planet Jupiter—which is governed, as noted elsewhere, by other angels as well.

Zechriel—one of 70 childbed amulet angels.

Zedekiel [Zadkiel]

Zedereza (Zedeesia, Zedezias)—a great luminary "by the pronouncement of whose name God will cause the sun and moon to be darkened." [*Rf.* Mathers, *The Greater Key of Solomon.*]

Zeffar—in Apollonius of Tyana, *The Nuctemeron,* the "genius of irrevocable choice." He also serves as one of the genii of the 9th hour.

Zehanpuryu'h ("this one sets free")—a great angelic prince; advocate general of Heaven and dispenser of divine mercy. With Michael he is weigher of the inerrable balances. Zehanpuryu'h is one of the crown princes of the Merkabah, with a rank higher than that of Metatron. [*Rf. 3 Enoch.*] In *Hechaloth Rabbati,* he is guardian of the 7th hall of the 7th Heaven.

Zeirna—genius of infirmities and one of the genii of the 5th hour. [*Rf.* Apollonius of Tyana, *The Nuctemeron.*]

Zekuniel—in Isaac ha-Cohen's tract "Emanations of the Left Side," Zekuniel is an alternate for Peli'iel as 2nd of the 10 holy sefiroth.

Zelebsel ("heart of God")—angel of the rainy season (in Enoch lore and in Schwab, *Vocabulaire* *de l'Angélologie*). Zelebsel is also one of 3 leaders of the months under the rulership of Melkejal.

Zephaniah (Zephemiah, Zephaniel—"Jehovah hides")—in rabbinic literature, chief of the order of ishim, which is the 2nd hierarchic order in the 10 orders of the cabala. [*Rf.* Ginzberg, *The Legends of the Jews* VI, 236.] Zephaniah, by the way, is a name for the witch (or, more correctly, the diviner) of Endor. [*See* Sedecla.]

Zephaniel—according to listing, in *Maseket Azilut*, of 10 hierarchic orders, Zephaniel is chief of the order of the ishim (*q.v.*). [*Rf. Jewish Encyclopedia*, "Angelology."]

Zephon ("a looking out")—guardian prince of Paradise; the 6th sefira; one of the cherubim. In *Paradise Lost* IV, 788 and 813, Gabriel dispatches Zephon, along with Ithuriel, to find Satan. They locate the "grieslie king" in the Garden of Eden on the point of tempting Eve. An illustration showing Zephon and Ithuriel confronting Satan appears in Hayley, *The Poetical Works of John Milton*.

Zerachiel (Verchiel, Suriel, Saraqael)—one of the 7 angels "who keep watch," as in *Enoch I* and *Esdras IV*. This would place Zerachiel in the camp of the grigori (*q.v.*). In Papus, *Traité Élémentaire de Science Occulte*, Zerachiel is a presiding angel of the sun. When equated with Verchiel (as he has been), Zerachiel is the angel of July and ruler of Leo in the zodiac.

Zerahiyah—one of the many names of the angel Metatron.

Zerahyahu—one of the many names of the angel Metatron.

Zeroel [Zeruch]

Zeruch (Zeruel, Zeroel, Cerviel—"arm of God")—an angel "set over strength." Zeruch bore up the arms of a warrior named Cerez or Kenaz in the battle with the Amorites, an incident related in *The Biblical Antiquities of Philo*. [*See* Nathanael.]

Zeruel [Zeruch]

Zethar—one of the angels of confusion. [*Rf.* Ginzberg, *The Legends of the Jews* IV, where Zethar is an "observer of immorality."]

Zevanion—in the cabala, an angel invoked in the conjuration of the Reed.

Zevtiyahu—one of the many names of the angel Metatron.

Zevudiel—in *Hechaloth Rabbati*, one of the 7 angelic guards of the 1st Heaven.

Zhsmael—an evil angel employed in conjuring rites for separating a husband from his wife. [*Rf.* M. Gaster, *The Sword of Moses*.]

Zianor—an angel invoked in the conjuration of Ink and Colors.

Zideon—like Zevanion, an angel invoked in the conjuration of the Reed.

Zi'iel—in *3 Enoch*, the angel "appointed over commotion."

Zikekiel—preceptor angel of Abraham (but *see* Zadkiel).

Zikiel (Ziqiel)—in *3 Enoch*, chief angel of comets and sparks (lightning). [*See* Akhibel.] In medieval Hebrew texts, Zikiel is in control of meteors. [*Rf. The Interpreter's Dictionary of the Bible*, "Angels."]

Zimimar (Zimmar)—"the lordly monarch of the North," a title given him by Shakespeare. [*Rf.* Spence, *An Encyclopaedia of Occultism*, p. 119.]

Ziv Hii—in Mandaean lore, one of the 4 *malki* (angels) of the North Star.

Zizuph—genius of mysteries and one of the genii of the 8th hour.

Zkzoromtiel—one of the *nomina barbara* in *The Sword of Moses*, where Zkzoromtiel is leader of the angels of ire.

Zlar—in Gollancz, *Clavicula Salomonis* (Key of Solomon), one of the "glorious and benevolent angels" who, when invoked, is solicited to share with the invocant the secret wisdom of the Creator.

Doré's illustration for *Paradise Lost* IV, showing the angels Ithuriel and Zephon on their way to earth to hunt the whereabouts of Satan. From Hayley, *The Poetical Works of John Milton*.

Zobiachel—angel of the planet Jupiter, according to Longfellow, *The Golden Legend*. In the cabala the angel of Jupiter is Zadkiel or Zachariel. The name Zobiachel occurs nowhere else than in Longfellow's work and may be a *hapax legomenon*.

Zogenethles—in gnosticism, an angelic power or aeon. [*Rf.* Doresse, *The Secret Books of the Egyptian Gnostics*, p. 85.]

Zohar ("splendor")—an angel invoked in the conjuration of the Reed. [*Rf.* Mathers, *The Greater Key of Solomon*.]

Zoharariel JHWH—in hechaloth lore, the name of one of the highest angels (if not the highest), or a secret name of God. Scholem, *Jewish Gnosticism, Merkabah Mysticism and Talmudic Tradition*, pp. 59–60, construes Zoharariel as "one of the principal objects of the Merkabah vision."

Zoigmiel—angel of the 9th hour of the day, serving under Vadriel. [*Rf.* Waite, *The Lemegeton*.]

Zomen—in occultism, an angel invoked in the exorcism of Wax. He is mentioned in the *Clavicula Salomonis*.

Zoniel—one of the 3 angelic messengers of the planet Saturn. [*Rf. The Secret Grimoire of Turiel*.]

Zonoei—in Chaldean mythology, the zonoei are planetary deities or intelligences; they are 3rd in order of celestial beings charged with the direction of the universe. [*Rf.* Aude, *Chaldean Oracles of Zoroaster*.]

Zophas—genius (angel) of pentacles and one of the genii of the 11th hour. [*Rf.* Apollonius of Tyana, *The Nuctemeron*.]

Zophiel or **Zaphiel** ("God's spy")—a spirit invoked in the prayer of the Master of the Art in Solomonic conjuration rites. When Michael bears his standard in battle, he has assisting him 2 chieftains, Zophiel being one of them (Zadkiel the other). [See *The Zohar* (Numbers 154a).] In *Paradise Lost* VI Zophiel reports to the heavenly hosts that the rebel crew are preparing a 2nd and fiercer attack. To Klopstock (*The Messiah*) Zophiel is the "herald of hell." He is the main character in the book-length poem entitled *Zophiel*, by the American poet Maria Del Occidente (Maria Gowen Brooks) who derived her inspiration from the story in the apocryphal *Book of Tobit*. Another character in the poem is the angel Raphael who also goes by the name of Hariph. In the poem, Zophiel is a fallen (but not evil) angel "with traces of his original virtue and beauty and the lingering hope of restoration to the presence of the Divinity."

Zoroel—in *The Testament of Solomon*, an angel who is able to circumvent the designs of Kumeatel, one of the 36 demons of disease (the decani). Zoroel is also mentioned in Shah, *The Secret Lore of Magic*.

Zorokothera or **Zorokothora** [Melchizedec]

Zortek—one of the angelic guards of the 1st Heaven. [*Rf. Pirke Hechaloth*.]

Zotiel ("little one of God")—in Enoch lore, a cherub sometimes identified as Johiel, guardian of Paradise. Enoch encountered Zotiel during his journey "beyond the Erythraean Sea." [Variant spellings: Zutiel, Zutel.]

Zouriel—in Jewish gnosticism, an angel whose name is found inscribed on magic amulets, along with the names of Gabriel, Michael, etc.

Zsneil—an evil angel cited in M. Gaster, *The Sword of Moses*. Zsneil is invoked to cure inflammation, dropsy, and other disorders.

Zuhair—in Mandaean lore, one of 10 *uthri* (angels) that follow the sun on its daily course.

Zuheyr—one of 2 *malki* (angels) in Mandaean lore whom the Great Life (i.e., God) sent down to help man in the performance of baptismal rites. [*Rf.* Drower, *The Mandaeans of Iraq and Iran*, p. 328.] The other *malki* was Zahrun (*q.v.*).

Zumech—"a most holy angel of God" invoked in magical operations. For details of invocation, see Mathers, *The Greater Key of Solomon*.

Zumiel—one of the 70 childbed amulet angels. [*Rf. The Book of the Angel Raziel*.]

Zuphlas—in ritual magic, a genius of forests; also one of the genii of the 11th hour. [*Rf.* Apollonius of Tyana, *The Nuctemeron.*]

Zuriel ("my rock is God")—prince of the order of principalities, ruler of the sign of Libra in the zodiac [*Rf.* Camfield, *A Theological Discourse of Angels*], and one of the 70 childbed amulet angels; also a curer of stupidity in man. When equated with Uriel, he is the angel of September. In Numbers 3:35, Zuriel is "chief of the house of the father of the families of Merari."

Musical cherubim. From Heywood, *The Hierarchy of the Blessèd Angels.*

Appendix

A complete list of appendix tables and illustrations appears in the Table of Contents, p. v.

THE ANGELIC SCRIPT

The Angelic Script, with variations of the Hebrew alphabet, from aleph to tau. From Ambelain, *La Kabbale Pratique*.

THE ORDERS OF THE CELESTIAL HIERARCHY

According to Various Sources and Authorities

ST. AMBROSE (in *Apologia Prophet David*, 5)
1. Seraphim
2. Cherubim
3. Dominations
4. Thrones
5. Principalities
6. Potentates (Powers)
7. Virtues
8. Archangels
9. Angels

ST. JEROME
1. Seraphim
2. Cherubim
3. Powers
4. Dominions (Dominations)
5. Thrones
6. Archangels
7. Angels

GREGORY THE GREAT (in *Homilia*)
1. Seraphim
2. Cherubim
3. Thrones
4. Dominations
5. Principalities
6. Powers
7. Virtues
8. Archangels
9. Angels

PSEUDO-DIONYSIUS
(in *Celestial Hierarchy*; also Thomas Aquinas in *Summa Theologica*)
1. Seraphim
2. Cherubim
3. Thrones
4. Dominations
5. Virtues
6. Powers
7. Principalities
8. Archangels
9. Angels

Constitutions of the Apostles
(in *Clementine Liturgy of the Mass*)
1. Seraphim
2. Cherubim
3. Aeons
4. Hosts
5. Powers
6. Authorities
7. Principalities
8. Thrones
9. Archangels
10. Angels
11. Dominions

ISIDORE OF SEVILLE (in *Etymologiarum*)*
1. Seraphim
2. Cherubim
3. Powers
4. Principalities
5. Virtues
6. Dominations
7. Thrones
8. Archangels
9. Angels

MOSES MAIMONIDES (in *Mishne Torah*)
1. Chaioth ha-Qadesh
2. Auphanim
3. Aralim (Erelim)
4. Chashmalim
5. Seraphim
6. Malachim
7. Elohim
8. Bene Elohim
9. Kerubim
10. Ishim

Continued

* *Note*: in Isidore of Seville's *De Ordine Creaturarum*, only 7 orders are listed, and the sequence runs thus: 1. Thrones; 2. Dominations; 3. Principalities; 4. Potentates (Powers); 5. Virtues; 6. Archangels; 7. Angels. The Seraphim are not given; the Cherubim are mentioned in a footnote.

The Zohar (Exodus 43a)

1. Malachim
2. Erelim
3. Seraphim
4. Hayyoth
5. Ophanim
6. Hamshalim
7. Elim
8. Elohim
9. Bene Elohim
10. Ishim

*Maseket Azilut**

1. Seraphim
2. Ofanim
3. Cherubim
4. Shinnanim
5. Tarshishim
6. Ishim
7. Hashmallim
8. Malakim
9. Bene Elohim
10. Arelim

JOHN OF DAMASCUS (*De Fide Orthodoxa*)

1. Seraphim
2. Cherubim
3. Thrones
4. Dominions
5. Powers
6. Authorities (Virtues)
7. Rulers (Principalities)
8. Archangels
9. Angels

Berith Menucha†

1. Arelim
2. Ishim
3. Bene Elohim
4. Malakim

5. Hashmallim
6. Tarshishim
7. Shinnanim
8. Cherubim
9. Ofanim
10. Seraphim

DANTE

1. Seraphim
2. Cherubim
3. Thrones
4. Dominations
5. Virtues
6. Powers
7. Archangels
8. Principalities
9. Angels

BARRETT, *The Magus*

1. Seraphim
2. Cherubim
3. Thrones
4. Dominations
5. Powers
6. Virtues
7. Principalities
8. Archangels
9. Angels
10. Innocents
11. Martyrs
12. Confessors

The erelim and the ishim are sometimes considered the same [*Rf. Revelation of Moses* in M. Gaster, *Studies and Texts in Folklore*, pp. 128–129.]

The erelim are derived from Isaiah 33:7. The elim are derived from Exodus 15:27 and Ezekiel 32:21.

Continued

* The chiefs of the orders given in *Maseket Azilut* are 1. Shemuel (Kemuel or Jehoel) for Seraphim; 2. Raphael and Ofaniel for Ofanim; 3. Cherubiel for Cherubim; 4. Zedekiel (Zadkiel) and Gabriel for Shinnanim; 5. Tarshiel and Sabriel for Tarshishim; 6. Zephaniel for Ishim; 7. Hashmal for Hashmallim; 8. Uzziel for Malakim; 9. Hofniel for Bene Elohim; 10. Michael for Arelim.

† It will be observed that in the *Berith Menucha* list, the Seraphim are ranked last (and 10th). The chiefs of the orders here are: 1. Michael for Arelim; 2. Zephaniah for Ishim; 3. Hofniel for Bene Elohim; 4. Uriel for Malakim; 5. Hashmal for Hashmallim; 6. Tarshish for Tarshishim; 7. Zadkiel for Shinnanim; 8. Cherub for Cherubim; 9. Raphael for Ofanim; 10. Jehoel for Seraphim.

The hashmallim (or hamshalim) are often equated with the order of dominations.

The hayyoths are equated with the cherubim (Ezekiel 20).

The ophanim in turn are equated with the cherubim; they are referred to as the "many-eyed ones" or "wheels."

The thrones are equated with the ofanim or arelim (erelim).

The malakim and the tarshishim are identified with the virtues.

The tafsarim (*3 Enoch*) constitute an order of angels grouped usually with the elim and erelim;

they are regarded as "greater than all the ministering angels who minister before the throne of glory."

The bene elohim (sons of God) are sometimes equated with the ishim. According to *The Zohar*, they belong to a subdivision of the order of thrones.

Other hierarchic orders, mentioned in various sources, religious and secular, include ardors, authorities, sanctities, voices, regents, apparitions, acclamations, sovereignties, gonfalons, warriors, etc.

THE SEVEN ARCHANGELS
According to Various Sources and Authorities

Enoch I (Ethiopic Enoch)
   (the earliest reference to the 7)
1. Uriel
2. Raphael
3. Raguel (Ruhiel, Ruagel, Ruahel)
4. Michael
5. Zerachiel (Araqael)
6. Gabriel
7. Remiel (Jeremiel, Jerahmeel)

3 Enoch (Hebrew Enoch)*
1. Mikael
2. Gabriel
3. Shatqiel
4. Baradiel
5. Shachaqiel
6. Baraqiel (Baradiel)
7. Sidriel (or Pazriel)

Testament of Solomon
1. Mikael
2. Gabriel
3. Uriel
4. Sabrael
5. Arael
6. Iaoth
7. Adonael

CHRISTIAN GNOSTICS
1. Michael
2. Gabriel
3. Raphael
4. Uriel (= Phanuel)
5. Barachiel
6. Sealtiel
7. Jehudiel

GREGORY THE GREAT
1. Michael
2. Gabriel
3. Raphael
4. Uriel
5. Simiel
6. Orifiel
7. Zachariel

PSEUDO-DIONYSIUS
1. Michael
2. Gabriel
3. Raphael
4. Uriel
5. Chamuel
6. Jophiel
7. Zadkiel

Continued

* In Odeberg's edition of *3 Enoch*, it is noted that "each of the 7 archangels is accompanied by 496,000 myriads of ministering angels."

IN GEONIC LORE

1. Michael
2. Gabriel
3. Raphael
4. Aniel
5. Kafziel
6. Samael
7. Zadkiel

IN TALISMANIC MAGIC

1. Zaphkiel
2. Zadkiel
3. Camael

4. Raphael
5. Haniel
6. Michael
7. Gabriel

IN *The Hierarchy of the Blessèd Angels*

1. Raphael
2. Gabriel
3. Chamuel
4. Michael
5. Adabiel
6. Haniel
7. Zaphiel

Other archangels mentioned as among the 7 include: Pravuil, Shepherd, Phanuel (equated with Uriel).

In Persian mythology, "the holy immortal ones," all of whom had the nature of angels, were: 1. Justice or Truth; 2. Right Order; 3. Obedience; 4. Prosperity; 5. Piety or Wisdom; 6. Health; 7. Immortality.

According to Muslim lore there are only 4 arch-angels: Gabriel, Michael, Azrael, Israfel. Usually 7, rather than 4, were favored because 7 is a more mystical number and because, as we read in Esther 1:14, there were "Seven princes who saw the king's (God's) face."

The Babylonians regarded the 7 planets as deities, and these (says W. O. E. Oesterley) were the prototype of the Judaeo-Christian archangels. The amesha spentas have also been regarded as the prototype.

THE RULING PRINCES OF THE NINE CELESTIAL ORDERS

SERAPHIM

Michael, Seraphiel, Jehoel, Uriel, Kemuel (Shemuel), Metatron, Nathanael, and Satan (before his fall)

CHERUBIM

Gabriel, Cherubiel, Ophaniel, Raphael, Uriel, Zophiel, and Satan (before his fall)

THRONES

Orifiel, Zaphkiel, Zabkiel, Jophiel (or Zophiel), Raziel

DOMINIONS (Dominations)

Zadkiel, Hashmal, Zacharael (Yahriel), Muriel

VIRTUES

Uzziel, Gabriel, Michael, Peliel, Barbiel, Sabriel, Haniel, Hamaliel, Tarshish

POWERS

Camael, Gabriel, Verchiel, and Satan (before his fall)

PRINCIPALITIES

Nisroc, Haniel, Requel, Cerviel, Amael

ARCHANGELS

Metatron, Raphael, Michael, Gabriel, Barbiel, Jehudiel, Barachiel, and Satan (before his fall)

ANGELS

Phaleg, Adnachiel (Advachiel), Gabriel, Chayyliel

THE ANGEL RULERS OF THE SEVEN HEAVENS

FIRST HEAVEN (Shamain or Shamayim)
Angel Ruler: Gabriel

SECOND HEAVEN (Raquie or Raqia)
Angel Rulers: Zachariel and Raphael

THIRD HEAVEN (Sagun or Shehaqim)
Angel Rulers: Anahel (chief); subordinate princes: Jabniel, Rabacyel, Dalquiel

FOURTH HEAVEN (Machonon or Machen)
Angel Ruler: Michael

FIFTH HEAVEN (Mathey or Machon)
Angel Ruler: Sandalphon or Sammael

SIXTH HEAVEN (Zebul)
Angel Rulers: Zachiel (chief); subordinate princes: Zebul (during the day); Sabath (during the night)

SEVENTH HEAVEN (Araboth)
Angel Ruler: Cassiel

[*Rf. The Sixth and Seventh Books of Moses*, 137; *The Book of the Angel Raziel*; de Abano, *The Heptameron*; Cornelius Agrippa, *Three Books of Occult Philosophy*.]

THE THRONE ANGELS

According to *The Book of the Angel Raziel*, the throne angels number 7. Other sources give the number as 4 or 70. Below are the 7 from *The Book of the Angel Raziel*. The other 15 listed are cabalistic throne angels and are drawn from *The Sixth and Seventh Books of Moses*. They are invoked in magical arts.

1. Gabriel
2. Fanuel (Penuel, Uriel, Feniel, Phanuel)
3. Michael
4. Uriel
5. Raphael
6. Israel
7. Uzziel (or Usiel)

1. Thronus
2. Tehom
3. Haseha
4. Amarzyom
5. Schawayt
6. Chuscha
7. Zawar
8. Yahel
9. Adoyahel
10. Schimuel
11. Achusaton
12. Schaddyl
13. Chamyel
14. Parymel
15. Chayo

THE SIXTY-FOUR ANGEL-WARDENS OF THE SEVEN CELESTIAL HALLS OR HEAVENS (HECHALOTH)

IN THE 1ST HEAVEN OR HALL

1. Suria
2. Tutrechial
3. Tutrusiai
4. Zortek
5. Mufgar
6. Ashrulyai
7. Sabriel
8. Zahabriel
9. Tandal
10. Shokad
11. Huzia
12. Deheboryn
13. Adririon
14. Khabiel (head supervisor)

Continued

15. Tashriel
16. Nahuriel
17. Jekusiel
18. Tufiel
19. Dahariel
20. Maskiel
21. Shoel
22. Sheviel

IN THE 2ND HEAVEN

23. Tagriel (chief)
24. Maspiel
25. Sahriel
26. Arfiel
27. Shahariel
28. Sakriel
29. Ragiel
30. Sehibiel

IN THE 3RD HEAVEN

31. Sheburiel (chief)
32. Retsutsiel
33. Shalmial
34. Savlial
35. Harhazial
36. Hadrial
37. Bezrial

IN THE 4TH HEAVEN

38. Pachdial (chief)
39. Gvurtial
40. Kzuial

[*Rf. Pirke Hechaloth.*]

41. Shchinial
42. Shtukial
43. Arvial (or Avial)
44. Kfial
45. Anfial

IN THE 5TH HEAVEN

46. Techial (chief)
47. Uzial
48. Gmial
49. Gamrial
50. Sefrial
51. Garfial
52. Grial
53. Drial
54. Paltrial

IN THE 6TH HEAVEN

55. Rumial
56. Katmial
57. Gehegial
58. Arsabrsbial
59. Egrumial
60. Parzial
61. Machkial (Mrgial, Mrgiviel)
62. Tufrial

IN THE 7TH HEAVEN

63. Zeburial
64. Tutrbebial

THE GOVERNING ANGELS
OF THE TWELVE MONTHS OF THE YEAR

JANUARY	Gabriel (or Cambiel)	JULY	Verchiel
FEBRUARY	Barchiel	AUGUST	Hamaliel
MARCH	Machidiel (or Malahidael)	SEPTEMBER	Uriel (or Zuriel)
APRIL	Asmodel	OCTOBER	Barbiel
MAY	Ambriel (or Ambiel)	NOVEMBER	Adnachiel (or Advachiel)
JUNE	Muriel	DECEMBER	Hanael (or Anael)

[*Rf. De Plancy, Dictionnaire Infernal, IV, 138.*]

SPIRITS, MESSENGERS, INTELLIGENCES OF THE SEVEN PLANETS

SUN

Spirits: Gabriel, Vianathraba, Corat
Messengers: Burchat, Suceratos, Capabile
Intelligences: Haludiel, Machasiel, Chassiel

JUPITER

Spirits: Setchiel, Chedusitaniel, Corael
Messengers: Turiel, Coniel, Babiel
Intelligences: Kadiel, Maltiel, Huphatriel, Estael

MOON

Spirits: Gabriel, Gabrael, Madios
Messengers: Anael, Pabael, Ustael
Intelligences: Uriel, Naromiel, Abuori

VENUS

Spirits: Thamael, Tenariel, Arragon
Messengers: Colzras, Peniel, Penael
Intelligences: Penat, Thiel, Rael, Teriapel

SATURN

Spirits: Sammael, Bachiel, Astel
Messengers: Sachiel, Zoniel, Hubaril
Intelligences: Mael, Orael, Valnum

MERCURY

Spirits: Mathlai, Tarmiel, Baraborat
Messengers: Raphael, Ramel, Doremiel
Intelligences: Aiediat, Modiat (Mediat),
                     Sugmonos, Sallales

Presiding Spirits of Jupiter: Sachiel, Castiel, Asasiel

Presiding Spirits of Mars: Sammael, Satael, Amabiel

Presiding Spirits of Venus: Anael, Rachiel, Sachiel

Presiding Spirits of Mercury: Raphael, Uriel, Seraphiel

[*Rf. The Secret Grimoire of Turiel,* 33–35, which omits listing the Spirits, Messengers, and Intelligences of Mars.]

THE ANGELIC GOVERNORS OF THE TWELVE SIGNS OF THE ZODIAC

Angel	*Sign*	*Angel*	*Sign*
Malahidael or Machidiel (Angel of March)	Aries (the Ram)	Barbiel (Angel of October)	Scorpio (the Scorpion)
Asmodel (Angel of April)	Taurus (the Bull)	Advachiel or Adnachiel (Angel of November)	Sagittarius (the Archer)
Ambriel (Angel of May)	Gemini (the Twins)	Hanael (Angel of December)	Capricorn (the Goat)
Muriel (Angel of June)	Cancer (the Crab)		
Verchiel (Angel of July)	Leo (the Lion)	Cambiel or Gabriel (Angel of January)	Aquarius (the Water-Carrier)
Hamaliel (Angel of August)	Virgo (the Virgin)	Barchiel (Angel of February)	Pisces (the Fishes)
Zuriel or Uriel (Angel of September)	Libra (the Scales)		

[*Rf.* Trithemius, *Of the Heavenly Intelligences*; cf. the 12 governors of the 12 signs of the zodiac in the astrological system of the Chaldeans: 1. Anu; 2. Bel; 3. Nuah; 4. Belit; 5. Sin; 6. Samas; 7. Bin; 8. Adar; 9. Marduk; 10. Nergal; 11. Istar; 12. Nebo. [*Rf.* Lenormant, *Chaldean Magic,* p. 119.]

THE ARCHANGELS AND ANGELS
OF THE SEVEN DAYS OF THE WEEK

Day	*Archangel*	*Angel*		*Day*	*Archangel*	*Angel*
MONDAY	Gabriel	Gabriel		FRIDAY	Haniel	Anael
TUESDAY	Khamael	Zamael		SATURDAY	Tzaphiel	Cassiel
WEDNESDAY	Michael	Raphael		SUNDAY	Raphael	Michael
THURSDAY	Tzaphiel	Sachiel				

Sunday	*Monday*	*Tuesday*	*Wednesday*	*Thursday*	*Friday*	*Saturday*
Michaēl	Gabriel	Camael	Raphaēl	Sachiel	Ana'el	Caſſiel
name of the 4.ᵗʰ Heaven Machen.	*name of the 1.ˢᵗ Heaven* Shamain.	*name of the 5 Heaven* Machon.	*name of the 2.ᵈ Heaven* Raquie.	*name of the 6.ᵗʰ Heaven* Zebul.	*name of the 3.ᵈ Heaven* Sagun.	*No Angels ruling above the 6.ᵗʰ Heaven*

A table showing the names of the angels governing the seven days of the week, along with their sigils, zodiacal signs, and the heavens ruled by these angels. From Barrett, *The Magus*.

[*Rf.* Shah, *Occultism, Its Theory and Practice*, p. 143; Barrett, *The Magus*, facing p. 105; Mathers, *The Greater Key of Solomon*, Table of the Planetary Hours, p. 7.]

THE ANGELIC GOVERNORS OF THE SEVEN PLANETS
CHIEF OF THE PLANETS: Rahatiel

according to Al-Barceloni

1. Raphael, over the Sun
2. Aniel, over Venus
3. Michael, over Mercury
4. Gabriel, over the Moon
5. Kafziel, over Saturn
6. Zadkiel, over Jupiter
7. Sammael, over Mars

according to Barrett, *The Magus*

1. Raphael or Michael, over the Sun
2. Anael or Haniel, over Venus
3. Michael or Raphael, over Mercury
4. Gabriel, over the Moon
5. Zaphiel or Orifiel, over Saturn
6. Zadkiel or Zachariel, over Jupiter
7. Camael or Zamael, over Mars

Longfellow in *The Golden Legend* gives the following list: 1. Raphael, over the Sun; 2. Gabriel, over the Moon; 3. Anael, the "angel of love," over Venus; 4. Zobiachel, over Jupiter; 5. Michael, over Mercury; 6. Uriel, over Mars; 7. Orifel, over Saturn. In angelology, Zobiachel is a *hapax legomenon* (he appears for the first time in *The Golden Legend* and in no other source).

THE GOVERNING ANGELS OF THE FOUR SEASONS

SPRING (Talvi)

Governing Angel: Spugliguel (head of the sign of Spring); serving angels: Amatiel, Caracasa, Core, Commissoros

SUMMER (Casmaran)

Governing Angel: Tubiel (head of the sign of Summer); serving angels: Gargatel, Gaviel, Tariel

AUTUMN (Ardarcel)

Governing Angel: Torquaret (head of the sign of Autumn); serving angels: Tarquam, Guabarel

WINTER (Farlas)

Governing Angel: Attarib (head of the sign of Winter); serving angels: Amabael, Cetarari (Ctarari)

[*Rf.* Barrett, *The Magus*, 108; Shah, *Occultism, Its Theory and Practice*, 43–44.]

THE ANGELS OF THE HOURS OF THE DAY AND NIGHT

Hours Day.	Angels and Planets ruling SUNDAY.	Angels and Planets ruling MONDAY.	Angels and Planets ruling TUESDAY.	Angels and Planets ruling WEDNESDAY.	Angels and Planets ruling THURSDAY.	Angels and Planets ruling FRIDAY.	Angels and Planets ruling SATURDAY.
	Day.	*Day.*	*Day.*	*Day.*	*Day.*	*Day.*	*Day.*
1	☉ Michael	☽ Gabriel	♂ Samael	☿ Raphael	♃ Sachiel	♀ Anael	♄ Cassiel
2	♀ Anael	♄ Cassiel	☉ Michael	☽ Gabriel	♂ Samael	☿ Raphael	♃ Sachiel
3	☿ Raphael	♃ Sachiel	♀ Anael	♄ Cassiel	☉ Michael	☽ Gabriel	♂ Samael
4	☽ Gabriel	♁ Samael	☿ Raphael	♃ Sachiel	♀ Anael	♄ Cassiel	☉ Michael
5	♄ Cassiel	☉ Michael	☽ Gabriel	♂ Samael	☿ Raphael	♃ Sachiel	♀ Anael
6	♃ Sachiel	♀ Anael	♄ Cassiel	☉ Michael	☽ Gabriel	♂ Samael	☿ Raphael
7	♂ Samael	☿ Raphael	♃ Sachiel	♀ Anael	♄ Cassiel	☉ Michael	☽ Gabriel
8	☉ Michael	☽ Gabriel	♁ Samael	☿ Raphael	♃ Sachiel	♀ Anael	♄ Cassiel
9	♀ Anael	♄ Cassiel	☉ Michael	☽ Gabriel	♂ Samael	☿ Raphael	♃ Sachiel
10	☿ Raphael	♃ Sachiel	♀ Anael	♄ Cassiel	○ Michael	☽ Gabriel	♂ Samael
11	☽ Gabriel	♂ Samael	☿ Raphael	♃ Sachael	♀ Anael	♄ Cassiel	☉ Michael
12	♄ Cassiel	☉ Michael	☽ Gabriel	♂ Samael	☿ Raphael	♃ Sachiel	♀ Anael
Hours Night	*Night.*	*Night.*	*Night.*	*Night.*	*Night.*	*Night.*	*Night.*
1	♃ Sachael	♀ Anael	♄ Cassiel	☉ Michael	☽ Gabriel	♂ Samael	☿ Raphael
2	♂ Samiel	☿ Raphael	♃ Sachiel	♀ Anael	♄ Cassiel	☉ Michael	☽ Gabriel
3	☉ Michael	☽ Gabriel	♂ Samael	☿ Raphael	♃ Sachiel	♀ Anael	♄ Cassiel
4	♀ Anael	♄ Cassiel	☉ Michael	☽ Gabriel	♂ Samael	☿ Raphael	♃ Sachiel
5	☿ Raphael	♃ Sachiel	♀ Anael	♄ Cassiel	☉ Michael	☽ Gabriel	♂ Samael
6	☽ Gabriel	♂ Samael	☿ Raphael	♃ Sachiel	♀ Anael	♄ Cassiel	☉ Michael
7	♄ Cassiel	☉ Michael	☽ Gabriel	♂ Samael	☿ Raphael	♃ Sachiel	♀ Anael
8	♃ Sachiel	♀ Anael	♄ Cassiel	☉ Michael	☽ Gabriel	♂ Samael	☿ Raphael
9	♂ Samael	☿ Raphael	♃ Sachiel	♀ Anael	♄ Cassiel	☉ Michael	☽ Gabriel
10	☉ Michael	☽ Gabriel	♂ Samael	☿ Raphael	♃ Sachiel	♀ Anael	♄ Cassiel
11	♀ Anael	♄ Cassiel	☉ Michael	☽ Gabriel	♂ Samael	☿ Raphael	♃ Sachiel
12	☿ Raphael	♃ Sachiel	♀ Anael	♄ Cassiel	☉ Michael	☽ Gabriel	♂ Samael

A table showing the hours of the day and night during which certain angels rule, along with the related zodiacal signs. From Barrett, *The Magus*.

THE SEVENTY-TWO ANGELS
BEARING THE MYSTICAL NAME OF GOD SHEMHAMPHORAE

The table consists of four horizontal bands of eighteen columns. Each column shows three rows of Hebrew letters forming the angelic name-root, a row bearing the divine suffix (יה or אל), and the angel's name beneath. The angel names, as printed (left to right) in each band, are:

Caliel	Leviah	Hakamiah	Hariel	Mebahel	Ieiazel	Hahaiah	Lauiah	Aladiah	Haziel	Cahethel	Achaiah	Lelahel	Mahasiah	Elemiah	Sitael	Ieliel	Vehuiah
Monadel	Chavakiah	Lehahiah	Iehuiah	Vasariah	Leeabel	Omael	Reiiel	Seehiah	Ierathel	Haaiah	Nithhaiah	Hahuiah	Melahel	Ieiaiel	Nelchael	Pahaliah	Leuuiah
Nithael	Nanael	Itnamiah	Hahaziah	Daniel	Vehuel	Mihael	Asaliah	Ariel	Saaliah	Idahiah	Vevaliah	Michael	Hahahel	Ihiazel	Rehael	Haamiah	Aniel
Mumiah	Hauiel	Ilbamiah	Rochel	Habuiah	Eiael	Meniel	Damabiah	Mehekiel	Annauel	Iahhel	Umabel	Mizrael	Harahel	Ieilael	Nemamaih	Poiel	Mbahiah

A table showing the seventy-two angels bearing the mystical name of God Shemhamphorae, according to the cabala. From Barrett, *The Magus.*

Shemhamphorae (1). The 72 names of God in the Hebrew tongue. From *The Sixth and Seventh Books of Moses.*

Shemhamphorae (2). The 72 names of God in the Hebrew tongue. From *The Sixth and Seventh Books of Moses.*

THE SEVENTY AMULET ANGELS INVOKED AT THE TIME OF CHILDBIRTH

Drawn from *The Book of the Angel Raziel*

1. Michael	19. Rachmiah	37. Chachmal	54. Tsirya
2. Gabriel	20. Katzhiel	38. Machnia*	55. Rigal
3. Raphael	21. Schachniel	39. Kaniel	56. Tsuria
4. Nuriel	22. Karkiel	40. Griel or Grial	57. Psisya
5. Kidumiel	23. Ahiel	41. Tzartak	58. Oriel
6. Malkiel*	24. Chaniel*	42. Ofiel	59. Samchia*
7. Tzadkiel	25. Lahal	43. Rachmiel	60. Machnia*
8. Padiel	26. Malchiel*	44. Sensenya	61. Kenunit
9. Zumiel	27. Shebniel	45. Udrgazyia	62. Yeruel
10. Chafriel	28. Rachsiel	46. Rsassiel	63. Tatrusia
11. Zuriel	29. Rumiel	47. Ramiel	64. Chaniel*
12. Ramuel	30. Kadmiel	48. Sniel	65. Zechriel
13. Yofiel	31. Kadal	49. Tahariel	66. Variel
14. Sturi (el?)	32. Chachmiel	50. Yezriel	67. Diniel
15. Gazriel	33. Ramal	51. Neria(h)	68. Gdiel or Gediel
16. Udriel	34. Katchiel	52. Samchia* (Samchiel)	69. Briel
17. Lahariel	35. Aniel	53. Ygal	70. Ahaniel
18. Chaskiel	36. Azriel		

* Repeats.

THE NAMES OF METATRON

The 76 names of Metatron given below are taken from *Sefer ha-Heshek*, a Hebrew tract published in Lemberg in 1865 and edited by I. M. Epstein. It appears that Metatron had other names besides, amounting to over 100 (*3 Enoch*, 48, gives 105). These additional appellatives include such familiar ones as Lad, Naar, Sar ha-Olam, Little Iao, Shaddai, Yoel, Surya, Yofiel, Pisgon, Sithriel, etc.

1. Tsahtsehiyah
2. Zerahyahu
3. Taftefiah
4. Hayat
5. Hashesiyah
6. Duvdeviyah
7. Yahsiyah
8. Palpeltiyah
9. Havhaviyah
10. Haviyahu
11. Veruah
12. Magirkon
13. Itmon
14. Batsran
15. Tishbash
16. Tishgash
17. Mitspad
18. Midrash
19. Matsmetsiyah
20. Patspetsiyah
21. Zevtiyahu
22. Miton
23. Adrigon
24. Metatron
25. Ruah Piskonit
26. Itatiyah
27. Tavtavel
28. Hadraniel
29. Tatriel
30. Ozah (Uzah)
31. Eved
32. Galiel
33. Tsaftsefiel
34. Hatspatsiel
35. Sagmagigrin
36. Yefefiah
37. Estes
38. Safkas
39. Saktas
40. Mivon
41. Asasiah
42. Avtsangosh
43. Margash
44. Atropatos
45. Tsaftsefiyah
46. Zerahiyah
47. Tamtemiyah
48. Adadiyah
49. Alaliayh
50. Tahsasiyah
51. Rasesiyah
52. Amisiyah
53. Hakham
54. Bibiyah
55. Tsavtsiyah
56. Tsaltseliyah
57. Kalkelmiyah
58. Hoveh Hayah
59. Yehovah Vehayah
60. Tetrasiyah
61. Uvayah
62. Shosoriyah
63. Vehofnehu
64. Yeshayah
65. Malmeliyah
66. Gale Raziya
67. Atatiyah
68. Emekmiyahu
69. Tsaltselim
70. Tsavniyah
71. Giatiyah
72. Parshiyah
73. Shaftiyah
74. Hasmiyah
75. Sharshiyah
76. Geviriyah

THE GREAT ARCHONS

The Archons ("rulers") are identified or equated with the Aeons. Gershom Scholem's definition of an archon is simply "great angel." In rabbinic lore, the great Archon is Shamshiel or Shemuiel, "mediator between the prayers of Israel and the princes of the 7th heaven."

IN THE OPHITIC (GNOSTIC) SYSTEM

Jaldabaoth
Jao
Sabaoth
Adonaios
Astanphaios
Ailoaios
Oraios

IN OTHER GNOSTIC SYSTEMS

Saklas (in Manicheanism, a chief demon)
Seth
David
Eloiein
Katspiel
Erathaol
Domiel

IN THE PAPYRI GRAECAE MAGICAE

Uriel
Michael
Raphael
Gabriel
Shamuil

[*Rf.* Danielou, *The Angels and Their Mission*; Gaynor, *Dictionary of Mysticism*; Doresse, *The Secret Books of the Egyptian Gnostics*; Scholem, *Major Trends in Jewish Mysticism*.]

THE CHIEF ANGEL PRINCES OF THE ALTITUDES
the Four Cardinal Points

CHIEFS OF THE 1ST ALTITUDE (or Chora)

Alimiel
Barachiel
Gabriel { carry in their hands a banner or flag with a red cross on it; carry a crown of rose flowers; speak with a low voice
Helison
Lebes

CHIEFS OF THE 3RD ALTITUDE (or Chora)

Eliphaniasai
Elomina
Gedobonai { form of little children or little women; dressed in green or silver color, with crown of bay leaves; leave a sweet perfume behind them
Gelomiros
Taranava

CHIEFS OF THE 2ND ALTITUDE (or Chora)

Aphiriza
Armon
Genon { form of young child dressed in satin; crown of red gilly flowers; face reddish
Geron
Gereimon

CHIEFS OF THE 4TH ALTITUDE (or Chora)

Barachiel*
Capitiel
Deliel { form of little men or boys, dressed in black, mixed with a dark green; in their hands they hold a bird "which is naked"
Gebiel
Gediel

* Barachiel appears to be a chief of both the 1st Altitude and the 4th Altitude. The Altitudes must be invoked according to their proper hour of the day and the month of the year; otherwise they cannot be summoned. [*Rf. The Almadel of Solomon*; Shah, *The Secret Lore of Magic*, 173ff.]

THE TWENTY-EIGHT ANGELS RULING
IN THE TWENTY-EIGHT MANSIONS OF THE MOON

1. Geniel	8. Amnediel	15. Atliel	22. Geliel
2. Enediel	9. Barbiel	16. Azeruel	23. Requiel
3. Anixiel	10. Ardifiel	17. Adriel	24. Abrinael
4. Azariel	11. Neciel	18. Egibiel	25. Aziel
5. Gabriel	12. Abdizuel	19. Amutiel	26. Tagriel
6. Dirachiel	13. Jazeriel	20. Kyriel	27. Atheniel
7. Scheliel	14. Ergediel	21. Bethnael	28. Amnixiel

[*Rf.* Barrett, *The Magus*, II, 57.]

THE ARCHANGELS OF THE HOLY SEFIROTH

1. Methattron (Metatron)	for Kether (Crown)	6. Mikhael	for Tiphereth (Beauty)
2. Ratziel (Raziel)	for Chokhmah (Wisdom)	7. Haniel	for Netzach (Victory)
3. Tzaphqiel	for Binah (Understanding)	8. Raphael	for Hod (Splendor)
4. Tzadqiel	for Chesed (Mercy)	9. Gabriel	for Yesod (Foundation)
5. Khamael	for Geburah (Strength)	10. Methattron (or the Shekinah)	for Malkuth (Kingdom)

[*Rf.* Mathers, *The Kabbalah Unveiled*.]

THE UNHOLY SEFIROTH

Emanations from the Left Side of God

1. Thaumiel — The averse sefira to Kether. Cortex: Cathariel

2. Chaigidiel — The averse sefira to Chochma. Cortex: Oghiel or Ghogiel

3. Sathariel (Sheireil) — The averse sefira to Binah

4. Gamchicoth (Gog Sheklah) — The averse sefira to Chesed. Cortex: Azariel

5. Golab — The averse sefira to Geburah. Cortex: Usiel

6. Togarini — The averse sefira to Tiphereth. Cortices: Zomiel and Belphegor

7. Harab Serap — The averse sefira to Netzach. Cortices: Theumiel and Baal Chanan

8. Sammael — The averse sefira to Hod. Cortices: Theuniel and Adramelek

9. Gamaliel — The averse sefira to Jesod. Cortex: Ogiel

10. Lilith — The averse sefira to Malkuth

[*Rf.* Waite, *The Holy Kabbalah.*]

THE WATCHERS

Known also as the Grigori

According to *The Book of Jubilees*, the Watchers are the sons of God (Genesis 6) sent from heaven to instruct the children of men; they fell after they descended to earth and cohabited with the daughters of men—for which act they were condemned (so legend reports) and became fallen angels. But not all Watchers descended: those that remained are the holy Watchers, and they reside in the 5th Heaven. The evil Watchers dwell either in the 3rd Heaven or in Hell.

1. **Armaros**
   Taught men the resolving of enchantments.

2. **Araqiel (Arakiel)**
   Taught men the signs of the earth.

3. **Azazel**
   Taught men to make knives, swords, shields; to devise ornaments, coloring tinctures for the beautifying of women, etc.

4. **Baraqijal (Baraqel)**
   Taught men astrology.

5. **Ezequeel (Ezekeel)**
   Taught men the knowledge of clouds.

6. **Gadreel**
   Introduced weapons of war to mortals.

7. **Kokabel (Kawkabel)**
   Taught the science of the constellations.

8. **Penemue**
   Instructed mankind in writing "and thereby many sinned from eternity to eternity and until this day. For man was not created for such a purpose."—*Enoch I,* 7:8. Penemue also taught children the "bitter and sweet, and the secrets of wisdom."

9. **Sariel**
   Taught men the course of the moon.

10. **Semjaza**
    Taught men enchantments, root-cuttings, etc.

11. **Shamshiel**
    Taught men the signs of the sun.

THE SARIM

Chief Celestial Angel-Princes

1. Akatriel (Akrasiel)
   Revealer of the divine mysteries and angel of proclamation; *cf.* Raziel.

2. Anafiel
   Chief of the crown judgment angels of the Merkabah.

3. Azbuga(h)
   One of the 8 great throne angels of judgment who clothes with the garment of righteousness those deemed worthy among the new arrivals in heaven.

4. Barakiel (Barkiel, Barbiel)
   Ruler of the order of seraphim, governor of the month of February, and one of the 7 archangels.

5. Camael (Kemuel)
   Chief of the order of powers; one of the holy sefiroth; personification of divine justice; among the 7 that stand in the presence of God.

6. Chayyiel
   Chief of the holy hayyoth (cherubim).

7. Gabriel
   Angel of annunciation, resurrection, mercy, and vengeance; ruling prince of the first heaven; chief of the angelic guards over paradise.

8. Galgaliel
   Eponymous head of the order of galgalim (chariots of the Merkabah); chief angel of the wheel of the sun.

9. Haniel (Anael)
   Chief of the orders of principalities and virtues; one of the 7 archangels; governor of December; reputed to have transported Enoch to heaven.

10. Iofiel (Yofiel, Zophiel)
    Preceptor angel of Shem; a prince of the Torah (like Yefefiah); one of the 7 archangels; chief of the order of thrones.

11. The Irin
    Twin angels who, together with the twin qaddisin, constitute the supreme judgment council of the heavenly court; among the 8 exalted hierarchs that enjoy a rank superior to that of Metatron.

12. Jehoel (Jaoel)
    Mediator of the ineffable name; prince of the presence.

13. Metatron (orig. Enoch)
    Chancellor of heaven; prince of the ministering angels; sustainer of mankind.

14. Michael
    Chief angel of the Lord; deliverer of the faithful; tutelary prince of Israel; angel of repentance, etc.

15. Phanuel (Raguel)
    Archangel of penance; prince of the presence; identified with Uriel and Ramiel.

16. The Qaddisin
    Twin angels who, together with the twin irin, constitute the supreme judgment council of the heavenly court.

17. Radueriel (Vretil)
    The recording angel; leader of the celestial choirs; creator of the lesser angels.

18. Raphael
    Angel of healing, science, and knowledge; one of the princes of the presence; regent of the sun.

19. Raziel (Galizur)
    Chief of the supreme mysteries; one of the archangelic governors of the Briatic world; preceptor angel of Adam, herald of deity, and reputed author of *The Book of the Angel Raziel*.

20. Rikbiel
    Chief of the divine chariot; prince of the Merkabah angels. *Continued*

21. Sopheriel Mehayye and

22. Sopheriel Memeth
Two of the supreme angels of the Merkabah (of which there are 8); keepers of the books of life and death.

23. Soqed Hozi
Keeper of the divine balances; one of the 8 supreme angels of the Merkabah; appointed by God to the Sword.

24. Sandalphon (originally Elijah)
Angel of power and glory; twin brother of Metatron.

25. Shemuil
The great archon, mediator between the prayers of Israel and the princes of the 7th heaven.

26. Suriel
Benevolent angel of death; instructor of Moses; a prince of the presence.

27. Tzadkiel
Angel of divine justice.

28. Uriel
Archangel of salvation; regent of the sun; overseer of Tartarus.

29. Yefefiah (Dina)
Angel of the Torah; instructed Moses in the mysteries of the cabala.

30. Zagzagel
Angel of wisdom; chief guard of the 4th heaven; angel of the burning bush.

THE ANGELS OF PUNISHMENT (MALAKE HABBALAH)

Over the seven divisions of hell

1. Kushiel ("rigid one of God")
2. Lahatiel ("flaming one of God")
3. Shoftiel ("judge of God")
4. Makatiel ("plague of God")
5. Hutriel ("rod of God")
6. Pusiel or Puriel ("fire of God")
7. Rogziel ("wrath of God")

The angels of punishment are under the leadership of archangels who in turn are under the rulership of the angel (angels) of death, according to *The Testament of Solomon.*

THE ARCHANGELS OF PUNISHMENT

1. Kezef (angel of wrath and destruction)
2. Af (angel of anger and the death of mortals)
3. Hemah (angel over the death of domestic animals)
4. Mashhit (angel over the death of children)
5. Meshabber (angel over the death of animals)

[*Rf.* Jellinek, *Beth ha-Midrasch.*]

THE NAMES OF LILITH

The prophet Elijah, according to legend, encountering Lilith, forced her to reveal to him the names she used in her various disguises when she worked her evil among mortals. She confessed to 17 names, and they are recorded in M. Gaster, *Studies and Texts in Folklore,* p. 1025:

1. Abeko
2. Abito
3. Amizo
4. Batna
5. Eilo
6. Ita
7. Izorpo
8. Kali
9. Kea

Continued

10. Kokos
11. Lilith
12. Odam
13. Partasah

14. Patrota
15. Podo
16. Satrina
17. Talto

In J. E. Hanauer, *Folk-Lore of the Holy Land*, a list of other names of Lilith is given:

1. Abro*
2. Abyzu
3. Ailo
4. Alu

5. Amiz*
6. Amizu*
7. Ardad Lili
8. Avitu*

9. Bituah*
10. Gallu
11. Gelou
12. Gilou
13. 'Ik*
14. 'Ils*
15. Kalee*
16. Kakash*
17. Kema*
18. Lamassu

19. Lilith*
20. Partashah*
21. Petrota*
22. Pods*
23. Raphi*
24. Satrina(h)*
25. Thiltho*
26. Zahriel
27. Zefonith

Those named followed by an asterisk (*) are from Hanauer's book. The others are from sundry sources.

THE FALLEN ANGELS

According to Revelation 12, the rebel host aggregated one-third of the angels in heaven. They fell for 9 days. Their number was estimated in the 15th century to have been 133,306,668 (the tabulation of Cardinal Bishop of Tusculum). *Enoch I* speaks of 200 apostates, but names only a score or so (allowing for variant spellings and duplications). The following are drawn from the Enoch listings, supplemented by lists from other sources in apocrypha, cabala, goetia, rabbinic, patristic, and secular writings.

1. Abbadona (once of the order of seraphim)
2. Adramelec
3. Agares (Agreas)
4. Amezyarak (Amiziras; also alternate for Semyaza)
5. Amy (once partly of the order of powers and partly of the order of angels)
6. Anmael (identified with Semyaza)
7. Arakiel (Araqiel)
8. Araziel
9. Ariel (once of the order of virtues)
10. Arioc(h)
11. Armaros (Abaros, Armers, Pharmaros)
12. Armen
13. Artaqifa (Arakiba)
14. Asbeel

15. Asmoday
16. Asmodeus (Sammael) (once of the order of seraphim)
17. Astaroth (once of the order of seraphim and of thrones)
18. Astoreth (Astarte)
19. Atarculph
20. Auza (Oza)
21. Azaradel
22. Azazel (once of the order of cherubim)
23. Azza
24. Azzael (Asael)

25. Balam (once of the order of dominations)
26. Baraqel (Barakel, Baraqijal)
27. Barbatos (once of the order of virtues)
28. Barbiel (once of the order of virtues)
29. Batarjal
30. Beelzebub (once of the order of cherubim)
31. Beliar (Belial) (once partly of the order of virtues and partly of the order of angels)
32. Busasejal
33. Byleth (Beleth) (once of the order of powers)
34. Balberith (once of the order of cherubim)

35. Caim (Caym) (once of the order of angels)
36. Carnivean (once of the order of powers)
37. Carreau (once of the order of powers)

Continued

38. Dagon
39. Danjal

40. Ezekeel (Ezequeel)

41. Flauros (Hauras)

42. Gaap (once of the order of potentates)
43. Gadreel
44. Gressil (once of the order of thrones)

45. Hakael
46. Hananel (Ananel)
47. Harut (Persian)

48. Iblis (Eblis, Haris) (Mohammedan Satan)
49. Ielahiah (once of the order of virtues)
50. Iuvart (once of the order of angels)

51. Jeqon
52. Jetrel

53. Kasdeja
54. Kawkabel (Kokabel)

55. Lau(v)iah (once partly of the order of thrones and partly of the order of cherubim)
56. Leviathan (once of the order of seraphim)
57. Lucifer (often, but erroneously, identified as Satan)

58. Mammon
59. Marchosias (once of the order of dominations)
60. Marut (Persian)
61. Mephistopheles
62. Meresin
63. Moloc(h)
64. Mulciber
65. Murmur (once partly of the order of thrones and partly of the order of angels)

66. Nelchael (once of the order of thrones)
67. Nilaihah (once of the order of dominations)

68. Oeillet (once of the order of dominations)
69. Olivier (once of the order of archangels)
70. Ouzza (Usiel)

71. Paimon (Paymon) (once of the order of dominations)

72. Penemue
73. Procell (once of the order of powers)
74. Pursan (Curson) (once of the order of virtues)

75. Raum (Raym) (once of the order of thrones)
76. Rimmon
77. Rosier (once of the order of dominations)
78. Rumael (Ramiel or Remiel)

79. Sammael (Satan, Asmodeus)
80. Samsaweel
81. Saraknyal
82. Sariel
83. Satan
84. Sealiah (once of the order of virtues)
85. Semyaza (Shemhazai, Azaziel) (once of the order of seraphim)
86. Senciner (once partly of the order of virtues and partly of the order of powers)
87. Shamshiel
88. Simapesiel
89. Sonneillon (once of the order of thrones)

90. Tabaet
91. Thammuz
92. Tumael
93. Turael
94. Turel

95. Urakabarameel
96. Usiel (Uzziel) (once of the order of virtues)

97. Verrier (once of the order of principalities)
98. Verrine (once of the order of thrones)
99. Vual (Vvall) (once of the order of powers)

100. Yomyael

101. Zavebe

also

102. Belphegor (Baal-Peor) (once of the order of principalities)
103. Forcas (Foras)

THE YEZIDIC ARCHANGELS
Prayed to in Yezidic Devil Worship

1. Shams-ed-din ("sun of the faith")
2. Fakr-ed-din ("the poor one of the faith")
3. Nasr-ed-din ("help of faith")
4. Sij-ed-din ("power of mercy")
5. Sheikh Ism ("power of mercy")
6. Sheikh Bakra ("power of mercy")
7. Kadir-Rahman ("power of mercy")

The invocation to the Yezidic archangels runs as follows:

"SOLE ALMIGHTY CREATOR OF HEAVEN, I INVOKE THEE THROUGH THE MEDIATION OF [HERE, THE NAMES OF THE HOLY 7]. . . . THOU DIDST CREATE THE SINNER ADAM, JESUS AND MARY [SIC]. . . . THOU ART THE FOUNTAIN OF JOY AND BEATITUDE. THOU HAST NO FACE; THY STATURE, MOVEMENTS AND SUBSTANCE ARE UNKNOWN . . . THOU HAST NEITHER FEATHERS, WINGS, ARMS, VOICE, NOR COLOR. . . ."

As J. G. R. Forlong says in *Encyclopedia of Religions* (from which the above is taken): "This is not devil worship but a good Theist's prayer."

THE SEALS OF THE SEVEN ANGELS

Seal of Aratron, the alchemist, who commanded seventeen millions six hundred and forty thousand spirits.

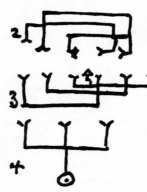

Seal of Bethor, who commanded twenty-nine thousand legions of spirits.

Seal of Phaleg, the War-lord.

Seal of Och, the alchemist, physician and magician.

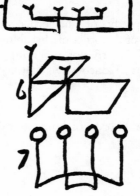

Seal of Hagith, transmuter of metals, and commander of four thousand legions of spirits.

Seal of Ophiel, who commanded one hundred thousand legions of spirits.

Seal of Phul, lord of the powers of the Moon and supreme lord of the waters.

The seals of the seven angels who rule over the 196 provinces of heaven. From the collection of ancient magical books reproduced in the works of Cornelius Agrippa.

THE MAGIC CIRCLE

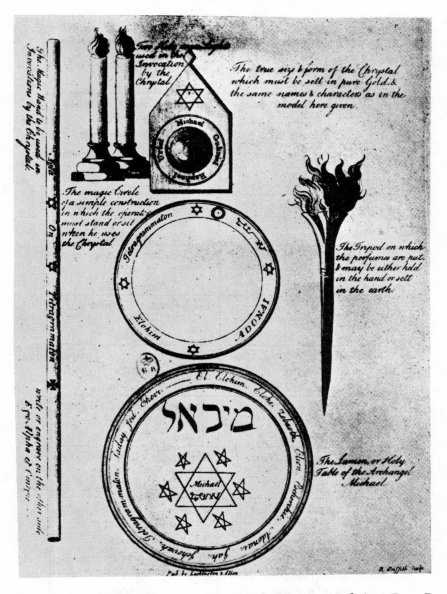

Magic circle and accessories for evocation in Solomonic magical rites. From Barrett, *The Magus.*

THE TEN RULING ANGELS AND THEIR ORDERS

INTELLIGENCE DES SPHÈRES	ORDRES DES BIENHEUREUX
Prince du Monde מטטרון: Mittatron	Séraphins Saints Animaux חיות הקודש Hakkodesch haioth
Courrier de Dieu רציאל: Ratsiel	Chérubins Roues אופנים: Ophanim
Contemplation de Dieu צפקיאל Tsaphkiel	Trônes Puissants אראלים: Erelim
Justice de Dieu צדקיאל Tsadkiel	Dominations Etincelants חשמלים Haschmalim
Punition de Dieu סמאל Sammael	Puissances Enflammés שרפים Seraphim
Qui est semblable à Dieu מיכאל, Michael	Vertus Rois מלכים Melachim
Grâce de Dieu חבניאל Hanniel	Principautés Dieux אלהים Eloïm
Médecin de Dieu רפאל Raphael	Archanges Enfants de Dieu אלהים בני Elohim Bene
Homme de Dieu גבריאל Gabriel	Anges Base des enfants כרובים Kerubim
Messie מטטרון: Mittatron	Ames bienheureuses Hommes אשים Ischim

A table showing the ten ruling angels or intelligences, and, in descending scale, the ten celestial orders, according to Hebrew cabala. From Ambelain, *La Kabbale Pratique*.

SIGILS, CHARTS, PACTS
also Invocations, Conjurations, Spells, Charms, and Exorcisms

in which angels are summoned to do the bidding of the invocant, or in which diabolic powers are
enjoined and/or exorcised usually in the name of God and His angels

CONJURATION OF THE SIXTH MYSTERY
WITH THE SEAL OF THE POWER-ANGELS

I, NN, a servant of God, desire, call upon, and conjure thee, Spirit Alymon, by the most dreadful words: Sather, Ehomo, Geno, Poro, Joehovah, Elohim, Volnah, Denach, Alonlam, Ophiel, Zophiel, Sophiel, Habriel, Eloha, Alesimus, Dileth, Melohim, and by the holiest words through which thou canst be conquered, that thou appear before me in a mild, beautiful, human form, and fulfil what I command thee, so surely as God will come to judge the living and the dead. Fiat, Fiat, Fiat.

The Seal of the Power Angels.

[*Rf. The Sixth and Seventh Books of Moses*, p. 11.]

CONJURATION OF THE GOOD SPIRITS

O you glorious and benevolent angels, Urzla, Zlar, Larzod, Arzal, who are the four angels of the East, I invoke you, adjure and call you forth to visible apparition in and through the great prevalent and divine name of the Most Holy God Erzla, and by the ineffable and efficacious virtues and power thereof, whereby you are governed and called forth, it being therefore absolutely necessary, pre-ordained, appointed and decreed. Now therefore I do most earnestly intreat and powerfully adjure you, O you benign angels Urzla, Zlar, Larzod, Arzal, in this potent name of your God Erzla to move and appear visibly, and show yourself to me in this crystal stone (or mirror) here before me.

And in and through the same, to transmit your ray to my sight and your voice to my ears that I may audibly hear you and plainly see you and include me in your mysteries wherefore I do most earnestly adjure you, O benevolent and amicable angels, Azla, in the most excellent name of your God, Erzla, and I as a servant of the highest do efficaciously invoke you to appear now perfectly visible to me, O you servants of mercy, come and show yourselves firmly unto me and let me partake of the secret wisdom of your creator. Amen.

[*Rf. Gollancz, Clavicula Salomonis.*]

A DEATH INCANTATION

I call thee, Evil Spirit, Cruel Spirit, Merciless Spirit; I call thee, who sittest in the cemetery and takest away healing from man. Go and place a knot in [N———'s] head, in his eyes, in his mouth, in his tongue, in his windpipe, and put poisonous water in his belly. If you do not go and put water in his belly, I shall send against you the evil angels Puziel, Guziel, Psdiel, Prsiel. I call thee and those six knots that you go quickly to [N   ], and put poisonous water in his belly, and kill [N   ] because I wish it. Amen, Amen. Selah.

[*Rf.* M. Gaster, *The Sword of Moses.*]

CONJURATION OF THE SWORD

Te Gladi, Vos Gladias, trea Nomine Sancto, Albrot, Abracadabra, Jehova elico. Estote meum castellumque praesidium contra omnium hostes, conspicuusque nonconspicuus, in quisque magiceum opum. Nomeno Sancto Saday, qui est in imperium magnum, et his alio nomine: Cados, Cados, Cados, Adonai, Elohi, Zena, Oth, Ochimanuel, primoque ultimo, Sapientia, Via, Vita, Virto, Principio, Oso, Oratie, Splendoro, Luce, Sol, Fono, Gloria, Mono, Porta, Vite, Lape, Scipio, Sacredo, Pravo, Messiah, Gladi in omnium meum negotia regnas et in illos res quem me resistunt, vincite. Amen.

[*Rf. Grimorium Verum.*]

The English translation, supposedly less effective than the Latin original, follows:

I conjure you, O Sword of Swords, by three Holy Names [given above]. Be my fortress and defence against all enemies, visible and invisible, in every magical work. By the Holy Name Saday, which is great in power, and by these other Names [given above], the First and the Last, Wisdom, Way, Life, Virtue, Chief, Mouth, Speech, Splendor, Light, Sun, Fountain, Glory, Mountain, Gate, Vine, Stone, Staff, Priest, Immortal Messiah: Sword, do you rule in all my affairs and prevail in those things which oppose me. Amen.

INVOCATION OF THE MYSTERY OF THE THIRD SEAL

I, NN, servant of God, desire, and call upon thee, and conjure thee, Tehor, by all the Holy Angels and Arch Angels, by the holy Michael, the holy Gabriel, Raphael, Uriel, Thronus, Dominations, Principalities, Virtues, Cherubim and Seraphim, and with unceasing voice I cry, Holy, Holy, Holy is the Lord God of Sabaoth, and by the most terrible words: Soab, Sother, Emmanuel, Hdon, Amathon, Mathay, Adonai, Eel, Eli, Eloy, Zoag, Dios, Anath, Tafa, Uabo, Tetragrammaton, Aglay, Josua, Jonas, Calpie, Calphas. Appear before me, NN, in a mild and human form, and do what I desire.

[*Rf. The Sixth and Seventh Books of Moses*, p. 9.]

INVOCATION FOR EXCITING LOVE IN THE HEART OF THE PERSON WHO IS THE OBJECT OF OUR DESIRE

with the help of the 137th Psalm

Pour oil from a white lily into a crystal goblet, recite the 137th Psalm over the cup and conclude by pronouncing the name of the angel *Anael*, the planetary spirit of Venus,* and the name of the person you love. Next write the name of the angel on a piece of cypress which you will dip in oil and tie the piece of cypress to your right arm. Then wait for a propitious moment to touch the right hand of the person with whom you are in love, and love will be awakened in his or her heart. The operation will be more powerful in effect if you perform it at dawn on the Friday following the new moon.

* Also spelt Hamiel, Haniel, Onoel—Ed.

[*Rf.* Christian, *History and Practice of Magic*, II, 439–440.]

SPELL FOR THE MANUFACTURE AND USE OF A MAGIC CARPET

Let a virgin girl weave a carpet of white and new wool, in the hour of the sun, when the moon is full, and when the sun is in Capricorn. Go into the country, to an uninhabited place, where you will suffer no disturbances; spread your carpet facing East and West, and, having made a circle to enclose it, hold your wand in the air, and call upon Michael toward the East, Raphael to the North, Gabriel to the West, and Miniel to the South. Then turn to the East and invoke the name of Agla. Take in your left hand the point of the carpet that is to the East, then turn toward the North and do the same; repeating it similarly for the South and the West, until you have raised all four corners. Then turning again toward the East, say, reverently:

Agla, Agla, Agla, Agla: O God Almighty, who art the life of the Universe, and who ruleth over the four divisions of its vast form by the strength and virtue of the four letters of Thy Holy Name: Tetragrammaton Yod He Vau He. Bless in Thy name this covering which I hold, as thou hast blessed the mantle of Elijah in the hands of Elisha; so that, being covered by Thy wings, nothing may be able,

[*Rf.* Shah, *Occultism, Its Theory and Practice.*]

to injure me, even as it is said "He shall hide thee under his wings, and beneath His feathers shall thou trust."

Then, fold it up, saying Recabustira, Cabustira, Bustira, Tira, Ra, A; and keep it carefully until you next need it. Choose a night of full or new moon. Go to a place where you will suffer no interruption, having written the following characters on a strip of azure blue virgin parchment with the feather of a dove:

Then prostrate yourself, after casting some incense on the fire; holding the wand in your left hand, the parchment in your right, say:

Vegale, Hamicata, Umsa, Terata, Yeh, Dah, Ma, Baxasoxa, Un, Horah, Himesere O God, Thou Vast One, send unto me the inspiration of Thy light, and make me to discover the secret thing which I ask of Thee, whatsoever such and such a thing may be. Make me to search it out, by the aid of Thy Holy Ministers Raziel, Tzaphniel, Matmoniel, Io.

A SPELL TO GUARANTEE POSSESSION
OF THE LOVED ONE

On a Friday, at the hour of Venus and before the sun rises, take from near a river or a pond a live frog which you will hang by its hind legs over a blazing fire. When it is burnt black, reduce it to a very fine powder in a stone mortar and wrap it in virgin parchment. This sachet must lie for three days under an altar where Mass is said. After the three days you must uncover it at the hour of Venus. The way to use this powder is to sprinkle it on flowers. Every girl or woman who smells them will then love you.

[*Rf.* Christian, *History and Practice of Magic* II, 412.]

Another Method

Stick on the head of a girl's or woman's bed, as near as possible to the place where her head rests, a piece of virgin parchment on which have already been written the names of Michael, Gabriel, Raphael. Invoke these three angels to inspire (here pronounce the name of the beloved) with a love for you equal to your own. That person will not be able to sleep without first thinking of you, and very soon love will dawn in her heart.

CONJURATION FOR THE EVOCATION OF A SPIRIT
ARMED WITH POWER FROM THE SUPREME MAJESTY

I do invocate, conjure, and command thee, O thou Spirit N (here interpolate the name of the Spirit desired to be invoked), to appear and to show thyself visibly unto me before this Circle in fair and comely shape, without any deformity or tortuosity; by the name and in the name of Iah and Vau, which Adam heard and spoke; and by the name of God, Agla, which Lot heard and was saved with his family; and by the name Ioth, which Jacob heard from the angel wrestling with him, and was delivered from the hand of Esau his brother; and by the name Anaphaxeton which Aaron heard and spake and was made wise; and by the name Zabaoth, which Moses named and all the rivers were turned into blood; and by the name Asher Ehyeh Oriston, which Moses named, and all the rivers brought forth frogs, and they ascended into the houses, destroying all things; and by the name Elion, which Moses named, and there was great hail such as had not been since the beginning of the world; and by the name Adonai, which Moses named, and there came up locusts, which appeared upon the whole land, and devoured all which the hail had left; and by the name Schema Amathia which Ioshua called upon, and the sun stayed his course; and by the name Alpha and Omega, which Daniel named and destroyed Bel and slew the Dragon; and in the name Emmanuel, which the three children, Shadrach, Meshach and Abed-nego, sang in the midst of the fiery furnace, and were delivered. . . . I do exorcise and command thee, by the four beasts before the throne, having eyes before and behind; by the holy angels of God. . . . I do potently exorcise thee that thou appearest here to fulfill my will in all things which seem good unto me. Wherefore, come thou, visibly, peaceably, and affably, now, without delay, to manifest that which I desire, speaking with a clear and perfect voice, intelligibly, and to mine understanding.

[*Rf.* Waite, *The Lemegeton.*]

THE SERPENT CONJURATION

I, N, do conjure thee, I Spirit N, by the living God, by the holy and all-ruling God who created from nothingness the heaven, the earth, the sea, and all things that are therein, in virtue of the Most Holy Sacrament of the Eucharist, and in the name of Jesus Christ, and by the power of this same Almighty Son of God who for us and for our redemption was crucified, suffered death, and was buried; who rose again on the third day and is now seated on the right hand of the Creator of the whole world, from whence he will come to judge the living and the dead; as also by the precious love of the Holy Spirit, perfect Trinity. I conjure thee within the circle, accursed one, by thy judgment, who didst dare to tempt God: I exorcise thee, Serpent, and I command thee to appear forthwith under a beautiful and well-favoured human form of soul and body, and to fulfil my behests without any deceit whatsoever, as also without mental reservation of any kind, by the great Names of the God of gods and Lord of lords, Adonay, Tetragrammaton, Jehova, Otheos [here, a dozen more divine names]. I conjure thee, Evil and Accursed Serpent, N, to appear at my will and pleasure, in this place, before this circle, without noise, deformity, or murmuring. I exorcise thee by the ineffable names of God, to wit, Gog and Magog, which I am unworthy to pronounce; Come hither, Come hither, Come hither. Accomplish my will and desire, without wile or falsehood. Otherwise St. Michael, the invisible Archangel, shall presently blast thee in the utmost depths of hell. Come, then, N, to do my will.

[*Rf. Grimoire of Honorius.*]

PRAYER

for binding and commanding angels "throwne downe from heaven"

I require thee, O Lord Jesus Christ, that thou give thy virtue and power over all thine angels which were throwne downe from heaven to deceive mankind, to draw them to me, to tie and bind them, and also to loose them, to command them to do all they can, and that by no means they contemne my voice or the words of my mouth. But that they obeie me and my saiengs, and feare me. I beseech thee by thine humanitie, mercie and grace, and I require thee, Adonay, Amay, Horta, Vegedora, Mitai, Hel, Suranat, Ysion, Ysesy, and by all thy holie names, and by all thine holie he-saints and she-saints, by all thine angels and archangels, powers, denominations and vertues, and by that name that Salomon did bind the divils, and shut them up, Elrach, Ebanher, Agle, Goth, Ioth, Othie, Venoch, Nabrat, and by all these holie names which are written in this booke, and by the vertues of them all, that thou enable me to congregate all thy spirits throwne down from heaven, that they may give me a true answer of all my demands, and that they satisfy all my requests, without the hurt of my bodie or soule, or any thing that is mine, through Our Lord Jesus Christ thy sonne, which liveth and reigneth with thee in the unitie of the Holie-Ghost, one God, world without end.

[*Rf. Reginald Scot, Discoverie of Witchcraft.*]

EXORCISM

where a blood pact has been entered into with the devil—by a sinner who has since repented

I exorcise thee, O impious Satan. In vain dost thou boast of this deed. I command thee to restore it as a proof before the whole world that when God receiveth a sinner, thou hast no longer any rule over his soul. I abjure thee, by him who expelled thee from thy stronghold, bereft thee of the arms which thou didst trust in, and distributed thy spoils. Return therefore this deed whereby this creature of God foolishly bound himself to thy service; return it, I say, in His name by whom thou art overcome. When thy power has come to nothing, presume not longer to retain this use-less document. By penitence already hath this creature of God restored himself to his true Lord, spurning thy yoke, hoping in the Divine mercy for defence against thine assaults.*

* The editor, Waite, remarks: "Whether this process was supposed to insure the return of the incriminating document or was held to cancel it does not appear and matters little, for what with the subtleties of the sorcerer and the assistance of the Church in the revocation of such acts and deeds, there was little chance for Infernus [i.e., the devil]." And Waite quotes this from De Plancy, *Dictionnaire Infernal*: "Spit three times on the ground and he (the devil) will have no power over you." In which case, adds Waite, "Black Magic, with all its grim theatricals, is the art of exploiting lost angels with impunity."

[*Rf.* A. E. Waite, *The Book of Black Magic and of Pacts.*]

Bibliography

All books in this Bibliography have been examined by the author in various libraries or private collections and the bibliographic data here given are as complete as possible. Where dates, publishers, and other matter are missing, their absence is not due to oversight but to incompleteness of title-page information in the originals. Further, apparent inconsistencies in titles or spellings are usually due to variant forms used by different publishers of the same or similar works.

A

Abano, Peter de. *The Heptameron*. In vol. 3 of the 10-vol. *Das Kloster*. Stuttgart and Leipzig: J. Scheible, 1846. Originally published as *Heptameron, seu Elementa Magica* (Magical Elements): Paris, 1567.

Abelson, J. *Jewish Mysticism*. London: G. Bell, 1913.

Abodah Zarah. A Talmudic tract contained in the 18-vol. Soncino *Talmud*. London, 1935–1952.

Abraham ben Isaac of Granada, *Berith Menucha*. Amsterdam: Judah Mordecai and Samuel b. Moses ha-Levi, 1648.

Abrahams, Israel (ed.). *The Book of Delight*. Philadelphia: The Jewish Publication Society of America, 1912.

———. *By-Paths in Hebraic Bookland*. Philadelphia: The Jewish Publication Society of America, 1920.

Abulafia, Abraham. *See* Berger, Abraham.

Abulafia, R. Todros ben Joseph. *Otsar ha-Kavod* (Treasury of Glory). Nowy Dwor (Poland): J. A. Krieger, 1879. An earlier edition published in 1808.

Acts of John. In James, *The Apocryphal New Testament*.

Acts of Paul. In James, *The Apocryphal New Testament*.

———. Tr. from the Coptic by Carl Schmidt. Leipzig: Hinrichs, 1904.

Acts of Peter. In C. Schmidt. *Koptisch-Gnostische Schiften*.

Also contained in the Akhmim Codex, papyrus, Egyptian Museum, Berlin.

Acts of Philip. In James, *The Apocryphal New Testament*. Also in vol. 8, *Ante-Nicene Fathers*. New York: Scribner. *See* Till, Walter C.

Acts of Pilate. In James, *The Apocryphal New Testament*. Also called the *Gospel of Nicodemus*.

Acts of Thomas, The. Vol. V of Supplements to *Novum Testamentum*. Intro., text, and commentary by A. F. J. Klijn. Leiden: E. J. Brill, 1962.

Adams, Hazard. *Blake and Yeats: The Contrary Vision*. Ithaca: Cornell U.P., 1955.

Admirable History of the Possession and Conversion of a Penitent Woman. *See* Michaelis, Sébastien.

AE (George William Russell). *The Candle of Vision*. New Hyde Park, New York: University Books, 1965.

Agrippa, Cornelius. *Three Books of Occult Philosophy*. (ed.) Willis F. Whitehead. Inwood, N.Y.: E. Loomis & Co. [1897]. Original English edition published in London, 1651.

———. *The Philosophy of Natural Magic* (first of Agrippa's three books of occult philosophy). (ed.) L. W. de Laurence, Chicago: de Laurence, Scott & Co., 1913.

Akiba, Rabbi. *Alphabet of Rabbi Akiba* (*Habdalah shel*

R. *Akiba*). Incl. in MS. Maggs No. 419 (1413 C.E.). New York: Library of Jewish Theological Seminary.

Albert, Thomas. *Manufacture of Christianity.* Philadelphia: Dorrance, 1946.

Albertus Magnus. *Les Admirables Secrets d'Albert le Grand.* Lyon: les Héritiers de Béringos Fratres, 1752.

——. *Albert the Great.* Adrian English and Philip Hereford. London: Burns [1933].

Albo, Joseph. *Sefer ha-'Ikkarim* (Book of Principles). 5 vols. (tr.) Isaac Husik. Philadelphia: The Jewish Publication Society of America, 1929-1930. Originally published in Venice, 1618.

Allegro, John M. *The Dead Sea Scrolls.* Harmondsworth, Middlesex, England: Penguin, 1957.

Almadel of Solomon. See Lemegeton, The.

Alphabet of Ben Sira. In Hebrew. (ed.) M. Steinschneider. Berlin: A. Friedlander, 1858. A 10th-century work containing earliest mention of Lilith.

Alphabet of Rabbi Akiba. See Akiba, Rabbi.

Alphonsus de Spina. *Fortalitium fidei.* Nuremberg: Anton Koberger [1485].

Ambelain, Robert. *La Kabbale Pratique.* Paris: Editions Niclaus, 1951.

——. *Le Martinique.* Paris: Editions Niclaus, 1946.

Ambrose, Isaac. "Ministrations and Communion with Angels." In *Compleat Works.* London, 1701.

Amulets and Talismans. See Budge, E. A. Wallis.

Ancient's Book of Magic, The. See de Claremont, Lewis.

Angels and Demons According to Lactantius. See Schneweis, Emil.

Anges. See Régamey, R. P.

Angoff, Charles. *Adventures in Heaven.* New York: Bernard Ackerman, 1945.

Annual of Leeds University Oriental Society, vol. IV. Leiden: E. J. Brill, 1964.

Ante-Nicene Fathers, The. American reprint of Edinburgh edition. 10 vols. (ed.) A. Cleveland Coxe. New York: Scribner, 1917-1925.

Ante-Nicene Fathers, The. (ed.) Alexander Roberts and James Donaldson. Buffalo: Christian Literature Pub. Co. 1886-1896.

Anthologie Persane (Persian Anthology). *See* Massé, Henri.

Apocalypse of Abraham, The. See Box, G. H.

Apocalypse of Baruch, The (The *Syriac Apocalypse* or *Baruch II*). *See* Charles, R. H.

——. *The Greek Apocalypse of Baruch* (*3 Baruch*). *See* Hughes, H. Maldwyn.

Apocalypse of Elias (*Die Hebräische Elias-Apokalypse*). *See* Buttenwieser, Moses; Steindorff, George.

Apocalypse of Moses. Known also as *The History of the Life of Adam and Eve. See* Conybeare, Frederick G.

Contained in Tischendorf, *Apocalypses Apocryphae.* Leipzig, 1866. Armenian title, *The Book of Adam.*

——. (ed.) Tischendorf, *Apocalypses Apocrypha.* Leipzig, 1866.

Apocalypse of Paul. A Coptic text. *See* Budge, E. A. Wallis; James, M. R.

Apocalypse of Peter. See extracts in James, *The Apocryphal New Testament.*

——. Part 2 in *Vision of Theophilus.* Cambridge, 1931.

Apocalypse of Salathiel. Embodied in *Fourth Ezra* (*q.v.*).

Apocalypse of Sophonias (Zephaniah). A lost pseudepigraphic book of Jewish origin, a fragment contained in Coptic MS. of Steindorff's *Apokalypse des Elias* (Leipzig, 1899). Clement of Alexandria cites a verse from the work. M. R. James quotes from it in *The Apocryphal New Testament.* [*Rf.*, "Zephaniah," vol. 10, *Universal Jewish Encyclopedia.*]

Apocrypha, The. Reprint of Nonesuch Press edition, 1924. New Hyde Park, N.Y.: University Books, 1962.

——. An American tr. by Edgar J. Goodspeed. Chicago: U. of Chicago Press, 1938.

——. (ed.) Manuel Komroff. New York: Tudor, 1936.

——. *Introduction to the Apocrypha.* Bruce M. Metzger. New York: Oxford U.P., 1957.

——. *Oxford Annotated Apocrypha.* (ed.) B. M. Metzger. New York: Oxford U.P., 1965.

Apocryphal New Testament, The. New York: Peter Eckler Pub. Co., 1927.

——. (ed.) M. R. James. Oxford: Clarendon, 1955.

Apocryphon of John. Also called *The Gospel of Mary,* and *The Secret Book of John.* (ed.) P. Labib in the *Coptic Gnostic Papyri in the Coptic Museum at Old Cairo.* Cairo, 1956. Also in C. Schmidt, *Koptisch-Gnostische Schriften.* Leipzig, 1905.

Apollonius of Tyana. *The Nuctemeron.* In Levi, *Transcendental Magic.* Philadelphia: McKay, 1923.

——. *The Life of Apollonius of Tyana.* By Philostratus. (tr.) F. C. Conybeare. New York, 1927.

——. by G. R. S. Mead. New Hyde Park, N.Y.: University Books [1966].

Apostolic Constitutions and Cognate Documents (Liturgy of the Mass called Clementina, etc.). (ed.) De Lacy O'Leary. London: Society for Promoting Christian Knowledge, 1906. An edition published in New York by Scribner, 1925.

Aquinas, St. Thomas. *Basic Writings* (comprising *Summa Theologica* and *Summa Contra Gentiles*). 2 vols. (ed.) Anton C. Pegis. New York: Random, 1941.

Arabic-English Lexicon. See Lane.

Arabic Gospel of the Infancy of the Saviour. In vol. 8 of *The Anti-Nicene Fathers.* New York: Scribner, 1925.

Aradi, Zsolt. *The Book of Miracles.* New York: Farrar, 1956.

Aramaic Incantation Texts from Nippur. See Montgomery.

Arbatel of Magic (De Magia Veterum). Basle, 1575; Frankfurt, 1686. In Scheible, *Das Kloster.*

Aristeas to Philocrates (Letter to Aristeas). (ed., tr.) Moses Hadas. New York: Harper; Philadelphia: Dropsie College, 1951.

Aristotle. *Basic Works.* (ed.) R. McKeon. New York: Random, 1941.

Arkhangelike or Book of the Archangels by Moses the Prophet. In *Poimandres* of Reitzenstein. Leipzig: G. B. Teubner, 1904.

Arnobius. *The Case Against the Pagans (Adversus Nationes).* (tr.) George E. McCracken. Westminster, Md.: Newman Press, 1949.

Arnold, Edwin. *The Light of Asia.* New York: A. L. Burt [1879].

Arnold, Hugh and Saint, Lawrence B. *Stained Glass of the Middle Ages in England and France.* London: A. & C. Black, 1925.

Ascension of Isaiah, The. See Box; Charles.

Ashmole, Elias. (ed.) *Theatrum chemicum britannicum.* A collection of articles by divers hands on hermetic mysteries. London: N. Brooke, 1652.

——(tr.). *Heavenly Intelligences,* by Trithemius.

Assumption of Moses, The (or *The Testament of Moses*). *See* Ferrar.

Aude, Sapere (tr.). *Chaldean Oracles of Zoroaster.* New York: Occult Research Press, n.d.

Augustine. *De Civitate Dei* (City of God). In the *Works of Aurelius Augustine.* (ed.) Marcus Dods. Edinburgh, 1888.

——. Extracts in Migne, *Patrologiae Latinae Completus.* Paris, 1844, 1864.

Ausable, Nathan (ed.). *A Treasury of Jewish Folklore.* New York: Crown Publishers, 1960.

Avigad, Nahman and Yadin, Yidael (tr.). *A Genesis Apocryphon.* Jerusalem: The Magnes Press, 1956.

Azrael and Other Poems. See Welsh.

B

Bach, Marcus. *Strange Sects and Curious Cults.* New York: Dodd, 1961.

Bamberger, Bernard J. *Fallen Angels.* Philadelphia: The Jewish Publication Society of America, 1952.

Banquet of the Ten Virgins. See Clark.

Baraita de Massechet Gehinnom. In Jellinek, *Beth ha-Mirasch.*

Bar-Khonai, Theodore. *The Book of Scholia (Liber Scholiorum).* Extracts in *Inscriptions Mandaites des Coupes de Khouabir.* Paris: H. Welter, 1898. An edition in German published in Berlin, 1905; an edition in Syriac, published in Paris, 1910.

Barnett, R. D. (tr.). *See* Dupont-Sommer.

Barnhart, Clarence L. (ed.). *The New Century Handbook of English Literature.* New York: Appleton [1956].

Barrett, Francis. *The Magus.* London: Lackington, Allen & Co., 1801.

Bartholomew the Apostle (Book of the Resurrection of Christ). In James, *The Apocryphal New Testament.*

Barton, George. "Origin of the Names of Angels." *Journal of Biblical Literature.* December 1912.

Baruch III (Baruch Apocalypse). *See* Hughes.

Basil, St. *The Ascetic Works of St. Basil.* (tr.) W. K. L. Clarke (*q.v.*).

——. *Letters and Select Works.* Nicene and Post-Nicene Fathers. New York: Christian Literature Co. 1887–1895.

Bate, H. N. *The Sibylline Oracles.* Books 3–4. London: Society for Promoting Christian Knowledge, 1937.

Baxter, Sylvester. *The Holy Grail.* Boston: Curtis & Cameron, 1904.

Beaumont, John. *Gleanings of Antiquities.* London: W. Taylor, 1724.

——. *An Historical, Physiological and Theological Treatise of Spirits.* London: Browne, Taylor, Smith, Coggan & Browne, 1705.

Beckford, William. *The History of the Caliph Vathek.* New York: J. Pott & Co., 1900.

Beer, J. B. *Coleridge the Visionary.* London: Chatto, 1959.

Begbie, Harold. *On the Side of the Angels.* London: Hodder, 1915.

Ben Horin, Meir. "The Ineffable." *Jewish Quarterly Review,* April 1956. Philadelphia: Dropsie College.

Bentwich, Norman. *Israel and her Neighbors.* London: Rider & Co., 1955.

——. *Philo-Judaeus of Alexandria.* Philadelphia: The Jewish Publication Society of America, 1910.

Benziger, James. *Images of Eternity.* Carbondale: Southern Illinois U.P., 1962.

Bereshith Rabba. 2 vols. in the 10-vol. *Midrash Rabba* (*q.v.*).

Berger, Abraham. "The Messianic Self-Consciousness of Abraham Abulafia." *Essays on Jewish Life and Thought.* New York: Columbia U.P., 1959.

Berith Menucha. See Abraham ben Isaac of Granada.

Bernard of Clairvaux. *de consideratione.* In Migne, *Patrologia Latina.* Vols. 182–185. Paris, 1854–55.

Bet Eked Sepharim (a bibliographical lexicon). Compiled by Chaim. B. Friedberg. Tel-Aviv, 1954.

Bevan, A. A. (tr., ed.). *The Hymn of the Soul*. Contained in the *Syriac Acts of Thomas*. Cambridge, 1897.

Bhagavad Gita. (tr.) Charles Johnston. London: John M. Watkins, 1965.

Bible, The. (tr.) James Moffatt. New York: Harper, 1935.

———. *The Authorized or King James Version*, with Apocrypha. London: Nonesuch Press, 1963.

———. *The New English Bible*. Oxford and Cambridge, 1961.

———. *New World Translation of the Hebrew Scriptures*. Brooklyn, N.Y.: Watch Tower Bible and Tract Society (Jehovah's Witnesses), 1953.

———. *New American Catholic Edition*. Old Testament, Douay Version. New York: Benziger Bros. [1952].

———. *The Holy Bible* (placed by The Gideons International). Chicago, 1958.

———. *The Interpreter's Bible*. 12 vols. New York-Abingdon-Cokesbury, 1951.

———. *Designed to Be Read as Living Literature*. E. S. Bates. New York: Simon and Schuster, 1936.

Bible Handbook, The. (ed.) G. W. Foote and W. P. Ball. London: Pioneer Press, 1953.

Biblical Antiquities of Philo, The. See James.

Bischoff, Erich. *Die Elemente der Kabbalah*. 2 vols. Berlin: H. Barsdorf, 1913–1920.

Bishop's Wife, The. See Nathan.

Bissell, Edwin C. *The Pentateuch*. New York: Scribner, 1885.

Black Pullet, The. A ritual of black magic. Paris, 1740. *See* Waite, *The Book of Ceremonial Magic*.

Black Raven, The. A Faustian manual. Lyons, 1469. *See* Waite, *The Book of Ceremonial Magic*.

Blake, William. *All Religions Are One*. A collection of maxims. Engraved. London, circa 1788.

———. *Complete Writings*. (ed.) Geoffrey Keynes. London: Nonesuch Press, 1957.

———. *Jerusalem*. In *Complete Writings*.

———. *The Poetry and Prose of William Blake*. (ed.) David V. Erdman. Garden City, N.Y.: Doubleday, 1965.

———. *Vala* (The Four Zoas). (ed.) H. M. Margouliouth. Oxford: Clarendon, 1956.

———. *Visions of the Daughters of Albion*. London: Printed by William Blake, 1793.

Blavatsky, H. P. *The Secret Doctrine*. 2 vols. Pasadina, Calif.: Theosophical U.P. [1952].

Bloch, Joshua. "Was There a Greek Version of the Apocalypse of Ezra?" Philadelphia: *Jewish Quarterly Review*, April, 1956.

Bloom, Harold. *Blake's Apocalypse*. Garden City, N.Y.: Doubleday, 1963.

———. *Shelley's Mythmaking*. New Haven: Yale U.P., 1959.

Bokser, Ben Zion. *From the World of the Cabbalah*. New York: Philosophical Library, 1954.

———. *Wisdom of the Talmud*. New York: Philosophical Library, 1951.

Bonner, Campbell. *Studies in Magical Amulets*. Ann Arbor, Mich.: U. of Michigan Press. Also, London: Oxford U.P., 1950.

Bonsirven, Joseph (tr.). *La Bible Apocryphe*. Introd. by Daniel-Rops. Paris, 1953.

Book of Adam and Eve, The. Also known as *The History of the Life of Adam and Eve* and as *The Conflict of Adam and Eve with Satan*. *See* Conybeare; Malan.

———. (tr.) L. S. A. Wells in Charles, *Apocrypha and Pseudepigrapha of the Old Testament*. London: Oxford U.P., 1913.

———. (tr.) S. C. Malan. London: Williams and Norgate, 1882. Also in *Lost Books of the Bible*. New York: Lewis Copeland, 1930.

The Book of the Angel Raziel (*Sepher Raziel*; also titled *Raziel ha-Malach*). Credited to Eleazer of Worms. In Hebrew: Warsaw, 1881. In English: MS. No. 3826, Sloane Coll., British Museum. An edition published in Amsterdam, 1701.

Book of Beliefs and Opinions, by Saadia Gaon. *See* Rosenblatt.

Book of Black Magic and of Pacts, The. *See* Waite.

Book of Ceremonial Magic, The. *See* Waite.

Book of Concealed Mystery. Part of *The Zohar*, contained in Mathers, *Kabbalah Denudata*.

The Book of Enoch. *See* Charles.

Book of Formation (see *Sefer Yetzirah*).

Book of the Great Logos According to the Mystery. A gnostic MS. in *Pistis Sophia*, summarized by Mead. *See* also the Bruce Codex, Bodleian Library, Oxford.

Book of James, or Protovangelium. In M. R. James, *The Apocryphal New Testament*. Oxford U.P., 1955. Also in Lightfoot, *Excluded Books of the New Testament*.

Book of Job. *See* Jastrow; Raymond.

Book of John the Baptist. A Mandaean scripture titled *Sidra D'Yahya*.

Book of John the Evangelist. In James, *The Apocryphal New Testament*. New York: Oxford U.P., 1955.

Book of Jubilees, The (or *The Little Genesis*). (tr.) R. H. Charles. London: Society for Promoting Christian Knowledge, 1917.

Book of Kuzari. *See* Judah ha Levi.

Book of Mary. *See* Guinan.

Book of Mormon, The. (tr.) Joseph Smith. Salt Lake City: The Church of Jesus Christ of Latter-day Saints, 1950.

Book of Old Testament Illustrations. Sydney C. Cockerell. Introd. M. R. James. New York: Cambridge U.P., 1927.

Book of Power, The. Subtitled "Cabbalistic Secrets of the Master Aptolcater, Mage of Adrianople." Tr. into English from Greek by J. D. A., 1724. Sections in Shah, *The Secret Lore of Magic.*

Book of Protection, The. See Gollancz.

Book of the Resurrection of Christ. See Bartholomew.

Book of the Sacred Magic of Abra-Melin, the Mage, The. See Mathers.

Book of Scholia, The. See Bar-Khonai.

Book of Spirits, The. See Grillot.

Book of Tobit, The. (tr.) Neubauer; Zimmermann.

Book of Wisdom, The. See Reider.

Books of the Maccabees. Books 1 and 2. (tr.) Sidney Tedesche. Books 3 and 4. (tr.) Moses Hadas. Philadelphia: Dropsie College/New York: Harper, 1954.

——. Book 4. (tr.) R. B. Townshend. In Charles, *Apocrypha and Pseudepigrapha of the Old Testament.*

——. In East and West Library. London, 1949.

Books of the Saviour. Extracts appended in *Pistis Sophia.*

Boswell, R. B. "The Evolution of Angels and Demons in Christian Theology." Open Court, vol. 14, No. 8, August 1900.

Botarel, Moses. *Mayan Hahochmah.* In *Sefer Yetzirah,* edition published in Mantua, 1562; Grodno, 1806, 1820; and Warsaw, 1884.

Bouisson, Maurice. *Magic, Its History and Principal Rites.* (tr.) G. Almayrac. New York: Dutton, 1961.

Box, G. H. (ed., tr.). *The Apocalypse of Abraham* (with J. I. Landsman). London: Society for Promoting Christian Knowledge, 1918.

——. *The Ascension of Isaiah.* Introd. London: Society for Promoting Christian Knowledge, 1917.

——. *The Book of Jubilees.* London: Society for Promoting Christian Knowledge [1927].

——. *The Ezra-Apocalypse.* London: Pitman, 1912; and Society for Promoting Christian Knowledge, 1917.

——. *Testament of Abraham.* London: Society for Promoting Christian Knowledge, 1927.

Brandt, A. J. H. W. *Mandaische Religion.* Leipzig: Hinrichs, 1912.

Braude, William G. (ed. tr.). *Midrash Tehillim* (Commentary on Psalms). 2 vols. New Haven: Yale U.P., 1959. An edition ed. by Buber, pub. in Wilna, 1892.

Brewer, E. Cobham. *A Dictionary of Miracles.* Philadelphia: Lippincott, 1884.

——. *Brewer's Dictionary of Phrase and Fable.* Philadelphia: Lippincott, 1930.

Broderick, Robert C. (ed.). *The Catholic Concise Encyclopedia.* New York: Simon and Schuster, 1956.

Brooks, E. W. *Joseph and Asenath.* London: Society for Promoting Christian Knowledge, 1918.

Brooks, Maria Gowen (Maria Del Occidente). *Zophiel; or The Bride of Seven.* Boston: Lee & Shepard, 1879.

Brotz, Howard. *The Black Jews of Harlem.* New York: The Free Press, 1964.

Browning, Robert. *Complete Poetic and Dramatic Works.* Cambridge, Mass.: Houghton, 1895.

Brownlee, W. H. "The Dead Sea Manual of Discipline." In *Bulletin of the American Schools of Oriental Research* (Basor). No. 10–12. Suppl. Studies. New Haven: Yale U.P., 1951.

Bruce Codex. British Museum.

Bruce Papyrus. Bodleian Library, Oxford.

Bruce, F. F. *Second Thoughts on the Dead Sea Scrolls.* Grand Rapids: Eerdmans, 1961.

Buber, Martin. *Erzählungen von engeln, gesistern und dämonem.* Berlin: Schocken, 1934. Tr. as *Tales of Angels, Spirits and Demons,* by David Antin and Jerome Rothenberg. New York: Hawks Well Press, 1938.

——. *Jewish Mysticism and the Legend of Baalshem.* London: Dent, 1931.

—— (ed.). *Midrash Lekah Tov. See Lekah Genesis.*

—— (ed.). *Midrash Tanhuma.* Wilna, 1885. Earlier editions of the text published in Warsaw, 1873, by N. D. Zisbert; and in Venice 1545.

——. *Tales of the Hasidim: The Early Masters and The Later Masters.* 2 vols. (tr.) Olga Marx. New York: Schocken [1961].

Buchanan, E. S. (tr.). *Gospel of John* (an apocryphon). London: C. F. Roworth, 1918.

Budge, E. A. Wallis. *Amulets and Talismans.* New Hyde Park, N.Y.: University Books, 1961.

——. *Book of the Dead.* London: Kegan Paul, 1898.

——. *Miscellaneous Texts* (containing *Apocalypse of Paul, Book of Bartholomew,* etc.). London: British Museum, 1913–15.

——. *Osiris.* Subtitled *The Egyptian Religion of Resurrection.* New Hyde Park, N.Y.: University Books [1961].

Bulfinch, Thomas. *The Age of Fable or The Beauties of Mythology.* New York: Heritage Press, 1942.

Bulley, Margaret. *Great Bible Pictures.* London: Batsford, 1957.

Bunyan, John. *Complete Works.* Philadelphia: Bradley, Garretson & Co., 1872.

Burrows, Millar. *The Dead Sea Scrolls.* New York: Viking, 1956.

Butler, E. M. *Ritual Magic*. New York: The Noonday Press, 1959.

Buttenweiser, Moses (ed.). *Apocalypse of Elias* (*Die Hebräische Elias-Apokalypse*). Leipzig: E. Pfeiffer, 1897. An edition edited by Georg Steindorf and published by Hinrichs in Leipzig, 1899.

C

Cabell, James Branch. *The Devil's Own Dear Son*. New York: Farrar, 1949.

———. *Jurgen*. New York: McBride, 1922.

———. *The Silver Stallion*. New York: McBride, 1928.

Cadbury, Henry J. *Jesus: What Manner of Man*. New York: Macmillan, 1948.

Caird, G. B. *Principalities and Powers*. Oxford: Clarendon, 1956.

Camfield, Benjamin. *A Theological Discourse of Angels*. London: H. Brome, 1678.

Canaanite Myths and Legends. *See* Driver.

Canonical Prayerbook of the Mandaeans, The. (tr.) E. S. Drower. Leiden: E. J. Brill, 1959.

Canticles Rabba. *See Midrash Rabba*.

Carpenter, Edward. *Pagan and Christian Creeds*. New York: Blue Ribbon Books, 1920.

Carus, Paul. *The History of the Devil*. Chicago: The Open Court Co., 1900.

Casey, R. P. (tr.). *Excerpts from Theodotus* (The *Excerpta ex Theodoto* of Clement of Alexandria). London: Christophers [1934].

Catholic Encyclopedia. "Gnosticism."

Ceram, C. W. *The Secrets of The Hittites*. (tr.) Richard and Clara Winston. New York: Knopf, 1956.

Chaldean Magic: Its Origin and Development. *See* Lenormant.

Chaldean Oracles of Zoroaster. *See* Aude.

Chandler, Walter M. *The Trial of Jesus*. 2 vols. New York: The Federal Book Co., 1925.

Charles, R. H. (ed., tr.). *The Syriac Apocalypse of Baruch* (*Baruch II*). London: Society for Promoting Christian Knowledge, 1918.

———. *The Apocrypha and Pseudepigrapha of the Old Testament*. 2 vols. Oxford: Clarendon, 1913.

———. *The Ascension of Isaiah*. London: A. & C. Black, 1900. Includes portions of *Martyrdom of Isaiah* and *The Vision of Isaiah*, as well as the *Testament of Hezekiah*. The Society for Promoting Christian Knowledge published an edition in 1919.

———. *The Book of Enoch* or *Enoch I*. Oxford: Clarendon, 1912.

———. *The Book of Jubilees*. London: Society for Promoting Christian Knowledge, 1927. Originally published in *Jewish Quarterly Review*, 1893–1894.

———. *The Book of the Secrets of Enoch* (*Enoch II* or *The Slavonic Enoch*). Oxford: Clarendon, 1896.

———. *Critical Commentary of the Revelation of St. John*. A volume in the 10-vol. American edition of *The Ante-Nicene Fathers*, ed. by A. Cleveland Coxe. New York: Scribner, 1917–1925.

———. *Fragments of a Zadokite Work*. Contained in *The Apocrypha and Pseudepigrapha of the Old Testament*.

———. *Testament of the Twelve Patriarchs*. Oxford: Clarendon, 1913.

Chase, Frederic H. Jr. (tr.). *Writings of John of Damascus*. New York: Fathers of the Church, 1958.

Chateaubriand, François. *Génie du Christianisme* (Genius of Christianity). Lyon: Ballanche Père, 1809.

Chivers, Thomas Holley. *Virginalia*. Philadelphia: Lippincott, 1853.

Christian Content of the Bible, The. *See* Gilbert.

Christian, Paul. *The History and Practice of Magic*. (ed.) Ross Nichols. 2 vols. New York: Citadel, 1963.

Chronicles of Jerahmeel. *See* Gaster, M.

Churchill, R. C. *Shakespeare and His Betters*. Bloomington, Ind.: Indiana U.P. [1959].

Churgin, Pinkhos (ed.). *Targum Ketubim*. New York: Horev, 1945.

———. *Targum Jonathan to the Prophets*. New Haven: Yale U.P. [1927].

Clark, W. R. (tr.). *Banquet of the Ten Virgins* of Methodius of Philippi. Buffalo: *Select Library of the Nicene and Post-Nicene Fathers of the Christian Church*, 1886–1890.

Clavicula Salomonis (Key of Solomon). *See* Gollancz.

Clayton, George. *Angelology*. New York: H. Kermot, 1851.

Clement of Alexandria. *Prophetic Eclogues, Homilies, Recognitions*, and *Stromata*. In *Anti-Nicene Fathers*. Vols. 2 and 8. New York: Scribner, 1925.

———. *The First Epistle and Second Epistle to the Corinthians*. In *The Apocryphal New Testament* (pub. by Eckler).

Clement, Clara Erskine. *Angels in Art*. Boston: L. C. Page & Co., 1898.

Clement, Robert J. "Forbidden Books and Christian Reunion." New York: *Columbia University Forum*, Summer 1963.

Cleugh, James (tr.). *In Search of Adam*. *See* Wendt.

Cockerell, Sydney C. *See Book of Old Testament Illustrations*.

Cohen, Chapman. *Foundations of Religion*. London: Pioneer Press, 1930.

———. *God and the Universe*. London: Pioneer Press, 1946.

——. *A Grammar of Freethought.* London: Pioneer Press, 1921.

——. *Primitive Survivals in Modern Thought.* London: Pioneer Press, 1935.

Colet, John. *Two Treatises on the Hierarchies of Dionysius.* (tr.) J. H. Lupton. London: G. Bell & Sons, 1869.

Cologne Bible, The. Cologne, 1478–1480.

Complete Book of Fortune. Anonymous. London: P. R. Gawthorn, Ltd. n.d.

Conder, C. R. *The Bible and the East.* Edinburgh: Blackwood, 1896.

Contra Celsum, see Origen.

Conybeare, Frederick G. "The Apocalypse of Moses" (titled in Greek MSS. *The History of the Life of Adam and Eve* and in Armenian MSS. as *The Book of Adam*). London: *Jewish Quarterly Review,* vol. 7, 1894.

——. "The Demonology of the New Testament." London: *Jewish Quarterly Review,* July 1896, pp. 576–608.

——. *Life of Apollonius of Tyana.* 2 vols. London: Heinemann, 1912.

——. *Myth, Magic, and Morals.* London: Watts & Co., 1909. Reissued as *Origins of Christianity.* New Hyde Park, N.Y.: University Books, 1958.

—— (ed.). *Philo About the Contemplative Life of the Fourth Book of the Treatise Concerning the Virtues.* Oxford, 1895.

—— (tr., ed.). "The Testament of Solomon." London: *Jewish Quarterly Review,* vol. 11, pp. 1–45, 1898.

Coomaraswamy, Ananda. *Buddha and the Gospel of Buddhism.* New Hyde Park, N.Y.: University Books, 1964.

Corcos, Josef (tr.). *Schiur Komah.* Livorno (Leghorn): J. Tubiano (1825?).

Cordovero, Moses. *The Palm Tree of Deborah.* (tr.) Louis Jacobs. London: Vallentine, Mitchell, 1960.

——. *Pardes Rimmonim* (Orchard of Pomegranates). Cracow, 1592.

Corte, Nicolas. *Who Is the Devil?* (tr. from the French) D. K. Pryce. New York: Hawthorn, 1959.

Cottrell, Leonard. *The Anvil of Civilization.* New York: New American Library, 1957.

"Covenant of the Community" (Manual of Discipline). Comments in Dupont-Sommer, *The Dead Sea Scrolls.* Oxford: Blackwell, 1954.

Crashaw, Richard. *Steps to the Temple.* Sacred Poems. London: Humphrey Moseley, 1646.

Craven, Thomas (ed.). *A Treasury of Art Masterpieces.* New York: Simon and Schuster, 1939.

Cruden, Alexander. *A Complete Concordance to the Holy Scriptures.* Hartford, Conn.: The S. S. Scranton Co. n.d.

Cumont, Franz. *Les Anges du paganisme.* Paris: "Revue de l'histoire des religions," tome 72, 1915.

——. *The Mysteries of Mithra.* (tr.) T. J. McCormack. London: Kegan Paul, 1903; Chicago: Open Court Pub. Co., 1910.

Curry, Walter Clyde. *Milton's Ontology, Cosmogony and Physics.* Lexington, Ky.: U. of Kentucky Press, 1966.

D

Dabistan, The. (tr.) David Shea and Anthony Troyer. New York: Tudor Pub. Co., 1937.

Danby, Rev. Herbert (tr.). *The Mishnah.* Oxford: Clarendon, 1933.

Danielou, Jean. *The Angels and Their Mission.* (tr.) David Heimann. Westminster, Md.: The Newman Press, 1957.

Daniels, Jonathan. *Clash of Angels.* New York: Brewer and Warren, 1930.

Dante Alighieri. *La Divina Commedia.* (ed.) Eugenio Camerini. Milan: Casa Editrice Sonzogno, 1930.

——. *The Divine Comedy.* (tr.) Lawrence Grant White. New York: Pantheon Books, 1958.

Darmesteter, J. (tr.). *Vendidad* (a Mazdean scripture). Included in *The Sacred Books of the East.*

Das buch Bahir. See Scholem.

Das Buch Beliel. See de Teramo.

Davenport, Basil. *Deals with the Devil.* New York: Dodd, 1958.

David-Neel, Alexandra. *Magic and Mystery in Tibet.* New Hyde Park, N.Y.: University Books, 1965.

Davidson, Gustav. "The Guise of Angels." *Tomorrow* (Eng.), Summer 1963.

——. "Metatron—Angel of the Divine Face." *New Dimensions* (Eng.), August 1964.

——. "The Named Angels in Scripture." In press.

——. "Poe's Israfel." In press.

——. "The Poets and the Angels." *The Literary Review,* Autumn 1965.

Davies, A. Powell. *The Meaning of the Dead Sea Scrolls.* New York: New American Library, 1956.

Dead Sea Scrolls, The. See Allegro, Bruce, Burrows, Davies, Dupont-Summer, Th. Gaster, Mansoor, Wilson.

de Bles, Arthur. *How to Distinguish the Saints in Art.* New York: Art Culture Publications, 1925.

de Claremont, Lewis. *The Ancient's Book of Magic.* New York: Dorene Pub. Co. [1936].

Deferrari, Roy J. *See* Eusebius.

de Jonge, M. (ed.). *Testament of the Twelve Patriarchs.* Leiden: E. J. Brill, 1964.

de Laurence, L. W. (ed.). *The Lesser Key of Solomon/ Goetia/The Book of Evil Spirits.* New York: Wehman Bros. [1916].

Del Occidente, Maria. *See* Brooks, Maria.

De Mirville, Marquis Eude. *Pneumatologie.* Paris: H. Vrayet de Surcy, 1854.

"Demonology of the New Testament." *See* Conybeare.

De Plancy, Collin. *Dictionnaire Infernal.* 4 vols. Paris: Librairie Universelle, 1825–1826. One-vol. ed., 1863, pub. in Paris by Plon.

——. *Le Diable Peint par Lui-Meme.* Paris: P. Mongie Aine, Libraire, 1819.

Des Sciences Occultes. See Salverte.

de Teramo, Jacobus. *Das buch Belial.* Augsberg, 1473.

Dialogues of St. Gregory the Great. (ed.) Henry T. Coleridge. London: Burns, 1874.

Dialogues of Plato. (tr.) B. Jowett. 2 vols. New York: Random, 1937.

Dictionary of the Bible, A. See Hastings; Schaff.

Dictionary of the Holy Bible, A. New York: American Tract Society, 1859.

Dictionary of Islam, A. See Hughes.

Dictionary of Miracles, A. See Brewer.

Dictionary of Mysticism. See Gaynor.

Dictionary of Mythology Folklore and Symbols. See Jobes.

Die Angelologie und Dämonologie des Korans. See Eickmann.

Die Elemente der Kabbalah. See Bischoff.

Dionysius the Areopagite. *The Mystical Theologie and The Celestiel Hierarchies.* (tr.) Editors of The Shrine of Wisdom. Surrey (Eng.): The Shrine of Wisdom, 1949.

——. *The Divine Names.* (tr.) Editors of The Shrine of Wisdom. Surrey (Eng.): The Shrine of Wisdom, 1957.

Discovery in the Judean Desert (The Dead Sea scrolls and their meaning). *See* Vermes.

Divine Pymander, The. See Hermes Trismegistus.

Dobbins, Dunstan. *Franciscan Mysticism.* New York: J. W. Wagner, Inc., 1927.

Dodds, E. R. (ed.). *The Elements of Theology* of Proclus. Oxford: Clarendon, 1963.

Doolittle, Hilda ("H. D."). *Tribute to the Angels.* New York and Oxford: Oxford U.P., 1945.

Doresse, Jean. *The Secret Books of the Egyptian Gnostics.* (tr. from the French) Philip Mairet. New York: Viking [1960].

Douce Apocalypse, The. Introd. by A. G. and W. O. Hassall. New York: Thomas Yoseloff [1961].

Driver, G. R. *Canaanite Myths and Legends.* Edinburgh: T. & T. Clark, 1956.

——. *The Hebrew Scrolls from the Neighborhood of Jericho and the Dead Sea.* London: Oxford U.P., 1951.

Drower, E. S. (ed.). *The Canonical Prayerbook of the Mandaeans.* Leiden: E. J. Brill, 1959.

—— (ed.). *The Coronation of the Great Sislam.* Leiden: E. J. Brill, 1962.

——. *The Mandaeans of Iraq and Iran.* Leiden: E. J. Brill, 1962.

Drummond, William (of Hawthornden). *Flowres of Sion.* Edinburgh: Andro Hart, 1630.

Dryden, John. *The State of Innocence.* In *The Dramatic Works of John Dryden.* (ed.) Montague Summers. 6 vols. London: The Nonesuch Press, 1931–1932.

Duff, Archibald. *The First and Second Books of Esdras.* London: Dent, 1903.

Dunlap, Knight. *Religion, Its Functions in Human Life.* New York: McGraw, 1946.

Dupont-Sommer, A. *The Dead Sea Scrolls.* (tr. from French) Margaret Rowley. Oxford: Basil Blackwell, 1954.

——. *The Jewish Sect of Qumran and the Essenes.* (tr. from the French) R. D. Barnett. New York: Macmillan, 1956.

Durant, Will. *The Story of Philosophy.* New York: Simon and Schuster, 1926, 1952.

E

Eickmann, Walther. *Die Angelologie und Dämonologie des Korans.* New York and Leipzig: Paul Eger, 1908.

Eisenmenger, Johann Andreas. *Tradition of the Jews* (*Entdecktes Judenthum*). 2 vols. (tr.) John Peter Strehelin. London: G. Smith, 1742–43.

Eleazor of Worms. *Hilkot Metatron.* British Museum MS. Add. 27199, fol. 114a.

——. *Sepher Raziel* (*Book of the Angel Raziel*). In Hebrew: Warsaw, 1881; in English: Ms. No. 3826, Sloane Coll., British Museum. An edition published in Amsterdam, 1701.

Emmet, C. W. (ed., tr.). *Third and Fourth Books of Maccabees.* London: Society for Promoting Christian Knowledge, 1917.

Empson, William. *Milton's God.* Norfolk, Conn.: New Directions, 1961.

Enchiridion of Pope Leo the Third. A collection of religious charms. Rome, 1660.

Encyclopaedia Britannica. "Angel" in 14th ed., vol. I, pp. 920–921. London-New York [1929].

Encyclopaedia Judaica. vols. A–L (no others published). Jakob Klatzkin. In German. Berlin: Verlag Eschkol [1928–   ].

Encyclopaedia of Occultism, An. See Spence.

Encyclopaedia of Religion and Ethics. See Hastings.

Encyclopedia of Witchcraft and Demonology, The. See Robbins.

Enelow, H. G. (ed.). *Mishnah of Rabbi Eliezer.* New York: Bloch, 1933.

Enoch I. See The Book of Enoch or *I Enoch.*

Enoch II. See The Book of the Secrets of Enoch.

3 Enoch, or *The Hebrew Book of Enoch.* (ed., tr.) Hugo Odeberg. New York: Cambridge U.P., 1928.

Epiphanius. *Penarion* (a work in Greek against heresy). German tr. in 5 vols. Leipzig: G. Dindorf, 1859–1863.

Epistle of St. Clement and *Second Epistle of St. Clement.* In *Excluded Books of the New Testament.* (tr.) J. B. Lightfoot (et al.). London: Nash and Grayson, 1927.

Epistle (or *Letter*) *to the Trallians. See* Ignatius (Martyr) of Antioch.

Erdman, David V. *Blake/Prophet Against Empire.* Princeton, N. J.: Princeton U.P., 1954.

Essentials of Demonology. See Langton.

Etheridge, J. W. (ed.). *Targum of Onkelos and Jonathan* (*q.v.*).

Eusebius, Pamphili. *Ecclesiastical History.* (ed.) E. Schwartz. 2 vols. Leipzig, 1905, 1909. (tr.) Roy J. Deferrari. 2 vols. New York: Fathers of the Church, 1953–1955.

——. *On the Theophania, or Divine Manifestation of Our Lord.* A Syriac version ed. by Samuel Lee. 2 vols. London: Society for the Publication of Oriental Texts, 1842.

"The Evolution of Angels and Demons." *See* Boswell.

Excerpts of Theodotus. See Casey. The Excerpts or Extracts are appended to *The Miscellanies* of Clement of Alexandria.

Excluded Books of the New Testament. See Lightfoot.

F

Fabricius, J. A. *Codex Apocryphus Novi Testamenti.* 3 parts. Hamburg: B. Schiller, 1703–1719.

Falasha Anthology. (tr.) Wolf Leslau. New Haven: Yale U.P., 1951.

Fathers of the Church, The. A New Translation. (ed.) Ludwig Schopp and others. New York: Cima Pub. Co.; Washington, D.C.: Catholic University of America Press; and New York: Fathers of the Church, Inc., 1947–1965.

Faust. See Kaufmann.

Fergusson, Francis. *Dante.* New York: Macmillan, 1966.

Ferm, Vergilius (ed.). *Ancient Religions.* New York: Philosophical Library, 1950.

Ferrar, William John (tr.). *The Assumption of Moses.* London: Society for Promoting Christian Knowledge, 1918.

——(ed.). *The Uncanonical Jewish Books.* London: Society for Promoting Christian Knowledge, 1918.

Finkelstein, Louis. *The Pharisees.* Vol. 1. Philadelphia: Jewish Publication Society of America, 1938.

First Book of Maccabees, The. See Tedesche.

Floyd, William. *Christianity Cross-Examined.* New York: Arbitrator Press, 1941.

Fludd, Robert. *The Compendious Apology.* Leyden, 1616.

——. *Cosmology of the Macrocosmos.* Frankfort, 1617, 1629.

——. *Mosaicall Philosophy.* London, 1659.

——. *Utriusque cosmi majoris et minoris historia.* 2 vols. Oppenheim, 1619.

Flusser, D. *The Apocryphal Book of the Ascension of Isaiah and the Dead Sea Sect.* Jerusalem: *Israel Exploration Journal,* III, 1953.

Fodor, Nandor. *Encyclopaedia of Psychic Science.* New Hyde Park, N.Y.: University Books [1966].

Follansbee, Eleanor. *Heavenly History.* Chicago: Covici, 1927.

Forerunners and Rivals of Christianity. See Legge.

Forlong, J. G. R. *Encyclopedia of Religions.* 3 vols. New Hyde Park, N.Y.: University Books, 1964.

Fosdick, Harry Emerson. *The Man from Nazareth.* New York: Harper, 1949.

——. *The Modern Use of the Bible.* New York: Macmillan, 1936.

Fourth Book of Ezra (*Ezra IV* or the *Apocalypse of Ezra*). Cambridge: R. L. Bensly, 1895.

Fragments of a Faith Forgotten. See Mead.

France, Anatole. *The Revolt of the Angels.* (tr.) Mrs. Wilfred Jackson. London: Lane, 1925.

Frank, Adolphe. *La Kabbale ou La Philosophie Religieuse des Hébreux.* Paris: Hachette et Cie., 1892. Eng. tr. by I. Sossnitz. New York: The Kabbalah Pub. Co., 1926.

Frazer, Sir James George. *The Golden Bough.* 1 vol. New York: Macmillan, 1951.

Fremantle, Ann (ed.). *A Treasury of Early Christianity.* New York: The New American Library [1960].

Friedlander, Gerald (tr.). *Pirke de Rabbi Eliezer.* New York: Herman Press, 1965.

Friedman, H. and Simon, M. (ed., tr.) *Midrash Rabba.* 10 vols. London: Soncino Press, 1961.

Friedmann, Meir (ed.). *Pesikta Rabbati.* Vienna: pvt. printed, 1880.

Fuller, J. F. C. *The Secret Wisdom of the Qabalah.* London: The Occult Book Society, n.d.

G

Gaffarel, Jacques. *Unheard-of Curiosities concerning the Talismanic Sculpture of the Persians*. (tr.) Edm. Chilmead. London, 1650.

Gales, R. L. "The Christian Lore of Angels." *National Review* (England), September, 1910, pp. 107–115.

Garinet, Jules. *Histoire de la Magie en France* (History of Magic in France). Paris: Foulon & Cie., 1818.

Gaster, Moses (ed., tr.). *The Asatir*. London: Royal Asiatic Society, 1927.

——. *The Chronicles of Jerahmeel*. London: Oriental Translation Fund, 1899.

——. "The Logos Ebraikos in the Magical Papyrus of Paris, and the Book of Enoch." London: *Journal of the Royal Asiatic Society*, 1901.

——. *Ma'aseh Book*. 2 vols. Philadelphia: The Jewish Publication Society of America, 1934.

——. *Schiur Komah*. In *Monatsschrift für Geschichte und Wissenschaft des Judenthums*; and in *Studies and Texts in Folklore*. London: Maggs Bros., 1925–1928.

——. *The Sword of Moses*. London: D. Nutt, 1896; also in *Studies and Texts in Folklore*.

——. *Wisdom of the Chaldeans*. Proceedings of the Society of Biblical Archaeology, 1900; also in *Studies and Texts in Folklore*.

Gaster, Theodor H. *The Dead Sea Scriptures*. Garden City, N.Y.: Doubleday, 1956.

——. *The Holy and the Profane*. New York: William Sloane Associates, 1955.

Gaynor, Frank. *Dictionary of Mysticism*. New York: Philosophical Library [1953].

Geffcken, J. (ed.). *Sibylline Oracles*. Leipzig, 1902.

Genesis Apocryphon, A. See Avigad and Yadin.

Gibb, H. A. R. and Kramers, J. H. (ed.). *A Shorter Encyclopaedia of Islam*. Leiden: E. J. Brill, 1961.

Gikatilla, Joseph Ben Abraham. *The Nut Garden* (*Ginnath Egoz*). Hanau: Eliezer b. Chayyim and Elijah b. Seligman Ulmo, 1614.

——. *Gate of Light* (*Shaare Orah*). Offenbach: Printed by Seligman Reis, 1715.

Gilberti, George Holley. *The Christian Content of the Bible*. New York: Macmillan, 1930.

Ginsburg, Christian D. *The Essenes/The Kaballah*. Two Essays. London: Routledge & Kegan Paul Ltd., 1956.

——. *The Kabbalah: Its Doctrines, Development, and Literature*. London: G. Routledge & Sons, 1920.

Ginzberg, Louis. *The Legends of the Jews*. 7 vols. Philadelphia: The Jewish Publication Society of America, 1954.

Girardius. *Parvi Lucii libellus de Mirabilibus naturae arcanis*, 1730. MS. in Bibliothèque de l'Arsenal, Paris. *See* Grillot, *Picture Museum of Sorcery, Magic and Alchemy*.

Glaser, Abram. *This World of Ours*. New York: Philosophical Library, 1955.

Glasson, T. Francis. *Greek Influence in Jewish Eschatology*. London: Society for Promoting Christian Knowledge, 1961.

Gleadow, Rupert. *Magic and Divination*. London: Faber [1941].

"Gnosticism" in *Catholic Encyclopedia*.

Gnosticism and Early Christianity. See Grant.

Goddard, John. "The Angels of the Jews, of the Christians, and of the New Church." Boston: *New Church Review*, vol. 13, 1906.

Godolphin, F. R. B. (ed.). *Great Classical Myths*. New York: Random (The Modern Library) [1964].

Gods/A Dictionary of the Deities of All Lands. See Redfield.

Goethe's *Faust. See* Kaufmann.

Goetia (*The Lesser Key of Solomon/Lemegeton*). *See* de Laurence.

Golden Legend, The. Jacobus de Voragine. Dresden, 1846. Originally published circa 1275.

——. By Henry Wadsworth Longfellow. A poem. Boston: Ticknor, Reed & Fields, 1851.

Goldin, Judah (ed., tr.). *The Fathers According to Rabbi Nathan*. New Haven: Yale U.P., 1955.

——. *The Living Talmud*. New York: New American Library, 1957.

Gollancz, Hermann (ed., tr.). *Book of the Key of Solomon* (*Sepher Maphteah Shelomo*). London: Oxford U.P., 1914.

——. *The Book of Protection*. London: Oxford U.P., 1912.

——. *Clavicula Salomonis* (Key of Solomon). Frankfurt: J. Kauffmann, 1903.

——. *Midrash of the Ten Jewish Martyrs* (in English). London: Luzac, 1908.

Goodspeed, Edgar J. *Modern Apocrypha*. Boston: The Beacon Press [1956].

Gordis, Robert. *Koheleth—The Man and His World*. New York: Jewish Theological Seminary of America, 1951.

——. *The Wisdom of Koheleth*. London: East and West Library, 1950.

Gospel of Barnabas. See Ragg.

Gospel of Bartholomew, The. See James.

Gospel of the Infancy of the Saviour. Tr. from the Arabic. In *The Ante-Nicene Fathers*. Vol. 8. New York: Scribner, 1917–1925.

Gospel of Mary. Known as *The Apocryphon of John*.

In *Lost Books of the Bible*. Also contained in the Akhmim Codex, papyrus, Egyptian Museum, Berlin, and in Schmidt. *Koptisch-Gnostische Schriften*.

Gospel of Nicodemus. Also called *Acts of Pilate*. In *Lost Books of the Bible* and in *Excluded Books of the New Testament*.

Gospel of Peter. See Harris.

Gospel of Peter and the Revelation of Peter. See Robinson and James; also Lightfoot.

Gospel of Philip. See Till.

Gospel of Pseudo-James or the Protevangelium. See Postel.

Gospel of Pseudo-Matthew. See James.

Gospel of Thomas. In vol. 8, *The Ante-Nicene Fathers*. New York: Scribner, 1925. Also in James, *The Apocryphal New Testament*.

——. *On the Secret Words of Jesus*. Appendix to Doresse, *The Secret Books of the Egyptian Gnostics*.

——. (tr. from the Coptic) A. Guillaumont, et al. Leiden: E. J. Brill, 1959.

——. (tr.) William R. Schoedel. In the *Secret Sayings of Jesus*. Garden City, N.Y.: Doubleday, 1960.

Gospel of Truth (Evangelium Veritatis). A Coptic MS. (ed., tr.) M. Malinine, H. C. Puech, and Gilles Quispel. Zurich: Rascher, 1956. MS. in Jung Codex XIII, Chenoboskion Library.

——. as *Das Evangelium der Wahrheit*. (ed.) Walter C. Till. Incl. in *Evangelien aus dem Nilsand*. Frankfurt-am-Main: H. Sheffler [1960].

Gospel of the Twelve Apostles (or the *Teaching of the Apostles*). See Harris.

Graetz, H. H. *Gnosticismus und Judenthum*. Breslau, 1846.

——. *History of the Jews*. 6 vols. Philadelphia: Jewish Publication Society of America [1891–1898].

Grand Grimoire, The. Excerpts in Waite, *The Book of Black Magic and of Pacts*.

Grant, Frederick C. (ed. with H. H. Rowley) Hastings, *Dictionary of the Bible*.

Grant, R. M. *Gnosticism and Early Christianity*. New York: Columbia U.P., 1959.

Graves, Kersey. *The World's Sixteen Crucified Saviors*. New York: The Truth Seeker Co. [1948].

Graves, Robert. *The Greek Myths*. 2 vols. Baltimore: Penguin, 1955.

——. *Hebrew Myths* (with Raphael Patai). Garden City, N.Y.: Doubleday, 1964.

——. *The White Goddess*. Garden City, N.Y.: Doubleday, 1958.

Gray, John. *The Krt Text in the Literature of Ras Shamra*. Leiden: E. J. Brill, 1964.

Great Books of the Western World. "Angels," vol. 1. Chicago: *Encyclopaedia Britannica*, 1952.

Great Dictionary of the Yiddish Language. (ed.) Judah A· Joffe and Yehudel Mark. New York: Yiddish Dictionary Committee, 1961.

Greater Hechaloth. See Hechaloth Lore.

Greek Influence on Jewish Eschatology. See Glasson.

Greene, H. C. (tr.). *Gospel of the Childhood of Jesus*. In Latin and English. New York: Scott & Thaw, 1904.

Gregory the Great. *Moralia* and *Momilia*. In Migne, *Patrologiae Latina*.

——. *Moralia*. Eng. tr., *Morals on the Book of Job*, 1844–1850.

Gregory Thaumaturgus. "Panegyric Addressed to Origen." In Fremantle, *A Treasury of Early Christianity*.

Grillot, Emile De Givry. *Witchcraft, Magic and Alchemy*. (tr.) J. Courtenay Locke. Boston: Houghton, 1931. Printed in Great Britain.

——. Same, under title *A Pictorial Anthology of Witchcraft, Magic and Alchemy*, New Hyde Park, N.Y.: University Books, 1958; and as *Picture Museum of Sorcery, Magic and Alchemy* in 1963 by same publisher.

Grimoire of Honorius. Attributed to Pope Honorius III. Rome 1760.

Grimorium Verum. "The True Clavicule of Solomon." Originally tr. from the Hebrew in 1517 by M. Plaingiere, in Memphis. Excerpts in Waite, *The Book of Black Magic and of Pacts*.

Grossmannus, C. A. O. See Philo.

Grundriss der iranischen Philologie. W. Geiger and E. Kuhn. 4 vols. Strassburg: K. J. Trübner [1895–1904].

Guignebert, Charles. *Ancient, Medieval and Modern Christianity*. New Hyde Park, N.Y.: University Books [1961].

——. *Jesus*. (tr.) S. H. Hooke. New Hyde Park, N.Y.: University Books [1956]. Edition in French, 1933.

——. *The Jewish World in the Time of Jesus*. Introd. Charles Francis Potter. New Hyde Park, N.Y.: University Books [1959]. Edition in French, 1935.

Guillet, Cephas. *The Forgotten Gospel*. Dobbs Ferry, N.Y.: The Clermont Press, 1940.

Guinan, Alastair (tr.). *The Book of Mary*. New York: Hawthorn, 1960.

Gurdjieff, G. *All and Everything/Beelzebub's Tales to His Grandson*. New York: Dutton, 1964.

Gurney, O. R. *The Hittites*. London: Penguin [1952].

H

Habdalah shel Rabbi Akiba. See Akiba.

Hadas, Moses (tr.). *Third and Fourth Books of Maccabees*. New York: Harper, 1953.

Halachoth Gedoloth (the Great Laws). R. Simeon Kayyara. A Geniza fragment of the 9th century. Venice, 1548. Edition published by Bernhard Levy in Bonn, 1937.

Halper, B. *Post-Biblical Hebrew Literature.* Philadelphia: The Jewish Publication Society of America, 1921.

Hamilton, Edith. *The Echo of Greece.* New York: Norton [1957].

——. *The Greek Way.* New York: Norton [1942].

——. *Mythology.* New York: New American Library, 1956.

Hammond, George. *A Discourse of Angels.* London, 1701.

Hamoy, Abraham. *Sefer Beth Din* (Book of the House of Judgment). Leghorn, 1858.

Hanauer, James Edward. *Folk-Lore of the Holy Land.* London: Duckworth, 1907.

Harding, Davis P. *The Club of Hercules.* Urbana, Ill.: U. of Illinois Press, 1962.

Harnack, Adolph. *History of Dogma.* (tr.) Neil Buchanan. 7 vols. (bound as 4). New York: Dover, 1961.

Harper, Samuel A. *Man's High Adventure.* Chicago: Ralph Fletcher Seymour, 1955.

Harris, J. Rendel (ed., tr.). *Gospel of Peter,* New York: J. Pott & Co., 1893. *Gospel of the Twelve Apostles* (or the *Teaching of the Apostles*). Baltimore: Johns Hopkins Press; also Cambridge: University Press, 1900.

——. *The Odes and Psalms of Solomon.* New York: Cambridge U.P., 1909 and 1911.

Harrison, Jane Ellen. *Epilegomena to the Study of Greek Religion.* New Hyde Park, New York: University Books, 1962.

Hartmann, Franz. *Magic, White and Black.* Chicago: Theosophical Pub., 1910.

Hassall, A. G. and W. O. (introd.) *Douce Apocalypse.*

Hastings, James. *Dictionary of the Bible.* Revised by F. C. Grant and H. H. Rowley. New York: Scribner, 1963.

——. *Encyclopaedia of Religion and Ethics.* Vol. IV. New York: Scribner, 1955.

Hawkes, Jacquetta (ed.). *World of the Past.* 2 vols. New York: Knopf, 1963.

Hawkins, Edward (ed.). *Poetical Works of John Milton.* 4 vols. London: Oxford U.P., 1824.

Hayley, William (ed.). *The Poetical Works of John Milton.* 3 vols. London: Boydell and Nicol, 1794.

Hazaz, Hayim. "The Seraph." *The Literary Review,* Spring 1958.

Heavenly History. See Follansbee.

Hebraic Literature. Tr. from Talmud, Midrashim. Kabbala. New York: Tudor, 1936.

Hebrew Amulets. See Schrire.

Hebrew Book of Enoch, The. See 3 Enoch.

Hebrew Myths. See Graves.

Hechaloth Lore:
Book of Hechaloth (Sefer Hechaloth). (tr.) A. Jellinek. Issued 1928 by Odeberg as *3 Enoch.* An incomplete MS. in Hebrew in Dropsie College Library, Philadelphia.

——. *Greater Hechaloth (Hechaloth Rabbati).* (tr.) Jellinek. Contained in *Beth ha-Midrasch* (1855); also, as *Pirke Hechaloth,* incl. by Wertheimer in 2-vol. *Bate Midrashot* (Jerusalem, 1950).

——. *Hechakoth Zoterathi.* Bodleian MS. Mich. 9, fol. 66a seqq.

——. *Lesser Hechaloth.* MS. in Hebrew, Bodleian Library, Oxford. Fol. 38a–46a. There is also an unpublished edition by Dr. Morton Smith.

——. *Pirke Hechaloth.* (ed.) Abraham b. Solomon Akra. Contained in *Arzei Levanon* (Cedars of Lebanon). Venice: Giovanni di Cara, 1601.

Herford, R. Travers (ed.) *Pirke Aboth.* Included in Charles, *Apocrypha and Pseudepigrapha of the Old Testament.*

Hermas Visions. See Shepherd of Hermas.

Hermes Trismegistus. *The Divine Pymander.* (ed.) Editors of the Shrine of Wisdom. Surrey (Eng.): The Shrine of Wisdom, 1955.

Herrera, E. Abraham Cohen. *Beth Elohim* (House of God). New York: Columbia University Library. Entry title, *Puerta del Cielo,* X86-H 42Q. An edition published in Amsterdam by Immanuel Benveniste, 1655.

Hertz, Joseph H. (tr.). *Pirke Aboth.* New York: Behrman, 1945.

Hervieux, Jacques (ed.). *The New Testament Apocrypha.* Tr. from the French by W. Hibberd. New York: Hawthorn, 1960.

Hesselgrave, Charles Everett. *The Hebrew Personification of Wisdom.* New York: G. E. Stechert & Co., 1910.

Heywood, Thomas. *The Hierarchy of the Blessèd Angels.* London: Adam Islip, 1635.

Higger, Michael (ed.). *Masekhtot Zeirot.* Contains *Masekheth Derekh Erets.* New York: Bloch Publishing Co., 1929.

Hilkot Metatron. See Eleazer of Worms.

Hinton, Richard W. (pseud.). *Arsenal for Skeptics.* New York: A. S. Barnes, 1961.

Hippolytus, Saint. *Philosophumena, or Refutation of All Heresies.* (Formerly attributed to Origen.) 2 vols. New York: Macmillan, 1921.

Hirschfield, Hartwig (ed.). *The Book of Kuzari*, by Judah ha Levi (*q.v.*).

History of Jewish Mysticism. See Müller.

History of the Life of Adam and Eve. See *Apocalypse of Moses* and *Book of Adam and Eve*.

History of Magic, The. See Levi.

History of Magic and Experimental Science, The. See Thorndike.

History and Practice of Magic, The. See Christian.

History of Ten Martyrs. In Jellinek's *Beth ha-Midrasch*. Contained also in *Midrash Konen*.

History of Witchcraft and Demonology, The. See Summers.

Holbein's Dance of Death. Contains 90 of Holbein's wood engravings illustrating the Bible. London: George Bell & Sons, 1878.

Höllenzwang of Dr. Faust. A general title of Faustian tracts to be found in Scheible's *Das Kloster* (vols. 2 and 5) and in his *Doctor Faust's Bücherschatz*.

Hughes, H. Maldwyn (ed.). *The Greek Apocalypse of Baruch (3 Baruch)*. In Charles, *Apocrypha and Pseudepigrapha of the Old Testament*.

Hughes, Thomas Patrick. *A Dictionary of Islam*. London: W. H. Allen & Co., 1885.

Hugo, Victor. *The Toilers of the Sea*. New York: Harper, 1866.

Husik, Isaac. *A History of Mediaeval Jewish Philosophy*. New York: Meridian Books/and Philadelphia: Jewish Publication Society, 1958.

——— (tr.). *Sefer ha-'Ikkarim* of Joseph Albo.

Huxley, Aldous. *The Devils of Loudon*. London: Chatto, 1952.

Hyde, Douglas. *A Literary History of Ireland*. London: T. F. Unwin, 1901.

Hyde, Thomas. *Historia Religionis Veterum Persarum*. Oxford, 1700.

Hymn of the Soul. See Bevan.

Hymn of Jesus, The. See Mead.

Hymnal of the Protestant Episcopal Church. New York: Nelson, 1920.

Hypostasis of the Archons (the Book of Norea). Coptic MS. apocryphon in the Chenoboskion Library. See comment in Doresse, *The Secret Books of the Egyptian Gnostics* (1960).

I

Iamblichus. *On the Mysteries of the Egyptians, Chaldeans, and Assyrians*. See Taylor, Thomas.

Idra Rabba. Incl. in *Kabbalah Denudata*.

Idra Zuta. Incl. in *Kabbalah Denudata*.

Ignatius (Martyr) of Antioch, also called Theophorus.

Letter to the Trallians. Buffalo: Christian Literature Pub. Co. *The Ante-Nicene Fathers*, 1885–1896. Also contained in *Lost Books of the Bible*.

In Search of Adam. See Wendt.

Interpreter's Bible, The. Commentary. (gen. ed.) George Arthur Buttrick. New York: Abingdon-Cokesbury Press [1951].

Interpreter's Dictionary of the Bible, The. "Angels." 4 vols. (ed.) George Arthur Buttrick. New York: Abingdon Press [1962].

Irenaeus, Saint. *Contra haereses*. Tr. of principal passages by F. R. Montgomery Hitchcock. London: Society for Promoting Christian Knowledge, 1916.

———. In vol. 7, Migne, *Patrologiae Graecae Cursus Completus*. Paris, 1857–1880.

Isaac ha-Cohen of Soria. "Emanations of the Left Side." A tract tr. from the Hebrew by Gershom Scholem in *Mada'e ha Yahadut* (vol. 2, pp. 164ff.), a periodical formerly published in Jerusalem.

Isherwood, Christopher. *Ramakrishna and His Disciples*. New York: Simon and Schuster, 1965.

Isidore of Seville. *Etymologiarum*. In Migne, *Patrologiae Latinae Completus*. Paris: 1844–1864.

Israelstam, J. and Slotki, J. J. (tr.). *Midrash Rabba Leviticus*, vol. 4. London: Soncino, 1961. An earlier edition pub. in 1939.

J

Jacobs, Joseph. *Jewish Contributions to Civilization*. Philadelphia: Jewish Publication Society, 1919.

James, M. R. (ed., tr.). *Acts of Paul, Acts of Philip, Apocalypse of Paul* (Vision of Paul), *Gospel of Pseudo-Matthew*. In *The Apocryphal New Testament*. Oxford: Clarendon, 1955.

———. *Apocrypha Anecdota*. New York: Cambridge U.P., 1893.

———. *Biblical Antiquities of Philo, The*. London: Society for Promoting Christian Knowledge, 1917.

———. *Gospel of Bartholomew, The*. In M. R. James, *The Apocryphal New Testament*. Oxford: Clarendon [1955].

———. *Gospel of the Infancy of Jesus Christ*. New York: Cambridge U.P., 1927.

———. *Lost Apocrypha of the Old Testament*. London: Society for Promoting Christian Knowledge, 1918.

———. "Recovery of the Apocryphon of Peter." *Church Quarterly Review*, vol. 80. London, 1915.

———. *Psalms and Odes of Solomon*; *Psalms of the Pharisees*, commonly called *Psalms of Solomon*. With H. E. Ryle. New York: Cambridge U.P., 1891.

——. *The Testament of Abraham.* New York: Cambridge U. P., 1892.

James, William. *The Varieties of Religious Experience.* New Hyde Park, N.Y.: University Books, 1963.

Jameson, Anna Brownell. *Legends of the Madonna.* London: Unit Library, 1903.

Jastrow, Marcus. *A Dictionary of the Targumin, the Talmud Babli and Yerushalmi, and the Midrashim Literature.* 2 vols. New York: Title Pub. Co., 1943.

Jastrow, Morris, Jr. *The Book of Job.* Philadelphia: Lippincott, 1920.

——. *Hebrew and Babylonian Traditions.* New York: Scribner, 1914.

Jayne, Walter Addison. *The Healing Gods of Ancient Civilizations.* New Hyde Park, New York: University Books, 1962.

Jellinek, Adolph (ed.). *Beth ha-Midrasch.* A collection of Midrashim, incl. parts of *3 Enoch, Alphabet of Rabbi Akiba, History of the Ten Martyrs, Midrash Petirat Mosheh,* etc. 7 vols. Jerusalem: Bamberger & Wehrmann, 1938. Earlier editions: Leipzig, 1853–1859; Vienna, 1873–1877.

—— (ed.). *Midrash Eleh Ezherah.* Leipzig, 1853.

Jewish Magic and Superstition. See Trachtenberg.

Jewish World in the Time of Jesus, The. See Guignebert.

Jobes, Gertrude. *Dictionary of Mythology Folklore and Symbols.* 2 vols. New York: The Scarecrow Press, 1961.

Joffe, Judah A. and Mark, Yehudel. *See Great Dictionary of the Yiddish Language.*

John of Damascus. *Exposition of the Orthodox Faith (De Fide Orthodoxa).* In Migne, *Patrologiae Graecae,* vol. 94, and *A Select Library of Nicene and Post-Nicene Fathers,* 2nd series.

——. *Writings of John of Damascus.* (tr.) Frederic H. Chase, Jr.

Jonson, Ben. *The Devil Is an Ass.* New York: Holt, 1905. Orig. pub. 1616.

Joseph and Asenath. Tr. from the Batiffol text by E.W. Brooks. London: Society for Promoting Christian Knowledge, 1918.

Josephus, Flavius. *The Works of Flavius Josephus.* Tr. from the Greek by William Whiston. Philadelphia: Lippincott, 1852.

Judah ha Levi. *The Book of Kuzari.* Tr. from the Arabic by Hartwig Hirschfeld. New York: Pardes Pub. House, 1946. Earlier edition published in London, 1905.

Jung, Leo. *Fallen Angels in Jewish, Christian and Mohammedan Literature.* Philadelphia: Dropsie College, 1926.

Justin Martyr. *Apology for the Christians.* In the *Writings of Justin Martyr* and *Athenagoras.* Tr. by M. Dods. London, 1857.

——. *The Dialogue with Trypho.* (tr.) A. L. Williams. New York: Macmillan, 1930. Also published by Christian Heritage: New York, 1909.

——. *The Theology of Justin Martyr.* E. R. Goodenough. In *Ante-Nicene Fathers.* New York: Scribner, 1917–1925.

K

Kabbalah Denudata (Kabbalah Unveiled). Incorporates the *Idra Rabba* and *Idra Zuta. See* Mathers.

Kaplan, M. M. *See* Luzzatto.

Karaite Anthology. See Nemoy.

Kaufmann, Walter (tr.). *Faust.* Garden City, N.Y.: Doubleday, 1961.

Kautsky, Karl. *Foundations of Christianity.* (tr.) Henry F. Mins. New York: S. A. Russell, 1953.

Kazwini, Zakariya ibn Muhammed. *Kosmographie.* 2 vols. (ed.) Ferdinand Wüstenfeld. In Arabic. Göttingen: Verlag der Dieterichschen Buchhandlung, 1849.

Kerubim in Semitic Religion and Art. See Lindsay.

Key to Faust's Threefold Harrowing of Hell. Otherwise known as *Key to the Black Raven.* In *Das Kloster.* Stuttgart: J. Scheible, 1846.

Key of Solomon. Usually titled *The Greater Key of Solomon. See* Gollancz; Mathers.

King, Charles William. *The Gnostics and Their Remains.* London: D. Nutt, 1887. An earlier edition published in London, 1864.

King, L. William. *Babylonian Magic and Sorcery.* London: Luzac & Co., 1896.

Kircher, Athanasius. *Oedipus Aegyptiacus.* 4 vols. Rome, 1652–1654.

——. *Voyage Ecstatique (Itinerarium Exstaticum).* Rome: Vitalis Mascardi, 1656.

Kleins Theologisches Wörterbuch. (ed.) Karl Rahner and Herbert Vorgrimler. Freiburg: Herder-Bucherei, 1963.

Kloster, Das. See Scheible.

Klopstock, Friedrich Gottlieb. *Der Messias.* Leipzig: G. J. Goschen, 1844.

——. *The Messiah.* (tr. in English) Joseph Collyer. New York: Duyckinck & Co., 1795. A translation by F. T. London was published in London by Longman, 1826.

Knight, Charles (ed.). *The Works of Shakespere.* 2 vols. London: Virtue & Co. [1870].

Knight, Margaret. *Morals without Religion & Other Essays.* London: Dennis Dobson, 1954.

Kohler, Kaufmann. "Pre-Talmudic Haggadah." *Jewish Quarterly Review*, pp. 399–419. Philadelphia: Dropsie College, 1895.

Kohut, Alexander. "Über die jüdische Angelologie und Dämonologie in ihrer Abhängigkeit von Parismus." Deutsche Morgenländische Gesellschaft Abhandl. Bd. 4, No. 3, pp. 1–105. Leipzig, 1886.

Koran, The. See Pickthall; Sale.

Kosmographie. See Kazwini.

Kramer, Samuel Noah. *From the Tablets of Sumer.* Colorado: The Falcon's Wing Press, 1956.

Kritzeck, James (ed.). *Anthology of Islamic Literature.* New York: Holt, 1964.

Kroner, Richard. *The Religious Function of Imagination.* New Haven: Yale U.P., 1941.

KRT Text in the Literature of Ras Shamra, The. (ed.) John Gray. 2nd ed. Leiden: E. J. Brill, 1964.

Kurth, Willi (ed.). *The Complete Woodcuts of Albrecht Dürer.* New York: Dover, 1963.

Kuzari (Book of). *See* Judah ha Levi.

L

Labarum, Constantine. *Pageantry, Popery, Pillage.* London: Charles J. Thynne, 1911.

Lamsa, George M. *My Neighbor Jesus.* New York: Harper, 1932.

Lanchester, H. C. O. (ed.). *Sibylline Oracles.* In Charles, *Apocrypha and Pseudepigrapha of the Old Testament.*

Lane, Edward William (ed.). *Arabic-English Lexicon.* London: Williams & Norgate, 1867.

Langton, Edward. *Essentials of Demonology.* London: The Epworth Press, 1949.

——. *Good and Evil Spirits.* London: Society for Promoting Christian Knowledge, 1942.

——. *Satan, a Portrait.* London: Skeffington, 1945.

Larousse Encyclopedia of Byzantine & Medieval Art. (gen. ed.) René Huyghe. New York: Prometheus Press, 1963.

—— *Encyclopedia of Mythology.* (int.) Robert Graves. New York: Prometheus Press, 1959.

Lauterbach, Jacob Z. (tr.). *Mekilta de-Rabbi Ishmael.* 3 vols. Philadelphia: The Jewish Publication Society of America, 1949.

Lawson, John Cuthbert. *Modern Greek Folklore and Ancient Greek Religion.* New Hyde Park, N.Y.: University Books, 1964.

Lea, Henry Charles. *Materials Toward a History of Witchcraft.* 3 vols. New York: Yoseleff [1957].

Leadbeater, C. W. *The Astral Plane.* India: The Theosophical Pub. House, 1963.

Legends of the Bible. See Ginzberg.

Legends of the Jews, The. See Ginzberg.

Legge, Francis. "The Names of Demons in the Magic Papyri." *Proceedings of the Society of Biblical Archaeology,* vol. 22, 1900.

——. *Forerunners and Rivals of Christianity.* New Hyde Park, N.Y.: University Books, 1964.

Lehrman, S. M. (tr.). *Midrash Rabba Exodus.* Included in *Midrash Rabba.*

Lekah Genesis. Tobiah b. Eliezer. vol. 1 of the 5-vol. *Midrash Lekah Tov.* (ed.) Martin Buber. Wilna: Widow Bros. & Romm, 1880.

Leland, Charles Godfrey. *Gypsy Sorcery and Fortune Telling.* New Hyde Park, N.Y.: University Books, 1962.

——. *Etruscan Magic and Occult Remedies.* New Hyde Park, N.Y.: University Books, 1963.

Lemegeton, The (The Lesser Key of Solomon). Subtitled "Goetia, the Book of Evil Spirits." Includes *The Almadel* and *The Pauline Art.* Brit. Mus. Sloane Coll. Ms. No. 3648. (ed.) L. W. de Laurence. New York: Wehman Bros. [1916].

Lenormant, Francois. *Chaldean Magic: Its Origin and Development.* Tr. from the French. London: Samuel Bagster & Sons [1877].

Le Sage, Alain Rene. *The Devil on Two Sticks.* New York: Paul Elder & Co. n.d. Originally published in 1707.

Lesser Hechaloth. Unpublished MS. in Jewish Theological Seminary, New York. Oxford Ms. No.1531, fol. 42b. Oxford University.

Lesser Key of Solomon, The. See The Lemegeton.

Levi, Eliphas (pseud. for Alphonse Louis Constant). *The History of Magic.* (tr.) A. E. Waite. London: Rider & Co., 1963.

——. *Le Livre d'Or.* Paris: Lavigne, 1842.

——. *Philosophie Occulte.* Paris: G. Balliere, 1862–1865.

——. *Transcendental Magic.* (tr.) A. E. Waite. Philadelphia: McKay, 1923.

Lewis, C. S. *The Screwtape Letters.* New York: Macmillan, 1959.

Lewy, Immanuel. *The Birth of the Bible.* New York: Bloch Pub. Co., 1950.

——. *The Growth of the Pentateuch.* New York: Bookman Associates, 1955.

Lhermitte, Jean. *True and False Possession.* (tr.) P. J. Hepburne-Scott. New York: Hawthorn Books, 1963.

Liber, Maurice. *Rashi.* Tr. from the French by Adele Szold. Philadelphia: Jewish Publication Society, 1906.

Library of Biblical and Theological Literature. (ed.) George

R. Crooks and John F. Hurst. 9 vols. New York: Eaton & Mains, 1890.

Life of Jesus, The. See Renan.

Light of Asia, The. See Arnold.

Lightfoot, J. B. (tr., with M. R. James, H. B. Swete, et al.). *Excluded Books of the New Testament.* Contains *Book of James; Gospel of Nicodemus* (1 and 2); *Gospel of Peter and the Revelation of Peter; Shepherd of Hermas,* etc. London: E. Nash and Grayson [1927?].

Lindsay, Frederic Nye. *Kerubim in Semitic Religion and Art.* New York, 1912. Thesis (Ph.D.), Columbia University.

Ling, Trevor. *The Significance of Satan in New Testament Demonology.* London: Society for Promoting Christian Knowledge, 1961.

Loisy, Alfred Firmin. *Birth of the Christian Religion* (and) *Origins of the New Testament.* Tr. from the French by L. P. Jacks. New Hyde Park, N.Y.: University Books, 1962.

Longfellow, Henry Wadsworth. *Poetical Works.* 6 vols. Boston: Houghton [1904].

Lost Books of the Bible and the Forgotten Books of Eden. Intro. by Frank Crane. New York: Lewis Copeland Co., 1930.

Loves of the Angels, The. See Moore, Thomas.

Luzzatto, M. H. *Mesillat Yesharim* (The Path of the Upright). (tr.) M. M. Kaplan. Philadelphia: Jewish Publication Society of America, 1936.

M

MacKaye, Percy. *Uriel and Other Poems.* Boston: Houghton, 1912.

Mackenzie, Donald A. *Egyptian Myth and Legend.* London: The Gresham Pub. Co. n.d.

——. *Myths of Babylonia and Assyria.* London: The Gresham Pub. Co. n.d.

——. *Myths of Crete & Pre-Hellenic Europe.* London: The Gresham Pub. Co. n.d.

MacVeagh, Rogers, & Costain. *Joshua.* Garden City, N.Y.: Doubleday, 1943.

Madách, Imre. *The Tragedy of Man.* Tr. from the Hungarian by J. C. W. Horne. Budapest: Corvina Press (1963).

Mada'e ha Yahadut. Vols. 1 and 2. A periodical published during 1926–1927 in Jerusalem at the Hebrew University.

Magia Naturalis et Innaturalis (a Faustian magic tract). Stuttgart: J. Scheible, 1849. Originally published in Passau, 1505.

Maimonides, Moses. *The Guide for the Perplexed.* (tr.)

M. Friedlander (from the Arabic). New York: Dover [1956].

Mishna Thora. See Maimonides.

——. *Mishna Thora. Yad ha-Hazakah.* (tr. in English) Simon Glazer. New York: Maimonides Pub. Co., 1922.

Malache Elyon. See Margouliath (compiler).

Malan, Solomon Caesar. *The Book of Adam and Eve,* also called *The Conflict of Adam and Eve with Satan.* Tr. from the Ethiopic. London: Williams & Norgate, 1882.

Malchus, Marius. *The Secret Grimoire of Turiel.* London: Aquarian Press, 1960.

Malleus Maleficarum (The Hammer of Witches). Fr. H. Kramer and Fr. J. Sprenger. (tr.) Montague Summers. London: John Rodker, 1928. First published in Cologne, 1489.

Mandaeans of Iraq and Iran, The. See Drower.

Manson, T. W. (ed.). *A Companion to the Bible.* Edinburgh: T. & T. Clark [1956].

Mansoor, Menahem. *The Dead Sea Scrolls.* Grand Rapids: Eerdmans, 1964.

——(tr.). *The Thanksgiving Hymns.* Grand Rapids: Eerdmans, 1961.

Manual of Discipline, The. See Brownlee, Wernberg-Møller.

Margouliath, Reuben. *Malache Elyon* (Angels on High). In Hebrew, Jerusalem: Mossad ha-Rav Koôk, 1945.

Maritain, Jacques. *The Range of Reason.* New York: Scribner, 1952.

Marlowe, Christopher. *The Tragical History of Doctor Faustus.* London: T. White, 1830. First published in London, 1604.

Martyrdom of Isaiah. Incl. in *The Ascension of Isaiah.*

Maseket Azilut. See Nazir; Wildman.

Maseket Derekh Erets. In *Masekhtot Zeirot* by Michael Higger (*q.v.*). This work mentions 390 heavens.

Maseket Gan Eden and Gehinnom. In Jellinek's *Beth ha-Midrasch.*

Massé, Henri. *Anthologie Persane* (Persian Anthology). Paris: Payot, 1950.

Massignon, Louis. "The Yezidis of Mount Sindjar." In *Satan* (New York: Sheed & Ward, 1952).

Masters, R. E. L. *Eros and Evil.* New York: Julian Press, 1962.

Martyrdom of Isaiah. See R. H. Charles.

Mathers, S. L. MacGregor (ed.). *The Almadel of Solomon* (part IV of *The Lemegeton* or *Lesser Key of Solomon*). London, 1889.

——. *The Book of the Sacred Magic of Abra-Melin in Mage.* Chicago: de Laurence Co., 1939.

——. *The Greater Key of Solomon.* London, 1889; Chicago: de Laurence, 1914.

——. *The Kabbalah Unveiled* (*Kabbalah Denudata*). Incorporates the *Idra Rabba* and *Idra Zuta.* London: George Redway, 1887.

McCabe, Joseph. *The Popes and Their Church.* New York: Freethought Press Association, 1953.

McCown, Chester (ed.). *The Testament of Solomon.* Leipzig: J. C. Hinrichs, 1922.

Mead, G. R. S. *Fragments of a Faith Forgotten.* Intro. by Kenneth Rexroth. New Hyde Park, New York: University Books (1960).

—— (tr.). *The Hymn of Jesus* (a mystery-ritual). London: John M. Watkins, 1963.

—— (tr.). *Pistis Sophia.* London: John M. Watkins, 1921.

—— (tr.). *Thrice-Greatest Hermes.* 3 vols. London: John M. Watkins, 1964.

Meaning of the Glorious Koran. (tr.) Mohammed M. Pickthall. New York: New American Library, 1954.

Methodius of Philippi (or of Olympus). *Banquet of the Ten Virgins, Convivia, Discourse on the Resurrection.* For a translation of the *Banquet of the Ten Virgins,* see Clark.

Michaelis, Sébastien. *Admirable History of the Possession and Conversion of a Penitent Woman.* London: William Aspley, 1613.

——. *Pneumenologie ou discours des esprits.* Paris, 1582; Douay, 1613.

Michelangelo, the Sculptures of. Foreword by Ludwig Goldscheider. Phaidon Edition. New York: Oxford U.P., 1940.

Michelet, Jules. *Satanism and Witchcraft.* New York: Citadel, 1939.

Midrash Abkir. In Jellinek. *Midrash of the Ten Commandments;* also in Buber, *ha-Shahar* (Vienna, 1883).

Midrash Aggada Exodus.

Midrash Eleh Ezkerah. See Jellinek.

Midrash Haggadol. Commentary on the Pentateuch. (ed.) Mordecai Margulies. In Hebrew. Jerusalem: Kook Pub., 1947.

Midrash Konen. In *Arzei Levanon* (Cedars of Lebanon). Venice, 1601. An edition published in Wilna, 1836. Also contained in *Ozar Midrashim* I.

Midrash Petirat Mosheh. In Jellinek's *Beth ha-Midrasch.*

Midrash Rabba Exodus. See Lehrman.

Midrash Rabba Leviticus. See Israelstam and Slotki.

Midrash Rabbah. See Friedman and Simon.

Midrash Tanhuma. See Buber.

Midrash Tehillim (Commentary of Psalms). *See* Braude.

Midrash of the Ten Commandments. See Jellinek.

Midrash of the Ten Jewish Martyrs. See Gollancz.

Mielziner, M. *Introduction to the Talmud.* New York: Funk and Wagnalls, 1903.

Migne, J. P. *Patrologiae Latinae Completus.* 221 vols. Paris, 1844–1864.

——. *Patrologiae Graecae Cursus Completus.* 161 vols. Paris, 1857–1880.

Mills, Lawrence Heyworth. "Philo's δυνέμεις [Dunameis] and the Amesha Spenta." London: *Royal Asiatic Society Journal,* pp. 553–568, 1901.

Milton, John. *Complete English Poetry.* (ed.) John T. Shawcross. Garden City, N.Y.: Doubleday, 1963.

——. *Complete Poetry and Selected Prose.* Intro. Cleanth Brooks. New York: Random, 1950.

——. *Paradise Lost. A Poem in Twelve Books.* London: Richard Bently, 1688.

——. *Poetical Works.* (ed.) William Hayley. 3 vols. London: Boydell and Nicol, 1794.

——. *Poetical Works.* (ed.) Edward Hawkins. 4 vols. London: Oxford U.P., 1824.

——. "The Reason of Church Government Urged against Prelaty." In *Works of John Milton.* 3 vols. New York: Columbia U.P., 1931.

Mishnah, The. See Danby.

Montefiore, C. C. and Loewe, H. (ed.). *A Rabbinic Anthology.* Philadelphia: Jewish Publication Society of America, 1960.

Montgomery, J. A. *Aramaic Incantation Texts from Nippur.* Philadelphia: U. of Pennsylvania Press, 1913.

Moore, George. *The Brook Kerith.* New York: Macmillan, 1926.

Moore, Thomas. *The Loves of the Angels.* London: Longman, 1823.

Morgenstern, J. "The Mythological Background of Psalm 82." Philadelphia: Hebrew Union College Annual, XIV, 29–126.

Morris, Harry. "Some Uses of Angel Iconography in English Literature." *Comparative Literature,* vol. X, no. 1, Winter, 1958.

Moses of Burgos. *The Left-hand Pillar. See* Gershom Scholem in *Mada'e ha Yahadut.* vol. II, 1927; and in *Tarbiz.* vol. II–V, 1931–1934.

Müller, Ernst. *History of Jewish Mysticism.* Oxford: East and West Library [1946].

——. *Der Sohar und seine Lehre.* Vienna: R. Löwit Verlag, 1920.

Myer, Isaac. *The Qabbalah.* Philadelphia: printed by the author, 1888.

Mysteries of the Quabalah. 2 vols. Written down by Seven Pupils of E. G. Chicago: The Yogi Publishing Society, 1922.

N

Narrative of Zosimus. In *The Testament of Abraham.* (tr.) W. A. Craigie. Buffalo: Christian Literature Pub. Co., *The Ante-Nicene Fathers,* 1885–1896.

Nash, Thomas. *Pierce Penilesse, His Supplication to the Divill.* London: Lane, 1924. Originally published in 1592.

Nathan, Robert. *The Bishop's Wife.* London: Victor Gollancz Ltd., 1928.

Nazir, Jacob. *Maseket Azilut.* In *Ozar Midrashim* I.

Nemoy, Leon (ed., tr.). *Karaite Anthology.* New Haven: Yale U.P., 1952.

Neubauer, Adolf (ed.). *The Book of Tobit.* Oxford: Clarendon, 1878.

Neumann, Henry. *The Dead Sea Scrolls.* New York: New York Society for Ethical Culture, 1956.

Neusner, Jacob. *A History of the Jews in Babylonia.* Leiden: E. J. Brill, 1965.

——. *A Life of Rabban Yohanan Ben Zakkai.* Leiden: E. J. Brill, 1962.

Newbold, W. R. "The Descent of Christ in the Odes of Solomon." *Journal of Biblical Literature,* December 1912.

New Century Handbook of English Literature, The. (ed.) Clarence L. Barnhart. New York: Appleton (1956).

New Jewish Encyclopedia. (ed.) David Bridger (with Samuel Wolk). 1 vol. New York: Behrman House, 1962.

Newman, Louis I. (ed. with S. Spitz). *The Hasidic Anthology.* New York: Schocken, 1963.

——(ed. with S. Spitz). *The Talmudic Anthology.* New York: Behrman House, 1947.

New Schaff-Herzog Encyclopedia of Religious Knowledge, The. (ed.) Samuel Macauley Jackson, et al. 12 vols. New York: Funk and Wagnalls, 1908–1912.

New Testament Apocrypha, The. See Hervieux; James.

Nicetas of Remesiana. "The Names and Titles of our Savior." Included in Fremantle, *A Treasury of Early Christianity.*

——. *Writings.* (tr.) Gerald G. Walsh. New York: Fathers of the Church, 1949.

Nichols, Ross (ed.). Paul Christian's *The History and Practice of Magic* (q.v.).

Nicholson, Reynold Alleyne. "An Early Arabic Version of the *Mir'aj* of Abu Yazid al-Bistami" in *Islamica* II, pp. 402–415. Leipzig: Braunlich, 1926.

Nigg, Walter. *The Heretics.* New York: Knopf, 1962.

Noveck, Simon (ed.). *Great Jewish Personalities in Ancient and Mediaeval Times.* New York: Farrar, 1959.

Nuctemeron, The (of Apollonius of Tyana). *See* Apollonius.

Nurni, Martin K. "Blake's Marriage of Heaven and Hell." In *Kent State University Bulletin* (Kent, Ohio), April, 1957.

O

Occultism. See Shah.

Odeberg, Hugo (ed., tr.). *3 Enoch or The Hebrew Book of Enoch.* New York: Cambridge U.P. 1928. A version of the Hechaloth.

Odes and Psalms of Solomon. See Harris. Included in *Lost Books of the Bible.*

"Odes of Solomon and the Pistis Sophia, The." *See* Worrell.

Oesterley, W. O. E. *An Introduction to the Apocrypha.* London: Society for Promoting Christian Knowledge, 1935.

——. "Belief in Angels and Demons." Vol. 1, *Judaism and Christianity.* London: Sheldon Press, 1937.

——. *The Jewish Doctrine of Mediation.* London: Skeffington, 1910.

——. *A Short Survey of the Literature of Rabbinical and Medieval Judaism* (with G. H. Box). London: Society for Promoting Christian Knowledge, 1920.

——. *The Wisdom of Ben-Sira* (Ecclesiasticus). London: Society for Promoting Christian Knowledge, 1916.

——(ed.). *The Wisdom of Solomon (Book of Wisdom).* London: Society for Promoting Christian Knowledge; New York: Macmillan, 1918.

——. *The Wisdom of Solomon (The Book of Wisdom).* London: Society for Promoting Christian Knowledge, 1917.

Oesterreich, Traugott Konstantin. *Occultism and Modern Science.* London: Methuen, 1923.

Oesterreicher, John M. (ed.). *The Bridge; A Yearbook of Judaeo-Christian Studies.* New York: Pantheon [1955].

Origen. *Contra Celsum.* (tr.) H. Chadwick. Cambridge (Eng.): University Press, 1953.

——. *de Principiis* and *Stromata.* In Migne, *Patrologiae Graeca.*

——. *Letter to Gregory Thaumaturgus.* In Fremantle, *A Treasury of Early Christianity.*

Orlinsky, Harry M. *Ancient Israel.* Ithaca: Cornell U.P., 1954.

——. "On the Present State of Proto-Septuagint Studies." Baltimore: *Journal of the American Oriental Society,* June 1941.

——. *The Septuagint.* Cincinnati: Union of American Hebrew Congregation, 1949.

——. *The So-Called "Suffering Servant" in Isaiah 53.* Cincinnati: Hebrew Union College Press, 1964.

Ouspensky, P. D. *In Search of the Miraculous.* New York: Harcourt, 1949.

——. *A New Model of the Universe.* New York: Knopf, 1948.

Oxford Cyclopedic Concordance, The. New York and London: Oxford U.P., 1947.

Ozar Midrashim. (ed.) J. D. Eisenstein. 2 vols. New York: Grossman's Hebrew Book Store, 1956.

P

Papini, Giovanni. *The Devil.* (tr.) Adrienne Foulke. New York: Dutton, 1954.

——. *Life of Christ.* (tr.) Dorothy Canfield Fisher. New York: Dell Publishing Co., 1951.

Papus (pseud. for Gerard Encausse). *Absolute Key to Occult Science.* (tr.) A. P. Morton. London: Chapman & Hall, 1892.

——. *Traité Élémentaire de Science Occulte.* Paris: P. Ollendorff, 1903.

—— (tr.). *Sepher Yetzirah.* Paris, 1887.

Paracelsus. *Four Treatises.* Tr. from the German by various hands. Baltimore: Johns Hopkins Press, 1941.

——. *The Prophecies of Paracelsus.* (tr.) J. K. London: Rider, 1915.

Paraphrase of Job.

Paraphrase of Shem (also called the *Paraphrase of Seth*). A Coptic Ms. In the Chenoboskion Library, Cairo.

Parente, Pascal P. *The Angels.* St. Meinrod, Ind.: Grail Publications [1957].

Parkes, James. *Judaism and Christianity.* Chicago: U. of Chicago Press, 1948.

Patrides, C. A. "Renaissance Views of Angels." New York: *Journal of the History of Ideas.* April–June, 1962.

Pauline Art, The. Part of *The Lemegeton.*

Payne, Robert. *The Holy Fire.* New York: Harper, 1957.

Pegis, Anton C. *See* Aquinas.

Persian Anthology. See Massé, *Anthologie Persane.*

Pesikta Rabbati. See Friedmann. A recension, published in 777, contains the *Revelation of Moses.*

Peter, John. *A Critique of Paradise Lost.* New York: Columbia U.P., 1960.

Peterson, Erik. *Das Buch von den Engeln.* Munich: Kösel-Verlag [1955].

Philo. *De Cherubinis ad Exod.* 25. (ed.) C. A. O. Grossmannus, Leipzig, 1856.

Philo-Judaeus of Alexandria. See Bentwich.

——. "Philo's δυνάμεις and the Amesha Spenta." *See* Mills.

——. *On the Contemplative Life. See* Tilden.

Philo-Lexikon/Handbuch des Judischen Wissens. Berlin: Philo Verlag, 1936.

Pickthall, Mohammed Marmaduke (tr.). *The Koran.* New York: New American Library, 1954.

Pictures from a Medieval Bible. See Strachan.

Pirke Aboth (Sayings of the Fathers). *See* Herford; Hertz; Taylor.

Pirke de Rabbi Eliezer. See Friedlander.

Pirke Hechaloth. See Hechaloth Lore.

Pistis Sophia. A gnostic gospel, containing extracts from *Books of the Saviour. See* Mead; also the Askew Codex, British Museum.

Poe, Edgar Allan. The Works of Edgar Allan Poe. 10 vols. New York and Pittsburg: The Colonial Co., 1903.

Pognon, Henri. *Inscriptions Mandaïtes des Coupes de Khouabir.* Paris: H. Welter, 1898.

——. *A Critical Biography. See* Quinn.

Portable Greek Reader. (ed.) W. H. Auden. New York: Viking, 1955.

Post-Biblical Hebrew Literature. See Halper.

Postel, William (tr.). *The Gospel of Pseudo-James or the Protovangelium.* In Latin. Basle: Bibliander, 1532.

——. *Key of Things Kept Secret from the Foundation of the World.* Originally published 1547 as *Absconditorum Clavis.* Tr. into French, 1899.

—— (tr.). *Sepher Yetzirah.* Paris: J. Ruelle, 1552.

Potter, Rev. Charles F. *Did Jesus Write This Book?* New Hyde Park, New York: University Books, 1965.

——. *The Last Years of Jesus Revealed.* New York: Fawcett, 1958.

Prayer of Joseph. A Jewish apocryphon cited in the works of Origen and Eusebius. Quoted in part of Ginzberg, *The Legends of the Jews.*

Preisendanz, K. (ed.). *Papyri Graecae Magicae.* 2 vols. Leipzig: B. G. Teubner, 1928–1931.

Prince of Darkness: A Witchcraft Anthology. London: John Westhouse, Ltd., 1946.

Proclus, Diadochus. *The Elements of Theology. See* Dodds.

Protevangelium. The Birth of Christ and the Perpetual Virgin Mary. By James the Lesser. [*Rf. Lost Books of the Bible.*]

Protevangelium of James. In vol. 8, *Ante-Nicene Fathers.* New York: Scribner, 1925.

Psalms of the Pharisees. See Psalms of Solomon.

Psalms of Solomon. (ed.) G. Buchanan Gray. In Charles, *Apocrypha and Pseudepigrapha of the Old Testment.* The work is also known as *Psalms of the Pharisees* and under this title was translated by H. E. Ryle and

M. R. James and published in Cambridge at the University Press, 1891.

Psellus, Michael. *Operations of Demons* (*Dialogus de energia seu operatione Daemonum*). Paris: G. Chaudiere. 1577. A later edition published in Paris in 1623.

Pseudo-Dionysii Areopagitae de Caelesti Hierarchia. Vol. 25 of *Textus Minores.* In Greek. Leiden: E. J. Brill, 1959.

Pseudo-Dionysius. *See* Dionysius the Areopagite.

Pseudo-Monarchia. See Wierus.

Q

Qabbalah, The. See Myer.

Quinn, Arthur Hobson. *Edgar Allan Poe, A Critical Biography.* New York: Appleton, 1941.

R

Rabbinic Anthology, A. See Montefiore and Loewe.

Radin, Max. *The Jews Among the Greeks and Romans.* Philadelphia: The Jewish Publication Society of America, 1915.

——. *The Life of the Jewish People in Biblical Times.* Philadelphia: The Jewish Publication Society of America, 1929.

Ragg, Lonsdale and Laura (ed., tr.). *Gospel of Barnabas.* Oxford: Clarendon, 1907. Also in vol. 8, *Ante-Nicene Fathers.* New York: Scribner, 1925.

Raskin, Saul. *Kabbalah, Book of Creation, The Zohar.* New York, 1952.

Raymond, Rossiter W. (ed.). *The Book of Job.* New York: Appleton, 1878.

Reade, Winwood. *The Martyrdom of Man.* Intro. by F. Legge. London: Kegan Paul, Trench, Trubner & Co. n.d.

Recognitions of Clement. See Clement of Alexandria.

Redfield, B. G. (ed.). *Gods/A Dictionary of the Deities of All Lands.* New York: Putnam, 1951.

Régamey, R. P. *Anges.* Paris: Éditions Pierre Tisné [1946].

——. *What Is an Angel?* (tr.) Dom Mark Pontifex. New York: Hawthorn, 1960.

Reider, Joseph. *The Holy Scriptures, Deuteronomy.* Philadelphia: The Jewish Publication Society of America, 1937.

—— (ed., tr.). *The Book of Wisdom.* New York: Harper, 1957.

Reitzenstein, Richard. *Poimandres.* Leipzig: B. G. Teubner, 1904. Contains the *Book of the Archangels* by *Moses the Prophet.*

——. *Studien zum antiken Synkretismus aus Iran und Greichenland.* Leipzig: B. G. Teubner, 1926.

Renan, Ernest. *The Life of Jesus.* London: Watts [1947].

Revelation of Adam to His Son Seth. A Coptic MS. in the Chenoboskion Library. Extracts quoted by Doresse in *Secret Books of the Egyptian Gnostics.*

Revelation of Esdras, Revelation of John, Revelation of Moses, Revelation of Paul. All in vol. 8, *Ante-Nicene Fathers.* New York: Scribner, 1925. *Revelation of Moses* appears also in *Yalkut Reubeni, Pesikta Rabbati,* and, as *Gedulath Mosheh,* in Jellinek's *Beth ha-Midrasch.*

Revelation of Moses. In M. Gaster, *Studies and Texts in Folklore;* also in *The Ante-Nicene Fathers,* Vol. 8. New York: Scribner, 1925. A recension contained in *Pesikta Rabbati,* pub. in 777.

Revelation of Peter. See Gospel of Peter.

Revelation of Rabbi ben Levi, The. In Jellinek, *Beth ha-Midrasch.*

Revelation of Stephen. Extracts in James, *The Apocryphal New Testament.*

Revelations of Zostrian (*Evangelium Veritatis*—Gospel of Truth). (ed.) M. Malinine. Jung Codex. Published by Puech and Quispel. Zurich: Rascher, 1956–1957.

Rieu, E. V. (tr.). *The Four Gospels.* Baltimore: Penguin, 1953.

Robbins, Rossell Hope. *The Encyclopedia of Witchcraft and Demonology.* New York: Crown [1959].

Robinson, J. A. and James, M. R. (ed.). *Gospel of Peter* and the *Revelation of Peter.* London: Clay, 1892.

Rosenblatt, Samuel (tr.). *The Book of Beliefs and Opinions* (by Saadiah Gaon). New Haven: Yale U.P., 1948.

Rosenroth, Knorr Von. *Kabbala Denudata.* Tr. from Latin by W. Wynn Westcott. A translation by S. L. Mathers was published in London, 1887, by George Redway. Early version appeared in 1677.

Roucek, Joseph S. (ed.). *Slavonic Encyclopedia.* New York: Philosophical Library, 1949.

Rowley, H. H. (ed. with Grant) *Hastings' Dictionary of the Bible.* New York: Harper [1955].

——. *The Relevance of Apocalyptic.* London, 1944.

—— (ed.). *The Zadokite Fragments and the Dead Sea Scrolls.* Oxford: Blackwell, 1955.

Rowley, Margaret (tr.). *See* Dupont-Sommer.

Runes, Dagobert D. *The Wisdom of the Kabbalah.* New York: Philosophical Library (1957).

S

Saadiah b. Joseph (Gaon). *Book of Beliefs and Opinions.* (tr.) Samuel Rosenblatt. New Haven: Yale U.P, 1948.

Sacred Books of the East. (ed.) Max Müller. 50 vols. Oxford: Clarendon, 1879–1910.

Sacred Book of the Invisible Great Spirit. In Doresse,

Trois livres gnostiques inédits. Virgiliae Christianae, 1948.

Sacred Magic of Abra-Melin the Mage, The. (tr.) S. L. MacGregor Mathers. Chicago: de Laurence Co., 1939.

Sale, George (tr., ed.). *The Koran.* Incl. "Preliminary Discourse." 5th ed. Philadelphia: Lippincott, 1860. Originally published in England, 1734.

Salkeld, John. *A Treatise of Angels.* London: Nathaniel Butter, 1613.

Saltus, Edgar. *The Lords of the Ghostland.* New York: Kennerley, 1907.

Salverte, Eusèbe. *Des Sciences Occultes.* 2 vols. Paris: Sedillot, 1829.

Sargent, Elizabeth. *Love Poems.* New York: New American Library [1966].

Satan. A collection of essays. (ed.) Bruno de Jesus-Marie. New York: Sheed & Ward, 1952.

Schaff, Philip (ed.). *A Dictionary of the Bible.* Philadelphia: American Sunday School Union, 1880.

——. (ed.) *A Select Library of Nicene and Post-Nicene Fathers of the Christian Church.* 14 vols. New York: The Christian Literature Co., 1886–1890. 2nd series (with Henry Wace). 14 vols. New York: The Christian Literature Co. 1890–1900.

Schechter, S. (tr.). *Aboth de Rabbi Nathan.* Vienna: M. Knöpflmacher, 1887.

——. *Documents of Jewish Sectaries.* Vol. 1, *Fragments of a Zadokite Work.* Cambridge: Cambridge U.P., 1910.

Scheible, J. (ed.). *Das Kloster.* 12 vols. Stuttgart and Leipzig, 1846.

——. *Dr. Faust's Bücherschatz.* Stuttgart, 1851.

—— (ed.). *The Sixth and Seventh Books of Moses.* Originally published in Stuttgart, 1849 under title *Das Sechste und Siebente buch Mosis,* vol. 6 in *Bibliothek der zauber geheimniss-und offenbarungs-bücher.* American edition published in Carbondale, Ill.: Egyptian Pub. Co. n.d.

Schiur Komah. See Corcos; M. Gaster; also *Ozar Midrashim.*

Schleiermacher, F. E. D. *Der Christliche Glaube.* Tr. as *The Christian Faith.* (ed.) H. R. MacIntosh and J. S. Stewart. Edinburgh: T. & T. Clark, 1960.

Schmidt, Carl (ed.). *Koptisch-gnostische Schriften.* 2 vols. Contains *Apocryphon of John, Wisdom of Jesus Christ, Acts of Peter, Gospel of Mary.* Leipzig, 1905. Another edition published in Berlin: Akademie-Verlag, 1954.

Schmidt, Nathaniel. *The Apocalypse of Noah and the Parable of Enoch.* Baltimore: Oriental Studies, 1926. An edition published in Leipzig, 1926. A copy is in the Jewish Theological Seminary, New York.

Schneweis, Emil. *Angels and Demons According to Lactantius.* Washington, D.C.: Catholic University of America Press, 1944.

Scholem, Gershom (tr.). *Das Buch Bahir.* Leipzig: W. Drugulin, 1923.

——. *Jewish Gnosticism, Merkabah Mysticism, and Talmudic Tradition.* New York: The Jewish Theological Seminary, 1960.

——. *Major Trends in Jewish Mysticism.* New York: Schocken, 1941.

——. *On the Kabbalah and its Symbolism.* (tr.) Ralph Manheim. New York: Schocken [1965].

Schönblum, Samuel. *Pirke Rabbenu ha-Kadosh.* Lemberg, 1877.

Schorer, Mark. *William Blake, the Politics of Vision.* New York: Holt, 1946.

Schrire, T. *Hebrew Amulets.* London: Routledge & Kegan Paul, 1966.

Schwab, Moïse. *Vocabulaire de l'Angélologie.* Paris: Academie des Inscriptions et Belles Lettres, 1897.

Schwartz, E. (ed.). *Ecclesiastical History* by Eusebius. *See* Eusebius.

Schweitzer, Albert. *The Quest of the Historical Jesus.* London: A. & C. Black, 1964. Originally published 1906.

Scot, Reginald. *Discoverie of Witchcraft.* London: A. Clarke, 1665. Repr., intro. Hugh Ross Williamson. Carbondale, Ill.: Southern Illinois [1964].

Scott, Sir Walter. *Letters on Demonology and Witchcraft.* London: John Murray, 1831.

Screwtape Letters, The. See Lewis.

Secret Books of the Egyptian Gnostics, The. See Doresse.

Secret Doctrine, The. See Blavatsky.

Secret Grimoire of Turiel, The. See Malchus.

Secret Lore of Magic, The. See Shah.

Secret Sayings of Jesus (The Gnostic Gospel of Thomas). Robert M. Grant and David Noel Freedman. Eng. tr. William R. Schoedel. Garden City, N.Y.: Doubleday, 1960.

Sefer ha-Heshek (Book of Desire). (ed.) I. M. Epstein. Lemberg, 1865.

Sefer Raziel. See The Book of the Angel Raziel.

Sefer Yetzirah (Book of Formation). (tr.) William Postel. Paris: J. Ruelle, 1552. Editions published by Stenring; Waite; Westcott.

Select Library of Nicene and Post-Nicene Fathers of the Christian Church. (ed.) Philip Schaff. 14 vols. New York: The Christian Literature Co., 1886–1890. 2nd series, 14 vols. (ed.) Philip Schaff and Henry Wace. New York: The Christian Literature Co., 1890–1900.

Seligmann, Kurt. *The History of Magic*. New York: Pantheon, 1948.

Semitic Magic. See Thompson.

Sha'ar ha-Heshek. Johann Alemanno. Leghorn, 1790.

Shah, Sirdar Ikbal Ali (ed.). *Book of Oriental Literature*. New York: Garden City Pub. Co., 1938.

——. *Occultism, Its Theory and Practice*. New York: Castle Books, n.d.

——. *The Secret Lore of Magic*. New York: Citadel, 1958.

Shakespeare and His Betters. See Churchill, R. C.

Shaw, George Bernard. *Back to Methusaleh*. New York: Brentano, 1921.

Shepherd of Hermas. A 2nd-century apocryphon. Contains the *Visions, Commands,* and *Similitudes*. In the *Lost Books of the Bible*.

——. (ed.) C. Taylor. 2 vols. London: Society for Promoting Christian Knowledge, 1903.

——. (ed.) Lightfoot, et al. In *Excluded Books of the New Testament*.

Short Dictionary of Mythology. See Woodcock.

Shorter Encyclopaedia of Islam. See Gibb and Kramers.

Sibinga, Joost Smit. *The Old Testament Text of Justin Martyr* (the Pentateuch). Leiden: E. J. Brill, 1963.

Sibylline Oracles. See Bate; Geffcken; Lanchester.

Silver, Abba Hillel. *A History of Messianic Speculation in Israel*. Boston: Beacon Press, 1959.

Singer, Isaac Bashevis. *Satan in Goray*. New York: Noonday Press, 1955.

——. *Short Friday*. New York: Farrar, 1964.

Sinistrari, Fr. Ludovico Maria. *Demoniality; or Incubi and Succubi*. Latin–English texts. Paris: Isidore Liseux, 1879.

Sinker, Robert (tr.). *Testament of the Twelve Patriarchs*. Edinburgh: T. and T. Clark, 1871.

Sixth and Seventh Books of Moses, The. See Scheible.

Slavonic Encyclopedia. See Roucek.

Smith, George D. *The Teaching of the Catholic Church*. 2 vols. New York: Macmillan, 1964.

Smith, Homer W. *Man and His Gods*. Boston: Little, Brown, 1952.

Smith, Joseph (tr.). *The Book of Mormon*. Salt Lake City: Church of Jesus Christ of Latter-Day Saints, 1950.

Snell, Joy. *The Ministry of Angels, Here and Beyond*. New York: Citadel, 1959.

Sode Raza. See Eleazer of Worms.

Sossnitz, I. (tr.). *La Kabbale ou La Philosophe Religieuse Hébrew. See* Franck.

Spence, Lewis. *An Encyclopaedia of Occultism*. New York: Strathmore Press, 1959.

Spenser, Edmund. "An Hymne of Heavenly Beautie" and "Hymne of Heavenly Love." In *The Complete Poetical Works of Edmund Spenser*. Boston and New York: Houghton, 1908.

——. "Of the Brood of Angels" from the *Amoretti*. Madison, N.J.: The Golden Hind Press, 1939.

Stace, Walter T. *The Teachings of the Mystics*. New York: New American Library, 1960.

Steindorff, Georg. *Apocalypse of Elias (Die Apokalypse des Elias)*. Leipzig: J. C. Hinrichs, 1899. *See* Buttenweiser.

Steiner, Rudolf. *Karmic Relationships*. (tr.) Georg Adams Kaufmann. London: Anthroposophical Pub. Co., 1929.

——. *The Mission of the Archangel Michael*. (tr.) Lisa D. Monges. New York: Anthroposophic Press, 1961.

——. *The Work of the Angels in Man's Astral Body*. London: Anthroposophical Pub. Co., 1960.

Steinschneider, M. (ed.). *Alphabet of Ben Sira*. Berlin: A. Friedlander, 1858.

Stenring, Knut (tr.). *Sefer Yetzirah (The Book of Formation)*. Philadelphia: McKay [1923].

Stevenson, Robert Louis. *Virginibus Puerisque*. New York: Scribner, 1897.

Story of Philosophy, The. See Durant.

Strachan, James. *Pictures from a Mediaeval Bible*. Boston: Beacon Press [1961].

Summers, Montague. *The History of Witchcraft and Demonology*. New Hyde Park, N.Y. University Books [1956].

——. *The Vampire in Europe*. New Hyde Park, New York: University Books [1961].

Sundberg, Albert C., Jr. *The Old Testament of the Early Church*. Cambridge, Mass.: Harvard U.P., 1964.

Svoboda, Karel. *La demonologie de Michael Psellos*. Berne: Philosophical Faculty, 1927.

Swedenborg, Emanuel. *Heaven and its Wonders and Hell*. New York: Swedenborg Foundation, 1956.

Sword of Moses, The. See Gaster, M.

T

Talmud, The. English text. 18 vols. London: The Soncino Press, 1961.

Talmud of Jerusalem. Preface by Dagobert D. Runes. New York: The Wisdom Library, 1956.

Talmudic Anthology, The. See Newman.

Targum Jonathan to the Prophets and *Targum Ketubim. See* Churgin.

Targum of Onkelos and Jonathan b. Uzziel on the Pentateuch. With fragments of the Jerusalem Targum. Tr.

from the Chaldee by J. W. Etheridge. 2 vols. London: Longman, 1862–1865.

Taylor, C. (tr.). *Pirke Aboth.* New York: Cambridge U.P., 1877 and 1897.

Taylor, Rev. C. *Shepherd of Hermas.* 2 vols. London: Society for Promoting Christian Knowledge, 1903.

Taylor, Thomas (tr.). *Iamblichus on the Mysteries of the Egyptians, Chaldeans, and Assyrians.* Chiswick: C. Whittingham, 1821. An edition published in Lyons, 1577.

Teaching of the Catholic Church, The. See G. D. Smith.

Tedesche, Sidney (tr.). *The First Book of Maccabees.* New York: Harper [1950].

——. *The Second Book of Maccabees.* (ed.) Solomon Zeitlin. New York: Harper [1954].

Tertullian, Q. S. F. *Adversus Marcionem* and *De Habitu Mulieb* (on women's apparel). In Ante-Nicene Christian Fathers Library. Edinburgh, 1869.

Testament of Abraham, The. See Box; Craigie; James.

Testament of Asher. In the *Testament of the Twelve Patriarchs.*

Testament of Job. In James, *Apocrypha Anecdota.*

——. (ed.) K. Kohler.

Testament of Judah. In the *Testament of the Twelve Patriarchs.*

Testament of Levi. In the *Testament of the Twelve Patriarchs.*

Testament of Moses. See The Assumption of Moses.

Testament of Naphtali. In the *Testament of the Twelve Patriarchs.*

Testament of Solomon, The. See Conybeare; McCown.

Testament of the Twelve Patriarchs. (ed.) R. H. Charles; de Jonge; Sinker. An edition also issued by the Society for Promoting Christian Knowledge: London, 1917.

Texts of the Saviour (also called the *Books of the Saviour*). Related to, and contained in, the *Pistis Sophia* texts.

The Thanksgiving Hymns. See Mansoor.

Theodotus. Excerpts from Theodotus' writings. In vol. 8 of *Ante-Nicene Fathers.* New York: Scribner, 1925.

Third and Fourth Books of Maccabees. See Emmet; also Hadas.

Thompson, R. Campbell. *Semitic Magic.* London: Luzac & Co., 1908.

Thorndike, Lynn. *The History of Magic and Experimental Science.* 3 vols. New York: Macmillan [1922–1934]. Vol. 3 has imprint of Columbia University Press.

Three Enoch (*3 Enoch* or the *Hebrew Book of Enoch*). *See* Odeberg.

Three Jewish Philosophers (Philo, Saadya Gaon, Jehuda Halevi). Lewy, Altmann, Heinemann. Philadelphia: Jewish Publication Society of America, 1960.

Thrice Greatest Hermes. See Mead.

Tilden, Frank William (tr.). *Philo Judaeus, on the Contemplative Life.* Bloomington: Indiana University Studies, vol. IX [1922].

Till, Walter C. (ed.). *Gospel of Philip.* Incl. in *Koptisch-Gnostische Schriften.* Berlin: Akademie-Verlag, 1954.

Tischendorf, L. T. C. *Apocalypses Apocryphae.* Contains *Acts of Pilate, Apocalypse of Moses, Apocalypse of Paul, Assumption of the Virgin, Gospel of Thomas,* etc. Leipzig, 1866.

Toplady, Augustus (tr.). *The Doctrine of Absolute Predestination.* From the Latin of Jerom Zanchius (or Zanchy). New York: Samuel Loudon, 1773. Earlier edition 1769.

Torah, The (Five Books of Moses). Tr. according to the Masoretic text. Philadelphia: Jewish Publication Society of America, 1962.

Torrey, C. C. *The Apocryphal Literature.* New Haven: Yale U.P., 1945.

Torrey, R. A. *Difficulties in the Bible.* New York: Revell, 1907.

Trachtenberg, Joshua. *Jewish Magic and Superstition.* New York: Behrman's Jewish Book House, 1939.

Transcendental Magic. See Levi.

Trattner, Ernest R. *The Autobiography of God.* New York: Scribner, 1930.

——. *Understanding the Talmud.* New York: Nelson, 1955.

——. *Unravelling the Book of Books,* New York: Scribner, 1929.

Treasury of Art Masterpieces, A. See Craven.

Treasury of Early Christianity, A. See Fremantle.

Treasury of Jewish Folklore. See Ausable.

Treatise of the Hechaloth (Massekheth Hekhaloth). Reprinted by A. Jellinek. Ger. tr. by August Wunsche in *Aus Israels Lehrhallen.* Leipzig: E. Pfeiffer, 1907.

Trithemius, Johannes. *Book of Secret Things.* Excerpts in Barrett, *The Magus.*

——. *Of the Heavenly Intelligences.* (tr.) Elias Ashmole. Included in William Lilly, *The World's Catastrophe.* London, 1647.

——. *Steganographia of Trithemius.* By John E. Bailey. London [1879].

U

Uncanonical Jewish Books. See Ferrar.

Underhill, Evelyn. *Mysticism.* New York: Dutton, 1912.

Universal Jewish Encyclopedia.

V

Valentinus, Basilius. *The Triumphal Chariot of Antimony.* London: Vincent Stuart, 1962.

Van der Loos, E. *The Miracles of Jesus*. Leiden: E. J. Brill, 1965.

Van Noppen, Leonard C. See *Vondel's Lucifer*.

Varga, Margit. *The Christmas Story*. New York: Dodd, 1946.

Vendidad Fragment, The. See Darmesteter.

Vermes, Geza. *Discovery in the Judean Desert*. New York: Desclee Co., 1956.

Verus Jesuitarum Libellus. In Scheible, *Dr. Faust's Bücherschatz*. Stuttgart, 1845.

——. Eng. tr. (still in MS.) by Major Herbert Irwin [1875].

Virginalia. See Chivers.

Visions of Ezekiel, The. A hechaloth text recovered from the Cairo Geniza. In Hebrew: *Reiyot Yehezkel*. See Wertheimer.

Vision of Isaiah. See Charles.

Vision of Paul (or *Apocalypse of Paul*). In James, *The Apocryphal New Testament*.

Voltaire, M. De. *Chinese Catechism, Dialogues and Philosophic Criticisms*. Contains article "Of Angels, Genii, and Devils." New York: Peter Eckler. n.d.

Vondel's Lucifer. (tr.) Leonard C. Van Noppen. Greensboro, N.C.: Charles L. Van Noppen, 1898.

W

Waite, Arthur Edward. *The Book of Black Magic and of Pacts*. London, 1898; Chicago: de Laurence Co., 1940. Subsequently issued as *The Book of Ceremonial Magic*.

——. *The Book of Ceremonial Magic*. New Hyde Park, N.Y.: University Books, 1961. Earlier edition published 1929. Contains extracts of *The Almadel of Solomon*.

—— (tr.). *The Book of Formation (Sefer Yetzirah)*. London: Rider, 1923.

——. *The Holy Kabbalah*. Intro. Kenneth Rexroth. New Hyde Park, N.Y.: University Books. n.d.

—— (tr.). *The Lemegeton*, or *The Lesser Key of Solomon*. New York: Wehman Bros., 1916.

——. *The Secret Doctrine in Israel*. New York: Occult Research Press, n.d.

—— (tr.). *Transcendental Magic* of Eliphas Levi.

——. *The Occult Sciences*. New York: Dutton, 1923.

Wall, J. Charles. *Devils*. London: Methuen, 1904.

Walsh, Gerald G. See Nicetas of Remesiana.

War Between the Sons of Light and the Sons of Darkness. See Yadin.

Watt, W. Montgomery. *The Faith and Practice of Al-Ghazali*. London: Allen & Unwin, 1953.

Welsh, Robert Gilbert. *Azrael and Other Poems*. New York and London: Appleton, 1925.

Wendt, Herbert. *In Search of Adam*. Tr. from the German by James Cleugh. Boston: Houghton, 1956.

Werblowsky, Raphael. *Joseph Caro, Lawyer and Mystic*. London: Oxford U.P., 1962.

Wernberg-Møller, P. (tr.). *The Manual of Discipline*. Grand Rapids: Eerdmans, 1957.

Wertheimer, Solomon A. *Bate Midrashot*. 2 vols. Includes (in vol. 1) *Pirke Hechaloth Rabbati* (Greater Hechaloth) and (in vol. 2) *Reiyot Yehezkel* (Visions of Ezekiel). Jerusalem: Mosad ha-Rav Kook [1950, 1953].

Wesley, John. *The Journal*. (ed.) N. Ratcliff. London: T. Nelson & Sons, 1940.

West, Robert H. *Milton and the Angels*. Athens, Ga.: U. of Georgia Press, 1955.

——. "The Names of Milton's Angels." In *Studies in Philology*, XLVII, 2, April, 1950.

Westcott, W. W. (tr.). *Book of Formation (Sefer Yetzirah)*. London: J. M. Watkins, 1911. Book originally published in Basle, 1547.

—— (ed.). *Collectanea Hermetica*. 9 vols. London: Theosophical Pub. Soc., 1893–1896.

—— (ed.). *Kabbala Denudata*. New York: Occult Research Press. n.d.

——. *An Introduction to the Study of the Kabalah*. London: J. M. Watkins [1926].

Westminster Historical Atlas to the Bible. (ed.) George Ernest Wright and Floyd Vivian Filson. Intro. William F. Albright. Philadelphia: Westminster, 1945.

Wheless, Joseph. *Is It God's Word?* Moscow, Idaho: published by "Psychiana," 1926.

White, Andrew Dickson. *A History of the Warfare of Science with Theology in Christendom*. 2 vols. New York: Dover, 1960. The same, in paperback, published by The Free Press, 1965.

Wierus (or Wier), Jean (or Joannes). *Cinque livres de l'imposture et tromperie des diables*. Paris, 1569.

——. *De Praestigiis daemonum*. Basle: Officina Oporiniana, 1563.

——. *Pseudo-Monarchia*. In *Opera Omnia*. Amsterdam, 1660.

Wildman, I. I. *Maseket Azilut*. Johannesburg, 1864. A cabalistic tract on the divine emanations (as the title denotes). An edition published in Jerusalem, 1932. A reprint in *Ozar Midrashim*. See Nazir.

William of Auvergne (Bishop of Paris). *De Universo*. Contained in his *Opera*. Paris and Orleans, 1674.

Williams, Charles. *War in Heaven*. New York: Pellegrini & Cudahy, 1950.

——. *Witchcraft*. New York: Meridian Books, 1959.

Wilson, Edmund. *The Scrolls from the Dead Sea.* New York: Oxford U.P., 1955.

Wilson, John. *Belphegor, or the Marriage of the Devil.* London, 1691.

Wisdom of Ben-Sira (Ecclesiasticus). See Oesterley.

Wisdom of the Chaldeans. See M. Gaster.

Wisdom of the Kabbalah, The. See Runes.

Wisdom of Solomon (The Book of Wisdom). See Oesterley.

Wood, Charles Erskine Scott. *Heavenly Discourse.* New York: Vanguard, 1942.

Woodcock, P. G. *Short Dictionary of Mythology.* New York: Philosophical Library [1953].

Woolley, Leonard. *A Forgotten Kingdom.* Baltimore: Penguin, 1953.

World of the Past, The. See Hawkes.

Worrell, W. H. "The Odes of Solomon and the Pistis Sophia." *The Journal of Theological Studies,* vol. 13. Oxford: Clarendon, 1912.

Wüstenfeld, Ferdinand. (ed.) Kazwini, *Kosmographie.*

Y

Yadin, Yigael (ed.). *War between the Sons of Light and the Sons of Darkness.* Jerusalem: The Bialik Institute, 1956.

Yalkut Hadash. (ed.) Israel ben Benjamin. Radziwilow (Poland): Jos. ben Mordecai, 1814.

Yalkut Reubeni (Hoshke). In Hebrew. Contains the *Revelation of Moses.* Prague, 1660. Other editions published by Immanuel ben Joseph Athias in Amsterdam, 1700; in Warsaw, 1892, by Lewin-Epstein.

Yalkut Shimoni. (ed.) Bezalel Landau. Jerusalem, 1960. A 2-vol. edition published in Warsaw, 1876–1877.

Yeats, W. B. *A Vision.* New York: Macmillan, 1961.

"The Yezidis of Mount Sindjar." *See* Massignon.

Young, Marguerite. *Angel in the Forest.* New York: Reynal & Hitchcock [1945].

Z

Zadokite Fragments and the Dead Sea Scrolls, The. See Rowley; Charles; Schechter.

———. (ed.) Solomon Zeitlin. Philadelphia: Dropsie College, 1952.

Zanchy, Jerome (Hieronymus). *The Doctrine of Absolute Predestination. See* Augustus Toplady. Earlier edition 1769.

———. *Opera Omnia Theologica.* 8 vols. Geneva, 1619.

Zeitlin, Solomon. "An Historical Study of the Canonization of the Hebrew Scriptures." Philadelphia: American Academy for Jewish Research. Proceedings for 1932.

———. *Who Crucified Jesus?* New York: Harper, 1942.

Zimmermann, Frank (tr.). *The Book of Tobit.* New York: Harper, 1958.

Zohar, The. (tr.) Harry Sperling and Maurice Simon. 5 vols. London: The Soncino Press, 1956.

———. (ed.) Gershom Scholem. 1 vol. New York: Schocken [1949].

Zophiel; or, The Bride of Seven. A book-length poem in 6 cantos. *See* Brooks, Maria Gowen.

About the Author

Gustav Davidson was the author and editor of a dozen books in drama, biography, poetry, and angelology, serving as a consultant in the latter field to Steuben Glass and the Kennedy Foundation. Poet, research bibliographer at the Library of Congress, University Fellow (Wroxton College, England), Mr. Davidson received many citations, prizes, and awards, including the Di Castagnola Award. At his death in 1971, Davidson was Secretary Emeritus of The Poetry Society of America.